Nothing is Impossible

This book covers most of Victor (Dusty) Miller's military service and all of his WWII Army flying career. During this time, he kept detailed diaries written within weeks of each operation. These personal first hand accounts, fresh in his mind, were augmented with pencil sketches. Many were actually drawn in the field of battle as in the case of the Arnhem and Rhine Crossing operations. Those original pencil drawings were the basis for his pen and ink renderings – which appear in this book. Almost immediately after demobilization, he started writing what was eventually to become this work, more a way of purging his experiences, rather than for publication.

The subject matter covers his initial training and three main operations in which he was involved: Sicily, Arnhem, and the Rhine Crossing. The book is a clear and vivid documentation of those airborne assaults.

Sicily was his first experience of battle where he describes the process of an ordinary man thrown into war and the first Allied mass experimental usage of gliders in warfare. The lessons learned there helped develop the use and tactics of airborne forces on D-Day.

The Arnhem section contains a detailed and harrowing account of that operation as seen by a glider pilot who was engaged in hand-to-hand fighting during the siege of the grounds of the Hartenstein Hotel and eventually the difficult withdrawal and retreat over the Rhine.

The final section covers his involvement in the largest WWII airborne operation in a single day while assaulting Germany proper on operation 'Varsity' – The Rhine Crossing.

Not mentioned in the author's diaries, this sketch by Victor Miller depicts a 'Tiger Tank' in Oosterbeek hit by a PIOT anti-tank weapon, which occurred on one of many patrols in which the author was a member. As the tank started to burn, the approximately six-man patrol removed themselves from the place of action before German troops could determine their exact position and retaliate.

Nothing is Impossible

by
Victor (Dusty) Miller

*A Glider Pilot's story of Sicily,
Arnhem and the Rhine Crossing*

Pen & Sword
AVIATION

In Memory

My dad Victor, was so affected and haunted by his war-time experiences that he tried to have his memoirs published just after the war; but for many reasons, it did not happen.

When we were children, Victor regaled us daily with his vivid memories of life during WWII. So in 1984 my brothers Peter and Timothy and I persuaded him to travel back to Arnhem and Hamminkeln to show us where he had landed, stood and fought. This was a very emotional experience for Victor, as it was his first visit to those sites since he was on the ground in 1944 and 1945.

Following this trip, we managed to convince him to reconsider publishing his memoirs. After considerable effort, and with the assistance of my brother Peter Miller and my Uncle John Curthew-Sanders, who both helped edit, collate and gather material revisiting his diaries, the original shortened book was published in 1994. Victor died in 1997 at the age of 78.

In 2013, with the up and coming 70th anniversary of the Battle of Arnhem in 2014, Peter and I thought that producing an updated version with the complete text from the original memoirs, including illustrations drawn by Victor and maps, would be worthwhile. We hoped that this book would provide a personal insight into those brave men who fought and died as heroes while serving in the Glider Pilot Regiment in WWII.

Peter spent many long months trawling through Victor's personal papers, updating the original work and laboriously restoring the illustrations my father created. We hoped this would produce a suitable tribute to Victor and all his comrades who fought so bravely in Sicily, Arnhem and the Rhine Crossing, especially his co-pilot at Arnhem Sgt Tom Hollingsworth, who did not survive the war.

Sadly – Peter died on the 27th of June 2014 – at the age of 57, after putting so much effort into preparing this revised edition, diligently working right up to the end.

I would like to dedicate this book to him. He really loved our father, and genuinely admired and respected all veterans from all wars, who are willing to lay down their lives for their country and their ideals.

Chris Miller

Oxted, England
July 2014

Nothing is Impossible

First published in 1994 by Spellmount Limited
The Old Rectory, Staplehurst, Kent, TN12 0AZ

and again in 2015 by
Pen and Sword Aviation

An imprint of
Pen & Sword Books Ltd
47 Church Street, Barnsley, South Yorkshire, S70 2AS

ISBN 978 1 47384 366 0

A CIP catalogue record for this book is
available from the British Library

Typeset in 10/12 pt. Palatino by
Moran Design Corporation

Printed and bound in England
By CPI Group (UK) Ltd, Croydon, CR0 4YY

Pen & Sword Books Ltd incorporates the Imprints of Pen & Sword Aviation,
Pen & Sword Family History, Pen & Sword Maritime, Pen & Sword Military,
Pen & Sword Discovery, Pen and Sword Fiction, Pen and Sword History,
Wharncliffe Local History, Wharncliffe True Crime, Wharncliffe Transport,
Pen & Sword Select, Pen & Sword Military Classics, Leo Cooper,
The Praetorian Press, Seaforth Publishing and Frontline Publishing.

For a complete list of Pen & Sword titles please contact
PEN & SWORD BOOKS LIMITED
47 Church Street, Barnsley, South Yorkshire, S70 2AS, England
E-mail: enquiries@pen-and-sword.co.uk
Website: www.pen-and-sword.co.uk

Contents

Preface..xi

Chapter 1   Early Army Life..15

Chapter 2   Glider Training 27

Chapter 3   North Africa..39

Chapter 4   Sicily...53

Chapter 5   Engagement 65

Chapter 6   Capture...86

Chapter 7   Return From Sicily 98

Chapter 8   Return To England 115

Chapter 9   Prelude To Arnhem.....................................127

Chapter 10   Arnhem..143

Chapter 11   Landing At Arnhem.....................................159

Chapter 12   Oosterbeek 177

Chapter 13   Three Days 193

Chapter 14   The Shrinking Circle...................................207

Chapter 15   The Sixth Day..218

Chapter 16   The First Hope 227

Chapter 17   How Much Longer?.....................................241

Chapter 18   Portents Of Doom 249

Chapter 19   Retreat Across The Rhine 256

Chapter 20   Out Of Arnhem...273

Chapter 21   Nijmegen - And Home 282

Chapter 22   Preparing For Wesel....................................291

Chapter 23   To The Rhine 304

Chapter 24   Landing Over The Rhine............................317

Chapter 25   On German Soil 334

Chapter 26   Hamminkeln..348

Chapter 27   Home Again 360

Epilogue 374

Afterword 376

Post Script 378

Appendix One 386

Appendix Two 389

Appendix Three 396

Acknowledgements 400

Preface

This is the story of a glider pilot, my story, in which I have tried to set down, faithfully and accurately, what I saw and felt during the three major Airborne operations in which I had the privilege of taking part. Battle is the severest test a man can be called upon to undergo; it can bring out the best in him - and the worst.

During the Second World War the British Airborne troops in Europe were made up of two divisions, the 1st and the 6th. In addition, smaller independent units were active in other theatres of the war, but of these I have little knowledge, and they do not come within the scope of this book.

An airborne division was taken into operation by two methods. One part dropped as paratroopers, and the other landed by glider. On certain operations, only one or the other was used. Practically all of the heavy equipment was landed by glider. Re-supply of the airborne force was carried out primarily by aircraft dropping supplies by parachute, although in some cases gliders were used to bring in further men and supplies.

The air-landing, or glider-borne, trooper was carried to the scene of action by glider and, in some rare instances, by plane. Air-landing troops, and the pilots of the gliders, carried no parachutes. The fate of the air-landing trooper was entirely in the hands of the two pilots who flew the glider, and of course in the hands of the pilots who flew the plane that towed it.

The glider-borne trooper landed with all his equipment at hand. If an infantry-man, he was ready for action the moment the glider came to a halt. If his task was with the artillery, it was only a matter of minutes before the piece of artillery and its towing vehicle was unloaded (often under fire from the moment of landing) from the same glider in which he himself had landed, and was then ready for immediate action. The glider pilots usually assisted in the unloading, unless they were busy defending against any counter-attack which may have developed. The pilots then accompanied their load in the attack on the initial objective. After this had been achieved, the pilots then made their way to their own squadron rendezvous for further orders.

The paratroopers were primarily infantrymen, with some light support, such as mortars, while the glider-borne troops were a mixture of infantrymen, artillerymen, anti-tank gunners and even tankmen (the Hamilcar glider was capable of carrying a light tank) and other units of a normal Army command.

The tasks of airborne troops were many and varied, but the one task that stood out in World War II was the capturing and holding of bridges over rivers, canals and adjoining strong points, in advance of Allied troops operating in a normal land role. The famous Arnhem Bridge operation (Market Garden) represented the deepest penetration behind enemy lines i.e. 64 miles in front of the 2nd Army's thrust from the Belgian-Dutch border—a link-up that only just failed a few miles short of the trapped British 1st Airborne Division in the Arnhem pocket. That operation has often been called 'The Bridge Too Far' and was the basis for the book and film of the same name.

There were three types of operational glider used in the Second World War by the Allies. The smallest of those was the American built WACO CG4A, also known as the Hadrian by the British forces. It was constructed of tubular steel covered with fabric. The seating capacity, including two pilots, was seventeen. An alternative load to fully armed soldiers and pilots was either a six-pounder anti-tank gun with crew, a 75mm howitzer, or a jeep with three to four men, sometimes more, depending upon the circumstances. The maximum permissible load was 3600 lbs.

The wingspan was about eighty feet and the machine had a free flight speed of about eighty mph with a full load. Stalling speed was in the neighbourhood of sixty mph with a full load. Next came the British-made Horsa, built by Airspeed Ltd.

The Horsa was, in my opinion and that of many other pilots, the finest glider that was ever built regarding handling characteristics, construction, and all-round usefulness. With a wingspan of eighty-eight feet and a length of sixty-seven feet, a rudder that towered twenty feet into the air and a tricycle undercarriage, she was an impressive sight. The design load capacity was 7000 lbs (exceeded many times on operations). The Horsa weighed the same itself, resulting in a maximum all-up weight of 14,000 lbs. Twenty-nine fully armed soldiers (a platoon) could be carried in addition to the pilot and co-pilot. The alternative loads were many. A six-pounder anti-tank gun and a towing jeep, together with the gun crew and jeep driver, was one such load. A jeep and fully laden trailer with several fully armed soldiers was yet another.

The Horsa had a free flight speed of over eighty mph and stalled with full flaps at around 65 to 70 mph fully loaded. The towing speed of a Horsa was about 145 mph, with a listed maximum towing speed of 170 mph. The maximum free flight speed, and diving speed, was 190 mph.

Lastly, we had the British-built Hamilcar, made by General Aircraft Ltd., the largest of all the gliders used during the War by the Allies, with a wingspan of 110 feet. The Hamilcar had an all-up weight of seventeen tons when fully loaded. Among the varied cargo she could carry was a nine-ton light tank (Tetrarch), or the extremely effective British seventeen-pounder anti-tank gun and its accompanying towing vehicle. The performance figures were very similar to that of the Horsa. Hamilcars were never produced in the same quantities as were the Horsa and the WACO CG4A however. The Hamilcar, like the Horsa, was built mainly of wood—laminated plywood covering wooden bulkheads; extremely strong in strength:weight ratio.

The controls of a glider were exactly the same as that of a powered aircraft except that, as there were no engines, there were no throttle controls and other controls and instruments that engines require. The glider has a control column, rudder bar, trimming controls, air brakes or flaps, brakes and lighting controls, just as in a powered plane. The instruments comprise a compass, altimeter, air speed indicator, air pressure gauge, rate of climb and descent indicator, artificial horizon and a rope blind flying instrument, known more familiarly to pilots as the 'angle dangle' or cable indicator, which was for use in maintaining the correct towing position behind the tug when flying in cloud.

The aircraft used for glider towing fell into two categories: twin and four-engined. The WACO CG4A was invariably towed by the American-built twin-engined C 47, known as the Dakota. The C 47 aircraft were the principal paratrooper and supply dropping planes used throughout the war. The British Airborne forces also used four-engined planes—Halifaxes and Stirlings of the RAF. In many fewer quantities, the twin-engined British built Albemarle also was used in British glider operations, being first used on the Sicilian operation as a glider tug. The Handley Page Halifax was the only plane really capable of towing the huge Hamilcar when it was carrying a full load.

Paratroopers were carried in all the above-named planes, but the C 47s were the most used for this purpose, partly due, I believe, to the fact that the heavier four-engined aircraft were more useful for towing gliders. Horsa and Hamilcar gliders were attached to the towing planes by means of a 300-foot hemp rope nearly an inch thick. In the case of the WACO CG4As, a nylon rope of lesser length was used. Through, or wound round, the tow rope was the intercom wire, which enabled the pilots of the glider and tug to communicate with each other. The rope could be released by either the plane crew or the glider pilot. Under normal circumstances, including operational flights, the glider pilot had the responsibility of releasing the glider from the rope when he judged that he was in the correct position to effect the pin-point landing planned. Only in an emergency did the tug crew ever release the rope from their end, such as when an engine failed on take-off, or for any other reason whereby the towing plane would be endangered by continuing to tow the glider.

The rope was released by the glider pilot pulling a red-knobbed lever, or pushing, according to the type of glider being flown. The tug pilot had a similar lever in his cockpit.

By day, the glider pilot flew by visual sight of the position and attitude of the tug. Whatever movement the towing plane made, the glider pilot had to react almost instantaneously and fly a corresponding movement. If he failed to follow the tug's course closely, the glider would be dragged roughly along by the plane until the glider pilot corrected and aligned the glider's flight with that of the towing aircraft. Naturally, failure to fly the glider in the correct position placed an enormous strain on the rope, and also on the tug, and this in turn put a severe strain on the tug pilots. A badly flown glider could swing the tail of the plane in a dangerous way, and could literally cause the towing plane to become uncontrollable and crash if on take-off, or in flight near the ground once airborne.

In bumpy weather, a long distance cross-country flight could be a nightmare. The glider would heave and lurch and roll around, and the tow rope would tighten and slacken. Only when we pulled the red-topped lever, and the glider broke away into free flight, did relief come and once again it would become a real pleasure to fly.

Night flying presented other difficulties not met with in daylight. The only advantage with night flying was that it was nearly always calm and we would speed through the air on tow as though sliding along well oiled rails. On a dark night it was impossible to discern the outline of the tug. We flew by reference to three lights on the towing plane – one on each wingtip and one on the fin. The only way one knew that the glider was in the correct flying position in relation to the tug was that the three lights should form a shallow 'V', with the rudder light at the bottom.

If one got out of position it was usually soon apparent, either by the 'V' taking on an odd shape, or by suddenly feeling the beat of the tug's slipstream. If one were unwary enough to get too low and well into the turbulent slipstream, it took great strength and rapid manipulation of the controls to bring the glider back onto an even keel and back into the correct towing position.

A green flashing light from the tail-gunner's turret, or the astrodome, of the tug was the usual signal to indicate that we were in the target area and it was time for us to release whenever we thought fit.

```
BEST POSITION ON TOW

To obtain the maximum rate of climb and range it is of
importance that, once steadily climbing conditions have been
reached and in level flight, the glider shall maintain the
correct position in relation to the tug flight path.
Recommended positions are as follows:

(i)    High Tow Position: Directly behind the tug and one half
       the wing span of the tug about it (with the relationship
       between the tug tailplane and mainplane) it is not
       sufficient to keep just clear of the slipstream.

(ii)   Low Tow Position: Directly behind the tug and one half
       the wing span of the tug below it. This position is to
       be preferred, except during initial climb, for the
       following reasons:

       (a) The glider tends to maintain position more naturally
           than in the high tow position.

       (b) The correct vertical position is such that the
           glider is just clear of the slipstream and can
           therefore be more precisely gauged.
```

Chapter 1

Early Army Life

Phase I – Stoughton Barracks Guildford

15th of January 1940 was my joining day in the Army; war had been declared on Germany three and a half months previous, and my papers had arrived about ten days before, directing me to report to Stoughton Barracks, Guildford, Surrey on the 15th of January.

I can well remember that day. It was cold and chilly, but I did not notice it that much. I left Thornton Heath Station at about 8.30 Hours and had to change at Clapham Junction Station for the Portsmouth train which had a halt at Guildford.

On reaching Clapham junction I found that I would have to wait about thirty minutes, so I wandered into the waiting room and dumped my haversack onto the floor. It was an old Army haversack and contained all my worldly possessions. As I glanced around the room, I noticed two other fellows sitting on the seats. Beside them were suitcases and packs, and some instinct told me that they were also bound for Stoughton Barracks. They seemed ready to enter into conversation so I asked them if they too were reporting to Guildford. They replied in the affirmative and from then on we entered into a lively conversation.

Our train rolled up and we entered a carriage. It was a pleasant run down through Esher, Cobham and Oxshott and as we entered Guildford we craned our necks in an endeavour to see our new home to be. Outside the station we found a number of other fellows who were waiting under the watchful eye of a sergeant in the Queen's Royal Regiment, who seemed to spend most of his time cracking jokes.

Shortly afterwards, two Aldershot & District buses drew up beside us and we crowded into them. Ten minutes later we came up Stoughton Road and turned in through the gates of the Queen's Royal Regiment barracks. As we passed by the old keep, and the iron gates shut behind us, jokes went around about us at last being imprisoned etc.

Our first step was to enter into the Guard Room and sit down where we could. Here we handed in all our particulars, i.e. number, name, etc. Up until now we had a national registration number, but now we were given our Army numbers (in my case No. 6093456).

After this long wait, we were shown our billets. Some were accommodated in the Old Stoughton Barracks themselves, whilst some of us were put into huts about 200 yards away. These huts proved very comfortable. Each one of the huts had a wireless set in each wing and we had folding spring beds with mattresses, sheets and four blankets.

Having explored our billets we were summoned by the sergeant who took us up to the Old Keep, which was apparently the store. Up the winding steps we went to the very top. From the slits in the side of the tower we had a magnificent outlook right across the town of Guildford two miles away and to the hills of the Hogs Back, the North Downs and St. Martha's Chapel. To the north, pine trees rose in profusion and the air smelt keen and bracing.

We collected our rifles and bayonets (thickly coated in grease), our battle dress, overcoat, toilet requisites and under this heavy load we staggered back to our huts.

How comical some of the lads looked with their Army caps perched on their heads and clad in their civilian clothes. After this, we all adjourned to the N.A.A.F.I. Canteen and had tea and cakes.

No one slept well that night, the new surroundings and coarse sheets and blankets saw to that. We laughed and talked for some time before dropping off into fitful dozings. I eventually feel asleep at about 1 o'clock the next morning.

I awoke to the sound of the bugle, and for several moments could not fathom where I was and then it all came back to me in a rush. I was in the Army now! That bugle meant, 'get out of bed'. Reveille was at 7.00 a.m., which was not so bad, no earlier in fact than I was used to in civilian life.

Most of us rolled out of bed sharp, but a few lingered. I made a dart for the ablutions; a really nice layout with porcelain bowls, hot and cold water, showers. A hot bathe and a cold shower soon brought one back to life. After this, was breakfast.

I was agreeably surprised with the menu, which I think consisted of porridge, marmalade or jam, followed by bacon, eggs and tomato. I must say, everyone seemed out to satisfy us. Mess orderlies hurried to and fro, and towards the end of the meal our Commanding Officer (Lt. Col. Pickering) came round asking 'Any complaints'? Needless to say, there were none.

We did very little that day, except for an address by the CO in the gym. He spoke of the fine tradition of the Queen's Royal Regiment, of its splendid achievements in the past and of its efforts in the last war, World War I.

Then soon after we got down to work and for weeks we pounded the barrack square, attended lectures and carried out ,exercises. We were taught ways of field craft and carried out route marches, learned to draw maps and make out range cards. We learned to lay and aim, the best firing positions, and the use of cover.

The first few days in January 1941 were very cold and out on the parade ground the wind was biting. Sometimes my hands seemed too cold to hold a rifle. 'Left right, left right, about turn, halt'! rang in our ears all day long, mixed in with the sergeant's sarcastic remarks.

We were always well off in respect of non-commissioned officers (NCO's), and our own Sargent was a really decent chap. Mind you, he could swear at us on parade, but off parade, you could not find a better man.

As January merged into February, the winds turned still colder and snow was indicated. We had become used to this sort of life now and when the snow did finally fall we were not so badly off. Almost before the snow reached a respectable depth, we were amongst it, snowballing for all our worth.

Shortly after the first fall of snow a great freeze set in and the parade ground was turned into ice like a sheet of glass, making parades impossible and our normal parade times were spent in the huts, listening to lectures and practicing loading positions, sight setting and several other things that could be carried out indoors.

Our huts were about 200 yards from the main barrack buildings down a slight slope and even the path here joining the two places was one slippery mess despite being composed of rough stones. One had to cling to the wall desperately when endeavoring to reach the barracks, and like everyone else, I found myself lying on my back.

This first snowfall of the year gradually thawed away, but shortly afterwards came a second and heavier fall. This snowfall came during the weekend and as usual a number of the recruits went home without passes on the Sunday. But they paid for it, for towards the evening a worse freeze than ever setin, bringing all road, and a great deal of rail traffic, to a halt; all those who had risked going home were caught out. Those living within 5 or 6 miles managed to walk back, suffering a great deal of hardship in doing so, but those who had traveled further afield—to London etc., were unlucky and failed to return that night. Of course the following morning the roll call showed all these absentees. Consequently, when they did turn-up, well, it was orders for them and a bit of being 'Confined to Barracks' by the CO

All this snow, together with dampness of our feet and wet clothes caused an epidemic of sore throats to arise and I was one of the first to catch this ailment. Every morning at 9 o'clock was the Sick Parade. For the next few days there was quite a crowd of us lining up outside the N.A.A.F.I.—our parading point.

After perhaps 30 minutes wait in a draughty corridor, one was taken into the Medical Inspection Room and stood in front of the Medical Officer, who would look at us with a calculating glance, ask us to open our mouths, peer down our throats and grunt. He would have a short word with the medical orderly, who would then lead us to another room where we would be given a glass of sweet tasting medicine.

The usual verdict was to take the medicine and then be fit for duty. That was my fate, so we were forced to tramp out of the gates, the cold air whistling down our throats and lungs as sore as hell, as we marched up Rydes Hill for a spot of field craft. There was very little we could do with all that snow on the ground, except make out target cards and take bearings. How thankful we were to get back to our billets and rest upon the beds, sucking throat tablets.

Our spirits rose, however, when it came to dinnertime and hot meals even though I experienced considerable difficulty swallowing food due to my sore throat.

Soon our initial training was passed, with plenty of physical training included in programmes for each day, from which I felt myself benefiting greatly. At first it seemed rather back-breaking, and our muscles ached for sometime after each bout of it, but later this effect wore off and I used to look forward to games of hockey, cricket etc.

Then shortly after the thawing of that severe January-February freeze the weather improved during March and April, and life became quite pleasant. The countryside around us discarded its bleak outlook and took on a gentler look as blossom and leaves started to come forth.

The sun shone forth from a cloudless blue sky for days on end, while the parade ground turned dry and dusty. How we sweated to the bellowing voice of our Sargent and the Sargent Major: 'Quick march, left, right, left, right. About turn. Swing those arms! Ri-i-i-ight turn. Halt. Leave those caps alone, even if they are falling off your heads'.

We rather looked forward to our field training. It meant getting away from the barrack square for some hours. We would march off down to the common through dusty lanes and across the gorse-covered slopes of Broad Street Common and Rydes Hill. The air seemed heavy and every time we stopped along the way, our one desire was to lie down in the grass under the blazing sky and doze off; but under the steely eye of our sergeant, we dared not try it.

It always used to be a great relief to reach our allotted positions where we could lie down under cover and just watch for the supposedly approaching enemy. The first few minutes our sergeant would explain to us what our objective would be this time. He would direct us to positions that gave a good field of fire over the area, and then march off with the less lucky part of the platoon who were going to represent the enemy that afternoon. They would march to a place about 1000 yards away and try to advance and take our positions without being seen.

About once a week, usually on a Saturday morning, a route march would be carried out, commencing during the first few weeks with a distance of about 4 to 5 miles; which was increased in later weeks to about 12 to 15 miles. Sometimes these were carried out in 'Field Service Marching Order' and at other times in 'Battle Order'.

From Saturday dinnertime, we were free for the remainder of the weekend. For those with special weekend passes proceeding away from Guildford was allowed. Those were issued at about the rate of one in every three weeks. For me, home was only 28 miles by road and 32 miles by rail, so I could be home in a short period of time when I had a pass. There were quite a number who went off home without a pass, just for the day. I did this two or three times. A bus left Guildford and went straight through to West Croydon just two miles from my home. This was the No. 408 (L.T.P.B.). There were too many 'red caps' (military police) in and around Guildford Station for one to get through, but for some reason or other they never paid any attention to the busses.

I had many a pleasant walk around Guildford and I often used to wander down through the town to the bridge over the River Wey and then take the towpath along the backs. Here I would laze for awhile and then proceed on to the foot of the hill that lead up the zigzag path to the summit, which gave a wide panoramic view to the south and ended at the ruins of St. Catherine's Chapel. Below, one could watch the twisting path of the river and see the boaters upon it. Across the valley rose Pewley Downs and St. Martha's Chapel, peering forth from her garment of foliage. Lying on the slopes of St. Catherine's Hill, I would often fall into a deep slumber under the influence of the blazing sun.

Other times, I would walk up the High Street of Guildford to the Tunsgate and turn off up Pewley Hill on to Pewley Downs with its lovely views away to the north, west and south. From here I would follow the footpath across the downs to the foot of the hill that leads up to St. Martha's Chapel, up through the beautifully wooded hills slopes until the spire came in sight. It was such a quaint church, hidden away miles from the nearest town, and over a mile from the nearest village. From the graveyard, one could get a magnificent view to the south, whilst on the right, the faint outlines of the Devil's Punchbowl and Hindhead could be seen. The pine trees clustered around the base of the chapel gave it exceptional beauty that made me briefly forget the uniform that clad my body. As I gazed wistfully from the crest, I idly wondered if I would ever gaze out from this beautiful spot again, or how long it might be if I ever did. As the sun would sink behind the distant hills and the cool evening breeze set in, I would wander back to the barracks lost in thought until the sudden echoing of the bugle brought me back to reality once more.

Phase II.

After 14 or 15 weeks of training at the main barracks, we moved down to the Queen's Camp about three-quarters miles from our now familiar hut homes. A footpath and a stretch of road connected these areas.

Queen's Camp had only recently been completed and contained its own road complex. All the huts were built of wood. It must have been a good mile and a half around the perimeter. The huts were exactly the same as we had up at the old barracks. The only difference was that we now had to sleep on the floor instead of a bed, but we got used to it in time.

Down here at the camp we had more advance training, but also went over the old courses we had already taken, which we used to get rather bored with, but it was really to our advantage.

Our route marches became longer varying from 12 to 15 miles a day, lasting from 9.00 a.m. to about 3.00 p.m. Down the dusty lanes through Sutton Pitch, Worpelsdon, Woking, Jacobs Well and the district around Pirbright; these were my favorite routes and they were not too bad with regard to hills. The sight of the village inns would bring exclamations of longing from our throats, especially when some old yokel would be sitting outside in the shade sipping a large glass of beer or cider. More than once when we would halt near some house or cottage, the inhabitants would bring out some refreshments. Usually our officer or NCOs would turn a blind eye to these going on.

We did a number of cross-country runs and I think about the time we were ready to leave Guildford, we had reached our upper limit of health and fitness.

Whitsunday was drawing nigh, when we heard the first rumour that we were moving shortly and would be moving to a coastal town preliminary to embarking for (a) China, b) India, c) Africa and finally d) France. It was amazing how those rumours flashed around and about such wildly separated places.

New kit was issued to us and our old leather equipment was handed in with Bren Web replacing it. The day before the Whitsun holiday we were packing our kit bags and packs etc., polishing brass and blancoeing webbing.

Whitsunday turned out to be a beautiful day—such a brilliant blue sky studded here and there with white puffy clouds that drifted lazily. At 10.00 hours we had to take down our kit bags and stack them near the transport. Then we returned to our huts, donned our equipment and paraded outside in threes, ready for inspection, before moving off. We were in F.S.M.O. and having been standing at ease for about half an hour in the sun, we were feeling uncomfortable. After one hour of this, our shoulders were aching like mad with straps cutting down on our collarbones. Then our commander spoke, telling us we were not moving off that day after all, but would go tomorrow instead and that we could dismiss, return to our billets, and rid ourselves of our equipment. In one way we were glad, just for the sake of removing our packs from our shoulders, but in another way we were disappointed.

After dinner we went down and collected our kit bags from the pile and lugged them back to our billets. Then our officer called us together and told us that we would be moving off for sure tomorrow; and so we went to bed that night full of expectation.

The next day came bright and sunny and again by 10.00 hours we were paraded ready to move off. Soon after parading the word of command came: 'Company, company, shun. Right turn. Quick march' and we were off. For the last time we marched out through the gates of the barracks. Somehow I felt a little sorry at leaving this place that had been my home for so many months. But getting into our stride and with songs on our lips, the past was soon forgotten and a new future lay ahead—but exactly what?

The two and a half miles march towards Guildford Station seemed quite short and we marched along with swinging strides that soon brought us to High Street, where people gave us a cheer and a smile. Everybody was in good spirits and when we arrived at the station we found our train already waiting. After a few orders we were clambering onboard. We were not overcrowded and I managed to get myself a corner seat with a view out of a window.

A chocolate girl was on the platform and in a short space of time we had bought her out; this, together with our haversack rations, promised a good meal. It was delightfully cool in the carriage after the heat of the ponding along the roads and we had all our windows pulled down to let in a nice breeze.

Just before moving off, our CO Col Pickering, came along the platform, walking the whole length of the train and wishing the occupants of each compartment separately, 'Good luck and bon voyage', and I could see from his face he was being very sincere in his wishes. I think he was almost on the verge of tears despite being an army man of many years. He was always a good fellow—strict and all that, but one of the best all the same.

A shrill whistle came from the engine and we began to move slowly out from the station; Col Pickering was still waving at us and saying 'Good luck'. As we pulled away, I peered out of the window for a last look at Stoughton Barracks. There was the old squat tower with the Queen's flag waving proudly above it. I watched as the last sign of the buildings had disappeared behind the trees, and then sat back to enjoy the trip to the coast. The train headed out through the town of Guildford alongside the river Wey and up the Tillingbourne Valley.

I was in high spirits as I watched the countryside flashing past the window. I took a last look at the spire of St. Martha's Chapel on the hill high above, surrounded by pine trees and foliage, and again wistfully wondered how long it might be before seeing that scene again. Soon after passing through Gomshall, I noticed the old firing range on the left where I had carried out my rifle and light machine gun training on open ranges, this was at Wescott. We headed on through

Dorking and Redhill, where we had a short wait while the locomotive was changed and we switched to another line before setting off to Brighton.

We heard a strong rumour that we were going to Seaford, East Sussex on the coast just east of Brighton. I began to think this was right as we branched off at Burgess Hill on the Lewes line, then I was sure. Soon the roofs of Lewes came into sight with the hill crowned by ruins of Lewes castle. We flashed through Lewes Station and out onto the Seaford line. Soon the long range of the South Downs was behind us as we approached our destination of Seaford. A ripple of excitement ran through the train as Seaford came in sight and the glint of the sea was visible; here we thought was a paradise indeed after the dusty parade ground at Guildford.

Phase III – Seaford

Drawing into Seaford Station, we tumbled quickly out of the carriages and assembled on the platform. After a few minutes of waiting, we marched out of the station and into the yards, where we again halted whilst our NCO's and Officers went into a huddle to sort out who was to have which billets in the evacuated civilian houses close to the sea front.

After a few minutes, our Corporal in charge came over to us and told us to get ready to move out. Slinging our rifles and endeavoring to heave our heavily loaded kitbags on our shoulders, we struggled off, hoping that we would not have to go far. I could not help laughing at one of our fellows named Mackrell, who was about 5' 4" in height. Despite frantic efforts to raise his kitbag onto his back, he failed to do so, and with muttered words of disgust, proceeded to march through Seaford dragging his kitbag in the dust of the road behind him. An officer tried to make him pick it up, but got no answer for his pains.

I was sweating profusely under my heavy load and the full beating down rays of the sun; it was a great relief when in less than five minutes, our Corporal called a halt in front of a house, which was just off the seafront. We could hear the rolling thunder of the sea about 50 yards away and sincerely hoped we would be allowed to have the rest of the afternoon off so that we could take a dip in the sea. It seemed too good to be true to have the sea less than a minute away and the town just about a three minute walk away, but it was indeed true.

The house we were to occupy was in fairly good repair. It was a four-story late Victorian or early Edwardian building with a basement and faced due west. On the second floor was a balcony with French windows opening into the room behind. I made a mental note that I must try to get into that room and have it as my billet.

Getting inside the building, I made a beeline for the room upstairs where the balcony was, calling to my friends to follow me. On entering the room I was quite pleased with it; when I stepped across to the French windows to open them and walked outside, I was delighted with the view. Just off to the left was the beach and the wide sweep of the Channel stretching away to Newhaven. On my right I could see right up the town. Newhaven was a picturesque cluster of buildings on the hillside of Newhaven Head, about two miles away by way of the beach and about three and a half miles by road.

The sun's rays sparkled on the dancing waves and I was tempted to immediately run down and take a plunge into the sea, but I was not sure of what orders we might get shortly. Making my way to the back of the house I glanced out of a window to get yet another pleasing sight of Seaford Head rising up about three quarters of a mile away, with a view of the Channel stretching away towards the French coast and Eastbourne.

I felt very happy indeed, and this was added to when we were informed that we could have a rest of the afternoon off. Out came our bathing kit and we headed straight off down to the sea. We were surprised to find the water so cold despite the heat of the sun, but I suppose it was rather early in the year for the sea to have warmed up.

After our dip in the sea, the remainder of the evening was spent looking around the town, although Seaford was not very large except where it spread out in residential districts. But with tree-lined roads, it was a pleasant place.

Our house, we now found out, was known as No. 4, West View, Seaford. Our dining hall was an old garage about three-to four-minute walk away from the billet, whilst our parade ground was the local cinema's car park, less than a three-minute walk for us and easily visible from the windows of the house, which came in useful at times.

That evening I witnessed a glorious sunset from the balcony. As the sun sunk down behind Newhaven Head in the west, the skies were tinted to a magnificent orange and red, which was reflected by the dancing waves of the Channel. The cool evening was most welcome after the heat of the day. I was able to see this beautiful sight for many more evenings to come, as during our stay here the weather was marvelous, with only the last three or four days changing to less idyllic weather.

I awoke the next morning with the dull murmuring of the sea in my ears and hurriedly dressed and walked down to the beach. It was a gorgeous fresh morning with hardly a soul about, with the sun showing faintly through the Channel's mist, glinting upon the slowing heaving waves, whilst overhead gulls screamed their morbid cry.

During the whole stay in Seaford, I was never tempted to stay in bed late on mornings, the keen air and the rolling of the waves always gave one the irresistible urge to leap out of bed and gaze across the Channel. My early morning thoughts as I gazed at the sea view always wandered to how long it would be before I would be sailing across those shimmering waters to the coast of France and what lay beyond – I knew my Brother Frank was over there already. I was longing to feel the soil of France beneath my feet.

There were about thirty of us billeted at the house. I shared my room with three others, whom, if I remember correctly, were Russell, Pier, Palmer and Pike (or 'Lofty' as we used to call him); he was a grave digger in peace time.

The first three days we did very little and most of our time was spent in collecting various items of kit from the Company stores. The following days were spent on some light training. Outside of our accommodation was a field; we would saunter over there with our rifles or a light machine gun to do weapons training. Our Corporal was rather a sport and when we used to arrive at the field, he would ask, 'What's this'?, pointing to the Bren gun and we would answer him. He would then reply by saying, 'Well, you know what it is and I know what it is, so what are we worrying about'? Forthwith, we would all lie on our backs and doze off in the heat of the sun.

These parades always came in the morning and after dinner, our officer would say: 'Well I think a bit of P.T. (Physical Training) is indicated'. We would change into our gym vests and shorts and report back in the Recreation Ground near the station. We would do a few loosening up exercises for about fifteen minutes and then play games for about half an hour, followed by a ten-minute break. After this the NCO in charge would say to us, 'Half of you can go swimming and the other half can stay here and play games until 4 o'clock'. The last parade should have lasted until 4.15, but Lance Corporal Bailey was one of the best, as I have mentioned before. Of course, all of us wanted to go swimming and in the end about three quarters of us would go swimming—or at least said we were going to. The other L/Cpl in charge of the swimming section would shut his eyes to us; on getting down to the beach we would immediately head back to our billets, change and go off to town.

Personally, I enjoyed entering the sea at about three in the afternoon. I could not swim, but that did not stop me from wading up to my chin, turn my back on the incoming sea and wait for a large wave to rush up so I could dive forward and be carried on up to the beach almost submerged the whole time.

Palmer, one of my roommates, was rather afraid to come out very far into the sea. He told us he had never been in the sea before. I used to try and tempt him to come out further with me, but I think he was suspicious that I had evil intentions of dunking him into the waves as they rolled in. Naturally, I had those very thoughts in my mind, but I never did manage to persuade him to get out of his depth, which was probably just as well.

During the evenings, we had no guard duties, as we were really a holding battalion on draft anyway, with nothing to actually guard. I often walked up the steep path to the crest of Seaford Head pausing now and then to cautiously approach the edge of the cliffs and peer over the top down to the rocks far below. The waves crashed and echoed against the foot of the steep face, whilst overhead swooping gulls screamed at each other.

From Seaford Head I would gaze out across the Channel and watch some slowly moving vessel come up over the horizon then disappear westwards in the direction of Brighton. As I looked out to sea, way to the right, the coast was clearly visible almost as far as Brighton, while to the left I could see as far as along as Beachy Head and the lighthouse. The Seven Sisters were only about two or three miles away along the coast standing out in all their brilliant white glory.

Twice I walked along the base of the downs as far as the base of the Seven Sisters, but owing to the wide lowlands of the Cuckmere Haven area, where the Cuckmere River runs into the sea, I was unable to get any farther. I would return just as the sun was setting in the west, throwing a crimson splash across Seaford Bay and giving the cliffs a tinge of gold as it threw deep shadows across the Downs. How wonderful Newhaven Harbour looked as the shadows of the evening crept across the bay and landscape, and thoughts of war were far from my mind. Only when I looked out across the Channel towards the unseen coast of France did my thoughts plummet me back to earth. I wondered what my younger brother Francis was doing at that very moment in France as part of the British Expeditionary Force. Why did we have to tarry here so long? How long before we set foot in France? But it was not to be.

Once I walked around the outskirts of Seaford and took a path across the Seaford Golf course, which brought me out onto Seaford Head; yet another wonderful walk. Another time I walked along the beach to almost as far as Newhaven and obtained a tea in a café on the way back. I did not get back until about 9.00 PM.

Then to my delight, shortly after this last long walk, our Major (Block I think), informed us we would be embarking for France. The thought pleased me, as I innocently thought I might get to see my brother. Most of the men did not like getting this news at all, but some, like me, were looking forward to this new phase of our Army life. We were also told we would not be getting any embarkation leave; he was sorry, but that was the order and we might be going any day now.

It was almost a holiday-like experience with warm blue skies and waters of the Channel for us to enjoy. Then the smoldering of war clouds over France flared up with the German 'Blitzkrieg' and the rapid invasion of Belgium, Holland and France commenced. Our Major called us together. And told us we would soon be over there, helping crush the 'Boche' with our comrades in arms. However, as the days wore by the news became more and more ominous. The rumours—startling rumours—began to fly about. Then came the great breakthrough by the fast moving modern tanks at Sedan, followed by the gigantic battle of tanks at Cambrai. Our Major called us together once more, and said in a rather pompous tone 'The boys are having a little trouble with the Boche at the moment, but we will soon fix that'.

Little did we know that the Armies of France and Britain were in full flight, covered by a magnificent 'rear guard actions' which staved off the full might of the German Panzer units from the main armies. This was the beginning of the end for France.

Soon after our Major's speech, we were told to hand in all our surplus kit at the company stores which was now the Bay Hotel Seaford and that we were to draw our overseas kit. It seemed that action was commencing at last. In went all our kit except for what we stood up in and a change of clothing. Even our boots, and brass brushes were withdrawn from us.

I can well remember how mad the fellows were when on the following morning we went round to our cooked food in the Bay Hotel and saw plies of battle dress blouses, caps, trousers, shirts etc., and worse still a huge piles of all our personal belongings all mixed up together. We had been informed that all our kitbags containing our personal belongings would be kept back and be sent to our respective homes when we embarked; but we could do nothing about it, although I did manage to retrieve a few items, such as a shorthand book, a scarf and one or two other odds and ends that I recognized in the pile.

The following evening, half our men marched off to the train station bound for Southampton and France, or so they thought. We were to follow the next day we were told. A thinly-veiled excitement ran through the ranks. France at last was to be our goal in a couple of days. The following day, we stood parade to move off to the station enroute for Southampton. We were then informed that we were not going after all! What was wrong? Rumours started to seep through that our men in France were in retreat, that even an evacuation was in progress, which seemed not just incredible, but impossible.

We went to bed that night with mixed feelings. I personally was bitterly disappointed at our embarkation being cancelled.

I awoke early next morning and something made me rise and walk across to the balcony that overlooked the sea. No—impossible—I could hardly believe my eyes! There before me stretching out to sea and over the horizon, and jamming into Newhaven Harbor some three miles away, were long lines of ships, barges, trawlers and every other type of seagoing vessel possible. A long line of motionless ships is a sight one sees only once in a lifetime, if then!

As I looked on, there was a reverberating explosion and a fountain of water shot heavenwards beside some ship that was attempting to creep into the harbour. The gunfire from the shore batteries warning the captain of the vessel to keep his turn at docking.

My roommates had been awakened by the sound of the shot. 'What is it?' they asked. I could only look on and mummer 'Impossible'.

'My God'! said one of them, 'What is it, an invasion'?

With thoughts running wildly through our heads we hurriedly dressed and ran down to the beach. There was already a large crowd on the front, despite the early hour. Amidst the many rumours, we eventually got the truth. The evacuation of our expeditionary force was taking place.

None of our British soldiers were arriving at Newhaven; these were all Belgian and French troops, we were informed. The remnants of British and French armies were swarming over the Channel to the sanctuary of the British Isles as the smashing attacks of fast moving German armoured divisions along with the coordinated support of the powerful 'Luftwaffe' crushed them. Even with witnessing the evidence of such a calamity, it was impossible for our minds to register the full horror of the situation. Fascinated, we continued to watch the long line of ships, most of which remained stationary.

This event was the only subject at breakfast. Most of my comrades could not credit it, but their hopes we soon shattered when our Major spoke to us. His voice was full of emotion. He said, 'My men, as you have probably seen for yourselves, we have been forced to evacuate France. The enemy have proved themselves almost armour plated and heavily armed—far above what was expected. You must be on your guard from now onwards, day and night. By night, you will patrol the coastline from Seaford Head to the beginning of Newhaven Bay. You will march in sixes with an NCO, and you will march up and down without rest, for we are but few here and it is highly probable that the 'Boche' will try to sweep across the Channel. You will not retreat from the beaches and must fight to the end with your bayonets if necessary. That is all'.

For some time a silence reigned and then a babble broke loose all around. How did we think we could hold them off if they did come across? When were they most likely to strike and where? These and a hundred other questions filled our conversation for most of the morning.

There were no parades all day, but in the evening we were called together and a certain number selected for the first night's patrols. This was the first guard duty I had done in weeks. It was then that a totally incredible situation was revealed. We were told that there was no ammunition whatsoever for the first night, but that it would be arriving on the morrow. In the meantime, we were to stave off any attack by the enemy with bayonets. We looked at each other in a half amused sort of way. Bayonets eh! Well we might as well get cracking, so the first patrol began its march.

When the ammunition did arrive, we were issued just five rounds of bullets each.

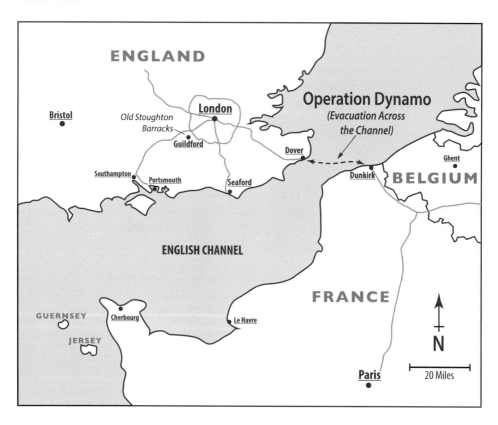

In a nine day period from 27 May–4 June, 338,226 Allied soldiers were evacuated from the beaches and harbour of Dunkirk, France. This included 139,997 French, Polish, and Belgian troops, together with a small number of Dutch soldiers, aboard 861 vessels, of which 243 were sunk. Known as Operation Dynamo, the life and death rescue galvanized the public, who freely assisted with 'little ships', private vessels such as fishing boats, pleasure cruisers, ferries and any number of private craft guided across the Channel by the navy. 'Dunkirk Spirit' refers to the solidarity of the British people in times of adversity.

Chapter 2

Glider Training

In 1940, after the successful use of airborne troops by the Germans in the low countries, and in particular the pin-point glider landings on the Maginot Line, the idea of forming a unit of glider pilots first came under discussion, introduced by the then Mr. Winston Churchill. By late 1940, experiments were being carried out, but at that time only peace-time sail-planes were available in one- or two-seater versions.

However, at the same time an order was given for 400 Hotspur gliders, the first real glider to be built for military use. The Hotspur was a midwing glider capable of carrying 13 to 15 passengers and 2 pilots who sat in tandem up near the nose of the glider. This glider became the one-and-only primary training glider used by the RAF for training glider pilots. From Hotspurs, the pilot converted onto the heavy operational Horsa and Hamilcar gliders. Before any glider training, however, the prospective glider pilot had to pass through an RAF elementary flying school full course (together with pupils destined for RAF squadrons) where he passed out solo on light powered aircraft. This was to enable him to master the art of flying before flying the larger and more unpredictable gliders in which he did not have the chance of opening the throttle again, if an approach had been misjudged, as was possible with the powered aircraft.

By November 1941 the experimental stage was over and it was decided that a start could be made on forming an operational unit. In the early days it was touch and go whether the new unit should come under the RAF (because of the flying skills required) or the Army (because of the land fighting role involved).

It was eventually decided that the unit would be an Army formation, and would be known henceforth as the Glider Pilot Regiment and would be part of the newly formed Army Air Corps. All this was still clouded in secrecy at the end of 1941 and the regiment was not actually formed officially until January 1942.

It was in November 1940 that I heard the first whispers about men being trained for glider flying. At that time, I was stationed in Spalding, Lincolnshire, in the intelligence section of the Brigade H.Q. of the 131 (Queen's) Infantry Brigade, which was part of the 44th Home Counties Division.

A message arrived one day early in November marked 'Secret' and a short while later a notice appeared on the Brigade H.Q.'s notice board to the effect that men were needed for training as glider pilots. The notice also stated that the information given therein was not for public notice, and was to be treated with the utmost secrecy.

Much to my surprise, this call for volunteers did not arouse much enthusiasm. I suspected the comparatively comfortable lot of most of the inmates of the H.Q. was much too attractive for those whose roots were deeply planted there.

Many an incredulous query was thrown at me during the following days when it was learned that I had applied for a transfer to this mysterious unit but, for myself, I was enthusiastic. I had followed closely the meagre reports of the success of the German airborne attacks in Holland during 1940 and, a month or so before the call for glider pilot volunteers had come in, a notice had appeared that volunteers were required to train as paratroopers. I had almost put my name in for that, but on carefully thinking the matter over, I realised that parachute jumping was not exactly what I had been waiting for.

For years before the war, flying had held me in its fascinating grip; not that I had ever been lucky enough to experience a flight. I had read books on flying by the score and at the outbreak of war had tried unsuccessfully, along with many other would-be fliers, to join the RAF. However, at the time I joined, the need for men to go into the army was particularly strong and it was not until a year or two later that attention was directed to obtaining men for air crew in the RAF. I, along with the others, had joined too early to be able to enter the service of my choice.

The interview that followed my application came to nothing and, with my enthusiasm a little dampened, I returned to Brigade H.Q. and resumed its monotonous routine. I had been told that I would be sent for in about two months time, but to me that seemed an interminable period.

I was not to hear or see anything about gliders again for over a year, when suddenly a new call came in for volunteers to train as glider pilots. My application was the first into the Brigade Major's tray, which he in due course forwarded with, I was given to understand from a source near to him, an excellent recommendation.

Within a week I was on my way to London for a physical and written examination. Our tests were exactly the same as those being given to civilians applying for air crew service with the RAF. In fact we intermingled and had to take our turn with the civilians, who curiously eyed our Army uniforms. I was jubilant at the end of the day when, after a final interview by several high-ranking RAF officers, I was told I had been selected and I could expect my transfer to be effective within a few weeks. I returned to the Brigade H.Q., which at that time was stationed in a small hamlet named Provender Norton near Faversham in Kent, with a feeling that this time I was really going places.

I was not wrong. Three weeks later to the day, on the 26th of March 1942, I was on my way to Tilshead on Salisbury Plain with an order detailing me to report to the H.Q. of the Glider Pilot Regiment and that furthermore, I was no longer a member of the Queen's Royal Regiment but of the Glider Pilot Regiment.

I arrived at Tilshead by night with about fifty other soldiers from various regiments of the British Army. We fifty, I am sure, represented a complete cross section of the British Army. Practically every regiment and corps was to be seen by looking at the shoulder markings of each man.

Tilshead was a pretty grim and isolated place with strict discipline and lots of Blanco, along with whitewash. This fact caused many of us to close our eyes in anguish and ask ourselves what had driven us to such mad steps. To me it was Guildford all over again, only worse. At Guildford, where I received my initial army training with the Queen's Royal Regiment, at least one was within a mile of a really beautiful town and its accompanying entertainments.

The days that followed bore out our first pangs of fear. Within a week several of the 'volunteers' had decided to withdraw their applications and had left for their old units. Two or three even left the very next day. I think the Officer-in-Charge's speech, given us on the day after we arrived, had something to do with their rapid retreat. Discipline (the soldier's bugbear), physical fitness, endurance and smartness formed the keynotes of his fiery speech, and that was enough for some. Many had been clerks in their old units or had held other administrative jobs, and I think the thought of gruelling route marches and hours of drill and gymnastics was more than they could bear. In all fairness to the administrative men who volunteered, many did stay and eventually passed with flying colours. To those who had transferred from infantry units, as I had, there appeared little difference from their normal routine life back with their battalions, and with the Glider Pilot Regiment there were several advantages outlined by the OC.

At first I found the life almost too strenuous, but gradually my body became more accustomed to the continuous exercise. I began to feel fitter and slowly I even began to like the life, although within myself I knew that I treated all this training as means to an end—flying.

Major Chatterton, our OC, was as good as his word. The food was excellent, as far as anyone could call Army food excellent. Time off was given ungrudgingly (a strange thing where the Army was concerned) and most weekends were free, with the added attraction of passes being made out to any place one cared to write on the application form.

Altogether, I was at Tilshead for four to five weeks, and then I was given a fortnight's leave. I returned to Tilshead to find that I had been posted to No. 21 Elementary Flying School RAF at Booker, near High Wycombe, in Bucks. I was elated. Not only was I going to fly but I had also been posted to the nearest aerodrome to London among those that had been allotted for flying training. The other aerodromes were at Derby, and near Abingdon in Oxfordshire. At Booker we would learn to fly on Tiger Moths and Miles Magisters, the standard trainers of the RAF.

It was a beautiful sunny day when we arrived at Booker and so jubilant was our party that, despite the long tiring march up the steep hill that leads the way out of High Wycombe town to Booker aerodrome, we were like a happy bunch of schoolboys after we had been assigned our huts and were settled in.

We were the first batch of Army men to be trained on this aerodrome which caused no little stir for several days both with the RAF men on the aerodrome and the inhabitants of Booker and High Wycombe. It was an unheard of thing for Army men to be training to become pilots, since all aerodromes and flying matters had been exclusively under the RAF. All airborne troops were drawn, as volunteers, from the existing armed forces - no civilians were accepted. We struck up a friendship with the RAF men that lived on long after our party had completed its course and had left for places farther afield.

Within three days of my arrival at Booker, I was undergoing my first lesson in flying. At last I had achieved my ambition. From that day onward I put my heart and soul into my work, both the flying side of the course, and on the ground schooling, which covered many subjects including navigation, engines, theory of flight, signals and aircraft construction.

The days passed faster than I wished. I knew that we were only due to stay for a period of two or three months which was the average time allotted by the RAF to complete the elementary flying course, which included both flying and classroom instruction. The weather was kind to us during the whole time we were there.

Day after day my instructor and I would rise smoothly from the green turf of Booker aerodrome and climb away into the blue. We would cavort over the green fields and hills of Buckinghamshire, a landscape spreading to the far horizon and patchwork quilt of many colours, looking beautiful in its summer cloak.

Over Princes Risborough, to the north of Booker, we would carry out aerobatics; spinning, looping and rolling in careless abandon, weaving in and out, around and through the huge cavernous valleys formed by the towering white cumulus clouds that rose for thousands of feet way up above our spreading wings. Only the steady roar of the engine accompanied us as we floated high over the peaceful landscape of Buckinghamshire.

Sometimes the roar of our engine would rise and then die away as went into an aerobatic manoeuvre. Then only the shrill whistle of the slipstream through the bracing wires of the Tiger Moth would play upon our ears.

With the Miles Magister, it was a heavier swish of air over the wing and around the fuselage as we headed earthward in a dive with the throttle closed. As we twisted about in aerobatics, the scenic patchwork quilt below would change position and wheel away to one side or over our heads as we slid onto our backs for loops or rolls, or entered a mad whirl with only the ground directly in front of the spinning propeller forming some intelligible pattern as we fell into a spin.

Then my great day arrived, the 31st of May 1942, when the instructor stepped out of the Tiger Moth's front cockpit, turned around and said, 'Well, she's all yours'! After just over nine hour's dual flight instruction, the moment had come for me to fly solo. It was the day I had been waiting for and yet, now that it was here, I had a sickly feeling in the pit of my stomach. With beating pulse, I watched the instructor slowly and methodically lock up the loose harness in the front cockpit, remove his parachute from the seat and step back. 'You OK'? he asked. I croaked a reply in the affirmative.

Almost in a daze I looked around to check for incoming and outgoing aircraft, opened the throttle and roared across the field. I lifted smoothly into the air, surprising myself, and the watching instructor also, no doubt, probably had all his fingers crossed. Once clear of the field, the empty cockpit suddenly stood out sharply in front. I was on my own this time. The beat of the engine was healthy, and the altimeter climbed steadily. I suddenly felt elated—I was flying solo at last! I had made it; but the thought remained that I wasn't back down on the ground yet, and that I still had a long way to go. The first turn was due, altimeter 1000 feet, into the left hand turn, trying to hold her steady. The horizon crept around the nose, the ninety degree landmark came up and I straightened out, flying cross wind as I had been instructed.

Like all other pupils on their first solo, I was practically blind to anybody else who was on the circuit; every nerve was concentrated on doing the correct turns and maintaining the correct courses. Well I knew the critical eye of the instructor down below would be following every yard of my flight, and no doubt he was troubled by the thought, 'Should I have sent him off solo'? Another turn and I was heading downwind. The turning point of the crosswind leg came up quickly—almost too quickly—travelling downwind as I was. This was the moment. I closed the throttle and continued to glide crosswind, the altimeter slid slowly back, the wind whistled through the struts—time to turn in now for the final run-in—the edge of the aerodrome was coming up rapidly. I was passing over the boundary at a nice height, the grass rising rapidly up to meet me, and beginning to slide past at an ever increasing speed.

Automatically I pumped the stick back and forth, and I was levelling off. The whistle of the wind through the struts died away into a gentle sigh as the speed fell off. A slight jolt, and I pulled the stick right back into my stomach as the wheels and tail skid hit the ground at much the same time. I was down. She rolled across the uneven surface of the field, gradually slowing to a stop.

Still following the instructor's words carefully, I swung her gently round cross wind and searched the sky and field for any signs of moving aircraft. Seeing none, I taxied over to the nearest boundary and wove my way back to the flight hut area from which I had started out an hour or so ago. I was relaxed now, and probably somewhat flushed with triumph.

With a final burst of throttle I turned the Tiger Moth into wind in the parking space, cut the motor, unfastened my belt with fumbling fingers and climbed clumsily out, laden down with the heavy bulk of a seat-type parachute. I walked with a grin over to some of my comrades, most of whom had not yet soloed, to be met with calls of 'nice work, Dusty', and so forth. The instructor was less informal with his criticism; just saying 'Not too bad—you'd better go and do a few more'.

Time sped by. By day we studied and flew hard; by night we played hard. The nearby town of High Wycombe was the place where we disported ourselves during the long summer evenings when we were not night flying.

Then the sad day arrived. We had completed the course, and there was no further reason why we should still plague High Wycombe.

After my leave was up I had to return to Tilshead, a terrible let-down after the easy-going and fascinating life at Booker. The bonds did not last long, however, for the call for glider pilots was urgent, and within a few days I found myself at Stoke Orchard aerodrome. On the evening of our arrival the aerodrome was strangely empty. The 'boys' had all departed into Cheltenham on a reconnaissance to check up on the pub and wench situation. From the stories one was still hearing at 1:00 a.m. Cheltenham had fulfilled their hopes.

At Stoke Orchard we were introduced to the Hotspur glider and, after the powered aircraft we had been flying, these machines of unknown quantity caused our hearts to sink. Their finish seemed crude, although we were to learn through experience that this apparent crudeness did not in any way detract from their performance as flying machines.

After the light touch of the Tiger and Magister, the controls of the Hotspur seemed heavy. Two hands were needed to move the control column, but this was modified at a later date, when frieze ailerons were fitted on to most models. We left the hangars after our first introductory lecture by an RAF pilot on the merits and demerits of the Hotspur in a not too happy mood, a mood, of course, which gave us a good excuse to make our way into Cheltenham that evening with all speed possible and find solace in a foaming glass of beer.

My first flight in a glider was quite an experience after having flown powered aircraft. The most noticeable feature was the absence of the engine noise that is always present in a powered plane. This was countered to a certain degree by the terrific drumming roar of the slipstream that filled the cockpit once we were airborne, when speed was creeping up over the 100-mph mark. Another surprise was the quite noticeable jerk experienced when the instructor pilot pulled the tow rope release knob for the first time. For a second I thought something had gone amiss and that we had lost a wing, as the rope in front parted from our locking device with a loud twang.

It is the free flight that is the most exhilarating part of flying a glider. Just a clean gentle roar of air past the perspex canopy, rising to a sharper whistle whenever we increased airspeed to go onto a turn or dive. Beautiful smooth landings were possible with these gliders, for the vision forwards and downwards as one landed was perfect. In time I began to become quite fond of the Hotspur and subsequent other glider models.

After we had soloed on the Hotspurs, we began to carry out more advanced tactics, among which was one known as the 'remote release'. After we had taken off, our tug would tow us in a steady climb which eventually ended around the 10,000 foot mark and at a pre-designated spot about fifteen to twenty miles from our home aerodrome in the upwind direction. This was so that on the return journey we would be flying downwind, that is, with the wind behind us and aiding our glider along. Upon arriving at the release point, we would circle once, give the OK to the pilot in the tug, and release. The rope would drop away, curling back towards the tail of the tug, which would go into a gentle left descending turn. We would continue on course, easing back on the stick to gain more height while we still had the excess speed from the tow.

The harsh roar would gradually die down as our speed fell from the towing speed of 130 mph to the natural free-flight gliding speed of 65 mph. Then only a smooth rasp of the slipstream past the canopy would break the silence. We would turn our nose onto the homeward course (worked out before leaving the aerodrome) and, with the aid of the compass and visual pinpointing of the ground below in conjunction with our map, settle down into a long steady glide. At 10,000 feet it was exquisitely calm and, with a little experimental trimming, most of the Hotspurs could fly hands-off for some distance.

Thousands of feet below, the rolling landscape of Gloucestershire hardly appeared to be moving. Little clusters of grey and red roofs indicated where villages nestled in folds and valleys. The skies around, more often than not, were half covered with white and grey masses of cumulus clouds whose shapes often changed even as one watched. It was awe-inspiring, gliding almost silently past the swirling masses of white, the sides of which towered up tens of thousands of feet above us. Mighty valleys were formed by the drifting clouds, valleys that beckoned to us to wheel into a turn and follow their twisting courses for mile upon mile.

But, flying as we were on rigid pre-arranged courses and with no engine to give us extended range, it was impossible to succumb to the temptation, strong as it was.

These remote releases were always practised on a clear day when the cloud base, if any, was a minimum of 9,000 to 10,000 feet. The tactical idea behind the plan was to enable gliders to release at a considerable distance (up to twenty miles) from their intended landing zones in enemy territory and glide almost silently down to a supposedly unsuspecting enemy. The only times this plan was ever used, as far as I know, was during the airborne landings on Sicily by night, when a few Horsa glider pilots were allotted the task of landing near and capturing the bridge over the river outside Syracuse, and the special landings on D-Day against gun batteries and bridges on the Normandy coast.

Even these operations called for only for a comparatively short glide from a remote release, somewhere in the neighbourhood of five miles. In later operations, remote releases were carried out, but again in a very restricted form, and nothing like the long distance glides we practised over the green fields of England.

Another advanced flying tactic we carried out in practice flights (an exercise discontinued shortly after we had completed our course) was one known as 'dive approach', an exercise I thoroughly enjoyed, and one which added real zest to flying the gliders, an opinion that I am sure was shared by most other pilots.

On this exercise, we were towed off by our tugs, which were Miles Masters, low-wing advanced trainers capable of a speed of over 200 mph when not towing a glider. We would carry out a normal circuit around the aerodrome, except that we climbed a little higher to about 1200 to 1500 feet. Having followed the usual turn across wind and another downwind, we would release on this last leg and continue on straight ahead, gradually losing speed until we were at our normal gliding speed of 65 mph. Instead of turning in onto the last crosswind leg preparatory to the final turn in to a normal landing, we would extend the downwind glide and turn when we were about a mile or so past the edge of the landing field. This would bring us onto the crosswind leg.

As we straightened out on the crosswind leg, the stick was eased forward, and the glider slid over into a dive. Farther and farther over went the stick. The horizon rose up and over our head. The fields, which had been stretching away ahead and on all sides, were suddenly staring us straight in our faces. The altimeter, which had been registering around 1200 to 1500 feet, began to unwind fast, and the needle slid rapidly back down in height. The gentle hiss of the slipstream rose higher and higher, changing fast into a drumming roar. The airspeed indicator hand swung up past the 65-mph mark and in a few seconds was registering well over 100 mph.

The ground rushed up faster and faster, the noise grew louder and louder, and the ASI (air speed indicator) hand climbed to around 140 to 150 mph, a high speed for a wooden-constructed glider. The altimeter hand was registering a height too low to read with 170 mph on the clock. We were relying on sight of the ground, which seemed to be coming awfully near. Then we eased back on the stick, with at the same time a gentle but firm turn to the left, the ground tilted, but still came nearer. The nose was coming up and veering round.

A ninety degree turn had to be judged, for by now the aerodrome boundary was no longer visible owing to the low height at which we were flying. Then we were around and level. Twenty to thirty feet below, the ground flashed by. Now that we were in level flight, we could ease down lower still, for we had no propeller to worry about striking the ground, as with the powered aircraft of that time. Down to ten feet we streaked over the ploughed fields, then a hedge, over a strip of grassland, sheep scattering in all directions.

A tall line of trees loomed up—gently back on the stick—or a degree or two of flap - up and over. The speed died away from over the 100 mph mark, and we looked ahead anxiously for signs of the aerodrome boundar coming into sight. Down to 70, still another unfamiliar field came up to meet us.

The roaring noise had died away—a warning. Then the familiar railway track would slide up to meet us. All pilots knew that the railway bordered the aerodrome. Up over the telephone wires, draped from post to post alongside the track, and stick forward once more. The green undulating grass of the flying field skimmed by under our wheels and a second later we were down, rumbling over the somewhat rough surface, gradually slowing to a halt where we would wait for the towing tractor to come out and pick us up. Then back to the starting lines for another tow and another flight.

Intermingled with the day flying, we had flying at night. When I first heard mentioned the prospects of night flying in a glider, I thought that the higher-ups were crazy. The idea of being towed around the night skies on a length of rope with no sight of the tug seemed beyond comprehension. Nevertheless, it was accomplished, but for some time after starting I had misgivings. After a while, like anything else that is practised, it became quite natural to be prowling around in the blackness of night but, undoubtedly, it called for terrific concentration, and proved quite a strain on the eyes.

Night flying was operated between dusk and dawn. If we were lucky we would be on a shift that started about 9.00 to 10.00 p.m. and finished up about 1.00 to 2.00 a.m., usually about a four-hour period.

A truck took us around the perimeter of the flying field until the appropriate take-off runway was reached. Here we jumped off, dragging our parachutes after us (parachutes were always carried on training flights, until we had earned our wings and were posted to an operational squadron, then they became a thing of the past). The field was always in darkness except for the dimly glowing lamps that marked the flare path and the various red and green guiding lights scattered around the field. The only noise came from the generator truck supplying the lighting, and of course the rumbling engines of the tugs, waiting to take us up into the black night skies.

We sat around a while chatting together until the officer in charge of night flying came up and assigned us off in pairs, as pilots and co-pilots. In due course we found ourselves climbing up into one of the grotesque-looking Hotspur gliders crouching in the shadows while a ground crew man fumbled around on a pre-flight check. Inside the cockpit, the only light was the greenish glow given off by the instruments on the dashboard.

A check on the controls, including the landing light, and we were then ready for our flight. Out on the runway, one of the Master aircraft impatiently rumbled away. A towing tractor hooked up to our fuselage and, with a winking torchlight to bid us on our way, we were towed slowly forward onto the runway behind the tug.

The towing rope was securely locked. The pale face of one of the ground crew came close to the perspex cockpit cover seeking the OK, which we gave. He in turn relayed this to the control caravan parked on one side of the runway at the take-off end. Seconds later, a green light flashed from the direction of the caravan. Out in front, the tug pilot opened up his throttle gently at first until the rope slack was taken up. A slight jerk and we rolled forward a few feet. Then the tug surged forward as the pilot opened up the throttle fully. A thunderous roar filled the air and we accelerated swiftly forward and away.

On either side, the long lines of lights marking the flarepath began to move past. Directly in front, the three lights marking the two wingtips and tail of the tug bounced and swayed. With swift rudder and stick movements, I tried to keep in a direct line behind the tug, and also keep our own wings level. Faster and faster the lights of the runway flashed by. The gentle swish of the airflow turned into a deep drumming. The controls suddenly became light but firm, full of response. We felt a surging lift, and the stick was eased back just enough to bring the glider about five feet off the ground. There I held it level until the tug in front became airborne also, when we would follow it steadily upward, always keeping slightly above the turbulent slipstream from the whirling blades of the propeller of the Master tug.

Our eyes continually flickered from the instrument panel to the swiftly shifting guiding lights of the towing plane and then back again. The airspeed mounted up. From the 65 mph registered when we eased off the ground, the airspeed needle crept up to 80 and then 90 mph when the tug became airborne also, and then a steady climb ensued.

Below our nose, the end of the flarepath slid away behind and we rose up into the blackness of the night sky. Only occasional lights from neglectful cottage and farm owners broke the vast blanket of darkness that spread out below. When the moon came up, however, various features of the landscape stood out, such as concrete roads and light cultivated fields against the shadowy masses of woods and blacked-out towns.

A normal daytime circuit was carried out. From the first left turn onwards the aerodrome was always in sight, unless there was a ground mist. As we banked around, the sparkling flarepath, some 1000 to 1500 feet below, tilted and changed shape. The rough shape of the aerodrome could be picked out by the red lights that shone from the roofs of hangars and other buildings that lay scattered around its perimeter. On the downwind leg a long steady green light beamed up towards us, indicating that it was in order for us to release and come in to land when we were ready.

The atmosphere inside the cockpit became a little tense, for this was the moment that called for excellent timing and concentration. In daytime, where the whole landscape was visible and height and distance judgment was easy, there was little cause for doubt. But at night, when it was practically impossible to judge distance accurately, it was a different story.

When by our calculations the appropriate spot was reached, the release lever was snapped back and we settled down into free flight. The three lights of the tug in front keeled away and disappeared below on our left.

The next few minutes called for a one hundred percent coordination of hands and eyes. The sky had to be scanned for other aircraft, the altimeter had to be watched (for dwindling height was precious to us) and, last but not least, the airspeed indicator had to be closely monitored. On top of this, the situation of the flare path, moving slowly by, had to be under our eyes all the time, except for the split seconds when the instruments were scanned. One or two guiding lights set outside of the flying field helped us in our calculations, for we knew that we had to be over these lights at certain heights to be gliding on a correct approach. The crosswind leg turn at about 800 feet was past, and directly 90 degrees to our left lay the edge of the field into which we would have to turn during the next few seconds.

Now was the time. The runway end was just in front on our left. Stick over to the left, and forward slightly, airspeed 70 in the turn. Straightening out now, with the flare path directly ahead. Apply flap, airspeed 65-mph. The glide-path indicating light registers green, telling us that we are OK. The red light atop the control caravan comes up on our left. The first two lights of the flare path are just ahead while directly in front the rest of the flare path stretches away over the darkened field.

Stick back. The sighing of the slipstream dies away. The flare path lights slide past on either side. The Hotspur drops, a gentle bump, one more little bump and we rumble over the grass, safely down. As speed slows down, we swing off the runway to one side, there to await the tractor which will tow us back to the starting line once more.

And so the course continued, and then the great day arrived when we sat for our examinations on the ground in those subjects we had been studying along with the flying side of our course. Earlier on, we had each been tested by the Chief Flying Instructor on our flying abilities, and as each time the instructor on landing breathed an 'OK', the pupil knew his trials were over and would make haste to catch the bus into Cheltenham to celebrate.

Once more we passed through the portals of Tilshead, but this time we were not so depressed, for we knew that we would be going on another two weeks' leave after we had attended our 'Wings Parade', a parade at which we would be given our wings and would listen to a complimentary speech by the Commander Glider Pilot Regiment. Not that our training was finished yet. After our leave we would have to report to an advanced flying training school where we would learn to handle the operational Horsa, and in due course be posted to an operational squadron.

The Wings Parade was a proud moment for us all. In true military style we were paraded hours before the officiating officer arrived, which left us hot and sweating in our carefully pressed uniforms. However, to make up for this long wait, our OC got us away in trucks in rapid time after the parade was over, and in less than one hour after the last pair of wings had been pinned on the last proud qualified pilot's chest, we were at Lavington Station, boarding the London-bound train. Many pairs of wings were sewn securely onto jackets even as the train bore us homeward.

The two weeks' leave passed, and soon we were rapidly approaching Salisbury once more where we would board a bus, not for Tilshead this time, but for a new camp that had been especially prepared. We knew it was only a transit camp as far as we were concerned, for I, with many another pilot, was due for more flying at an early date.

A few days later, early in November, I found myself among fifty men who clambered up over the tailboard of a lorry that would be taking us to the station at Salisbury on the first part of our journey to our next flying school at Brize Norton aerodrome, about fourteen miles outside Oxford.

At Brize Norton, our principal task was to fly Horsa gliders. Until now, our efforts had been somewhat confined to flying comparatively small aircraft and gliders. The Horsa was classed as a large flying machine, and could not be thrown around like the machines we had been flying up until then.

From a pilot's point of view, Brize Norton was an excellent aerodrome. The surface was very good, and the area covered by it was more than ample for our purpose.

From the moment I saw the Horsa, I knew that I would always be happy to fly it. My first sight of the interior only served to strengthen my original impression. There was ample room in the cockpit, where the pilot and co-pilot could sit side by side. The all-round view from the cockpit was excellent. The controls felt smooth and firm and the whole set-up gave me a feeling of confidence.

In flight, most of the Horsas I flew handled as well as they looked. Trimming could be adjusted to give the maximum comfort in flying, except on one or two whose controls would never be good, no matter how hard the ground crew worked on them.

The course called for a certain number of hours of flying by day and by night and followed much the same pattern as that carried out on the Hotspurs, except that no dive approaches were included in the syllabus. For tugs we had the ancient Armstrong Whitleys, twin-engined aircraft, which refused to tow our gliders at more than 120 mph except in exceptional circumstances. A lightly loaded glider was not much of a problem to them, but a fully laden Horsa was almost more than they could manage. However, they were steady aircraft, and ideal for the job of training. They were also used extensively in the training drops of paratroopers.

The Horsa glider was fitted with a tricycle undercarriage, which I found a most desirable feature. The two main landing wheels were jettisoned, but the nose wheel was a permanent fixture. The original idea was that the glider pilot jettisoned the undercarriage when coming in to land on enemy territory, with the theory that the drag of the fuselage (on fixed skids) on the ground would slow up the glider considerably.

This idea was not practicable for large operations with gliders landing by the score, almost at the same time, and perhaps on the same field. Where possibly two or three gliders were to be used on a special operation by themselves, the undercarriage dropping idea would be reasonably feasible. But when large numbers of gliders were to land in the same field, the problem arose that the landing gliders coming in might misjudge the approach, land short and thus block up the landing run for the rest of the gliders following in.

By retaining the undercarriage and wheels, any pilot who found himself landing short could avoid using the brakes and let the glider run up the field, or turn off sideways under its own impetus, and only apply brakes when he estimated that he was no longer blocking the approach for the remaining gliders. This was the method proved essential during mass landings in large-scale operations during the war.

We completed the Heavy Conversion Course shortly before the end of the year, and early 1943 found us moving around from aerodrome to aerodrome, doing odd bits of flying here and there. Flying was very restricted, however, as most of the gliders and tugs were being used on the very aerodromes we had left, where more and more glider pilots were being trained.

Chapter 3

North Africa

We were lounging around on Chilbolton aerodrome near Andover, Hants, one day in February 1943, doing nothing but watching a squadron of Hurricanes which had arrived the day after we had, a week ago, and had taken over all flying on the field on an exercise, when a message arrived that set us all agog. We were to be given two weeks embarkation leave immediately, after which we would proceed overseas to an unspecified destination. One minute we had been lazing on the grass, gazing up into the blue cloudless sky and cursing the presence of the Hurricanes; the next, everybody was on their feet, with an excitement on their faces that had been missing for many months. At last something was happening.

Feverish packing took place the next day, followed by a quick visit back to Fargo, our recently allotted camp near Amesbury in Wiltshire, well inside the Salisbury Plain belt.

The two week embarkation leave soon passed and it was with mixed feelings that I boarded the train at the Waterloo rail terminus in London that would whisk me away to Salisbury in Wiltshire and finally back at Fargo. Arriving at Fargo in the dark did not help to disperse my feelings. In one way I was elated, in another sad. There was no way of telling how long this spell of overseas service would last; just as long as the war, I felt, and that might be years and years.

In true Army fashion, we were paraded in the early hours of the morning the day we left Fargo. It was about 3.00 a.m. I believe, and we were taken in trucks in great secrecy to a branch line that was not normally used. Here, after an hours' wait, we boarded a darkened train that came hissing into the siding where we sat around shivering in the cold night air.

Daylight found us well on the way north. We had heard the port of Greenock mentioned, which is where we finally slid to a halt the following afternoon. No time was lost. We detrained, marched across a pier onto a small tug-cum-transport boat which left a few minutes later, heading out towards one of many large ships that were moored in and around the harbour. As we transferred to one of the huge towering boats, I caught the name 'Boissevain' in small letters up on the bow. She turned out to be a Dutch passenger/cargo vessel, and it was not long before she had been firmly condemned by all who traveled on our trip as the 'Hell Ship'.

Men were crammed into every possible corner. By night we almost stifled in the sweat-laden air that hung like an invisible blanket over the interior of the ship. The food, when we eventually got it, was not bad, but invariably cold by the time a place had been found in the mess room to eat it. Life on board was one continual lining up for food. Almost as soon as breakfast was finished, it was time to join the long snaking queue that was already forming for the midday meal.

The trip was uneventful, except for a scourge of stomach trouble that ran amok among us all. This was apart from seasickness, which hardly affected me but for nasty headaches at times.

Almost the whole of every day was spent on deck in order to recover from nights in the fetid sealed innards of the heaving ship. The convoy, spread out in all directions as far as the distant horizon, was an impressive sight. On the outskirts, ahead of the moving mass of ships, the greyhound-like destroyers darted hither and thither like hunting hounds hot on the trail.

On the sixth night out, a red glow showed intermittently in the sky ahead of us. Hours later, the glow began to appear as a flashing light. Gibraltar lay ahead. It was in the early hours of the morning that we actually passed through the Straits, and the spreading dawn some time later found us moving over the calm waters of the Mediterranean Sea. For a day and night longer, we continued on an easterly course, always carrying out the prescribed zigzagging hour after hour, a necessary precaution for almost every mile of the journey from England to our still unknown destination.

Enemy U-boats lurked everywhere from the far North Atlantic down through to the South Atlantic and also in the Mediterranean, ever watchful for any unwary merchantman forced by unforeseen circumstances to lag behind the convoys.

During the first day of our entering the Mediterranean, we received official confirmation of the rumours that we had already heard to the effect that we were bound for Oran in Algeria, French North Africa. I was jubilant, for I had always yearned to see that part of the world, and here I was less than 24 hours sailing from it. Actually, I would have preferred to go further along the African coast to the Middle East, but the Near East also had its mystery and I was happy—that is— as happy as a soldier can be heading for a strange country with a very uncertain future.

In North Africa, the battle with the Afrika Corps was still raging, but it was nearing its end. The British Eighth Army was up against the line at Enfidaville at the foot of the mountains some sixty miles from Tunis, while in the British Army area and the American area troops were nearer still to Tunis.

From the moment I heard that Oran was our destination, I felt certain we were due for an operation taking part in the final battle, culminating in the defeat of the Axis Forces in North Africa. I had visions of an airborne landing on the outskirts of Tunis with our men joining in the last battle in Tunisia and, being ignorant of all the horror and destruction of action, I was excited. Later, this enthusiasm was to be considerably dampened after my first operation in Sicily.

That day, the decks became crowded and remained so until far into the night for, late in the afternoon, we caught our first glimpse of the coast of Morocco. The mountainous coastline, looking magnificent against the blue of the Mediterranean, fulfilled all my dreams that I had ever had of North Africa. The multi-coloured cliffs rose for thousands of feet in some parts, and the peaks disappeared inland in a seemingly never-ending chain. Fluffy snow-white balls of cumulus clouds hung around some of the higher peaks, adding to the glory of the already breathtaking sight.

As evening closed in, with a sky such as only North Africa can produce, we swung around in a gentle curve and headed into the harbour of a tiny port called Mors el Kabir just outside the main port of Oran. Against the background of the rising mountains, the city of Oran reflected many colours in the evening sunlight, but white predominated. From far out in the bay, Oran presented an alluring sight but we were to learn too well that the clean white-walled houses that nestled so beautifully against the darker hills, in many cases, hid a filth and smell that was almost unbelievable. The houses funnelled up for hundreds of feet, following the road out over the towering hills behind. Great modern buildings, architecturally graceful in their own right, were to be seen in profusion. Yes, in many ways Oran was a great city.

As we edged further still into the bay, we passed the sunken rusting hulks of the once proud fighting ships of the French Navy. This was the outcome of the great battle that had taken place between the British and French ships after the downfall of France, when the French fleet was in the balance between becoming the property of Germany under the Vichy Government or of allying itself with the British and American fleets.

As dusk fell, the city on the hills took on another miraculous look. Twinkling lights began to appear until, when the full cloak of night had fallen, Oran was a blazing mass of lights. Under ordinary circumstances this would have meant nothing to us, but having been so accustomed to the rigid, total black-out enforced everywhere in England during the past three years, the brilliantly lit city of Oran looked almost incredible. In a peculiar way, this sight evoked in everyone without exception a jubilation such as is witnessed only on very rare occasions among Army men.

None of us really went to bed that night. At 3.00 a.m. we were to commence disembarking, and the lights of Oran held us in their fascinating spell until well after midnight. There was little sense in bedding down for a matter of an hour or two. Furthermore, even at the early morning hour it was, a feeling of alertness that pervaded us all.

The only real glimpse of Oran we got was from the back of a speeding truck that took us out of the docks, through the main street and up the winding hill on the road to Mascara, some sixty miles inland. It was an invigorating ride, sometimes dangerous, as we plunged down mountain roads that skirted great black bottomless-looking gulches and swung violently around hairpin bends, the cold night air rushing by, numbing us almost to the bone. The early morning mists were still swirling around when we finally turned into what had been originally intended to be a German POW camp, but which was now to be our home for an undetermined period.

Our camp was among the bleak hills that form the Atlas Mountains. The nearest place of habitation was a village named Tizi, which lay about seven miles out from the town of Mascara, which was visible from Tizi across the narrow plain that cut between two ranges of hills. We arrived at the time of the heavy seasonal rains, and again and again we were washed out of our tents while the rain slashed down from the dark scudding clouds that raced across the night sky. In the mornings, after the mists had evaporated and the sun had burst through, the quagmires left by the torrential rains of the night before would dry up in an hour or so, taking away with them the miserable memories of the night before.

There was no such thing as a glider to be found when we first arrived in Africa. Six months before, the Allies had invaded this very same coast and since then all their efforts had been put into pouring all the aircraft they could into North Africa. But the planes they needed were fighters and bombers, not gliders, and undoubtedly the fact that we were an unknown quantity at that time put us at the bottom of any priority list.

However, we were not idle, and many hours were spent each day on route marches across the mountains and on tactical exercises and physical training until the sweat ran down our bodies in streams and all muscles ached from strenuous exertions.

Many of us were chafing at the bit. Just over the border in Tunisia, fighting was still raging. The Afrika Corps was fighting desperately to stave off the flood of Allied troops that beat upon them from all sides. Here we were at Tizi fooling around at war while only a few hours flying distance away a real war was being fought out in earnest. The battle did not last long, however, for the German and Italian troops were rapidly crumbling before the Allied assault, and May 13th found the remnants of the Afrika Corps surrendering out on the Cap Bon peninsular. The war in Africa was over.

For a while I wondered why we were out here. It seemed to me that we had missed the boat. A stagnancy set in. Every night found the camp empty, except for those on duty, while the village of Tizi, and especially the town of Mascara, echoed with the singing of our men while the North African wines flowed freely in the estaminets. Mascara offered small variety of entertainment and most of it was of a very dubious character. Any sane-minded person thought twice about taking advantage of some of the charms Mascara had to offer.

Transport was nonexistent when we first landed and we had to rely on the generosity of the American drivers, which was invariably forthcoming. Inevitably the road from Mascara and Tizi was dotted with lurching and swaying figures endeavouring to find the route back through the darkness, hampered by drink-befuddled brains, not that every person ended up that way. While a goodly number took their entertainment in moderation, there was an increasing tendency for even the levelheaded to slip off the straight and narrow more and more often.

Then one day, word came through that a number of WACO gliders had been landed at Oran in crates. Furthermore, there was no one with them except for a few technicians. Apparently, no provision had been made for men to be there to assemble them. However, our CO Col G. Chatterton was not to be outdone. In his words, 'If there is no one there to build them, we'll do it ourselves'. And his orders were carried out. A detachment was sent to an airfield outside Oran and within a short time these men, who had never assembled a glider before in their lives, had turned out the first glider complete and ready for air test and, what is more, it actually flew.

Back at Tizi, an airstrip was built and we moved our camp alongside it on the far side of the road. A few days later, the first C47 arrived over the camp, towing a

WACO glider. Great excitement pervaded us all; at last we were coming into our own. Critical eyes watched the glider come in to land. If that glider pilot had cracked up the WACO, I am sure he would have been torn limb from limb by his colleagues on the ground watching him land. The glider itself caused great excitement and it was carefully examined by all after it had been towed back to a dispersal point.

The WACO was an entirely new machine to us. Opinion varied, but on the whole we were satisfied with its appearance and by the report on its flying characteristics, as given to us by the pilots who had flown the glider in from Algeria's Maison Blanc airfield.

The gliders began arriving in increasing numbers and soon we were running through a planned programme. It was great to be flying again, and the mountainous and somewhat harsh landscape (except where cultivation had been put into effect) opened a new vista before us.

In June, a number of glider pilots, including myself, were dispatched to another aerodrome about a hundred miles away named Relizane. We found Relizane much to our liking. Not only was it a one-time French field, with permanent buildings for living quarters (the first since arriving in North Africa), but it was also within two miles of the town of Relizane, which, as far as French North African towns go, was quite acceptable.

As in the Mascara area, we were still under American Forces here. The British 1st Army was some hundreds of miles further east towards Tunisia.

The food, as always in American areas, was excellent. Plenty of transport was available and a solid friendship sprang up between the USAF men and ourselves although, most of the time the glider pilots went about in their own little cliques.

Flying training continued. By now, we were very familiar with the WACO glider and had mastered the technique of flying her under all circumstances, although I must say that we never did, in my opinion, undergo sufficient operational training including mass landings by day and night. We did carry out a very limited number of mass landings by day with a fair degree of success, but not once did we carry out a night landing exercise with more than two gliders. This undoubtedly contributed to the failure of the Sicilian landings, which were carried out by night. When I say failure, I do not wish to give the impression that the whole operation failed. In point of fact, the main objective was captured, held for the required number of hours, and several more. Although eventually lost to the enemy, it left him too little time to destroy it before the Eighth Army, coming overland, re-took it after having been held up for several hours longer than had been anticipated. However, from the point of the actual landing of the gliders in their specified positions, it was a failure.

Training flying, however, was considerably restricted by the small number of gliders and towing aircraft available. Programmes were drawn up that allowed only half a days flying per crew, and even less than that by night. We also helped in the maintenance of the gliders, as the ground crew were too few to give the gliders the 100% maintenance they required.

As I have said before, the Glider Pilot Regiment was hardly yet recognised by the War Office, being an entirely new unit, as yet untried in battle, and no doubt they looked upon us as something that had been forced upon them, and had to be put up with. They were fully occupied with supplying, maintaining and operating land armies that had been tried and proved in battle, especially at this time when the whole of North Africa had just been rid of the German Afrika Corps. Furthermore, fresh from the flush of this victory, they were deeply engaged in planning the next stab at the enemy over the Mediterranean.

British ground crews were nonexistent on Relizane aerodrome, as it was an American flying field, and the American Air force had allotted only the usual ground crews to service the towing planes, plus one or two men for the gliders, a totally inadequate force for the task.

While one half of the pilots flew during the day, the other half were more or less free. We had a first rate OC leading our squadron; he was a man who called upon us to put our backs into a job while it lasted but; when there was nothing further to do, he went out of his way to assist us in every way to make our spare time pleasant.

Captain Boyd, otherwise known as 'Blubberhead', did his best to relieve the boredom that was likely to set in when a whole day or more went by without flying. He could have given us numerous petty tasks to do, but Captain Boyd, with clear understanding of the position we were in, went about things in the right way. Every afternoon at about 2.00 p.m., a truck would be ready to take all those not on duty to the lovely beaches at Mostaganem, about sixty-five miles away, fringing the deep blue Mediterranean Sea. The weather in June was exceptionally hot, and the men appreciated Capt. B's thoughtfulness.

The long dusty ride in the back of a 2-1/2 ton truck was amply repaid by the long hours spent sprawled out by the tepid waters of the Mediterranean on the golden-white sands of a perfect little bay, set aside especially for the military about a mile outside of the town. Here we could gorge on grapes and nuts sold by the bare-footed Arab boys who flitted up and down the stretch of sands naming what they had for sale in their quaint English, picked up from the troops. They also offered other means of entertainment which they could lead us to in the town if we were so disposed to take advantage. A few did, but most of us preferred to bask on the sands under the scorching rays of the North African sun and listen to the music of the lapping waves, or fling ourselves around with careless abandon in the beckoning waters, gleaming with myriad reflections from the sun that darkened our bodies day by day to a deep brown, which gave us a feeling of being fitter thanwe had ever been before in our lives.

A snack in the Red Cross building, set up by some pleasant American women with the aid of some local French girls, would be followed by the long ride home, usually at the hands of a driver who was known by the name 'The Madman', due to the fact that we always considered it a miracle that we arrived back at the camp in one piece. Up hill and down dale, 'The Madman' hurtled, with his foot forever hard pressed down on the accelerator, through slumbering white-walled, French-Arab villages with a roar that would bring out the wildly waving half-naked children, their screams for 'gum' and 'cigarettes' lost in the swirl of dust and the deafening shriek of the wind. Down the shady poplar-lined roads leading out of the villages, swinging round corners with the thought that the truck must roll over this time forever present in our heads, and then the eventual relief as we swung in through the airfield gates, sliding to a halt with a jerk—the 'Madman' had completed another run safely. Only once was he involved in a slight collision, which was amazing, considering the number of narrow shaves we experienced each time.

Owing to the forced pace of the training with inadequate equipment, we had a few tragedies. One towing plane hit a nearby mountain during night flying, burst into flames and exploded. We saw the mass of flames and, even from where we were five miles away, we could make out the intensity of the fire which seemed to roll down the mountainside like a blazing river. We lost two crews of gliders also during training in the Relizane area, both during night flying.

Towards the end of June, we had a sudden order to get ready to fly our gliders out of Relizane in Algeria into an area near Sousse in Tunisia, some 700 miles away over the Atlas Mountains. This, of course, caused a great deal of speculation and no little excitement for, although Algeria and Tunisia are on the same continent, they are different countries, both under French rule at that time.

It was, if I remember rightly, the end of June when we actually took off from Relizane for the last time and headed out in an easterly direction. Most of the way we would be flying over the Atlas Mountains, but nowhere enroute were we called upon to go higher than 6000 feet, unless we wandered off course.

It was still dark when we finally managed to locate our glider, but soon dawn broke and in due course we were rising from the dusty runway of the airfield and climbing steadily up to the prearranged height at which we were to fly. I was flying co-pilot to Captain Boucher-Giles. Some time before, we had agreed to team up for the rest of the time that we would be flying together in 3 Squadron. This was our first really long-distance flight together, and certainly the longest flight the Squadron had ever attempted in WACO gliders. In the fuselage of the glider we had a pile of old junk belonging to Capt. BG including an old table, boxes and piles of bags, as well as my kitbags. Perched on top of all this sat Capt. BG's batman, our only passenger.

It was a wonderful day with cloudless blue skies, but the burning heat of the sun coming through the perspex windows of our cockpit made our position almost intolerable. I wore a topee (pith helmet), hoping to protect myself from some of the heat and glare.

We discovered we had trouble from the start in the form of a failing engine on the Albemarle tug. Capt. BG and I hung on for over two hours with the Albemarle giving us a hell of a time. Its starboard motor continued to operate in an extremely uneven manner for the next two hours, causing the tug to swoop and dive from time to time in a very disturbing way. Naturally, we caught the reaction on our end of the rope, and for the last ten minutes before we cut loose, I expected the nylon rope to part with the ominous twang that informs you that it has taken all the rough usage that it intends to.

Capt. BG hit the release when we had been thrown up into a very precarious position, caused by the tug's starboard engine deciding nearly to quit, which in turn made the tug flip up, over and down to the port side. Our glider, on the end of the rope, was tossed up and over onto one side despite all my efforts to hold her straight. Then Capt. BG decided that we had better cut loose into free flight.

It was a desolate spot in which to make a forced landing. The predominant landmark that caught my eye, as we circled around looking for a clear space in which to set down, was a huge salt lake on our starboard about five miles away.

The general area was desolate—sandy scrub which stretched away southward to the Sahara Desert with no sign of habitation whatsoever. Ahead of us loomed a yet higher range of the Atlas Mountains, over which I am sure that our tug, with one of its engines failing, could never have towed us.

We set down with the loss of one side of the undercarriage, but no injuries. We had found a comparatively level stretch of ground, but it was covered with large anthills, one of which caught the starboard undercarriage and wheel, which we left behind embedded deeply in the anthill, while we slid on to come to a halt in a cloud of dust.

I thought we had landed way out in the wilds, but amazingly, a few minutes later, along came a man in the uniform of a French soldier. Apparently, away over a rise some little distance behind us was situated a POW camp with very few prisoners, which accounts for the fact that we did not see it from the air.

We were informed that five miles away was a road that would take us into the nearest village that was another ten miles along the road and went under the name of M'sila. It was mainly an Arab village, but a few French officials also lived there.

Our French soldier led us over a hillock and down into the POW camp, where we were introduced to the Commandant and the rest of the Frenchmen there. They were very excited over our arrival, while the German prisoners stared at us in stolid silence. We spoke to one or two of them, but the Frenchmen did not seem too keen on this.

The OC had a car and BG arranged to go into M'sila, where he could use a phone to get onto the nearest RAF aerodrome that the Camp CO informed us was more than 100 miles away over the Atlas Mountains. Their car disappeared down the road in a cloud of dust and I was left to the mercy of a very voluble French NCO who knew but little English. I made friends with him for life by giving him two bars of Lux toilet soap. Apparently good soap was nonexistent in this part of the country.

Living up to the usual hospitality of the French, the NCO first sent out an Arab soldier to mount guard over our glider and then produced a row of bottles. That sign needed no translation and within a comparatively short time several empty bottles were littering the floor of the building we were sitting in, while with me life began to look very rosy.

BG arrived back to spoil the fun and actually had the nerve to suggest that I had been drinking heavily. As a matter of fact, at that time, I did not mind what anybody said, and was willing to agree with whatever they cared to say.

BG had not arrived back alone for, on emerging from the building in which I had been having such a pleasant time, I found several cars drawn up in addition to that of the Camp Commandant. An odd assortment of people met my gaze. About three children were playing around one of the cars, while a group of women and men stood around chatting among themselves. I learned from BG that most of the officials from M'sila had come over, bringing their wives and children, to see our glider.

We took them over the rise to where our WACO lay, one wing low, among the anthills. We did not allow anyone inside, but everyone took good stock of the glider from the outside and asked many questions, some of which we answered and some we didn't.

It was around about this time that I noticed that one of the women, the prettiest among them, was continually looking in my direction, and it wasn't the drink making me think that. I immediately lost interest in answering questions about the glider and transferred my attention elsewhere.

The party broke up and BG and I were driven back into M'sila by the Camp Commandant. There we were taken to the local inn and put up. Most of the village consisted of mud-walled buildings inhabited by the Arabs, but there were a few French Colonial houses scattered throughout, mostly at one end. The whole village turned out with the Arabs running alongside our car clamouring for everything from soap to chewing gum; it was evident that at some time previous, British or American troops had been through the village.

The inn turned out to be a very clean place, quite well furnished. We were given a room that really belonged to a French officer, who at that time was away someplace. BG and I intended to share the only bed, but the batman would have to sleep on the floor.

After a thorough wash down, we were informed that a meal awaited us. Such a meal I had not tasted for many a month consisting of things that I thought never existed in North Africa. We were served the meal outside in the courtyard that was overlooked on all four sides by balconies and rooms of the inn. During the meal, I became conscious of somebody staring down at us, and quickly glancing around and up, I caught a glimpse of the pretty woman again.

Up until now I had felt rather sore at our mishap, but now I wasn't so sure. The future didn't look so bleak after all. More than once I looked up at the balcony to receive a warm smile from the same spot, and began to wonder whether BG would be bothered with two of us sleeping in the bed that night.

After the delicious meal, we went back into our room to unpack our bags. BG was surprised at the effort I put into polishing my boots, a habit he had never noticed before.

It was late afternoon now and I was chafing at the bit while BG dozed on the bed. Then suddenly from outside came the noise of an Army truck pulling up. I crossed to the door just in time to see an RAF driver climb down from his truck and who, on seeing me said, 'I suppose you are one of the pilots I have come to pick up?,' while eyeing my Army wings strangely, for they were unknown in his parts. I could have killed him quite cheerfully, but instead said, 'You had better come in and see Capt. BG; he may not want to be leaving tonight.'

Within me I knew that BG would welcome the opportunity of driving on to an RAF 'drome, but with all due respects to him, he wasn't as young as I was, and furthermore he was married.

Just as I feared, BG was ready to start off immediately and within half an hour we were standing beside the truck saying goodbye to mine host and some French officials. The women were conspicuous by their absence and, with a frustrated feeling within me, we started up and drove off up through the dusty village to the usual accompaniment of 'chewing gum' and 'cigarettes' and outstretched filthy children's hands.

Another RAF truck had arrived with several ground crew to dismantle the glider just before we left and I left them in the hands of the French officials who promised to take them out to our damaged machine. The carcass of our glider, with wings and tail removed, would be towed through the village and out over the mountains to the airfield near Setif, to which we ourselves were going.

With my proposed amorous adventure killed before it had even started, I resigned myself to the long arduous trip over the mountains that stretched away ahead of us, barring any direct route to the town of Setif, wherein lay the airfield for which we were bound. The rugged beauty of the trip soon made me forget my evening of pleasure that had been nipped in the bud, and I gazed fascinated at the breathtaking landscape unreeling before my eyes. Some hours later, as the shadows of evening were well advanced, we rolled in through the airfield entrance and a short while later I was ensconced in comfortable quarters, with an RAF corporal running to and fro for me with an enthusiasm that I had never seen before with the RAF.

BG caught a plane back to Mascara that same night, and I was left alone. A whole week went by before I heard or saw anything to do with the Glider Pilot Regiment. Then one day, after I was really feeling fed up with nothing to do, several of my colleagues turned up in a jeep and a small truck on which was piled a motor cycle. I had arranged to go out into the town of Setif (as I had each day for the past week) with some RAF air crew fellows to see what sort of wine they brewed in this neighbourhood, but the coming of the trucks made me forget that. Nice as the rest had been, I was longing to be among my own friends again.

It took us nearly a week to reach the Sousse area by road. It was a wonderful journey that took us over some of the highest peaks. Always, we were among the mountains, until at last we came down out of Algeria onto the plains that stretched towards Tunis. On the way, we passed the towns of Guelma, and Constantine with its beautiful bridge spanning the gorge that links the city with the road eastward. Through the Cork Forest that hugged the hills for scores of miles, up long twisting climbs, with hairpin bends that hung over drops that vanished hundreds of feet down. Sometimes the rolling peaks were bare and harsh looking, at other times they were covered with a thick verdant green mass of trees that filled every gully and niche.

The highest peaks were tinged with snow although we ourselves, following the main road, never passed through any, but away on either side, the brown summits would be flecked with white. A thousand times I cursed myself for not having a camera as some breathtaking sight would unfurl itself before us as we breasted a long climb and poised for a moment before falling into the downward sweep that would end in another long twisting rise ahead.

On through Souk-Ahras, until the last swoop brought us down onto the plain that led towards Beja. I had been riding the motorcycle the day we passed through the last of the mountains and it was late afternoon as we began to speed along the level plain on the last lap to Tunis. I had not ridden more than a mile along the road before I hit a very unevenly filled-in shell hole. Before I knew it, I was hurled through the air to end up skating along the loose surfaced road on my hands and thigh.

That evening found me sitting disconsolately in the seat next to the jeep driver with both hands heavily bandaged and a burning pain in my thigh, where no little skin had been burned off sliding along the road. My hands were both raw along one side, but I knew that within a week or two I would be fit and well again for flying. Little did I know it, but I was due to be flying in less than one week, and furthermore it would be on an operation.

We spent half a day in Tunis and then hurried off on our last lap to the airfield camp outside Sousse, about 70 miles further on. I was looking forward to arriving at the camp, for my hands and leg did not feel too good, and there I thought I would get good attention and a rest. I was due for a shock however, for the camp had had its trouble also, against which mine was to appear but a pinprick

Late in the afternoon, we swung down the hill that leads into Sousse. Sousse had suffered at the hands of the Allied bombers during the recent campaign and, down by the station, the crossroads were an uneven mass of pocked earth where bombs had ripped the road apart.

We climbed up out through the town to the summit of the hill whereon stands the old Arab Casbah. Below and behind I caught a last glimpse of the blue Mediterranean before we coasted down the slope that led inland towards the distant Holy City of Kairouan. Hot waves of air swept up from the scorched roadway, almost stifling us, as we roared along in the jeep, past the huddled cluttering of Arab mud buildings and cactus lined roads, past groves of neatly set out olive trees that were to become a familiar sight for us for some months ahead. We continued over a bridge, alongside which lay an overturned tank, its tracks pointing skyward, a relic of the battles that had been fought here a short while ago.

We came to a village where the road forked. We called out to an MP (Military Policeman) standing nearby, who informed us that the place was called M'saken and was entirely Arab, with the usual board indicating that there was a danger of typhus in the village and warning soldiers not to linger.

We asked the MP if he knew of our regiment being in the neighbourhood but he replied that he did not know of any such unit. We drove out onto the open road that leads down to the famous Roman amphitheatre of El Djem. For miles, we drove swiftly along the burnished highway over a desolate stretch, with barren undulating ground falling away on each side. We breasted a rise and there ahead of us, still some ten miles away, rose the colossal structure of the amphitheatre. The road led straight as a die towards El Djem, following the course of the ancient Roman highway.

Fifteen minutes later we were threading our way into the dirty looking Arab village that hugs the base of the amphitheatre. The Arabs swarmed out with their usual cries for baksheesh, but we had little to spare after our long journey.

We passed through the village without having seen anyone in uniform. On the far outskirts we stopped to hold a conference. Just at that moment, an Army truck hove into view and, hailing it, we managed to obtain the information from the driver that he had seen some of our men camped out on the road between M'saken and Kairouan. We heaped dire curses on the head of the MP in M'saken who had sent us down the wrong road and hurriedly returned through El Djem to retrace our way back to M'saken.

As we approached the village some time later, we noticed a rising column of black smoke billowing up into the blue late afternoon sky, and I remarked to my friend alongside that it must be some fire. In the centre of M'saken we found an MP on duty, but not our old friend who had misdirected us. He barred the way to the road that led to Kairouan and told us that we could not go through as there had been a bad explosion a few miles down the road where an ammunition dump had blown up. We explained our position and said it was imperative that we joined our Squadron without further delay. He let us through.

We drove swiftly along the undulating road bordered by verdant groves of olive trees. Suddenly I had a premonition. I felt sure that the explosion must be connected with our camp somehow.

The cloud of smoke was drifting by over our heads and an acrid stench filled our nostrils—the smell of cordite and other explosives. We slowed down as we approached the densest area and suddenly, on our left, caught a glimpse of some tents, among the tents moved men with the familiar red berets. We had found our squadron. Driving off the road, we followed a sandy, dusty track that led towards the tents.

The explosion must have been near, I could see. Odd shell and mortar cases began to litter the ground ahead of us. We came up to a group of men among whom I recognised a lieutenant. He saw us at the same time and let out a cry of welcome. Hurrying over to meet him, we were greeted warmly. I asked what had happened, for the men were walking around as though in a daze.

'Oh,' he replied, 'our reserve ammunition dump blew up half an hour ago and destroyed nearly all our camp. Well, make yourselves at home under one of the trees', he continued, and dashed off to carry on with the work of salvage.

We left the jeep and wandered into the nearby olive grove where our camp had been pitched. A scene of desolation met our gaze. Smouldering pieces of what had been tents lay at the feet of the trees in the shallow irrigation ditches. Burned and blackened bits of equipment lay everywhere, including twisted remnants of rifles and Sten guns. Scorched and burnt paper lying in piles indicated where the Squadron Office had once been. The stench of explosives filled the air, while the ground around was littered in a profusion of unexploded shells, grenades and mortar bombs, intermingled with twisted pieces of ammunition boxes. The olive trees themselves in many instances were blackened stumps.

Truly the squadron area had been blasted. Most of the men did not seem to know what was happening and the grove was filled with bent and slowly moving forms trying to gather what little they could find of their personal belongings.

I learned that there had been two explosions, the second following closely on the heels of the first, blasting skywards in a terrific concussion of smoke and thunder and raining earthwards seconds later, scattering destruction for hundreds of yards around. It had come like the first clap of a thunderstorm to the men. Some had flung themselves flat as the blast tore its way through the lines of trees followed by the rain of unexploded missiles, while others had fled far from the grove and did not return until long after the last of the minor explosions had died away.

By a miracle, no-one had been killed although several were hurt and at least one man was temporarily blinded for several weeks by the initial blast that had swept through the grove.

Whether it was an accident or sabotage no one knew, but it was strange that it should have occurred just at the time that our first operation was being planned, as I was to learn later on that evening.

That night I slept under one of the remaining olive trees, with a blanket wrapped around me, and the starry African sky for a roof.

Operation Ladbroke

Operation Ladbroke was a glider landing of British Airborne forces near Syracuse, Sicily, that began on 9 July 1943 as part of the Allied invasion of the island. This was the first Allied mission using large numbers of gliders. The operation was carried out from Tunisia by the 1st Airlanding Brigade, with a force of 136 Wacos and eight Horsas. The objective was to establish a large invasion force on the ground near the town of Syracuse, secure the Ponte Grande Bridge and take control of the city itself with its vital docks and strategic command of Mediterranean sea lanes. Ladbroke was the beginning of the full-scale invasion of Sicily known as Operation Husky, one of the largest Allied operations of WWII, in which the Allies took Sicily from the Axis Powers. Husky eventually drove Axis forces from the island, opening the sea lanes and ultimately Italian dictator Benito was toppled from power.

V Miller Ladbroke Operational details:

- Glider chalk No.110
- Glider: WACO
- Departure airfield; Airfield F, Goubrine No.2 North of M'Saken, Tunisia
- 1st Pilot: Capt Boucher-Giles
- 2nd Pilot: Sgt V. Miller

- Unit carried: 'H' Company 1st Battalion Border Regiment.
- Tug Aircraft: Albermile
- Tug Aircraft No. P1389, 38 Wing RAF
- Pilot: Squadron Leader Bartram , 296 Squadron
- Landing Zone: Field E

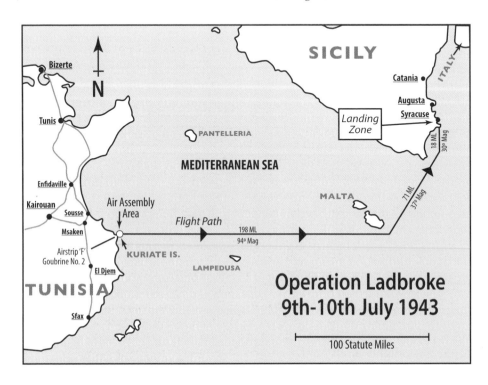

Chapter 4

Sicily

The next day, July 8th, I spent in feverish activity, including an early call on the M.O. who had to give his permission for me to be allowed to go on the operation owing to my hand being injured and still in bandages. I managed to persuade him to let me go, although he wasn't very keen on the idea as he was under the impression that I would not be able to have full control over the glider.

I sought out Capt. BG, my co-pilot and captain/First Pilot of our glider and he was very pleased to learn I would be coming along with him.

The rest of the day was spent in trying to get the right equipment, arms, rations and so forth out of the quartermaster who, owing to the explosion, was in no mood to hand out odd bits of equipment to me. However, due to the losses of material for the operation suffered by most of the men, I was only one among many continually pestering the storeman, who was almost demented before the day was half through.

I had learned the evening before that we were due to take part in an airborne operation against Sicily on the night of the 9/10th of July; now that was tomorrow. The time left to re-equip us all was fantastically little and had it not been for the imperative urgency of the situation, whereby the whole operation depended upon us glider pilots being able to fly our gliders into Sicily; the Q.M. would have turned around and said that it was impossible.

Normally, at least one week was allowed for the stores to be passed down from the Divisional dumps and in turn issued out to the men, and here we were with less than 24 hours before take-off with most of us deficient of some type of equipment, arms or ammunition.

To add to my confusion, I had missed all the detailed briefings that had been going on for the last few days. I had not seen one map or photograph of the area we were due to land in. Usually, we glider pilots were allowed to study the landing zones for hours if we wished. This would include ample information, such as enlarged oblique and vertical photographs that showed up every detail of the target areas.

I managed only once to pin Capt. BG down for about ten minutes when he explained as best he could the general plan for the landing and loaned me one of his few maps to study. He also told me that I would have a few hours to study the layout maps and photographs out on the airfield tomorrow before we took off.

In between times of collecting battle equipment (officially termed as G 1098 stores), I tried to glean more of the plan from the other pilots, some of whom were most helpful.

From what BG had told me, I learned that the operation was to be a night one and was to be carried out by what light of the moon would be available. There would be no lights at all on the ground to guide us in. The landings were timed to coincide with the altitude of the moon being between 20 and 30 degrees. This apparently would be the most favourable time. The moon would be about three quarters full and, provided no clouds came up to obscure the landscape, we had a reasonable chance of picking out our landing grounds, which were confined to fairly large fields.

The main objective for the Air-landing Brigade was the seizure of the bridge over the river and canal about a mile outside the town of Syracuse on the eastern coast of Sicily. The bridge was to be held for approximately twelve hours, if all went well, when forward seaborne units of the British Eighth Army, which was landing about twenty miles down the coast about three hours after our landing, could be expected to make contact with us on the bridge. We would join in with them to capture the town itself, after which our task would be finished.

The Quartermaster did wonders and before late afternoon we were ready and fully equipped. I myself was in a sweat with the ceaseless rushing to and fro I had had to do, and was thankful when every round, every piece of equipment and the rations were packed in their appropriate place and then I could sink down under the tree where I had made my bed the night before. Here I rested until the trucks arrived to take us out to our respective airstrips where the gliders were already marshalled for the take-off.

Long shadows from the swiftly sinking North African sun were already creeping across the scrub-filled slopes and geometrically spaced olive groves when the trucks arrived. As usual, they were an hour or so late. Now we would not arrive at the airstrips until after darkness had fallen and locating the airstrips would be no easy matter, for the crimson flecked skies already showed signs of clouding over, which would mean an almost impenetrable blackness once the sun slid over the eastern horizon to its well-earned rest. Furthermore, our drivers were not very familiar with the routes.

However, with the philosophical outlook of the soldier, we climbed up over the tailboards of the trucks, and left our fate in the hands of the drivers, and settled down for an uncomfortable ride to the airstrips. No one seemed to know how far away the strip was to which our own particular truck was headed.

In the rapidly descending twilight, our truck moved away down the dusty track, while the administrative staff waved to us, wishing us luck on our venture.

As we lurched off the track onto the metalled road, I took one last look backward at the little knot of dim figures still waving and wondered whether I would see them all again, for tomorrow would bring me under my baptism of fire and no one could foretell the future. For the first time since I had learned of the operation, I felt pangs of apprehension, but these quickly passed as we roared away down the road to our strip and the waiting gliders. The first airborne operation of the Allies was about to begin.

It took us the best part of an hour to locate our strip, for at one time our driver was hopelessly lost. Then we felt ourselves bumping over uneven ground, groping through blackness, while occasionally voices came to our ears as we slowed up by a sentry post. In the impenetrable blackness of the truck, unaided by any natural light from the outside night, I gathered that we had at last found our strip.

The driver came around and lowered the tailboard. Thankfully, we jumped to the ground, stretching our aching legs and flapping our arms to bring back into circulation the blood that seemed to have been temporarily slowed up by the cold of the African night.

Here the darkness was broken by beams of light issuing from the open flaps of tents scattered around. We were told that a hot meal was awaiting us in the mess tent and that an RAF corporal would lead us to it. We needed no second bidding and a few minutes later were gratefully gulping down the hot stew provided by the RAF cooks.

After the meal, I met BG outside and he informed me that all pilots were to sleep in their gliders that night ready for tomorrow. It took us nearly an hour to locate our glider but eventually we found it way down the end of the marshalled line. I carefully checked on the figure 110 scrawled on the nose in chalk for, once I had settled down for the night, I did not want to have some lout trampling all over me telling me I was in the wrong glider.

BG and I laid our blankets down on the floor of the WACO and within a few minutes I was fast asleep, for the day had been a tiring one.

I was awakened by someone banging on the door of the glider and calling out 'OK, fellows, seven am'. Despite the cold outside, I felt snug inside the blanket rolled around me but, hearing BG stirring, I cursed to myself and cast aside the blanket. I did not have to dress, for I had slept fully clothed except for my boots; BG had done likewise. It was still dark outside, although a faint tinge of daylight was showing on the horizon. The air was keen and cold and soon removed the sleepiness from my eyes.

Taking our mess tins, we wandered over through the half darkness to where several open air ovens were sending their flames licking out into the darkness, lighting up the surrounding area. I could see that already a goodly number of our men were milling around there with mess tins and eating irons clanking impatiently.

We sat around in the half light as near the warming effects of the stoves as we could. Our CO Col Chatterton, moved around full of bantering talk, although at that time of the morning the men's appreciation was limited. The breakfast of Vienna sausages, powdered egg and mashed potatoes tasted good, while the tea, which at any other time when we would have been in full possession of our faculties would have tasted vile, seemed to be the best we had ever had, at least it was hot, and helped to drive out the chill from our bones. The air was damp and wafted around in a thin mist-like swirl.

With the coming of daylight I had a wash and a shave and then went over with BG to check our glider. She seemed in perfect order, and stank in the usual fashion of varnish and scorched paint which the rapidly rising sun, already sending out rays of heat, did nothing to improve.

We went along to the briefing tent about 10.00 a.m. for a final brief, which was mainly concerned with the weather. It seemed as though we were fairly lucky as regards the moon; there should be no cloud to obscure our vision at the vital moment of landing. We were to release at 1300 feet about half a mile offshore, glide in over the coast to one side of a jutting headland and set down in the field allotted us.

There would be some flack from the port of Syracuse, and possibly a few night fighters. A considerable number of searchlights were in the vicinity but, our gunner of the Albemarle tug, which was due to tow us, assured us that he would shoot out any that came up in our direction. I left the briefing tent feeling very confident and excited, and a little apprehensive.

Our loads arrived in a long column of trucks and jeeps, some of which were towing six-pounder guns. I knew we had been given a load that consisted of a six-pounder gun and its crew. The towing jeep for the gun would be in another glider near which we hoped to land on the landing zone. The two could then become one unit on the ground and the anti-tank gun would be ready to be towed into action immediately.

The column of trucks drew up alongside our gliders and I went forward to meet them. On the side of each truck was scrawled a number which corresponded with the number chalked on each glider. I soon picked out the jeep with number 110 chalked on it. I shouted and waved and the driver waved back, started up and headed towards me towing a six-pounder gun behind. I introduced myself to the sergeant in charge and within a few minutes the gun was unhooked and being slowly edged in under the raised nose of the WACO glider into the interior of the fuselage, where a wave of hot stuffy air greeted the sweating men tugging at the gun.

Within half an hour we had lashed the gun down securely onto troughs that lay close along the sides of the glider, and boxes of ammunition were passed in and stowed away. I then supervised the lowering of the nose compartment, which had been swung upwards and locked in that position until the glider's load had been well and truly chained down. A swing of the locking lever and we were all set.

I wandered off back to the Officer's mess tent, where a barrel of red wine was being uncorked in honour of our departure. I was satisfied with two glasses; BG refused to take more than one. Light bantering talk flashed between the glider pilots and the tug pilots and their crews.

Outside, the African sun beat mercilessly down on the parched strip and the massed air armada. Inside the tent the air was hot and stuffy and it was a relief when we emerged from the dim light of the tent out into the bright sunlight.

The airstrip had been laid down across the barren ground that lies between M'saken and El Djem (Airstrip F - Goubrine No 2) and consisted of a combination of hard packed mud and sand runways. Whenever an aircraft took off, a column of light brown Tunisian dust would billow upwards in the wake of the speeding aircraft, blotting out the sun for yards on each side of the runway. The dust would either waft away or settle gently down on the runway only to be stirred up again by the swirling propellers of yet another plane taking off.

It was now six o'clock and we were due off at 7.00 p.m. - one hour's time. A feeling of tension was already spreading round, and I found myself constantly glancing at my watch while the minutes dragged by. At 6.30 p.m. all the loads were ordered over to the vicinity of the gliders. Then, bless the cooks and the thoughtful officer who had so ordered, a truck started driving from glider to glider with a huge urn of tea—just the thing to steady one's nerves for the rapidly approaching take-off. No other man coming round could have been more popular at that moment than the one who doled out the hot, strong, sweet, brew into our mess tins and chipped enamel cups.

Even as we sipped the steaming liquid, despite the terrific heat of the sun, a coughing roar broke out from the first tug to warm up its engines. All heads turned in the direction of the sound and everyone suddenly went quiet. I felt my heart beat a little faster. I glanced at my watch and noted the time of 6.45 p.m. Only fifteen minutes to take-off. Behind the Albemarle, whose twin engines were being revved up, a cloud of dust was swirling steadily and odd pieces of paper were whipped up in the slipstream and sent whirling away across the sparse grass-covered airfield. Fascinated, I watched the whirling blades of the propellers glinting in the sunlight. The Albemarle trembled against the chocks and brakes like a dog straining at its leash. The roar of the engines worked up to a crescendo of thunder as the pilot advanced the throttles to their limit long enough to test the magnetos, and then the deafening roar faded away until the engines were barely ticking over. Another plane took up the cacophony of sound, and yet another, until the very air vibrated with the defiant thunder of scores of motors raising their voices to the blue expanse of sky above. A swirling maelstrom of dust was everywhere.

One of the Air-landing Troops' officers was running from group to group gesticulating for them to enter the gliders. I walked swiftly over to mine and found BG already there going through a final check-up. The men were already clambering in and I counted three; they were the complete crew of the gun, which we had lashed down inside the glider.

Perspiration, which had been soaking steadily into my shirt, began to increase as I clambered in. I greeted the men who replied enthusiastically—they were raring to go—although I suspected that they were to undergo a severe mental strain, for this was the first airborne attempt on a large scale ever to be made by the British, and the degree of success could only be guessed.

BG was fumbling with his straps when I entered the cockpit and sank down into the right hand seat. The scorching rays of the sun burnt their way through the perspex windows of the cockpit and the whole interior felt like a glass house that has full heat switched on. I buckled on my safety belt, secured my Sten gun into a safe position where it would be unlikely to break loose, pulled out the one map we had been issued for the flight and studied our projected course. This would take us over the African coast between Sousse and Sfax and out over the Mediterranean Sea to Malta. We would go around the island keeping it to port, by which time it would be dark, and then almost due north until we came up to Sicily. From there we would follow the coast northwards until it was time for us to turn to port over our pre-determined release point, cut loose and glide down to our landing zone

The flight looked so short on the map, but I knew that it meant three hours or so flying time, and mostly by night. We were to fly at 300 feet altitude to avoid radar detection once we had crossed the North African coast and remain at that height until we were within a few miles of our release point. Then we would climb up to the 1300-foot mark ready for the pull-off.

As I mused over the route, I heard the first tug moving out onto the runway and glanced up. The first glider was also being moved forward towards where one of the ground crew was waiting to hitch up the towing rope to the nose of the WACO.

About two hundred feet farther up the runway, another ground crewman stood with the far end of the rope ready to hook up to the tail of the Albemarle tug.

I shot a glance at my watch. One minute to seven. We were really on the dot. The first combination would be off on the stroke of seven.

The jeep which had towed the first glider onto the runway was unhooked and turning to come swiftly back to hitch up to another glider. I watched with fascination as the ground crew plugged the rope into the top of the glider's nose. On the other end, the rope had already been snapped into place under the rear of the Albemarle's belly. A man was waving a yellow disc and the blades of the Albemarle's propellers whirled faster.

The fog of dust increased behind the tug as she slowly moved forward. The rope became taut and the WACO slid forward a few feet. The throttles were opened fully and the tug disappeared behind the wall of dust it had itself created. The glider swiftly followed, towed remorselessly along until it too became only faintly discernible through the swirling dust. The thundering roar of the Albemarle racing down the runway was drowned out by the next tug moving out onto the runway together with the second glider being towed forward by the jeep.

From out of the pall of dust, the first combination emerged at the end of the runway, climbing slowly away. The first glider was airborne and the operation had begun.

Within 75 seconds, the next combination was disappearing into the brown swirling cloud and yet another was making its way out onto the runway.

As each tug and glider moved up a position, I felt the band of tension across my chest grow tighter and tighter while my pulse raced faster and faster. I licked my parched lips and blinked the sweat out of my eyes. Shooting a look at BG's tense face, I noticed how he gripped the wheel as though it meant his very life. As captain of the glider, BG was responsible for the takeoff and the landing, when that time arrived. En route we would each have spells at the controls, although most of the flying would fall on me, as BG needed to be fresh and ready for the landing which would be the most dangerous moment of all.

Before I realised it, it was our turn. One minute we were stationary; the next, a jeep was hooked on and we were moving out onto the runway. Our tug was swinging round in front, presenting its tail directly towards us, while the ground crew affixed the rope under its belly.

We were lined up on the Albemarle's tail, shuddering in the blast of its slipstream. Our ground crew was leaning over the perspex windshield and ramming home the rope plug. Then he was gone and the controller on our port was waving his yellow flag. I noticed dimly that most of the administrative staff of the RAF and our own drivers were waving from the edge of the runway. I gave them the thumbs up and then quickly turned my eyes forward as we lurched forward under the first pull of the tug. The rope quivered like a live being. BG had the wheel forward to bring the tail up.

We gathered speed and the fog churned up by our tug swirled backwards and upwards, and within a hundred yards, the tail of the Albemarle was almost obliterated. BG came back on the wheel as the tail lifted. Out in front, the tug had disappeared into the wall of dust and BG superbly held her dead behind the

Albemarle by sheer flying ability and solely by means of the swaying rope that disappeared into the light brown cloud in front.

The airspeed swung up to 50 mph and I prayed for the figure 75 mph to come up, for then BG could lift her up out of the cloud with luck and we could then orient our wings once more. The dim outline of the runway flashed by underneath while a drumming roar began to echo throughout the glider. A wing dropped and BG brought it back level as we rose and fell in the turbulent slipstream. The noise was now deafening in the confined space of the cockpit and the ASI needle swung up and hovered around the 75 mph mark. BG eased back on the wheel and we shot up through the worst of the dust. Ahead, the faint outline of the Albemarle was discernible and we descended down to within about ten to fifteen feet of the runway to give the tug a chance to get its tail down and then climb. The ASI needle flickered around the 100 mph mark, and crept above. The Albemarle suddenly appeared clearly, climbing rapidly out of the murk and we followed her up into the clear sky ahead.

The worst part was over, until we reached the Sicilian shores. The massed green foliage of an olive grove skirting the air strip flashed by under our wheels, dropping farther and farther away as we gained altitude.

It was terribly bumpy, and the glider lurched and swayed under the influence of the swiftly rising columns of hot air swirling up from the arid, scrub-covered land below. Following BG's swift hand signals, I trimmed back on the elevator tabs until I got the thumbs up signal from him. The glider rode a little better now, but more and more vicious bumps threw us all over the sky. Out in front the Albemarle dipped and rose, dropping one wing then the other. The rope slackened and tightened in an alarming manner and I would not have been one bit surprised to see it part suddenly under the terrible strain.

The heat inside the cockpit was becoming almost intolerable. Through the perspex the sun burnt with a savage intensity, causing the sweat to run down my face and neck in steady rivulets and my eyes to be drawn into a painful squint.

Our altimeter was registering over a thousand feet and still we climbed in a large spiral following the combination in front. This circling and gaining height would go on until the whole squadron was airborne and in formation. Then we would have to rendezvous with other squadrons already rising from other airstrips.

It was not difficult to pick out our airstrip as we swept round in a circle. The cloud of dust that hung over the field could be seen from far away, rising for over a thousand feet before dispersing.

Now we were at two thousand feet and levelling off. Our airspeed indicator was fluctuating between the 110- and 125-mph marks, while the rate of climb indicator swung crazily up and down as we rode the severe thermals that tossed us around incessantly.

I looked at BG, who still had the controls. His face was streaked with perspiration and he looked white and drawn. His arms and fingers worked unceasingly on the wheel—from one side to the other and back and forth as he fought to ride the bumps and keep behind the tug. On the rudder bar, his feet were straining first left and right seeking to keep the nose from skidding around. How well I knew what a fight he had on his hands.

I glanced around at the gunners in the rear, and received several sickly grins. I felt extremely sorry for them, for I knew that back there in the fuselage they were having a worse time than we were. At least we had something to occupy us and take our minds off the awful stomach heaving motions to a certain degree.

At one point we hit a shocking bump that sent me rocketing out of the seat with only the safety belt preventing me from being hurled against the top of the cockpit. As it was, my head struck hard against the top of the perspex covering which was only about six inches to a foot above us in normal positions. The whole glider shuddered with the impact and a sound like a giant striking the bottom of the glider echoed throughout. Behind us, the heavy six-pounder gun, weighing about a ton, literally leaped clear of the floor, snatching fiercely at its chains. If it had broken loose it would have meant the end of us all. A fraction of a second later it crashed back down into its troughs, raising a blinding cloud of dust from the floor of the cockpit and from the rear.

For a moment, BG almost lost control of the glider and it shivered as though in agony. Then we were back on normal keel again. BG was showing the strain and I tapped him on the arm indicating that I was ready to take over if he was exhausted, but he shook his head, managed a grin, and continued the fight.

At last, the combination in front turned out towards the coast and thankfully we followed. Once over the sea, I knew that it would be much calmer.

We left the shimmering salt lakes that lay inland behind us, while ahead the blue Mediterranean beckoned us on. Between us and the sea lay a panorama of olive groves and dry scrub covered slopes, dotted here and there with little clusters of dirty white buildings occupied by the Arabs.

It was 8.15 p.m. when we crossed the coast in the neighbourhood of Sousse. The town lay quiet and peaceful, its white buildings reflecting the late afternoon sun in a way that was almost dazzling, a whiteness that hid the filth and poverty that lay underneath. I looked at the beaches with a feeling almost of sadness, remembering those lovely days at Mostaganem a short while ago.

Then the sparkling waves of the deep blue Mediterranean were below us while the golden sands slid away swiftly behind. We immediately descended to the 300-foot mark in order to try and avoid any enemy radar that might be sweeping the approaches to Sicily.

The noise in the cockpit had settled down to a dull roar while the air became smooth, and I knew that the last of the bumps was finished. Ahead of us stretched an imposing armada of gliders and tugs and, even as I watched, a line of Halifaxes towing the huge British-built Horsa gliders drew up and passed us on our port side. Among those gliders would be the parties that would have the task of landing almost on top of the bridges over the river outside Syracuse. They were to seize and hold them until the main landing parties of the airborne could come up and reinforce them.

BG tapped me on the arm and I took over. The glider was flying beautifully now that we were out of the turbulence over the land. I felt better now that I was actually handling the WACO. I glanced down at the sea and watched the shadow of our glider skimming over the waves almost immediately below us and to one side. It was then that I noticed how cold the Mediterranean looked. White caps were flecking the waves and it no longer appeared calm. I prayed that we would not be forced down into that inhospitable water. I knew that we would be flying over it for 300 miles and that there would be no ships in the vicinity until we neared Sicily itself, when we would pass over or near the invasion fleet that was carrying the Eighth Army troops.

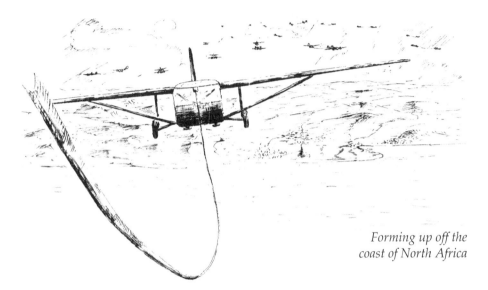

Forming up off the coast of North Africa

We droned on over the water and I noticed that it was beginning to become dark. In another 30 minutes night would be upon us and then we would have over an hour of following the dancing pinpoints of our tug's guide lights.

As the sky darkened more and more, the combinations in front became indistinct and finally vanished altogether, leaving me with a lonely feeling as though lost, although in my heart of hearts I knew that around us the rest of the armada was moving steadily along on its purposeful course.

I began to worry about seeing the tug, for night was almost upon us and our towing plane was becoming less and less visible. Suddenly, just as I was about to ask BG to request them to switch on their lights, the three pinpoints glowed out in the darkness and I was able to line up on them.

From the position in which I was flying, the three lights formed a shallow 'V', a 'V' which danced tantalizingly from side to side and up and down as the tug passed over undulating masses of warmer and cooler air.

I took a firmer grip on the wheel and strained my eyes into the darkness ahead, following faithfully the antics of the wil-o'-the-whisps tug in front. From time to time, despite my careful efforts, the restless lights would prove too difficult to follow and I would feel the turbulent bumps that indicated I was out of position and in the tug's slipstream. That called for some swift manipulation of the controls to get back on an even keel before the position became too bad.

Time passed by and my eyes began to ache with the strain of watching the almost invisible lights of the tug. I glanced swiftly down at the dashboard, weirdly illuminated by the green glow from the radium painted figures on the dials. The airspeed registered a steady 125 mph. It was impossible to pick out the exact height on the coarsely calibrated altimeter. Some gliders had sensitive altimeters fitted that showed the height within ten feet, but not the type I was flying.

In the split second that I took my eyes off the swaying lights of the tug, we lost position badly. In a moment we were being slewed up and around by the vicious backwash of the propellers of the Albemarle, while the roar in the cockpit increased as the full blast of the slipstream smashed against the fabric-covered sides of the WACO. Wildly I strained my eyes into the darkness seeking the madly gyrating lights of the tug. I caught a glimpse of them way down on our port side and flung the wheel forward and over in that direction. The glider bucked in the turmoil of the slipstream and fought hard against the controls. Then the lights were shooting up and at the same time we emerged out of the backwash into smoother air.

The sweat ran down my neck rolling on down my chest and back with the effort I had put into brute strength movements on the wheel and rudder bar. The shallow 'V' of lights gradually slid into the correct place and then I held her steady once more. I felt limp and exhausted and cursed myself for ever taking my aching eyes off the tug's lights for one moment. BG shouted across, 'That was a near one', and I nodded my head in agreement. How I blessed the strength of that rope that stretched way into the darkness to the rear of the tug.

BG shouted something about Malta on the port and at the same time I watched the lights in front tilt in that direction. I followed through carefully; so engrossed was I in keeping that position that I never did get a glimpse of the island, although later BG told me that very few lights were showing to indicate where the island lay in the inky blackness.

We were now on our last leg, with the possibility of night fighter attacks. I looked at BG with the idea of handing over to him for a while but he was bent forward, his face a ghastly green in the eerie dashboard lighting, while he studied the map. Quickly I returned my gaze to the lights in front. I didn't want a second dose of entering the tug's slipstream. Wearily I continued to hold the glider on course while my eyes almost cried out for a chance to close for just a few seconds. I was feeling very tired and a numbness was filling my head. If only I could have slept. I shook my head violently, blinked my red rimmed eyes, and cursed softly to myself.

The air began to become bumpy again and more and more effort had to be put in to keep our WACO in line with the swaying and dipping lights in front.

The minutes passed with BG still peering closely at the map by the glow from the luminous instruments. Out of the corner of my left eye I watched him glancing from the map to the blackness of the night outside on the port side. Suddenly he stiffened, peering intently through the perspex side window. Then he turned and shouted wildly above the thunderous roar that filled the cockpit, 'Sicily coming up on our port'. He pointed vaguely with his finger to where I had estimated the island would be, but I dared not take my eyes off the lights in front even for one second to take a look in the direction that BG had indicated.

The moon was just beginning to creep up over the horizon, and through the faintly illuminated night I suddenly made out a dark mass rising out of the pale, almost imperceptible, waters. Sicily at last! Not a light showed on the land and not a searchlight sent its revealing beam skyward. We must have been flying a mile or two off the coast and quite within audible range of the land patrols that must have been on guard throughout the island, but nothing stirred.

My heart started beating a little faster and, despite the cold of the night, I felt perspiration soaking into my shirt, while beads formed on my forehead and started to run down my cheeks. My lungs began to feel constricted, while some of the dullness that had infiltrated my head vanished. It wouldn't be long now.

I gripped the wheel harder with palms that had suddenly become sticky and the ridge of the wheel cut into my hands with the fierce grip I applied. Still we flew on parallel with the coast with the uneasy feeling that night fighters might come sneaking out of the surrounding darkness any moment, against which we would be almost defenceless.

Then, way out ahead, the blackness of the night suddenly took on a faint reddish tinge. It was a tinge that flickered up and down and caused my pulse to beat even faster. The thunder of noise within the glider seemed to fall and rise when the rope slackened and tightened as I leaned forward from my braced position and stared intently out past the guiding lights of the tug. Every minute of flight brought us nearer to the tinge which was turning into a distinctive glow.

I flashed a look at BG and at the same moment he looked across at me. He did not need to shout the name Syracuse, for I was certain that the red glow ahead could only come from that area.

Now, as we drew nearer, I could distinguish the golden tracers curving upwards and the reddish explosions from the high explosive anti-aircraft shells. Searchlight beams were breaking out and sweeping the night sky, already bearing the reflections from fires on the ground. We were climbing rapidly from the 300- to 400-foot mark we had been flying at since we left the North African coast and, about a mile from where the greedy tracers were criss-crossing in the sky, we reached an altitude of 1500 feet, 200 feet higher than had been suggested back in the briefing tent. There was a reason for this, as I was to learn on my return to North Africa later.

The rush of air past the WACO drowned out any noise the flak may have made. The next minute we were among the hungry fingers of the flashing tracers and at the same time a purplish-coloured searchlight burst forth and pinpointed us squarely in its blinding beam. The interior of the cabin became like daylight and I fought to pick out the lights of the tug in front. We were held for less than five seconds and then the light went out. The sudden transition back to darkness, except for other searchlights playing to and fro near us, was almost too much for my eyes. Desperately I tried to hold the WACO to where I thought we should be in relation to the tug. Red and yellow tracers streaked past the side window of the cockpit. Out of the corner of my eye I saw BG with one hand poised over the release lever.

Another searchlight beam swept around towards us and at the same moment BG, who had been staring tensely through the port window, slammed hard against the release lever. The tow rope dropped away. There was a bang and a rush of air as the field telephone was pulled through the canopy—we had not disconnected it before release. We were riding free. Instinctively I eased back on the wheel slightly to lose excessive flying speed, and perhaps in automatic reaction to climb clear of the searchlight beam that was swinging towards us. Our speed fell away and so did the roar of the slipstream. Now the thump of the exploding shells drummed through the sides of the cabin in muffled grunts, although most of it was light A.A. and could do little damage unless it burst really near.

Directly ahead, a fountain of tracers seemed to float up slowly towards our nose and a split second later were flashing past only a little way in front. At the same time BG called out in the now comparative quiet 'OK, turn in'. I needed no second bidding and wheeled into a sharp turn to port w,hile the frightening tracers slid off to the right.

The dim outline of the coast swung round towards our nose as we keeled over and I straightened out. The searchlights were behind us now, as were the curving tracers. Immediately in front, the edge of the cliffs stood out quite clearly against the dark waters of the sea. Inland, about half a mile ahead, I could see two fires burning fiercely. I felt pangs of worry, for it seemed to me that the lights coincided exactly with our landing ground and I had the uneasy feeling that the enemy must have known we were coming and had lit the fires in order to illuminate us as we touched down. They could then fire on us at will before we could stop and jump out to take up defensive positions. My thoughts were chaotic while a dull hammering drummed within my head and at the same time I sought to blink the perspiration out of my eyes.

I snapped a glance at the airspeed indicator and noticed that we were doing 90 mph, still too fast. The altimeter, as well as I could read on the coarse calibrations, showed 1000 feet, a little high.

BG tapped me on the arm and I relinquished my grip on the wheel and took my feet off the rudder bar. It was up to BG now, but I still had a task to perform and a very important one at that. It would be my job to operate the lift spoilers on the wings and also read out the airspeed and height at frequent intervals to BG in order to help him judge the approach better, for the dim light of the moon, which incidentally had become partly obscured, was little to land by.

I chanted the airspeed of 100 mph and a height of 600 feet through the dull roar that filled the cockpit. I had to lean right forward to take the readings, for the figures on the altimeter were very indistinct. Still, we sailed on down through the night to our landing zone, undisturbed now by flak or searchlights. Again I shouted out the figures to BG, 100 mph, 400 feet. I shot a quick look out through the perspex in front and in that split second I saw we were passing over three distinctive fields that I remembered from the photos back in North Africa as bordering the field in which we actually had to land. Dead ahead appeared a faint white outline that indicated an open space. On each side and on the far end, dark masses indicated trees, and these we would have to avoid at all costs. I had great faith in Capt. BG's capabilities of landing, although I knew at 100 mph we were gliding a little fast by about 10 mph, but undoubtedly BG was trying to get down on the dim white spot.

Once more I called out a reading of 100 mph, 200 feet. It was the last thing I remembered for a while, for the next second there came an exploding crash and a brilliant red flash seemed to tear my head apart. A noise like thunder filled my ears and blackness descended as I was hurled into oblivion.

Chapter 5

Engagement

I came to with the smell of torn and burnt metal in my nostrils and shocking stabs of pain passing through my head. I pulled my head out of the remains of the dashboard and fought to draw air into my tortured lungs. Something, I felt, was pinning me down for I could not move, or else I had broken nearly every bone in my body. I found that I could move my arms and, in the agony of pain, I pushed against the remains of the nose. A haze of dust filled the cockpit. Dimly I heard BG calling out to me,

'Are you all right?', but I could not reply. After my first effort to push myself up and out of the wreckage, I collapsed back again and lay sprawled in the shattered seat. Behind in the fuselage I could hear someone groaning and BG was stumbling out of his seat crying out, 'I'm coming'.

I lay there incapable of moving while I heard BG struggling to get the injured man who had been groaning out onto the ground. I summoned up my strength again and pulled myself out of the tangle, half crawling.

There was a crack of something ripping through the fabric of the wrecked glider followed almost instantaneously by the loud report of a rifle. We were being fired on. That did more than anything to clear my numbed brain and I staggered to a torn opening in the side of the glider and fell onto the ground below. By now I could talk and I called out to BG in a tense, pain-filled voice,

'Where are you, Sir'? Back came BG's voice from the other side, 'Over here. Are you OK'?

I replied in the affirmative. Another shot snapped through the body of the glider and I crawled around to the other side where BG was half crouched over one of the gunners sprawled out on the ground, groaning in pain. BG, and another man who crouched beside him, had pulled the injured man under one of the wings in the shadows, for the moon had now burst forth in all its revealing light.

A strong wind was blowing, and the torn and tattered fabric was fluttering and slapping on the glider. It lay like some grotesque monster of the prehistoric age, the nose tilted up into the air at an angle where it had almost broken away from the rest of the body except for some twisted tubular construction. Part of the underside of the body had been ripped clean away and I could see pieces of it scattered along the gouged earth for some fifty yards. One wing drooped as though in agony and the undercarriage had all but vanished, ground up underneath the body as we had ripped over the soil of the ploughed field in which we had landed.

A third shot whistled by and struck the earth with a dull thump and suddenly I remembered my Sten gun. Stealthily, I crawled back into the black interior of the glider to find my weapon.

I groped around among the tangle of splintered woodwork and, more by luck than judgement, felt my fingers close over the barrel of my Sten. I felt further along, seeking the bandolier of ammunition that should have been near the gun, but could not find it.

Author's WACO - Heavy Landing

My eyes were becoming accustomed to the gloom in the cockpit, and through the torn slashes in the fabric, the pale moonlight gave a feeble illumination. I came to the conclusion that the bandolier was no longer in the cockpit but lay somewhere underneath the ripped up flooring. I tried to find my haversack that held grenades and my rations but again met with no luck.

Abandoning hope, I crawled out again into the open. Looking back along the furrowed earth marking the trail of the glider from where it had struck the ground, I espied several indistinct pieces of wreckage and decided I would check up to see if my haversack was among them. I struck lucky in the first few yards for there, lying among some splintered woodwork, I found my haversack intact. I searched further, hoping to find my bandolier but without success.

Creeping back to the group under the wing, I reported to BG my situation regarding ammunition. BG had a rifle and bayonet, but his ammunition was .303 and mine was 9 mm, which meant that I had only the one magazine on my Sten and one grenade.

I was now feeling a little better, although waves of pain swept up my back every time I moved and my stunning headache still persisted. I looked around, lying in the shadow of the wing, to take stock of our position. The rifleman seemed to have disappeared, for no further shots came our way.

At the far end of the field over which we had passed, flames from a fire on the far side of the trees were leaping skyward. It was one of the two fires I had seen burning while on the way down.

From the opposite end of the field, and beyond, the heavy crash of a Bren gun beat out on the night air, while in between the bursts came the spiteful crack of rifles and an occasional thud of an exploding hand grenade.

Out towards the coast, searchlights and tracers were combing the night sky, for gliders were still coming in. The sky was slightly cloudy, but from most of it shone myriads of twinkling stars, while the moon disappeared and reappeared at intervals behind the few clouds that scudded by in the high wind.

I listened to the gentle whine of a glider that seemed to be circling rather fast. Searchlight beams swept over and round and suddenly one caught the glider in its revealing light. Immediately, a second searchlight darted across the sky, also pinning the glider in its beam. Golden tracers arched swiftly up from first one point and then another and yet another, until the wheeling glider was caught in the crossfire of at least four streams of tracers, all reaching up eagerly to tear it out of the night sky. I watched in fascination as the pilot threw the glider almost up on one wing in a vertical turn while the whistle of the slipstream rose higher and higher. The dull thud of the anti-aircraft guns echoed across the field. Then the glider fell into a steep diving turn and in a second had slipped out of the hungry fingers of hot steel that played upon its body and sought to send it crashing earthward to destruction.

I could still follow the flight of the glider by the ugly high-pitched shrill whine that told me the pilot was coming in too fast, much too fast. The noise grew louder and something flickered past overhead, momentarily silhouetted against the star-studded sky. With a last rush of sound, the machine disappeared over the far end of the field and for a moment silence reigned, to be followed by the sound of a terrible rending crash. The flak had claimed its victim after all.

Before the sound of the crash had fully died away, I was aware of another machine slicing down out of the dark sky with a softer wail. With my ears, I followed the course of the glider coming lower and lower, until that too faded out of earshot. Again came the sound of a shocking impact followed by an uncanny silence, broken only by the sound of distant firing from several different directions.

I felt sick at heart and hurled silent curses into the rising wind. Out over the sea I could hear the last of the towing planes turning back on their homeward course. Good luck to them, I thought. They have done their job; ours is just beginning.

The searchlights were going out one by one, and only one stream of golden tracers climbed slowly into the blackness, way over towards the port of Syracuse.

Behind the trees, the fire was dying down into a red glow. A smattering of gunfire was coming from a distance that I estimated to be about half a mile beyond the fire. From time to time, other firing would echo across the moonlit fields, indicating that some of our men were in contact with the enemy, probably isolated outposts.

Still we lay under the shadow of the wing. The injured man had lapsed into silence. I looked at BG and asked him in a whisper 'What next?'. I did not relish the idea of remaining out here in the centre of a moonlit field, a perfect target if the enemy should bring up a heavy machine gun.

BG replied that we had better wait a short while and see if the moon would go down and cloak our movements across the open field. I nodded in agreement, for we would be perfect silhouettes against the whitish soil of the field, although I was uneasy about lingering too long.

We waited another fifteen minutes and to our agonised gaze, the moon did not appear to budge an inch towards the horizon. Then BG said, 'The next time a cloud obscures the moon, we'll make a break for it. We'll leave one man with the injured sergeant and take the other with us. We must make for the bridge, which lies about three miles away'. I agreed, and lay there waiting for the signal from BG.

An isolated cloud came up edging towards the moon. A minute later, a long black shadow stole across the field. BG signalled. We all rose to our feet, bid the man we were leaving behind with the sergeant farewell, and moved off across the field, heading for the far corner. We moved swiftly, for we wanted to get into the shadows of the hedge before the moon broke forth again from behind the concealing cloud. We made it and sank down against a stone wall bordered by a hedge. In the shelter of the wall, BG drew out his map of the area, studying it by means of a well-shielded torch. It was impossible for me to see it as well, owing to the thin ray of light that BG was using, so I left it to him for a decision.

The wind rustled the hedge in a very unpleasant way and several times I peered cautiously in the direction of some sound, ever expecting a shadowy form to be creeping up on us. Nothing happened. We crouched there while BG pored over his map.

'OK Sergeant,' he suddenly whispered, 'I think I know where we are.' He took another last look at the map and then said 'Let's go.'

BG moved off, keeping close in alongside the hedge. I followed at about a ten-foot interval, while ten feet behind me, the third man took up the rear. I slung my Sten gun over my shoulder, but kept the grenade firmly in my right hand, ready to pull the pin instantly should a situation arise to warrant it.

We came to a thick wall about four feet high and without hesitation BG clambered over it, the loose stones rattling down with a noise that seemed terribly loud to me. I quickly followed him and motioned to the third man to do likewise. We crossed the field, for now the moon was low on the horizon and obscured by clouds, and we came up against another wall. BG peered over and beckoned to me.

'It's a road, but I think we'll still keep on the inside of the wall for safety's sake'.

I nodded and we set off skirting along the wall. We were in what seemed to be an orchard and I longed to cross over to the trees and find out if there was any fruit on them, for I was parched and yearned to moisten my lips. To make it worse, I was a mass of aches, although the keen night air was beginning to disperse the wracking headache I had been suffering.

We passed over another wall and began to stumble over what appeared to be, by the feel, round objects. BG whispered for a halt and gratefully I sank down. I felt around and soon encountered one of the spherical objects. Pushing the leaves aside, I wrenched the ball free. I tapped it with my Sten and guessed that it must be a melon. Thankfully, I struck at it with the metal butt of the gun and broke through the outer skin. Ripping the melon open, I was fully occupied for the next few minutes. Never had a melon tasted better. By now it was almost pitch dark and I could not see what I was eating, but that didn't worry me, for it tasted fine.

With my thirst quenched I was ready to start off again, but BG had other ideas. He was looking at the luminous dial of his watch and said, 'It's two a.m. At 2.15 the

RAF are due over, and they're going to bomb the docks at Syracuse as a diversionary attack. We may as well wait here and watch it as we should only be about a mile or two from the outskirts of the town',

I didn't mind, for it meant a little more rest for my pain-wracked back and head. We lay there in silence, sprawled on the cold ground. While we were waiting, BG told me that he hadn't been able to see the ground clearly as we came in to land and consequently had not levelled off in time. When I had called out 200 feet, as per the altimeter, we must have been down to about 50, but at the rate we were descending, the lag on the altimeter would have been considerable. Furthermore, the change in weather (unpredicted by the Met. man back in Africa) may have considerably altered the setting of the altimeter as this instrument works on barometric pressure, and unless compensation is made during flight, the reading will be out if the weather has changed. Also, owing to the roar of the slipstream, BG found difficulty in hearing my figures despite the way I had shouted them out.

BG was continually looking at his watch. For my part I thought it would be rather interesting to be able to watch our own men bombing an enemy port. Up until now, I had always been on the receiving end in England. I prayed that our men would be in good form, for I wanted to see the enemy really hurt after what I had seen earlier on.

At precisely 2.12 a.m. we heard the first droning in the night sky. A minute later the plane was overhead., By the sound of the motors I guessed the plane to be of the Vickers Wellington type, a twin engined bomber which had built a very good reputation for taking punishment as well as giving it.

Other planes were following close in on the heels of the first. All seemed to be cruising leisurely along and so far no AA had opened up on them. Perhaps the Italians were lying quiet, hoping that the flyers would not be able to find their targets.

A dull roar was filling the skies now and suddenly, away over to where we had estimated the port of Syracuse to be, the first flares blossomed forth over the town. They were a brilliant yellow. They hung in a cluster of three almost motionless, for the strong wind had long since died down.

It was as if the signal had been given for the Italian AA to open up. From the direction of the port came the first distinct grunt of a gun firing, followed by several others. Almost instantaneously, the shells burst with rolling thunder across the heavens. Searchlights switched on, swaying to and fro, seeking the unseen enemy that droned unhurriedly over the port.

Scores of flares were now illuminating the surrounding landscape. Our own field in which we were crouched, became lit as if by daylight, and I could now see distinctly long cultivated rows of trees which indicated that we were actually in an orchard. Around its edges I could see the rounded objects which I knew, from the snack that I had just had a short while ago, to be melons.

Above the throb of the engines, I heard the whistle of the first bombs going down. A moment's silence, then the earth rumbled and vibrated with the concussion of high explosives. I estimated that they had fallen a good mile away, probably in the dock area.

I heard one bomber diving down through the night sky, its engine note rising higher and higher. It levelled off and began to climb. The earth shook as the bombs gouged great holes in the ground.

One stick of bombs dropped not far away from where we were staring cautiously out of the cover of the hedge. For a moment the wail rose to a crescendo, and then they were gone. Across the fields, a red glare lit the sky and silhouetted the black outlines of trees and hedges for an instant. A line of rocking explosions passed through the earth in waves, giving the impression that the earth was convulsed with agony under the stabbing impact of the high explosives. That was one batch of bombs that had gone wide of the target.

From the direction of the port, the sky was tinged with red, but not as much as I had anticipated. I got the impression that the RAF had used mostly high explosive bombs, and very few incendiaries.

The raid was dying out now. The sound of motors was fading away out towards the sea and fewer and fewer tracers were arching up into the still flare-ridden sky. The searchlights had gone out and quiet settled over the area once more. From time to time, the sounds of scattered firing from ground troops echoed over the fields, but even this was limited.

We waited until the last flare had flickered out and then we emerged from our shelter and set off again, hugging the wall and hedge. The field was still slightly illuminated by some fires that burned away in the direction of Syracuse, which helped us to pick our way along.

We came upon a gap in the wall and BG halted, then beckoned me on. I in turn signalled to the third man to follow. Together we crouched down and listened to BG suggesting that we dart over the gap one by one. Then he decided otherwise. We would all go over together. It was only about twenty yards to the next section of the wall and all sounded quiet.

At a word from BG, we slipped out into the open and moved across. We had not covered more than five yards when, from immediately ahead and round the bend in the road, came the sound of rapidly approaching footsteps. At the same moment, I saw dim shapes coming directly towards the gap, but on the road side of the wall. We all sank down motionless on the ground. I cursed the luck that had chosen that moment for the passing figures to reach the gap just as we had begun to cross it. The bend in the road must have shielded the sounds of their marching, even though we had listened carefully.

I lay on the ground while I felt the sweat beginning to run down my face despite the cold of the night. My breathing became heavy and short with the agony of the wait, while the figures loomed larger and larger as they started to cross the gap with swift paces. I remained motionless, my arms out in front with my right hand holding the grenade and my left forefinger closed round the pin. With staring eyes, I tried to pierce the dim light to get a glimpse of the uniforms of the flitting shapes. I knew they must be soldiers by the sound of their hobnailed boots on the roadway and by the spaced line in which they were marching.

The clatter of their boots on the hard road filled my ears as the leaders passed on. Then I heard a voice shout out in the file of men. 'There's someone on the ground on our left.' The words were in English but all the same I was almost petrified, for all the figures had suddenly fallen into a crouch and I could dimly see weapons being aimed in our direction. Together we called out, 'Friends, we are English—hold it'! The figures still crouched and then someone replied, 'Come on out over here with your hands up'. I put the grenade and Sten gun down on the ground and BG and the third man laid their rifles down. We rose to our feet and moved forward, arms well up. We came to the foremost figure who, on seeing our uniforms and hearing us identify ourselves, said, 'OK'.

We went back for our arms and returned to the halted column. They had already identified themselves as men of the Border Regiment whom our squadron had brought in our gliders. They were heading for the bridge, which they hoped to reach before daylight. They had no officer with them so BG took over command from the Sgt. Major who had been leading them.

The column consisted of about twenty men, and BG and I took our places at the head. With a quiet word of command, we set off at a smart pace down the dark roadway. Every moment I expected to be ambushed as we hurried down the tree and wall-lined lane. We did not have time to put scouts out on either side of the road, for already it was not far off dawn and we hoped to reach the bridge by then, or at least, shortly afterwards.

I had obtained from one of the men a spare Sten gun magazine and at last I felt safer, for one grenade and one magazine in the Sten gun would be of little use should we run into enemy resistance. I cursed the loss in the crash of my bandolier of spare Sten magazines.

For about a mile, we continued down the road without incident and, as we neared a sharp bend which took us off at a right angle, I realised that the first rays of dawn were beginning to show. We would never make the bridge before broad daylight I now knew, remembering from a glimpse of the map I had obtained before we set off with the column that I had reckoned on it being at least two miles away, possibly more. We were now on a lane that ran parallel with the sea, which was another quarter of a mile further on over some rough commonland. It was just light enough now to make out the cold-looking waters lying under a faint mist. Suddenly, out of the mist came the distant thunder of speeding aircraft. Without stopping, we turned our heads towards the open sea just in time to see two fighter planes which, through the dim half light, I made out to be either Hurricanes or Spitfires. The latter, I believe, come streaking along flying very low, about fifty feet off the surface and parallel with the coast. At the same moment they opened up with their machine guns, and the tearing rasp shattered the early dawn with a thunderous noise as they attacked what I presumed to be the docks and boats in the harbour. In a few seconds they were gone without a shot being fired at them. Quietness descended once more, but that incident gave me the feeling that we had not been forgotten and that we were still part of a gigantic invasion now under way.

The road suddenly turned inland again and we continued our rapid marching without pause. We had hardly traversed more than a hundred yards when the quiet was torn asunder by the harsh stutter of a machine gun firing and a burst of bullets swished and snapped down the centre of the road just to one side of our column. Instantly, we all dived for the side of the road and sprawled down full length. There were no ditches alongside the road and we were forced to lie on top of the ground.

A second burst hammered out and again the ugly whispering of the bullets flailed my ears.

I peered ahead into the half light but could see nothing. Probably the gun was firing down the centre of the road on fixed lines, for ones' vision was restricted to about 100 yards at the moment, although every second it grew lighter and lighter.

It was this last fact that caused me to ask BG what we were going to do, for I did not relish the idea at all of lying out on the road with no cover whatsoever, waiting for it to get light enough that the enemy could eventually pick us out visually.

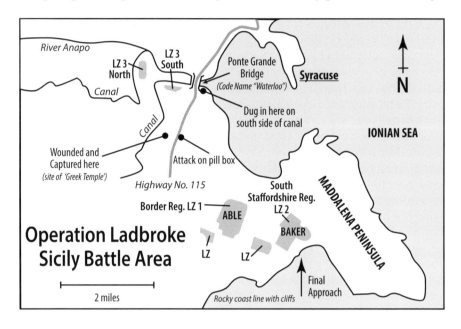

BG ordered us to scatter out in the fields on either side of the road. On the opposite side, there appeared to be a farmhouse set in an orchard. BG told me to follow and darted across the road, through the gate and into the orchard. I plunged across a few seconds later.

At a word from BG, I took up a position behind one of the trees covering the space through the orchard straight ahead. I laid the grenade down by the bole of the tree, ready for instant use, and sighted my Sten at the gap in the trees. Daylight was rapidly breaking out and a chilly mist rose up from the ground and soaked through my battle dress. The coldness numbed me to the bone, but that was the least of my worries. Ahead was a dangerous enemy who could kill, and he had to be watched, and eliminated, if we were to advance.

On our right, the heavy shattering roar of a Bren gun broke through the lighter hammering of the enemy machine gun. Red tracers darted through the trees from the muzzle of the Bren and I tried to pick up the spot where they were striking in order to get a line on the enemy, but the thick growth of the trees prevented my seeing anything. A few minutes later the firing stopped. I waited, still staring away in front and to both sides but nothing happened.

A word of command was softly passed around the orchard to the effect that we were moving off again. I still did not know what had happened, and whether or not the enemy post had been destroyed. As we made a detour around the orchard, I came to the conclusion that we were bypassing the enemy post, for it was our job to get to the vital bridge and not to be delayed by skirmishes en route unless it was absolutely necessary.

We struck off across another field and a few minutes later came to another road, down which we turned. By now it was broad daylight and, looking back down the column, I was pleasantly surprised to see that we had picked up other stragglers during the march and that we now numbered nearer thirty than twenty. Among the men that had tagged on to us was a glider pilot who had been hit in the stomach and who was being pulled along in one of the light airborne trailers carried by our troops in the gliders. He was quite cheerful, despite the ugly look of the crimson stain that spread all over the towel someone had wrapped around his middle as an improvised bandage.

We opened our ranks a little more, now that it was daylight, to lessen losses if by some chance we should be ambushed, and marched swiftly up the road. Suddenly, the man in the rear of the column shouted and the column halted. We all turned around after having slid into the shelter of the wall alongside the road. Coming up the road in our rear was a lone cyclist. He dismounted when about a hundred yards short of our rear and continued to walk on towards us. I could now see that he was an Italian soldier with his rifle slung over his back in such away that he could never have reached it before being riddled with bullets from the column, all of which had their weapons trained on him. A Bren gunner near me snarled,

'Stand back, I'll riddle the bastard'.

BG intervened as he required a prisoner for interrogation. Reluctantly, the Bren gunner lowered his gun while the cyclist came on. He appeared quite unperturbed and was smiling all over his swarthy face.

Two men pounced on him as he drew level with the rear of the column. One took his bicycle and the other wrenched off his rifle. The man who had the Italian's cycle searched the bag attached to the rear and withdrew triumphantly a bottle of red wine. The rifle was smashed against the road and left by the hedgerow as we set off again with the Italian under guard of the rear two men. He seemed to be very pleased at being captured and kept talking away volubly, although no one understood him.

Away ahead of us, I could make out the sound of firing, which grew louder as we made good speed in that direction. It was the sound of a fast firing machine gun challenged by the heavier thunder of one of our Bren guns, and intermingled with these there was the heavy crack of .303 rifles.

We gradually climbed a hill and came out on the crest. BG signalled a halt and we sank down on the grassy edge of the road. It was beginning to get warm and I was glad of the rest. Ahead of us I could make out another batch of our men in their red berets. We had contacted more of our soldiers.

While I rested, BG went forward and started talking to an officer of the other party and, taking advantage, I relaxed and closed my eyes. Most of the pains caused by the crash of the night before had worn off, but I still found it painful to lie down flat on my back; nevertheless I did so and closed my eyes against the rising Sicilian sun. Across the valley from our crest came echoing the bursts of enemy machine gun fire but, lying where we were, they could not touch us. I wondered where all this would lead to and how the main landing force of the 8th Army was getting on with their sea-borne landings. In another few hours they would be at the bridge also, if they kept up to their anticipated schedule. If we did not get a move on, they might reach the bridge before we did.

BG came back and we got up while he indicated the small valley that stretched down from our crest and then rose up to another crest on the far side. The valley was covered with a lemon grove with neatly laid out trees in rows. On the summit of the hill on the far side, there stood a large concrete tower, painted in checks. It rose up some twenty to thirty feet above the trees and bushes and had small slits cut out of the walls.

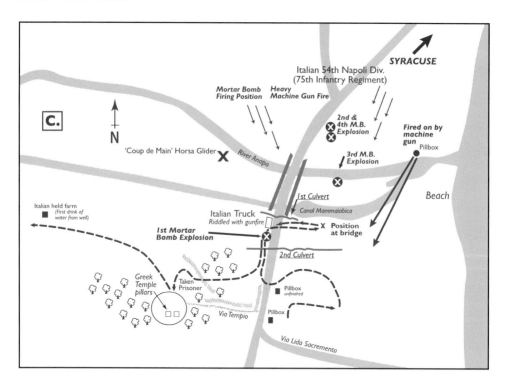

'We,' said BG, 'are going to attack that pillbox from the crest here via the lemon grove. While we're attacking it frontally, another party's going to attack from the flank. After we've overcome the pillbox, we'll continue on to the bridge, which is about a mile further on.' He asked for any questions. We had none.

I felt my heart beating a little faster, for this would be my first attack under fire and I was not looking forward to it very much; but at the same time, it had a peculiar attraction for me that I could not explain. After the attack, I was never again subjected to this peculiar attraction. Once sampled, I found that there was nothing attractive at all about attacking an enemy pillbox.

We spread out in a long line behind the wall and, at a given signal from BG, scrambled over and down into the shelter of the lemon trees on the slope.

Some had been detailed to stay behind and give us covering fire as we advanced through the grove. They were already firing, and the shots passed over our heads towards the concrete stronghold of the enemy.

BG endeavoured to keep the line somewhat straight but inevitably some lagged. We dodged from tree to tree and I myself hung grimly onto BG's tail, a little to his right.

Between the trees there were shallow troughs of earth, probably for irrigation purposes, but I kept an eye on them for possible cover should the enemy pin us down. Up until now we had been lucky, for either the enemy had not seen us come over the wall or else he could not pick us out under the sheltering foliage of the trees.

We had almost reached the bottom of the sheltering valley when the first burst of machine gun fire tore through the trees. The bullets swished by just over our heads, snapping loudly as they passed through the leaves and boughs or thudded into the tree trunks. I, along with the rest, flung myself down behind the nearest tree at this bellicose outburst from the enemy. The burst stopped and BG called out for us to advance and keep up with him. Again the enemy flayed the grove, sweeping his fire from one side to the other in a burst lasting about five to seven seconds. Again the ugly snapping came that caused me to cringe down behind another tree and find what little cover I could in the shallow ditches alongside the trees.

It was my first time under fire, apart from the few insignificant shots just after we had crashed, and I did not like it at all.

The pillbox was invisible to us as yet, and undoubtedly we also were invisible to the enemy machine gunners, who were sweeping the grove in hopes of getting some of us with lucky shots. All the same, it was an uncomfortable feeling being fired upon and not being able to retaliate.

We were now climbing up the far side of the slope and, as I had an idea of how long the bursts lasted and how long a gap lay between each burst, I was able to dart forward somewhere in BG's rear and keep up. Again and again the enemy bursts would scythe through the grove, crackling and snapping and sending the leaves down in showers fluttering to the ground, while chips of bark would fly off under the invisible stroke of the lead. Other bullets would ricochet off with an ugly snarl that would cause my inside to curl up in an agony of anticipation of being hit.

Now ahead of us loomed a wall about three feet high while beyond it I could make out the base of the pillbox tower. It lay less than a hundred yards away, but to get to it we would have to break out of the grove, climb over the wall and cross about twenty yards of open ground. Things were happening so quickly I had little time to dwell upon the situation. BG was up on one knee about ten yards from the wall, calling and waving us on. I was nearest to him and the rest of the line was at least another ten yards behind me, still darting from tree to tree.

BG didn't seem to have any nerves and I spurred myself on to catch him up, but before I could reach him, he was off again, and reached the wall. Even as he did so, I caught a glimpse of red bereted men running half crouched around the base of the pillbox. The flanking party had already reached there. I heard the thud of a bursting grenade and then the men were doubling back for the cover of the nearby trees on our left. Something was shouted from man to man and I saw BG call back and wave an acknowledgement.

Then he turned to me and shouted out, 'It's all over; get back to the road. Get going now. Head for that mound on the left behind you where we'll be out of the line of fire.' The word was passed on and those at the rear, who had the shortest distance to go, were already on their way.

Despite the grenade that must have been flung inside the tower, somehow the enemy continued to fire and the grove echoed with the crash and whine of bullets. In between the bursts, I doubled back towards the mound pointed out by BG. This time I was travelling faster than I had been when going forward. The clacking of the unseen bullets through the avenue of trees spurred me on as nothing else could have done.

Panting, I flung myself down on the ground behind the cover of the mound and waited for BG, who arrived a few seconds later looking all in. I felt little better. In one way I was very disappointed at our failure and in another rather glad that we did not have to cross into the open. The men lay there breathing hard, but still on the alert. The enemy firing continued to sweep the grove, but the target within had gone.

I never did find out why we had given up the attack on the pillbox but, judging from the actions of the men I had seen around its base, I would say that there was no easy way of getting in, and hanging around that place out in the open was simply asking for it. It was no ordinary type of pillbox with conventional entrances from what I had seen of it.

After a few minutes rest, BG gave the order to follow him and we stumbled off through the undergrowth, skirting around the mound just below the summit. We came out of the tangled undergrowth and trees and found ourselves looking down a long slope that ended up in flat heathland, reaching towards the sea after another half a mile or so. On the slopes before us lay row after row of tomatoes ripening in the hot Sicilian sun.

A mist still hung over the water, obscuring any view there may have been of boats off the coast, more than a mile out. I could make out a pillbox near the water's edge, but could see no signs of life around it.

BG went forward onto the open ground and spread his map out. I went with him, and together we studied the layout and endeavoured to orientate the map with the ground in front of us.

As we did so, we again heard the swish of bullets passing above our heads and at the same instant, we heard the distant barking of a machine gun. The sound came from the direction of the pillbox down on the water's edge. The enemy gunners must have spotted us as we came out of the trees.

However, the shots passed over our heads by at least ten feet and, apart from startling us for the moment, had little effect, although of course we withdrew into the cover of the trees.

From just inside the thicket I eyed the tomatoes hungrily. Then I made up my mind and, keeping well down, I edged out towards the nearest row. The gunner must have seen me, for another burst sighed passing over my head and the slope echoed with the hammering from the pillbox. Again the shots were high, and I continued on. I snatched half a dozen tomatoes from the plants and then edged back to the trees. Back in the shelter of the foliage, I shared out my spoils, and then ravenously ate my share of the luscious ripe tomatoes.

We did not stop long and a few minutes later emerged from the trees and marched off, keeping well spaced. This must have annoyed the gunner for he opened up again with no more result than before. We rounded the hillock and climbed off at a tangent until we had reached the crest, where we came upon a half built pillbox. We could see that it was empty as we approached it and soon ensconced ourselves in and around it.

I went forward a few paces with BG and we found ourselves looking out across a valley. About a mile away, we picked out the Ponte Grande bridge we had come so far to seize and hold. BG peered through his glasses and then passed them to me. Looking through the powerful lenses, I could make out several men walking over and around it with the familiar red berets on their heads. I was surprised, for I had expected to come upon a raging battle at and near the bridge. Down there, not a shot was being fired, although to the rear and on both sides of us, desultory bursts of firing were continually echoing across the fields and groves.

Beyond the bridge I could make out the outskirts of Syracuse. Between the bridge and the town lay an open stretch of commonland with a farm or two scattered around.

A road led down from somewhere on our left and emerged out into the valley before curving towards the bridge. In a field on the left of the road, about two hundred yards from the bridge and about fifty yards from a farmhouse, a Horsa glider lay with its nose buried in a ditch and the tail pointing to the sky. Apart from the mishap of running into a ditch, the glider appeared intact. It was obviously one of the coup-de-main party's gliders who had been designated to land in the fields on either side of the bridge, capture it, and withdraw and destroy the charges that the enemy had inserted ready to demolish the bridge if capture appeared imminent. It looked as though the landing party had been successful, for the bridge was intact and held by our men.

We felt elated and set off immediately towards the bridge. We reached the road where it passed through a cutting and, after sliding down for some twenty feet, landed up in a heap on the road. Forming up, we marched down through the cutting, emerging into the open after about two hundred yards.

The enemy machine gunner in the pillbox on the coast harassed us again, and we turned off the road to the left where an embankment sloped down and afforded complete protection from the gunner. We spread out for safety's sake in case the enemy should start using mortars or artillery, and a few minutes later we reached the bridge where our party was warmly welcomed by the officer in charge. Apparently, he had very few men on the bridge and was extremely worried. Our arrival helped a lot, but it was still not enough. With us, he had about 60 men under his command, whereas the whole Air-landing Brigade (about 1200 men) had been allotted the task of defending the bridge, including other objectives of course, such as the port of Syracuse. No one seemed to have any clear picture of what had happened to the hundreds of men who had taken off from the North African coast, but we were all hopeful and in high spirits. I even forgot my aches and pains.

We learned from the officer in charge that an attack from the direction of the town of Syracuse was expected to materialise at any minute. I was surprised that no counterattack had been made by the enemy since our men had first captured the bridge before midnight. We also learned that at least two Horsa gliders had landed near the bridge, which had been captured after a brief engagement with the defending Italians. The charge under the bridge had been withdrawn and the danger of it being blown was averted. Unfortunately, one of the two gliders had been hit by flak and had crashed and burned by the trees bordering the river. All on board had been killed.

From the banks on either side of the bridge and facing the town came the sound of men digging in. The banks, I noticed, were covered in undergrowth and lined with trees giving quite good cover.

BG went forward to the far bank facing Syracuse and held consultation with the other officers already there. I leaned against the parapet of the bridge, talking with another glider pilot whom I had recognised on reaching there. As we talked, I heard a sudden shout, and the next moment an officer appeared at the end of the bridge calling out,

'This looks like it. There are some lorries coming out of the town. Get to your positions.'

Gazing towards the town, I made out two lorries edging out. The officer came up to me and asked if I had an assigned post, to which I replied in the negative.

'OK', he replied. 'Go out in front beyond the bridge towards the town, and take up a position in one of the farm buildings there; you will go with him', he continued, addressing the other glider pilot.

'Right, sir.' I replied, and prepared to move off.

Just at that moment BG came quickly over the bridge.

'Where are you going?' he asked of me. I explained and he crossed over to the officer who was talking with another sergeant and said, 'If you don't mind, I would like to have Sergeant Miller with me.' The officer agreed immediately, and I placed myself at BG's disposal.

There came another shout from the front bank to the effect that the Italians had dismounted from the lorries and were deploying. BG sprinted for the front bank, calling to me to get onto the rear bank and start digging in. He would follow me over in a few minutes. I started to clamber over the parapet, followed by the other sergeant.

We could not go directly off the road onto the bank, for the enemy had laid a thick barbed wire defence at that point. Sgt. Cawood and I made our way along the bank for a few feet, and then got down. Sgt. Cawood was in possession of an entrenching tool and was soon making use of it. Mine had been lost in the crash and I could only lie and wait until Sgt. Cawood could lend me his.

The sound of digging in on the far bank increased and I felt lost. Then came the first whine of enemy bullets. I was below the crest of the bank and facing inland away from the fire, but even so, I instinctively ducked at the first shots. These were high, but that was soon remedied. Bullets began to thud into the bank just above my head, while others ricocheted with a murderous hum off the tree trunks that grew in some profusion along all the banks.

Now some of our own .303 rifles were crashing forth in retaliation and occasionally the Brens, of which we only seemed to have two, would thunder out their song. The acrid smell of cordite began to drift on the air.

All I could do was lie patiently and cover the open space of heathland that spread from our bank to the sea and up to the slopes of the hill we had come down earlier. The bank curved away slightly towards Syracuse about fifty yards from where I lay and the undergrowth growing thereon created a blind spot, as far as I was concerned. No other troops were dug in on this side around the bend and an enemy could have stolen up on us from that point with the greatest of ease, shielded by the profusion of foliage. I continued to survey the open landscape away from the town of Syracuse.

Away on the same hilltop that we ourselves had come from, I suddenly noticed the movement of men. I stiffened and sighted my Sten, although the range was too far for effective firing. I watched the figures making their way around the hill, skirting the tomato field. Then they came out into the open and I saw the almost invisible dots of red on their heads. I knew they were our men and relaxed a little, but I still watched them closely, just in case.

At that moment, the machine gun in the pillbox on the coast chose to open up on the little group of men spread out in single file. I saw them pause for moment, as the distant stutter of the machine gun drifted across the open heathland. Then they moved on at a steady pace. The machine gun persisted with its steady burst, and so did the men. Eventually they crossed the road and vanished out of sight of the gunner. I watch them steadily approach the bridge, still spread out in single file, and saw one of our men near the bridge wave his arms and hail them. They replied and hurried up to the bridge, where they were warmly greeted.

All this time, an incessant firing had been coming from the outskirts of the town and our men were replying, but to a lesser degree. Ammunition had to be conserved by our side for our supplies were limited to that which we had on us - no more could be brought up.

I called across to Sgt. Cawood to get a move on with his digging and received a soldier's typical reply. I felt restless and wished I was out on the front bank where at least I could get a crack at the enemy and have something to occupy my mind. Lying here listening to the sigh and snap of the enemy bullets without being able to retaliate was not very morale boosting. I considered for one moment opening up on the distant pillbox, but better judgement won through and I thus avoided wasting ammunition.

Then to my amazement a speeding object caught my eye coming down the road out of the cutting on the hillside. It was a lorry and instantly I knew it was not one of ours, for we were only carrying jeeps on this operation and this truck was somewhat larger. I pushed my Sten forward in the lorry's direction and carefully sighted on it. It was still half a mile away and was slowing down as it approached the bridge.

I hesitated to open fire, for there was a chance that some of our own men might have captured an Italian lorry. I could make out some men sitting in the body of it which was open, but could not be sure of their uniform as yet.

Nearer and nearer drew the lorry and then, when it was about two hundred yards from the bridge, I recognised that at least one of the men was a civilian and old at that. Two others by his side were wearing the familiar Italian soft caps of the Army. I could not see through the reflection of the windscreen to identify the man inside the cab, but I had seen enough.

The lorry had almost stopped at the bridge and the men were peering inquiringly over the side of the lorry. I held my fire, for I was under the impression that our men, who were dug in right by the roadside on the river bank, had signalled them to stop and had them covered.

There came a shattering roar of firing from the bridge end and the lorry swerved off the road, while the windscreen dissolved into a thousand fragments. The engine roared for a moment then died and the lorry jerked to a halt on the grass verge. Again spiteful cracks and the crash of rifle fire. Screams rent the air from the lorry and I saw one of the soft capped men topple over and droop across its side. The old man stood swaying on his feet, his two arms thrust skyward, while cries of fear and agony poured from his lips. Another short burst and he spun around, his old battered civilian hat flying off at a tangent while he fell forward inside the truck body. The firing stopped and for a moment I felt sickened by this wanton killing of what seemed to be an old harmless civilian, who probably had hitch-hiked a lift off the lorry. But this was total war involving civilians as well as soldiers, whether we liked it or not.

I watched one of our Red Cross men dart across the bridge, bent double to avoid the fire that was still being directed against us by the enemy advancing from the town. As I watched him moving around the wreckage of the lorry, stopping and looking and sometimes doing something to the unseen figures, the thought of how futile war was came over me for a brief instant. A few minutes ago, his fellows had been killing and maiming the same men who were now being tended by the Red Cross soldier.

I had little time to dwell upon these thoughts for a new sound arrived like a clap of thunder that twisted my nerves in a sudden awful expectation. It was the noise of the first mortar bomb I had ever heard fired in my direction.

The mortar bomb screamed by over the bridge and burst two hundred yards away on the open heathland. The sharp rending explosion, and the stab of crimson tinged flame through the swirling grey smoke, caused me to cringe well down on the unyielding earth.

A sudden silence followed the explosion and then the small arms fire continued. With a new urgency in my voice, I called out to Sgt. Cawood to let me have his entrenching tool as soon as possible. His reply was to dig faster and deeper. Anxiously I gazed around for some sort of cover from the red hot slivers of steel that would erupt from the bursting bombs along the bank once the enemy got our range, which would not be long. Again the sudden nerve chilling wail and again a rocking explosion—this time just off the end of the bridge. More grey smoke curled lazily upwards from the torn earth.

At the foot of the bank I spied a weed-filled ditch and there and then I made up my mind I would dive for cover if that mortaring became more accurate, for a mortar bomb is a deadly thing that will tear a man to shreds if it lands a short distance from its target.

I began to feel the sweat trickling down my face and rubbed it off with my sleeve; but it was of little use, for the combination of the hot Sicilian sun and the nervous tension caused by the mortaring bathed my body in a sweat that increased every second.

The next mortar bomb was on target. It came with shattering suddenness. There was a short sharp scream that grated upon my ear drums and the next second a shocking steel-tearing explosion filled the air. From across the narrow river, less than twenty yards away, earth and grey smoke spued skywards and moments later the spine chilling whirr of flailing shrapnel, red hot from the recent explosion, filled the air. I flattened myself out along the ground and dug my fingers in as the searing metal smacked into the earth and cracked against the tree. For a few seconds, an uncanny silence hung over the bank, and then a number of cries and groans fell upon my ears. I heard others shouting for the first aid man. The small arms firing broke out afresh and for a few minutes there was peace from the mortar.

I thought of diving into the ditch away from the murderous blast of the mortar bombs, but realised on second thoughts that if I went into that bramble covered ditch I would be unable to cover the rear with my firing as it would certainly be impossible for me to see more than a few feet. No, it was definitely out, unless the bombs started to actually fall on the rear bank, then I would be in it and quick.

Again the harsh rending scream through the air and again the ground shook with the impact of the bomb. I buried my head a second before the impact while my body twisted up tautly in horrible anticipation. Immediately after the explosion, I looked up and saw a similar pall of smoke rising from the trees on the far bank. 'Oh God', I thought, 'how much longer before they raise the range on to our side'? The singing of jagged pieces of shrapnel raining from the sky caused me to force my head down once again while I curled up into what I faintly hoped to be as small a target as possible. The hot slivers of steel beat into the ground around me and whined away into the distance, but again I was lucky, although I began to think, through the chaos of my thoughts, that my luck could not hold out much longer. If only I had a hole to drop into it would make all the difference. I called out to Sgt. Cawood again for the loan of his entrenching tool and he called back that he had almost finished.

I returned my gaze to the open heathland again, and then up to the hill. More men, about ten, were coming around the hillside. These too had red berets on their heads. I felt a little better but still hugged the ground in anticipation of the next bomb.

I heard it coming, but I knew by the note that this time it was not heading directly for the bank. The bomb moaned by well overhead and a few moments later I saw a burst of scarlet and a puff of grey smoke break out on the side of the hill alongside the moving line of men heading our way.

Seconds later, a muffled grunt of the explosion echoed across the open ground. I was sorry for the men there but grateful in one way that the enemy had lifted their mortaring from us.

The little figures of our men emerged from behind the smoke of the explosion and appeared to be running for some trees. Another mortar bomb hurried by overhead on its deadly journey. Another red flash accompanied by smoke shot skyward while the dull note of the explosion drifted back to our ears. This time they had been even further out in their aim and now their targets had disappeared into the shelter of some trees.

The pillbox on the water's edge had been adding its chatter against the running figures, but had now stopped. I could not help but wonder why the pillbox had not opened up on the bridge here in support of the attack from the town itself, and could only surmise that there was no communication between it and the forces in the town.

Even as I stared at the pillbox, I saw a geyser of water spurt up alongside it. A sharp explosion echoed across. Someone was shelling the pillbox, either from the sea of from the interior. I felt a surge of elation as another explosion followed a plume of smoke jetting skywards alongside the pillbox. A little group of figures darted out from the opening in the side of the pillbox and hurried off in a crouched position along the sands, half obscured from view by a slight bank. They were too far away to hit with the short range Sten gun I had, and I cursed my luck, but restrained the impulse to press home the trigger and waste precious ammunition, although at the time I felt as though I would never use any up, the way things were with me at the moment.

The bushes about a hundred yards away on my left towards the mouth of the river stirred visibly and I caught a glimpse of enemy uniforms and swung my Sten around. This time I did not wait, but squeezed the trigger. I knew my bullets were raking the bushes, but nothing else happened apart from a couple of answering single shots, and I fired again. Then all went quiet. I flattened out even more, realising that I was in a very exposed position.

A rising note in the sky took my attention from the bushes. Lifting my eyes to the cloudless blue sky, I watched two fighter planes boring down towards the bridge. They were flying at about two thousand feet when I first saw them, but this height rapidly diminished as they swept down in a shallow dive. At about 500 feet they levelled off and I could now make out that they were Italian Machii 2002's, planes very similar to our own Hurricanes. One of the planes was trailing a long spume of white misty cloud behind it which I believed to be glycol from his cooling system. They were both in a hurry and flashed by over the bridge without firing a shot and disappeared towards Syracuse. I had lain motionless as the fighters approached, after shouting out a warning to others on the banks. Now as they roared past, I raised myself to make sure that they kept on going, and that they did not turn around for a sneak attack. They did not return.

The rifle and machine gun fire had settled down to intermittent bursts and shots while the mortar bombs fell at infrequent intervals on the bank facing the town. As each tearing explosion mushroomed upwards, I would cringe lower on the ground as the accompanying rain of shrapnel hummed and whirred through the air.

From the hill at our rear, several more red-bereted men appeared and began making their way down the road towards the bridge. The mortar lifted its range and again a missile wailed across the heavens to burst with a distant explosion alongside the road about fifty yards from the trotting party. As the red-flecked smoke shot up from the tortured earth, the men flung themselves down. The next instant they were on their feet, running off the road towards the shelter of the embankment. The enemy sent another bomb on its arching flight over towards the now unseen men. From behind the embankment where they had fled, smoke suddenly billowed up and a reverberating crash rolled across the open ground. Then from our own bank there came a thud, and I could see a black object climbing rapidly up into the sky. We were now also firing a mortar. I wondered why we had not retaliated on the enemy before now, seeing that we had a mortar ourselves.

The answer followed swiftly on my thoughts, for I saw a cloud of smoke roll swiftly up from a point behind the embankment where I estimated our men to be. Another thud from our bank and a second mortar shell curved upward then down. This one fell a little nearer towards the bridge. A second blanket of smoke started to billow forth from the point of impact. Now I knew why we had not been firing at the enemy. We appeared to have only smoke mortar bombs to fire and no high explosive ones. By firing the smoke bombs in the direction of our men behind the embankment, the men on the bridge hoped to give them cover so they could make a dash for the bridge. Within a few minutes, the men whom I had first spotted up on the hill were doubling along out of the smoke just short of the bridge. I was glad that they had made it. That made about 90 men in our force, still very few compared with the 1200 men who started out.

The enemy mortar gave us no respite and every now and then a bomb would fall on the banks. As each one fell, Sgt. Cawood would dig in a little deeper and I never got a chance to use his entrenching tool, not that I blamed him, for I think that I would have done the same if I had been in his position. The only consolation I had was that practically all the enemy mortar fire was falling on the front bank; but even so, each one sent its share of hot metal slivering across the river.

I continued to cover the rear, but nothing stirred out on the open heathland or up in the hills in the hinterland.

From the direction of the harbour, three quarters of a mile away, an engine broke into life. For a while it continued to thunder away in a steady note, then the noise grew higher and higher, until suddenly over the trees about half a mile away an old flying boat rose up into the air. It climbed slowly curving around towards the bridge. I recognised it as an ancient Cant Z 501 of Italian make. As it drew near the bridge, still at an altitude of not more than three or four hundred feet, one of our Bren guns opened up with its heavy beat. The flying boat seemed to stagger, levelled off, and suddenly turned away and headed back for the harbour. That was the last we ever saw of it.

The enemy firing seemed to be increasing and the whine of bullets became almost continuous. Our firing appeared to be decreasing somewhat and I began to feel a little anxious, longing to hear a report of some sort on the position. I did not have long to wait.

My attention on the hills behind was suddenly dragged away by the sound of splashing in the river just behind me. Swiftly I turned and crawled up the bank almost to the summit while I trained my Sten in the direction of the noise. Sgt.

Cawood did likewise. A dripping figure carrying a rifle appeared over the crest and instantly I recognised him as one of our men. I relaxed my finger on the trigger. Another man with water running down his clothes followed closely on the heels of the first. Together they slipped swiftly over the brink while the bullets snapped past. They dropped down alongside and I noticed that the first man was a sergeant from one of the regiments we had carried in. He seemed rather agitated and was panting with his exertions.

Alarmed, I asked him what was wrong. He struggled for breath and then replied that he had been ordered over this side as the front could not be held much longer. He also stated that the rest of the men were following him over at intervals. We were to move off under the bridge and then back up alongside the road until we reached the crest of the hill where we would take up new positions. I replied that Captain BG, my immediate superior, was over the front bank and that I ought to wait for him. The sergeant said no, that we were all to get moving to avoid congestion.

Sgt. Cawood had been listening in, and we agreed that all had better get going if those were the orders. We thinned out into a single file and doubled up to the bridge. Underneath the bridge, and parallel with the river, there ran a culvert through which we crawled. This brought us out on the far side of the road. Finding a ditch running up alongside the road, we turned up it with me taking up the rear, and four others in front. The ditch was not deep enough to give us complete cover and, as we began to climb the slope, we became exposed to the enemy. Bullets began to thud and whistle past.

I urged the man in front to greater speed for, being in the rear, I stood the greatest chance of being hit. We kept going, half doubled up to make ourselves as small a target as possible. I began to pant with the exertion and my back began to hurt again. The bullets came faster and we had to dive under a low bridge that ran under the road to our left. We paused there for a moment to regain our breath. The underneath of the bridge was one mass of gluey mud, but no water. I moved to the opening, ploughing through mud that came up well over my ankles. Cautiously, I peered out and tried to take stock of our position. I could see no sign of the enemy. Something cracked against the stonework a few inches from my head and ricocheted off into space with an ugly hum. I tumbled back in the mud, cursing myself for a fool. Somebody had the opening covered.

After a brief discussion, we decided to push on, sniper or no sniper. We darted out as fast as the glue-like mud would permit, one after the other at about two yards' interval. For a moment, we all crouched in the ditch, and then set off again half doubled up. We covered about twenty yards before the enemy spotted us again. Bullets cracked past and we spurted on faster. Ahead was a bend with some trees growing down to the edge of the ditch, and that meant cover from view for us. Something jerked at my heel and I winced as the hot lead ripped off a chunk from my boot. I almost caught up with the fellows in front, and then we were leaping out of the ditch into the shelter of the trees. Exhausted, I sank down behind the thick trunk of a towering tree. The breath wheezed through my lungs while a searing pain stabbed at my chest. I lay there sobbing for air, and with a dull anger burning within me against the enemy gunners.

As soon as I had got back my breath, I crawled to the edge of the trees and swept the countryside with a careful gaze, making sure that I could see without being seen. I could not see the bridge owing to the formation of the ground, but could see beyond it towards Syracuse. In vain, I searched for signs of some moving object or tell-tale spurt of smoke. I retired into the shadows of the trees and lay sprawled out again, trying to regain some strength.

My head was spinning with the heat of the near midday sun and with the after effects of the crash. My back throbbed with a regular pulse of pain while my throat felt like dried parchment. I would have given a lot for a long cool drink of water right then.

I asked the sergeant who had come over the river what he had in mind now. As he was an Infantry sergeant, and had also received the order to withdraw, Sgt. Cawood and I had more or less placed ourselves under his command, although we were of equivalent rank.

After a brief discussion, the sergeant reiterated that his orders were to take up position on the hill overlooking the bridge. We decided to push on towards the top of the hill and take up positions there. Pulling ourselves to our feet we set off slowly, weaving through the trees in single file and keeping well on the alert. Away in the valley on our right I could still see the lone Horsa glider tilted up in the ditch. No one moved around it.

Ahead of us, about two hundred yards away and out in the clear away from the trees, I espied some ancient looking ruins, which I took to be either Roman or Greek, or possibly some more modern copy.

We reached the weathered stones and I felt sure that they were genuine, although to me at that moment it was just a passing interest. At any other time I would have been keenly interested in the ruins, but now I was too exhausted to study them closely.

Among the ruins we found several comparatively newly dug trenches. The enemy must have intended this to be a strong point of some sort. This, we decided, would be our position. They commanded a fine view from the summit of the hill although, due to long grass growing all around, the field of fire was somewhat restricted when we were actually down inside the trenches, which were all of about four feet deep. We would clear away the grass from the immediate front as soon as we had rested, but just now we were all too tired to do a thing except slump down gratefully into the ready-made holes. Foolishly, we neglected to put a man out on watch, for all seemed quiet around us, a mistake for which we were to pay dearly.

Chapter 6

Capture

I lay in the bottom of the trench, my eyes closed, seeking a place where I could rest my aching body in some sort of comfort for just a few minutes before we began the task of clearing the grass away.

I felt despondent. Everything seemed to have gone wrong, and where would it end? Why had the Eighth Army not turned up at the appointed hour? We ourselves had been on the bridge for several hours after the time Montgomery's men had been due at the bridge. To me, on my first operation, the thing was impossible to untangle; the future was unforeseeable. I lay there in a half daze of exhaustion.

I must have dozed off when suddenly I was roused by the sound of bullets thudding and cracking into the parapet of the trench. I opened my eyes and slowly raised myself. My body felt like lead. Dimly, I saw the sergeant who had led us up here pull himself up sharply and peer over the edge of the trench. The next second his head jerked back, and he spun round and toppled down in the trench, his lifeless body half doubled up and jammed down in between the trench sides.

With a body that did not seem to belong to me, I pushed myself off the ledge I had been leaning on and slowly straightened up. Even as I did so, the whole trench seemed to erupt in smoke and flame while a stunning concussion smashed through. I felt a blow like a hammer hit my left thigh, but felt no pain. My ears rang with the explosion, while my eyes were blurred. Faintly through the murk of smoke and half consciousness, I saw one of our men throw back his arm and then hurl something over the edge of the trench. A few seconds later white smoke billowed up around our position mingling in with the grey of the explosion, which somehow I guessed to be caused by a hand grenade.

The explosion seemed to have numbed me, for I could not move, although in a dim way I could see two of our men, bent double, climbing up over the rear of the trench. Next moment they were gone, and I was alone.

Frantically, I forced the cloudiness that fogged my thoughts away. Glancing around the trench, I found only the dead sergeant for a companion. He was lying half across me with a bullet hole in the middle of his forehead. I could hear shouts and rifles cracking. I reached up and pulled myself over the edge. I looked around. Immediately in front, about twenty yards away, a soldier was aiming his rifle at me. I brought my Sten gun up, pressing the trigger as I did so. The gun jumped and pulled away up and to the right as the bullets stuttered forth. Then it stopped dead. Something hummed angrily past my head. The Italian had dropped to the ground although I do not think I had hit him in my hurry of firing, even though the range was so short.

Madly, I pressed the trigger again, as I felt my left leg buckle. Nothing happened. I had used up the last of my ammunition. I was down on one knee, while hornet after hornet of lead flailed the air around and thudded into the ground. My head was spinning and I could not see straight. The thought of being taken prisoner, or worse, killed, drove me on in desperation.

Pulling myself up onto my feet, out of the trench, I turned to stagger away, away anywhere from invisible death that was striking for me. As I ran, zigzagging madly, my leg gave way again. I could not make out what was wrong, for in those few intense action-packed seconds since I had first been jerked into wakefulness by the sounds of firing, I had not realised that the grenade had hit me with its flying fragments all up my left thigh, and momentarily blasted me unconscious.

I half crawled and half ran towards one of the ruined pillars of stone, hoping to find salvation behind its thickness. As from afar, I heard the spiteful crack of rifles, and realised that something was beating into the ground on both sides of me.

It was an agony to breathe, but desperation drove me on. Now I was at the pillar, and thankfully half fell and half crawled around it. I lay there sobbing for breath. A thousand thoughts flashed through my head, none of which made sense. Fearfully, I looked around. The whole of the rear was open, and nothing offered cover to me. I prayed that they would not get around to the back—a forlorn hope indeed. I then noticed one of our men sprawled out behind another pillar about six feet away. He was staring at me with a funny expression. He pointed towards his stomach, and I followed his finger. A dark red stain spread all over the lower part of his battle dress. Pulling himself up into a sitting position, with one hand over the stain, he crawled over to me. I could see he was in great pain. My haversack was still on my back, and I told him to open it up and pull out the towel.

This was the end. We would have to surrender. The firing had stopped, and the soldier pulled and tugged at the haversack until he managed to tear out the towel. I took it from him, and began to raise myself on one knee, first of all pushing out the towel to one side of the pillar and waving it about. Nothing happened, so I gradually followed the towel out with my head. About ten feet away was an enemy soldier in a half crouched position, his rifle at the ready but not aimed. He saw me waving the towel, and to my horror quickly raised his rifle, took aim and fired. The bullet struck the column right alongside my face, ricocheted off, tore part of the moustache from my upper lip and whined away into the distance.

I fell back in a panic. To me this seemed the end. They were taking no prisoners. My thoughts welled up inside me. I had felt no pain from the shot, only a deep agony of despair. I was to die here on this lonely Sicilian hilltop, and my body would be tossed carelessly into some half dug grave. Never again would I see home. In those seconds, I died a hundred deaths. No, oh God no, it couldn't be so. Wildly I glanced round behind. Even as I did so, a light machine gun opened up. The shots came from the rear and shattered just above my head on the column. Chips of stone flew off in all directions as under the strokes of an invisible hammer. A terrible chatter filled the air. No, the bastards wouldn't get me, they wouldn't.

I heaved myself up and tried to run away from the direction that the machine gun fire was coming, but I ran into more rifle fire. Again, by a miracle, the shots sighed and swished past but none hit me. I was falling forward again. An agony of thoughts flashed across my mind. The ground came up to meet me. Something red-coloured rolled under me. There was a brilliant and blinding scarlet flash, a rocking explosion that seemed to burst my head apart, and I hit the ground in an oblivion of grey-black smoke. I was not completely out, and could feel a terrible pain tearing at my face. I couldn't feel my mouth, and felt sure that it had been blown clean off.

With the little feeling I had left in my body I tensed myself up, waiting for the burning thrust of an enemy bayonet into my back that would bring a final oblivion. Death was at hand. They had got me after all. A wave of darkness seemed to engulf me, and I knew no more until I came to and found myself staring up into a ring of flushed faces, mostly bearded, looking down at me with hate-filled eyes. A ring of bayonets was thrust within a few inches of my face, while one of them was pushing a pistol hard against my right temple. I muttered something through a bloody mouth, and feebly raised a hand to push the revolver away, an act that might well have cost me my life, but at that time I did not know what I was doing. An exited chatter of strange voices beat against my ears, and once again I lay there waiting for the end, caring little, wanting only restful oblivion.

I felt hands roughly tearing at my clothes, searching, fumbling hands, but I was past caring; let the vultures take what they could find – I would have no use for it where I was going.

Somebody dragged me upright by the scruff of my collar, and shook me. My head suffered stabs of pain, and I cried out. I was flung down again.

Slowly some semblance of consciousness returned to me. I stared dazedly around at the ring of unfriendly faces. They were standing back examining their spoils. Through the agony of my pain, I began to realise that I was still alive, and a strange exaltation overcame me. A moment later I thought that maybe it was just a respite. The Italians closed in again, their faces still angry. One motioned to me to get up. Painfully I dragged myself upright. I received a rough shove from behind that sent me staggering forward. My head was in a whirl, and my face one mass of pain. My left leg was beginning to hurt also, and it took a great effort to limp along. I thought I would fall again but caught myself, and swayed forward under the prod of a bayonet.

The soldiers were still talking excitedly among themselves as they marched me across the open space away from the ruins. I could not think straight. Raising my right hand to my mouth, I felt a swollen mass. The blood ran down between my fingers. All my teeth seemed to be intact, much to my amazement, but I shuddered to think what my face really looked like. Perhaps it was lucky that I could not dwell upon that thought. The uncertainty of what was going to happen next beat through the fog that choked my head.

We were approaching the far end of the field, and suddenly I felt alarm well up within me, for I could see that I was being marched straight towards a number of freshly dug holes. I tried to think more clearly. Had they spared me in the heat of battle, only to shoot me in cold blood now? The urgency of the situation pierced through the dulling cloudiness that fogged my thoughts. Furtively, I shot a look to the left and then to the right. Out of the corner of my eye I could see that at least six men were tailing along close behind me. I would never be able to break clean away before one or all of them brought me down with a scythe of burning lead, but better that than to die standing over a freshly dug grave.

The holes loomed nearer, and then I saw figures moving around in one or two of them. It was the enemy's positions from which they had attacked us. Shouts came from these men to the ones escorting me. There was a brisk cross-fire of talk between them all as we drew level with the trenches. I braced myself to run if the Italians showed any signs of lining me up, not that I would have got far on my shrapnel-ridden leg. Then, to my relief, we were past the holes in the ground, and the escort was goading me to stagger along faster.

Up until then I had thought I was alone, but now I realised that at least two more of our men were being marched along behind me. I turned my head and shot a quick glance back. One I recognised as the soldier who had been wounded in the stomach. At the sight of him lurching and swaying along with my towel still pressed to his crimson-stained middle, I forgot some of my own pains, for I could see that he was worse off than I was. Behind him limped another of our men. He had been hit in the shoulder as well as the leg, and his arm hung almost useless by his side.

A rough push forced me to look to the front again. I felt a dreadful weariness overcoming me, and I felt that I could not go on much longer; but at the same time I felt a surging hope rising within me. I felt more confident that the Italians were not intending to kill us off. If they had been thinking of that, they would have done it long ago, and would not have marched us so far. I almost became cheerful despite the agony of pain that swept over me, and the dreadful thirst that tortured my swollen and bleeding lips and parched throat.

The afternoon sun beat down mercilessly, adding to the discomfort I was already suffering. The stabbing pain in my left leg was becoming almost unbearable, although I was comforted by the thought that no bones could be broken, otherwise I would not have been able to walk the way I had.

We were now descending a long slope, at the base of which I could see a number of farm buildings. Perhaps this would be the end of our trek for the time being, at least I prayed so.

More Italian soldiers came out to meet us as we passed through a gate into a yard belonging to the main building. A sorry looking party we must have looked. The soldiers gathered around and stared at us in curiosity, but said nothing. We sank down on the ground as soon as we halted. I lay there half in a coma, caring little what happened next. I felt that I would die for the want of a drink.

I lay in the cooling shadow of a huge spreading tree, and closed my eyes. Dimly, I could hear the sounds of battle eddying and swirling in the surrounding countryside. It was very restricted, however, and came in spasmodic bursts. At that moment I cared little of what was happening—all I wanted was water and sleep. I could even forget the pain, and the attention my wounds needed, if I was left in peace to sleep.

I heard the rattle of equipment, and looked up slowly. A few feet away, an Italian soldier was drinking from a tilted water bottle. The sight almost drove me mad. Through parched and swollen lips, I croaked to him the one word I knew in Italian, 'Aqua'.

He looked at me, and then shrugged his shoulders and said something that sounded like 'Fini', and illustrated his words by turning the bottle upside down, showing me that it was empty. Then he said something else to me, and beckoned. I staggered to my feet, and followed him across the yard. He picked up a bucket en route which lay against the wall of the farmhouse. I spurred myself on after him. He crossed the yard again, and the next moment I found myself looking at the heavenly vision of a well. The soldier turned a handle. With much creaking, a bucket suddenly came into sight, with water slopping out all around.

My mouth tightened in anticipation, and I could hardy control myself from lunging forward and seizing it. The Italian unhooked the bucket and tipped the contents into the one he had brought across. The gurgle of the water almost drove me insane. Then he passed the bucket across to me. I grabbed it desperately, and with trembling hands raised it to my lips. I tried to drink, but found I couldn't get the rim into my swollen mouth. I plunged my whole face in and sucked the most beautiful cold water I had ever tasted. The coldness of the water made my head spin, but heedlessly I drew mouthful after mouthful into my parched throat, ignoring the tearing pain of my lacerated lips. After I had quenched my thirst to a degree that I never thought was possible, I upended the bucket and poured the rest over my head. I leaned against the stone wall of the well, while my head spun around and around. Then the effects wore off and, feeling more alive than dead as I had felt before the drink, I lay down again, and watched the others taking their share.

We did not stay in the farmyard long. An NCO came across and motioned for us to rise again. Wearily, I stumbled to my feet in company with the other two prisoners. We were marched out onto a dusty lane down which we limped, prodded on by the Italians who were uneasily gazing around as though they expected to be ambushed at any moment. I was terribly tired, but felt much better now that my thirst had been quenched. My leg had gone stiff, and a gnawing pain bit into my thigh. A dark crust of congealed blood had formed around the slashed cloth of my trousers, but so far I had not had the opportunity to look at my thigh to see what damage had been actually done to me. I also dreaded the thought of looking into a mirror at my battered face.

We rounded a bend in the lane and came upon a cottage outside of which was draped a Red Cross flag. I felt hope flare up within me as we approached the little building, half covered by a luxuriant growth of creepers. Perhaps we would be left inside where we could rest.

Outside the cottage was an old farm cart of the two-wheeled variety minus a horse. On the cart was something that I first took to be an old bundle of rags but, as we drew near, I could make out that it was an Italian soldier lying there, dreadfully wounded. Incoherent words fell from his bloody lips in a weak jumble. He was sprawled out, his uniform covered all over with splotches of scarlet, where the cruel hot steel had ripped him apart. He looked as though he had been either caught by a nearby exploding shell, or by a prolonged burst of machine gun fire. Even though he was my enemy, a feeling of pity welled up within me.

The Italians snarled something at us, and pushed us on past the cart and the cottage. Evidently they did not intend to give us any medical aid yet. The pain-wracked mumbles of the wounded soldier faded as we passed on down the dusty lane.

I was beginning to feel faint again under the heat of the burning sun that gave us no respite. A thundering headache joined in the stabbing pain that was already beating through my head. I blinked the never ending stream of sweat out of my eyes, and tried to close them for a moment against the red veiling mist that was continuously trying to cloud them. But one cannot sweep away the red mist of pain just by blinking.

We came to where a lemon grove bordered the roadway and, to my great relief, we turned off into it. The thin foliage of the trees gave little shelter from the sun, but at least we had come to a halt. We appeared to be in some sort of Italian encampment. They were standing around in groups, and most of them came forward to stare at us as we sank down in a little heap under one of the trees. The men were indifferent towards us, but definitely somewhat curious. I asked one of them if he had any 'aqua'. He smiled and said something which I took to be no, for he shrugged his shoulders, and at the same time turned his water bottle upside down to indicate that it was empty.

An officer pushed his way through the soldiers, and stood before us with his legs widespread. He reminded me of pictures I had seen of Mussolini. For a minute he stared at us then, in very halting English, asked me where we had come from. I shrugged my shoulders, and pretended I did not understand him, which was half true anyway. He asked how many men were dropped the night before. Again I shrugged my shoulders and looked perplexed. He half smiled, and turned away. When he had gone, the Italians crowded in. Some of them seemed as though they wanted to talk to us.

Suddenly, I thought of the man with the bullet in his stomach. I beckoned one of the Italians forward, and pointed to the towel, stained a dirty blackish red, which the man still had pressed against his stomach. He pulled the towel away as two of the Italians bent over. An ugly looking dark rimmed hole was visible just above his right groin, and I did not like the look of it at all, for it appeared to me as though infection was setting in. I tried to explain in English to them that he needed attention. They looked sympathetic for, although they did not understand a word I said, I think they got the hang of it from the way I was gesticulating. However, they shook their heads, and shrugged their shoulders, and that was as far as I got.

Something came in with a short wicked rasp about two hundred yards away, and a violent explosion ripped the air. I hugged the ground under the lemon tree, while the Italians fell flat, clawing their way to the meagre shelter of the nearest tree. I could hear heavy clods of earth raining down in the not too far distance, accompanied by the sound of breaking branches.

I began to feel uneasy. This would be no place to be if our men suspected, or knew, that the enemy had an HQ here. Tired as I was, I would sooner be on the march than be here if our soldiers started to shell the area.

Another missile came grinding in, somewhat nearer this time. The ground shook with the concussion, and again came the thuds of clods of earth falling out of the sky. This time there was the ominous whirr of shrapnel mixed in. More branches snapped under the vicious slivers of hot steel as they speared earthwards.

The Italians were looking rather frightened now, and they were gazing around fearfully as though expecting the next shell to come screaming down in their very midst here in the grove. I was rather uncertain myself, and not a little scared, for there was no cover anywhere.

I could now hear the sounds of motors running and, out of the surrounding trees, lorries driven by the Italians came bucking and lurching onto the roadway about fifty yards away. The Italians near us started to pick up their packs and blanket rolls. One stood, or rather half crouched guard over us, his rifle pointing continuously in our direction.

Excited cries were echoing throughout the grove, and I could hear the sound of orders being bellowed around. With an almost paralysing suddenness, the heavy crash of a Bren gun thundered out not more than three or four hundred yards away. I could hear the bullets cracking through the trees about fifty yards away on my right. I half started up. A sudden hope flared up within me. The guarding Italian snarled something out to me and pushed his rifle another inch forward. I sank back. The guard was really alarmed, and he kept his eyes on us.

One of the Italian officers came running over towards us, shouting to the guard. He in turn motioned to us to get up, which we did. The Bren gun was beating out in regular bursts, the shots echoing through the grove. A bullet ricocheted away among the trees.

The guard motioned us towards the road where one of the lorries had halted. Bent double, we started for the truck. Bullets from some of the Italian rifles were whistling across the clearings and down the avenues of trees, but in the main they were on the run. I saw them clambering hurriedly onto the lorries, some of which were moving off before they were fully loaded, while the Italians running behind shouted their curses into the air.

We reached our lorry, which was an open one. The driver shouted something to our guard, and appeared to be cursing us. Spurred on by the prodding bayonet, we clambered up over the tailboard of the ancient, decrepit lorry. The guard climbed on after us together with another soldier. They went to the far end of the truck, keeping us covered.

The driver clashed the gears in his hurry to move off, and let in the clutch violently, throwing us all to the floor. A wave of pain ran through my leg. I lay on the floor as we lurched madly away, swinging off the road for an instant, bumping over the uneven ground bordering the road to avoid another truck that had stalled there. The noise of the firing was lost in the roar of the motor. Back onto the road and away from the direction of the firing we sped, our speed mounting every second, while the wind roared by with ever increasing intensity. We had to slow down, however, for we had quickly caught up with the line of trucks ahead.

We were now out of the grove and sweeping down an open road. Never in all my life had I ever seen such a panic as that which had occurred in the grove. I was almost forced to smile at the thought of it, although I was somewhat sad at the thought of being so near to our own men and yet so far away. As I eased myself onto one of the lorry's sides, the full force of my situation enveloped me, and I felt very despondent. I was a POW and might be for many years to come. It would be a long time before the confirmation that I was a POW would reach home. The column moved on spasmodically, most of the vehicles being almost nose to tail instead of spread out in orderly fashion.

I turned my eyes to the front, and suddenly felt weak, for heading straight down the convoy was an aeroplane that I recognised almost instantly as a Spitfire. The outline of the fighter loomed up larger and larger with terrible rapidity.

I gesticulated madly towards it for the benefit of the guards. They looked scared, and half crouched down while shouting wildly to the driver. I cowered down behind the cab, for the fighter was upon us, bracing myself for the curtain of lead I felt certain would strike from the speeding plane. A black shape flashed for an instant in my restricted vision and then was gone. I pulled myself up, and then fell back as another shape streaked past low overhead.

The Spitfire behind us was wheeling up into a sharp turn, and the second plane was following, which I now recognised as a German Focke-Wolf 190. Now I knew why there had been no sheet of flaming lead tearing through the crowded vehicles. Possibly the pilot had not seen the convoy, for it was obvious that he was intent on giving the pursuing enemy fighter the slip. I breathed a sigh of relief, as the two planes curved around and disappeared from sight behind a low hill, while praying that the Spitfire would not return, for that one plane could cause havoc among the convoy if he really got down to it. AA defences did not seem to exist, from what I could make out.

The two guards and we prisoners kept a nervous eye on the skies. With a sudden jerk, our lorry stopped. As one guard jumped off and crouched down alongside the lorry, the other kept one eye on us and one on the sky. Nothing happened, and the second guard dropped off the lorry while the first one kept us covered. Alongside the road ran a ditch, and the first soldier doubled over to it and crouched down, covering us from his shielded position.

I stood up in the truck, and made signs that we too should be allowed out into the shelter of the ditch. I knew that if an air attack came, we would not have many seconds to seek shelter. At first, the guards shook their heads and waved their rifles menacingly, but I persisted, and in the end they beckoned us out. I needed no second bidding along with the two other prisoners and, painful as it was to my leg, I cocked my good one over the side of the lorry and lowered myself down. We sat by the edge of the ditch with the two Italians keeping a wary eye on us.

The column remained halted. The driver had long since abandoned his cab for the shelter of the ditch. The minutes went by and then an officer came down the road and spoke to the two guards. They answered him quickly, and then turned to us. With their rifles they motioned us up and forward. I groaned to myself, for it looked as though we were in for another march, and I felt all but dead.

Past the stationary line of lorries we limped. We got hostile stares from some of the soldiers lying in the ditch, and not a few curses also. A short way past the leading lorry, we turned off the road up a farm track that led through an orchard. The way was uneven and I staggered more than ever. Trenches had been dug among the trees, and a heavy machine gun had been set up commanding a field of fire that covered the road and well beyond the far side. The Italians behind the gun stared at us curiously, but said nothing.

We reached a farm building set well back in the rear of the orchard and were halted in the centre of the yard. Without waiting for any indication from the guards, I sank down on the hard, sun-baked earth utterly exhausted. The other two men did likewise. My throat was terribly dry again, and I yearned for a long cool drink such as I had had from the well back at the previous farm.

A very young looking soldier came over, smiling all over his face. He said something in Italian, and I shrugged my shoulders. He stood there, evidently keen to talk to us. Perhaps he felt pity for the three begrimed, bloodstained and bearded POWs we were. I asked him for water and he replied with a stream of words, smiling even more. He hurried away around the farm building and I tried to lick my swollen lips in anticipation. Returning a few minutes later with a long face, he made signs that we were out of luck. He was genuinely sorry, of that I am sure. I groaned to myself, and nodded. He motioned towards the farm and he ran across to the walls of the farm and pointed to the shadow which offered some shelter from the sun. I caught on and, with the other two, moved over to the cooling shade of the wall.

We were not left long in peace. Hardly had we settled down when along came an officer with three men. We were herded together again and went stumbling out of the yard down a rutted dusty lane. At the bottom of the lane we found ourselves on a metalled road. We turned right and, keeping well into a stone wall, headed off in the direction of what I took to be Syracuse. About a mile away, I could see a number of houses which appeared to be the outskirts of a town.

Intermittent sounds of battle drifted across the fields, and our escort looked distinctly worried. We were pushed on about five to ten feet ahead of the guards, who were continually shooting uneasy glances from side to side as we hurried along as best we could. I kept glancing back at the guards, for I still did not entirely trust them, and their trigger fingers looked very itchy.

We all dived close in to the wall as something wailed across the sky ahead, rising to a sudden scream as the shell plummeted down into one of the fields lining the road on our left. It burst a good two hundred yards away, but at this stage my nerve was not very strong, as with the others, and I flattened myself out in a shallow depression against the wall.

The officer got up and shouted something to the guards. With reluctant looks they also raised themselves from the prone position, and I followed. Keeping even closer to the wall, and with nerves tensed in expectancy, we moved off. I ached in every bone, and wondered at the endurance that kept me going—perhaps because I had no alternative. My legs tried to buckle at every step and my left thigh throbbed with a deep pain.

Again the rushing roar of a shell coming in, this time nearer. Again we flung ourselves down against the scanty cover of the wall. I saw dirty grey smoke, tinged with scarlet, erupt skywards from the field on our left, and the next moment the ugly whirr of shrapnel fanned down from the sky. Hugging the ground closer, I dug my fingers in as the shrapnel thudded home into the earth and cracked sharply against the stone wall. The thunder of the explosion beat against my eardrums, adding to the dull pain that was already pulsating through my head. Then we were on our feet again and pushing forward.

Judging by the direction from which the shell had come, I guessed that it must be our Navy shelling from out at sea. I did not feel particularly friendly towards the Navy at that moment, for the shells were not falling on any special target as far as I could see. The only things in range appeared to be our good selves and our escort, and they looked far from pleased about it.

A third shell sighed across with a queer rustling sound that ended up in a short sharp scream. We were already down before the concussion beat across the road, and smoke flowered upwards, flecked with red. Unseen slivers of red-hot metal flailed down, but this time they were a little farther away. Wasting no time, we pulled ourselves up and hurried as fast as our wounds would let us go to get beyond the target area, prompted by the agitated curses of the guards.

With startling suddenness, a group of Italian soldiers came rushing out of the field where the last shell had fallen. They were shouting among themselves and numbered six or seven. They looked panic stricken and some of them dazed. The leading man spotted us being herded down the road and, mouthing what I took to be curses, raised his rifle and sighted on me. I got ready to plunge for the shallow depression by the roadside, but was saved the trouble when one of the other men said something to him, and pulled down the rifle. We hurried by under the baleful glares of the man who would have shot us.

The officer with us ran across the road ahead and we were pushed after him. He turned into the field from whence the party of startled Italians had just dashed —he very field in which the last shell had fallen. I was not a little perturbed, but had no other option but to follow.

Bent double, I hobbled along as fast as my wounded leg would permit. The others followed quickly. The field sloped upwards but, despite that, I forced myself on, although every part of my body cried out for a rest. We got through the field before the next shell came in on its errand of destruction. This time we kept on going and did not dive for cover. The sooner we put a good distance between that field and ourselves the better off we would be.

We had come out into a vast open space, and ahead of us I could see what appeared to me to be an old Roman or Greek amphitheatre almost overgrown with grass. We were given no respite and marched on towards the foot of the amphitheatre. Now that we had passed out of the danger of the shelling, the urge that had driven me on suddenly went. I stumbled and pitched forward. One of the guards yelled at me as I lay face downwards on the dried grass. Wave after wave of exhaustion passed over me. A red mist swam before my closed eyes, while my breath wheezed through my tortured lungs. My heart was beating as though it would burst out of my chest, while my swollen face did not seem to belong to me anymore. My leg had gone numb except for throbs of pain, which came and went in a never-ending cycle. I could not go on.

Something pricked my back. Forcing my head around, I opened my eyes. One of the guards motioned at me furiously with his bayonet-tipped rifle. I stumbled to my feet. The amphitheatre seemed to be revolving slowly around, and I fought to bring it into focus. I felt the agony of thirst would drive me mad.

We reached the base of the amphitheatre, and I could now see that it stretched up endlessly out of sight. I couldn't do it. I leaned against the first ridge. The officer halted the party, and I slid to the ground where I lay caring little what happened, as long as I was left alone. Gradually the tearing pain faded from my lungs, and my breathing became normal. The shocking chaos of pain that whirled within my head persisted, while my body appeared to have become numb and dead to me.

I do not know how long we rested, probably not more than five minutes. As if in a mist, I remember the officer setting off on the nightmare climb, while the guards prodded us into action. I pulled myself up slowly from ridge to ridge. Turning for a moment, half on my knees to seize a respite, I found that the man with the wound in his stomach was also hardly making it. I reached down and gave him my arm, and tried to help him up, although it was all I could do to drag my own battered body from ridge to ridge.

We continued on, me helping the wounded man whenever I could summon up strength to do so. My head spun, while again and again a red mist threatened to envelop me into oblivion, but by a miracle I fought it off time after time. Halfway up, we passed some civilians sheltering in little caves hewn out of the ridges. I hardly noticed them and furthermore did not care. They stared sullenly at us as we staggered up past them.

Then, as if in a dream, we came over the top of the last ridge, but ahead stretched a long gradual slope that appeared to have no end. I sobbed for breath. Would this nightmare climb never end? Without a pause we stumbled on.

To me, the slope had taken on the appearance of a gigantic green blur that pitched from side to side. More than once, I found myself on my knees, forcing myself up and on. Nothing seemed to make sense anymore, as my mind hovered on the brink of deep oblivion.

Somehow, we reached the summit, and the deadening strain on my legs eased off a little. I found myself lurching out onto a road. We turned to the right while I fought to focus my eyes on the white walled houses that bordered the roadway.

As we drew level with the first gateway, our conducting officer called out an order and the guards halted. I slumped to the ground, leaning my tortured back against one of the massive posts that flanked the gateway on either side. My swimming head sank down on my chest, and I closed my eyes.

Somebody shook my shoulder. I looked up into the face of the officer. He made motions of lifting something to his mouth and said, 'Aqua'. I nodded as vigorously as I could, then let my head drop forward again. I heard the footsteps of the officer going up the gravelled drive towards the house, and waited with hope in my breast. In a few minutes I heard footsteps returning. I forced my head up. The officer was coming through the gateway with a large urn in his hands. With water-starved eyes, I watched it as he passed it down to the man who was wounded in the groin. He greedily gulped vast mouthfuls of the liquid and with anguished eyes I saw a few drops spill from the edge to the ground. He lowered the urn and passed it over to the other wounded man. Again I watched with a greed that must have been ill-concealed to the guards watching. The second man finished and turned to pass it on to me.

With eager hands, I reached out and almost snatched the urn from him. With shaking hands I raised the urn to my blood caked, swollen lips. The swelling had gone down a little and, despite the pain, I forced my lips against the rim and sucked in all I could. Some of the water spilled down my chin and ran on down my neck, but I did not care. My head reeled with the sudden contact of the wonderful cold water coursing down my throat. I drank deeply, and at that moment could have cared for nothing else, not the best wines in the world, but the quenching water that slaked my burning thirst.

I drank till I thought my stomach would burst. Then I laid the urn aside. My head cleared and, except for the multitude of pains that wracked my body, I felt a new man. Looking around, I spoke with the other two men. They both felt incredibly better after their deep drink of the cold refreshing water.

Chapter 7

Return from Sicily

I gazed around at the houses and noticed that they were very large. The one nearest us was a beautiful masterpiece of architecture and the grounds were laid out in a most attractive manner. Even as I stared into the grounds, I saw the officer returning again down the path in company with a bustling little civilian. They came up to our wounded group and, on seeing us, the civilian threw up his hands in horror.

We must have looked worse than I had realised. He came over to me and said in broken English that he was French, and that furthermore he was a doctor. I thanked him for the water, and he waved his hands as though to say it was absolutely nothing. I pointed to the man who had the towel still wrapped around his stomach. The doctor went over to him and bent down. The towel was eased away and he carried out a swift examination. He gently replaced the towel, and turning to the other man, quickly checked him over. Then he came back to me.

He looked at my mouth, and then at my leg, shaking his head all the time. Fumbling in his pocket, he pulled out a small bottle and some cotton wool. He found a small sliver of wood and wrapped the cotton wool around it, following this up by dipping the whole into the bottle. Finally he turned to me and, taking my face in his hands, began to try and clean away the dirt and congealed blood from my mouth. It was agony, gentle as he was, but as he worked I felt my lips become lighter as he eased off the hardened dry blood. He stood back, and I found I could open my mouth a little more; I thanked him as much as I could.

Suddenly, he turned to the officer who had been watching the operation and let loose a flood of French which I could not understand. He accompanied his speech by much waving of his arms. He looked really angry. I got the impression that he was telling the officer off for not having seen that we got medical aid before this. And what was more, the officer was taking it all with hardly a protest. In the end, the officer shrugged his shoulders, upon which the doctor immediately turned around and darted off back up the drive to the house. I wondered what was happening, but didn't really care so long as we were left to sprawl out in peace. I looked at the officer, who was staring down at us, half expecting him to order us up on our feet again. Instead, with quite a friendly grin, he motioned for us to stay where we were. He then followed the doctor up the drive into the house.

We were left alone except for the guard, which seemed to have grown to about six men now. They stood and leaned against the wall, staring at us curiously, but making no move to try to speak.

I closed my eyes and relaxed my aching body against the hard unyielding roadway, resting my head and back against the stone wall.

As I lay thus, I thought I had begun to dream for distinctly, through my befuddled thoughts, I heard an American voice talking away. It grew in intensity, and gradually it beat into my brain that it was actually someone speaking. I opened my eyes, and saw that a second group of Italian soldiers had joined our guard. From among them I could hear the drawling voice that was unmistakably American.

One of the soldiers was coming forward saying 'How are you fellows?' In my dazed state, I looked at him half comprehendingly. He continued, 'I lived in America for fifteen years, and happened to be back here on a visit in 1940 when the war broke out, and Mussolini yanked me into his Goddamned army.' He was all smiles, and banged us on our backs in a none too gentle fashion. Even though he was our enemy, I felt strangely elated to hear someone talking English with hardly a trace of accent.

'Well, so long. I've got to be on my way with the rest. See you later'. With that parting rejoinder he was gone, and I was still wondering whether I had heard correctly, or was getting delirious. I closed my eyes and opened them again. Yes, it must have been real, for I could see the soldier along with the rest of his party just disappearing around a bend in the road.

I looked at the guard. The intrusion seemed to have broken the ice, for some of them were closing in and appeared quite friendly. Some of them were grinning in a half hearted way. One fumbled in his pocket and pulled out a packet of cigarettes, which he passed around to us. The others took one gratefully, but I refused, for my mouth was so painful.

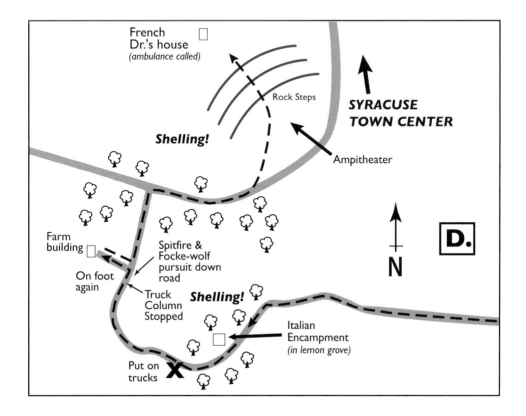

There was a noise on the gravel, and the next moment the little French doctor came flying out of the drive mounted on a bicycle. He waved to us and shouted out something. Next moment he was pedalling furiously away down the road towards what I estimated to be the centre of Syracuse. The officer came crunching down the drive on foot after him. He still seemed friendly but aloof. He stood to one side while the guard, who had drawn back a little at the sight of their officer returning, closed in again. Their officer appeared not to mind them trying to talk to us, even though neither of us knew what the other was talking about.

The officer came over and pulled three lemons out of his pocket which he proffered to us. We all took them and thanked him as best we could. He nodded and stepped back to muse on his own again. The minutes passed, and I began to feel a little better. The rest was bringing as fair a recovery as was possible under the circumstances.

About ten minutes after the doctor had ridden away, an ambulance came around the corner. It was a beautiful white civilian one and idly I watched it approaching. I was a little surprised when it pulled up alongside us. The doors opened and a nurse descended followed by the little doctor. I could have blessed him. He must have cycled off especially to fetch an ambulance for us. In his quaint English, he told us to get in and that we would be driven to hospital. We thanked him as best we could, but he waved it all aside. He was all smiles as the doors of the ambulance in the rear closed behind us, and shouted something about good luck.

Through the windows of the rear doors, we could see him waving away as the ambulance started up and smoothly sped away down the road towards the town. Even the guard waved as we left, and for a brief moment I forgot the throbbing pains that engulfed practically all my body. I leaned back against the side of the ambulance and wearily looked at the nurse who rode with us. One armed guard also accompanied us, and he sat staring without comment. We purred on through the streets, and I closed my eyes.

A few minutes later we slowed to a stop. The doors were opened and we lowered ourselves out with the helping hand of the nurse. I looked around and found that we had stopped in front of a beautiful hospital. A tree lined drive led up to the entrance, which itself was magnificent. Faint as I was, I could not help admiring the graceful architecture of the building.

We were led up the broad steps into a room where we sat down. It was heavenly to be able to perform that civilised action, small as it was, after the last forty-eight-hour ordeal. We did not have to wait long. Another nurse came and beckoned to us. Rising up, we limped after her out along a broad corridor. She directed one of the men into a room, and then led the other man and myself on. We were both taken into the same room, and I was promptly put onto an operating table.

A nurse unlaced my boots, and tugged and strained to get them off. At any other time I would have been ashamed at the state of my feet, mud-encrusted, dirty and grimy as they were from the time when we had sought shelter under the bridge in the thick, glue-like mud. My socks had stuck to my feet, and she had to use considerable force to peel them off.

Next, my trousers were gently removed, and the doctor started to examine my leg. I twisted my eyes downward to catch a glimpse of what damage had been done. As far as I could make out, there were six shrapnel wounds in my left thigh. They were not very large, but looked rather nasty. From two of them I could see slivers of glinting metal protruding, for which I was thankful, for it meant that they had not penetrated very deep. The edges of the wounds had taken on a greenish tinge, and I felt uneasy on that point with visions of gangrene rising before my eyes. A nurse passed the doctor a pair of large tweezers and I closed my eyes. I felt a tearing pain in my flesh as he gently removed one piece of metal. He probed deeper and I winced. One by one, my wounds were probed and I could hear the metallic clink as piece after piece of shrapnel dropped onto a container on the tray. At one time it particularly hurt as he dug and twisted among the torn flesh. Apparently, no local anaesthetic was available, or else I am sure he would have used it. I felt the perspiration gathering on my brow and gripped the edge of the table with my hands.

Then he was through, and I felt my leg being bandaged up. I looked across at the other man who had been hit in the groin. Another doctor was still examining him. His stomach was bared, and I could see where the bullet had struck home. Red, angry-looking flesh had risen in the form of a mound around the point of entrance of the bullet. The rim of the hole had turned a dark red while the surrounding flesh was covered with coagulated blood, now almost black.

The doctor was bending over my face now, while a nurse continued to bandage up my leg. He peered closely at my mouth, and then applied something on a piece of cotton wool. It burnt like hell as he dabbed away. Then he attacked my upper lip with a large cut-throat type razor and, minus any lather, commenced to hack at my already mutilated moustache. The hairs resisted and caused agony as the still swollen lip was pulled first one way and then the other. He stepped back and a nurse wiped a wet flannel all over my face, removing some of the filth and grime that had embedded itself. The cool contact of the flannel was gratifying. The doctor said something to the nurse, turned around and left the room. She strapped a pad across my lip with adhesive plaster. I lay there as more and more bandage was wrapped around my leg from groin to knee, which had gone terribly stiff with a dull ache beating away from toe to the upper part of my thigh.

One of the nurses eased me up, and a stretcher was wheeled over. I was gently lifted off the table onto the stretcher. I remembered my trousers, and gestured towards the almost unrecognisable garment, ripped and muddied. The nurse bent down, picked up the soggy mass with a smile and placed it on the stretcher. I was wheeled off out of the operating room down several corridors. We turned into a large ward, which was empty except for the two men already there. The two nurses eased me off the stretcher. and I half hopped and half fell onto the bed, which incidentally consisted of a mattress and one blanket, but quite comfortable. I lay back and closed my eyes, for my head was spinning and my body felt one mass of aches and pains.

I rested thus for some time and then, feeling a little better, opened my eyes and began to take stock of my surroundings. I looked at the man in the bed next to mine. He looked at me. The recognition was mutual. He was a fellow glider pilot by the name of Sgt. C. I did not know him very well, but had spoken to him from time to time. Actually he was from another squadron.

I asked him what had happened to him. He told me that he had been flying one of the Horsas detailed to glide in over the harbour and land near the bridge. Searchlights had pinpointed their glider, and a few moments later they had been hit by flak. The glider had gone into a dive out of control. Some of the flak had hit Sgt. C in the legs and he was all but unconscious when the glider plunged into the waters of the Ponte Grande harbour. The Italians had picked him up out of the water a short while later and he had ended up in the hospital. He did not know what had been the fate of the other occupants of the glider. He turned back the blanket and showed me the bandages that were swathed around both legs. Even though they had been put on in depth, an ugly dark stain had spread over and was seeping out, especially from his left leg. He did not think that he would ever fly again, and I was inclined to agree with him.

We lay back and listened to the sounds of guns, light and heavy, rumbling and barking in the distance. Perhaps it was the Eighth Army advancing on Syracuse at last. We hoped so, although we were afraid that we might be evacuated if they came too close.

Towards evening there came the roar of low flying aircraft. They thundered down over the roof of the hospital. Machine gun fire crackled, and the quick pulsating grunt of light AA broke forth. We cringed down in our beds, shielding our faces with the blankets, for the ward was one mass of huge windows with large panes of glass. Something smashed through one of the windows, and broken glass tinkled to the floor. The planes zoomed down and up. The thundering concussion of bombs falling about half a mile away rocked the building. Another machine skimmed low over the roof and was gone.

I never heard the bomb come. There was a mushroom of dirty, grey, black smoke rising upwards outside one of the windows. The thunder of the explosion was deafening. A wave of concussion beat across the room. Through the thinness of my blanket I heard a cascade of glass crashing to the floor and outside. Gingerly, I lifted my face from the shielding blanket. Smoke still billowed up outside, and for a moment I thought the place was on fire. Then the smoke subsided. I felt shaken. When I had entered the hospital I had at least thought we would be somewhat immune from attacks.

The last of the planes had gone, and a contrasting silence descended. We talked amongst ourselves of many things, mostly of England and our chances of getting back there.

A short while later a number of Italians were brought in. From the cries of pain emanating from some of them, they had been hurt pretty badly. They were taken off the stretchers and put into bed. Most of them quietened down, but one persisted in moaning without pause, and kept breaking out into a torrent of Italian. They had been put at the far end of the ward. Two or three more came limping in, but they seemed only slightly wounded. Each was allotted a bed at the far end.

The less wounded Italians were staring down towards our end curiously. After a short while, one of them slowly limped down the ward, and paused uncertainly by our beds. Another Italian drifted down and joined the first. One of them fumbled in his pocket, and pulled out a wallet. Then he said something to one of our men, who did not understand him, and shrugged his shoulders. The Italian moved closer and sat down on a bed adjoining the man he had addressed. He opened his wallet and drew out a number of photographs, which he pushed towards our man. The soldier took them slowly, and looked through them, while the Italian watched eagerly. Then he began pointing to each one and tried to explain who the persons in the photograph were.

Gradually the ice thawed between us all, and another Italian came over to my bed; he also appeared to carry numerous photographs of people who, I gathered, were his wife, children, mother and so on. We, of course, had nothing to show in return, for the Italians who had captured us had stripped us of everything. It passed the time away to look at the photographs and try and carry on a conversation, which nobody understood anyhow.

There were several nuns helping in the ward and they were all smiles to us. While we were being shown photographs, one of them came into the ward bearing a tray with steaming bowls of spaghetti and tomatoes. I had not realised how hungry I was until I saw the contents of the bowls. Now my stomach positively craved food. I thanked the nun as best I could and, along with the others, ate ravenously. I asked the nun for some water, and she nodded and hurried away. A few minutes later she returned bearing a glass of water which I drank thirstily.

The hot food had a wonderful effect upon me. Even some of the aches and pains seemed to vanish. I could have eaten much more, but didn't like to ask, for I had a hunch that there was not a great deal of food about. I did however ask for some more water, but the nun spread her hands and in very broken English explained that the RAF had bombed last night and had smashed the water mains, hence no more water. The glass I had had came from their precious store in the hospital. I did not press for any more.

Jokingly, I turned to one of the Italian soldiers and said 'Vino' which I thought stood for wine. He looked at me for a moment and then smiled, saying something to me thar I did not understand and limped quickly out of the ward. In a few minutes he returned triumphantly bearing a large bottle of red wine. I was surprised, for I had not really expected to receive any. I opened the bottle and took a goodly swig, then passed it on to the next bed and so the bottle made its rounds. The Italians seemed delighted that they had pleased us.

Later that afternoon, a German officer, accompanied by some Italian medical staff, entered our ward. It became apparent that the German officer was selecting those who could walk to take away as prisoners of war. I didn't want to be shipped off to some POW camp so fiddled with the bandages on my leg to spread them out a bit and then laid back with my eyes closed and feigned semi-consciousness. The officer came round to me, flipped the blanket back and saw my leg and said, 'Nein'! and walked away. I felt very relieved.

Night fell quickly and I suddenly felt tired. The noise of battle had almost died away, but I was too far gone to worry about anything. I slept deeply that night, and I do not think that even a raid would have awakened me. As a matter of fact, next morning I was told that there had been a raid that night. It seemed to have been directed against the harbour, although by whose planes no one seemed to know.

I felt much better after the night's sleep, although my leg still throbbed painfully, as did my mouth. No breakfast was forthcoming, and by mid-morning I was really famished.

All seemed to have gone quiet outside. I wondered what had happened. Had our men been driven back, or what? About midday I was put at rest regarding that point. I was dozing quietly away when I was awakened by the familiar sounds of English voices. I sat up in bed and listened intently.

The door opened and in came a procession of English and Italian officers. They came straight over to our beds, and a man with the rank of Colonel asked who we were. I must admit I was rather suspicious. I thought perhaps that the Italians were pulling a fast one with Italian soldiers dressed up in English uniforms to obtain information from us. I knew it was useless to deny that we were airborne troops— our red berets had already told the Italians that much. I replied that we were from the Airborne, but did not mention any units. That seemed to satisfy him anyway.

He asked how we had been treated, and I replied, 'As well as could be expected under the circumstances'. The colonel was very cheerful, and said he would send up some cigarettes. I was so elated at the thought that they were probably English (their accent was too perfect for an Italian to copy, as the prolonged conversation had revealed), that I forgot to mention that food would be welcome also. An old, dirty-looking Italian civilian was acting as interpreter between our officers and the Italians, and he had listened in anxiously to our reply about treatment. He was all smiles and repeated our words to the Italian doctors, who also had been looking rather worried. They in turn looked considerably relieved.

The procession moved out of the ward with the Colonel informing us, over his shoulder, that he would get us out of the hospital and onto a ship during the day. That was wonderful news to us. An excited conversation broke out after they had left. Even the Italians appeared elated, due probably to the uncertainty of the situation being cleared up; I could find no other reason.

A short while later, a corporal returned to the ward with a number of packets of cigarettes which he distributed among our men. I had to refuse mine, for my mouth would not permit any smoking, much as I longed for a few puffs. The corporal left with the assurance that we would be shifted out of the hospital some time that day. There was a hospital ship out in the bay right now loading up.

Evening closed in bringing with it a short sharp raid by enemy planes mostly directed against the harbour, where I gathered several of our ships were anchored. We could hear the planes thunder down amid a cacophony of AA fire. Distant explosions made the windows rattle in their frames, while loose glass from the previous raid fell to the floor with a tinkle. I would not be sorry to be out of this building. The enemy did not always show respect for hospitals, and it even appeared that he singled them out at times.

A soldier dropped in later on to say that we would not be taken out today as the Germans had bombed and sunk the hospital ship in the harbour despite the fact that she was brilliantly lit up. We felt bitter against the Germans for that deed, not because of the delay vented upon us in that hospital, but for the sake of the men, already wounded once, who must have been hurled into the waters or trapped in the sinking vessel. After the nervous and physical fatigue which we had undergone the last two days, most of us in the ward reversed our keenness to get aboard a hospital ship. For my part, I felt distinctly safer on dry land. Well, we could only wait and see—we had no power over whether we went on board a ship or not.

The town appeared to be firmly in our hands, and from what I had learned from the corporal earlier on, our troops had pushed well beyond. I gave up hope of being moved that night and fell off into an uneasy slumber in which I saw the whole operation all over again. I woke up with a start to find myself drenched with sweat. The horror of the night before last rose before me time and time again before the first faint light of dawn heralded a new day.

About mid morning a group of our men entered the ward with stretchers and told us that we were really off this time. I was rolled onto a stretcher and taken down the stairs, along a corridor and into a room, where I was properly tagged by one of our medical units. Then I was lifted once more, and a few minutes later I was lying on a comfortable stretcher bed inside a military ambulance. Two more men joined me on stretchers. The ambulance doors were closed and we moved off. I half sat up, trying to get a glimpse of the town as we passed down the hill towards the docks. Tumbled masonry was everywhere from what I could see through the small windows. I noticed a number of Sicilians picking their way through the rubble, little bundles slung over their shoulders. Their faces were expressionless. Out on the broad quay we drove, broadened I think by the Allied bombing which had demolished a large number of buildings during their periodical raids.

We stopped, and a few moments later the doors were opened by the cheery faced driver and we were lifted down. I got off my stretcher and, with the help of one of the attendants, limped over to the edge of the quay, alongside which were moored a number of small landing craft. Willing hands assisted me down some steps. On the deck of the landing craft were a number of stretchers laid out in rows, some of which were occupied. I was shown one, and sank down feeling quite weak after that small effort.

The landing craft rose and fell gently on the lapping waters. I began to feel the effects of the hot Sicilian sun. The sides of the landing craft, which were of steel sheets, felt extremely hot under my hands.

The minutes went by and we made no move. Somehow I did not feel oversafe in this steel cockle shell, and I longed to hear the motor break into life. I asked one of the Navy fellows if we were moving off soon. He replied that several more ambulances would have to bring their loads down first. The landing craft had to leave full each time, as the hospital ship to which we were bound lay some ten miles down the coast. The Navy was not taking any chances this time. I settled down, shielding the glare of the sun from my eyes as best I could.

As I lay, half asleep, I suddenly heard the menacing drone of aircraft. I half sat up, and looked up into the blue cloudless sky. My vision was very restricted by the sides of the landing craft. The roar grew louder and then I saw them. A flight of Italian R.E. 2000s, with their unmistakable elliptical wings and radial engines, curving around over the port in perfect formation not more than two or three thousand feet up. At the same moment, some gunners must have awakened to the fact that they were enemy, for the rhythmic thumping of a Bofors gun beat out upon the air, to be joined a moment later by more.

Puffs of smoke burst in the air near the formation. They continued their lazy circling, passing directly over the harbour. My uneasiness increased. I would hate to be caught inside one of these hollow steel shells if they decided to drop bombs, even if they were light ones. Something seemed to tell me that it would not take much of a hole to sink a landing craft of this type. The sides would afford some protection against machine gun fire if they strafed, but a bomb hitting squarely would be another proposition entirely.

The wounded upon the stretchers gazed up at the fighters. Some appeared unconcerned, others expressed their apprehension. The AA fire increased, and the formation began to break up. They peeled off into dives, but to my great relief they headed out and away from the harbour. The noise of the AA died down, and the planes did not return.

We waited another hour or so while ambulance after ambulance brought in its load of broken humanity. One of the sailors returned from a looting expedition into the town carrying a large number of parasols and umbrellas which he promptly passed down to the wounded in order that they could keep the heat of the sun off to some degree. He was welcomed with cheers. He also carried an enormous volume written in English on navigation, for which he received a number of jeers from fellow sailors. The funniest thing of all was the ancient black silk top hat he wore, acquired from a house facing the harbour, so he informed us. It did not go at all with the sailor's outfit on the rest of his body, but it caused some merriment among us.

With startling suddenness, the landing craft vibrated from stem to stern as the powerful engine broke into life. I breathed a sigh of relief and thankfully watched the sailors on the quay above casting off. With gently throbbing engines we edged away from the stone quay. The nose swung slowly round and we headed out across the harbour, threading our way between moored ships and wrecks that dotted the waters. The harbour was wonderfully calm and we glided smoothly along with only the slightest indication of roll.

I lay back and listened to the healthy beat of the engines as we picked up speed. As we passed out of the shelter of the harbour, the landing craft began to pitch and roll in the most alarming manner. The steel plates strained and creaked, and to my non-nautical mind, it seemed that that boat must gradually fall apart.

I half pulled myself up and tried to peer out over the sides, but just couldn't make it. Not that I needed to, for the pitching and rolling was becoming so bad that from time to time I could see the distant coast appear over the rim of the boat as we rolled heavily shorewards. From the fragmentary glimpses I caught of the Sicilian coast, all seemed peaceful, with the rolling landscape lying serene under the almost cloudless blue skies. No signs of battle could be discerned from the distance that we were out from the shore. We were holding a course parallel with the coast, and I soon lost interest in the pitching landscape. I lay there, my stomach rebelling against the unruly movement of the landing craft, and hoped that we would not have too far to go.

We must have been travelling for about half an hour before I heard the engines being throttled back while we swung in a large circle. I half raised myself again, and caught a glimpse of the side of a ship, painted white, towering high above us. One moment it was there, the next it was gone as we dipped down into a trough. I could hear voices shouting, and the engines were opened and closed several times as we manoeuvred alongside the ship.

We lay in the lee of the hospital ship while a cage was lowered down. Stretcher after stretcher was lifted away from the landing craft and hoisted up onto the deck of the motionless ship. Then came my turn. I was assisted into the strange looking cage, and the next moment the landing craft dropped away below, still wallowing and grating against the sides of the huge ship. The cage reached the deck level, swung in and gently dropped to the boards. I hobbled out and was assisted by a nurse who left me in a ward after assigning a bunk to me. Before leaving, she gave me a package marked with the insignia of the Red Cross.

I sat on my bunk and opened up the gift. Inside were a razor, blades and soap. I limped over to the ablutions and, despite the painful pulling of the bandages stuck well into my wounds, washed and shaved for the first time in many days. I dared not use the showers owing to the wealth of bandages that swathed my left leg. Returning to my bunk, I sank gratefully down thereon.

Those of us that could limp along somehow were summoned to the messroom adjoining the ward, and were served an excellent meal. Never had food tasted so good to me, the first real man-sized meal I had tasted for many a day. Returning to my bunk, I fell fast asleep, only to wake up late that night. The ward was quiet, and only a few low lights burned.

The sweat was heavy on my brow, while I felt my heart beating within my chest. Only a moment before, I had again been in the midst of the horror of the hill above Syracuse. I tried to sleep again, and succeeded, only to awaken later on with the same dream tumbling through my head, and my body trembling while beads of perspiration rolled down my brow and face. The orderly spotted me the second time, and he must have seen something in my face that demanded attention, for he brought over a strong sleeping draught that kept me in oblivion until late the following morning.

It was only the dull throb of the engines that indicated we were moving at all. But for that, I would have thought we were motionless. My wounds were dressed, and I was ordered not to leave my bunk. I lay there, but could think of nothing but the last few days, my mind a chaos of thoughts.

That same afternoon, we arrived at Tripoli and anchored in the harbour amidst the desolation of bombed and sunken craft. As we were transferred from the ship into waiting ambulances, I caught a glimpse of the pulverised quaysides. The Allies had certainly blasted the dock area of Mussolini's capital of the once-proud colony of Italy.

We drove off through the graceful architecture of the town, and out onto the open road beyond, on the way to Homs. I remember thinking how lovely the laid-out date plantations looked, flanking the road as we drove through the village of Tajura. The road was well built, and our ambulance sped smoothly along. We passed through another village, but I could not see the name of it. Half a mile beyond, we slowed up and turned off to the right onto the sandy soil that flanked the road on either side. We stopped. The doors were opened and I descended in company with three others.

A vista of tents set amid the Tripolitanian sandy scrub met my gaze. A board proclaimed the settlement as the 106th South African General Hospital. We checked in and were then shown our respective tents, which were splendidly equipped with beds and other paraphernalia.

Somehow, a feeling of safety at last settled over me as I lay on my bed that evening. All was quiet except for the occasional rumble of a truck heading down the road outside. Through a loudspeaker affixed to one of the tent poles, the gentle strains of music flowed forth. I nuzzled down in the white sheets, although I knew that the coming night would bring no restful sleep. I knew that I was to be haunted by nightmares that would steadfastly refuse me peace and quiet, and I waited.

I spent seven weeks at the 106th, and the staff were most kind to us all the whole time. Daily my wounds were tended. Patiently the nurse would unroll the yards of bandages that swathed my thigh, remove the scabs that fought hard to form over the gouged flesh, clean out the wounds with a peculiar yellowish looking lotion, and bandage them up again. It was pretty painful while it lasted, but gradually they all healed but one, which one day gave up a further piece of shrapnel, a very small piece however.

On one occasion, I sneaked out and limped across the road down to the water's edge of the sparkling blue Mediterranean. Daily I was hearing its praise from those fortunate enough to be able to go swimming. How warm the water was! How lovely to browse on the sands afterwards!

I picked my way down past some old rusty barbed wire, and came to the water's edge. The waves swirled gently in, and foamed white where they met the sands. I stood on a nearby rock and gazed down into the transparent depths, and longed to plunge into the blue green waters, cursing the bandages that still held me chained. I lingered until the sun went down in a flame of crimson and orange over the western horizon, and the cool of evening followed rapidly in on the heat of the dying day. Meandering slowly back to the tent, I was met by a reproving sister who hustled me back into bed.

The days passed by in a blaze of sunshine, making the finely-grained sand red hot beneath the naked sole. At night, the silvery African moon would steal silently across the night sky amidst the company of brightly twinkling stars, casting a pale cold light that turned the sands white. I would sit by the open flap of the tent and let my thoughts wander to home, usually by selecting out the Pole Star and roughly calculating the direction in which England lay.

Over the radio came the news of the conquest of Sicily, and then the fall of Mussolini and the surrender of Italy. We all got excited over that last bit of news, for it looked as if the war might come to an end quite soon. How we deluded ourselves. Mid August saw me with only one wound still unhealed. I was a little surprised one day when I was summoned to the O.C's tent and told that I would be leaving that day. I was surprised for almost invariably, as men left the wards, they were automatically transferred to the convalescent area which adjoined our hospital. There they stayed for at least a week while they were gradually brought back onto trim again.

He asked me if I felt alright and I replied in the affirmative, but mentioned that I still had one bandage on. He replied that that would be OK, so I left with my papers, and the same afternoon an ambulance took me with two others out of the camp and back along the road we had come up seven weeks earlier. Through the palm flanked road to Tajura and on to Tripoli. We did not stop in Tripoli, but passed straight through.

About five miles beyond Tripoli, on the road to Zavia, we turned off into a wired-in enclosure set amid rolling sand dunes. I stepped down from the ambulance and surveyed the scattered tents and the notice board which informed me that this was a transit camp. The ambulance left, and the others who had ridden in the ambulance were told to cross the road and go to another part of the camp among the infantry. I stayed on this side of the road.

An orderly showed me to my tent and left. It was bare except for a pile of kit made up, which indicated that I at least had company. I spread my ground sheet out on the sandy soil and laid my blanket atop. Feeling a little tired after my efforts, I realised how weak even a short spell in bed can leave one. I sat down among my kit and rested, musing as to the future.

A short while later, the only other occupant of the tent arrived back. He was a corporal of the Regular army. We chatted about various things, and I learned from him the meal times and so forth. Being an old soldier of the infantry, he regarded airborne warfare as completely out of place in war, and plugged for the land armies a hundred per cent. We argued in a friendly way, and each ended up convinced that his was the real force that counted!

That evening at dinner, eaten on the ruins of an old factory about ten minutes' limping walk away, I ran into an old friend from my original regiment, the Queen's Royal Regiment, whom I had not seen in three years. I had recognised him instantly. We talked over old times. He was going back to England, owing to his nerves being no longer very good after a bad do during the Eight Army's campaign across North Africa earlier in the year. I never saw him again after that meeting.

The next day I went down to the office to learn how long I could expect to be here in the camp. They replied to the effect that it might be one to five or more days. They couldn't tell for sure as it was not often that trucks came in that were going as far as Sousse in Tunisia.

My leg was beginning to act up on me again. That same afternoon, the open wound that had been still bandaged swelled up. Evidently sand and dirt had seeped through the bandage and had inflamed it. There was little I could do until the following morning when sick parade was held. I cursed my luck, for I had wanted to spend the evening in Tripoli. I was one of the very few left in camp that evening; the rest had either walked or hitchhiked in to Tripoli to sample its dubious pleasures.

I slept little that night with the gnawing agony that increasingly pained my thigh. I was up early next morning and, forgoing breakfast, I set off down the road, hobbling as best I could, for no transport was available. The first aid station lay nearly a mile away, and the sweat was pouring off me when I eventually limped up to the entrance. During the whole of the walk, the bandages had been constantly tearing at the wound, for they had been stuck fast into the pus and scab that had formed over the raw flesh. The movement of my leg muscles as I hobbled along caused the bandages to pull at every step, causing severe pain.

The medical aide examined my leg carefully, after slowly removing the bandages. The last roll bared the naked flesh, and I was a little alarmed at the inflamed and pus-ridden wound that was revealed. I had never seen it so swollen before. The aide cleaned it out and the swelling went down somewhat. He re-bandaged my thigh and remarked that if it was not better tomorrow, he would put me in hospital. I limped back to the camp trying to hold the bandages still with both hands wrapped firmly round my thigh. I was all in when I reached my tent.

The next day my leg had swollen up again, but not quite so badly. I prepared to go down to the first aid post once more. Before I could set out, an orderly came over to my tent and informed me that there was an empty tank-carrying transport leaving for Sousse in about an hour's time and I could take that if I was ready. I made up my mind immediately that I would take the transport; I'd be better off back with my old squadron.

It was about four to five hundred miles to Sousse by road, and the tank transport would take about four days to do the journey. At least I would get a magnificent view from the open flat top of the transport. I piled my small amount of kit and blankets onto the vehicle, and waited for its departure.

We only travelled twenty miles or so that day as we had made a late start. We slept alongside the huge bulk of the tank carrier with the stars overhead for a roof. My leg pained me, but I managed to get in a fair night's sleep.

The next day, we rolled westward along the coastal road with the blue Mediterranean Sea nearly always in sight about a mile away on our right. Cloudless skies accompanied us, and I really began to enjoy the trip despite my troublesome leg. I gazed with unrestricted vision upon the sometimes almost pure white sand dunes studded with majestic palms that lay between the road and the sea.

It was cloudless, very hot, and the sun beat down without a break. There was absolutely no shade at all on the open body of the tank carrier, and the only way to keep a little cool was to stand up and let the slipstream play over one's body, stripped as we were to the waist. Even so, the stream of air would come back as a hot blast from the black tarmac road, while tiny particles of sand and dust that were swirled up by the wheels of the transporter would strike stinging blows on our naked flesh.

We passed on through the villages of Zuara and Farma and, a short way beyond the latter village, we came to the border between Tripolitania and Tunisia. The only visible sign that showed that we had left Tunisia was a straggle of barbed wire that stretched away on either side as far as the eye could see. No one stood guard there now, while on either side lay undulating, scrub-covered semi-desert. There was, however, a distinct feel that we had crossed from one country to another. The road from Tripoli to the border had been wonderfully engineered and built by the Italians. The moment we crossed into Tunisia, we entered upon a road that was in very bad repair. Potholes were everywhere for the first few miles, but it gradually improved. But never again did we traverse a length of road comparable to that in Tripolitania.

Our carrier jolted on, and late afternoon we came to a halt on the brow of a hill above the town of Ben Gardane. There was a transit area where trucks could pull in for the night, but no shelter was available. We lit a fire alongside the transport, and prepared our evening meal, which consisted of bully beef and biscuits cooked up into a strange looking mess. We also had the inevitable tea.

After the meal, I sat on the truck and wistfully looked down and away at the white buildings of Ben Gardane and the beckoning waters of the sparkling sea. On the crest of the hill, graceful palms stood out on the skyline, surrounded by golden white sands. The two drivers and the rest of the men who had been travelling on the transport had left for the town to spend an evening therein. I had to stay behind, for my leg was too painful, and I could never have made the walk into the town which lay over a mile away.

On the right of the town I had a birdseye view of the aerodrome, and I idly watched the planes taking off and landing until the dusk of evening settled in. A few scattered lights marked where the town lay. I unrolled my blankets, laid them out alongside the carrier, and dozed.

At 8.00 am the next day, we roared out of that area, and wound our way down the long hill into Ben Gardane. We rolled through the town without a halt and up a slight hill the other side.

Midday found us passing through Medenine up a short steep hill. White buildings of the French inhabitants peeped through verdant green foliage of palms and other trees. A church tower dominated the scene. We passed the dwellings of the Arabs, built in strange tier-like form on the side of the hill as we climbed out of the village.

About thirty miles further on, we approached Mareth, scene of a vicious battle between the Eighth Army and the Afrika Corps earlier on in the year. The village was sprawled out on the slopes of a hill and, as we wound up through the centre amid a luscious growth of palms, I could see signs of the recent battle. The white walls of nearby buildings were pitted and torn where bursting steel and lead had gouged out great chunks in a mad fury. Beyond the village, at the top of the hill, we passed a military cemetery on our left. The rows of wooden crosses bore mute witness of the savage battle that had once raged there. The Battle of the Mareth Line had been front-page news when it was being fought, but no print could bring home the full impact of death and destruction as did the battered village of Mareth and the silent rows of crosses outside on the hillside where the winds would whistle over them in a mournful dirge in the coming winter and those thereafter.

In vain, I looked for signs of the formidable Mareth Line thrown up by the Afrika Corps, and earlier still by the French before the war had started. The only signs I saw were a few well-sited pillboxes and part of an anti-tank trap. No doubt the soldiers who had taken part in the Battle of Mareth could have enlightened me, that is, those who did not now lie under the cold earth back on the hillside. Probably a great deal of the more conspicuous signs had been cleared away, or blasted during the advance. Furthermore, it was a well known fact among military men that the line had been skilfully camouflaged, so perhaps it was there in front of me all the time, only I was not able to see it.

We rumbled on along the dusty road that leads towards Gabes. I was surprised at the lack of traffic on the road, for this was the main coastal arterial road. The only conclusion I could come to was that all our effort was being concentrated in Sicily at the moment.

Throughout the long ride, we had been constantly passing by bullet-ridden and burned-out wrecks of cars, lorries and tanks. Hardly more than a quarter of a mile during almost the whole of the four- to five-hundred mile ride was passed without one or sometimes groups of six or seven vehicles together, pushed off the road in a jumbled mass and left just as they were during the days of the sweeping advance of the triumphant Eighth Army.

More than once we passed the rusting carcasses of ambulances, conspicuously marked by glaring Red Crosses, their slashed and torn bodywork bearing witness to the ruthlessness of the enemy. Only once did I see an Italian ambulance that had been the victim of an attack, all the rest were British. Obviously strafing aircraft had been responsible for most of the rusting and broken hulks lying by the roadside. Now they lay there, the aftermath of battle, like weird prehistoric monsters, scattered along the lonely roadside for hundreds of miles, rotting under the African sun; the remnants of the once proud Afrika Corps.

Occasionally we passed crashed aircraft, mainly German. I would have liked to have investigated them, but they lay well off the main road in all cases, and unseen death in the form of mines lay everywhere along the route. Thousands of mines had been dug up, and they lay in great piles alongside the road edges, but thousands more still laid in wait for the unwary, buried under the sandy borders of the roadside and in the scrub beyond. No chances could be taken.

It was late afternoon when we came in sight of Gabes with its gleaming white walls against the backdrop of the deep blue Mediterranean. We stopped about a mile short of the town and turned off into a sandy waste area where we halted. The area had been cleared of mines and was being used as a staging point. No other vehicles were using it that night.

A short way over the brow of a hill we espied a clump of palms surrounding an Arab dwelling and, with the thought of eggs in our heads, we set off. The pace was slow owing to my bandaged and still-painful leg. We came upon a little Arab girl of about twelve or so, who stared at us doubtfully. We gave her a piece of chocolate and tried to make her understand that we wished to buy some eggs. At that moment we heard someone shouting and, looking up, I saw an Arab woman, dressed in flowing robes that looked none too clean, come hurrying out of the mud building amid the palms. In one hand she carried a long pole with a scythe-like knife attached. With glittering eyes she bore down upon us. We carried out a hasty retreat, without even asking about eggs. Evidently she thought her young daughter was in grave danger, and I realised it was useless arguing.

We returned to the transport empty-handed and resigned ourselves to another meal of bully beef and tea. Before the moon had hardly risen high, I was asleep despite the nagging pain in my leg.

Punctually at 8.00 a.m. next morning we set off down the road to Sfax. We were skirting around what is known as the Gulf of Gabes, and the endless sweep of rolling sand dunes and the accompanying sparkling sea were nearly always in sight.

That evening we rolled into Sfax, and here we found that the transport was going no further. I dropped my blankets and kit off as the transport stopped outside the transit camp, which was the one-time Sports Pavilion of the French and situated in the outskirts of the town. I was assigned a room and after washing, eating and making my bed down, decided that, leg or no leg, I was off onto the town centre.

The next day I was informed that I would be finishing the rest of the journey by train to Sousse. I would rather have gone by road, but with the philosophy of a soldier, I accepted the fact that I was to go by train.

At the camp, I met another fellow from our squadron, and together we prowled the town of Sfax, visiting one cafe after another, mostly drinking down the foul concoction that passed for vin rouge. More by instinct than by sight, we returned to the camp that night.

It was late morning on the following day that we boarded the train for Sousse. As usual, we were travelling fourth class in the wagons labelled '40 men or 10 horses'. We kept the big sliding doors of the wagon open to keep it well ventilated, although the wagon itself was surprisingly clean for a French goods wagon.

The distance from Sfax to Sousse by rail was about one hundred miles, but it took us all of seven hours to cover it. Every twenty miles or so, whenever we came upon an Arab settlement, the driver would stop, alight, and disappear for twenty minutes or half an hour. After the second halt, we got wise to him, and whenever the train stopped thereafter, one of us would be down before the train had actually halted, and would be running like mad up to the engine cab. We would then ask him to open his valve and release some hot water. The none-too-clean looking liquid would come gurgling out of a pipe near the rails, while clouds of steam would surround the engine. The water was then conveyed back to our wagon, and planted upon a fire already started on the track alongside. In about five minutes or less we would all be enjoying a slightly rancid oily tasting, but hot, mug of tea. This procedure was adopted all the way into Sousse. We ourselves didn't care how long the driver stopped, for we were in no hurry.

In due course, we puffed into the station yards at Sousse. It was evening, and we had to wait until we could hitchhike our way along the road to M'saken. My orders, however, were not to go direct to my squadron, but to report to a transit camp halfway between Sousse and M'saken. It took me some time to locate the camp in the gathering twilight, but finally I did so. After reporting in, I thankfully dumped my kit down on the earthy floor of the tent assigned me. Tomorrow, with luck, I would join my squadron, and there perhaps I would get the proper medical attention my leg needed.

It was midday the following day before a jeep arrived from my squadron camp. The driver, whom I knew of old, greeted me warmly. After checking out of the transit camp office, I climbed into the jeep and, with roaring engine, we swung out of the olive grove which housed the camp.

I felt fine. At last I was on the last lap to what was home to me. The smooth macadam road unwound before us rapidly as we passed through the village of M'saken, and out onto the road to Kairouan. A few minutes later we topped the rise that lay before our tented encampment half a mile further on.

The jeep slowed up, we swung off onto the sandy track that I had left many weeks ago, full of confidence, on the first leg of the Sicilian operation. Before we came to a halt, I saw Lieutenant Mockridge ambling along with his familiar gait. He saw me almost at the same moment, and his face split into a wide grin. Hurrying over as I stepped down from the jeep, he grabbed my hand and shook it furiously. He asked where the hell I had been, and briefly I told him. He was very glad to see me back.

Chapter 8

Return to England

Captain Boucher-Giles was in the camp at this moment, which was good news to me. Several other old comrades spotted me during my limping walk to the squadron office to report in. I was plagued with questions. Some thought I had been killed. (I learned later that one fellow had actually sworn that he had seen me topple into the river, shot through the head. Luckily, the report from the hospital in Sicily had arrived in time to prevent the false report of my death being forwarded on to England).

I was allotted a tent with several other fellows, and made myself comfortable. Later that afternoon I sought Capt. BG. He was delighted to see me, and to learn what had happened to me after I had last seen him on the bridge. I told him all as briefly as possible, and especially told him how bad I had felt when, on arriving at the hilltop, I had heard desultory firing still going on down at the bridge. He in turn told me what had happened to himself.

He told me that an order to pull out had been given by an officer who had no right to issue it. Incidentally, I never heard this confirmed by any other source, official or private, although Capt. BG was not one to make a statement that had any element of untruth in it. In the end, the few left holding the front bank who had not been able to fall back over the river were forced to surrender, being released some hours later by the leading Eighth Army patrols. The bridge was intact, the enemy being unable to blow it as our men had destroyed the charges.

He was rather concerned over my leg, and advised me to report to the Medical Officer in the morning. I had intended to do that in any case.

It was now mid August, and rumours were rife. Another operation was pending, but no one knew where, although it did not take much imagination to envisage that Italy was involved.

The next day I reported sick and, for the first time since I had left Tripoli, my leg felt considerably better after treatment by the MO. He told me that if it was not any better during the next two or three days, I would have to go into hospital again.

My leg did not improve within the stipulated period, and one morning I was transported to a hospital that lay just up and over the ridge that faced M'saken. I was there for two weeks or so, and they found that the non-healing of my leg was due to a small piece of shrapnel still embedded in the flesh. It was removed, and with that the pain went quickly. This time, they hung onto me until the wound was completely healed up and only a healthy scab remained. I returned to camp with the feeling that at last my leg wound was healed.

The camp was in a turmoil when I returned. Apparently something was on. There was talk of Italy, but no one seemed to know exactly where they were bound, but bound they were, for some destination unknown. Full G 1098 kit was being issued. Ammunition and arms were carefully checked. One point stood out: no gliders were being used on this operation. Wherever the men were going, it was by sea. To me, it did not seem feasible to use airborne troops for such a mission, but I was not in possession of the full facts, and did not realise the overall strategy involved.

I tried to get permission to go along, for my old squadron, with which I had been for so long, was leaving with the party. In its place, here in Africa, was being left No. 4 Squadron which had only recently come out of England and I felt among strangers, although there were others like myself of No. 3 Squadron who had been wounded and were being transferred to No. 4. They also would not be going on the operation.

No permission was forthcoming for me to go, and I was told that I would definitely be remaining here in North Africa. It was rather disappointing, but there was nothing I could do. One ray of brightness prevailed, Capt. BG had been awarded the Distinguished Flying Cross for his part in the Sicily operation, an award he richly deserved, and of which he could justifiably be proud.

With mixed feelings I watched 3 Sqn. parade, ready to move. The date was around September 4 - 5th. They all seemed in high spirits and, as they clambered up into the trucks that would take them off on the first leg of their journey, I felt pangs of regret at not being able to accompany them. I stood watching the trucks until the last one vanished down the dusty track through the olive grove. Somewhat sadly, I returned to my tent, and lay there in loneliness until the heat of the African afternoon sun sent me into an uneasy sleep.

A few days later, I was given four days leave to spend at a rest camp that had been established on the shores of the Mediterranean at a summer resort named Hamman Lif not far from Tunis. One afternoon, along with two other fellows, I flung my kit into a jeep, and minutes later we were speeding smoothly down the road to M'saken and Sousse. We covered the ninety miles to the rest camp in a few hours after passing through Enfidaville and Hammamet. We paused in the wide tree-lined main street of Enfidaville and partook of a few glasses of vin rouge. Enfidaville had been the final point of advance made by the Eighth Army during their triumphant sweep across North Africa, and the town still bore scars of the battle that had been fought there.

It was a pleasant drive on to Hamman Lif under the blue cloudless skies, with glimpses of the sparkling sea on our right for most of the journey. It was hot, but a slight breeze set up by the forward movement of the jeep was enough to make one think that life was really worth living. Due to my bandaged leg, I had not been able to take a dip in the sea since before the operation on Sicily; but now, for the next four days, I would be able to swim all I wanted.

Our rest camp was situated in the well laid out grounds of a large house. We lived in tents, and the waters of the Mediterranean lapped up to within fifty yards of where we lay. Those four days were heaven. No one bothered us. We could do just as we pleased, and go where we liked, within reason—not that I wanted to wander far from the cooling waters of the sea. We rose when we felt like doing so, and the meal times were as we wanted them, for we cooked in little groups, having been issued with rations for each day.

The four days passed by quickly, far quicker than I wanted. Faint hopes that had lain within our breasts regarding the possibility of the Squadron Headquarters forgetting we were at the camp were shattered when a truck arrived punctually to take us back to Sousse.

Back at camp there was little we could do. There seemed to be an atmosphere of unrest and uncertainty pervading the area. Gradually a form of training was introduced, but it was a very mild one. In the mornings we were given lectures and physical training. Sometimes we carried out limited route marches, lasting a few hours. Flying was non-existent. At night, about once a week, we carried out marches by compass, which were quite fun in their way. It was the afternoons, I must confess, that appealed to me most of all. Practically every afternoon, at about two o'clock, we were free and then I was off into Sousse in the company of Sgt. A. Webb, one of the men that shared my tent.

We would walk down to the roadside and, more often than not by diligent thumb waving, we would find ourselves riding into Sousse in the back of an open truck. I always found that ride exhilarating. We would stand up near the front of the body and lean against the cab. The wind would rush by in a cooling stream. The tyres would whine on the road underneath. Blue skies with occasional clouds would smile down from above, while the sun's rays would burn our faces to a deep reddish brown. The powerful motor would roar loudly as we sped up hill and down dale, thundering through the little Arab encampments en route. The Arabs themselves, in their flowing dirty robes, would wave as we rushed by. Tucked inside our shirts would be our towels and bathing shorts.

The last short climb would bring us to the crest of the hill where the outskirts of Sousse began, and the casbah sprawled its sunbaked walls by the road. For a moment we would catch a glimpse of the town of Sousse spread out below and the deep blue sea beyond, flecked with white caps. The old white walls of the town always filled me with a strange elation. The spire of the large French church would rear up like a beckoning finger. Then we would be clattering down the winding road, past the Arabs with their barrows laden high with fruit and nuts of all types. The peculiar smell that hangs over all French-Arab towns would fill my nostrils.

We would usually drop off by the wrecked station yard and cross over the partially repaired bombed square; down the main street, buying nuts en route, and then straight out onto the wide sweep of golden sands which curved away into the distance on both sides. Dimly on our left, if it was a clear day, one could faintly make out the outline of Cap Bon Peninsular jutting far out to sea scores of miles to the north. Beyond the peninsula lay Tunis.

We would spend happy hours lazing on the burning sands and wallowing around in the cool waters, diving off the small shipwreck that lay about a hundred yards out at high tide. From the sides of the ship one could look straight down through the clear waters to the sandy bed below. Back on the sands we would devour the nuts and grapes from the endless streams of dirty bare-footed Arab boys that plagued the beach shouting their wares and also suddenly breaking into a weird English to ask whether we were interested in meeting their 'sisters', of whom they seemed to have an endless number. For my part, I preferred the cooling breeze off the Mediterranean and warm sands beneath my stripped body to the stuffy foetid smelling dens of the Arab boys' 'homes'. That went for Sgt. Webb also.

In the evening, before dusk set in, we would be busy thumbing our way back out of Sousse to camp. This was not difficult while daylight lasted, but extremely so once darkness fell.

We learned that No. 3 Sqn., in company with other airborne troops, had landed at Taranto in Italy, thus taking part in the invasion of that country. We heard garbled accounts of what had happened, but on the whole we did not find out much, and gradually their existence faded to the back of our minds. Soldiers make new friends quickly.

September passed into November, and the weather turned somewhat colder. Sgt. Webb and I still paid visits down to Sousse most afternoons and persisted with our bathing, although the water was nowhere near so pleasant as it had been the month before. The sky was becoming more overcast with clouds, and occasional rain squalls would beat down with discomforting results, both in the camp and out. By the second week in November, the bad weather had really set in. Swirling dust storms would be the forewarners of torrential downpours that more than once collapsed and flooded our tents, sometimes in the dark early hours of the morning. Shivering and miserable, we would try to seek shelter in the larger marquee tents, with our sodden blankets tucked underneath our arms. More often than not, the marquees were also in a partially collapsed state, but did afford some protection.

Many times as I lay listening to the beating rain slashing against the trembling cover of our tent, I would think of the many stone buildings in Sousse that could have afforded us warmth and dryness against these downpours, and wondered why nothing was ever done about it. Probably there were no empty places that we could use. At night the ground in the camp area would become a sodden mass of ankle deep mud, while turbulent streams of water would sweep down between the lines of tents. Yes, it was rather a miserable period for us all.

Within an hour or two of the sun coming up, all would be dry again, and there would be no sign to show that rain had ever fallen the night before. By midday, the ground was dry enough to send up dusty swirls whenever one moved about.

We were not at all sorry to learn that some of us would be going into Tunis for another three days leave. As I had not had my full quota, I was in the first batch sent off.

The run to Sousse was not quite so pleasant as the one I had made to Hamman Lif, but I did not mind. We were to be billeted right in the centre of Tunis in what had once been a hotel. After the somewhat drab existence we had been leading, despite the natural attractions of Sousse, I could not help but feel a little excited as we drove past the large airfield outside Tunis and saw before me the sprawling suburbs of the city. There we would find entertainment of all sorts, including films, theatres, cafes and so forth. I had not seen a film for over six months, and then it had only been one out in the open under the night sky near Relizane.

It was a real treat to be passing through streets where impatient trams clattered their way over tracks and numerous cars, driven by excitable Frenchmen, continually blared their horns. And, what was more, there were hundreds of well turned out women, practically all of them French with, however, a sprinkling of

American service girls. It was great to be back in civilisation once more, even if it was only for three days.

I have no need to dwell upon those three days, except to say that I had a most wonderful time. The cooks at our hotel were excellent and I am sure that they must have had more than the normal rations to be able to give us what they did. We returned to our camp at Sousse feeling new men, but also rather depressed at having to leave such a place and come back to the rain-swept tented area. Strangely enough, in Tunis it had not rained once during the three days. The first day back at camp ominous black clouds rolled up towards evening, a foreboding as to what we were in for that night.

However, I need not have worried, for there was great news in store for us the day after my return from Tunis. We were to move. Furthermore, there was a persistent rumour that ran like wildfire round the camp that this move would eventually either take us home or to India. The odds were about even on both spots. Much as we wanted to fight and get the war over, there was not one man who did not, in his heart, fervently hope that the boat, if and when we did board it, would turn westward towards Gibraltar and not eastward towards the Suez.

For two days we were kept in suspense, and then our CO paraded us together and informed us that we were moving off in two days' time. No indication was given as to where we were going, but the CO seemed to have a satisfied smile on his face the whole time he was talking, which I took to be a good sign, bearing in mind the rumours.

The parade broke up, and excited little groups made their way back to the tents. Packing had to begin immediately and the kitbags stacked in an orderly manner near the truck parking lot. We needed no spurring.

That same afternoon, the kitbags were taken away and placed in a divisional dump about a mile down the road to M'saken. We were left to our own devices for the next two days. No move was indicated at the end of the two days, and all we learned was that we would be leaving any day.

Then the great day arrived and, late in the morning, we clambered up into the trucks and rolled out on the road to Tunis, leaving a somewhat unhappy rear party behind.

We were all in great spirits, and sang songs by the score. We rumbled through Sousse for the last time to the shrieks of ragged Arab children who held out their hands for 'cigarettes' and 'gum'. Being in high spirits, our men showered them with both. Soon the trucks swung out through the town, past the sprawling Arab cemetery, and along the open road.

Being in convoy, we took far longer than we had on the leave trip to Tunis. It was evening by the time we reached the outskirts of the city, and it was strange to see many lights twinkling away in only a partial blackout. Bypassing the centre, we eventually drew up alongside a stretch of railway track that seemed to have no connection with a station.

The sky had clouded up, and we knew that a downpour was pending. We hoped they would assign us our wagons so that we could bed down for the night before we got soaked through.

Our kit had been unloaded and lay in great piles along the shadowy tracks. A line of railway wagons that we thought must have been meant for us suddenly came to life and, headed by a snorting engine, disappeared into the darkness, leaving just empty rails in both directions.

The inevitable rainfall commenced. Large drops heralded the downpour. Cursing, we huddled together under a few leafless trees, leaving our kitbags out to bear the brunt of the rain. Miserably, I looked at the puddles forming alongside the glistening rails, reflecting the few lights that lay scattered alongside the tracks.

About half an hour later, we heard the sound of an approaching engine. With a great hissing of steam, the locomotive slid past us hauling a long line of goods wagons. With squealing brakes it came to a halt. After a few minutes' consultation with an official, our CO learned that this was the train meant for us.

In ten minutes we had stacked all the kit aboard, and we ourselves were seeking shelter inside the wagons where we each 'pegged' out our piece of the flooring by flinging our kit down in the spot appearing most acceptable. Although the French had painted the numbers '40 Homs' on the outside, we restricted the number to 19, thus allowing ourselves a little more room than French soldiers would have had.

Outside, the rain drizzled down. With a sharp jerk, we were off. Gathering speed, we steamed on through the wet night, leaving us with painful memories of our last sight of Tunis. In a short while, I had accustomed myself to the hardness and the rolling motion of the truck floor, and I fell into an uneasy slumber. Within me, I had a certain feeling of contentment, despite being rather damp and a little dispirited.

The morning dawned clear and fine with a cloudless blue sky. We breakfasted on tinned sausage and tea, heated by means of a fire carefully lit on a metal sheet in the open doorway of the goods wagon. The scenery was magnificent, and I began to enjoy the trip. Our engine chugged its way up long and twisting gradients that wound through the rugged mountains of the Cork Forest area. Some of the distant mountains were topped with glistening white snow, adding to the wonder of the panoramic landscape spread out before us.

Whenever we came to an Arab settlement, sometimes hidden away in the verdant slopes of the mountains, our locomotive would grind to a halt with squealing brakes. We would then carry out the same procedures as we had done on the railway journey from Sfax to Sousse. One man would quickly jump down and hurry up front to the engine. The engineer was most obliging, and would open the valve to send out a stream of boiling water into the tin can held ready near the great driving wheels. Making tea was then a matter of two minutes or so. We were lucky in having fair stocks of tea with us, and never once did we lack this item, despite the numerous stops en route.

All day long we slowly climbed, ever turning first one way and then the other. By late evening we were commencing to descend, and the whole line of trucks would sway madly from side to side as we swept around bends, while the clatter of the wheels over the steel rails would rise to a crescendo. That evening, we passed through Constantine, but saw nothing of it.

During the hours of darkness we continued on, lulled into sleep by the ceaseless drumming of the wheels on the tracks beneath our floorboards. Once I was awakened by the terrific lurching and swaying of our truck. For a moment I was a little scared, as the wheels were squealing and protesting as we plunged down and around a sharp curve. Then we straightened out once more and, to the rapid clicking below, I again fell asleep.

A large part of the following day was spent in a siding between Constantine and Setif. It gave us an opportunity to stretch our legs, for which we were grateful. We also had a chance to purchase fruit and eggs from the ragged, dirty-looking Arabs who besieged the train from end to end the whole time we were halted.

Evening found us clattering on towards Algiers. It was a strange sight whenever I looked out through the huge open sliding doors to see, stretching away in front towards the head of the train, a long line of twinkling lights made by the tins filled with coke and wood that the occupants of each truck had hanging outside their open doors. The slipstream from the speeding train kept the fires going strongly the whole time. Whenever a wagon load of men decided it was time for a cup of tea, the fire was hauled in and mess tins put upon the leaping flames. I was surprised to learn, at the end of the journey that we had only one mishap through these fires swinging so freely, and rather dangerously, outside the wagons.

The next day found us steaming down towards Algiers on the last lap of our journey. We arrived during the evening, and after the usual wait of at least half an hour, detrained. Humping our kitbags, and with full marching equipment, we set off for the transit camp, which we found to be the sports arena of Algiers.

I shall always remember the discomfort and agony of the march from the station goods yard to the camp. The arena lay about two miles from the station. Without a kitbag, it would have been nothing, but under the terrific weight of the tightly filled bags, it was just plain hell. The final blow was the march up the short but exceedingly steep cobblestone hill to the arena entrance. It took me some time to recover from the march, but that night I slept happily on one of the open benches that encircled the sports ground below. The jutting roof of the stand protected us from a slight fall of rain during the night.

The next day we learned we would be embarking onto a ship in the harbour. It still seemed fifty-fifty that the boat would either head for England of India. We kept our fingers crossed.

We rose early next day, eager to be off, whatsoever the ultimate destination. During the day, our enthusiasm was slightly dampened when word went round that an officer had flown over from Italy to pick up a few reinforcements for No. 3 Squadron in Italy. The news spread like wildfire, and there was great anxiety and consternation on many faces that morning. With the possibility of being home in a couple of weeks, the thought of being sent somewhere else would be a heavy blow. However, word also spread quickly that we were definitely going home, except for those selected for Italy. Rumours were rife. We heard later in the morning that a few more crews would be wanted for duty in India for sure.

Officers scurried to and fro, and within an hour several crews learned their fate. The rake-in also accounted for a few of the administrative staff. As soon as the men learned the worst, they hurried outside into Algiers to drown their disappointment. I must admit that I felt a great relief when all the men had been selected, and I was not slow in slipping out with Sgt. Webb into town, where we made a few purchases.

Time, however, limited our exploration of the city, and we only managed to get in two hours or so.

Late afternoon, we were paraded in the centre of the arena and the roll was called. This was one roll call that no one missed. Great secrecy had surrounded the departure of the airborne troops from North Africa. Before we left the Sousse area, we had to take down all insignia, including our pilot's wings, even our rank indication, in order that no enemy sympathisers could identify us. Instead of our own red berets, we wore the standard army field service khaki caps. Now, as we stood under the hot late afternoon sun, awaiting the word that would start us off on the march down to the dockside and home, our Squadron Sergeant Major made one of the biggest blunders of his life.

Drawing himself up, and bringing all the force of his vocal chords to bear (among other things, no doubt, to impress the few interested French civilians who were watching us from the outside through the gates) he shouted '4 Squadron, Glider Pilot Regiment Squadron, shu-u-u-n'.

We jumped to attention, but I do not think that one man, except for the few half drunken fellows that were being supported by their comrades, missed the serious implication of the Sergeant Major's blunder. He himself had realised his terrible mistake almost as soon as the words had left his lips. His face turned a deep scarlet, and for a moment he was dumbstruck. A few sniggers went down the line, but the Sergeant Major made a splendid recovery, and called for silence. As though nothing had happened, the Officer Commanding gave the word of command to march off. I never did hear what sort of severe dressing down the Sergeant Major got, but that he got one I am absolutely certain. After all our measures of security to avoid identification, the Sergeant Major shouts to all the world that our regiment was in the vicinity, and it would not have taken an enemy agent or sympathiser another half hour to learn that we were embarking onto a ship for somewhere.

It was a great moment for us all as we marched out through the gates of the arena. An air of gaiety pervaded the column. The only men who did not seem to be enjoying the march were the drunks. They had been out into Algiers earlier on in the day. Most of them were being supported by their comrades, and at least one was being virtually dragged along. The officers had closed their eyes to this very unmilitary-like parading, for they also no doubt were filled with exhilaration at the thought of going home again.

We sang as we marched along down through the town. Curious French people waved and the children followed us along all the streets, hanging onto our flanks like young vultures waiting for the pickings flung away in the form of cigarettes and sweets.

We approached the dock area, and all began speculating as to which of the many ships anchored there we would be embarking on. One authoritative source stated that we would be going on the largest ship there. I looked at the boat indicated and saw that she was indeed the largest vessel, the only one in fact sporting three funnels. Word came down the ranks confirming the first rumour. Furthermore, we learned the name of the boat, which was the famous 'Monarch of Bermuda', a pre-war cruise ship.

I was pleasantly surprised at the accommodation we were given. I still had fresh in my memory the extremely bad accommodation we had been given on the Dutch boat 'The Boissewain' when we had come out to North Africa earlier on in the year. In the 'Monarch', we pilots had been allotted cabins which had bunks for about six to eight men, which was indeed a luxury after the decks and holds of the 'Boissewain', which had been literally crawling with men, like a rotten fruit overrun by maggots. The decks lower down were rather crowded, but not quite as bad as it had been on the Dutch boat.

We moved during the night, and next morning found us anchored outside the harbour. We were to form part of quite a large convoy consisting of about twenty-six ships, and even now all were taking up their positions. Late afternoon we got under way, and I leaned on the rail along with many others taking a last look at the rugged shores surrounding Algiers. The city lay sprawled against the background of hills, and looked very attractive with its modern and ancient buildings, mainly white, glistening in the sun.

Just before going to bed, after taking one last look at the twinkling lights of Algiers reflected in the harbour waters, I heard the engines throb into life. The whole convoy sailed away in the night, and morning found us ploughing steadily through the calm waters of the Mediterranean, always following the inevitable pattern of zigzagging to lessen the chance of presenting a good target to any unsuspected U-Boat that might have slipped past the vigilant searching by the destroyers escorting the convoy.

I always found it exhilarating to lean over the rails and listen to the wash of the water as our ship lifted its prow, and then nosed down once more to send the spray flying high, filling the air with a salty tang. For hours I would watch the ceaseless swirling wall of foam playing around the bows of the ship as she nosed remorselessly on. At night I was fascinated by the wondrous trail of phosphorescence that curved away behind our stern, churned into a frothy gleam by the turbulent action of the ship's propellers.

Overhead, the glittering stars of the African sky would pivot first one way and the other as we pursued our tortuous course. No moon hung in the dark skies, which was in our favour. No lights shone forth from the tightly closed portholes, while a glowing cigarette end in the shadows on the decks meant an instant Courts Martial.

During the hours of darkness of the second night out, we passed through the Straits of Gibraltar. It was actually the early hours of the morning and I did not trouble to rise, as some did, to catch a last glimpse of the red flashing light that marked the Rock out in the sea of blackness.

Morning found us well out in the Atlantic, steaming steadily westward. The waters were considerably rougher than the Mediterranean had been. The ship began to creak and groan, as the plates took on the greater stress. We had sailed on the 28th November, and it was anticipated that we would be home well before Christmas, which put us all in great spirits.

The blue, almost cloudless, skies off North Africa had given place to the dirty grey blanket of cloud for which the North Atlantic is famous at this time of year. The farther we bored westward, the rougher the seas seemed to get. That night, I oriented myself by the Pole Star, and was quite surprised to find us still heading almost due west. We certainly seemed bent on giving the Bay of Biscay and its marauding Focke Wolfe Condors and Junkers 88s a wide berth. These enemy planes scouted out far beyond the Bay most days, and were very troublesome to many a convoy with their shadowing tactics and radio contacts with the hunting German U-Boats skulking beneath the waters of the Atlantic.

It was on the afternoon of the second day out from Gibraltar that the great shock came. I was embroiled in a heated discussion with the other occupants of the cabin. In the middle of a sentence, there came a thunderous crash. The whole ship shivered and lurched heavily over. We were on the port side of the ship, and it was this side that was going down.

Through the glass of the porthole I saw the sea tilting up towards us. Our speech had been cut as with a knife. The faces of the others in the cabin had gone pale as no doubt had mine. I had been sitting on the edge of the bunk with my feet dangling over. The next second I was hurled to the floor. As I scrambled up, there came a second grinding crash, which shook the ship again. Our side of the ship, which had been recovering from the blow and was rising up to level keel again, tilted once more, and again I saw the waters rising towards the porthole.

Seconds after the first crash, we had all grabbed our lifebelts and made for the door, but common sense and discipline intervened, and we returned to stand by our bunks. The second crash and jerk threw us around once more. We riveted our eyes on the door, waiting for the alarm bell to send out its strident clanging that would summon us up on deck to the lifeboat positions that we had practised many times during the past days. Nothing happened. We all felt certain that we must have been torpedoed, and yet calm seemed to reign throughout the ship.

The minutes passed by, and I noticed that the ship had slowly righted herself. The engines had stopped, and we were wallowing in the heavy sea. The sound of clattering footsteps on the stairway outside our cabin announced the entrance of one of the naval men. With a cheerful face he told us not to worry, that we had only been rammed by one of the other boats on the convoy. Her steering had apparently gone out of commission and she had swung in, cutting through our starboard side. Two or three cabins had been badly damaged, and we had been holed beneath the waterline, but there was nothing to fear.

We continued to list to port quite heavily, moving sluggishly from side to side in the swell. The ship vibrated as the engines rumbled into life again. Slowly we swung clear of the convoy and our hopes fell suddenly to zero as we started to head back on the opposite direction to that taken by the convoy. A destroyer raced up alongside us, her lamp sending out a swift message to our captain.

All that afternoon and evening, we retraced our course back towards Gibraltar. A gloom had settled over most of the ship. It looked as though we had lost our chance of getting home in time for Christmas. We ploughed on at a greatly reduced speed, listing more and more heavily to port.

That night we anchored just outside of the harbour at Gibraltar. Next day, I went up on deck feeling rather disconsolate and gazed out on the island fortress. The towering heights of the island dwarfed the town spread out at its base. There was no outward sign of its intricate defences which seemed to us to be surprising when I looked at the almost adjoining country of Spain. On that mainland, I could see several cities sprawled out along the rugged coastline. The white buildings lent a picturesque air to an already beautiful coastline.

Aircraft were constantly taking off and landing on the airfield, which lay at the foot of the highest point of the island. To avoid flying over Spanish territory, the aircraft had to execute turns almost as soon as their wheels were clear of the ground.

We moved into the harbour proper that day, and work was begun at once to make temporary repairs on the huge gash in the ship's side.

We remained at Gibraltar for over two weeks until it seemed that all hope of reaching England by Christmas had faded away. Wistfully we thought of the convoy, which must have reached England several days ago. Day after day, we stared impatiently out over the rails at the Island fortress of Gibraltar, and the mountainous country of Spain. Because of security, we were not allowed ashore; otherwise we might not have fretted so much.

It came as a great surprise to us one day when we steamed out of the harbour. No one seemed to know whether we were really on our way or not. We had already steamed outside the harbour once before, but that had turned out to be a test run. This time it was the real thing. In the gathering twilight, we slipped out between the outer defences and soon the red flashing light of the island had faded far behind, although we picked up the glow even after the direct beam had vanished down beneath the horizon.

For an escort, we had four destroyers. I was amazed, because I had only seen about that number when we were part of the whole convoy earlier on. The destroyers took up positions: one a little way ahead, one on the port and one on the starboard side, and the other one to the rear on either side. The only reason I could think of for our being given so many boats as escort was that they were due to head for England in any case.

Despite the heavy list to port, we made excellent speed, although I understood that our ship was very much lower in the water than it would have been had there been no damage.

It was only a week to Christmas, and there was great speculation as to whether we would get home in time. The weather had turned for the worse, and heavy seas assailed the ship while overcast skies stretched away to the horizon. Squalls of rain swept the deck from time to time. The eternal zigzagging course was followed, keeping in perfect unison with the escorting destroyers.

Daily over the radio came the news that the U-Boat campaign had been stepped up in the North Atlantic. The enemy submarines were now hunting in what was called 'wolf packs', and were harrying convoys for days on end, but not without loss to themselves.

Day after day, night after night, we pursued our creaking course. We headed deeply into the west before turning north. The blanket of cloud that hung over us nearly the whole time prevented me from making a rough calculation of the course we were following, but as it grew colder and colder, I knew that we must be making a wide sweep far to the north in an endeavour to keep clear of the enemy wolf packs.

One day, through the lowering overcast, a Flying Fortress swooped down over us and proceeded to circle around in great sweeps. Half the time, the aircraft was shrouded in rain-swept clouds and only appeared from time to time when we followed its ever circling course with appraising eyes.

It was a great day when the word flashed around that land was in sight. Actually, it was the northernmost tip of Ireland. And then a few hours later we caught our first glimpse of Scotland showing faintly through the mist that hung over the coastline. I think that all of us felt the same thankfulness at the sight of those green fields and the rising hills behind for the first time after so long an absence. The ship fairly exuded gaiety, and the rails were lined with happy faces gazing landward, inwardly cursing the slow methodical progress of the mighty ship beneath them.

We did not dock in the rain-swept port of Liverpool until the next day. Not one of us cared a hoot for the teeming rain that swept down as we disembarked. What matter what happened, we were home, weren't we? That was the general tenor of the excited talk as we carried our heavy kitbags down the gangplank, while on shore a band played welcoming music that lent a lilt to our step.

The next day was Christmas Eve and, thanks to the Royal and Merchant Navies, we spent Christmas Day at our respective homes.

North Africa and Sicily were far behind. The dusty plains of Tunisia, the forest-clad slopes of Algeria, and the cultivated valleys with their white walled buildings huddled under the heat of the North African sun. Sicily with its bitter memories, and sun baked fields under which would forever lie the bodies of many of my comrades who fell during July 9th and 10th. The blue lapping waters of the Mediterranean Sea that had claimed so many that rain-swept night. The rotting shreds of our gliders would bear mute testimony for years to come of the first large scale airborne operation of the Allies—an operation that was both victorious and defeated. Defeated not by the action of the enemy, but by the elements over which we had no control and partially by the ignorance of what was needed, which could only be learned by experience.

Chapter 9

Prelude to Arnhem

January 1944 found my flight stationed at Shrewton flying field in Wiltshire. We remained there for nearly a month doing a refresher course on the old faithful Tiger Moth.

It was strange at first to feel a throttle under my hand after the long period of motorless flight on gliders. I was quite perturbed at the thought that I might have completely lost my touch where powered aircraft were concerned, but I need not have worried. My check-out under the eye of an RAF instructor was uneventful, and, to my joy, I found that within a few minutes of taking off, I felt that I had never been away from the cramped cockpit of the Tiger Moth. In fact, I discovered that once I had adjusted myself to the different gliding angle of the Tiger against that of the gliders, I was bringing off amazingly good three-point spot landings; this boosted my spirits one hundred per cent for, although motorless flight had certain attractions, there was always the longing for powered flight, and I think that I can safely speak for practically all glider pilots. The long spell on gliders had improved my technique of spot landings considerably.

The weather was bitterly cold most of the time and the open cockpit of the Tiger did nothing to alleviate this discomfort. We flew with our thick overcoats on, sometimes over padded flying suits. Nevertheless, the thrill of flying the Tiger once more repaid us many times over for the physical discomfort suffered.

At the end of January we moved to Thruxton, a Horsa glider flying field in Hampshire. I was sorry to leave the Tigers at Shrewton, but orders were orders. I had not flown a Horsa for over a year, and I was looking forward to sitting behind the controls of one of these giant machines. Our first flight was a cross-country one to Lincoln and back, and I was really pleased to be on this type again after the WACO in North Africa.

Flying was very restricted at Thruxton, and I was not surprised when we received orders to move once more. This time we were really moving out of the West Country. Our new airfield was to be Leicester East. I had never been up in that direction before and Leicester East was a fine place, except that we did no flying. There was plenty of time off, and we had a very good time during the evenings in the local village and the city of Leicester itself. I even managed to get a weekend pass for home, although we were there for less than three weeks. We all guessed that it was too good to be true, and were having too much fun at Leicester, not that we wanted to dodge flying; on the contrary, we would have welcomed it with open arms.

Early in March, I took off from Leicester East for the West Country once more. Our destination was the airfield of Fairford fifteen miles or so east of Oxford and twelve miles north of Swindon. We had heard fairly favourable reports on the airfield, but its disadvantage seemed to be in its inaccessibility to nearby towns for the evening's entertainment. From the flying point of view it was excellent with a fine surface, and the accommodation was reputedly good.

It was a rough flight down and my stomach rebelled more than once. The ever delightful English countryside slid slowly past underneath and made a pleasant diversion from the violent rolling and bumping.

Glimpses of the spires of Oxford indicated that our trip was almost over, and I cannot say that I was very sorry when we finally broke away from our towing plane, wheeled around the airfield once, and then swooped down onto the beautiful stretch of runway that ran southwest across the vast expanse of grass.

We soon made ourselves at home, and it was just as well, for we were to be stationed at Fairford for many months to come. Flying training was stepped up in earnest, and numerous cross country mass flights were practised. On most of these mass-landing flights, 75% to 90% of the squadron took part. We were now formed onto 'G' Squadron. Actually, we had been formed while at Leicester East, but this was the first time that we were flying once more as a squadron.

At first, these cross country mass landings were fairly precarious affairs, with one or two crashes inevitably involved, but as we practised, we gained confidence, and by the end of May, our squadron was becoming very proficient.

Undoubtedly, these mass landings called for first class precision flying, especially at the point of touchdown. We did not realise it at the time, but these exercises were the forerunners to the invasion of France, where their pattern was applied to actual practice in forthcoming operations against the enemy.

Usually, briefings would take place either the day before, or on the actual day of the flight.

The gliders and tugs would be marshalled ready the day before in lines on either side of the runway to be used. Sometimes the weather would force a cancellation for a day or even more.

Usually the takeoff time would be in early morning and, at shortly spaced intervals of about one minute, combination after combination would roar off the far end of the runway and climb slowly away. At a prearranged turning point, the long column would slowly swing around and head back on the first leg of the course which would take them over the airfield they had just left. By the time the first aircraft was crossing over the field, the last combination would have taken to the air and nearly all the squadron would be more or less formed up in their correct positions.

Most of the flights were timed for about one-and-a-half to two and a half hours, (about the time calculated for the actual D-Day operation to come).

About one third of the way around the many-legged course, all the squadrons which had taken off from widely dispersed airfields would converge on a pre-arranged rendezvous. Then the whole mighty air fleet would thunder on towards one of the home aerodromes selected for the mass landing.

Ten miles from the landing zone, the navigator in the tug would start to chant out the diminishing miles or minutes from the zone.

Then, when the gliders were within striking distance of the zone, a green lamp would flash out from the astro-dome or tail gunner's turret of the tug, and thereafter it was the responsibility of the glider pilot to release when he thought fit.

Through the perspex of the cockpit the glider pilots would see the predetermined airfield loom up nearer and nearer. The combination ahead would be breaking into two parts, the gliders wheeling away after releasing the connecting rope and the tugs diving gently off in the opposite direction still trailing the flailing rope. The rope would later be released at some designated airfield for recovery for further use.

These were tense moments. The sky would be filled with the great black Horsas swooping around, seeking the best approach position, and at the same time trying to hold some semblance of the planned order of landing. Despite the careful briefing, more often than not, gliders would cut in from their line of flight, crossing over in front, or from above, or underneath, especially on the last leg in, on the final approach.

Like a flock of crows spotting a ripe cornfield from the air, the mass of black Horsas would swoop down into the green field, and in a few minutes the ground would be covered with motionless, forbidding looking machines, disgorging men and equipment from their bellies.

Rarely did a mass landing go off without incident. Luckily most of them were not at all serious, merely involving locked wingtips and damaged tail assemblies, when one or both gliders were unable to swerve from their course as they rolled swiftly over the ground after the touchdown. Sometimes the accident was more serious, and the impatiently waiting 'Blood Wagon' would leap forward and race over to the scene of tangled matchwood.

After the show was over, usually on the following day, our Squadron Commander would go over the whole exercise again in the briefing room, pointing out mistakes. As time went by, we became more and more proficient, and accidents occurred less and less often.

In May, these exercises reached a climax, and at the beginning of that month we started to carry out concentrated training on night exercises with an emphasis on moonlight landings where the aerodromes were entirely devoid of landing lights, and with only a few red lights to mark the positions of high buildings and the hangars. No lights marked the runway, which had to be picked out with the aid of the moon or half moon, not at all an easy task, especially when a ground mist was in the making.

These moonlight landings culminated in two mass landing exercises known as Dingo I and Dingo II. These were made to determine whether a successful moonlight landing could be made (a point that was no doubt still under discussion, based on the outcome of the Sicilian moonlight landings the previous year), or as a precautionary measure in case the general overall plan of the invasion of Europe (of which we were still ignorant) called for night landings at short notice.

Exercise Dingo II took place on the night of May 8th, a short while after Dingo I had been executed. I, with Sergeant Hollingsworth who had been permanently attached as my co-pilot, was not on Dingo I. Reports from some of my hut mates who had taken part on it indicated that it had not gone off too badly, although most of them reported a little difficulty in actually picking out the exact area they had been allotted to land in, despite the fact that a green 'T' giving wind direction had been illuminating the landing zone.

The general plan of Dingo II was that about thirty minutes before we touched down, a detachment of paratroopers would land and lay out a green landing 'T' (using smoke flares) which would indicate the direction of the wind and so the direction in which we would have to land our gliders. Approximately one hundred gliders were to take part. Navigation lights could be switched on just before we cast off to minimise any accidents, especially as they would indicate to the gliders still in the air the position of those already landed.

The airfield selected for the landing was Netheravon in Wiltshire, itself a paratroop and gliding station. Each squadron was allocated a section of the airfield in which to land. In turn, each flight was allotted a place in that squadron's area in which to concentrate, and each glider was given an area to land in or near. If the leading gliders landed in their correct position, there would be no trouble for the others following them up. If, however, the first gliders to go in muffed their spot landings, it was going to make things uncomfortable for the rest of the lift, because the clear run-in would not be available. Such was the position on the evening of May 8th.

It was dark when we took off, and the moon was still well down, but by the time we had completed our many-legged flight it would have risen enough to shed its full light on our landing zone.

We had been given the latest estimate of the wind direction and speed at the landing area, which more or less fixed for us the approach we would have to carry out.

The flight was scheduled to last two hours and twenty minutes. The initial leg lay over the blacked-out Midlands with very little moonlight to aid us in identifying turning points. The air was calm, and little effort was needed to hold the giant Horsa steady behind the tug, although it was, as usual, very tiring, watching the three tiny positioning lights marking the tug ahead.

It was impossible to pick out any of the other combinations, although from time to time I caught a glimpse of tiny lights away ahead, which could have been stars, or the guiding lights of other gliders and tugs. However, I could not help but sense the presence of the huge armada which was steadily droning on over the sleeping countryside below.

More than once we passed avenues of bright lights indicating airfields from which either training or operational aircraft were taking off or landing. It was always a comforting sight because, although our ropes were strong, they had been known to break under a severe strain. A long glide down into the black depths below with little indication of the landscape would be a nightmare, and the odds were that one would end up in a fatal crash unless the moon was high enough to give fair illumination of the ground. At no time did we take parachutes either on training or on operations, hence our feeling of gratitude to the sparkling lights of the friendly runways appearing from time to time, where we knew we might find sanctuary if, by some mischance, the rope broke.

On through the night we roared, the dull thunder of the slipstream beating an endless song against my tired brain. Sergeant Tom Hollingsworth and I took twenty minute spells at the controls. It was always a relief to hand over to Tom after my twenty minute period was up. I could then sit back and close my eyes for a while, or gaze out into the inky blackness of the night sky. I had every confidence in Tom for, although he had but few hours on Horsas, I had long since sensed he was a born flyer.

The metallic voice of the navigator coming over the intercom from the tug roused me. 'Ten minutes to go, Matchbox'. I flicked the switch and repeated his sentence. My head cleared as if by magic. With straining eyes I peered out into the blackness that enveloped the cockpit. Despite the fact that the moon was well up, I could make out very little of the landscape that moved past slowly underneath our wings nearly three thousand feet below.

Again that old tensing of the throat and constriction of the chest yhat I always felt as the target area grew near, both on exercises and on actual operations.

The minutes crept by with the tug navigator chanting off the time from the target with regular monotony. We were down to two minutes and I could still see no sign of the expected illuminated 'T'. Just as the voice of the navigator chanted out the last minute I caught a glimpse of a green mist-like illumination on our starboard, about two miles ahead. It was faint but enough to show me the general location of the landing zone.

Tom flew the glider while I leaned forward, trying to determine our distance from the landing area, with one hand resting lightly on the release lever that would send us off into free flight the moment I pulled it.

The voice of the navigator was dimly echoing in my head informing me to pull off when I thought fit. I hardly heard him. The drumming and thunder of the slipstream seemed to have risen to a crescendo. An inner voice kept calling, 'Now, now' while another cried, 'Not yet, not yet—hold on a moment longer'. Despite the cold of the night, the perspiration dripped slowly down my face, while my lips seemed glued together by a terrible dryness. 'Damn the 'T', which way is it facing'? The misty mass of green lights was now almost on our starboard. I snapped back the lever, and the glider quivered as the unseen rope fell away from our wings. The lights of the tug tilted and disappeared down on our left. I took over from Tom, without taking my eyes off the elusive ghostly green lights. Our speed dropped away from the towing speed of 145 mph. The roar of the slipstream died down to a mere whisper as the airspeed indicator slid back to 85 mph.

I almost forced my eyes from their sockets as I strained through the night sky to try and determine which way the 'T' faced. Then it stood out clearly from behind the faint mist that had been covering it. 'Hell!', I muttered to myself, for I could see that it was facing the opposite way to that which we had been briefed. That meant the wind had changed and we would have to land from the opposite direction to that planned.

Already I could see a large number of navigation lights gleaming down on the field, indicating that the leading gliders were already down. I prayed that they had landed more or less correctly and that they had left sufficient space for the remainder to set down in.

The altimeter was unwinding fast. We were already down to two thousand feet and still on the upwind leg. I shot glances from side to side, above and below, checking for other machines, for I knew that the sky above Netheravon would be full of wheeling gliders, invisible in the darkness except for their red, white and green navigation lights. Tom also scanned the sky on his side.

I swept into a gentle turn that took us downwind. We were rather close to the boundary or, rather, where I judged the boundary to be, for there were no lights to show the outline of the field. I swept the area below with a worried gaze, for it appeared to me that the gliders on the ground had landed in a rather haphazard way. As we came lower, with the altimeter nearing the one-thousand mark, I could make out the dim outline of the field.

In vain, I swept the area for a clear lane in which I might make a landing. The upwind end of the aerodrome was now parallel with us. I would have to turn on the final crosswind leg at any moment, but still I could see no clear space that would give a reasonable run and roll over the ground. Even as I watched, more red and green lights entered the already congested area, indicating that more and more gliders were piling into the chaos below.

At 800 feet, a height that was lower than usual for a turn into cross wind, I heeled the Horsa over. Below on our starboard the mass of lights on the ground tilted up. I levelled off, anxiously flickering my gaze alternately from the altimeter that was now registering below 600 feet and the seemingly hopelessly congested field of lights on our right.

It was my last chance to find a clear run-in, but I found it impossible. At 400 feet I made the final turn-in and braced myself for what I knew would be a touch and go landing. I glanced at the airspeed dial—70 mph! I called out to Tom to take his feet off the rudder bar, and to hang on. The edge of the field slipped by underneath. At the same moment, I saw a blaze of light shoot out from the far end of the field at about the same height as we were. Instantly, I knew a glider was coming in from the opposite direction, perhaps more than one. The pilot had switched on his light in an effort to aid him in picking out a clear space, if such a thing could be found.

Ahead I saw what appeared to be an unobstructed area, small, but enough to set down and lose a fair amount of speed before we hit one of scores of gliders scattered all over the field. Suddenly, as I levelled off about twenty feet above the ground, a glider loomed up towards us, a glider devoid of landing lights, which accounted for my not having seen it before. I hauled back on the wheel, but our flying speed was too low to lift us. The sighing of the slipstream died away; I saw a huge expanse of wing underneath our nose. There was a tearing rending crash; our glider shuddered, and the nose dropped. Part of the cockpit flooring disappeared from beneath our feet. I caught a glimpse of the airspeed needle juddering around the 50- to 60-mph mark, and then we were past.

We struck the ground heavily despite the fact I had the wheel all the way back. It was a spine jerking crash. We careened on across the turf, and our port wing smashed through another motionless glider on the ground. The impact on the port side dragged us around and we slid along half broadside, coming to a halt amid a horrible smell of ripped dope-covered fabric. I was snapped forward by the impact, but by good luck I hit nothing. The safety belt held me well. I turned to Tom and found that he was a little shaken but uninjured. We had been very fortunate, considering the congested area in which we had to land.

Tom and I crawled out of the wreckage that had once been the cockpit. We stood up, but an ominous rushing sound made us drop to our knees. The vague shape of a Horsa slid over our heads. Seconds later, we heard the sound of crunching matchwood. Tom was fumbling around looking for a cigarette lighter he had dropped. I took the opportunity to walk around the glider. Locked underneath the shattered undercarriage was half the wing torn from the glider we had first struck. Splintered plywood lay everywhere amongst the gouged earth.

Another Horsa came sighing in through the darkness. We vaguely saw her touch down and bound across the field and vanish into the gloom. A landing light split the darkness as yet another glider swooped down into the chaos below. This glider was coming in from the opposite direction to the first two, and swiftly behind followed further indistinct black shapes filling the air with their low-pitched whistle. More gliders ploughed in from the other end of the airfield. It seemed a miracle to me that none crashed head on, coming in as they were from opposite directions.

We stayed by our own wrecked glider, not daring to try and reach the edge of the airfield. From time to time, in these few action packed minutes, the sound of breaking wood and metal crashed out on the night air.

On our right, and a hundred feet away, the green lights of the 'T' burned with a smoky glow. Our glider had stopped more or less in the position that had been assigned to us, but not in the anticipated condition.

The last of the gliders had drifted in, except for one that was still being towed in a circle above the aerodrome. Undoubtedly the pilot was very worried as to his chances of setting down in one piece among the multitude of lights that must have appeared to him to take up every available foot of landing space.

Some figures loomed up from the direction of the vague shape of the watch tower on the edge of the field. We had been informed that a number of VIPs would be watching our landing from the security of the watch tower, and were now, presumably, coming out to inspect the results.

Tom and I were standing by the nose of our glider when one of the figures broke away from the main group and came over to us. We stood watching him as he inspected the shattered remains of our Horsa. Then he turned to us and said, 'Where have they taken the poor fellows'? We smilingly assured him that they had been taken nowhere as yet for we were the two pilots who had been flying the machine. He was rather taken aback, for he had fully expected to learn that the pilots had been seriously injured, if not killed. He congratulated us on our escape and moved on to the next wrecked glider.

We headed off across the field towards the watch tower where we knew our lorries would be waiting to take us back to our home base. We ourselves were surprised to learn next day that there had been no serious injuries suffered by anyone during the landing, despite the fact that there had been numerous crashes.

Dingo II ended the mass night landings, and we began to concentrate on day mass landings. Among them was Exercise Exeter, which went off very well.

At the beginning of June, there seemed to be a great deal of activity going on. Our Squadron Commander was continually disappearing for conferences. All exercises stopped, and even local flying was cut down to a minimum.

Royal Air Force mechanics began giving all gliders and tugs intensive checks. Everyone sensed something was in the wind but nobody knew what.

About the 2nd of June, all leave was stopped and the following day not a single man could even step outside to the local village. Two of our flights were detailed to report to the briefing room which was a Nissen hut that had been carefully guarded for the last two days.

Speculation spread as they remained inside the room for a long period. All the higher ranking officers seemed to be going about with an air of mystery, and in many cases with harassed expressions.

We knew something important was on, and somehow by instinct we knew that it was the big show this time, but where it was to take place was anyone's guess.

My flight was not in on the briefing, and I was burning with curiosity when the hut eventually disgorged its inmates. They were all talking excitedly among themselves in very guarded tones, but when they came within earshot of the rest of us, they shut up completely.

On the 4th of June, all the gliders were massed. Some had already been loaded with anti-tank six-pounder guns, trailers, 75mm howitzers, Bofors guns and jeeps among a varied assortment of cargoes. The empty ones merely awaited the arrival of troops who, unlike the guns and jeeps, could be loaded very quickly.

The troops arrived early on the 4th, and on that day the glider pilots involved in the operation (still unknown to us as D-Day) received what was intended as their final briefing, apart from one giving a last-minute weather prediction.

The following day, the 5th, everything was set for the takeoff, which was due sometime in the afternoon, but nothing happened. We learned that the operation had been deferred for 24 hours.

The skies looked a little stormy, with clouds scudding across. However, that night the roar of aircraft heading out brought me hurrying outside in company with the rest. It was a wonderful sight, the low flying formations passing overhead, with their red, white and green navigation lights moving against the black cloudy sky. It was too dark for me to identify the aircraft.

By now, we who were not taking part in the operation knew that the invasion was to be made on the Normandy coast. We could not get hold of any maps as these were carefully guarded, and we were not allowed in the briefing room; therefore the name Ouistreham meant nothing to us from the point of trying to visualise exactly where the landing would take place.

The delay must have put a terrific strain on the men taking part in the landings. The West Wall, Festung Europa, was an unknown quantity, but there was no doubt whatsoever that it was a very formidable line of defensive positions, and an invasion would not be a walk-over.

The next day, the 6th of June, the troops entered the gliders once more. It was mid-afternoon, and the whole of the aerodrome personnel who weren't on duty had gathered near the huge armada of marshalled tugs and gliders. Lorries and jeeps were everywhere, dashing up to and away from, the long line of waiting gliders.

With Tom, I walked down the rows of gliders saying goodbye to all I could see. All the glider pilots had been instructed to smear on black cream which would help to make them invisible in the coming darkness. The troops, however, had not done this, and our pilots made a strange contrast to them.

Even though I was not going on this trip, I could not help but get caught up in the terribly tense atmosphere that pervaded the airfield. I felt a lump in my throat every time I saw a familiar pilot checking up on his glider's controls or carefully checking over his weapons. Their camouflaged smocks bulged with the shapes of hand grenades and extra ammunition. Some faces wore a look of excitement, some were wearing a forced look of cheerfulness, while others appeared grave.

The thunder of the tugs' engines warming up almost hurt the eardrums, while the slipstream from their whirling propeller blades tried hard to spin us round or knock us over.

The glider pilots were summoned to the leading glider where Major Croot gave out his last minute instructions. For a few minutes they huddled together, and then dispersed. This time they made straight for their individual gliders and climbed up inside, pulling the portable steps up after them. Sliding doors swung down and closed. We fellow pilots watching knew that the great moment was at hand.

White billowing clouds sailed majestically across the skies. Gaps of bright blue were plentiful and, all in all, the weather appeared favourable.

A green light from a flashing Aldis lamp winked out at the leading tug, which then rolled slowly forward onto the runway, swung around and halted. The first glider was already being towed forward by a tractor even before the huge Stirling tug had quivered to a halt.

The RAF ground crew dashed forward with the ends of the towing rope. Two men plugged one end into the rear of the tug, while more men, standing on steps, plugged the yoke end into the two plug holes located underneath each wing on either side of the cockpit. Then the ground crew melted away from both machines. The four engines of the Stirling rose to a thunderous roar, and gradually the rope slack was taken up. With beating heart and moist eyes, I watched the combination move slowly forward, gathering speed every second. With the rest of the watchers, I waved good luck to the two figures seen through the perspex of the glider's cockpit. I saw a hand raised in return salute and then they were gone, racing down the concrete runway to lift into the air three quarters of the way down the seemingly endless path. Our squadron was off to play its part in the invasion of France.

Combination after combination followed swiftly in the wake of the first, the gliders with a variety of comments and figures scrawled in chalk on their sides and cockpits. One after the other they flashed down the runway with the names of each pilot dimly registering on my brain as they faded away into the distance.

I waited until the last combination had disappeared into the late afternoon sky, and the twin black specks no longer moved across a heaven that had suddenly become sombre as though it had become aware of the grim task that faced those men thundering through the air on that June day.

With a heavy heart, and with still fresh memories of Sicily in my mind, I walked slowly back to our hut with Tom keeping a silent vigil by my side.

The next day we learned the plan of the D-Day operation concerning the airborne.

At 0200 hours in the early morning of June 6th, 'Coup de Main' parties were dispatched in six gliders to seize and hold the bridges over the River Orne and the Canal de Caen in Normandy. Later we learned that all but one of the gliders had been highly successful in reaching their objectives which involved surprise landings.

Thirty minutes later, paratroopers of the 3rd and 5th Parachute Brigades began to drop east of the Orne River to reinforce the bridges already seized by the glider troops. The paratroopers also captured the coastal gun battery near Merville. Later on, they successfully carried out tasks involving the blowing of bridges over the Rivers Dives, Varaville, Bures and Troarn.

The British 3rd Division, assaulting from the sea, was to link up with the airborne troops on the Benouville Bridges over the canal and river. The 1st Commando Brigade, also assaulting from the sea, was to capture the port of Ouistreham and then link up with the 'Coup de Main' parties of the airborne troops. The bulk of the airborne troops were due to arrive later in the afternoon.

At 2100 hours the main force of gliders, including my squadron, arrived to reinforce the bridges.

Within 48 hours, the glider pilots were on their way back to England by sea, their task accomplished beyond expectation, and definitely with far fewer losses than was estimated by the High Command.

The troops of the 6th Airborne Division flown in by the glider pilots carried on the fight approximately another month before being withdrawn. They had had to beat off numerous savage counter-attacks on the bridges by well-equipped Panzer units and first class infantry, but not without loss.

Upon the return of the two flights of our squadron that had taken part in the operation, we were amazed to learn of their extremely light casualties. As far as I can remember, our total loss of pilots was four out of thirty four glider crews consisting of seventy two pilots, which, considering the magnitude of the operation involved, was almost unbelievable.

However, it must not be taken that the landings were a walkover for the airborne troops as a whole. Other squadrons suffered very heavy casualties, and bitter fighting evolved. Despite the light losses of our squadron, the fact emerged that many of them had been engaged in sharp fighting. Furthermore, great tribute is due to the skill of their landings, for a large number of the fields selected were covered with well dug in thick poles, (known as Rommel's Asparagus) many of which caused severe damage to gliders landing in the fields where they had been installed. Many of the poles had wires strung between them, and there were also reports that mines and other explosives were attached to some of the wires.

To bring in a glider, constructed mainly of wood, touching down at a speed of around 70 mph with the momentum of the heavy loads carried, right in among a mass of unyielding poles, undoubtedly called for a skill and courage of which the glider pilots were justly proud.

Tribute must also be paid to the soldiers who went along as passengers. The soldiers had to sit and wait for what was coming to them, knowing that their fate was not in their own hands but in those of the two pilots guiding the glider down among the uncertainty of obstructed fields. From those fields, small arms fire, and in many cases, light flak, was reaching up hungrily to destroy the invaders. To me, the men in the body of the glider behind the pilots had even more courage than those in front who knew what was happening and could do something to avert disaster. The passengers were powerless until they were safely down on the ground.

After the triumphant return of our two flights, we fully expected to take our turn in an operation to expand the rather narrow bridgehead that existed for some time after the initial landings in Normandy, but no such operations took place; gradually the feeling of tenseness, which had prevailed with us ever since the week before D-Day, died down. In one way I felt frustrated, and inexplicably in another way I felt relieved. I believe this feeling was quite common among most of our pilots due, I am sure, to the terribly long anticipatory waiting periods, periods that left the mind to run riot. Always I underwent those torturing thoughts right up to the moment of takeoff, and then they were a thing of the past. At the moment just before approaching the target area, when my hand was reaching for the red-topped release lever, those thoughts would flash through my mind again, to be instantly forgotten in the overpowering urgency of the moment—the task of landing on our assigned targets.

The weeks passed by with routine flying. Then suddenly the camp air again began to thicken with the excitement and anticipation of an operation. The camp was sealed off. Rumours ran rife. The usual irritating routine was followed once more—drawing rations, new equipment, arms, ammunition, and then the first briefing to reveal our destination.

In the crowded Nissen hut, carefully guarded outside as usual, our Squadron Commander, with a cheerful and satisfied smile, informed us that another 'do' was on. He explained, as we already knew from newspaper reports, that on the British front a large quantity of enemy armour had been concentrated, especially around Caen. To help the British 2nd Army break through and destroy that armour, the airborne were to be dropped south of Caen, well behind enemy lines, and form what our Commander Glider Pilot Colonel Chatterton was often known to call 'the cork in the bottle'.

We were, in fact, to prevent the escape south of the German armour and, of course, infantry. In other words, we were to drop astride the retreat routes of the Germans. This retreat was expected to take place automatically after 2nd Army troops had forced the flanks of the enemy back, thus endangering their withdrawal and escape.

We could, he went on to say, expect to meet with very strong resistance from the ground forces, and furthermore, the enemy was known to have concentrated strong anti-aircraft defences in and near our landing areas. Minefields might hamper landings although that could be considered a minor worry. Poles in the fields might be expected to cause some trouble. Apart from these interferences, we should be able to carry out the tasks assigned to us up to the expectations of the High Command.

Many expressive glances were flashed all over the room between the men. There was not one man who did not realise the implications behind the light-hearted briefing of the Squadron Commander.

Maps were issued and further briefings followed, going into more detailed reports as to the enemy divisions with which we would meet, and the word Panzer occurred more than once, indicating that there must be a considerable force of enemy armour in the area.

We all left the hut, a very thoughtful group. Even the men who had not yet taken part in any operation seemed to understand that it would be no walkover.

Out on the airfield, intense activity was in progress. The great black Horsas were being towed into position bordering the runways. The rising and falling note of the massive towing Stirlings' engines beat out on the air. The quartermaster's hut was already besieged by a throng of men seeking stores of all types.

The operation was due for the day after next and the landing would be a daylight one, late afternoon in the style of the main D-Day operation.

That night there was a feverish cleaning of weapons and checking Sten guns and their magazines. On the beds, grenades were spilled out, with the fuses being checked.

A light chatter ran around the room, but the tense atmosphere belied the cheerfulness. Other men were writing letters in a long and careful manner which was normally absent from their hurried scrawls on other days. A fog of tobacco smoke filled the hut, and I walked out into the darkness, drawing in deep breaths of clean fresh air, an uncertain stream of thoughts running through my head. Two days—they would soon pass by—and then out over the Channel and over the coast to an uncertain fate.

The following day was occupied with further briefings and drawing of more kit. Some of the men were still a little hazy from their visit to the Mess bar the night before.

Those whose gliders had been loaded with guns and jeeps and suchlike gave the chains that held them down another thorough check. Controls were carefully gone over, while some, with painstaking care, chalked multi-coloured sketches on the sides of the glider cockpits - girls of all shapes figured prominently in this not always artistic work.

The evening before the operation closed with a sunset of blood red glory, as if to hint at the fire and agony we would have to undergo.

The lights burned deep into the night. Reveille was at 0400 hours and most inmates saw no reason to put the lights out. Others like myself tried to seize some sleep in the hot foetid atmosphere under the glare of the naked bulbs, but refreshing sleep was impossible. In one corner, the slap, slap of cards kept up a steady noise until 2.00 a.m.

Just before 3.30 a.m. one of the orderlies looked into the hut and sleepily said, 'The op has been cancelled'.

Almost at the same time, the harsh metallic voice of the Tannoy system echoed out through the hut area, giving the news in a more disguised way with, 'The cricket match for tomorrow has been cancelled'.

It was a simple code form used to mislead any civilians who might be abroad that night in the vicinity of the airfield and to whom the message might be carried on the wind. For a moment there was silence, then a babble of voices. Everyone was wide awake. Curses and exclamations of relief filled the smoke-ridden hut.

The exclamations of relief did not so much indicate how glad we were that the operation was off, for we were always ready to do our part, but were due to the fact that we could close our heavy eyes in earnest, knowing that no one was going to rouse us at some ungodly hour. At that time of the morning there was little enthusiasm except for deep sleep, no matter how much we might have been looking forward to taking off the previous day when in full possession of our faculties.

We slept well on into late morning, for no one bothered to disturb us at the usual hour. The following day, all machines were towed back to their dispersal area and the proposed operation was a thing of the past.

That afternoon we were assembled to learn why the operation had been cancelled. Apparently more and more flak had been poured into the proposed landing areas, making an airborne operation out of the question, except with the risk of very heavy losses, which in turn would have made us prey to the heavy concentration of enemy armour.

All of us felt that it was a terrific let down after the immense mental and physical build-up that had been going on for the past few days. The inevitable mad let-up followed with the local towns and villages experiencing the outlet of our men's spirits in the pubs. Many resorted to other forms of entertainment to release the safety valve that had been held down at such high pressure during the preceding days. I personally chose the pub that night, arriving back at camp in the early hours of the morning, huddled down in the seat of Tom's little but powerful MG which he drove more by instinct than vision back to the airfield. Yes, it had been a wonderful evening, I thought, as I stumbled over the threshold of our hut, and tried to focus my eyes on which one of the still empty beds was mine. I slept like a log.

From that time onward, we were alerted several times during the coming months for operations that never materialised. In each case, days of preparation were filled with endless briefings, and marshalling of gliders. Guns, jeeps and trailers were loaded, and then unloaded. In most cases, the order of cancellation came only a matter of an hour of two before take-off in the early hours of the cold mornings. Again and again we were braced for something that never came off. The cancellations were always followed by a mass exodus from the airfield the same evening, and the saying 'Wine, women and song' was never more true, as each man sought out his particular way of blowing off steam.

After the proposed Caen drop, the next alert was for an operation on St. Malo on the Normandy coast, in an effort to seize the port. This was planned for the 9/10th July 1944. For some reason, never fully explained to us, it was abandoned. I did hear one rumour that the operation called for some glider landings on the beaches themselves, but how true that was I do not know. It certainly would have drawn considerable casualties, of that I am sure, for undoubtedly the beaches and the adjoining fields would have been well covered by fire from light and heavy guns of the well defended port.

Early in August 1944, a large Allied airborne landing was planned for a spectacular drop on the road to Paris in the area of Versailles. Our particular landing area was close to the town of Ramboillet, bordered by wooded country.

At this time, General Patton was driving the enemy swiftly back in a retreat that would take the Germans through the Versailles area. As usual, the plan for the airborne was that they should form 'The Cork in the Bottle'. In other words, we were to land astride the escape route and try to prevent the enemy armour and infantry from getting away.

To us this had an unusual appeal, for the very words Versailles and Paris were magic. We had visions of entering these two places after the battle was over, Paris especially, as its world renowned reputation as the soldiers' paradise lured us on.

It is, I must confess, the first operation we had been briefed for that held the 100% approval of the men. I had never seen them so enthusiastic before, and that went for me as well. What we weren't going to do to Paris was nobody's business! The operation was far more complex than any planned so far. In the first place, our squadron was to be towed by an American squadron flying Dakotas. In the second place, our squadron had to leave its main base at Fairford temporarily and move over to the American troop-carrying squadrons' airfield at Ramsbury in Wiltshire, about thirty miles away. The latter was a refreshing break for us, for the advance party had reported the usual excellent American food available, including two or more eggs for breakfast, all the sugar and milk we could want, plenty of chicken, and many other delicacies such as we had not seen since we were in North Africa with an American troop carrying command there.

To see our lorry loads of men moving off out of Fairford for Ramsbury, one would have thought they were going on a picnic, which they were, in point of fact, with regard to the food side of the question. This would be the operation of operations. Never could men have gone into an action of that sort feeling more confident and gay than our men were feeling that bright sunny day when we rode over the hills through Swindon to Ramsbury.

We pitched our tents in a wooded copse alongside the aerodrome, and for the next three days, while we waited for the signal for takeoff, I must confess we all gorged ourselves full in a most disgraceful way on food that never was, or is ever likely to be, part of British Army, Air Force or Navy rations.

During the first three days we had several briefings in company with the American tug pilots who were a fine lot of men. We were all amused at the very informal method of briefing that was carried out by our American friends, and in a way we missed our own, which we thought was a more thorough way of briefing. However, by the end of the third day, we had a pretty good idea of what lay in front of us.

We checked out our gliders again and again, marshalled out on the wide expanse of the well laid out airfield. The weather was fair, except for a sharp fall of rain that beat down one afternoon, driving under the canvas shelter of our tents.

We were due off on the fourth day, but the operation was postponed for twenty four hours. We sat in our tents and waited. The next day we were ready again. After many consultations, during which time no one seemed to know what was going on, in true Army style, we were informed that the operation was off for good. Most of the men were really fed up with this news. All visions of Gay Paree faded from their minds. We cursed our luck, the High Command and the enemy.

Our Squadron Commander was as fed up as we were and readily gave his consent to the usual mass exodus from the camp. The nearest town was Hungerford, and that night its sleepy streets resounded with the gaiety of us pilots, and the

American boys, such as had not been heard for a long while, despite the fact that soldiers were roaming its streets in their hundreds night after night. To the outsider, it may seem senseless the way our men drank and sought other pleasures after each let-down, but to us it was the only thing to do, rather than let the pent-up nervousness ease its way out slowly degree by degree in the loneliness of our huts.

Back once more at Fairford, we fell into the old routine – local flying, ground and physical training. Summer was well advanced now and it would not be long before the first autumnal tints set in.

On 15th August news reached us that airborne landings in conjunction with sea landings had taken place on the southern coast of France. The airborne troops, consisting of paratroops and glider-borne troops, dropped down in the area between Toulon and Cannes on the Riviera Coast. Later, I learned that my old squadron had flown the gliders in to land among the poles that were scattered over the landing ground. No. 3 Squadron was known as the Independent Squadron when later it began operating out of Italy. I did hear that some or all had operated out of the Island of Corsica, but never saw any written confirmation of that rumour. The landings 'Operation Dragoon' were very successful.

Towards the end of August, we were again fully alerted and briefed for an operation in Belgium. Again, the gliders were marshalled ready with their eager loads. We attended briefing after briefing until we knew the landing zones by heart. The area selected for the operation was around Tournai in the Escaut River bend in Belgium. The intention as usual was to operate offensively against the retreating enemy who were being driven rapidly back in this particular sector by 30th Corps of the 2nd Army. Once more, the 'Cork in the Bottle' operation was being eagerly anticipated by the High Command. Our Commander, Colonel Chatterton, had every faith that the cork would hold once we had established ourselves. Without exception, I think, all glider pilots had great faith in Colonel Chatterton and would never question a decision reached by him at any time. If he said we would form a 'cork' and hold that cork firmly in the bottle, that order would be carried out to the utmost ability of our men. However, none of us were under any illusion as to the formidable task that the order presented.

We were scheduled to take off at dawn on 1st September, which would have meant landings around 10.00 to 11.00 a.m. However, less than two hours before takeoff, the oft repeated phrase 'operation cancelled' was passed from hut to hut, and once again yet another well planned and prepared airborne operation was but a dream of the past. We learned later that 30th Corps had advanced so quickly that they had overrun our proposed landing zones.

Operation Market Garden

Operation Market Garden was an ill-fated military operation lasting nine days, from 17-25 September 1944. The objective was to achieve an entry into Germany over the Lower Rhine by seizing the bridges across the Maas (Meuse River) and two arms of the Rhine (the Waal and the Lower Rhine) as well as several smaller canals and tributaries. The operation made large-scale use of airborne forces. Paratroopers were dropped in the Netherlands to secure key bridges and towns along the Allied axis of advance. Farthest north, the British 1st Airborne Division, supported by men of the Glider Pilot Regiment and the Polish 1st Independent Parachute Brigade, landed at Arnhem to secure bridges across the Nederrijn. Expecting light resistance from the Germans, British XXX Corps planned to reach the British airborne forces within two to three days.

MARKET was the airborne side of the operation, and the GPR would deliver the troops, weapons and equipment of the 1st Airborne into Arnhem using nearly 700 gliders; 658 Airspeed Horsas, 29 General Aircraft Hamilcars and 10 CG4-A Waco (Hadrians). It was the largest airborne operation of the war, and involved three lifts over the first three days of the operation. The first lift involved 359 gliders, the second 297, and the final 44 taking off as part of the third.

V. Miller Operational details:

- Glider chalk No. : 431-440
- Serial No. : B18
- Glider: Horsa Mk1
- Glider Squadron: 'G' Squadron
- Airborn Block No. : 56
- Departure airfield: Fairford, England

- 1st Pilot: Sgt V. Miller
- 2nd Pilot: Sgt Tom Hollingsworth
- Unit: HQ. 1st A/B Div.
- Flight: 24 Flight
- Tug Squadron: 190 Squadron R.A.F.

Chapter 10

Arnhem

ARNHEM, the name of that never to be forgotten little Dutch town near the German border astride the Lower Rhine, is where one of the most savage battles of the war was fought. This pleasant historic town and its suburb of Oosterbeek were to suffer great devastation during the nine days that the men of the British 1st Airborne Division engaged the enemy in fighting that raged in the streets, on the railway tracks, in the woods and fields and in the beautifully laid out gardens of the houses in Oosterbeek. Savage hand-to-hand battles were fought to the bitter end, while the almost ceaseless and practically unopposed shelling and mortaring by the enemy took heavy toll of our men.

Many places around Arnhem will remain forever indelibly imprinted in my memory. The ploughed fields where I touched down after a three hour flight from my home base in England on the first day of the operation, Sunday 17th September 1944. The little Dutch farm nestling in the far corner of the field, with the occupants dashing out to welcome us with open arms and genuine smiles of thankfulness. The thickly wooded plantation in which lay the asylum, a building which later was to burn furiously from the mortar shells that sent me cringing into the narrow slit trenches. The nightmare of watching the inmates of the asylum walking in a helpless daze, their flapping white night-clothes bringing an eerie atmosphere to the deepening shadows of evening spreading through already shadowy woods, lit only by the hungry flames burning in the asylum building. The Hartenstein Hotel that lay beside the road that ran eastwards from Renkum through Oosterbeek to Arnhem that was to be our Divisional Headquarters and also the centre of that hell of enemy mortar and shell bombardment that raked the grounds of the old, solidly built house. The withdrawal, nine days later across the Lower Rhine river under enemy fire on that dark, cold and wet night when the woods around burned and smouldered with a deep angry reddish glare fired by the rain of explosives from both our own and German lines.

Some 10,000 men set out confident, jovial and in high spirits on that final morning of 17th September 1944 – from which just over 2,000 came back across the Rhine nine days later, shocked, dazed and exhausted, but not demoralised – forced to steal away into the dark, rainy night and abandon their comrades who lay dead or too wounded to move. Between 7,000 and 8,000 never found their way back over the river on that night. Over 1300 lay dead among the softly falling leaves of autumn, and under the piled rubble of Oosterbeek and Arnhem.

Months later, in March 1945, the survivors who withdrew back over the Rhine under fire, in company with thousands more, fell upon the enemy once again to wreak revenge for the terrible punishment inflicted on them during those nine days of agony – nine days of almost ceaseless shelling, mortaring and machine gunning, and of fighting off prowling, heavily armed tanks. Even the Luftwaffe was thrown in from time to time but, thank God, only on a small scale.

Six months later, on 23rd March 1945, the triumphant 6th Airborne Division together with the American 17th Airborne Division struck at the enemy again over the Rhine, this time on German soil. Victory was undisputed as the enemy collapsed into utter chaos under the impact of the mighty black cloud of the Airborne as they flew over the Rhine to descend by the thousands in the fields of Germany northwest of Wesel, destroying or capturing the enemy wherever they met him. But that was in March, six months hence, and this was September 1944.

Summer was on the wane when we first received an indication that an operation was in the offing. During the past weeks, we had been taking advantage of the excellent weather to carry out further practise mass landings. Almost every second week found the skies above the peaceful West of England countryside darkened with armadas of tugs and gliders moving steadily across at regularly spaced intervals in long purposeful columns.

Squadrons of Hamilcars took their place in these huge streams, although the Horsas predominated. The mighty Hamilcars were capable of carrying a small tank, or a large seventeen-pounder piece of artillery with its accompanying vehicle, a tremendous asset to airborne troops who always had to face superior forces of enemy artillery and tanks.

Replacements from the Normandy operation, both gliders and men, had long since arrived. Our squadron was now the proud possessor of several Mark II Horsas, which had the modified cockpit and nose that swung open rapidly to allow any wheeled or tracked vehicle to unload in an astonishingly short space of time, once the landing had been effected. This was a great improvement over the old Mark I, in which the whole tail unit had to be unbolted and lifted clear before the cargoes inside could be unloaded, a Herculean task for any number of men less than five.

The planning of Operation 'Market Garden' called for an extremely bold stroke, with a glittering prize as a reward if it was successful. This prize was no less than the capture and retention of three bridges over three very strategic rivers, and other smaller bridges over intermediate canals. The three bridges in order of advance were the Maas at Grave, the Waal at Nijmegen and the Nieder, or Lower Rhine, at Arnhem. With these three bridges in our hands, the British Second Army, poised ready on the Belgian-Dutch border, could plunge forward and, after crossing the last bridge at Arnhem, burst out over the great North German plain beyond with very few strategic barriers to bar the way to Berlin.

The drop at Arnhem meant that we would be over sixty miles ahead of the front line of the British 2nd Army or, in other words, we would be over sixty miles behind enemy lines, which would in fact represent the deepest penetration of all the Allied airborne drops since the Normandy invasion.

The United States' 101st Airborne Division was to drop in the areas of Son and Vehgel, with the object of capturing and holding the bridges over the Wilhelmina and Willemsvaart Canals. Son was just north of Eindoven, and represented the nearest dropping area to the front line of the 2nd Army, which would be about twenty five miles away on the Belgian-Dutch border. The moment the first Allied

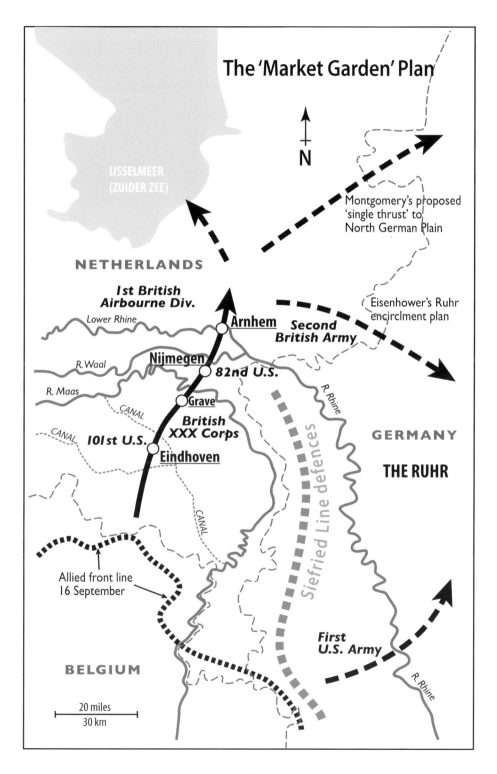

The 'Market Garden' Plan

N

IJSSELMEER (ZUIDER ZEE)

NETHERLANDS

1st British Airbourne Div.

Lower Rhine

Arnhem

Montgomery's proposed 'single thrust' to North German Plain

Second British Army

Eisenhower's Ruhr encirclment plan

Nijmegen

R. Waal

82nd U.S.

R. Maas

Grave

CANAL

British XXX Corps

R. Rhine

CANAL

101st U.S.

Eindhoven

GERMANY

THE RUHR

Siefried Line defences

CANAL

Allied front line 16 September

First U.S. Army

BELGIUM

R. Rhine

20 miles
30 km

air units passed over the front line, the signal for the general ground attack would be given. It was estimated that the Guard's Armoured Division, which would be spearheading the 2nd Army, would establish contact with the United States 101st Airborne division later the same day.

Next in order of distance from the front line of the 2nd Army would be the dropping zones of the United States' 82nd Airborne Division. Their objectives were the bridges over the rivers Maas at Grave, and Waal at Nijmegen.

Grave was approximately twenty miles beyond Vehgel and Nijmegen another twelve to fifteen miles further on.

Finally, the British 1st Airborne Division was allotted the two bridges at Arnhem, one a railway, and the other – the main target – a road bridge. At this point the Lower Rhine is about a quarter of a mile across, and the current flows swiftly between the fairly steep banks. Arnhem was roughly twelve miles further north of Nijmegen, or between sixty and seventy miles from the 2nd Army's jumping off point.

It was estimated by our High Command that the British 2nd Army spearheads would contact us within forty-eight to seventy-two hours from the time of our landings. If things went wrong, there was a chance that we might have to hold out for a little while longer, certainly not more than four or five days, as that would represent our limits of endurance against a numerically superior enemy with plenty of heavy weapons.

Five days. That's what they thought, and so did we. I do not think that one man present would have believed it could he have foreseen it would not be seventy- two hours, or four or even five days, but nine, before we would see the faces of 2nd Army men, and then only because the 1st Airborne Division was to be forced to extricate itself from the encircling enemy and fight its way out and across to the south bank of the Lower Rhine, thus giving up our foothold over that river.

From the moment we entered the long Nissen hut used for briefings, we were confined to camp for obvious security reasons. The day was 15th September 1944, two days before the actual takeoff. With all the briefings and subsequent cancellations of several previous operations since D-Day in June, there was a somewhat disbelieving air among us all as to whether this newly planned operation would really come off.

Putting us all at our ease, and with the word to smoke if we so wished, our Squadron Commander proceeded to outline our squadron's particular part in the landings.

The date of the operation was to be Sunday 17th of September and would be in two lifts. Takeoff would be at between 7.00 and 7.30 a.m., just after first light. Landing time at the landing zone would be around 10.30 a.m., thus involving a three-to three-and-a-half-hour flight. The Meteorological Officer indicated that the prevailing good weather would hold. This prophecy was met with the usual sceptical comments. About 500 gliders would be involved in the operation, the importance of which, our Squadron Commander went on to say, could not be over stressed.

The landing zones on Ginkel Heath and the surrounding fields would lie in an area about eight miles to the west of Arnhem. This was necessary because of the heavy concentration of anti-aircraft guns in and around the outskirts of the town. The suburb of Oosterbeek was only about four to five miles away from the Arnhem bridges, while the nearest village was Heelsum on the Renkum-Arnhem road. The landing zones lay astride the railway, and this line would in fact represent the dividing line between squadron zones. Pointing to some excellent aerial photographs, our Squadron Commander indicated with a pointer, the ploughed fields in which our squadron was to land. On the adjoining Ginkel Heath, a squadron of Hamilcars would be setting down.

The landing would be made in two separate lifts. The men of the first lift could expect contact with the enemy the moment they touched down and would have to come out of the gliders with their weapons ready for instant use. The second lift, scheduled for the next day, should find things easier, with the landing zones firmly in the hands of the men of the first lift. I saw from the blackboard that Sergeant Hollingsworth and I were assigned to the first lift.

Opposition by enemy aircraft should be negligible, probably nonexistent, as our fighter aircraft and bombers would be paying visits to all enemy airfields in the vicinity, and even some in Germany itself would be thoroughly bombed and strafed. We could expect some light flak over the town of S'Hertogenbosch, and also from the landing areas.

Our Squadron Commander continued with his briefing, going into detail on certain points. Some minutes later, he indicated that he was finished and that we were at liberty to come up on the platform and study all maps and aerial photographs at close hand.

Sergeant Hollingsworth and I studied our particular landing field minutely. I noticed that tall trees bordered both ends of the field. This factor would shorten our already none too long landing run considerably. At the far end of the field in one corner was a farmhouse, a good point of reference when approaching and landing. On our left as we would come in were two prominently shaped woods in the form of a triangle with the apexes meeting. The photographs were of immense help to us, as we were to learn later. One copy of each photograph and appropriate maps were issued to all crew before we filed out of the hut, blinking in the bright sunlight that shone serenely down on our busy airfield.

The rest of the day was devoted to drawing all the necessary equipment for the operation. When I entered our hut, I found that each man's bed was piled with ammunition of all kinds, plus boxes of forty-eight-hour rations that we always carried on such operations. Piats (anti-tank weapons) and Bren guns lay scattered over the floor with their accompanying cases of bombs and magazines. Grenades were being carefully primed, and each cartridge for the Brens was cleaned before being inserted into the magazines. The men were taking no chances after the Squadron Commander's warning about immediate action on landing.

Sergeant Hollingsworth and I had been detailed to act as one of the Piat anti-tank crews after we had effected our landing, having completed our air task. To me, the Piat was, and always will be, a heavy clumsy-looking anti-tank weapon, but quite effective nonetheless. We had been issued three cases of bombs for the Piat, containing a total of nine bombs, the whole presenting a substantial weight. In addition, we both carried a Sten gun with its accompanying eight magazines, each magazine holding thirty-two rounds, plus two Bren gun magazines, each loaded with twenty-eight rounds of ammunition. Last but not least, we were each issued with four Number Thirty-Six hand grenades, and two phosphorus grenades. We jokingly remarked that between us we had enough ammunition to stave off a company attack supported by tanks.

Much letter writing was done that night before adjourning to the mess for a few drinks. The atmosphere there was one of suppressed excitement, and the beer and liquor flowed freely.

On the whole, we had been more favourably impressed with the planning of this forthcoming operation than any so far. From all accounts, we could see nothing but success ahead. If only a corner of the veil hiding the future could have been lifted to allow us to catch a glimpse of the coming nine days, we would have had a rude shock.

The next day our load arrived, a jeep and its trailer. I was still unaware of the exact load I was to take in and its role in the operation. A long line of anti-tank six-pounder guns bumped its way across the field towed by the versatile jeeps. These and seventy five millimetre howitzers were wheeled up the ramps into the fuselage of the Mark 1 gliders. Sweating crews heaved and lifted the jeeps around the bulkheads near the entrance in the side of the Mark 1 Horsas, followed by the long-barrelled six-pounder guns, seventy-five millimetre howitzers or trailers. All were lashed firmly down to the floor by chains with wheels locked in troughs laid lengthways down the fuselage.

I was dripping with perspiration by the time we had chained down our own particular jeep and trailer. I was curious to know who I was taking in, but had to be patient. Finally we were able to step back and ease our aching backs with the feeling of a job well done. It had to be well done, for if ever one of those vehicles broke loose in flight, disaster would follow swiftly in the form of an uncontrollable plunge earthwards.

That afternoon, during a further briefing, I learned more about what my load was to be. With mixed feelings I listened to the Squadron Commander say, 'Staff, in addition to your military load you will have a Colonel of Divisional Signals with you and the press, the official Army photographer, the public relations men, plus a few other soldiers. The war correspondent's name is Alan Wood of the Daily Express. The BBC man is Stanley Maxted. The public relations officer is Major Oliver. The army photographer is a Sergeant Smith. You'd better get hold of them when they arrive later on this afternoon and introduce yourself.'

Needless to say, I received a severe kidding from the rest of the squadron. Some thought I was extremely lucky, others thought 'Bad luck!' My feelings were mixed. On one hand I felt quite excited at carrying such an interesting load; on the other, I realised I would not have the advantage of having all army-trained fighting men to help unload the equipment from the glider after touchdown, an act that would probably call for speed and skill, if we were to evade the enemy fire that would, in all probability, meet us the moment we landed.

I had the pleasure of meeting my load within the hour. Curiously they only asked a few questions, even though for most it was their first glider flight.

Sergeant Webb, a one-time glider pilot who had taken part in the Sicilian operation with me, but who had since been grounded owing to trouble with his eyesight, was doing me the great honour of accompanying me as one of the passengers on this operation. Such was his keenness to take part that he had obtained special permission from the Squadron Commander to come along, not without argument, but he had won through. Personally, I was very pleased he was flying with us for he would be invaluable at the landing to help remove the huge tail unit in order that we would be able to safely unload our cargo. Game old Arthur, he paid for his volunteering, being wounded and eventually taken prisoner during the ensuing battle.

The mess was a popular spot that night. For my part, I drank sparingly, for I knew the coming day would place a severe mental and physical strain upon us, and I wanted to be 100% fit to meet it.

I went to bed that night with a feeling of dark foreboding hanging over the field. I slept but lightly, and was awake when the orderly came round switching on the lights at 5.00 am. Tired-eyed, I rose along with the others. It was pitch black outside, and rather chilly. This was it. This was D-Day once more. No cancellation this time. A strange silence hung over the wash house that morning. Some did not trouble to shave. I removed my beard under the light of the dim bulbs that burned, one at each end of the cold water basins, and a broken sliver of mirror that I had carried with me for many months. Strange how one can become so attached to a broken piece of glass, I thought idly as I tugged at the resisting beard. Well, it was coming with me on this operation. Maybe I would find a better piece in Holland.

Breakfast was a little livelier. As was customary on the day of an operation, two fresh eggs and bacon were served instead of the usual odd looking powdered egg mixtures normally offered us everyday. The WAAFS smiled in a sad way as each one of us filed past to collect our breakfasts. The tea was strong, sweet and hot. They were seeing us off in style. I waved across to our tug crew who had almost finished their breakfast and were preparing to hurry over to a last minute briefing. We would join them in fifteen minutes to hear the final weather forecast.

Tom, who I had left in bed still half asleep when I went to breakfast, appeared in a rather dishevelled state just as I has finished eating. Bleary eyed, he sat down beside me and ate hungrily. Telling him I would see him in the briefing room, I left and made my way back to our hut to pick up my equipment. It was empty when I arrived, and for a moment I looked around wondering how many would come back to claim their beds after the operation. Brushing these thoughts aside, I bent down and lifted up my strap equipment, slipping it over my shoulders. Even with only the pouches, it weighed heavily. I slung my Sten gun, picked up the terribly weighty rucksack, put on my steel helmet, took one last look around and stepped outside. The first faint glint of daylight was lighting the eastern horizon. The air was clean and cool after the stuffy, smoke-laden atmosphere of the hut.

I walked swiftly over to the briefing room and went inside. Most of our men were already there, perched on stools and table tops. Mingled with the camouflaged smocks of the glider pilots was the blue of the RAF aircrews who would be towing us away within the hour.

Tom walked in about thirty seconds before the first briefing officer began to speak. There was little new. The military situation remained unchanged. The weather would be as perfect as could be expected. Some cloud from our base to the east coast, and then a cloudless sky over the North Sea until we crossed the Dutch coast. We could then expect scattered cloud right up to the landing zones. The route would be as planned. Thirty minutes out due west, and then back over Fairford airfield in a formed-up line. On past Oxford to Hatfield, north of London. From there to Aldeburgh on the East Anglian coast and out across the North Sea. We should cross the coast of Holland at the Island of Schouvern (which would be mostly under water). On to Vehgel, where we would turn almost due north straight for our landing zones around Oosterbeek.

I caught a glimpse of Alan Wood as we left the briefing hut. Outside, the dawn was taking a firm grip. Trucks were waiting to take us to the marshalled line of gliders. The fast ride around the perimeter track in the cold air blasted away the last cobwebs from my brain. We were really going this time. This would be my first operation since that fatal landing in Sicily. Great strides had been made since then – this one would be successful – it had to be. Sunday, 17th September 1944, a day that I was to remember for the rest of my life.

The truck stopped. We got down and walked along the line of gliders, looking grim and ominous in their black paint against the rapidly lightening sky. The smell of dope, peculiar to wooden-built flying machines, permeated the air. On the far side of the runway, the giant Stirling four-engined towing planes squatted, straining at the chocks as their great engines rumbled in a healthy roar, vibrating the very air with powerful voices, as if urging us to hurry, hurry into the maelstrom of battle.

Seeing this great display of air power, I could not help but marvel at the energy, time and material that had gone into this planned operation. In less than four hours the enemy would be feeling the weight of this mighty armada.

Sergeant Tom Hollingsworth and I checked all controls carefully. We went over the lashings holding down the jeep and trailer with minute care. Then we were satisfied.

I glanced at my watch – 7.00 a.m. – fifteen minutes to takeoff of the first combination. I stepped back out through the cockpit doorway and descended the short ladder to the ground. Looking around I noticed my load together in a group. Walking over to them, I bid them good morning. They replied cheerfully. An air force photographer was taking shots of our group and I was asked to point out to a spot on one of our maps indicating Arnhem, while the camera buzzed away.

It was almost broad daylight now, and already the cold of the early morning was fading. The engines of the tugs had gone silent after their preliminary warming up, and I lay down on the dewy grass basking in the morning sun.

An engine coughed and broke into a steady roar, followed by another and yet another, until the air once more was filled with their thunder. Men began moving towards their gliders. This was it. I raised myself and walked with Tom over to the glider. We were silent.

I watched our load climb aboard and saw that they were seated correctly, checking their safety belts. We shook hands with Sergeant Arthur Webb, and saw him through the rear door. He would be separated from us during the flight by the bulk of the jeep and trailer. He wished us luck in our landing, and I caught a last glimpse of his smiling face as he slid the door down and locked it. Good old Arthur, always willing to take a chance, always ready to do his part. A staunch pal who would never let anyone down. A veteran of the Sicilian operation.

As I climbed up the short steps into the fuselage for the last time before takeoff, I saw that the first tug was already moving out of line onto the runway with rumbling motors. At the same moment, the leading glider was also being towed forward onto the runway by a tractor.

I pulled the steps in after me and closed down the door, double checking the locks. I gave the men seated in the fuselage a grin as I went through to the cockpit. One of the men was nonchalantly eating an apple and reading the Sunday paper with no more concern, outwardly at any rate, than he would have exhibited on an exercise. Alan Wood grinned and nodded as I told him we would be off in about three minutes.

Sliding down into the left-hand seat, I swung the safety harness over my shoulders and across my legs, making sure that there was very little play, just in case we landed badly. Tom, in the right-hand seat, was already strapped in. He was busy moving the controls in all directions, checking for their smooth action. When he had finished, I took hold of the duplicated wheel and rudder bar and tried them out. They responded easily. I checked the altimeter, setting it at zero, glanced at the air pressure in the bottles which operate the flaps, correctly registered at 140 lb. OK, I pulled once at the red-topped release lever to make sure it was not sticking. All was well.

The cockpit was stuffy despite the fact that I had all the small windows open. Well, the air blast once we were flying would clear that. I looked over the carefully folded maps to make sure they were in the right order; there might not be time to sort them out en route.

The rising thunder of motors beat in through the walls of the cockpit. The first combination was rolling down the runway gathering speed every second. I could not see the takeoff owing to the mass of stationary gliders obstructing my view. The second combination was already on the runway with the ground crew working feverishly to ram the rope plugs into the corresponding sockets in the glider and tug. And then they were off. Timing was perfect. Everybody worked with a will to keep the despatching up to schedule.

Only two more gliders remained in front of us. It wouldn't be long now. I looked at my watch. 7.25 a.m. We should be airborne by 7.30 a.m. if all went well.

A tractor came racing up towards us, swung round sharply and then backed up under our nose. A man lifted the connecting bar and I felt our glider vibrate as he rammed home the securing pin.

Only one glider remained in front now, and that was beginning to move forward towards the runway. Fascinated, I watched it swing round onto the runway. Its parent tug was already there, the great blades of its swirling propellers glinting in the morning sunlight.

I saw the controller on the side raise his yellow disc, and then snap it down sharply. The tug shuddered with the opening of its throttles, and moved forward. At the same moment our tractor moved us off with a jerk. The glider and tug on the runway were racing off, gaining speed rapidly. We swung quickly into the space just vacated. Shooting a glance back through the doorway, I gave the thumbs-up to the two passengers who were visible. They returned the sign accompanied by weak grins. I thought their faces looked a little pale, but no doubt mine did also.

Looking through the perspex, I watched two ground crew plugging the rope into the sockets of our wings. Ahead, two more men were locking the far end of the rope into the tail of the Stirling tug. Our glider vibrated under the backwash of the slipstream from the spinning airscrews ahead. The combination that had taken off ahead of us was climbing rapidly up over the end of the runway, the glider dipping and swaying in the slipstream of the tug hauling it forward and upward.

My lips had gone dry. It was useless licking them with my tongue; that was parched too. I could feel my forehead wet with perspiration and my hands sticky with sweat. A hammer seemed to have started madly beating away in my chest. Another beat dully on my temples.

The controller stood with the yellow disc above his head. I looked at Tom. Nodding OK at the controller, I raised my left thumb. Down flashed the yellow disc. I stared at the tug ahead which was creeping forward, slowly taking up the slack of the rope.

The rope tautened. Dimly I heard the pilot of the tug call over the intercom 'Brakes off, Number Two!' I automatically slipped off the lever. We rolled forward under the pull of the tug. Shooting a glance out to one side, I saw the line of men and WAAFs waving farewell. I raised one arm in reply, and then switched my eyes back to the tug, the tail of which was swinging violently from side to side. I kicked the rudder one way and then the other to take the strain off the Stirling pilot. Glider and tug lined up. Keeping the wheel forward, I watched the airspeed creep up, forty, fifty, sixty mph. The dull roar of the slipstream beat into the cockpit.

The tail of the Stirling lifted gradually off the ground. Levelling off, I hugged the runway ten feet up. The Horsa trembled under the upward impact of the tug's slipstream beating up from the runway. Strength was needed to hold her level at this point. One wing dipped, over went the wheel and it lifted back to level. The thunder of the slipstream made talking out of the question. I signalled to Tom with one hand to trim back, and he obeyed instantly, easing the pressure on the wheel. I grinned my thanks, and hung squarely behind the tug, now lifting free of the ground. Our airspeed clocked 110 mph as the hedge bordering the end of the runway loomed into sight, moving swiftly towards and then below us. We were climbing rapidly, and a moment later the hedge, and the road bordering it, slid by underneath – we were away.

It was bumpy up to 500 feet despite it being early morning. At that height I handed over to Tom, and sank back gratefully to relax for a few minutes. Fairford village passed by below and to our right, the old stone buildings and the square church tower looking a picture in the early morning sunlight.

Our flight gradually became smoother as we climbed higher into the blue cumulus-studded sky. At 2,500 feet we levelled out. This height was to be maintained all the way to the landing zones, unless cloud or enemy action decreed otherwise. We continued to head due west. After fifteen minutes we turned onto a reciprocal course and headed back for the aerodrome, the whole squadron forming up into a predetermined pattern of pairs in echelon to starboard. We were already catching up with the combination in front with whom we were to pair off. The glider and tug ahead dipped and rose constantly, gracefully riding what little bumps there were.

Below, the peaceful Gloucestershire countryside moved slowly by with little villages of grey stone peeping out from the long rolling folds in the hills. Sometimes, all of the villages except the church spire would be hidden beneath a white blanket of mist through which the spire would rise like a symbol. Yes, life below had nothing in common with us that bright morning. In those little grey stone buildings beneath our spreading wings, people lay sleeping, still unaware of the mighty armada forming up above them, and its grim task ahead. For a moment, I felt envious of those people lying there so distant from the maelstrom of war.

I came out of my reverie as we went into a gradual turn. We were on our way back to our rendezvous over the airfield. As we came out of the turn, I signalled to Tom that I would take a spell at the wheel. He gave me the thumbs-up sign and relinquished his grip on the wheel as I took over. I began to feel exhilarated. Here we were, thousands of feet above the earth, part of a huge airborne army that soon would be crossing the North Sea to descend on the enemy. One more step towards ending the war and returning to home. Return to home! Yes, I hoped so, if all went well this time.

We were flying about five hundred to a thousand feet below the base of massive white cumulus clouds, which were beginning to appear in increasing quantities. I marvelled at their size. The towering walls billowed up for thousands of feet above us. Mighty caverns wended their way through those majestic silent wonders, caverns that beckoned us to investigate and explore their heavenly grandeur. But not today - our task could wait for none of that. The realm of fantasy was not for us - grim reality lay ahead.

Now, I could make out our home base over two thousand feet below. The last of the gliders had left. Only the reserve gliders lay scattered around its perimeter; and then it was gone, disappearing under the cockpit nose. We were on the first leg of the operation. The village of Lechlade, with its slender church tower, passed by to port. I picked out the Nags Head Inn on the Wantage road where Tom and I had spent many a happy evening. If we got back safely from this do, the Nags Head would see us again for a real celebration. Good old Lechlade sprawled around the Thames tributary known as the Isis, in which we had swum many a time. I felt somewhat sad for a minute, and then the mood passed.

Owing to the thickening cloud, I never did get the glimpse of the north eastern suburbs of London for which I had hoped. The green fields of Essex meandered by underneath. The dull roaring monotony of the slipstream drummed into my head. Our tug dipped and rolled, with ourselves forever following its motion to keep undue strain from being placed on the rope. I carefully followed our progress on the map, not because I feared getting lost over the British countryside, but because I wanted to get into the feel of it for the ultra-careful reading I would have to do as we neared our target area.

As we approached the east coast, we ran into a clear patch of weather, and suddenly the land seemed to drop away, and the grey of the sea materialised. My heart beat a little faster at this sight, our last glimpse of England. I searched for the town of Aldeburgh over which we would be passing, and there it was. We were not too high to prevent my seeing the large number of black specks gathered in the streets below, people hurrying to their churches, no doubt, pausing en route to glance up at our impressive armada. I kept my gaze on this last outpost of England until the leading edge of the wing situated just behind the cockpit eventually cut it off from sight. Below stretched the inhospitable looking North Sea, grey and cold. I prayed that our rope would not break during the sea crossing. We had been told, however, that rescue boats would be patrolling our route, and that did give some comfort.

The army photographer left his seat and came forward to take some shots through the perspex windows of the cockpit. This little interval served to break the monotony of the flight. Ahead, flying at slightly varying altitudes, the long line of gliders and tugs stretched away into the distance. Except for a very gradual rise and fall by the combinations, the whole armada seemed poised motionless in space. The air was wonderfully calm over the grey waters. From time to time the waves below would reflect a bright sparkle as the tossing crests caught the sunlight.

A feeling of satisfaction came over me. Rummaging around, I found the oversize army issue Thermos flask we had brought along filled with tea. I poured out a cupful for Tom as he sat at the controls, his movements almost imperceptible due to the calm. He flew with one hand while sipping at the hot brew. I sat back and, gazing on the majesty of our aerial fleet, drank my tea. The endless roar of the slipstream no longer seemed painful to my ears. It was smooth and steady now, not jarring as it had been when we had been riding the air pockets over the land. I passed the flask back through the connecting door to our passengers, who accepted it with great pleasure. Even at the comparatively low height of 2,500 feet, it was somewhat chilly back in the fuselage. Here in the cockpit, we caught the heat of the sun's rays, almost to the point of being uncomfortable.

Below, a Hamilcar slid up and past us, towed by one of the squat Halifax four-engined tugs, which were the only ones that could do a satisfactory job of towing those heavy artillery-laden gliders.

To ease my cramped muscles, I snapped off my safety harness and stepped back into the fuselage to chat with our passengers. They all appeared cheerful, except for one man who was a little airsick.

I went back to the cockpit and took over from Tom for a spell. He in turn slid out of his harness and went back into the fuselage to stretch his legs.

I felt fine with my hands resting lightly on the wheel, and feet placed lightly on the rudder bar. If the rest of the flight was as smooth as this, it would be a treat.

Something flashed up alongside for a second and then was gone. Startled, I glanced down after the disappearing machine. Like a thunderbolt, the Typhoon streaked seaward for over a thousand feet before levelling off and climbing again. Another swept up alongside. A second later, the pilot flipped over showing the belly of his fighter for a brief instant before plunging down out of sight. A third Typhoon closed in to within ten feet of our wingtip. The pilot waved and I responded, and then he too was gone. A feeling of elation swept over me. Our escort of fighters were now with us. I looked upwards and saw a huge formation of fighters cruising along a few thousand feet higher. Looking down, I spotted yet another large flight silhouetted against the waters of the North Sea.

Tom and I exchanged smiles like a pair of happy schoolboys. We shouted back the news to our passengers to help make them feel good as well. They craned their necks trying to see out through the rather small round porthole type windows with which the Horsa is fitted.

I turned my eyes to the front again. In the far distance the sky seemed to merge with the grey seas in an indefinite line. I glanced at my watch, and noted that nearly thirty minutes had elapsed since we had crossed the English coast at Aldeburgh. Making a swift calculation on the basis of a ground speed of 140 mph, I estimated that we had another twenty minutes to go before we would first sight the island of Shouven off the Dutch coast, that was unless the island had been so inundated by sea water (after the Germans had breached the dykes and flooded most, or all of it) that no sign would be visible to tell us that we were over the island.

I checked the instruments. Airspeed needle remaining steadily at 145 mph. Altitude registering 2,800 feet, three hundred feet higher than the briefed height. Well, that didn't mean anything. Our pilot had probably made that adjustment to keep out of the turbulent slipstream hurled back by the scattered combinations out ahead. Air pressure normal. All seemed OK. I looked at the compass and noted our course was around 110 degrees.

Signalling to Tom, I handed over to him, and carried out a more careful check of the instruments than had been allowed by the rapid glance I had just given them.

I reached for the area map and began to study it closely. I tried to memorise the track as much as possible. We should pass almost over the little town of Haamstede two miles after landfall was made at the island of Shouven.

In ten minutes we would be there – our first glimpse of Holland. The minutes ticked by. The glider rode smoothly on the calm air, only a gentle wallowing and the thunder of the slipstream to remind us that we were really moving through the skies at something like 140 mph.

Now! Shouven should be showing up. I felt the odd tightening in my chest. I longed for a cold drink to pour down my parched throat. What would meet us at Shouven! Had the enemy much flak, mounted, as we had heard, on little outposts in the midst of the flooded countryside? Would enemy fighters suddenly bore into the attack? Well, our fighter escort should take care of that contingency, though I feared some enemy fighters would be bound to get through to destroy or damage some of the defenceless gliders swaying helplessly on the ends of their 300 foot ropes.

Intently, I peered down and forward through the perspex. Where the devil was the island? Perhaps I was out in my rough estimations. We roared on steadily. Another minute passed. I could feel the blood pounding in my ears, almost drowning out the noise of the slipstream playing hard against the fuselage. If only the island would appear.

Ah! There it was. We were almost vertically over the coastline before I spotted it. Through the flood waters, I could make out what had once been the dykes guarding the island from the sea's onrush. I raised my eyes and stared hard inland. Now I could see the rooftops of villages peering out from the destructive inundation willfully brought about by the enemy. Occasional trees sent their bare crests up out of the still grey waters. No sign of life could be discerned among the desolation below. In one way I was glad, for it was unlikely that enemy flak batteries could be operating amongst the floods.

I lifted my eyes to the mighty air armada stretched out ahead. Nothing seemed to be interfering with them, and yet the leaders must be over dry land by now. Yes, there was the Dutch coast proper. I could make out the dull black line sharply etched against the limit of the floodwaters. Almost before I realised it, we were over the coastline ourselves. I picked out the village of Steenbergen on our right. From a dirty black sludge of mud, the landscape was turning green and verdant looking. The great flat farmlands stretched away into the misty horizon.

Fascinated, I gazed down at a road, alongside which, nearly three thousand feet above, our course took us. Even at that height, I was able to pick out an enemy roadblock, with the white and black striped poles alongside. I could clearly see a car stopped by the roadblock, and smiled to myself at the thought of what consternation those below must have been feeling, watching our great stream of black, menacing aircraft moving steadily and purposefully through the Dutch skies that mid-September morning.

Fifteen minutes passed by as we flew unmolested over the pretty Dutch countryside. Then ahead, ominous black and grey puffs of smoke appeared in the heavens. Flak! We drew nearer and I could see that some of our combinations were carrying out evasive action. I glanced back at the men in the fuselage behind. Alan Wood and the army photographer were standing up. I beckoned them forward, mouthing the word 'flak'. They came forward peering between the shoulders of Tom and me. The photographer began filming.

More and more puffs of smoke broke out like an ugly rash in the sky immediately in ahead of us. My tug took no notice, and continued to fly a steady course. Well, I thought, if he can do that, so can we, not that we had much alternative, since we were attached to his tail by only 300 feet of rope, our only means of propulsion. On our left, I could make out the town of S'Hertogenbosch. It was the flak defences of this town that were taking shots at us, not that it was unduly heavy, far from it.

Even as I stared down at the ground, trying to pick out the batteries that were firing at us, I saw two Typhoons peel off into a dive and go streaking down towards a little group of buildings. I saw them easing up out of their dives, and at the same moment, flame and grey smoke shot up from the buildings. Billowing black smoke followed. More and more small fires appeared, accompanied by climbing columns of smoke. Good old Tiffys – they were doing their work. Real close co-operation. It gave me a feeling of grim satisfaction to see those batteries going up in smoke and flame. I felt the perspiration breaking out on my forehead and could feel my shirt, saturated with sweat, lying a limp sodden mass against my spine, down which ran rivulets of perspiration. All the time, my inside was half screwed up anticipating hot steel smashing up at any moment through the thin wooden flooring of the glider.

The blossoming smoke puffs began to fall behind and I breathed silently in relief. S'Hertogenbosch was behind us now, and its defending flak. At that moment the glider shuddered. Something beat upon it with the rapidity of a woodpecker. It came from back inside the fuselage. Instantly, I hunched and tensed. Next moment, the thrusting steel fingers of the enemy were gone. I licked my parched lips. The controls continued to function normally. Well, if we got nothing worse than that, we wouldn't have anything to worry about. Looking at Tom, I saw his face was white and tense, but he was holding the Horsa steady. I turned my eyes to the map; wouldn't do to lose our position too much. Another five minutes and we should be at our last turning point, Vehgel.

I remember idly thinking how much prettier and wooded the country was getting as we progressed deeper and deeper into Holland. No more flak marred the skies ahead, and I thankfully remembered the words of the briefing officer when he had said 'If you keep within the three mile corridor along which the route has been laid, you should meet practically no flak. Our fighters have been clearing this corridor for the past week, so don't stray outside, and you'll be OK.'

Away up ahead I could see the leaders of the stream turning to port. That must be Vehgel. Only about thirty miles to go to Arnhem, or about twelve minutes' flying time. We rounded Vehgel, following closely the combination in front. I took over from Tom for a short spell before I would return the controls to him for a last minute map read right up to the target area where, just before pull-off, I would again take over again for the landing.

Below on our right ran the main road from Eindoven through Vehgel and Nijmegen to Arnhem. Concentrating on following our tug, I could not take even a second off to glance down and see what enemy activity, if any, was going on.

Our tug, with ourselves accompanying it, began to wallow and roll as if wearying from the long physical effort involved. I blinked the sweat out of my eyes. Ahead, a thin strip of winding water appeared. The Maas, the first of three rivers we would have to fly over, the last being the Lower Rhine, the bridges over which were our objectives.

I stole a glance from the swinging tail of the tug and peered at the river. A feeling of surprise swept over me at the peaceful sight it presented. Nothing stirred on its surface, but the bridge at Grave was beyond my vision, and that no doubt would have been a busy sight, as an alarmed enemy would be on the alert.

I found myself gripping the wheel tensely. I tried to ease off, but the fever of anticipation, excitement and mental strain was too much. Every nerve was strung taut like a finely tuned piano wire. Perspiration oozed from every pore, running down my cheeks and getting in my eyes. Time and time again, I blinked my eyes to drive away the sweat that threatened to block my sight. My lips were parched beyond belief, and my throat was rough and dry. My eyes ached with the constant demanding strain of the flight. A dull headache beat into my brain adding to the pulsating thump in my temples. The squeezing band around my lungs tightened a little more.

The railway line from S'Hertogenbosch to Nijmegen loomed up and then disappeared under our nose. Another river, like a silver streak athwart our course, drew nearer and nearer; the Waal River, spanned by the bridge at Nijmegen which lay out of sight on our starboard. This river, like the Maas, appeared deserted, except for one or two barges moored along its banks.

As we crossed the river, I handed over to Tom for the last time before I took over finally for the landing.

In one hand I held the vertical photograph of the landing area, issued to each crew. In the other, I held my carefully folded map showing in detail the approaches to the Arnhem area.

Road by road, hamlet by hamlet I followed our course. Only ten miles to go - about four minutes. Every muscle and nerve had gone taut beyond imagination. Names on the map appeared and dropped back; Ewijk, Valburg, Lienden. The thunder of the slipstream had faded back into my subconscious - only dimly could I feel it beating on my eardrums. Every village, every lane stood out clearly before my searching eyes.

Another minute gone, three to go. I looked up from my alternate scanning of the ground below and the map. The leaders of the stream were already pulling off, and I could see the tugs diving and wheeling away underneath them some five to ten miles ahead.

Yes, there was the Lower Rhine directly in front and below. So calm; unbelievably calm. I lifted my eyes from the rapidly approaching river and gazed beyond, seeking to pick out my own particular field from the scores that spread before us in a panoramic view. Where were the triangular shaped woods, and the little farm nestling in the far corner? Vaguely, I sensed the river sliding by under our nose. Three miles from the river was our landing area.

There was the farm! Yes, there was no doubt about it, and the woods too! We were dead on course. Bless the tug pilots up front. We wouldn't have to veer an inch from our course, just pull off and go straight in when we were the right distance out. Any second now. The voice of the navigator on the Stirling came over the wire. I hardly heard him. 'OK number two, when you're ready.' 'OK number one, thanks.' I croaked in reply. 'Good luck number two - out.'

My hand slid over the red topped rope release lever. The field loomed nearer. Height 2,500 feet, exactly right. Airspeed 145 mph.

I snapped back the release, and we were free. Tom looked at me. I nodded, and took over the wheel. The roar of the slipstream died down quickly as our airspeed fell off. Our tug disappeared down and away to port, the rope flapping and flailing in its wake. That would be dropped among the enemy as a parting gift before the tug turned onto its homeward course.

Chapter 11

Landing at Arnhem

The airspeed needle slid back, 120, 110, 100 mph.

'Half flap!' I snapped out to Tom, who had been ready with his left hand poised over the flap control. Instantly the lever went down. For a moment the glider bucked as the great flaps descending from underneath each wing clashed with the airstream. The speed instantly dropped to ninety, then eighty mph. I eased the wheel forward a little. The airspeed crept up to eighty five mph. I tried to hold it there. The altimeter hand was unwinding down the dial as though it had gone mad. Already we were down to just under 1500 feet. The trees bordering the edge of our landing field were less than a mile away. The little red roofed farmhouse stood out clearly, a wonderful guiding landing mark.

My LZ in Sight

I reminded Tom to look out for gliders on his side. One slid across and above us, less than fifty yards away. I cursed him as he swung in on the same course. Another glider seemed to be drifting slowly but surely directly into us from starboard. I don't think the pilot even saw us, so intent was he on getting down into the field.

I eased the wheel forward, we nosed over slightly and passed underneath the glider. Its great black shape flashed by about twenty feet above our cockpit, too close for my liking. I tried to blink the sweat out of my eyes, with little success.

The field was very close now. Already I could see several gliders motionless with little figures darting around them. One glider was sliding to a halt in a cloud of dust. In my intense concentration to set down in one piece in our allotted field, I never had a chance to wonder if the enemy were firing at us or not – not that we could have done much about it in any case.

Full flap! The tops of the trees were rushing up to meet us. They seemed a heck of a height to me, and the landing run beyond them was not very long. At the far end of the field, across the line of flight, ran another line of tall trees. Well, it meant setting down in between, and no mistakes could be made – there wasn't room.

For a second, my eyes flickered to the airspeed. Eighty mph. There were the tree tops leaping up towards our floor boards. I eased back a fraction on the wheel. Then the mass of foliage was gone, slipping past under our wings. Now the ground was rushing up to take their place. Another glider was coming in alongside. Back on the wheel. We levelled. The wheels hit once. We bounced about three feet, came down again and held. Tom had already slammed on the brakes, holding on to them as though his very life depended upon the action, which quite possibly it did. The glider we had been following in had touched down a hundred yards in front, and was swinging off. We careened across the ploughed field. Dust rose up and was whipped past the cockpit. The line of trees at the far end loomed nearer and nearer. I gritted my teeth. The airspeed dropped rapidly. Sixty, fifty, forty. The wheels sinking into the soft earth helped slow us up far quicker than would have been possible on grassland.

I relaxed slightly as we ground towards a halt. Before the glider had stopped rolling I turned my head and shouted 'OK, boys!' to the passengers in the rear. Then I released the wheel and let it fall forward. We weren't doing any more than fifteen to twenty mph, and at that low speed I had no more control over her anyway.

I tore at my harness release pins, and hurled the shoulder straps to one side. Now we had stopped, short of the tall heavy-looking line of trees by fifty yards. I flicked aside the straps over my legs, reached forward for the maps and photos and stuffed them into the front of my camouflage smock. From the rear I heard the sounds of the two doors being raised up. A blast of cool air swept in through the cockpit. I had but one thought, to get out of the glider before one of two things, or possibly both, happened, which was either another glider landing on top of or crashing into us which was highly probable, or enemy fire coming down upon us.

In the peculiar silence that had followed our landing, after the continuous deafening roar of the slipstream, I heard the distant crackle of small arms fire. The fight was on. I spurred myself forward. Tom was already out through the connecting door. As I forced myself up from the seat, I snapped up the flap lever – a purely automatic movement, considered essential on exercises, but rather superfluous on an operation. The flaps rose with the sound of escaping compressed air. It startled me for a moment, accustomed as I was to hearing it.

I snatched at my webbing equipment and Sten gun, snatched up my rucksack and plunged through the connecting doorway into the fuselage. It was empty. I was the last man out and didn't pause, but jumped straight out through the open ramp door, hitting the ground four feet below rather hard, tripped and sprawled forward onto the earthy soil of Holland.

I looked up, pushing my Sten gun forward at the ready, and glanced around. The others were already in firing positions, forming a defensive circle around the glider as per laid down instructions.

The firing was still hammering out from the enemy amongst the trees. We seemed to have hit it lucky, for a calm lay over our area, only an occasional bullet whistling over. The remainder of the gliders were still coming in and made a heart-lifting sight. The sky appeared full of the black, wheeling shapes. Most of the tugs had already turned on their homeward course, but a few were still visible, turning away to port, trailing their long flailing ropes behind.

The Hamilcars were heading for the field next to ours, and most of the firing was coming from what I judged to be the far side of their landing ground. Thick hedges and trees hid the field itself from view.

I watched one Horsa coming into our field. It came in over the trees too fast and with one wing low as the pilot tried to straighten out of a slight turn. Fascinated, I watched as the glider struck heavily. A cloud of dust spurted up into the air, and the whole undercarriage on the port side buckled. The wing tip missed the ground by inches as the machine careened around and plunged almost sideways across the ploughed field, practically hidden by the cloud of dust it had raised. I heard the sound of splintering matchwood. The glider ground to a halt and men poured out of it, apparently none the worse for the rough landing.

From the far side of the trees came a terrific sound of more breaking wood. It sounded serious, almost like a thunderclap. Pulling myself together, I called to the others to help unload the glider. Arthur Webb, after complimenting Tom and me on our landing, pulled himself up inside the rear of the glider and started to release the four bolts that held the tail onto the main part of the fuselage. The rest of us, some after considerable prompting, took up the strain of the tail unit and the rear part of the fuselage. Together with our passengers, I put my shoulder under the sloping body, and a few minutes later felt its weight as Arthur released the bolts and cut the connecting control cables. The weight bore down heavily and I felt that my back would break. We managed to ease the section away from the main fuselage about an inch, and then it jammed.

With the sweat running down our faces and bodies, we madly wrestled to break the tail unit free, but in vain. I cursed and swore along with the rest. More than once the skin was ripped from my hands as I fought to release the jammed unit. The rattle of gunfire was spreading nearer every minute. Damn, and damn again, I thought.

Then, suddenly, it was free, and we staggered back clear of the main body. Still bearing the weight of the tail unit and rear half of the body, we moved it to one side and then, at a word from me, everyone released their hold and jumped clear. The great piece of glider fell to the ground amid a cloud of dust.

We all hurried back to the rear of the glider where now the gaping hole would enable us to drive the jeep and trailer out and down onto the ground. Two ramps, about three feet long, were rushed around from the front of the glider, one end laid against the glider floor while the other was placed on the ground. I shouted to the jeep driver to start up. The chains holding the jeep and trailer had long since been released by the driver. The jeep's engine burst into life, and slowly it moved forward. The next moment it was plunging down the ramp, the trailer bumping after. At last our load was off.

I suddenly felt weak, and leaned against the halted jeep. The mental and physical strain of the flight, combined with the recent strength-draining battle with the rear end of the glider, had taken its toll. I fought for breath, and wiped the streaming perspiration away from my face with the sleeve of my camouflage smock.

All round the field other crews were busy unloading their Horsas. They, like us, were struggling to free their tail units. Others, having already completed their unloading task, were marching or driving away across the field in jeeps, all without interference from the enemy.

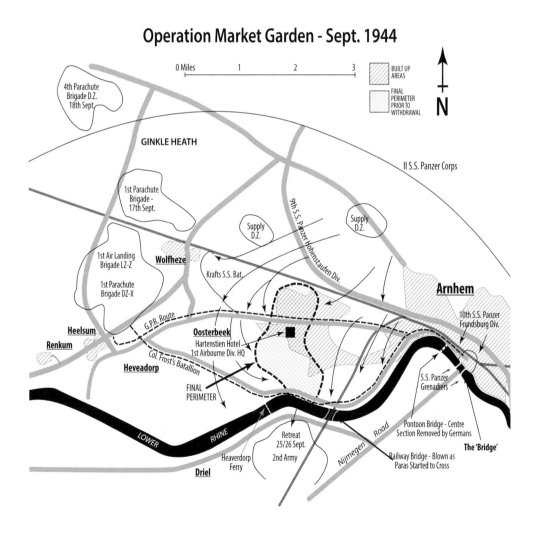

Operation Market Garden - Sept. 1944

I pulled myself together and clambered up inside our glider, checking to see if anything had been left behind. I threw out a couple of boxes I found lying in the main fuselage.

A low thunder in the distance brought me outside once more. Dropping to the ground, I turned my head towards the sound. Once more the sky was becoming clouded with scores of flying machines. They were coming from the same direction as we had. If they continued their present course, they would pass over the fields flanking ours, on the opposite side of the tree lined field in which the Hamilcars had landed.

As they came on, I could see that they had no gliders behind them, and instantly I knew – paratroopers. Good for them, here right on the dot, about thirty minutes after our landing.

In company with others in our field, I stood still, fascinated by the overpowering spectacle of scores of machines bearing down, flying at about six or seven hundred feet. Twin engined Dakotas – the most widely used of our paratroop dropping machines. The roar of their motors filled the air with a menacing thunder. Now the leaders were almost parallel with us, and at that moment the first of the paratroopers came tumbling through open doors in the Dakota's sides. Twisting and turning as the slipstream hit them, they plunged earthwards. The chutes blossomed over the little figures, and their rapid descent slowed. More and more figures plummeted earthwards, mingled with spinning supplies also falling in basket and cylinder form, swinging from side to side like giant pendulums in the sky.

The heavens filled with hundreds of multi-coloured 'chutes silhouetted against the cloud flecked blue sky. Red, yellow, green, blue and others, camouflaged in a fantasy of colour, drifting silently down. Still the air armada droned on overhead. Still more silk burst forth to add their glory to the mass of colour, carrying men and their supplies into battle.

More than one supply-laden 'chute failed to open, and the combination would speed earthwards, twisting madly in what is termed a 'Roman Candle' to crash suddenly and violently into the unyielding soil.

Only once did I see a man's 'chute fail to open. He fell, turning over and over in a great curving arc until he struck the ground with a distinct thud. His crumpled, motionless body lay in an unrecognisable heap. We did not trouble to go over, for we knew that he was past human aid; he had paid the price of war before even coming into direct contact with the enemy.

A desultory fire was being directed against the paratroopers as they floated down, but I think the range was too great to have been very effective.

The last of the long line of Dakotas dropped its load, and then turned for home in the wake of the forerunners. The rumble of their motors faded gradually away, but some of their seeds still drifted aimlessly down, falling in the field mainly, but some ended up in the tall trees that bordered it, while others draped over fences, the silk billowing in the breeze. As the paratroopers hit the ground, they rolled over, sprang to their feet and wrestled with the shrouds of their parachutes. Breaking free, they methodically went about collecting their arms and forming up. Within minutes, columns of paratroopers were marching away to their objectives. By that time, we had clambered up onto the jeep and trailer, and were bumping across the rough ploughed field towards the little farm in the far corner.

The farm dwellers were all gathered outside, waving madly to every jeep that thundered away down the dusty track that led past their farmhouse. As we passed they shouted, their faces wreathed in smiles. We waved back, and then the farm receded as we raced towards a dark looking mass of trees, part of the plantation that, I knew from our briefings, housed the asylum.

We turned down a sandy track running alongside the plantation, and I flattened myself out on top of the jeep, my Sten at the ready. I had heard firing coming from the direction of the wood while we had been unloading, and did not wish to present myself as a target more than was necessary.

On our right was the field selected for the Hamilcar landings. There they were, scattered everywhere, along with many Horsas. I made a rough count as we jolted down the track, and estimated there were about forty gliders in that particular part of Ginkel Heath. A few had been damaged in landing; some had collided after landing as shattered wings indicated. One Hamilcar had gone over on its back. Later I learned that both pilots had been killed, which was not surprising considering the heavy loads they were carrying.

Slowing down, we turned off into the gloom of the fir plantation. As we threaded our way along, following a narrow track, I noticed that already a large number of jeeps, six and seventeen-pounder guns and their towing vehicles were parked in amongst the trees on both sides. It was a cheering sight. The large seventeen-pounders had been brought in by the Hamilcars. Yes, it was quite a formidable armament – a far cry from that which we had taken into Sicily nearly eighteen months ago.

Our jeep stopped near a group of men and vehicles, and we all dismounted. For the time being, Sergeant Hollingsworth, Sergeant Webb and I would stay with our load. As soon as things became organised, we would join our squadron at a pre-arranged rendezvous and take our place in the defensive or offensive role assigned to us according to Divisional plans.

Alan Wood, Stanley Maxted and the Army photographer wandered off, so Arthur, Tom and I seated ourselves and proceeded to discuss the recent events. For my part, I felt satisfied knowing we had delivered our load safely to our exact landing zone. Their future was in their own hands from now on. Despite a certain weariness, I felt exhilarated.

The distant clatter of gunfire rose and fell, echoing across the fields. The nearest, I estimated, was not closer than a quarter of a mile away, nothing to worry about. I looked at my watch, and was surprised to see that it was already midday. Strangely, I did not feel hungry as yet, even though it was nearly six hours since I had last tasted food. I lay back on a grassy bank and closed my eyes, endeavouring to calm the turmoil that raged within my head.

Half an hour went by thus, until the sound of digging brought me to. I sat up. Most of the men were busy excavating trenches. I suggested to the others that we should do the same, since we might be in this spot for some time to come.

Unstrapping our entrenching tools, we looked around for a suitable area that would give us cover, and as good a field of fire as could be expected in the closely wooded plantation.

I soon learned that digging a slit trench was going to be a very laborious job, for the soil was extremely sandy, and as fast as one spadeful was removed, another fell in. For half an hour I sweated and dug, breaking off for ten minutes, then digging again. Tom was looking down disgustedly at the hole he had scraped out, hardly more than a foot deep. Arthur had gone down to about two feet and still was not satisfied, naturally enough. We dug on in silence, and in due course, with about four feet to my credit, I called it a day. Arthur and Tom did likewise, and we all stretched out luxuriously in our new, if somewhat temporary, homes. It is strange how even a shallow trench can give one so much added confidence and feeling of security, a security which is a fact against flying splinters of red hot shrapnel.

I suggested tea to the others, and I didn't have to repeat my suggestion. Within fifteen minutes we were drinking a delicious brew.

'Is this all there is to an operation?' asked Tom.

'We do not know what the future holds for us,' I replied, 'but you can be pretty sure that something is going to happen soon.'

After the brew, we decided to go on a tour of the area, and accordingly set out. Perhaps we would find out what was happening. No one in the vicinity seemed to know. We followed the sandy track deeper into the woods, and suddenly came upon our old friend the Army camera man, posing several laughing nurses for some snaps.

'Just the people' the sergeant called out. 'Come over here and put your arms around the girls. I want to get some good shots.'

We didn't need any second bidding and the nurses were only too eager to reciprocate.

When the sergeant was satisfied, we moved on. In a little glen, just short of the asylum building, we found a little group of our men guarding a German soldier. He had been wounded in the arm and a scarlet rivulet of blood was coursing down over his wrist. He looked rather nervous and despondent. One of the guards leaned forward and offered him a cigarette, which the prisoner accepted cautiously. He drew in deeply and expelled the smoke through his nostrils. At that moment a captain arrived and, seeing the German smoking, nearly threw a fit. 'Who the hell gave that bastard a cigarette?' Remembering my own experience in Sicily as a prisoner, I could not help feeling sorry for the German.

Suddenly, the sharp rattle of small arms fire burst out nearby, coming from the direction of our slit trenches. Calling on the others to follow, I ran back towards the sound, slipping from tree to tree, with my Sten gun at the ready.

Back at our area, we found everybody on the alert, but the firing was coming from a spot some two hundred yards farther on.

'Shall we go out and have a look?' I asked Arthur.

'OK, Dusty.', he replied. We moved slowly forward taking cover behind each tree in our path. At this point there was little undergrowth and despite the abundance of trees, one could see for at least fifty yards ahead. The echoing crash of gunfire had stopped, but we still edged forward with extreme caution. I glanced back. We had come two hundred yards and the woods still stretched away without a break on all sides. Each getting down behind a tree, we slowly scanned the surrounding area. Nothing stirred and nothing appeared unusual. We remained still for about five minutes and then started to withdraw back again to where the rest of our group were waiting.

Hardly had we reached our silt trenches when a sound broke out that froze me to the spot for an instant. It resembled the noise of a car skidding along at high speed with wheels locked. Whoooosh, whooosh, whooosh. Three times, one after the other, each followed by a faint whistle, growing louder every split second, until it reached a screaming roar. By that time I was at the bottom of my slit trench. The first rushing missile plunged into the earth about fifty yards away; a shaking explosion following. The ground trembled and the sand cascaded down the sides of the trench. The second and third missiles wailed down close behind; again and again the earth shook. More sand spilled down my neck, while the sound of falling branches reached my ears. An acrid smell floated across the clearing.

I started to raise my head, but jammed it down again, as a second trio of mortar bombs left the not too distant muzzles of the enemy mortars in a spine chilling screech. Again the faint whistles grew louder and louder. Again the angry screams and the resultant explosions. This time they fell a little further away and, from the resulting sounds, they must have scored hits on the asylum, by the noise of falling masonry reaching my ears.

Almost before the sounds of the explosions died away, a third batch of bombs shrieked down. The earth rocked once more and a further landslide occurred down the sides of my slit trench. I tried to force myself deeper into the soft earth while shrapnel rained down outside. A silence descended over the wood. The smell of burning reached my nostrils. Peering over the trench rim, I saw flickering flames and billowing smoke rising from over the direction of the asylum. 'The swine, the bloody swine', I thought to myself.

I sat up on the edge of the slit trench and wiped the sweat off my brow. Tom's face appeared over the edge of his hole.

'Well Tom, it's not so quiet after all, eh?', I could not help saying. He looked rather white as, no doubt, did I. Arthur added his comments on the enemy as he emerged from his slit trench.

Alan Wood, the Daily Express Reporter who, before the mortaring had begun, had been contentedly typing away perched on a mound of newly turned earth beside his trench, also raised himself up and without more ado resumed typing. In the distance, bursts of machine gun fire drifted across, mingled with the sharp crack of rifles and the occasional hollow thud of bursting grenades. I wondered how long we would remain in this position before we were summoned to take our turn engaging the enemy.

Dusk was rapidly spreading its cloak over the countryside. Here in the already dark woods, it appeared to descend even quicker. All around, men were making a last effort to deepen their holes before complete darkness set in. I hacked away at my hole with the rest, spurred on by the recent mortaring. Who could tell whether the enemy would begin shelling and mortaring in real earnest? A deep slit trench was the answer - no point in becoming a casualty through negligence.

Despite the chill of this evening, I was wringing wet with perspiration by the time I was satisfied with my efforts. Now I felt I could rest in comfort. I relaxed, leaning against the sides of my hole. Away in front the burning asylum smouldered with an angry looking reddish glare.

Suddenly I stiffened – something white flitted through the trees. Darkness had almost closed in, making visibility very poor. Another white-clad figure moved slowly forward and I felt my scalp tingle.

Whispering a warning to Tom and Arthur in their nearby holes, I eased my Sten gun forward. I relaxed slightly as I heard voices among the trees in front where the white forms had been, and went tense again as one of the queer figures appeared from behind a tree less than ten yards away. I strained my eyes and, as the figure drew near, I could see that it was old and bent. Still watching closely, I allowed it to draw nearer.

I still could not make out exactly what it was except that it was human. The figure was laughing away to itself and when it was less than ten feet away, the glow from the burning asylum lit up their features. A shock went through me as the wrinkled face of an old woman was revealed. I stood up. The figure drew back, as I lowered my Sten and she smiled, then threw back her head and laughed insanely. By then I realised that she must have been an inmate of the asylum, either let out or broken loose. I felt a wave of pity for her and also a burning hatred for the Germans that had caused such misery to be forced upon this helpless old woman.

Another figure appeared out of the gloom and, as the light played upon her, I could see that she was a nurse. She called out to the old woman, who in turn ran off into the darkness, holding her long, voluminous skirts up as she did went.

More voices came through the trees and a column of weird white-clothed men and women filed passed my trench, silhouetted against the evil glow of the smouldering buildings. Several nurses were herding them forward. I was standing up outside my trench now and the nurses, as well as some of the insane, smiled warmly at me. Then they were gone, fading away into the night. It was the last time I saw them. I could not help but shiver as I sat down on the edge of my hole.

'Gee, I could do with a cup of tea' Tom's voice floated across in a whisper.

'So could I' I replied, suddenly feeling the cold more than ever.

Except for a few spasmodic bursts of firing, the night had been quiet. Tired as I was, it was too early to think of sleep. Besides, I wanted to know what was happening. I soon found out, for in less than five minutes word was passed around for all men of 'G' Squadron to rendezvous on the path preparatory to moving off. I did not need a second bidding, for I wanted to join my squadron as soon as possible.

I picked up two cases of the Piat bombs we had brought with us and Tom took the Piat while Arthur also picked up a case of bombs. We made our way to the entrance of the plantation along the narrow twisting sandy track. I could hear the rumble of trucks on the move and once we had to step aside into the trees to let through a jeep towing a six-pounder.

At the entrance, I found quite a number of our squadron gathered. Greetings varied according to the individual, but all were happy to see each other, even men who normally did not get on well together. It is strange how imminent danger can bring men together closely, men who wouldn't lift a finger to help each other under ordinary circumstances.

At a word of command, we marched over into the ploughed field in which the Horsas and Hamilcars lay, their giant bat-like shapes looking grotesque in what little light the stars shed. It was rough going over the upturned earth, and all around me men stumbled and swore.

We did not go far. Somewhere near the centre of the field we halted and the officer in command gathered us around and explained that we would be spending the night here. It had been generally agreed among the officers that it would be safer to move out of the woods, in case the enemy took it into his head to shell the place during the night, as undoubtedly he knew we had moved in there during the afternoon.

Wolfheze - A Hamilcar Safely Down

I was assigned a section of men under me and told to start digging in. We were forming a perimeter of defence in the centre of which would be our headquarters. Following the order of our officer in command, I went out into the darkness to contact some seventeen-pounder crews, who were about a hundred yards in front of us. We would have to be careful of our field of fire or else we would be firing upon our own men if a counterattack developed in the hours of darkness. I had some difficulty in locating them, for there was practically no visibility at all, only the faint gleam from the stars to aid me.

Half an hour later, I came back to where Tom and Arthur were busy digging in. They had almost finished their hole and very kindly suggested they would help me, for which I was very grateful. I set the guards with orders to keep a very strict watch and to call me if they were in any doubt whatsoever. I lay back in my trench and talked quietly with Tom and Arthur. It was cold and damp. A mist seemed to be rising from the ground, which did not help matters at all. The night was quiet except for the distant sound of firing coming from where I estimated Arnhem to be. I fell into a fitful sleep from which I was awakened in the early hours of the morning to take my turn at watch and to check on our positions.

It was terribly cold as I moved quietly from post to post. All guards appeared on the alert and more than once I had to proceed with caution after the challenge from one of the sentries unseen in the enveloping darkness.

I was thankful when the first light appeared in the east and a new day was heralded in. Objects began to appear in the misty grey light spreading rapidly over the countryside, and the grotesque shapes of the crashed gliders took on a more earthly appearance.

LZ   Morning of the 18th

Simultaneously with the first light of dawn, came the first crash of gun fire. The distant rat-tat-tat of machine guns increased in tempo. The rattle of small arms spread like wildfire over the countryside. For some minutes the firing raged fiercely and then gradually faded away. It was the usual dawn outburst to which we were to become accustomed during the next eight days.

Our own area remained strangely quiet, except for a small engagement being fought out on the edge of the woods we had left the previous night. I watched the spot in the swiftly growing daylight. It was about half a mile away, possibly more. Small puffs of smoke, followed by sharp explosions, indicated that grenades were being used. Then that too died down. From the direction of Arnhem itself, the sounds of firing continued, but that was several miles away, and seemed remote.

The warmth of the morning sun helped drive the stiffness and cold out of my body. I felt tired and dirty and longed for water to wash away the dirt that caked my face and gritted my eyes. Already a goodly growth was sprouting from my chin, but the thought of something hot to eat and drink soon drove thoughts of cleanliness from my mind – there was nothing I could do about washing anyhow. Tom, Arthur and I soon had a pan of hot water ready and, from our meagre stocks of tea, we poured in enough to make a really strong brew, of which we felt sorely in need. We mixed some porridge and heated that up too.

It was really amazing the difference the hot tea and a bite of food made. I felt a new man, although I still longed for a wash, but that was out of the question.

After a breakfast, enjoyed by all, I set about cleaning my Sten gun into which sandy soil persisted in penetrating. The magazines also managed to accumulate large quantities of sand, which would have prevented their springs from operating effectively.

While in the middle of cleaning out one of the magazines, word was passed round to get ready to move off. I hastily pieced the magazine together, taking care however to insert the cartridges correctly.

Once more I strapped on my rucksack, slung my Sten, and picked up two cases of Piat bombs, one in each hand. Columns of men were already filing past us down onto the sandy track bordering the plantation. Five minutes later we marched off, but not far. In fact it was merely to the opposite side of the field in which we already were. We passed through a gap in the hedge and found ourselves in a larger field, which was really a stretch of heathland, covered plentifully in heather. Here we were ordered to halt and spread out.

As in the ploughed field, gliders lay everywhere, silent and deserted, some twisted, almost unrecognisable, splintered wrecks. Close by me lay a Hamilcar, intact, its gaping jaw revealing an empty dark interior. Curiously, I looked at the chalked name on the side. 'Olive' No 317. I wondered if I knew the pilots that had flown it in. It had been a successful landing; that was obvious. Feeling in my pockets, I drew out some sheets of paper and pencils and commenced, quickly and roughly, sketching all the gliders within my vision that were near enough to show detail. We remained there for fifteen minutes and I was able to do at least three sketches which I brought back to England and later copied in ink.

Unloaded
Hamilcar
Olive No.317

The order was given to rise once again and minutes later we were back on the sandy track, this time marching away in earnest. From the direction of Arnhem a continuous sound of firing drifted over the landscape. On our right, towards the unseen village of Renkum, another battle seemed to be taking place on a smaller scale.

We reached the edge of the plantation and the end of the sandy track. Turning right, we tramped off down a dirt road, or more accurately, a dirt track. The going was rough, for we were forced to keep close to the sides in order to let through the great seventeen-pounder guns towed by their composite trucks, and the more agile jeeps towing trailers and six-pounder guns. As each vehicle passed it enveloped us in a cloud of brown dust. More than once I stumbled in the rutted road edge, but it could not dampen my elation as I watched our heavy weapons rolling by to take up their supporting positions.

I began to feel the heat of the morning sun and the discomfort of a parched throat and lips. Overhead the blue, almost cloudless, sky smiled down as if giving her blessing. Looking up I prayed that this weather would continue. We could then expect first class air support.

The road ahead descended steadily down a slope, turning to the left over a stream about half a mile away. The road then mounted a hill where, on the crest, I could see the bright red roofs of the village of Heelsum, which lay across the Renkum - Oosterbeek - Arnhem Road. A long column of men and vehicles was following the road down and then up. A cloud of dust hung over the entire length. As we drew nearer the stream, I looked longingly at it, wishing we could stop for just a few minutes to bathe our faces and feet. On over the bridge we marched and commenced the short but sharp ascent to the village.

The Piat bombs I was carrying slung from each hand began to weigh heavier and heavier. The straps of my rucksack cut deeper and deeper into my collar bones. I kept hunching my shoulders in an endeavour to ease the pain, but with little effect. The sweat began to roll down my face as we toiled up the slope, and I tilted my helmet back to try to catch what little breeze I could to cool my burning forehead and face.

We had now reached the outskirts of the village. Tired as I was, I could not help but admire the trim little houses, set in their picturesque gardens. Everything looked so green and fresh. Most of the inhabitants seemed to be standing at their gates or were walking alongside, offering apples to the long line of dusty, thirsty soldiers. I eagerly accepted one from a girl who ran up alongside me and I smilingly expressed my thanks.

Just before we reached the junction of the main road to Arnhem, the order to halt passed down the line and gratefully I sank down on the grass verge lining the road. I lay full out on my back to ease the burden of the rucksack.

Then those good people of Heelsum came bursting forth with, joy of joys, brimming pails and jugs of cold clear water together with pails of apples. With faces wreathed in smiles, they hurried from group to group, dipping cups and glasses into the slopping pails of water and passing them along with piles of apples. I took the opportunity of filling my water bottle with the fresh water and, with disregard for the rule of not drinking water on the march, I drank my fill, but took care to do it slowly. I was only sorry that I could not repay the kind and thoughtful people of Heelsum, although I think our presence was more than ample repayment to them. Little did they realise that, in just over a week, they again would be under the iron heel of the enemy, and many would pay dearly for their helping hands extended to us today.

We did not stop for more than five minutes, but I was thankful for those few we did have. At a command we arose again and, shouldering our weapons, moved off with accompanying cheers from the villagers. We waved them goodbye and with lighter hearts turned onto the main Renkum - Arnhem road to Oosterbeek.

The road stretched away straight and level. As we marched, the houses of Heelsum grew fewer and fewer and finally we were out in a wooded section. If it were not for the grim task that faced us, I could have found time to admire the beauty of the landscape. Left, right, left, right down the road we proceeded at a swift pace that sent the perspiration running down my face, neck and back in never ending rivulets. The muscles in my legs began to hurt with the speed of the march. Once we passed some wrecked German war material, our first glimpse of battle.

About a mile after we had left the outskirts of Heelsum behind we were ordered off the road among the trees, and automatically we took up firing positions. Where I had stepped off the road, along with Tom, were piles of newly cut logs, and I lay down behind a low pile, which formed fair cover and yet permitted excellent observation and field of fire.

Our Flight Officer came around and informed us that a report had been received that about 200 Germans were approaching through the wood to our positions and we were to engage them as and when they presented a target.

I lay there peering intently over about a hundred yards of grassland that bordered the wood. Anyone coming out from the woods would have to cross the open stretch, and that would be too bad for them. Other men were deployed on the far side of the road and then quiet settled over the area.

Five minutes passed and, except for the sound of the occasional jeep racing by up the road, nothing stirred. Tom suddenly nudged me and pointed back towards the road. About six men in civilian clothes, with pieces of orange cloth around their arms, were talking with our Flight Officer. Men of Holland's underground were already appearing to take part in the coming battle. They were a game lot.

We continued to divide our attention between the civilians and the wood in front. Both intrigued us. Then the civilians left our Flight Commander and came over towards us. Sprawled out behind the logs, I smiled a welcome. To my surprise, one of them said in perfect English,

'I am glad you have come. May we join you?'

'By all means.' I replied. Four of the men moved off further along our line, but two remained and crouched down behind us. One asked if we were thirsty, I replied in the affirmative.

'I will be back in one minute.' he replied and hurried off down the road. Tom and I chatted with the other man, keeping a careful watch on the woods in between snatches of conversation. It was almost pathetic the way the Dutchman kept reiterating how glad he was that we had come at last. I almost began to feel like a hero. He had no weapon but expressed his view that it would not be long before he came into possession of a rifle, to which I heartily agreed.

The man who had gone off returned with two bottles under his arms. Smiling, he passed one to me, explaining that it was lime water. I tasted it and it proved very strong but very thirst quenching.

In the middle of a swig, the first enemy shot cracked over, whining away into the distance. I hurriedly rolled over and peered out. Somebody called for the bottle. I took one more swallow and passed it along. The Dutchman had dropped down onto one knee, still in a very exposed position in my opinion.

Further shots hissed by, but I searched the woods in vain – I couldn't see a damn thing. Something cracked nearby into the log behind which I lay. I hunched a little lower. Some of our men were replying to the enemy fire now, but still I could not pick out any movement or sign that might indicate the enemy. Feeling somebody pushing the bottle back into my hand, I raised it to my lips without taking my eyes off the woods. The rat! It was empty. Tossing the bottle aside, I promptly forgot that such a thing as lime water existed.

I thought I saw a bush move and took a quick shot, but could not tell with what result for nothing stirred. The firing died down and, two minutes later, silence had settled once again. Either the enemy was lying doggo, or else he had withdrawn. Well, we could only wait for orders.

Suddenly, I went tense as a small figure emerged from the woods, hands held high in the air. I was puzzled for a moment, for it looked like a young boy to me, and it was. As he drew nearer, I could see that he was a civilian. The Dutchman with us stood up and called out something. The boy shouted back, and veered towards us, his hands still held high.

'What does he want?' I asked.

'I don't know yet.' the Dutchman replied. The boy came up to us, panting with his efforts. He lowered his hands and talked rapidly to the Dutchman. Our Flight Officer came up to enquire what it was all about. The Dutchman translated the boy's message which was as follows: 'The Germans in the wood want to surrender; are we prepared to accept?'

'OK, tell them to come out with their hands up.' replied our officer. The underground man translated to the boy, who smiled and hurried off back the way he had come.

I could not help but admire the courage of that young boy travelling between the lines apparently unafraid, and willing to take so many risks.

Within five minutes, the boy reappeared at the edge of the woods once more. Doubling across the open space, he came to a panting halt beside the underground man. Anxiously, we watched their two faces, for it was obvious that something was wrong.

After listening to the boy, the Dutchman turned to us and said 'The Germans have gone. It looks as though they have changed their minds.' The boy looked disappointed, and we asked the Dutchman to thank him for his brave efforts. This, when translated, brought a smile to his pale face.

Still no word came to move off. I lay back and relaxed, talking with the two Dutchmen. They told us of their trials and tribulations under the Germans. Some of it did not make very nice listening.

A movement in the garden across the road caught my eye. Looking up, I saw an old lady crossing over the road with a tray in her hands. She went up to the group of soldiers in the next defensive position to ours and, in quite good English, said,

'I thought you would like some coffee.'

At first the men refused, knowing that all food and drink was in short supply in Holland. She, however, pointed out that the coffee was already made and would only go to waste if they did not drink it. They took the beautifully made, dainty, cups in their great clumsy dirty hands and, as though inspired by the delicate ware in their hands, drank as though back in their own dining rooms at home, trying to bring to the fore their best party manners.

Then the old woman turned to us and asked if we also would like some coffee. We thanked her warmly, but refused. She insisted however, and hurried back to her house set amid the trees. In less than two minutes she was back, bearing a second tray of steaming coffee. With many thanks, we accepted this kindness and drank thirstily. The coffee was not of the best, in fact I strongly suspected that it was either all acorn, or at least 90% of it. But it was hot and life-giving.

Handing back my empty cup, I again heartily thanked her. It was not only the coffee that warmed my body, but the sincere gratitude displayed in her kindness towards us. It really gave one a sound reason for being here in Holland among the enemy. Before she returned to her house, she told us that she had a son in the Dutch Navy. He had fled Holland before the Germans had fully occupied it, and was now in England, or at any rate, with the English. I watched her bent figure re-cross the road for the last time, and disappear into her house.

Hardly had she done so than there came the low roar of aircraft approaching. From where I was lying, about ten feet off the road, my vision upwards was obscured by the thick foliage of the many trees that grew in profusion along the roadside.

One of our men got up and walked over to the road. The thunder of motors was close now. I watched him looking up; then he looked across at us and waved his arms. 'Hurricanes – our planes!' Somehow, the note of the engines sounded strange to me – they certainly weren't Hurricanes – on that I would have bet my life. They were circling now, and sounded rather low. I got up and hurried over to the road. Looking up, I saw the first aircraft turning in a wide sweep, at less than a thousand feet. One glimpse was enough.

I turned and called out 'Enemy aircraft overhead'. Those were no Hurricanes. I had not been teaching aircraft recognition for over a year for nothing. I watched the evil snub-nosed aircraft continue its turn. A Focke-Wolf 190, Germany's latest fighter. A second FW appeared over the tree tops, and yet another. Soon, I counted at least ten swinging around in a wide circle, like vultures scanning the ground below for victims. The air was filled with their thunder. Lower and lower they swing, their black crosses now plainly visible. I never took my eyes off the circle. Then I saw the leader's nose tilt over. I didn't wait any longer, but flung myself towards the scanty shelter of the logs. As I dropped, I told the others what aircraft they were, not that it really mattered – the fact that they were enemy was enough.

I wormed myself down as far as possible, almost moving the logs with my efforts. The roar of motors filled the air as the planes bored in. Their machine guns opened up with a shattering blast. Leaves fluttered to the ground all around. I flinched instinctively, and tried to push myself under the logs. It was then I realised what poor cover they gave. I rolled over towards the thickest tree I could see. As I looked skyward for a moment, I saw a black shape flash by overhead travelling at a terrific speed. The heavy thunder of his guns beat down. I tried to bring my Sten gun up to fire, but the plane was gone. I heard another motor approaching. Lunging for the tree, I squirmed down lengthways behind it. Again the blast of machine gun fire came. Away on my left I heard the corresponding clatter faintly above the noise of engines and machine guns as the raking bullets slashed and ripped through branches, leaves and trunks.

Occasionally, I heard the retaliatory bark of a Bren gun burst as one of our men caught a glimpse of the speeding planes through gaps in the foliage. Panting, I tried to make myself as small as possible, and wished deeply that a convenient hole was nearby.

They were coming in again – just glimpses through the gaps on the trees – no time to target on them. I cringed lower. This time they swept down several hundred yards to my right. Again their guns flailed the area. The perspiration ran down my face. More approaching motors. I pulled my head into what I thought was the centre, and naturally the thickest part, of the trunk. The 190 passed over in a long drawn-out scream and then was gone without firing his guns.

The planes didn't come back to strafe again, but I could still hear their motors. I relaxed, and pulled myself up, dodging over to a nearby clearing. Looking up, I saw the fighters circling once more at the height they had first appeared. Twice, as if in contempt, they flew around. It was useless wasting ammunition on them - they were too high and too far away. In fact, I was greatly relieved when they turned away, and the note of their engines swiftly faded.

Nobody appeared hurt anyway. Later I learned that they had been after the guns mostly, some distance away, but undoubtedly some of the pilots had preferred us as a target. Now that they had gone, I felt good once more, and my self confidence returned in full.

A whistle blew, the signal to prepare to march off. We all gathered on the roadside. Tom took up position behind me, and on another whistle we moved forward. It was hotter now, and in a few minutes I was really beginning to sweat in earnest. Our officer set a fast pace, which caused my leg muscles to hurt considerably after about ten minutes.

From the direction of Arnhem, away ahead of us, came the constant sounds of battle. Every step brought us nearer and nearer. We came to the crossroads signposted on the left to the village of Wolfhezen. Pushed off onto the grass verge was the remains of an ambushed German Staff car. We had halted momentarily at the crossroad, and I looked at the first German casualties we had come across. The car had been riddled by machine gun bullets. The windscreen no longer existed except for a few jagged edges embedded in the frame. Lying stretched out on their backs, as if resting, were the three bodies of the occupants. They looked ghastly, almost like waxwork effigies, their white faces in sharp contrast to the immaculately cut field grey uniforms trimmed with scarlet. From the corner of their mouths thin trickles of blood ran down their faces. Only a bloody stump remained where the hand of one of the men had once been. The three corpses were a reminder that death lurked everywhere, waiting to strike without warning. These were the first dead men I had seen since Sicily, and it wasn't a pretty sight.

'OK men, forward.' Our Flight Commander's voice broke in on my thoughts. A scene of death such as that which I had just witnessed always has a sobering effect on men. It was some minutes before we broke into conversation again. In the coming days, the scene was to become an everyday occurrence, and was then taken for granted. It is always the first one that comes as a shock. Thereafter, it has less effect.

It was now late afternoon, and I began to wonder where we would end up. We had left the macadam road behind us now, and were marching over stone setts. More and more signs of battle were becoming apparent – still-smoking houses – occasional wrecked equipment, pushed into the gutter.

The sound of firing was breaking through quite loudly now and I braced myself, expecting to hear the rasping hum of bullets raking the road at any moment. We tramped on, nearing a village that I knew from my map must be Oosterbeek, a suburb of Arnhem. Houses were becoming more numerous. Just inside the village we halted. Fighting seemed to be going on in the far end of the village, which was hidden around a bend about a quarter of a mile farther on.

Wearily, I leaned on a stone wall at the side of the road. The firing grew in intensity. Now and then the sharp explosion of a grenade would sound above the rattle of machine guns and the crack of rifles. The shadows of evening were just beginning to steal in. In another half an hour it would be dark.

Chapter 12
Oosterbeek

A little way ahead on our right were the grounds of a large house. I looked at the well-kept grounds separated from the road by finely wrought iron railings. Half hidden by trees and set back from the railings was the large stone house. I did not realise it then, but I was looking at the ill-fated Hartenstein Hotel, which was to be Divisional Headquarters and, incidentally, the centre of a rain of shelling and mortaring for many days to come. Furthermore, I, together with my flight, would be in that area until the night when we were to withdraw to the river and to the 2nd Army which, through no fault of their own, were stopped from reaching and relieving us. They were at that moment still about sixty miles away on the Belgian-Dutch border, slowly edging forward.

'On your feet.' The command rang out softly. This is it, I thought, straight in. Well, that's what we're here for. I fell into line with the rest.

'Forward!' I pushed my tired legs on, and stepped out along with the rest. Fifty yards ahead was a turning to the left down which ran a narrow lane, bordered by fairly large houses in good-sized gardens. Just ahead lay what was to be the much fought-over Oosterbeek crossroads. To my surprise, we turned off right through the open wrought iron gates of the stone house I had been admiring a few moments before.

I noticed two six-pounder anti-tank guns covering the approach up the drive. They also covered the lane branching off the main road down which enemy tanks could quite possibly come, as well as along the main road along which we had come. The crews had dug slit trenches alongside their guns, and were sitting on the edges talking among themselves. The line halted, and our Flight Commander told us to fall out. We thankfully sank down on the smooth lawn. I slipped off my rucksack and rubbed my sore shoulders.

Lying back, I listened to the sounds of battle taking place not more than two hundred yards away. It grew in intensity as the shades of night rapidly set in. The blasts of heavy machine guns shattered the air, intermingled with the tearing, terribly fast roar of the German light automatics, and the spiteful crack of our own Stens. Frequently, the thunderous explosion of a hand grenade detonating in a confined space would burst forth. Whenever this happened, the sky would light up, momentarily silhouetting the house and trees.

Our Flight Commander came over and told us to dig in for the night. We could rest after the appropriate guards had been put out, but must be ready for instant action, should the need arise during the night. Judging from the noise around, I wouldn't have been surprised at being called upon to repel an attack at any time.

Tom and I had been lying down near a towering coniferous tree, and we decided we would dig in under the outer spread of its mighty boughs. That position would give us a fairly good field of fire up the drive, and also afford some protection if it rained. The rest of our flight spread themselves around, the majority choosing, as we had done, the shelter of the huge spreading branches.

I un-strapped my entrenching tool and began to hack away at the ground. It was now fully dark, but enough light was being given by several buildings that were burning across the road around which most of the fighting seemed to be taking place. Despite the darkness of the night, the firing did not let up. In fact, the tempo had increased. More than once I flinched as stray tracer bullets, glowing in the darkness, flashed by and sometimes slashed through the foliage of our tree. Their deadly whisper served to spur me on to dig faster and faster.

No one spoke, and the only sound was the dull thud of spades and entrenching tools striking the soft earth. In a short while, despite the cold of the night, I felt the perspiration streaming down my face and back. Tom worked diligently alongside, digging his own trench. Occasionally, through my panting efforts, I chatted away with him, although I could only catch glimpses of his face whenever the flickering flames from across the road flared up.

And then my trench was ready. I tried it for fit, and considered it OK – not quite as deep as I would have liked – but nevertheless it afforded protection against small arms fire as well as could be expected for the time and energy spent and gave a good field of fire.

I lay back full length, resting my weary body and regaining my breath. Overhead, stray tracers continued to fly by like fireflies in the night, their ugly whirr discernible above the chaos of firing in the village. The red glow appeared to be gaining ground and, raising myself up, I peered over the edge of the trench. Yes, the fires were spreading. Billowing black clouds of smoke intermingled with the dancing flames.

For a moment, I felt almost afraid, and then the feeling was gone, to be replaced by a desperate urge to go to the aid of the men fighting so bravely amongst those burning buildings and tumbling masonry. Men were dying in agony not two hundred yards away, their life smashed from their bodies by the flying lead and red hot steel; men fighting desperately to hold off a determined enemy who was using every means at his disposal to drive them forth and destroy them totally.

Then the moment passed, and I knew that we were here as part of a plan, and that we would be used as and when the higher command decreed, and not before. Wearily, I sank down again, placing my helmet under my head in such a position that it afforded a kind of pillow. I closed my eyes against the criss-crossing tracers and the sullen fires, but I could not blot out the savage noise of battle. It was cold, and I huddled down in an attempt to find some little warmth in my inhospitable earthy hole. The pine needles gave off a fresh scent which, unfortunately, was polluted by the occasional drifting clouds of acrid smoke from the fires outside the park area and the smell of explosives.

I was convinced I would never be able to seize any sleep that night with the cold gnawing at my bones and the thunder of battle in my ears but I did, in the early hours of the morning. I came to with a start when I felt a hand shaking me. I blinked my tired eyes and tried to clear the fog that blanketed my brain. It was cold, very cold. That was the first thing I noticed. Then I realised how quiet it had become, although occasional bursts of fire still shattered the darkness. I looked at my watch – 5.00 a.m. – God, I must have slept for longer than I had anticipated. The figure who had been shaking me had gone.

I blew on my cold hands and pulled myself up. I felt terribly stiff and numbed throughout. With cold fingers I rubbed my eyes trying to shift the grit that had accumulated on my eyelids. Another figure loomed up and whispered in a voice that I recognised as that of our Flight Commander.

'Stand to. Are you all awake?'

'Yes, Sir', I replied. I leaned over into the adjoining trench. 'You awake, Tom?', I whispered. No reply. I reached down and gave him a rough shake.

'OK, Dusty, I'm awake,' came back Tom's voice.

'Come on, get up Tom. It's stand to.' I continued, giving him another shake. Every shake I gave him seemed to wake me up a little more each time, so I continued the treatment. At last Tom, despairing, stirred in his hole. He pulled himself up complaining bitterly about the cold, to which I agreed.

I turned my attention towards where I knew the road lay and peered out into the darkness with eyes that wanted to close and bring me peaceful sleep. No one can think clearly under such conditions, of that I am sure. A strange quiet had spread over the area. It was a false quiet, that I knew, and I was right. It was merely the lull before the storm. It is at this time of transition from darkness to light that both sides are on the alert, for it is a favourite time for an attack, with misty figures likely to come looming out of the darkness in an effort to take the enemy unawares.

As the first faint light of the dawn tinged the eastern horizon, a splutter of shots ran around the village. Within seconds it had increased in intensity. Once more the savage beat of machine guns and the heavy single shots of rifles tore the air asunder. I gripped my Sten gun tighter, and strove to extend my still night-restricted vision even further. I prayed for daylight to come quickly, but the dawn would not be hurried.

Still-smouldering fires from the night before tended to light up the night-obscured roadway. I strained my eyes towards that point. More and more men joined in the firing. Machine guns fought retaliatory duels. First one burst of heavy fire from our guns, then the lighter, and more harsh, reply of the enemy's, followed by a merging of the two, rising to a furious climactic last-second burst. These individual duels, multiplied many times, served to split the very air with their thunder. Stray tracer bullets hissed and whirred through the tree's foliage – red and golden trails ricocheted and darted above our heads.

For several minutes the fury of the battle raged and then began to diminish. Within fifteen minutes all was quiet except for spasmodic outbursts from time to time. The sky lightened rapidly, pushing back the uncertainty of the night. I began to see clearly beyond the iron railing. Across the road, the sullen, smouldering house embers became lost in the spreading daylight. I breathed more freely.

Dirty begrimed figures began to emerge from their holes in the ground. I pulled myself up and over the trench rim and straightened my stiff legs and back. Well, this was the beginning of our third day at Arnhem, and for a moment I was lost in thought, trying to determine what might happen to us. The sight of one of the men lighting a small fire soon brought me to earth.

Tom and I dug some of the small circular heating tablets we carried out of

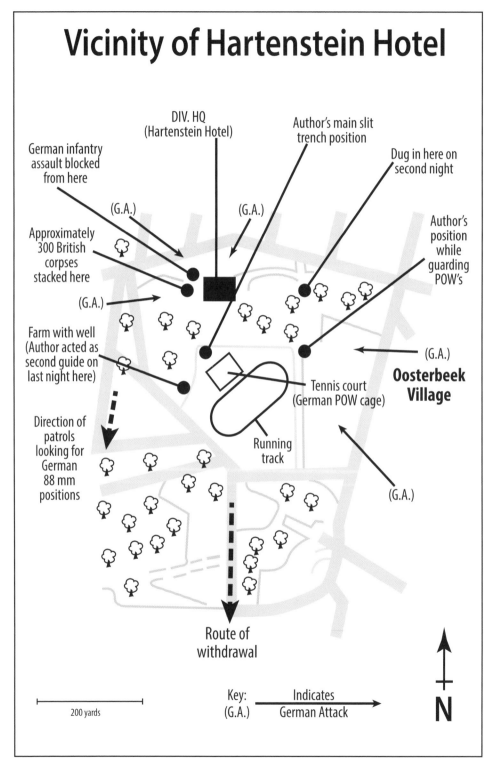

Vicinity of Hartenstein Hotel

DIV. HQ
(Hartenstein Hotel)

Author's main slit
trench position

German infantry
assault blocked
from here

Dug in here on
second night

(G.A.)

(G.A.)

Author's
position
while
guarding
POW's

Approximately
300 British
corpses
stacked here

(G.A.)

Farm with well
(Author acted as
second guide on
last night here)

(G.A.)

**Oosterbeek
Village**

Tennis court
(German POW cage)

Direction of
patrols
looking for
German
88 mm
positions

Running
track

(G.A.)

Route of
withdrawal

200 yards

Key: Indicates
(G.A.)   German Attack

N

our haversacks, together with tea and a tin of sausages. Within a few minutes the water was bubbling away in one of my mess tin sections. Tom was busy trying to fry the sausages, or at least heat them. Altogether, it was a delicious breakfast. We exchanged bantering talk with our comrades nearby, who were also busy preparing their own breakfasts.

As I ate, I took time off to look around at the grounds of the large house; they were well laid out. The drive was beautifully gravelled, but already it was being cut up by the wheels of many vehicles. The house, of which I could catch a glimpse through the many trees that grew in profusion all over the grounds, appeared very sedate looking. I was curious and wanted to have a look inside, but that pleasure was denied me.

Sometimes an extra prolonged burst of firing would cause us to glance apprehensively towards the source, which more often than not, was the village itself. I wondered vaguely how long it would be before we too would be fighting among the houses in the village. I wondered too how the battle was going in general – no one seemed to know. I was beginning to feel that the whole thing would be over before we could even get a shot in, that was if the advancing 2nd Army arrived more or less on schedule, forty eight to seventy two hours, we had been told. Well, we had been here for forty hours.

A voice calling out, 'Get ready to move off!', broke in on my idle thoughts.

'Now where the hell are we going?' asked Tom of no one in particular. We packed up quickly.

Our Flight Commander called us over to where he was standing on the rutted gravel drive.

'Well chaps,' he informed us, 'we aren't going far. Just over to the grounds on the other side of the house. We are going to form a defence line around Divisional HQ.'

Without more ado our flight set off. I looked curiously at the house as we marched past. The airborne divisional flag hung outside on a pole. Men were hurrying in and out of the massive doorway. Jeeps arrived and departed one after the other.

A hundred yards or so past the house, down a slope, the path skirted a bank covered with bushes and trees. We halted. 'This is it' announced our Flight Commander. 'Dig in somewhere here - either on the bank or here on the lawn.' With Tom, I clambered up the bank, which was not more than four feet high. I looked back at the lawn and then out in the opposite direction. I decided there and then that I favoured the bank. For one thing, there was quite a good field of fire over what appeared to be a running track for a distance of at least a hundred yards. Beyond the track lay a thick fir wood.

On the left, close to the bank, lay a large tennis court that was to be used later as a prisoner of war cage for enemy personnel captured in the battle. Opposite the tennis court, on the far side of the track and against an extended hedge, was a large wooden pavilion. A smaller hut lay just outside the court entrance, about twenty yards from where I stood. Behind us was the path down which we had just marched and beyond that the well laid-out lawns studded, with majestic trees and huge rhododendron bushes, the whole soon to be scarred and slashed by an almost continuous artillery and mortar bombardment for days on end. The house was plainly visible between the scattered trees. It was a magnificent building, and I made up my mind to sketch it as soon as I could, the situation permitting.

I slipped off my rucksack and unstrapped my faithful entrenching tool. The spot I selected was just below the top of the bank and underneath the spreading boughs of a large tree. This was an error that I was to rue a hundred times over. I hacked at the long grass that grew profusely all over the bank. Soon I was scooping out the soft soil underneath. It appeared to be a mixture of sand and earth, and came out quite easily.

Tom drifted away looking for water while I dug on. Arthur Webb appeared by my side suddenly and started to give me a hand. Within an hour we had dug a deep hole with the aid of a shovel we had borrowed from the party digging another trench alongside ours. We rested on our labours, the sweat streaming down. Curiously, I noted that the first of the prisoners had arrived in the tennis court. There were about ten of them, all gathered together in a sullen looking group.

At that moment Tom returned, informing me that he would not be remaining with me, as he had decided on another spot about twenty yards away on the lawn and that furthermore he had two German prisoners digging his trench for him. I kidded him over his laziness as he walked back to see how his trench was shaping. 'Well,' said Arthur, 'seeing Tom's moved out, I may as well move in.'

'OK with me, Arthur' I replied. I was, in fact, very glad to have him with me. A one-man trench can be an awfully lonely place, especially when things get hot. We proceeded to make ourselves as comfortable as circumstances permitted. I laid my Sten gun on the earth thrown up in front after making sure that the field of fire was as good as I had first supposed. We rested back in our trench, speculating on the way things were going, listening to the almost constant sound of small arms fire coming from the direction of Oosterbeek village about two hundred yards away, just outside the park. I could detect a new sound that had not been prominent before, that of mortar bombs or shells bursting in and around the village.

Then their range shifted. With nerves that had suddenly gone taut, I heard the first bomb wail over. I followed its flight by sound until it screamed down some two hundred yards away into the fir tree woods beyond the running track. Even at that distance, I felt the earth tremble with the concussion. Another followed swiftly in, also falling in the woods. I watched the two columns of dirty grey black smoke rise over the tree tops amid the sound of tumbling branches.

Little did I know at that time, but those were the first heralds of a nerve shattering bombardment that was to beat down upon us right up to the night we were to fall back across the river many days hence. I looked at Arthur. He grimaced in return. Well, as long as they fell that distance off, we would have nothing to worry about, but would they?

We waited anxiously for further bombs, but none followed. They did, however, continue to fall on the far side of the village, about four or five hundred yards away. I felt sorry for our men, crouching in their slit trenches over there, fighting the enemy with their rifles and machine guns, and hoped that some of the explosions we heard were from our own mortars.

As the lull seemed more or less permanent, Arthur and I decided we would give the local grounds the once over, and have a look at the prisoners on the tennis court. Picking up our Stens, we left our holes and stepped down onto the path. Already, the lovely lawn was pockmarked with numerous slit trenches.

We walked up the path towards the house, seeing many familiar faces. From each trench we got a greeting corresponding to its occupants. I stopped for several minutes by one large slit trench where I found housed Alan Wood of the Daily Express, Stanley Maxted of the BBC and Major Oliver the PRO, my passengers on the flight to Arnhem. They were pleased to see us, especially Major Oliver. I shall always remember him, for all through those long and trying days at Arnhem, he had nothing but a cheerful word, despite the fact that he was wounded twice by flying shrapnel from the murderous barrage rained down by the enemy.

Nearly every day, he came over to our trench to give us the latest news of how things were going, scanty though it was through no fault of his own. Several times he gave us tins of food during the week when he learned that we had all but nothing left to eat.

We moved on to the tennis courts to find that it now contained a fair number of prisoners. Even as we walked up to the entrance, three more of the 'master race' came stumbling in, prodded on by the barrel of a Sten gun held by one of our men. All the prisoners looked rather frightened, and did not appear loath to answer any questions that our officer in charge of the tennis court barked at them.

They were thoroughly searched and then herded in through the entrance of the court where they immediately became the centre of interest among the prisoners already there. I looked at the tennis court, which had obviously been first class before we arrived. The once smooth surface was cut to pieces by zigzag lines of trenches dug by the prisoners as a precaution against mortaring and shelling, a precaution that was to repay them a hundred times during the coming days and nights.

Noticing a considerable amount of activity around the small wooden hut, I crossed over with Arthur and found inside a sink complete with running water. Men were shaving and washing in every corner of its confined space. We didn't linger but hurried back to our slit trench for our washing and shaving gear. As I climbed out of my hole, I snatched up my precious water bottle and, following hard on the heels of Arthur, was soon back at the hut.

It was a godsend, sluicing my face and upper half of my body with the cold running water. Shaving was not an easy job, but my face looked fairly passable by the time I had finished, and I felt a new person. Taking my refilled water bottle, I returned to our trench. Finding an empty biscuit tin nearby, I hurried back to the hut to fill the tin with the clear cold water. Now Arthur and I really felt we were ready for anything.

We stood on the lawn talking with some hut mates of ours who had dug in there, but not for long. Above the sound of small arms, which now seemed to be coming not only from the direction of the village but from positions that almost encircled us, there came the harsh wail of mortar bombs in flight. Within two seconds, Arthur and I were inside our trench, crouching low. They screamed on down into the fir tree wood across from the running rack. Shock waves beat across the ground as the bombs exploded with a thunderous roar. Another batch was on its way before the echoes of the first died away. Again the awful dirge wailed across the heavens, rising to a short sharp scream as the bombs plummeted earthward, once more into the woods. I looked over the rim of my trench towards where they had fallen. A cloud of black smoke hung over the tree tops. The acrid stench of explosives drifted across.

The range lifted and the next salvo whispered across to fall at least a quarter of a mile away beyond the wood. The dull roar of their explosions made the ground tremble gently. For some time, the mortar bombs continued to rain down at intervals of about one minute. The range stayed far away so we had nothing to fear, but I always felt a tingling down my spine as I listened to the sighing path of the missiles. The small arms fire also seemed to increase in tempo. Quite a battle appeared to be in progress down in the woods between the river and us, while fighting in the village nearby continued with unabated fury.

Our Flight Commander came around to warn us to be careful about firing as a few of our men were dug in on the far side of the running track almost directly in front of us. A short way beyond them was the enemy line, so we were to watch with particular care the fir wood through which it was highly probable the enemy would try and infiltrate. Then he was gone, leaving us to our thoughts. Since the enemy mortar fire was at times falling into the wood, I did not think the enemy themselves would relish making their way through it, nevertheless one never knew, besides, the mortar fire falling there was not much, and hardly a deterrent to a determined enemy.

The mortar fire suddenly stopped, and even the small arms fire decreased somewhat as the day drew on. Our Flight Commander paid us a second visit to inform us that we could expect a re-supply drop by the RAF sometime in the afternoon. That was heartening news, not only from the point of view of supplies, but also of morale. Surrounded as we were in enemy-held country, with our nearest ground units anywhere up to sixty miles away, the sight of the RAF would be a tremendous morale booster.

With re-supply due in any time, Arthur and I decided that we would open up one of our few tins of food we were carefully hoarding. Within a few minutes, a can of water was boiling ready for a small handful of tea to be deposited therein, while some Vienna sausage sent out a fragrant scent from another mess tin balanced precariously on the metal cross pieces supplied with each packet of tablet fuel.

That meal was delicious. Hardly had we finished than I heard a faint drone in the sky. Arthur heard it at the same moment. We grinned at each other - this was probably the re-supply group coming in. Together, we hurriedly clambered out of our trench and walked out onto the running track, where our view would be less obscured by the dense foliage that hung down over the bank.

All around, the firing had gone strangely silent, as though both the enemy and ourselves were waiting to see what the next move was. Men began to gather on the lawn and on the track. The low thunder came nearer, intermingled with the heavy cough of anti-aircraft fire in the sky. I strained my eyes towards the limited horizon offered us in the tree-studded grounds. The noise of the motors indicated that the aircraft were very close. The AA grew louder also. Now the enemy was adding machine gun and light AA fire to the medium AA that we had heard at first.

Then the first Dakota came into view, flying slowly but surely at not more than six or seven hundred feet. I could see the open door in the side of the fuselage. Tracers arched up and struck home, some ricocheting away, but most seemed to go right on in. More Dakotas followed closely in, until the restricted space over our heads was filled with them. Why the hell don't they drop the supplies now, I kept thinking, don't go too far or else we will lose them all to the enemy.

As if in answer to my thoughts, the first container appeared, tumbling away from the open door. The long static lines tautened, and a bright red parachute blossomed forth. A stream of containers and baskets spilled out after the first, until they were swinging in a long colourful line astern of the Dakota.

Plane after plane dropped its load from heights varying between three and eight hundred feet, until the sky was filled with a mass of coloured chutes swinging gently from side to side as they floated earthward. As though the majestic sight had filled them with a maniacal hate, the enemy increased his barrage. More and more tracers curved upward seeking their prey. Grey puffs of bursting AA shells appeared among the aircraft moving steadily along their pre-determined course. And then the first Dakota was hit. With a tightening throat, I watched the hungry flames lick out, rapidly gaining ground, until the belly was an entire mass of flame. The crew never had a chance as the plane nosed gradually over and fell with a dull roar not more than a quarter mile away. The thunder of the ground fire increased as if the enemy were spurred on by their victory.

Another Dakota reared up as if in agony. Again the tell-tale stream of smoke spewed out, followed quickly by the leaping flames. Then there came a distant explosion, felt more than heard above the angry thunder of the flak. A black oily pall of smoke rose up over the last resting place of a brave crew. Still they came on. More planes. More parachutes. More red tracers darting upward.

I watched two converging fingers of tracer close in and strike the tail unit of a Dakota that was flying especially low. Pieces fell off, spinning and tumbling earthward. The Dakota staggered, but kept on going. The dispatcher continued to heave out the containers. More coloured silk filled the air. The enraged enemy directed much of their small arms fire against the slowly drifting parachutes in an endeavour to rip apart the silk and send the containers and baskets plummeting down into their own lines. I cursed the enemy and cursed them again as another Dakota suddenly started earthwards, both engines dead

Suddenly I felt a feeling of elation as a new type of aircraft came into view. Stirlings! Four engined Stirlings, probably from our own towing squadrons. Hoarse cheers went up from parched throats around me as the Stirlings droned on through the curtain of fire. The round gaping holes in their floors spewed forth containers and baskets. In an agony of suspense, I watched the tracers claw up at the leader and disappear into his belly. Another curving arc of tracer hosed up at him. These struck viciously at his two starboard motors. One stopped and an ominous trail of smoke began.

I ducked for the shelter of a tree as one of the containers came spinning down end over end trailing behind a useless parachute, unopened. The container fell straight towards where I had been standing. As I flung myself down I heard it smash into the ground.

I shot a glance up at the Stirling. Thank God, she was still going. The smoke had stopped – so had the engine – but the other three were working still, although one was coughing and spluttering. Fascinated, I watched the machine, having completed its job, turn slowly towards home, climbing little by little.

Still the Stirlings came on, containers and baskets cascading down from open bomb bays and through the round parachute dropping holes. The fury of the Germans' AA reached a crescendo as tracers criss-crossed and heavier AA burst in dirty grey puffs. Tears entered my eyes as I watched a courageous effort, such an effort as I had never before witnessed in all my life, and hoped I never would again.

A Stirling faltered and began its downward journey. This time, even though it was terribly low, I saw the white silk of the crew's parachutes open out underneath and behind the falling bomber. Thank Heaven, I thought as I watched them drift down over the far side of the woods.

The Stirling hit, leaving a huge black smoke cloud rising into the sky to mark its last resting place. Then the drop was over; the last of the aircraft had turned for home and the last of their seeds floated gently earthwards, carrying their cargoes of war beneath. Some fell faster and faster as the small arms fire found them, slashing the silk to pieces.

The drone of the departing aircraft died away. I felt suddenly tired as I looked around the running track. At least four containers had fallen there and already a jeep was driving over the grass towards them. I walked over with Arthur and helped cut the cords and hoist the heavy containers onto the jeep. We retained a parachute each, knowing that they would afford protection against the cold during the night to come. Many of the 'chutes were caught up in the trees in and around the park; they would be cut down later.

The ominous silence which had followed the departure of the Dakotas and Stirlings was once again shattered by the fury of both enemy and our troops as the ground fighting re-commenced, and soon the whole area was afire once more.

Arthur and I sat in our trench discussing the recent supply drop. We damned the fate that chained us to this spot where we could do nothing to try and stem the firing that had reached up and torn down so many of the courageous RAF crews who had flown through a hell of fire, attempting to bring fresh supplies of ammunition and food to the beleaguered British 1st Airborne below. We learned later that much of the drop had fallen into the enemy lines – a savage quirk of fate.

On the perimeter, the machine guns tapped out their song of death, punctuated by the distant cough of exploding grenades and the heavier thunder of mortar bombs. In the nearby village, the battle raged harder and faster as the afternoon wore on.

Then to my surprise there came again the rumble of motors in the distant sky. Surely not another supply drop, I thought? The vicious sound of firing died down. Once more an ominous quiet settled over the area. AA began to burst in the sky, unseen from our foliage-covered slit trench. The roar of motors grew stronger. The chattering bursts from enemy machine guns chimed in and I saw red tracers darting upwards, curving away at the still unseen aircraft.

We climbed quickly out of our hole and stepped over to the track. I stared away over towards the far side of the Arnhem road. The enemy's AA barrage increased

Crowded Skies Above LZ

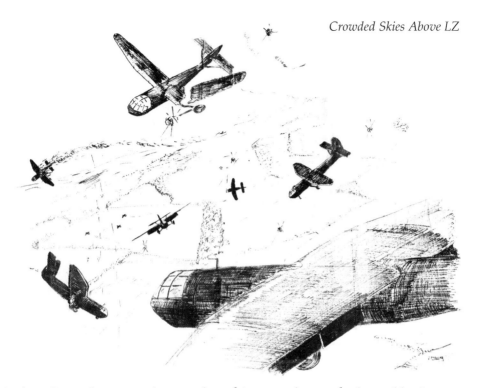

in fury. Long drawn out bursts of machine gun fire crashed out, blasting away like scores of giant riveting machines. Then the leading aircraft, a Stirling, came into view, but this was no supply drop in the sense of parachuted supplies, for the Stirling was towing a glider. Reinforcements were arriving. This was something new to us. Nobody had mentioned that another lift was due in. Actually, we learned later that they were Poles of the Parachute Brigade who should have been landed at an earlier date.

Right at that moment I felt terribly sorry for them. I watched the tow rope fall away from the glider's wings. The tug turned away for home and the glider continued on, losing speed prior to making its landing approach.

I watched the glider slowing down. Suddenly, it seemed to shudder as light flak bored into its fuselage. The pilot swung into a steep turn. The flaps came down, and it started diving steeply for earth but apparently under control. It disappeared down behind the woods towards the area around the village of Wolfhezen. More Stirlings and Horsa gliders were filling the air over Oosterbeek. The woods around echoed and re-echoed with the chatter of enemy machine guns and blasts of the heavier guns. Flashing tracers crossed and criss-crossed as they sought to tear out of the skies the men who had come to aid us.

I watched the huge black gliders wheeling around over the haze of battle and I knew that they were having difficulty picking out their landing zones. More than one jerked convulsively as the hungry fingers of steel gouged at their bodies. With a sickening feeling I saw one Horsa half roll over and begin a downward plunge from which there could be no recovery, and for a moment I lived through the horror that the two pilots were undergoing – that was if they were still alive to so suffer. The glider hit too far away to be heard. The heavy woods prevented me seeing the final impact that must have shattered the glider into a thousand pieces of splintered matchwood.

Reinforcements
Landing at Arnhem

The Stirlings, which appeared in my restricted vision to have got through practically unscathed, turned away and the roar of their engines gradually faded away. Overhead the gliders continued to circle and dive, although most of them were already down by now, safely or otherwise. As the last Horsa dived down behind the distant woods, the enemy fire diminished. Now only a blank sky looked down, a sky that at first had been comparatively blue, but which was now covered with a thin layer of low cloud caused by the accumulated smoke from the high explosives.

Arthur and I walked slowly back to our trench, both expressing how glad we were that we had come in on the first lift. It would be no joke, diving through those flak-ridden skies with nothing to strike back with, just having to sit there and take it. I wondered how many had come through without being hit in some way or another and would not have cared to put the figure very high – the AA had been very concentrated.

Then the battle resumed with ground firing by both sides. It was as if the pent-up fury of both the enemy and our men was expelled against each other with the utmost hate. From the wooded depths towards the river, the vicious burrrrps of the enemy light machine guns ripped the air with their short murderous blasts. Our own Brens reciprocated with their heavier anger. The sharp snapping crackle of Sten guns echoed throughout the clearings, their clatter rising to a crescendo that could be heard clearly above the thunder of the Brens. Bursting grenades added to the chaos of sound beating in on us as we slumped in our trenches unable to join battle, yet we were but a few hundred yards from the nearest firing.

Slowly the cacophony of sound diminished until only spasmodic firing flickered along the perimeter. However, the enemy mortaring and shelling began to make itself felt even more. At first the bombs and shells shrilled sharply overhead, bursting in the woods to the south towards the river. Then they crept closer. Their ugly wails became more menacing. As the minutes wore on the range shortened until they were screaming down into the fir wood just across the running track from us. The acrid smell of explosives drifted across.

I prayed for evening to hurry in for up until now the enemy had always slackened his shelling and mortaring at night. I looked at the sky, already taking on the first hue of evening. Another hour should see darkness enveloping us all which might bring respite to some, if not all.

Arthur and I decided that we had better start preparing something to eat and drink immediately before darkness set in, for then fires and lights of any description were obviously forbidden. Already the temperature had dropped sharply and the chill of the evening was making itself felt. A good strong cup of tea was the answer, and this was forthcoming. I opened up my forty-eight-hour food pack for we had no further tins. The pack contained some useful items, including several sweets, cigarettes, and even two sheets of toilet paper had been included by the thoughtful person who had drawn up the original plans for concentrated food packs for use in the field.

We felt better after the hot beverage and blessed the man who had thought up the little heating tablets that eliminated the need for a fire to be built out of sticks. We leaned back in our six foot long trench, my legs crossing over Arthur's. Our quarters were cramped. The slit trench measured no more than two feet six inches in width and was about four feet deep. It was impossible to turn on one's side, or stretch out. When we could doze, we just lay back with the upper half of our bodies upright and our heads just below the rim of the trench. A helmet was our pillow, and each one's feet rested on the stomach of the other, but most of the time one of us was always on guard in the trench, Sten gun at the ready. Every time a shell fell near our trench, the earth sides would cascade down, the loose soil running down my neck. I knew my body must be filthy by now but also knew that I could do nothing about it.

As we hunched down in our home in the ground, we talked of many things, stopping only when a missile came rasping in with a louder than usual shriek to burst just across the far side of the running track. Together we would mutter 'The bastards.'

It was the neighing of a horse that brought us both up on our feet to look over the edge of our trench. I looked around but could see nothing. Together with Arthur, I clambered out of the trench, glad of an excuse for doing so. Again the neighing, which appeared to come from the lawn. Stepping down from the bank we crossed over the path. There was a horse tethered to a pole on the far side of the lawn. Another shell fluttered over with a deep sobbing sound. The horse whinnied pitifully. We walked towards it to find another soldier already there. He looked at us and said that he was going to take it into the nearby rhododendrons and shoot it; he couldn't bear to see it suffering so. If the shelling got worse, and they started to drop in the park itself, the horse would probably get hit anyway and could die in agony. We agreed, and watched him lead the animal away.

The first bomb to fall right into the lawn area screamed down as if the departure of the horse was a signal for the shifting of the enemy's mortar range. Arthur and I flung ourselves down as the missile burst near the edge of the road which lay at the rear of our position and parallel with the main Renkum - Oosterbeek - Arnhem road. Shrapnel hummed angrily all around, the flying hot metal striking the ground with a dull thumping sound. No sooner had the rain of shrapnel ceased than we were on our way back to the shelter of our slit trench with all possible speed. Panting, we dropped down between its earthy walls, thankful for its protective sides.

Hardly had we done so than a flight of mortar bombs wailed on past. The ground trembled as they crashed down somewhere on the lawn behind us. Again the menacing whirr of spinning shrapnel came that made me squeeze myself down even deeper, with my tin hat set at an angle which, I fervently hoped, would help to shield me from any stray pieces that might come slashing into our hole.

The tempo of the barrage increased, and flight after flight of mortar bombs straddled the park. Some fell on the far side but others struck less than twenty yards away. Each time they burst, the tortured ground would tremble as if from the strokes of a mighty hammer. The earth fell in cascades down the sides of our hole.

'Hell,' said Arthur, 'they really seemed to have found us now.' To which I could not help but agree.

One bomb shrilled across seemingly low over our heads, and a resounding explosion came from the running track in front of us. Again, hot slivers of steel raked past overhead, striking into the tree branches spread over us. Leaves fluttered down, some falling directly into our hole. I idly picked one up and examined it in an effort to take my mind off the barrage.

More than once one of the bombs came in with a short rasping shriek, indicating that it was about to land in the close vicinity, burst with a louder than usual blast up in the trees scattered throughout the park. The flailing shrapnel would rain down on the area immediately below, and it was then that I realised our mistake in digging our trench beneath the cover of the huge tree spreading over our heads.

Then, as suddenly as it has started, the barrage stopped. I licked my dry lips and reached outside for my water bottle and took a long drink. Arthur did likewise.

We stood up and looked out. The shades of evening were well advanced and whereas the mortaring had ceased, the small arms fire had increased around the whole perimeter as the inevitable 'Stand to' period arrived. To the south, the woods echoed with the shattering blasts of machine gun fire. In Oosterbeek, the fight went on unceasingly. In the gathering dusk, the burning embers in the village silhouetted the trees of the park. The sour smell of explosives hung over the grounds from the recent mortaring, and the cold of the approaching night could be felt stealing over us relentlessly. I shivered and drew a ripped piece of parachute fabric around me.

With the rest of the men in our line of defence, we peered out into the gathering gloom over the running track. The fir wood loomed forbiddingly across the way. This was the hour of danger from attack if one was to materialise. We would be standing to until darkness had set in and the guards had taken over the vigil.

From the dusk behind us, on the path bordering the lawn, I heard the Flight Commander's voice float out calling Arthur and me by name. I answered and he replied telling us that we were to proceed at once to the tennis court and take over a twenty-four hour period of guarding the prisoners. We acknowledged the order and the Flight Commander returned to his trench.

'Well, I suppose we might just as well be there as here.' I said to Arthur as we gathered our equipment and checked our weapons and ammunition.

'Just let one of those bastards try and escape,' said Arthur. 'I'm just in the mood for knocking them off.' He had my hearty agreement on that point.

In a way, I was sorry to leave our slit trench. I had become rather fond of it, despite the cramped quarters. Well, we could return to it after our spell of watching. Pulling ourselves up out of the hole, we stepped onto the path. The last light of day was fading as we made our way up towards the court. I noticed that more than one tree had been struck during the recent mortaring, for several smashed branches lay across our path and leaves lay everywhere in a carpet.

We reached the entrance to the court and crossed over to the nearest slit trench which covered the prisoners. We asked if the two men entrenched therein were waiting for a relief, to which they replied 'Yes.' They seemed quite keen to get back to their own trench and a minute later we were occupying a well-dug slit trench from which the whole of the court could be observed, at least when it was daylight. We had learned that a similar trench existed on each corner of the court and that two others were covering the sides, as an extra precaution, both of which contained Bren guns.

The court appeared deserted but we had been informed by the men we had relieved that there were quite a few prisoners in the zigzag trenches now hidden by the enveloping darkness. Arthur and I worked out a rough rota as to who would go on watch and when. Then we settled down for the night.

On the perimeter the firing had died down, but vicious bursts of shots would break out periodically, especially in the village which lay about two hundred yards away to the north. Whenever a grenade burst the skyline would light up with a deep crimson flash that would sometimes be the birth of a fire that would burn for some minutes before darkness descended again.

The night wore on, and a cold one at that. I got in some fitful sleep between the times when I was awakened by Arthur telling me that my two hour period of watch was due. With tired, dirt-rimmed eyes, I would sweep my gaze constantly over the tennis court. Sometimes I would carry on a whispered conversation with the guard in the next trench on the adjacent corner of the court about thirty yards away. When the cold began to numb my feet, I would clamber out of the trench and patrol between the two.

Occasionally, a shell or mortar bomb would wail harshly across the sky to burst in the distant woods towards the river. For a second, the flash would appear over the dark mass of trees and then die away. I could not think what had happened to the 2nd Army. I listened intently whenever silence settled over the area for any sound what would indicate their presence somewhere to the south over the Rhine river, but in vain.

It was a night that dragged out, and I was glad when the whispered word was passed around for 'stand to' for then I knew that a new day was at hand. I awoke Arthur, and together we shivered in the still enshrouding darkness. An almost uncanny silence hung over the area, a silence that I knew would soon be shattered by the blast of gunfire, the forerunner of another day's battle.

Chapter 13

Three Days

I forced my tired eyes open another fraction of an inch. As the uneasy dawn of a new day sent in its first faint glimmer of grey, I grew more and more alert. The grey gave way to an indistinct pink in the east, and Wednesday 20th September 1944 was born. Simultaneously with the first tinge of morning light, the air was split by the jarring crash of gunfire on the perimeter. Within seconds, the blast of hate spread like a flame on a quick burning fuse. Bleary and dirt-rimmed eyed men, minds still clouded with sleep, pressed triggers with savage satisfaction and hatred in their hearts, a bitter hatred for the men facing them unseen in the undergrowth and in buildings, men who had been the cause of their being in this very predicament due to their lust for power.

Heavy explosions following close on the heels of whining shells and mortar bombs added to the confusion of sound, bringing home the grim realisation that we were in for another day of bombardment. The fury of the fire increased with the spreading light of day. At times the small arms seemed so close that I felt I could have joined in, then the sound would drift off. Judging by the mounting fury of chattering machine-guns and cracking rifles from the road leading in from Arnhem, the enemy must have been putting in a counter-attack.

For nearly an hour after the first signs of dawn, until it was broad daylight, the pressure did not ease; then it tailed off and settled down onto the usual steady exchange of fire, indicating that both sides were recovering from the early morning efforts.

With the easing off of the fire, the prisoners in the court began to show themselves. A sorry looking lot they were, too. I noticed soon that they had been segregated into two parties. At the far end of the court were the true German soldiers, some of the SS included. At our end, there appeared to be a mixture of Germans of the Luftwaffe, anti-aircraft and satellite troops.

The lower grade troops at our end were obviously trying to be friendly for they nodded at us whenever they caught our eyes. The SS troops, whenever they walked down near the entrance a few feet from where we were entrenched, stared coldly at us. We reciprocated their feelings in our expressions.

I stepped out of our trench and moved around to the side of the court. There, in a separate trench dug outside the tennis court, I came across the first German officer I had seen in this area. He was standing upright, his head and shoulders above the rim of the trench, looking straight ahead at nothing in particular. Without moving a muscle he just gazed out, his hands clasped behind his rigid back. He was the first prisoner I had seen wearing a steel helmet or even in possession of one. I stared at him for a moment but he ignored me. I looked closer at his face, which was as though carved out of wood. If I had searched among a thousand prisoners, I am sure that I would never have seen anyone more the image of the typical Prussian officer. Cruelty and contempt showed on every line of his face. He was a big man, well built, and his uniform was immaculate despite a night in the slit trench.

I left him and walked back to my trench. He was still in the same position when I looked back a few minutes later. I promptly forgot him when the first shells of the day to fall in the park were heralded by a long-drawn out wail that ended in an earth-shaking explosion. Breaking branches crashed earthward, and I heard cries for the stretcher bearers. The enemy had drawn blood with their first shells. A pall of dirty grey-black smoke hung over the blasted trenches.

Another batch bored in with a short rasping shriek, falling nearer the tennis court. I ducked as the ground shook under the impact of the high explosives. Again the familiar menacing buzz of shrapnel filled the air. Peering over the trench rim, I saw that the shells had fallen squarely in the centre of the running track. The court had suddenly become deserted as all the prisoners had gone to earth in a hurry, except for one – the Prussian-like officer who still stared stolidly out into space. For a moment I felt a twinge of admiration for his indifference.

The morning wore on with the shelling and mortaring continuing spasmodically. By midday the barrage had eased off considerably and I was able to leave my trench with a feeling of confidence. The prisoners came out of their holes and sat around the tennis court. For the purposes of sanitation they were let out of the court, but only two at a time. To reach the latrine area they had to pass the Prussian-like officer who still stood immobile in his slit trench, looking grimly away across the running track towards the fir wood as if expecting relief to come smashing through the trees at any moment.

I watched some of the men slouch past him without even saluting. When this happened he would move his head and stare grimly at them, but make no comment. If a man did salute him, he returned his greeting promptly. A few of the SS men gave him the Hitler salute as they passed him. I was interested to see that he totally ignored them.

Sometimes the prisoners under the escort of a guard would come doubling back, their under clothing still half drawn up. The invariable cause for this undignified behaviour was the arrival of a shell or mortar bomb in the vicinity. I could not help but smile, despite the grim warning in those rocking explosions, at the sight of those frightened men tripping and stumbling as they fought to tighten their belts and reach the comparative safety of their slit trenches.

It was frustrating, standing there watching the prisoners, while the men at the perimeter a short distance away continued to blast defiance at the enemy who sought to force their way through our thin line. In fact I found the whole operation somewhat tedious having seen only dead Germans and prisoners. The inaction was trying beyond description to the nerves. More than once I felt like slipping away towards the village a few hundred yards away to join my comrades on the perimeter. At least the move would break the monotony of being caged in a hole while the enemy sent his shells and mortar bombs over with almost regular destructiveness, raking the paths over the park. However, since we had been ordered to guard the prisoners, moving was out of the question.

Around two o'clock we heated up some food. The shelling had all but ceased, and I felt good again. The prisoners clustered around the nearby wire fence and asked for food. We had no option but to ignore their pleas – not that I felt like giving them anything even if we had more than we wanted.

Leaving Arthur in the trench, I walked into the tennis court itself. The prisoners nearest us grinned in a half-hearted way, but the nearer I got to the far end the more hostile the atmosphere became until, by the time I had reached the SS section, I was beset by looks of hatred. God knows what those swine would have done to me if I had been in their position with them as my captors.

On the way back down the opposite side, I came across a hunched figure looking like a boy judging by his size. I stopped and examined him. He was dressed in civilian clothes and crouched against the wire netting, his head buried in his arms. He must have sensed my presence for he suddenly looked up and I found myself looking into the face of an oriental. It came as quite a shock. His face was badly bruised and cut, but I could find no sympathy for him. I looked at him for a moment longer, then moved on.

Returning to the trench, I dropped down beside Arthur who was staring out disconsolately over the tennis court. Apparently Arthur didn't like it here any more than I did.

Two of our men suddenly appeared at our trench, and informed us that they were taking over. Arthur and I didn't waste any time; we picked up our weapons and rucksacks and promptly quit the trench, handing over with the greatest of pleasure.

I called out to Major Oliver as we passed his hole in the ground, asking him for the latest news. He replied that there was very little except for the fact that the Germans were believed to be bringing up something like a hundred tanks from the north. I thanked him and moved off towards our trench, discussing the charming bit of news just imparted to us. Tanks! We hadn't one in the whole division. Bren carriers yes, but they could hardly be classed even as an ultra light tank.

Anyhow, I cheered myself up with the thought of our six and seventeen-pounder anti-tank guns we had seen the day we landed. Little did I know it but a large proportion of those had already been put out of action by the enemy, and ammunition for the rest was getting very low.

We were glad to find that our trench had not been occupied in our absence, since we did not relish the thought of digging another. It was like being back home again to sink down into our own hole once more. Sergeant Bob Pavett in the next trench greeted us with his usual bantering query of, 'Where have you been, Dusty, you old bastard?' smiling all over his face. Poor old Bob. He was to be killed several months later during the Rhine crossing. Just now he was in fair spirits – more than the average person at any rate.

Leaving Arthur, I started out to see if I could find my co-pilot Sergeant Tom Hollingsworth, as I had not seen him since the day before when he had been watching over three prisoners digging him a fine trench. Hardly had I got out onto the path when Captain Walchli, our Flight Commander, beckoned me over to his trench, grinning all over his face.

'Ah, Staff, just the man I want,' was his greeting.

'Now what?' I replied with a feeling of uneasiness stealing over me. Whenever

Captain Walchli smiled like that there was some job on hand, as I knew of old.

'There's a little patrol heading out in a few minutes. I'm sure you would like to go on it, wouldn't you?' With the thought of getting out of the park before me, I replied with alacrity, although I would have given a lot for a few hours rest first.

'OK, Staff, report up to the officer outside the main entrance of the house. He'll be there in a few minutes. Take plenty of ammunition.' Still grinning, he sank back into his hole. I liked Captain Walchli; as a matter of fact, I do not know of anyone in our squadron who didn't.

I returned to my hole to find that Arthur was missing. Picking up my Sten gun I checked the magazines. I didn't trouble to take my rucksack. I didn't want that heavy impediment on my back if things were going to happen. However, I did attach my entrenching tool onto my straps, and then I was ready. I glanced at my watch – nearly two o'clock. Well, we had plenty of time and I hoped that we would be back before dark.

Shouldering my Sten gun I walked off up the path towards the house. A lone shell moaned across the heavens and fell with a reverberating crash in the woods towards the river. I passed the entrance to the tennis courts, and kept on going. Broken branches lay everywhere. As I walked, I kept a wary eye open for the nearest hole into which I could dive if any of the enemy's missiles should start to fall too close. I noticed that more than one slit trench had been turned into a grave by direct or close hits. A jeep lay on its side burned out; the stench of burned rubber still hung on the air. The metal sides had been slashed by the flying slivers from the shell burst that had started the conflagration.

Just past the burned-out hulk of the jeep, a soldier emerged from an almost invisible hole on the lawn alongside the path. Immediately I recognised him as Tom Hollingsworth and I hailed him warmly. I learned that he had had several narrow escapes, especially from the shell that had set the jeep afire. I also learned from him that he also was detailed for the patrol to which I had been assigned. I welcomed the news for it was good to know that I would be accompanied by at least one person whom I knew.

Together we approached the house. Outside the main entrance were gathered several men who, we found out, were also part of the patrol. We stood talking amongst ourselves at the foot of the stone steps alongside which hung the divisional flag, the Pegasus on the maroon background.

Nobody knew what the patrol was about so we just had to wait until the patrol officer arrived. The men looked tired and dirty but their spirits were high. I hoped that I looked as unconcerned as they did. I knew that within each one there must have been some fear as to what the outcome of the patrol would be.

A screaming roar, like the noise of a giant express train approaching, broke in on my thoughts. I flung myself down with the others on the gravel close to the wall underneath the window. With a last-second screech that froze the blood, the shell plummeted to earth on the lawn just across from the entrance. Close as my face was to the ground I caught a glimpse of smoke and dirt rising skyward. I dug my fingers into the gravel as glass from the already shattered window overhead tinkled down. Then came the whirring and hissing of shrapnel; red hot metal raining down, striking all around. I drew my neck in as much as possible, hoping that nothing would strike me on the unprotected nape which was exposed through my helmet being tilted forward.

I began to raise myself up, only to drop again as another batch came wailing in. Again the ground rocked with the concussion of the explosions that sent more dirt and smoke leaping skywards. I felt the perspiration running down my face and huddled closer to the somewhat doubtful shelter of the wall.

Silence followed. I think that the lighter sound of small arms fire was unable to register on my ears, which were still ringing from the bursts. We got up again. Most of the men looked a little pale and the atmosphere was strained until someone came out with 'Where the hell is that idiot of a patrol leader?' in a loud voice.

'Here I am, chaps,' came a cheerful voice from the top of the steps. An embarrassed silence settled over the group, broken by the lieutenant who quickly came down the steps.

'Sorry to have kept you out here in the open but I couldn't get away' he said. 'Well, here's the 'gen'. We have to go out to the perimeter towards the river and possibly beyond to search out likely open spaces where the enemy might establish his eighty eight millimetre artillery during the hours of darkness. We have to mark those spaces down on our maps and, if the enemy does place any guns there, I want you same fellows to come out again and see that they are removed. So make sure that you take in the territory we cover, so you will be able to find it easily again if necessary. OK. Any questions?'

Apparently we had none, which seemed to satisfy him. He glanced at his watch and remarked that our jeep should be here by now. Well, at least we wouldn't have to march down, not that it was any distance but a jeep was always welcome. While we waited for the jeep, the enemy sent in a few more mortar bombs close enough to make us crouch down once again in the shelter of the house wall. I wasn't sorry to leave the park. The inactivity and the feeling of being a target for the enemy gunners and not being able to hit back was getting me down.

As the noise of the explosions faded away I could hear the radio operator in the basement of the house close by, carrying on speaking in the low and measured tones used by all radio operators. For a moment I felt envious of him, sitting down there in a well-protected basement surrounded by sandbags as additional protection; then the thought left my head as a jeep came racing up the gravel drive to draw up with a screech of brakes.

Our officer called out asking the driver if he was detailed for the patrol, to which the driver replied 'That's right, Sir; all aboard, it ain't healthy around here.' We scrambled up and I found a precarious position near the back. I counted six of us, excluding the driver.

Leaving the park, we turned off the main Renkum - Oosterbeek road to the left and I knew that we were skirting the far side of the park. It was a pretty but narrow lane, that much impression I managed to gain through eyes that watered in the blast of the slipstream.

A minute later we turned off to the right down an even narrower lane that twisted down a slope. Thick fir woods lay on either side, and automatically I flattened myself out as much as possible for we had been warned that those woods harboured numerous snipers. I knew also that we must be fast approaching the perimeter for the enemy by now had squeezed us into quite a small pocket. Still, we plunged on down the hill. I became uneasy thinking for the moment that perhaps our driver had lost himself and was taking us out into no-mans-land in full view of the enemy.

Jeep Patrol Near Oosterbeek

With a sudden jerk, the jeep swept around a bend and stopped. For a moment I swayed with the thrust and recoil. The engine stopped the same instant. In the momentary ensuing silence there came the distinct whistle and crack of bullets striking home among the nearby trees. I left the jeep in such a hurry that I also left part of my trousers behind that had caught on a projection on the jeep. The ripping sound of cloth hardly registered itself at that moment. I had one thought only, to get down under cover. It wasn't until later that I became aware that I had also ripped my leg in addition to the trousers.

With the rest of the patrol, I crawled for the shelter of the nearest tree trunk and lay down behind it, my heart thumping madly with the sudden exertion and the mental tension. The driver hurriedly backed his jeep into the shelter of the trees off the road.

Peering out ahead, I found that the road swung round a dell that stretched away for about two hundred yards. On the far upward slope lay a house. I eased my Sten into a position that covered the house and intervening space for some instinct told me that that was where the shots had come from.

'That's right, mate, that's where the swine are', came a voice from just in front to my left. I started and looked closer. Then I made out the grinning face of a soldier in the familiar airborne helmet looking at me from over the rim of a carefully camouflaged trench. He had a Bren gun trained on the dell while he leaned casually back, his hands in his pockets. Catching the mood of his banter, I asked him how he liked it here. At that moment the lieutenant in charge of the patrol approached the man and began talking to him. I couldn't hear what they were saying, but I saw the man point to the house across the dell. No other firing had followed the shots that had greeted us and I began to feel more at home. It was then that I felt a burning on the inside of my leg, and discovered that a sharp projection on a jeep can make quite a painful gash.

The lieutenant called us to him and I cautiously rose and, half crouching, scuttled across to where he was standing. The others followed suit. In the shelter of the trees we all stood up and listened to what he had to tell us.

'We are going to follow this path along that more or less follows the line of the perimeter. We shouldn't run into anything for a while but keep your eyes skinned. OK, follow me at about ten foot intervals. You, Staff,' he said, 'Keep right behind me.' I acknowledged his order, and followed him into the heavy, dark forbidding woods which seemed full of evil that late September day.

The track wound along through the trees. An uneasy silence hung over the wood, full of ominous foreboding. My clothes stuck close to my body as the sweat oozed from my pores. I wiped the sweat from my brow as I swept the thick and close-growing trees with all the penetrating gaze I could muster. Only the distant muffled sound of small arms fire penetrated the deep woods. Most of it seemed to be coming from the direction of Oosterbeek whence we had just come and down nearer the river behind us.

I followed the lieutenant at the prescribed interval, from whose form I scarcely took my eyes even though I covered each side with quick glances. I noted that his camouflage smock merged in well with the foliage surrounding us. The path beneath our feet was covered with a thick layer of pine needles which helped to deaden our footsteps. Whenever a man inadvertently stepped on a rotten dry twig, the sound of the crack seemed like a clap of thunder to our straining ears. The man responsible would be on the receiving end of numerous black looks and unvoiced damnation.

The uneasy quiet was suddenly broken by a faint soft whistle that grew louder every second. God, even here, I thought as the whistle changed to a short sharp shriek. I plunged behind the nearest tree. As if by magic the path was suddenly deserted. The ground shook under the impact of the high explosives. I buried my head in the soft pine needles as the spine-chilling whisper of spinning shrapnel followed, intermingled with the crash of falling branches. I looked up as the noise died away. An ugly pall of black smoke drifted in between the tree trunks a short distance away. As it cleared the ripped and broken trees became visible. Again the soft whisper and again the sudden express train-like roar followed by the shuddering explosion that brought more branches tumbling down. The acrid stench of high explosives filled my nostrils and burned its way down into my lungs. Red hot steel tore its way in all directions with a vicious hum, falling with a dull thud into the carpet of pine needles. Why whoever it was had chosen to shell this particular part of the woods, which appeared deserted to us, I could not think. I only hoped they would stop and then, as if in answer to my wish, the shelling ceased.

'Right, chaps, you all OK?' came the lieutenant's voice. No one seemed hurt in any way and we assembled on the path again. 'Right, let's be off', he continued. Without more ado we took up our positions and moved off into the gloom of the woods, which stretched ahead of us in a seemingly never-ending mass.

We came to a larger than usual open space and halted. While the officer marked his map, we took up positions under cover and scanned the opposite side of the clearing. We did not stay long and continued the march. As we proceeded from clearing to clearing I began to feel quite confident but did not relax my vigil.

We turned off the path towards where I estimated the enemy lines to lie. The further we progressed, the more oppressive the atmosphere became. I felt in my bones that we were heading for trouble. I think the lieutenant felt it also for he whispered back, 'Keep your eyes peeled until we get back to the road.' I passed the word back down the line and then concentrated more closely on the almost impenetrable undergrowth and trees that seemed to close in all around us.

Reaching a bend in the trail, the officer raised his arm. Immediately the whole line sank down to one side of the track. At the same instant the reverberating crash of gunfire, stunning in its suddenness, broke out ahead. Bullets hissed and cracked through the undergrowth. I clawed my way towards the nearest thick tree trunk. My muscles had twisted themselves up into tense hard balls and I felt my stomach tighten. Almost without pause the enemy's fire continued. The sharp tearing roar of a light automatic weapon added its nerve-breaking voice to the echoing thunder of fire. A shower of leaves and twigs came falling down from over my head. Instinctively I pulled my head in as one of the twigs fell on the nape of my neck.

I eased myself to one side of the tree, pushing my Sten gun forward with hands that trembled in the most unaccountable manner. My palms had become sticky with sweat. The clatter of gunfire continued. In vain I searched the undergrowth ahead for some sign that would indicate the enemy's position. On my right flank I dimly heard the crack of a Sten gun retaliating against the enemy. One of our men had spotted something. The heavier bark of a .303 rifle added to the chaos of sound. Somebody threw a grenade which burst with a thunderous crash away ahead of us. For a moment the enemy's fire stopped only to resume a few moments later.

I saw the undergrowth move a fraction about a hundred yards away through a gap in the trees. I sighted quickly and pressed home the trigger. The Sten jumped as a stream of lead spurted out. Automatically, I fired in short bursts. The smell of cordite whipped back and stung my nostrils. I hardly heard the quick snapping blast of fire. Above the roar of gunfire I could hear shouts and screams in German. Before I realised it the magazine was empty. I ripped it off and flung it to one side, fumbling inside my left pouch for a fresh loaded one which I quickly snapped onto the Sten.

Then I realised that the firing had stopped. I waited, the breath labouring in my lungs, not only from the physical action but mainly from the mental strain which had set my heart thumping in a mad burst of speed. I lay there, feeling a little weak, with eyes peering on the alert for the slightest movement, half expecting to feel the murderous slash of hot lead ripping into my body at any second. I would have given a lot for a slit trench no matter how shallow at that moment. Lying behind the tree, I felt naked.

I noticed that my ears were ringing but gradually they cleared. I swallowed a lump that had arisen in my throat and licked my lips. An silence had settled over the path. I had an uneasy feeling that perhaps the enemy was even at that moment slithering through the undergrowth around to one side. I rolled over and twisted my body around to cover that side as well as the path.

The minutes passed. I just lay there waiting, moving as little as possible, for well I knew how a moving man can give himself away with even the slightest movement to an enemy, whereas if he had remained still, in all probability he would never be seen. With these thoughts running through my mind I watched and waited.

I began to think that all the others must have been killed and didn't relish the idea of being alone in these enemy-infested woods. Then I heard the officer's voice come whispering over from my left.

'You OK, Staff?'

In a voice as steady as I could muster I replied, 'Yes, Sir, nothing wrong with me.'

'Right, Staff', he went on, 'Have a look round and find out what's happened to the others.'

Leaving the slight shelter of my tree, I doubled over across the path in the direction from where I had heard the Sten guns chatter during the engagement. I dropped down alongside a bush and called out softly. A voice answered from the brush. I learned that they were two of the men who had formed part of the patrol. They informed me that another man was lying ten feet or so further on and that he was also OK. That left two men to locate. Doubling from tree to tree and eventually across the path I returned to my old spot. From there I made my way across to where I estimated the lieutenant ought to be.

He rose up suddenly in front of me, so suddenly in fact that I half brought up my Sten before recognising him. I reported the number of men I had located to which he replied, 'That's OK, Staff, the other two are out here on my flank – we seemed to have got off without a scratch. Now go back to the men on the far side of the path and bring them out. Go down the path about a hundred yards and wait just off it.'

I doubled back across the path, half expecting to hear the blast of gunfire as I did so, but nothing stirred. I rounded up the men and together we moved quietly back down alongside the path, keeping a good interval in case the enemy should spot us and open up again. At a point I judged to be a hundred yards, I halted the men and we sank down facing in different directions to give all round observation. I didn't intend to get caught napping. A few minutes later, I heard a faint rustling across the path in the undergrowth. A bush was slowly parted and I found myself looking at the lieutenant, although he couldn't see me. I called out softly to him and he broke out of his shelter with two men behind him. Once more he took over and we marched quietly away down the path, keeping close in to one side. I was more alert than ever as we made our way through the woods.

Once again I became aware of the distant drumming of fire on the far side of the perimeter. Occasionally, the firing would break out close by, where I knew the southern part of the perimeter to lie. Beyond that line lay the river and somewhere south of its far banks I hoped the 2nd Army was advancing to link up with us. I did not know it, but the Guards Division, in conjunction with the U.S. 82nd Airborne Division, were still engaged in fierce fighting north of Nijmegen and in fact they had only just managed to capture the bridge over the River Maas at that town. Tenacious fighting by the enemy was holding them up despite their desperate and gallant efforts to relieve us.

We suddenly broke out of the woods and found ourselves on a macadam lane. The lieutenant consulted his map and said,

'I think this is the lane where our jeep is.'

Keeping close to the bank, we moved cautiously down the lane. We came to a crossroad and went straight over and there, just ahead, we saw the jeep still tucked away among the trees off the road. The driver was sitting on the grass alongside and caught sight of us at the same moment.

We reached the jeep and without a word clambered onto it. The driver started the motor and looked at the lieutenant for permission to go. At that moment two figures came bursting out of the wood whom I recognised instantly as British. As they came closer I could see that they were greatly perturbed, agitation written all over their faces. They hurried up to the jeep and I could see that they had been running. I noticed that they had no weapons with them and became even more curious.

'What the devil's wrong with you two?' snapped out the lieutenant. They paused to regain their breath and then one of them gasped out,

'Snipers, there must be scores of them. Couldn't move for being shot at. Never got a glimpse of them either. Couldn't shoot back.'

'Where are your rifles?' went on the lieutenant.

'Back in the woods,' one of the men replied rather shamefacedly, 'just over there.' He pointed towards the edge of the woods.

'Go and pick them up – what the hell are you leaving them there for?' shouted the lieutenant. The men turned and re-crossed the road. As they did so the lieutenant called out after them,

'Now get back into the woods where you were.' He then nodded to the driver who immediately engaged gear, swung out onto the lane and sped back the way we had come about an hour before.

As we raced up between the banks that bordered the lane, I thought of the two men and could not help but feel a little sorry for them. Well I understood their fear of those deep dark woods with death ready to strike them down at any moment.

I crouched lower on the jeep as we turned off up the lane that led to the main Oosterbeek - Arnhem road. The roar of the wind blotted out all other sound. Our driver slowed down as we approached a spot where a tree had been blasted down over the lane. We bumped our way over the shattered boughs that had been stripped of all leaves by the blast of high explosives. With the slowing down of the racing motor, I became aware of the sharp rattle of small arms fire from the far side of the park on our right and also the deafening explosion of bursting mortar bombs. I began to look forward to seeing my hole again, at least it presented a reasonable amount of shelter. We swung hurriedly around into the main road and sped along past the iron railings that skirted the Hartenstein Hotel. I peered over the driver's shoulder as we began to swing across into the entrance to the park. I caught a glimpse of the main street of Oosterbeek. Drifting smoke obscured most of the far end. Not a soul was to be seen on the streets – most of the men were entrenched in the gardens or inside the houses. Then we were inside the park and squealing over the gravelled driveway. We halted with a jerk outside the main entrance and thankfully I slid off.

'Right chaps,' said the lieutenant, 'if I send out a message for men to tackle any eighty eight millimetre guns, I'll want you all here within five minutes.' Tom and I made our way down the path that had been churned up at intervals by the shelling. We had to clamber over more than one broken and mangled tree that lay across the path. The body of one of our men lay pinned down under a trunk. I knew from the queer twisted way in which he lay that he would never again want any human aid. Tom dived away into his hole with a farewell word.

The lull that had been lying over the park since I had jumped down off the jeep was broken by the throaty roar of a shell spinning in. I crouched near the ground even though I knew that it would pass well over my head. It burst in the woods beyond the running track. Another followed in fast and I broke into a run to cover the last fifty yards to my trench.

Thankfully I tumbled into it as the echoing crash of the second shell beat over my head. I lay slumped in the bottom of my hole feeling suddenly weak and tired. I fought to ease my breathing from the recent sprint, wiping the sweat off my grimy face. I reached out for my water bottle which lay on the floor of the trench. Greedily, I gulped down the cool water and sprinkled a little over my hot brow.

It was then I realised that Arthur was missing and assumed that he also has been directed out onto a patrol. I looked up at the sky and realised that evening was about to set in. In under an hour, night would be upon us again.

Closing my eyes I leaned back, feeling much better after the refreshing drink of water. I opened them again almost immediately as my ears caught the distant rumble of aircraft motors above the clatter of fire in the village and the surrounding woodland. For a moment I listened carefully: a re-supply, perhaps? I pulled myself up out of the trench and walked out onto the track in order to obtain a clearer view of the sky. No, there was something different and ominous in the motor notes I could hear coming rapidly nearer. The man from the next trench joined me. Bill Pavett turned to me saying,

'Well, Dusty, you old bugger, you know a lot about aircraft - what are they?'
'I'm not sure, Bill,' I replied 'but I'm certain they aren't ours, and another thing, I'm pretty sure they're fighters.'

We stood there straining eyes and ears, half hoping that they were our planes although I knew it was a vain hope. The motors of German aircraft have a peculiar beat that brands them immediately even when they are not visible. I still maintain that, despite many an argument with those who are certain that it is not possible to differentiate between our aircraft and the enemy's, that it is possible to distinguish by sound.

The first machine slid into sight from behind the obscuring horizon of trees. I recognised it instantly – a German Focke – Wolf 190. It was flying at about one thousand feet, no higher. We didn't wait to see any more but headed for our respective trenches. For one thing we did not want to give our positions away and secondly, there is nothing like a good slit trench for protection against low flying aircraft strafing all before them.

Once inside the safety of my trench I turned and looked up again although the branches overhead prevented a view directly upwards. The fighter came onto view again, swinging around in a wide circle. Another was following close behind, followed by another and yet another until at least seven were circling, their port wings tilted earthwards, the stark black crosses plainly visible.

Our Flight Commander called out loudly 'No firing to give away positions.' I followed the circling planes closely, fascinated by the powerful looking fighters, Germany's latest.

They passed out of sight and swept around the far side of the village. Then I heard the note of their motors rising. Here they come, I thought, and sank down as far as I could. The roar grew louder and nearer. Like a giant trip hammer the first blast of gunfire swept the area. Short bursts of machine gun fire raked the park and the village intermingled with the thundering motors of the diving aircraft.

Most of the attack seemed to be directed against the far side of the park some hundred yards away, but more than once a burst of fire scythed down over my head, crackling through nearby trees. Sometimes a bullet would ricochet off a tree with an angry hum. The planes came in again and this time the ugly short sharp explosions of anti-personnel bombs joined in with the vibrant clatter of the machine guns. I tried to squeeze lower down into the trench.

Somewhere in the distance I heard a Bren gun stutter into life. Another joined in, adding to the clamour. I had a sudden urge to stand up in my trench and try and get a few shots in with my Sten gun although I knew that the chances of achieving a hit were negligible. I stood up and gazed at the narrow strip of sky visible between the spreading branches.

I heard the roar of an approaching plane and tensed, gazing fixedly at the narrow strip of sky, lining up the sights of the Sten as I did so. The thunder grew louder. The fighter's guns blazed out with a sound that reminded me of a giant strip of canvas being ripped apart. Now the plane was almost overhead, but not quite. It must have passed to one side of the small gap of sky visible to me, then it was gone. Cursing, I sat down again in the shelter of my trench.

The planes did not come back. Forming up again, they circled leisurely around the area for another minute or so and then the noise of their motors grew fainter and fainter. I laid my Sten down on the brink of the trench and took another swig of water to slake my dry throat.

At that moment Arthur appeared and dropped down into the trench. I asked him where he had been and he replied to get some water, not up at the hut by the tennis court but at the well of a farm that he had found down the back lane that bordered the park. He had been forced to take cover by the farm when the fighters came in to strafe.

The cold of evening was beginning to make itself felt and I anxiously scanned the sky, for it had clouded over and looked as though it might rain. As we had no shelter whatsoever, apart from the spreading boughs of the tree overhead, we would be in for a thoroughly unpleasant wet night. We made up our minds there and then that we would have some tea from our dwindling supply before darkness

Cardwell's Keep, the former home of the Queens Royal Regiment, Guildford, Surrey. *Copyright C. Miller*

Troops await to board a WACO CG4A glider in Tunisia for Operation Ladbroke – 9th July 1943. *Copyright IWM CN 1002*

Author's sketch of his own glider crash landed near Syracuse, Sicily 9th July 1943. *Copyright V. Miller*

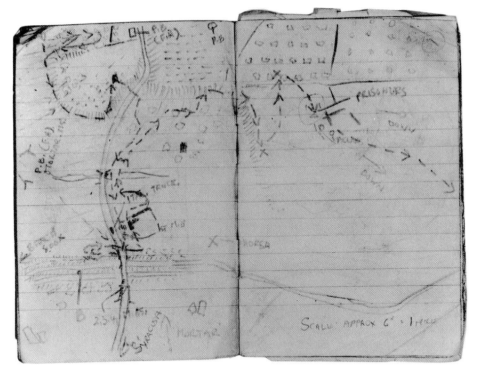

Sketch map from the author's diary drawn a week after his landing in Sicily, showing the area around the Ponte Grande. *Copyright V. Miller*

Sketch map, showing the area around the Ponte Grande. *Copyright V. Miller*

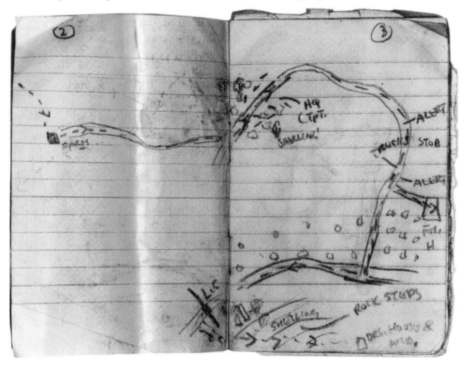

G Squadron, Glider Pilot Regiment, the author is in the middle row, 7th from left with his co-pilot Tom Hollingsworth top row 5th from left. *Copyright V. Miller*

Author 2nd from left with Tom Holligsworth far left, RAF Fairford, Gloucestershire, Summer 1944. *Copyright V. Miller*

Author's log book showing the page for operation Market Garden. *Copyright V. Miller*

Author at the controls of his Horsa glider on route to Arnhem. *Copyright IWM*

Sgt Tom Holligsworth at the controls of of his Horsa glider on route to Arnhem. *Copyright IWM*

Photo taken by Sgt Smith through the author's cockpit, showing flak bursting just below the Stirling tug as they cross the Dutch coast on their way to Arnhem. *Copyright IWM BU 1160*

RAF reconnaissance photo taken on 17th September 1944, showing the author's Horsa in the bottom left of the main landing zone field. *Copyright IWM CL1173*

Above: 14:00 hrs on Sunday 17th September, the author was filmed by Sgt Walker near Wolfhezen Asylum, right to left – Maj Oliver, author, nurse, Sgt Webb. *Copyright IWM*

The author marched past this scene with the body of Major General Kussin who was ambushed at the crossroads near Wolfhezen. *Copyright IWM BU 1155*

The Daily Express war correspondent Alan Wood, one of the author's passengers, sits typing a dispatch in Oosterbeek, 18th September 1944. *Copyright IWM BU 1146*

View of the tennis court in the grounds of the Hartenstein Hotel. The author was dug by the fir trees top right of this photo. *Copyright IWM BU 1144*

1st Airborne Division soldiers in the grounds of the Hartenstein Hotel use parachutes to signal allied supply aircraft, 23rd September 1944. *Copyright IWM BU1119*

Author's own copy of a reconnaissance showing the Landing Zone near Hamminkeln, Germany. *Copyright V. Miller*

Irene Reimann a captured German Luft-Nachricheten Regiment 201 telephonist, who the author spoke to for a while. *Copyright IWM BU 1096*

Nazi Party armband and membership book taken as a souvenir by the author from the inn keeper Hans Neu in Hamminkeln. *Photo copyright Moran Design*

set in to prohibit a fire. It was an excellent brew. We had to drink the tea quickly for our aluminium mess tins cooled off the liquid in a matter of two or three minutes.

Half an hour before dark we stood to. We leaned against the trench side, peering out into the slowly enveloping blackness, ever watchful. The bursts of gunfire on the perimeter increased in tempo as if each side was seizing the last faint dying rays of daylight, trying to destroy each other before the black shroud of night obscured their targets.

The enemy continued to hurl in shells and mortar bombs sporadically. They came in, sighing unseen across the heavens, to burst deep within the woods across the little lane behind us, or sometimes they would come screeching in with a noise that sent us both ducking beneath the rim of our trench. Loose earth would cascade down as the ground trembled beneath the bursting missiles. The ugly hum of steel fragments would cause us both to cringe even lower, if it were possible. For the first time I began to calculate mentally the chances of one shell eventually coming down on top of us. It seemed impossible to me that they could continue to fall in the area without either subjecting us to a close hit, or a direct one.

The firing seemed most intense in Oosterbeek village. The enemy's automatic machine pistols blasted forth terribly fast with a tearing note that meant certain death for whoever was caught for one second in its deadly stream of lead. Their heavier machine guns, MG 34s, added a thunder that could be heard above all else. On our side, our excellent light machine guns, the Brens, beat out their retaliatory defiance, supported by the short sharp spiteful bursts of the Stens and the heavier distinctive crack of the .303 rifles. Adding to the cacophony of sound were the intermittent explosions from hand grenades and the larger, more prominent bursts of the mortars and shells adding to the shambles. As darkness closed in, the flashes from the explosions lit up the skyline more and more.

And then night spread her cloak over the scene of devastation and as if in obedience most of the firing died down, except for that in the village. There the house to house fighting continued. In the woods towards the river, both sides seemed to have called it quits for the day. Beyond the fir wood, over the running track, sporadic firing continued.

Arthur and I lay back in our trench stretching our legs as much as possible. I closed my tired eyes and then we talked to each other. As usual, we touched on the subject as to what had happened to the 2nd Army. We had now been here over three days, eighty hours to be precise, and still there was no sign or word that they were anywhere near.

It turned cold and we were glad of the enveloping fabric of the supply parachute. Our Flight Commander paid us a visit to inform us that sentries had been arranged and that we must get what sleep we could. We would soon be awakened if matters warranted it. Within me I knew that I would not be able to sleep continuously. Maybe after another day or so, the craving for sleep might overcome all obstacles but tonight I felt uneasy.

The hours went by and I began to doze. I came to with a start. Glancing at the illuminated dial of my watch I noticed that it was nearly midnight. I listened, wondering what had awakened me. The perimeter seemed quiet except for occasional bursts of firing around and in the village. Then I heard a new sound.

It was the sound of a heavy tracked vehicle moving around on the far side of the fir wood. Tanks! Its engine roared for an instant at high pitch and then died down into a steady rumble. Another seemed to be moving near it. I eased myself up and stared out into the blackness across the track. Down in the trench, Arthur slept on, breathing heavily. Again I heard the clanking and squeaking of tracks and the straining motors driving the steel-clad monsters forward about two hundred or so yards away. The noise appeared to be moving across in front of us.

I hardly noticed the purposeful wail of two shells that droned across the night skies to fall about three hundred yards away in the woods to the south. I shivered as I stood peering hard out into the almost impenetrable blackness. The clanking and the roaring motors stopped. I knew that we had no tanks of any kind; the only tracked vehicles we had brought in were light Bren gun carriers, and their noise was nothing like that which I had just heard. Undoubtedly they were enemy tanks prowling out here, probably on the shady lanes that twisted through the thick woods.

I knew that no attack would develop by the enemy tanks, for their roles are strictly daylight ones, except in exceptional circumstances such as a night pursuit of a retreating enemy column. For those tanks to operate against us in the darkness through lanes and roads that wound through the thick woods would have been suicidal. They were probably moving into positions within their own lines, readying for a dawn attack. Nevertheless the sound of clanking tracks and rumbling motors in the dead of night was not a pleasant one.

It grew colder and I drew the parachute shroud closer around my stiff limbs and huddled down in our hole. The air was saturated with a thick earthy smell, mixed with the smell of burnt cordite. A silence hung over the park area and despite the occasional blast of gunfire around the village, I fell into a fitful sleep.

Chapter 14

The Shrinking Circle

I awoke before dawn; it was the morning of September 21st, our 5th day here. There was a peculiar expectancy in the air. A misty dampness seeped through the parachute and my battle dress. My feet were stiff with cold as were my arms and legs. I looked at my watch. – 4.30 a.m. I closed my eyes and tried to rest my head which felt as if it were stuffed with enormous balls of cotton wool. An ache beat continuously across the back of my eyes which were gritted and sore. Standing up, I beat my arms and stared out painfully into the darkness.

I stared out in the direction from which the 2nd Army were supposed to be coming. I thought I heard the distant rumble of guns from beyond the river. Occasionally a dim distant light flickered on the horizon over the tops of the trees that crowded the park. Then the noise stopped and I thought that I must have been hearing something that did not exist.

The expected gunfire broke out abruptly. It was the short sharp burst of an enemy machine pistol, long drawn out, that proved to be the signal for a general flare-up all along the perimeter. The village echoed and re-echoed with rocking explosions. In the woods to the south gunfire, like a myriad trip hammers, joined in the thunder that shattered the dawn.

I heard the clanking of tracks from the same spot as the night before. Heavy motors rumbled into life, straining and failing as the tank crews swung them first one way and then the other. A few heavy guns thundered out with short reverberating explosions. The noise of the tanks continued for a few moments and then died away. Mentally, I took my hat off to the crews of the six and seventeen-pounder anti-tank guns who were engaging the enemy tanks. Seldom had the gun crews time to dig in when mobility was required to fight a numerically superior enemy.

More than once they were forced to fight at close quarters, firing point blank over open sights at the advancing lumbering steel giants until either they blasted the enemy tank to a halt or were blasted themselves. In addition, they had to brave the rain of mortar bombs and shells that were always seeking out their positions. Yes, theirs was an unenviable position, hunting and being hunted in turn. I know I used to view with disfavour the arrival of the six-pounders in our area, for I knew that inevitably the enemy would send his barrage over the park in search of them; but in our hearts the thought that the poor devils had no chance of keeping their heads down as we could always remained foremost in our minds.

Unlike previous days, the firing did not die down as quickly as usual. The violent tempo of the battle continued with almost unabated fury. Out there in the woods and in the village, men were dying every minute under the lethal streams of hot lead and flying steel fragments that filled the air with their constant barrage.

The shelling and mortaring of Hartenstein Park began early that day. Arthur and I crouched in our tiny sheltering hole as missile after missile descended on the park. Explosion followed explosion as the messengers of death shrieked in. Trees, already gouged and slashed, were struck again, the red hot steel ripping the bark and digging deep onto the wood. The spiteful whine of shrapnel filled the air. The ground trembled in agony as shell after shell bored in to explode with terrifying force, leaving a mark like a festering sore, burned and smoking at the edges. Earth would cascade down after being thrown skyward by the tearing blasts. The pungent odour of high explosives became more and more noticeable, and nearer-than-usual bursts sent dirty grey black smoke drifting over our trench.

The morning wore on and at last the shelling eased. As soon as Arthur and I deemed it safe, we left the shelter of our trench and stretched our legs. I walked out onto the lawn. Still-smouldering scars lay everywhere. Shattered branches lay in profusion, especially across the path which bordered the long line of trees that followed the line of our bank down towards where I understood the farm to lie. Several whole trees had fallen athwart the path, testifying to the severity of the bombardment.

Two men were busy rolling a corpse into a blanket about fifty yards away. They were German prisoners brought under guard especially from the tennis court. They went about their task grimly silent, in a rather scared way as though they expected reprisals from the men under whom they were working. From the expressions on our men's faces the prisoners had every reason to be worried, although they had little to fear in point of fact for our men adhered strictly to the terms of the Geneva Convention. As I watched the body being borne away I felt extremely hateful towards the Germans. A few minutes later I saw them rolling up another corpse which they staggered away with towards the house. I guessed that a cemetery must have been established somewhere on the far side of the house. Later I was to see it.

Returning to the trench, we checked over our almost non-existent rations. We still had enough tea left for at least three more brews but of tinned rations there were none. We broke open the last of our forty eight hour ration packs and I sucked one of the sweets. Carefully we set up our portable tablet-fired stove on the rim of the trench in a hole scooped out of the parapet of turned earth. After much persuasion we managed to get the blue flame to light, flickering around the white circular piece of solid fuel. Even the tablets were getting low for I counted only four more in the container. I sincerely hoped that the next supply drop would be more successful otherwise we were going to be somewhat hungry if the 2nd Army did not reach us shortly. I watched the repulsive looking mixture of tea, milk powder and sugar gradually come to the boil.

Meanwhile my thoughts turned to the 2nd Army. I had long ago, in company with Arthur, sensed that something had gone wrong with the plan for the 2nd Army to lunge forward the day we landed and link up with us within forty eight hours. Sunday midday, Monday, Tuesday, Wednesday and now Thursday afternoon. Yes, something was amiss. And where was the air force? Not once had we seen any of our fighters or bombers, only our own close support supply droppers, Dakotas, Stirlings and Halifaxes.

I learned later, when we had returned to England, that that gallant Army was fighting grimly to break through the strong line of defences the enemy had thrown up between Arnhem and Nijmegen. The Germans had established a strong anti-tank defence at the village of Bessam, north of Nijmegen, astride the main road. At the same time we also learned that on the 21st, the enemy had captured the point known as the Heaversdorp Ferry across the Rhine, immediately south of where we were fighting at Oosterbeek, thus cutting us off completely from the river.

While we were sipping our tea, Major Oliver came across and told us with his inevitable cheerfulness that the Polish Parachute Brigade were dropping during the afternoon on the far side of the river near the village of Elst. They were going to ferry themselves across the river to reinforce us. At the same time, he asked us whether we had plenty of rations. I told him how we stood and he suggested I go with him back to his trench and he would see what he could do.

Major Oliver and the press had built themselves an excellent trench the top of which was covered with the trunks of some of the smaller trees felled during the recent shelling. Earth had been piled on top and on the whole they had a pretty strong shelter. Major Oliver disappeared down into the blackness of the trench and a few seconds later returned and handed me at least three tins containing sausages and bully beef. I thanked him heartily and hurried back to our own trench. Sliding down into the hole I held up the tins triumphantly for Arthur's inspection. 'Good for you, Dusty.' was his reply.

Our rising spirits were quickly dampened with a distant thud followed by a whistle which grew and grew with alarming rapidity. With a climactic screech the missile ploughed into the lawn behind us. The ground shook under the violent concussion. Earth showered down the side of our hole as I tried to squeeze lower and lower. Steel fragments whipped and hummed through the air. A second shell came in on the heels of the first. The sound of falling branches followed. The nauseating stench of high explosives permeated our hole. I tilted my steel helmet forward over my eyes for the ever-present fear of being blinded by flying shrapnel drove out thoughts of being hit elsewhere.

We lay there for several minutes while shell after shell whined in with evil wails culminating in shattering explosions. Once I heard screams follow the arrival of one of the shells. I half rose up but dropped again as a further screech filled my ears. Earth showered over the trench. I felt tired and weak as I wiped away the beads of sweat that formed on my forehead. God, I thought, how much more of this can we stand? One of those damn shells is bound to get us in the end. Arthur, sprawled in the opposite end of the trench, stared back at me with a face that was etched with grime and lines of tiredness.

A little while later the shelling began to ease off, and I decided that it was high time that I refilled my water bottle and also the large biscuit tin that formed our reserve. Arthur suggested that I wait a little longer, as it was a good three hundred yards or so down the path to the farmyard where lay the well. However, the combined urge of securing some water together with a strong desire to escape from our hole for a few minutes made up my mind.

Taking our water bottles and the tin, together with my Sten gun, I pulled myself up out of the trench and moved off down the path. My eyes roved incessantly from one side of the path to the other, always seeking the nearest trench into which I could dive if my ears picked up the first distant whisper of an approaching missile.

The park was taking on an even more devastated look. More than once I was forced off the track to make a detour around a fallen tree. Some of the shell and mortar craters still emitted faint swirls of smoke and the pungent odour of high explosives. One slit trench near the path had received an almost direct hit. The sides had caved in and a man's twisted legs protruded out from the pile of recently churned earth.

As I neared the bottom of the path one of our men stuck his head out of his trench and asked me if I was going down to the well. I told him yes. 'Well, you had better watch out. Jerry has some snipers covering it. He got two men earlier today' was his rejoinder. That almost turned me back but our water was nearly gone and we had to have some soon. It might be harder still to get it if I left it until tomorrow.

I came to the end of the path, turned into the farmyard, dropped to the ground and scanned the area. On my right stood the farmhouse, its roof badly damaged by a shell burst. Across the yard lay a hayrick. Beyond that lay an open ploughed field, sloping gently uphill. No one was in sight. The well was on my left. It was the usual sort with the wooden structure over the round stone mouth. The woodwork was riddled with bullet holes and slashed by flying fragments of steel, but it still stood.

I rose and doubled over, dropping down behind the low stone parapet of the well, keeping it between myself and the open ploughed field fringed with trees for I suspected that that was where the enemy snipers must be if they were still in the vicinity.

The bucket stood on the stone wall just above my head. That too had numerous bullet holes through it and I began to doubt the feasibility of filling and hauling it to the top before all the water drained out. I gave the bucket a push and it fell away down the well. The rope unwound without any difficulty despite the battered condition of the wooden drum around which it was wound.

I reached up and tried to turn the handle from where I crouched but found I could hardly move it. At that moment I heard the familiar wail and promptly let go the handle and flattened myself as close to the stone wall as I could. The missile flailed across over the farm and fell on the far side of the road some hundred yards away. The ground vibrated as the mortar bomb exploded with a sharp concussion. Silence followed except for the distant rattle of small arms fire towards the village.

To hell with this, I thought. I am not going to get caught out here if they start putting down more stuff. I stood up and put two hands on the handle, winding the bucket up as fast as I could. It was hard going, with the drum wheezing and protesting all the time. The whole wooden structure swayed to and fro to such an extent that I thought it might collapse at any moment.

The bucket appeared over the rim and I cursed as I saw the water spurting out in jets from the numerous holes. I pushed the tin under two of the jets and my water bottle under another. The rest of the water just spilled out onto the ground. It was murky looking but it would do. I gained the impression that the well was just about drying up.

Owing to the large amount of water escaping I found that I had only half filled the tin although my water bottle was full. Noting that the water showed signs of disappearing for good in the well, I decided to wait just long enough to obtain another bucketful and sent it tumbling back down into the well.

As I did so I heard my name called out and looking up saw my old friend Sergeant Harry Cole peering around a tree that bordered the path down which I had come.

'Is it OK out there, Dusty?' he called out.

'It seems to be,' I replied, 'although I was warned that snipers are supposed to be covering the well, but nothing has happened as yet.'

Seeing Harry there raised my spirits and I started talking jovially to him as he hurried over to the well with two other men whom I did not know tailing after him.

'A little hot around here, isn't it, Harry?' I said with a laugh.

'You old devil,' Harry retorted, 'you always find something to laugh about. I don't see anything funny about it. I reckon we've had it.'

'Yes, it looks that way,' I replied, suddenly feeling thoughtful. By this time I had brought up the second bucket and bent down to pull my tin nearer. I never got that far for a shell screamed in. I have never seen anyone move so fast as Harry did at that moment. One second he was facing me, casting nervous glances around, seeking out possible shelter in case of trouble, as we all were I suppose. The next, I caught a glimpse of him jumping and turning in the air at the same time. With uncanny accuracy, he disappeared into a slit trench by the farmhouse wall. All this I noticed in the second or so it took me to dive behind the well wall.

The shell fell with a screaming roar just short of the yard. Grey black smoke billowed up from behind a line of trees that bordered the farmyard. The ground shook savagely under the impact. I clawed my way round to the other side of the well, putting the wall between me and the burst even as the fragments hummed down and around.

Pulling myself together, I jumped up and began furiously to wind the bucket up once more, which had immediately fallen back into the depths of the well when I had let go of the handle. As the bucket reached the top again Harry appeared at my side.

'OK, grab what you can,' I said, 'because I'm getting out of here now.' I was feeling a little shaken up by the near miss and had a sudden urge to see the inside of my trench again.

With my tin now three quarters full and the water bottle full to the brim, I set off back trying not to spill any enroute although all my instincts called upon me to run like hell for my hole. I prayed inwardly that I would be granted just two minutes to reach the comparative safety of the trench. My wish was granted and it was with deep relief that I set down the tin of water carefully on the edge of the trench and dropped inside while Arthur peered up at me with an inquiring look.

'Good for you, Dusty.' was his only comment. I made quick use of some of the water to slake my thirst which had suddenly come upon me in the last five minutes. 'I've got some news for you, Dusty,' continued Arthur, 'there's going to be another supply drop this afternoon.'

'Good,' I replied, 'I hope we have better luck this time. From what Major Oliver told me most of the last drop went to the enemy – through no fault of the RAF fellows, of course. Those poor devils went through hell to try and get the stuff to us.'

The mortaring was beginning to increase again. They were coming in several at a time, close behind each other. One would moan across to fall in the fir wood or the woods across the road on the far side of the farm, while another would scream down unpleasantly close. The sound of falling branches after the shaking explosions was becoming more frequent; they were really beginning to range in on the park. Once my rucksack, which I had placed just outside on the rim of the trench, came flying in. For a moment I thought that we had been hit.

To while away the time, I examined the ripped and slashed fabric. I opened the pack and pulled out the contents. I found the flashlamp had been shattered by a piece of shrapnel and was useless. I tossed it outside. The spare clothing was also torn and ripped by flying fragments of steel but was still useable. I found one of the pieces of jagged steel embedded in a compass. Needless to say, the compass was useless. Turning the fragment over, I mentally figured how many square inches of flesh it could have ripped off one of us if it had come into the trench instead of striking my rucksack just outside. I also realised that the rucksack might have been the medium that had prevented the shrapnel from entering our hole and promptly replaced it on the rim of the trench.

Towards late afternoon the firing tailed off, but a new sound took its place; the distant grunt of anti-aircraft fire. The re-supply drop was nearing. Our Flight Commander came running over calling out for everyone to get out his Celanese yellow triangle, our recognition cloths. I heard him calling out to someone to light up the smoke signal.

Dragging out our triangles, Arthur and I clambered up out of the trench. We moved out onto the running track so that our waving would be seen to the best advantage. On the lawn, a billowing cloud of orange-coloured smoke was beginning to rise.

A nerve-tingling rumble began to make itself felt as the air armada drew nearer. The small arms fire on the perimeter decreased rapidly until only sporadic bursts broke through the ever-growing thunder of motors. The AA increased its fury.

Feeling that my view was still too restricted, I doubled up towards the tennis court and further out onto the running track. I stopped near the wire fence surrounding the court. Inside, the prisoners were climbing out of their trenches. They either knew or sensed that something unusual was about to happen, probably by the sudden appearance of our men from all the trenches in the park, all with yellow triangles in their hands, all staring upwards. On the lawn, the cloud of orange smoke billowed higher and spread out but I doubted still whether it would be of much help to the airmen. It was too small and too low to be seen easily especially by men enduring the curtain of flak that must have been going up, judging by the sound of machine guns and heavier guns that filled the skies with their sudden explosions.

With beating heart I peered intently at the tops of the trees that crowded the park, waiting for the first aircraft to come into view. I shot a glance at the prisoners. They were gesticulating and calling out to one another. Some even looked pleased. Possibly they thought the aircraft were German. I turned my head back again just in time to see the first aircraft, a Stirling, slide into view. Her bomb bays gaped open, the containers clearly visible.

Even as I watched, the containers fell away from the Stirling's belly and plummeted down. Coloured silk billowed out and their falls were checked. Beneath the long line of chutes the containers swung gently to and fro. At the same moment, the Stirling seemed to jerk forward as the pilot threw open the throttles to try and escape the stream of tracers that rushed up towards him but they sprayed the Stirling from end to end. For a moment the plane staggered, righted and climbed away with one engine dead. Three motors thundered defiance at the enemy gunners below and then she passed out of my view beyond the park.

Suddenly the sky seemed filled with planes. The AA grew to a crescendo that seemed to split the very air. Darting red and gold tracers rushed hungrily upwards, seeking the black giants that cruised unswervingly across the cloudy sky, some less than five hundred feet up. Across the battle-scarred park and village they droned, disgorging their belly loads of multi-coloured silk and life-saving cargoes to the men who watched and waited below. Thousands of square yards of silk were floating in the sky.

The formations, though more compact than on the previous drop, were still far too spread out and I knew for sure that large quantities of the supplies were falling into enemy hands. I waved my yellow triangle madly, hoping and praying that it would catch the notice of some eagle-eyed pilot or navigator. Other men on the track and on the lawn were doing likewise. The orange smoke still persisted in swirling around but always failing to surmount the trees thus making it practically ineffective.

Resupply Drop Over Oosterbeek

Still the supply droppers came on. Black puffs of AA filled the sky around the gallant flyers – a sudden blinding flash and a machine was gone. Curving tracers caressed the exposed vitals of the black machines, seeking to claw them earthwards. Spinning pieces of black metal broke away from more than one aircraft as the tracers tore home.

Now the sky was a mass of blossoming multi-coloured chutes; red, yellow, blue, green and camouflaged, all swaying and sailing slowly downwards – too slowly, for the enemy machine guns were cutting some to ribbons as they drifted down towards the park. As the silk became more and more rent, the speed of the fall would increase, the chute would progressively collapse and end up a fluttering rag, no longer capable of supporting the precious container of food and ammunition.

Sometimes an occasional white chute would come floating down indicating that a fortunate airman had managed to bail out of a stricken machine. Through the maelstrom of fire over Oosterbeek to a future storm of steel on the ground came these gallant men.

The first wave had passed and in came the next. The familiar shape of the Dakota was predominant in this wave. I watched one with a constricted heart as under the savage blast of AA it appeared to go completely out of control. First it dived almost to treetop level then it climbed almost to the stalling point, then into a steep turn, another dive and then finally began to climb slowly away just above stalling point. The enemy gunners harassed it all the way until it was out of sight.

Another Dakota, approaching almost directly overhead, received a stream of red tracer in her wing roots and belly. An ominous flame flickered forth, tiny in its beginning but rapid in its growth. Sick at heart, I watched the tiny flame take on the proportions of a fiery comet that enveloped almost the whole of the lower half of the fuselage and trailed out behind the tail section. In vain I waited for the crew to bail out. The plane was now down to about three hundred feet, far too low for anyone to jump.

With almost unbelieving eyes I clearly saw, through the curtain of fire, the dispatcher at the open doorway furiously pushing out the baskets and containers. I found myself muttering 'Jump! Jump!' as the dispatcher stopped thrusting forth the containers for they had now passed beyond the park area. Instead the Dakota, still trailing a fiery tail, went into a tight left-hand turn and came curving back for another run in. Mesmerised, I watched her sweep across, now down to something like two hundred feet, a flaming inferno from nose to tail.

Through the smoke and flame that swirled around inside the doorway more containers and baskets tumbled forth. The inevitable end came as she nosed over further and further, the roar of the fire lost amidst the chaotic thunder of gunfire. Then she was gone, down behind the trees towards Arnhem and the river, only an oily column of smoke arising to mark the resting place of a brave crew who had died that we might have the chance to live. I felt like crying for a moment, overwhelmed by an act of heroism that could never be surpassed. Later on, after our return to England, I learned that the pilot of the Dakota, Flight Lieutenant Lord, had been awarded a posthumous Victoria Cross.

I looked across at the prisoners. They were no longer gesticulating or calling out. They, too, had been overwhelmed by what they had seen even though the men who had died were their enemies. Their faces had a numbed look to them. It remained in my memory, a vivid scene of men in ill-fitting and unkempt uniforms staring towards the last resting place of that plane with a look that could only mean awe and outright admiration.

I turned my face to the sky once more as the Dakotas came on, still bent on completing their task. More coloured silk filled the air. More chattering machine guns played their tracers over the floating containers, leaving many flapping and spinning earthwards, unfortunately mostly into enemy lines.

One of the containers under its supporting chute came floating down right into the centre of the prisoner's cage. It landed with a crash and immediately, without any word of command, the prisoners fell upon it and dragged it towards the exit where two of our men stood guard, perhaps thinking that they too would benefit from its contents in the long run.

A jeep pulled up outside the court and the prisoners were directed to load the container and chute into it, which they did with great alacrity. The jeep continued off onto the running track and picked up two more containers. Some of the chutes had tangled in the trees that bordered the track and the containers hung motionless beneath. Men were already climbing the trees with knives to cut the shrouds and let the containers fall to earth.

The main stream of the supply droppers had passed by now and only a few stragglers remained. They came under the concerted fire of the gunners below. Dimly I heard the thunder of the AA as I watched the tracers curving upwards in a fountain of red fire, probing and tearing. The eighty eight millimetre guns grunted and barked, sending their lethal high explosives bursting among the few remaining aircraft.

Again one of the Dakotas caught the full blast of a shell. A sullen red rose blossomed in its belly, turning quickly into a fiery comet. God, how those Dakotas could burn. The machine half rolled and plunged in about a mile away. An oily pall of black smoke rose in a gigantic column from the distant woods.

I thought it was all over and had begun to walk back to my trench when a renewed burst of firing made me pause and stare upwards. Over the tops of the trees came a lone Stirling. One engine was still, the propeller idle. The bomb bays were open and empty, testifying that the crew had done their job. The plane was turning onto the homeward run as she passed over the park. Tracers flared up and buried themselves in the wings and then moved slowly along to the body. Still she rumbled on, turning slowly. In a last burst of fury the enemy directed everything against her but the game machine defied them all and, with motors that sounded very uneven in their running, she limped off back towards the Rhine and home.

The last of the chutes had drifted down and now once more the sky was bare except for the tell-tale layer of smoke left by the bursting shells that had brought death to so many. I walked slowly back to my trench to find Arthur already there.

A kind of reaction set in after the excitement and emotion of the last few minutes and I sat hunched up in our trench feeling rather despondent. Arthur felt the same. In one way we should have been in high spirits, with the new supplies parachuted in; that is, the limited amount that I felt sure had fallen in our area. However, I think that our witnessing the awful price that the RAF had paid to deliver the supplies had taken away any jubilation we might have felt.

The uneasy silence that had followed the departure of the last aircraft was shattered once more as the men on the perimeter again unleashed their fury against each other. A fresh batch of mortar bombs wailed over and past to explode down in the woods in the direction of the river.

I sighed deeply and looked up at Arthur saying 'Well, what now?'

'I don't know,' replied Arthur. 'We don't seem to be getting anywhere, do we?'

'If only they would move us around, away from this accursed spot!' I went on. 'The monotony of sitting here as a target for the enemy's artillery is getting me down.'

Arthur thoroughly agreed on that point. Whenever we felt down at heel, the remedy was always a brew up and from our almost non-existent store of tea powder we rationed out a small heap and emptied it into Arthur's mess tin which was already on the small burner. After the tea I felt considerably better.

In an hour darkness would be upon us. I felt I had to stretch my cramped limbs once more before night made it dangerous to move around. On the path by the lawn I breathed deeply of the evening air. It was cool but tainted with the smell of burnt explosives, and I walked a little way down the path towards the well.

I stopped by one of the trenches dug in along the bank like our own. Two men occupied it. One was slumped at the bottom looking utterly worn out. The other leaned against the rim of the trench and stared dully at me. Both were begrimed with red-rimmed eyes and torn uniforms. The man standing appeared to be near breaking point for he muttered away, half to himself and half to me,

'It's no good – we've had it, it's no good, we've had it.' I saw the paratrooper's insignia on his shoulder and asked him where he had been.

'We've just got in from Arnhem. All our officers have been killed, and most of the men. God, it was awful. We managed to fight our way back to Oosterbeek.' I tried to cheer him up but was not very successful. A few of the Poles who had dropped yesterday were there also, digging in alongside.

A flight of mortar bombs fell on the far side of the park and I made my way back to our cramped quarters, feeling much better after being away from the confines of the trench, even though only for a few minutes.

We watched the deepening shadows steal relentlessly in as the sun dropped beneath the western horizon. Standing to, I listened to the firing intensify. At one time it drew very close from a direction just east of the village, but then it wavered and fell back again. Another enemy counter-attack driven off, I noted mentally.

And now the black night was upon us. Another day at Arnhem had passed without any sign of relief from the 2nd Army. I had almost lost count of the days and it took quite an effort to remember what day it was. In battle, one day merges in with another – every day is just like the last. This applies particularly so to the infantry proper, whose campaigns drag on for weeks and months. It was noticeable even to us, with our short operations of only a few days in length.

In the early hours of the morning I fell into a fitful slumber from which I frequently awoke when a burst of machine gun fire, longer than usual, was fired by a nervous finger and watchful eye into the surrounding night. Sometimes a bursting shell would light up the limited horizon of our trench with a momentary reddish glare. The distant explosion would break upon my eardrums seconds later. It was the wailing and moaning of these missiles on their errand of destruction that caused my body to shiver involuntarily. I could feel Arthur doing likewise and we both attributed it to the coldness of the night although, in our heart of hearts, we knew that the cold was but one contributing factor to our trembles. With our legs tangled with each others', the shaking and trembling was most noticeable.

Just before dawn, I awoke from one of my uneasy slumbers. I heard someone whispering 'Stand to.' I shook Arthur who started out of his fitful sleep. I kept watch while Arthur, although awake, still stayed huddled down in the comparative warmth of the trench. This was a practise we followed every morning and evening, each taking it in turn to keep watch unless word had been passed around to keep especially alert when we both peered out into the almost impenetrable blackness together.

Once again I heard the ominous clanking of tank tracks and the rise and fall of the motors as the steel clad giants manoeuvred around for position, from which to launch a dawn attack no doubt. The squeaking and rattling made the muscles of my stomach tauten up for more than once they sounded terribly close. I had an idea that our perimeter had been reduced even more during the last forty eight hours.

Something like a fiery comet rose silently up over the black mass of woods directly over the running track. Curving over, it lit the darkness up with its vivid red path until it plunged earthwards again, leaving the night blacker than ever. I could not be sure whether it was a flame thrower in action or some form of rocket weapon. No explosion followed, so I assumed it to be the former. I felt my hair tingling on my scalp at the thought of that incandescent tongue of flame leaping forward to burn all in its path.

The first grey of dawn was accompanied by the initial bursts of firing of the new day. Our sixth at Arnhem, Friday 22nd September. The sixth day; the grim circle shrinking, our rations dwindling, our losses increasing and no news of relief. Not a sound or a sign of relief from hell.

Chapter 15

The Sixth Day

It took me some time to decide that this dawn was our sixth day of siege, Friday, September 22nd, for my head was thick and woolly from lack of proper sleep. My eyes felt like balls of fire as I moved them around in red-rimmed sockets. I would have given much to have been able to close them in some peaceful spot and sleep, sleep, sleep.

I was thankful when full daylight had broken at last and we could relax. It is strange how sleepiness will fall away like a cloak once it is broad daylight. My hands and feet were numb with cold, for the dampness of dawn seemed to have seeped deep into my bones. Waves of pain shot down my cramped legs as I pulled myself up and out of the trench. I walked around a little and the pain soon wore off, but the stiffness remained.

Sniffing the cold morning air, we lit one of our last remaining fuel tablets and used up all but a little of our tea mixture. I hoped we would get some of the rations that had been dropped the day before.

We mixed a vile concoction of porridge also, and hoped that it would fill our bellies. I was reluctant to open the two tins given us by Major Oliver for I was not sure of the future chances of rations.

Just as I was beginning to enjoy life once more, with something hot inside me, the enemy had to spoil it by sending in his first shells of the day. They fell on the far side of the house, but their distant moan and the subsequent explosions served to drop my spirits by several points, for it was a reminder that we had another grim day ahead of us during which we would be subjected to the enemy's wrath conveyed to us through the medium of high explosives and flying steel.

I slid off the rim of the trench on which I had been sitting enjoying the after effects of breakfast, such as it was. Down inside the shelter of our trench, Arthur and I looked at each other with expressions that needed no embellishment of words to indicate their meaning.

I noticed one thing that I had not heard on the previous days, a distant boom, boom of the guns being fired. A short silence would follow, then the rapid high-pitched scream of something travelling incredibly fast. The last-minute roaring shriek, and finally the shocking impact of bursting high explosives in the vicinity, varying in degree according to the nearness of the strike. The artillery must have moved somewhat nearer for us to be hearing the firing of the guns.

Again and again the rushing sound of shells filled the air, but each time they fell up near the house, much to our relief. From time to time batches of mortar bombs howled overhead, falling in their scattered pattern mostly in the fir woods and, very occasionally, on the running track. I had an awful feeling of being boxed in. With shells to one side and mortar bombs on the other, if either decided to alter its range we would be for it.

After about an hour of shelling, the barrage eased up. At the same time I heard the sound of jeep motors. I raised myself up, thankful for the chance to move my limbs. A line of jeeps was coming down the running track from the direction of the house and the tennis courts. They roared up level and passed on, dispersing themselves around the field. One stopped about twenty yards away under the camouflaging cover of a large tree. I felt uneasy, for I had an idea that the jeeps had moved over from the spot that was being shelled earlier on. If the enemy discovered they were here, the barrage would accordingly be raised and we would be on the receiving end.

Half an hour passed and I began to think I had been unduly alarmed, when I again changed my mind – very quickly. It was the distant double boom that did it. Instinctively I cringed lower in our hole, sensing that we were really in for it.

Intolerable moments ticked by as we waited in suspense for an indication as to where the shells were going – and we found out. They came boring in, with a noise like an underground train. I tried to flatten myself even lower, but the contents of the pockets of my smock prevented the last half inch.

The high pitched shriek of rushing air ended with a series of violent concussions as they burst dead on the running track. The earth heaved like a live being stricken with a mortal wound. Shocking blast waves swept over our trench. Outside, red hot splintered fragments of steel flailed the area, humming and whirring with an evil dirge, ripping and slashing all within their path.

An uncanny silence reigned for a few seconds and then moans and cries rang out. The enemy had scored on their first try. I forced myself up on trembling limbs only to fall back again as I picked up the distant boom, boom again.

I clawed for the bottom of our hole, with Arthur keeping close company, and we lay there tensely. Again the shrill scream as the missiles descended towards us. I felt my stomach muscles twist up in an agony of suspense. Once more the earth rocked. More flying shrapnel, striking with a dull thucking sound into the trees and ground around us. Smoke from the first shells drifted in, bringing with it a throat-searing, pungent smell of high explosives. As the noise died away, I again heard the cries and moans of the wounded. In addition, I could hear the ugly cracking of a fire burning.

A third batch howled in. Away on our right, one burst in the air as it struck a tree. The thunder of the explosion hurt my ears. The tree fell with a tremendous cracking and snapping noise, adding to the chaos.

The next few minutes were a nightmare, as shell after shell screamed in. We grovelled in the bottom of our hole, trying to force our way down further after each explosion. The air filled with the almost constant noise of shrapnel humming viciously down, making the hair stand on end at the base of my scalp whenever a piece whirred sharply across the mouth of our trench.

Then, as suddenly as it had begun, the barrage stopped. For a few moments I lay limp and trembling. Outside, the crackling of a fire continued. Somewhere a man was alternately moaning and sobbing in agony. I pulled myself up and dazedly looked around. About fifty yards away, the remnants of a jeep burnt in a drifting cloud of smoke. Another jeep lay half buried under a tree that had been slashed almost in half by the high explosives.

Several men were working away near the shattered jeeps. Even as I watched, a man, or what was left of a man, was rolled onto one of the stretchers. He screamed as they moved him. The men lifted the stretcher aboard a jeep, which drove away slowly towards the house and the make-shift hospital with its moaning wreckage of a human being.

I slumped down once again, feeling sick at heart. Would there be no end to it all? Now the searching shells had found a new target in the woods across the lane towards the river. I felt sorry for the men on the receiving end, but had no illusions as to where I would wish the shells to be falling.

Later that afternoon, a heartening, if not very helpful, episode occurred. We had long since recovered from the recent shelling and were standing up, leaning against the rim of our trench talking, of all things, about flowers and vegetables, which may not have been so strange after all, because Arthur in civilian life had been, if I remember rightly, a market gardener.

Without warning, we both suddenly heard the roar of aircraft motors almost directly overhead. Throwing caution to the wind, we climbed out and stepped into the open. Looking up, I saw three Mustangs – army co-operation fighters, the first friendly fighter aircraft we had seen since we had bid farewell to our escort last Sunday, six days ago.

It gave our morale a terrific boost. Wildly we waved our yellow Celanese triangles and cheered madly, even though the pilots could not hear us.

The three fighters circled lazily around, one behind the other, for several minutes, and then flew off altogether. I had an idea that, as they were army co-operation planes, they may have been over to spot for the artillery, and if that was the case, the 2nd Army must have been getting pretty close.

On our return to England, I learned that the 2nd Army was in fact very close at that moment. The 43rd Division, which was spearheading the attack with the Guards Armoured Brigade, had been held up outside Elst, but a small column had managed to make a detour around that village and fight their way to the bank of the river on the south side, about three to four miles from where we were as the crow flies. But that was as far as they could get. To all intents and purposes, we were still cut completely off from the 2nd Army. At the river bank, the small column from the 42nd Division had joined up with some Polish Paratroopers, who had dropped on the south side of the river the day before. They also were subject to heavy and close fire from the enemy.

After the planes had flown away, the intermittent mortaring and shelling commenced again. While the three fighters had been over, the enemy had kept rather quiet, although their appearance in no way distracted the enemy and our men on the perimeter from keeping up the small arms fire, which continued with little respite, day in and day out.

As we sat on the edge of our trench, with one ear ever cocked ready for the warning whistle of an approaching shell, I detected a furious increase of small arms fire coming from over the far side of the house. It seemed to gain tempo every passing minute and it really sounded as though the enemy were putting in a determined counter-attack.

Even as we listened, our Flight Commander came over to us with a worried expression on his face.

'OK fellows, get your weapons ready. We've got to move over to the far side of the house to new positions. It looks as though the enemy are breaking through and we have to hold them off. They mustn't reach the house at any cost. Don't bother to bring your packs. Meet here in two minutes' time'. After making that statement he passed on to the next trench.

I stuffed the two tins of sausages we had left, together with the last heap of tea powder, into my smock. I checked over my Sten and the magazines and turned to our Piat, which had lain there unused ever since we came into the park. Just at that moment, our Flight Commander returned in company with a sergeant of the paratroopers.

'Ah, I see you have a Piat, Staff,' were his first words.

'Yes, Sir,' I replied. 'I'm bringing it along with me.'

'I'm sorry, Staff, but you can't do that,' he retorted. 'The sergeant here has to take it back with him to another position which is threatened by tanks, but you stay here, I want you with us'. With mixed feelings I handed the Piat over to the sergeant.

In one way I had been glad to know that we had such a weapon with us in case the enemy did break through the thin forward ring of men who were but two to three hundred yards in front of us. On the other hand, I had felt somewhat guilty having such a lethal weapon lying here in idleness when in all probability it was urgently needed on many parts of the perimeter. The sergeant left with the Piat and the three cases of bombs.

'Hurry up, men'. I heard our Flight Commander call out. Arthur and I doubled over to where he stood by his trench. About twenty men were there. Without another word, our Flight Commander doubled away up the path towards the house, with the rest of us following at intervals.

We picked our way through the debris that was strewn along the whole length of the path; past the burnt out jeep I had seen heading out on patrol, past caved-in trenches and fallen trees. From some of the intact slit trenches men peered out at us with puzzled eyes, for normally no man was seen out of his hole unless it was for very urgent reasons, and here were twenty odd men, doubling up the path as fast as the devastation would allow.

The duel of small arms fire grew in intensity as we approached the house. An occasional shell sobbing over caused all eyes to dart furtively around to note the nearest hole in the ground. We reached the house and made our way around the left hand side. Our Flight Commander led us across to a line of trenches about a hundred yards or so beyond the house and on the edge of the grounds. With the sound of gunfire clattering ahead, I hurriedly dropped into the nearest trench with the rest doing likewise. I soon got out again, for although the holes were nicely dug, many were completely lacking a field of fire, for a huge tree had been blasted down in front of them.

Tearing and hacking at the branches, I managed to clear myself a reasonable field of fire. I found myself looking out over what I believe was called the 'Deer Park'. Less than a hundred feet away, three pyramidal piles of bodies had been formed, each about twenty feet high, with about a hundred bodies in each. Even there the bodies found no peace, as I saw that shells kept on dropping among the heaps, scattering bodies or parts of bodies over the surrounding ground.

Further to the right, in the more open ground, was the Divisional cemetery. Line upon line of blanket shrouded forms were laid out alongside the freshly dug holes. Even those that had been interred were not immune from the effects of the bombardment. Shells were continually falling into the area, blowing new craters open and sometimes the graves, scattering bits of the bodies all over the place. I felt an acute depression descend upon me as I wondered if this was the way it was going to end for us all.

Even as I watched I heard the distant moan of a mortar bomb. I ducked below the trench rim as it howled down into the Deer Park. Another followed in, but burst further over. As the noise of the explosions died away, I lifted up my head in time to see a pall of smoke hovering over a spot near to the corpses.

I quickly lost interest in the scene in front as the noise of battle increased out on the far side of the Deer Park, in what I took to be a wooded plantation. Now and again a stray bullet would hiss over and away but, try as I might, I could see no sign of movement ahead.

Hearing the sound of someone approaching from the direction of the house, I turned my head and saw two German prisoners, under the guard of one of our men, staggering towards us, carrying between them a blanket that sagged ominously. As they passed nearby to go to into the Deer Park, I caught a glimpse of a pair of lifeless booted feet dangling from one end of the blanket. The gaiters and the little of the khaki trousers I could see identified the corpse as British.

The two Germans cast us scared looks as they staggered by with their heavy burden, picking their way through the shattered branches and churned up earth and passed into the cemetery. They shot apprehensive glances skyward every few feet, as though expecting to be smitten down any second by shells of their own countrymen. The guard prodded them on in silence. I felt a wave of savage hatred pass through me as I watched them lower the lifeless enshrouded corpse to the earth alongside a waiting pile of shattered flesh and bone encased in blankets, stained with blood already turning black.

The trio emerged from the Deer Park and hurried back in the direction from whence they had come; in search of further gruesome burdens no doubt. Whenever the shelling eased off, the burying parties made their rounds. The backlog of burials seemed to me to be mounting.

I looked around. On our right about fifty yards away lay the main Arnhem - Oosterbeek road, separated from us by iron railings. On the far side of the road and a little behind us lay some large houses, most of which had been damaged and some burned down. Many were reported to be held by our men and some by the enemy – and they housed snipers. I made a mental note not to expose my head in that direction any more than was absolutely necessary.

From the direction of the woods and along the main Oosterbeek - Arnhem road came the sound of a tracked vehicle travelling fast. It was moving much too fast for a tank, which left only one explanation, that it was a Bren gun carrier of our own troops. It could have possibly been a German half track, but the sound of the motor was somewhat familiar. The tracks squealed harshly on the road surface as it rounded the bend. Cautiously I peered over the rim of my trench towards the iron railings and the road. A Bren gun carrier flashed into view and vanished towards the park entrance. I had an idea it was coming in for more ammunition to be taken back to the hard-pressed men in the woods beyond the Deer Park.

Two or three minutes later I again heard the sound of an approaching Bren gun carrier. I raised myself up further this time. The high pitched roar of its engine blotted out all other sounds. The tracks grated on the bend and then she was in view travelling at what I judged to be maximum speed. The next second, the Bren gun carrier disappeared in a sheet of flame that shot skyward tinged with smoke. A shattering explosion filled the air. Before I could drop down, a blast wave swept over the trench, knocking me down. My ear drums hurt with the shock of the explosion. There were only two explanations as far as I could make out, sprawled in the bottom of the trench. One was that a lucky enemy shell or mortar bomb had scored a direct hit, or else some ammunition on board had gone up for some reason or another. I favoured the former. I never heard the approach of the shell or bomb, probably due to the noise made by the Bren gun carrier's motor. A minute later I looked over rim of my trench towards where the Bren gun carrier had been. Nothing seemed to be left of it.

In front of me, the firing seemed to be dying down and I began to wonder whose side had won the engagement. An almost deathly silence now hung over that part of the front. I increased my vigilant watch over the cemetery, but nothing stirred.

Suddenly from the direction of the Oosterbeek-Arnhem road, shattering bursts of machine gun fire echoed louder than ever. I peered intently in the direction of the thunder of small arms fire – then from among the rubble of tumbled masonry I observed a fleeting movement and at the same time bullets raked across the top of my hole, crackling and ricocheting among the branches of the fallen trees.

The half crouched figures of German soldiers darted among the ruins and instinctively I aimed and fired at the nearest, who jerked and then fell forward – the others dropping instantly to earth. Again the figures rose and advanced, seeking cover as they came on. Alongside me I could hear the snap of a Sten gun and the heavy crack of rifles spitefully hitting back at the German fire. Through the thunder of firing I could hear screamed shouts in German as they came on. Sweat poured off my face. I aimed and fired again, and at the same time the heavy thunder of a Bren gun joined the cacophony of gunfire. The figures in front suddenly broke and ran back dodging for cover.

I breathed deeply as the fire died down and wiped the perspiration from my face – still keeping a sharp lookout. Spasmodic firing continued, but the immediate danger seemed to have passed.

Suddenly I felt tired, terribly tired, but knew we had to go on until relief came – but when? Heavy firing broke out on my left, and I squinted in its direction. The firing reached a crescendo and then just as quickly died down.

Our Flight Commander stood up and said. 'Right chaps, we can go back now. It seems the flap is over. Let's get going'. Men sprouted from the holes around and we quickly doubled away back past the house. Somehow, for no real good reason, I felt more secure on the far side of the house. It is strange I had become so attached to that particular piece of ground.

The mortaring and shelling had subsided somewhat, but we did not linger on the few hundred yards that lay between us and our holes. Hardly had we settled down when the noise of aircraft again filled the air. This time, however, they did not sound like the engines of our Mustangs. In thirty seconds my suspicions were confirmed.

A line of evil looking Focke-Wolf 190s slid across the sky at not more than a thousand feet. With motors throttled back, they went into a large circle, flying leisurely around as though seeking out the best targets for the day. Being a keen student of all types of aircraft, I found a strange pleasure in examining them as closely as the distance permitted and, strangely enough, it was keenness regarding all types of aircraft, which incidentally had begun long before the war, that eliminated the fear I might otherwise have felt.

The circling line passed out of sight behind the tops of the trees over the far side of the village. I heard the note of the motors change as they nosed over. That was the signal for me to disappear below the rim of my trench.

'What sort are they?' asked Arthur, as I settled down as low as possible. I told him and then we both listened for the first opening blast of machine gun fire from the raiders.

The shattering roar of gunfire accompanied by the thunder of speeding engines filled the air, as the first fighter swept low over the area. Another fighter followed in fast. I tried to ease down another half inch without success.

'Not so interested now.' chuckled Arthur.

'All in good time.' I managed to grin back at him.

'The bastards.' was Arthur's reply.

From the noise of the firing, and the sound of the diving motors, I had an idea that the Divisional Headquarters in the house was on the receiving end of a good deal of what the enemy were giving us.

Time and time again, they dived in to rake the park and surrounding woods. Only once did I catch a fleeting glimpse of one of the machines as it levelled off and climbed out of sight once again. If I had been standing up in my trench, there was a slim chance I might have got a crack at it, but it would have been doubtful.

Then abruptly the attack stopped. I suppose the pilots had used up all their ammunition. They resumed circling the area again and once more I felt it safe to stand up and give them the once over. A minute later they were gone, their ever-fading motors being the only reminder that an attack had been made.

With a start, I suddenly realised that it was almost evening. We had got through another day unscathed.

'What about opening another tin of sausages; I'm damned hungry.' I heard Arthur say. It was then that I became aware of how hungry I was.

'That's a good idea, Arthur,' I replied. 'But what about tea? There's only enough left for one more brew up.'

'Well,' went on Arthur, 'I heard someone talking about some rations being dealt out. Let's try Captain Walchli.' Together we climbed out and walked over to his trench.

'Any rations going, Sir?' we asked.

'We are just fixing them up now.' he replied. 'We are dividing them up right this moment, such as they are.'

'Any tea?' I went on.

'Not much, but we will find you a little. No fuel tablets, though'.

By this time, others had sensed something was on and a growing crowd of six or seven men had gathered around Captain Walchli's trench.

'Steady chaps.' he called out. 'Don't bunch or one shell will fix the lot of you and then I'll have all the rations.'

'Over my dead body.' replied one of the men.

'That's just what I meant!' Captain Walchli retorted quickly. We all laughed at the pun being turned against the hungry sergeant, who took it in good part.

We got our rations at last: four cracker type biscuits, a smear of jam, a minute piece of cheese and about enough tea mixture to make three brew-ups. The last item was the most important to us.

'Nothing else until tomorrow, unless more rations are sent down from the house.'

'We might not have any tomorrow.' I heard Captain Walchli add under his breath, as he handed the rations out.

Triumphantly we bore the spoils back to our trench. At least we were assured some hot tea for a little while yet. The only problem was the fuel tablets, but we would get around that OK There was plenty of splintered wood around.

As we brewed up our tea and heated the can of sausages we had decided to open, we heard remarks coming from the nearby trenches indicating that a general cooking session was being held.

It was noticeable that spirits were of the highest order whenever a mess tin of tea was being heated up. As long as a British soldier can have his hot tea – and a smoke if possibletogether with a small bite of food, he is happy.

The chill of the evening set in, warning us of yet another cold night ahead. Before the word to 'Stand to' was passed around, I took my Sten gun to pieces, together with the magazines. I found that this had to be done frequently, for the sandy soil seeped into the mechanism, especially the springs of the magazines, where it prevented their working. With a piece of the parachute which we had in our trench, I wiped off the clinging particles of grit. A careful oiling and I again assembled the gun and magazines. I knew that within a few hours it would be just as bad again, but this time of the day was a critical one, and heaven help the soldier whose gun or magazines jammed at the crucial moment – there was no margin for error.

As evening merged into night, the almost ceaseless rattle of small arms fire decreased, until only sporadic bursts jarred out on the night air. The shelling and mortaring practically ceased also and after 'Stand down' I relaxed back in our hole thankful for the relative quiet of the night. My eyes pained me so much that I took some of my precious water and dabbed them with a damp cloth. I made up my mind that I was going to have a wash and shave if possible the next day, come what may.

I loosened the laces of my boots and eased my feet around inside them. I remembered that it was almost a week since I had taken them off. Well, my feet didn't feel too bad, just a little stiff. Arthur and I talked a little, until I fell off into a fitful slumber that could hardly be called sleep. The least explosion would automatically snap my eyes open. For some reason I was uneasy that night.

I was awakened by Arthur shaking my shoulder and saying,

'Come on, Dusty, wake up – it's stand to.' I felt stiff and sore. It was still pitch black outside.

'To hell with stand to.' I muttered.

Again Arthur shook me. 'Come on, Dusty, wake up. I'll stand watch, but keep awake.' I opened my eyes and rubbed my gritty eyelids, but still slumped there in a state of stupor. I knew that I only had to poke my head up over the rim into the colder outside air and I would feel a little better, but the effort was too much, so I lay there with my head resting against the earthy walls of our trench, feeling about as terrible as I ever had.

Slowly the first grey light of dawn crept over the park. I watched it from the comparative comfort of the bottom of my trench. Arthur's silhouette grew clearer and clearer.

Chapter 16

The First Hope

Saturday, September 23rd, the dawn of our seventh day. Forty-eight hours, they had said ... The seventh day and still no sign of relief. It took some time to concentrate and to decide the date. What the hell am I doing here, I thought. If I were back in England I would probably be dreaming still, dreaming of the pass waiting for me in the flight office for a weekend at home. I moved my legs and winced at the pain caused by the cramped position in which I had been resting. As I moved my head the usual rivulet of loose soil ran down behind my collar and continued down my spine. Heck, I thought, there must be quite a pile of dirt down there by now.

'Come on, Dusty, you'd better get up now.' Arthur's voice floated softly down to me.

'OK, Arthur,' I replied, 'You've broken into my pleasant daydreams, so I may as well get up.' It was painful straightening out. I shivered as the cold air played upon my face as I pulled myself up and leaned against the side of the trench. It was damp too, and I sniffed several times.

'God,' I went on, 'It's a miracle we don't all get pneumonia. At least I'm thankful that it hasn't rained yet. See anything?' I asked Arthur.

'Not a thing.' he replied. My mouth tasted vile, and I took a swig from my water bottle. It was very cold and gave me a feeling of freshness that quenched the parched tongue that clung to the roof of my mouth.

I looked out into the grey of the morning. The line of trees on the far side of the running track were just becoming visible. It was quiet and peaceful. Not one shot shattered the stillness of the air. I knew, however, that thousands of eyes were peering out into the breaking dawn, seeking to catch a glimpse of a target. One jumpy finger pressing home a trigger could set the whole perimeter aflame with gunfire. It was just a matter of time.

Once I heard a tank motor break into life. For a while it idled, then revved up. Steel tracks squeaked and clanked as it moved around. Then it stopped. The motor was switched off, and silence fell again.

But not for long. The anticipated burst of machine gun fire rang out harshly over the woods, still grey and forbidding in the early dawn. The clamour of fire spread like an ignited gunpowder fuse. It served to clear my brain a little more. I stared across at the woods with a more penetrating look, searching for any signs of movement, but nothing stirred.

Broad daylight was a long time coming, but soon the sun was sending its warming rays across the track once more. What would this day bring? More shelling? More mortaring? Patrols, or perhaps relief?

We stood down shortly afterwards, and I told Arthur of my intentions of having a wash and a shave.

'OK, Dusty,' he replied, 'but it will probably mean another visit to the well later on.'

I didn't waste any time, for I wanted to get done before any shelling started in earnest. The relief due to the wash was astonishing. It prompted me to shave. This was a painful procedure, with the many days' growth and the cold water, but I made a passable job. I felt ten times better and was ready for the tea that Arthur had been busy brewing up. I remember thinking how little water a man needs for a wash and shave.

The enemy tried to spoil our breakfast by starting shelling, most of which, however, passed well over our heads down towards the river. We cleaned our mess tins with leaves from the tea, water being too precious to consume doing that task. A shave was permissible, but not the washing up of mess tins, we had decided.

We sat back and relaxed, but not for long. Our Flight Commander Captain Walchli paid us a visit. He was smiling in a way that I always knew meant something was in the wind. I was right.

'Did any of you go out on that patrol a few days ago to look for eighty-eight millimetre gun sites?' he asked.

'Yes,' I replied.

'Well, you're wanted again up at the house. You are to report to the same officer as before, OK?'. I acknowledged the order and Captain Walchli moved off seeking fresh victims.

'I'll come with you, Dusty.' said Arthur. Trust Arthur not to shirk anything. He hadn't been on the other patrol so he had no cause to come along if he didn't wish to.

We picked our way up the now familiar path and arrived outside the house. This time the officer arrived punctually. I counted three others. A couple were missing. Well, I wasn't surprised, and Arthur had made up for the loss of one. Tom was present, I noticed, and we greeted each other warmly.

A jeep was ready waiting and we piled aboard. As we did so, the officer explained what was on. Apparently, they had had a report that one of the sites we had reconnoitred the other day was now occupied by a piece of artillery, and we had to see about it. I looked at Arthur and he looked at me. Words weren't necessary.

I looked up anxiously at the sky as the jeep started up. I didn't like riding on jeeps because they made too much noise and you couldn't hear firing if it was coming in at you.

We started off with a jerk as usual that nearly pitched me off. Down the gravel drive and out onto the road we roared, swinging again down the lane that skirted the park. Near the farm, we turned off right and descended a lane hemmed in by dense woods.

The wind whipped and tore at us as we raced on. We didn't go far, and with squealing tyres drew up in the shade of a large tree. I left the jeep in a hurry because I wasn't sure how near to the front line we had been dropped. Away on our right a Bren gun hammered out, and was answered by the whip-like snarl of an enemy machine pistol. The woods echoed the shots again and again.

The lieutenant knelt on the grass and studied his map. Then he turned and said something to the jeep driver who jumped into his machine with alacrity and drove quickly back up the lane.

'I've sent him back a hundred yards or so.' said the officer, seeing us eyeing the retreating jeep. Some hundred yards! I thought to myself as the jeep rounded a bend out of sight – not that I blamed the driver.

'You all ready?' continued the officer, 'Then follow me.' With a feeling of deep apprehension, I followed him at a reasonable interval into the dark forbidding woods. Arthur was behind me. We both held our Sten guns at the ready. With thumping heart, I sent looks darting from side to side. Remembering our last patrol there, I knew that the utmost vigilance was needed should we encounter the enemy again.

We came to a spot where two paths crossed, and the officer signalled a halt. I sank quickly down on one side of the path behind the dubious cover of a young tree. The pleasing scent of pine permeated my nostrils, while the thick carpet of fallen pine needles felt soft underneath compared with the hard earth bottom of our trench back in the park.

The lieutenant signalled us on, and I rose swiftly, making sure that I did not lose sight of him. He was the only one with a map that was of a large enough scale to be able to find our way through the woods. We kept going. Once I was startled as gunfire clattered away on one side a short distance away. I half expected some of the stray bullets to come ricocheting through the trees.

Again the officer signalled a halt. We got down again. Then he signalled me forward. I doubled up to him and sank down alongside.

'There it is.' he said.

I looked ahead and saw a large clearing, which I scanned closely.

'Well, there's nothing here.' I remarked.

'That's right,' he replied, 'someone must have been nervous and thought they saw something when they sent in that report.' We again studied the clearing and the bordering trees. Nothing stirred. The officer noted down some remarks on the edge of his map.

I found myself listening to the sound of muffled explosions coming from behind in the direction of the park and Oosterbeek. 'Gee,' I said to the lieutenant, 'in one way it sounds worse from down here.' He listened and nodded in agreement. Bam, bam, bam, went the Bren gun behind us again. Brrrrrrp, roared the German light automatic in reply.

'OK, let's get back.' said the officer.

We all moved back out of sight of the clearing and then stood up. The officer took his place at the head of the single file of men again and we set off back.

We reached the road without any trouble. Walking ahead up the road, keeping well into the side, the lieutenant stopped and signalled at the bend. We heard the jeep's engine start up and, at the same time, he beckoned us on. We reached him just after the jeep did. The driver swung around and we climbed aboard.

The wind roared past my ears as we drove swiftly back up the lane. I flattened myself out on the jeep as we neared the farmhouse, for I still connected snipers with it, although I had seen or heard nothing to indicate that they were there when I had fetched the water.

I wasn't sorry when we drove in through the iron gates of the park again. Dropping to the ground we didn't linger, but Tom and I bid the lieutenant goodbye and hurried back to our trenches. Little did I know that that would be the last time I saw my good friend and mate Tom. 'I'll send for you again if I need you.' were his parting words.

As Arthur and I passed Major Oliver's trench, he hailed us. 'I've got some news for you. Keep your heads down around about three p.m. The 2nd Army is going to put down an artillery barrage, and a few of their shells might go astray.' We thanked him and continued on to our trench. That was great news. It meant the 2nd Army must be somewhere in the vicinity. Why, they would probably get through to us tomorrow! Yes, the news was great. It gave us great pleasure to pass on the information to those who had not heard, though there were not many.

We huddled down in our trench once more. Time and time again, whenever I returned from a trip outside the immediate area, I had a feeling of being in a place of security once I was down between the four earthy walls of the slit trench. Only when missiles began to fall uncomfortably close did I feel that the trench wasn't so invulnerable after all.

Arthur and I talked of the coming barrage, and hoped that the gunners had fairly accurate information of the situation around Oosterbeek. Being shelled by our own troops would be ten times worse than being shelled by the enemy. Deaths caused by one's own comrades always had the effect of lowering morale among troops more than anything else.

Half an hour had passed before the shells came in. The only thing was that they weren't British shells. The enemy were off again. The air was filled with rasping shrieks as salvos of shells came in every few minutes. The ground trembled violently under the tearing blasts. Judging from the way they were falling, I had an idea that the enemy was raking the park and surrounding area in methodical sweeps. First, a salvo would scream down way over the lane behind us. Then the next would fall a little nearer the park itself. Another batch would burst full on the park, and finally, a salvo would burst away beyond the tennis court.

Time and time again this process would be repeated. As the salvos fell nearer and nearer, we would try and force ourselves lower and lower. My legs would start an uncontrollable trembling, and I would feel Arthur's doing likewise.

It was on about the fourth creeping path of salvos that Arthur was hit. One of the shells came screaming in on its purposeful arc. It plunged in with a roar onto the running track. The earth heaved, and loose soil showered down the sides of the trench. I cringed even lower as the ugly hum of shrapnel broke ominously through the deafness that momentarily blocked my ears.

Suddenly, Arthur jerked convulsively and cried out. I looked quickly up from the position in which I had bent my head to avoid a chance hit in the head. Arthur's face, less than three feet from mine, had gone a deep grey. With his left hand he clasped his right forearm and elbow. His face twisted in pain.

'Where are you hit?' I asked, 'Is it bad?'

'Here in the arm, and God, it hurts.' replied Arthur in a faint voice. He looked as though he was going to pass out at any moment.

'Let me put a field dressing on it.' I suggested. Arthur shook his head, and moaned a little.

'It'll be best.' I went on, but again Arthur shook his head. An ugly dark stain was spreading over the arm of his smock. He hung his head on his chest and hugged the injured arm.

Another salvo whined in and we both hunched lower. Up until now I had thought our trench practically foolproof apart from a very near or direct hit. Now I knew different. I made a mental note to get some cover over our hole at the first opportunity. I kicked myself for not having done it before. The salvo burst further up the path near the tennis court.

'OK, Arthur,' I went on, 'as soon as the shelling eases, I'll help you up to the house where the first aid post is.' He feebly nodded his head. I wished he would let me put on a field dressing.

Another two or three minutes passed and I heard the next salvo fall way up on the other side of the park. This seemed the time.

'Ready, Arthur?' I asked.

'OK, Dusty.' he replied in a low voice. I got up, helping Arthur to raise himself. Quickly I pulled myself out of the trench. Arthur found it rather hard to get out, even with my help. We set off up the path towards the house, Arthur putting his good arm around my shoulder and leaning nearly all his weight on me.

As we passed the Flight Commander's trench, I called out to him and told him what had happened and where we were going.

'OK, Staff.' he replied, and then his head disappeared beneath the ground again.

The Eight Day in the grounds
of the Hartenstein Hotel

231

The park looked strangely deserted. Not a head showed above the slit trenches scattered around. We had to carefully pick our way through the debris, for the least jerk seemed to pain Arthur considerably. Smoke drifted from several shell craters. Anxiously, I scanned the sky in anticipation. I heard a shell moan over and fall way down in the woods. Perhaps it was a signal for another creeping string of shells to start off. We hurried a little more, for we both dreaded the thought of being caught out in the open. We made sure our path followed a route that took us past nearby trenches that could be utilised in an emergency.

I was thankful when at last we reached the shelter of Hartenstein Hotel. We found the entrance to the cellars outside which hung a Red Cross flag. Arthur was getting heavier and heavier, and I was glad to pass him over to a stretcher bearer who met us at the bottom of the steps.

It was dark down there, lit by a lantern and some candles. I caught a glimpse of row after row of wounded men lying on the floor packed closely together. The stench of antiseptics hung heavily on the air. More than one man was groaning and mumbling in pain. Once a man cried out in sheer agony. Peering through the dim light shed by the lamp, I saw him lying there on his stomach.

I winced as I looked, for the whole of his back was ripped and slashed, while the blood had coagulated into a black mass around the edges of the wounds. Another man standing near me said, 'I just helped bring him in; a shell burst in a tree near his hole and the shrapnel rained down on him.'

Hell, I thought, I am going to get some cover over my trench since it looks as though we are going to be stuck here for some time yet.

'All right, you two, you can get back now.' I became aware of one of the medical officers talking to us, rather sharply I thought, but then it was understandable with the hell they were working in down here and, naturally enough, they didn't want any more men than was absolutely necessary in a place where a person could hardly move around. I turned and walked out towards the steps that led up into the open air.

I started to walk up and changed my mind in a hurry when I heard the awful whooooooosh of mortar bombs flailing in. I almost fell back down the steps in my haste. The bombs burst with sharp explosions somewhere close by outside. I started up the steps again. As I did so, I heard someone yell out, 'Get those jeeps the hell out of it, otherwise we won't have any left.' The jeeps' engines roared into life. Again I was foiled as another salvo screeched in. The jeeps kept going, but I didn't. I dropped onto the steps. Again rocking explosions and whirring shrapnel. I shivered, thinking of Arthur and the man I had seen screaming in pain on the floor back in the cellar.

Forcing myself into action, I scrambled to my feet again and lunged up the steps. For a moment I paused. Smoke was drifting over the gravel drive of the house where the mortar bombs had recently fallen. I took one look and then ran, bent double, for my trench.

I threaded my way down with all speed, as though the Devil himself was at my heels. Way behind me something exploded which only served to give wings to my feet. I tumbled into my trench with all the breath knocked out of me, and fumbled for my water bottle, taking a deep swig.

Regaining my breath, I looked out. I felt strangely lonely without Arthur's company. It was going to be hateful sitting in this trench all alone. Good old Arthur, I'll be missing you. The trench, which I had come to regard with affection as a faithful friend, suddenly became repulsive to me. I no longer wanted to stay in it. Well, Hell, I wouldn't, I would find someone else who was also occupying a trench by himself.

However, I had my mind made up for me finally when the Flight Commander appeared above my head on the rim of the trench.

'Will you go up and relieve one of the men guarding the prisoners, Staff?' he said.

'I certainly will.' I replied, only too glad of an excuse to leave my trench for another.

I collected together my ripped and torn rucksack, slung my Sten and set off for the tennis court. Arriving there without the hindrance of any more mortaring or shelling, I found a man waiting to leave one of the two trenches set facing the entrance to the court. He seemed only too pleased to be leaving the spot, informing me that quite a few shells had landed within a few feet of the trenches and had, moreover, killed one of our men who still lay across the way. I took over the guard and dropped down into the vacated trench.

Looking across at the other trench about ten to twelve yards away, I saw the body of the man killed earlier on, still lying there face down, half buried by leaves and shattered branches. As I looked, a man stirred in the trench alongside which the body lay, and with a glad feeling, I recognised him as Sergeant Louis Levy, a fellow glider pilot, whom I knew pretty well.

Louis smiled across at me and called out a welcome, to which I replied with heartfelt pleasure. It was good to see someone I knew. I didn't feel so strange and lonely now.

'Who's the corpse?' I said, nodding towards the body. Louis's face went grave and he replied, 'It's poor old Jock.'

'What, not old Jock, surely?' I exclaimed, hardly believing my ears, for he was the sort of person whom one felt would never get killed.

'It's him all right,' went on Louis, 'As far as I can make out, a shell burst near the trench and slightly wounded him in the back. He thought he would go up to the first-aid post, and wouldn't wait until the shelling eased off. He got out of the trench OK, took about six paces, when another shell came in. He never knew what hit him.'

I felt bad over Jock. I had been very friendly with him, and he was one of the best, everyone liked him.

'Is anyone going to come and pick him up?' I asked, a futile query perhaps.

'Not that I know of.' replied Louis.

An ominous wail sent us both down in our trenches. The shell burst across the track in the fir woods. I stood up again, and told Louis about Arthur. He was genuinely sorry. I think Louis was lonely too, for he fell in readily with my suggestion of sticking together from now on. For my part, I was pleased, for I knew Louis to be a reliable, conscientious man.

I told him of the expected barrage. Louis seemed to have heard of it also. I looked at my watch and realised that it was nearer four than three o'clock. Calling across to Louis, I told him so.

'I know,' he replied, 'somehow, I don't think that we are going to have any barrage, unless of course', he added with a wry smile, 'it's the enemy's.'

I turned my attention to the tennis court. It looked strangely deserted. All the prisoners were sheltering deep down inside their trenches, which criss crossed the court in all directions. I could see no sign of the Prussian-like officer. Evidently he had decided that it wasn't wise to leave one's head exposed all the time. Opposite Louis' trench I noticed that a shell had blown a large hole in the wire netting, made possibly by the same shell that had stricken Jock.

An episode was about to occur which would bring me as near to death as at any time during the operation. I had been idly chatting away across the yards that separated Louis from me, when a louder than usual scream of an approaching shell sent us to earth.

The shell passed straight over and howled on down, bursting with a violent concussion about two hundred yards away in among the fir trees. I lifted my head a moment later in time to see a billowing cloud of grey smoke rise above the tree tops.

Almost a minute passed before the next one announced its approach with a distant sharp whistle growing louder and louder in an incredibly short time. Two soldiers who had been hurrying past jumped for my trench. They tumbled in as I squeezed down to one side. Falling with a final shriek, the shell sent shock waves through the earth. Sandy soil spilled down the trench sides. Again I peered over the rim. This time the shell had fallen somewhat nearer on the far side of the running track. I felt the hair tingle at the base of my scalp as I noticed that the second pall of smoke lay directly in line with the first, whose smoke had all but drifted away now. Hell, I thought, if they keep on like this they will straddle right over my trench, and possibly on it. Boom, boom came the double thud of a gun. I sank down again, every nerve taut, waiting for the tell-tale scream. The shell came in, terribly fast, much too close above our trench for my liking. The resultant explosion shook the trench violently, sending more sand then ever cascading down.

Almost afraid to look, I forced myself up. I felt the perspiration break out on my forehead, as I looked upon the rolling cloud of smoke. Even nearer this time, and still on an almost straight line.

I felt a mad desire to leap out of the trench and flee from what seemed to me the inexorable line of shells bearing down with precision on my trench. The other two men were also staring at the tell-tale drifting smoke. Boom, boom again. Oh, God, no, I thought. We crammed into the bottom of the trench, huddling close to each other as though seeking protection by doing so.

I knew instinctively that the coming shell was meant for us. For a moment I heard a thin, high pitched whistle, rising almost instantaneously to an all-pervading roar, higher than the brain could fully register. The muscles in my body tied themselves up in knots. I clawed deeper at the trench bottom.

For a moment, a terrible pressure seemed to bear down on my spine, followed by a shocking explosion, felt more than heard, that ripped my whole world wide open. An instantaneous flash of scarlet followed by an all-enveloping cloud of blackness passed over me. Something seemed to be pulling and heaving at my legs as the wave of concussion swept over and on. My chest pained for a moment, and my throat and nose were filled with the searing pungent odour of high explosives. This is the end, I thought, as my head spun round and round inside.

And then my head cleared. My eyes focused, and I found that the leaden weight around my legs and thighs was sandy soil. The sides of the trench had collapsed inwards. It was still dark, but I realised that it was caused by the drifting pall of smoke that swirled around over the trench. I lay there for a moment without being able to concentrate my thoughts on anything. The smoke cleared, and I saw the other two men were dazedly pulling themselves upright. They appeared unhurt. Unhurt! I pulled myself together, clawing at the heap of sandy soil that pinned down my legs, dragged myself up, and felt my legs, arms and chest. I seemed all right, but I still couldn't think straight.

The two men didn't say a word, but I saw them climb up out of the trench and stagger away towards the nearby path. I dimly heard another roaring coming over and slid down in a heap, waiting while I felt my whole body tremble as if from an ague. A muffled explosion penetrated my befuddled brain.

I got up again and leaned against the trench side feeling a little sick, more from the pungent fumes than anything else, I think. I found myself looking into a crater, the edge of which came within almost an arm's length of where I stood. Staring at the crater, from which whisps of smoke still rose, I stupidly tried to figure why the trench had not been blown right in.

From across the way, I heard somebody calling and, looking round, I saw Louis peering over his trench.

'Are you OK, Dusty?' he asked anxiously.

'Yes, I think so.' I found myself replying.

'Come in here, Dusty.' went on Louis. I scrambled up out and plunged across the intervening space and almost fell on top of him. I was still shaking.

'God, that was near.' I remember saying.

For some minutes I sat there, while a headache that had come on gradually disappeared. I then realised that I had no rucksack and no Sten. Wearily I pulled myself up and looked across the gap. I shivered, and sank back again with more perspiration breaking out all over me as I heard the distant boom, boom. A feeling of terror knifed through my body as the muscles in my stomach, and across my chest, tightened.

The shells sobbed down into the far side of the park and I felt myself conquering the awful tension in which I appeared to be bound. Even so, the tremors of the explosion were echoed in my legs. My clothes, from my socks up to the collar of my battle dress, were sodden with sweat and clung tenaciously to every bit of skin they touched.

I summoned up my courage and almost threw myself out of the trench and across the few yards that separated Louis' trench from my recent one. I jumped into the hole that was half filled with the loose sandy soil hurled in by the recent explosion. Feverishly, I clawed away at the soil piled in the bottom. I found a corner of my rucksack and pulled with all the desperate strength I could muster. It came free, showering sand on all directions. I clawed around further searching for the Sten and then, like a ray of light bursting through the darkness, I remembered. I had left it on the rim of the trench when I had first entered it.

I went to raise myself up, but instead cringed lower as the soft but persistent whistle of something heading over fast broke in on my turmoil of thoughts. The noise shrilled past overhead and ended in a sharp explosion over in the fir wood. I got up again and looked over the trench rim. From a pile of freshly turned soil, I spotted the barrel of my Sten poking out. Reaching forward I tugged, pulling it free, only to mutter a curse to myself and toss it to one side. It had been bent around almost ninety degrees by the bursting shell.

Abandoning the trench, I half slid across the ground back to Louis', dragging the rucksack with me. At least I had salvaged something. It shouldn't be hard to find another weapon no longer needed by its previous owner.

At the moment I did not feel like leaving the shelter of my new home. Perhaps in a few minutes' time I would feel much better and go off on a search for a weapon. I sagged back in the trench and talked with Louis about our prospects.

After chatting with him for half an hour, I began to feel much better and informed him that I would be off to seek some sort of weapon. The shelling and mortaring had returned to intermittent episodes, and I was reasonably safe in emerging from my shelter. However, I didn't intend to wander far.

I didn't have to. Just across the way from us, I came to a trench containing two military policemen. Casually, I mentioned to them that I was looking for a weapon as mine had been destroyed.

'You've struck the jackpot.' one of them replied to my surprise. 'We've got several here – take your choice.' He reached down into his trench and brought out a rifle and an American type carbine. The carbine intrigued me. It looked a nice weapon and, moreover, was considerably lighter than the .303 rifle. I took it and thanked them. All they could give me in the way of ammunition, however, were several clip-on magazines containing a number of cartridges. Possibly it wasn't a very wise choice from the ammunition point of view but, nevertheless, I wanted the carbine.

As I turned away, I almost dropped it with astonishment. From out of a nearby trench, a figure was climbing, not that it should have been a sight to cause astonishment except for one fact, and that was that the figure was a woman in a German uniform. I stared hard, thinking that I was seeing things, but the vision still persisted. No soldier could have grown hair that long in the comparatively short time that we had been here.

She turned and looked at me and half smiled in an uncertain way. Her features were, if anything, slightly Asiatic, caused I believe, by the way her eyes slanted a little. She had a figure that was a trifle on the fat side, but not enough to destroy the favourable shape she presented.

A second figure was climbing out of the trench behind her, and I couldn't help smiling, it was Staff Sergeant Joe Clark. He spotted me at the same moment and grinned in a knowing way.

'What the devil are you doing in a trench with a woman at a time like this?' I asked in sheer amazement.

'Hi-ya, Dusty.' replied Joe. 'Gee, what a job I've been landed with, watching a dame. Still, it's not bad at times.'

'But what the devil is she doing here? Who is she?' I went on.

'Well, Dusty, old man,' continued Joe, 'it's like this. The dame's a German WAAF. Apparently, she was on leave when we dropped, and some of the boys roped her in. Now she's got to stop here with us because she's seen too much to let her go back, otherwise we would send her back to her own lines. And so,' Joe went on, 'I get stuck with her, and have to sleep, eat and live in the same trench with her, and what's more, I have to take her places when she wants to go – just like I'm doing now.'

'Why, you old ram,' I couldn't help saying, 'trust you to get landed with a job like that, trust you. Where does she come from, anyway? Have you asked her?'
'Nope, she and I can't speak the same lingo, but we don't have to worry about words, do we?' he turned and leered again at the girl. She smiled back at him, although I knew she couldn't understand a word he was saying.

'Where do you live in Germany?' I asked her in the best German I could muster. It probably sounded atrocious to her, but she understood. Smilingly, she replied that she didn't come from Germany, but East Prussia.

'OK, Dusty,' broke in Joe, 'we gotta be going, otherwise the I.O. in the trench over there will start getting nasty.'

I had an idea that Joe thought he might lose the WAAF if we lingered much more. They moved off towards a copse of trees, with Joe throwing many an uneasy glance up at the sky.

I returned to my slit trench feeling safer now that I had a weapon. I never saw the WAAF again, but I do know that Joe got back to England safely.

Looking out, I was sobered up quickly. Less than three feet away lay the booted feet of Jock.

I tore my gaze from him and stared out over the trees towards where I knew the river to lie. Where was the 2nd Army? For a while my thoughts ran wild. Damn it, if something isn't done soon we'll all be corpses like poor old Jock. Where the hell was our artillery? Weren't they supposed to put down a barrage on those swine who had been hurling in shells and mortar bombs at their will for the last five or six days?

I fought down the rising tide of despondency and tried to talk sanely with Louis. He wasn't so happy himself, but he looked quite calm. A philosophic sort of fellow was Louis. Gradually, I felt myself regaining confidence.

The afternoon wore on. Only when I peered over the rim of the trench to see Jock's boots did I feel my spirits flag, but after a time I found myself surveying the mortal remains of Jock without emotion even though he'd been a friend.

As the shelling had become so sporadic, I decided that it was high time we found some wood to cover over our trench. Louis was in full agreement. I looked at the shed by the tennis court entrance. It had been riddled with flying splinters from shell and mortar bursts and looked as though it would fall down at any moment. Louis shook his head and told me that it was being kept for the purpose of putting in all the belongings of the prisoners. To hell with them, I thought, but refrained from tearing some of the planking off it. Instead, I got out and searched the area.

I found an old folding wooden chair and a few planks of splintered wood. I also collected together some of the smaller branches that had been blasted from the trees. Louis and I set to work.

I had been looking at the sky for some time, noticing that it had clouded over considerably, and I had an idea that it was going to rain in the not too distant future. This made me all the more determined to build a shelter over our heads. In my rucksack I found my waterproof gas cape. This made an ideal rain shelter spread out over the chair which we laid across the top of the hole. On top of that, we spread some branches, and then shovelled on earth to the depth of nearly a foot. One end was left open so that the view of the prisoners would be unrestricted. We then piled on more branches criss-cross fashion. We knew that it wouldn't stand anything like a direct hit, but I did believe that it would stop flying fragments of shrapnel from entering the trench. We both felt one hundred per cent safer once the job was done. We checked our food supplies. Louis had two cans of sausages and I had one. We both had some tea, which we pooled. Water was the only thing that was really short. My bottle was all but empty, and the can was about half full. Enough for today, we reckoned.

I sat in the dark shelter of the covered end of the trench while Louis took a turn at watching out of the open end. I heard someone speaking to him and recognised Lieutenant Palmer. 'Will one of you men give us a hand with Jock here?'

'I will' came back Louis without hesitation. He clambered out of the trench, and I took his place at on guard. I watched them roll the already stiff form of Jock into a blanket, then they staggered away up the path with their heavy burden. Mentally, I bid farewell to Jock as his body was borne away to its resting place. I hoped that they would not get caught in any shelling, for shells were still coming in, even if at a lesser rate.

Louis wasn't gone long, but I thought he looked a little more pale than he had been. Not that I blamed him, I didn't feel so good about it myself, and I hadn't carried Jock away as Louis had. We didn't say a word for some time. Louis was an extra special friend of Jock's.

It would soon be evening, I thought as I looked at the sky through the intertwining branches overhead. How much longer? I thought. I had lost all sense of time. I was beginning to get past the worrying stage. I had resigned myself to an indefinite stay until the shells coming in would eliminate us one by one, until it would be only a park of the dead.

The powerful roar of aero motors brought Louis and me on the alert. They were fast and light, and I knew them to be fighters, but whose? As the noise grew louder, I was positive that they were friendly. Half a minute later my supposition was confirmed. Three squat looking Typhoons crossed over the battle area at around a thousand feet. I felt elated.

My spirits soared wildly as I watched the powerful fighters swing into a wide circle. As they passed overhead, I noticed that they were equipped with a battery of rockets under each wing. Joy of joy! If only they would fire those rockets down on the enemy gun positions!

Louis' face split into a happy smile, while from nearby trenches I heard excited voices. Looking at the court, I saw some of the prisoners had left the shelter of their trenches to come and gaze upwards. One of them called out to us asking in broken English if they were British.

'Yes,' I replied, and I couldn't help adding, 'And I hope the hell they knock the living daylights out of your 'Kamaraden'.' He managed a feeble grin, and I think he got the idea alright.

The three Typhoons continued to circle, as though leisurely seeking out their targets. The enemy remained strangely quiet. Only once did I hear a machine gun clatter out, which didn't cause the fighters to deviate one foot. I suppose the enemy didn't wish to give their positions away.

These were different from the slow lumbering unarmed supply-dropping planes. These could hit back, hard. Harder than the enemy could hit them. No, it didn't suit Jerry at all. It gave me a deep sadistic pleasure to think of the enemy crouching in their trenches by their guns, each hoping that the Typhoons wouldn't attack his particular area.

I watched the leader nose over into a shallow dive. For a moment I was worried, for it appeared to be coming straight down at us. I fervently hoped that the pilot was well aware of just how the lines stood, but the fighter passed on with a low roar. A machine gun on the ground, in the direction that the fighter was heading, broke out with a harsh chatter. The Typhoon kept going.

Fascinated, I watched and waited. The rockets left the wings. They shot out ahead of the plane, leaving a trail of whitish-grey smoke. An awful tearing, rushing sound filled the air. The machine gun stopped, as if the crew had dived for shelter. The roar of the rockets in flight grew louder. The long thin trails of smoke raced ahead of the plane towards the ground and disappeared down into the fir wood.

The Typhoon arched upwards and climbed rapidly away. The rockets exploded with a vast tearing explosion. Black smoke rolled skywards over the treetops. The ground shook, even though the rockets had burst some distance away. 'Take that, you bastards. Die, you bastards, die.' I added as the second Typhoon levelled out of its dive. The tell-tale trails of smoke marked the rocket's line of flight. The Typhoon curved over and up. 'Good for you, boys, good for you.' I found myself shouting. Louis, his face lit up, also shouted into the air.

The second batch of rockets burst over the woods in a rolling thunder. More smoke shot skywards. I took a moment off to glance at the prisoners. They were standing there, grave of face, muttering amongst themselves. I had an idea that they were very glad that they were not on the receiving end.

'Well, damn you,' I couldn't help bursting out at them, 'what do you think of that?' They knew what I meant, for the English speaking one said 'Terrible, terrible.'

The third Typhoon delivered its cargo of death and again the men around cheered – that is, all except the prisoners. I watched the three Typhoons circle around, and was preparing to bid them a mental farewell, when the leader went into another dive.

'Here they come again!' I shouted to no-one in particular.

No machine gun fire met them this time. Again the spine-tingling hiss and roar of the rockets flashing through the air for their targets: again the shattering blasts.

The second and third Typhoons swept down in their unhurried dives, and more missiles added their thunder to the chaos that already reigned.

Then the Typhoons were finished. Once again, they circled the destruction they had wrought. I was sorry to see them turn for home, but they had done a wonderful job, not only for the amount of physical damage they had inflicted on the enemy, but from the point of view of morale. It had given us new hope. No longer did I feel a forgotten man. Although I knew in my heart of hearts that the 2nd Army were straining to reach us with all their power, this actual demonstration had driven home that point sharply. Actions speak louder than words.

Chapter 17

How Much Longer?

As if to vent his rage for the damage wrought upon him by the Typhoon attack, the enemy commenced a brisk shelling. On the perimeter, the small arms firing reached a new pitch. It was almost 'Stand-to' time anyway, I thought. We were due for the usual flare-up at any moment, and the fact that it had started a quarter of an hour earlier made little difference. The firing grew to a maniacal intensity, as though both sides had been spurred on by the recent air-to-ground action.

I listened to the terribly fast tearing roar of the enemy's light machine guns and automatic weapons. Somehow, these always sounded far worse than the slower beat of the heavier machine guns. Those light automatics could almost tear a man in half with a prolonged burst.

The coming of darkness forced the sharp engagement to an early termination. Men fought on, however, from time to time, in the woods between us and the river, and in the shattered village of Oosterbeek. Sometimes, a stray red tracer would dart across over the park, which disclosed no movement.

We heard the clanking and squealing tracks of the giant Tiger tanks as they prowled restlessly somewhere around the fir wood. Their toiling motors rose and fell on the night air as they crept around the perimeter; ugly death-dealing monsters, seeking a breach in the line. Too vulnerable to be risked in an all-out night attack, they fought by day, but moved very often by night to new positions within their own lines.

In the early hours of the morning, I fell into a fitful sleep. At the open end of the trench, Louis kept a ceaseless vigil on the prisoners, more so tonight because we had been warned the SS men might make a break for it. An extra Bren gun had been posted to one side of the tennis court to cover this eventuality. I awoke with a start to hear a vicious outbreak of firing in the village, two hundred yards or so away. The incessant chatter of machine guns blasted away. Grenades coughed their deep explosions, lighting up the restricted horizon of our trench.

'What the hell's going on?' I asked sleepily of Louis.

'I don't know,' he replied, 'but they have been having a right go for the last five minutes. I don't know how you slept through it.'

I got up, shivering in the cold, after looking at my watch.

'OK, Louis, I'll take over now, I've only ten minutes to go in any case.'

The hours of darkness wore on. The shattering fire died down as the hour of dawn approached. I shook Louis ready for the 'Stand-to'. He grunted something, pulled himself together and came out into the cold night air from the almost as cold shelter of the roofed-in section of the trench.

Together, we stared out into the tennis court, the outline of which was beginning to show itself with the grey light of dawn. I rubbed my sore eyelids, trying to prevent myself from falling asleep. It turned colder, and I gently shuffled my numbed feet and rubbed my hands together to try and bring some life back into them. The stubborn dawn slowly but surely drove back the shroud of night.

Louis' hunched form suddenly turned and, in a low voice said, 'Do you know what, Dusty, I've been counting the days. It's Sunday today, a day of peace and quiet.'

'That's what you think,' I couldn't help replying. 'Sunday, eh?' I went on, 'This time last week we were just preparing for the take-off.'

Brrrrrrp. The rasping burst from one of the enemy's automatic machine pistols shattered the dawn. Away down by the river a Bren beat heavily on the morning air. 'Nice and quiet and peaceful, eh?' I grinned at Louis through the half light.

Across the tennis court, the line of trees and the pavilion were taking shape. I passed my tongue over rough lips. My mouth tasted vile. Reaching for my water bottle, I drank the last remaining portion. It was icy cold, but wonderfully refreshing. Louis took a swig from his bottle.

'It'll have to be a visit to the well, I'm afraid.' I said to him. He nodded in reply. The customary 'Stand-to' battle around the perimeter had fought itself to a halt by the time broad daylight had set in. Sporadic firing, however, continued to ripple around the perimeter throughout the morning.

Breakfast consisted of some broken-up tinned sausage and tea. It tasted wonderful, and the gnawing pangs of hunger fled. Two or three of the prisoners leaned against the wire of the tennis court and looked hungrily at us. We ignored them for our rations were short enough as it was. We didn't know when we would be receiving our next ration of food ourselves.

About mid-morning, the enemy commenced their shelling again. The rise in morale caused by a good hot breakfast quickly ebbed as we crouched down in our trench, listening to the nerve-straining screams and wails of the missiles streaking in, culminating in shuddering explosions, first far away, then near, and then away again, and finally back in the park.

By midday, my nerves had gone unbelievably taut. For the first time, I felt violent emotions raging within me. I am sure that my face showed it, too. I didn't know how much more I could stand, and yet outwardly I strove hard not to show it, although I am not sure that I fully succeeded.

I looked at Louis' pale face, and knew that he too was undergoing a fearsome strain, as was every other man in the area. For the men on the actual perimeter, now down to less than two hundred yards away at its furthest point, it was even worse, although they may not have had to withstand so much shelling and mortaring, due to their nearness to the enemy lines, but what they missed in the heavy stuff, they made up for in sudden death from the belching muzzles of the enemy's small arms weapons.

During the early afternoon, the almost ceaseless shelling and mortaring had eased off, and feeling utterly worn out I stood up in our trench once more. Some of the prisoners were emerging from their trenches also. I watched one of our men go into the court and appear a few minutes later, escorting several Germans who were carrying between them two galvanised iron tubs. Ah, I thought, they're heading down to the well. I called out to the escorting guard and asked them if they were going down for water.

'That's right, do you want any brought back, Staff?' he obligingly offered, 'Give your bottle to one of these bastards.'

I beckoned one of the prisoners over and handed him my water bottle. In the best German I could muster I told him to fill it and bring it back safely – or else... He seemed only too pleased to be able to do something for me. The party hurried off down the path, casting apprehensive glances around as they did so.

Feeling better, I leaned against the trench and talked with Louis. Time went by, and I began to wonder about my bottle. It was one of my most precious possessions. Perhaps I had been a fool for giving it to the German, perhaps I should have gone myself with the party. I was downright uneasy until I saw them coming back.

Getting out of the trench, I waited expectantly by the entrance to the court. The men came stumbling along with the now heavy water-filled tubs. I stood plainly in view so that my German could see me. For the life of me, I couldn't remember which one it was, but I had relied on his recognising me. I thought they looked pretty grim as they filed past. The guard broke off and turned away to his trench as the last prisoner passed through.

'Hey,' I shouted out. They all stopped, lowering the tubs to the ground and turned around. 'Where the hell's my bottle?' I bawled out in English without thinking. They all looked blankly at me. I asked again in German that was not particularly good, I suppose. They spread their hands and one of two of them muttered.

'Now come on, which of you bastards has got my bottle?' I went on, feeling a little alarmed and angry. One of the prisoners stepped forward and said slowly in German, as far as I could understand,

'One man is dead, perhaps he has your bottle, down at the well.'

For a moment I stared at him, and then turned and hurried over to where I had seen the guard disappear into a trench. I asked him about the bottle.

'Oh, you, yes, I forgot all about it in the excitement down at the well. I had forgotten that you had given a bottle to one of the prisoners. Yes, one of them got his down at the well, by one of his own bloody snipers, too.'

'Well, I'll be damned, 'I said, 'of all the men to get shot, it has to be the one that was carrying my bottle. OK, thanks, I'll go down there and pick it up, that is, if it's still there.' I felt pretty sore over the loss of that bottle.

Hurrying over to Louis, I told him where I was going and set off down the path. I made my way around the fallen trees, feeling terribly exposed, for I could hear mortar bombs falling short on the far side of the house, and I remembered my last visit down to the well.

As I neared the bottom of the path a soldier popped up as had one the last time I had been hurrying down that path.

'Where're you going, Staff?' he asked.

'Why?' I paused to say.

'Well, you'd better be careful if you're going to the well. Snipers are still around, and they just got one of their own men who was down here for water.'

'Yes, I know, and that fellow had my water bottle too, and still has.'

I thanked him for his warning and went on round into the farmyard. I bent double as I peered around. Ah! there he was. Lying against the wall of the house was the uniformed figure of the prisoner. He lay on his back with his arms almost straight down by his sides. Doubling over to him, I noticed the ugly red stain on his left side. A small trickle of blood trailed from his mouth. I thought I saw his eyes move in his ashen wax-like face, but I guess I was wrong.

Feverishly I searched around for my bottle. Damn, I thought, where the hell did he put it? I felt the perspiration break out all over me as I crouched beside the corpse. I felt alone and more exposed than I had been on the trek down the path.

I was about to give up when I noticed the corked top of my water bottle projecting from underneath one side of the body. I pushed hard and managed to half roll him over. With one hand I tugged the bottle out. It was full, I could tell by the weight. I took one last look at the man who had died for his country, slowly stiffening in a torn and mud-caked uniform, stained with his life's blood. I could summon up no pity for him, for I had a vision of Jock before me, and the other corpses lined up in the cemetery over by the house.

I half rose to my feet and dashed into the shelter of the hedge bordering the path. The ground trembled under my feet as a salvo of bombs erupted in smoke and flame over by the house. For a moment I dropped to the ground, and almost in the same moment rose again, as I realised that they were too far away to affect me.

I arrived at our trench panting from the physical and mental exertions. I felt weak, and slumped in the trench fighting to regain my breath. Something shrilled in with a shattering roar. The sound of tumbling branches followed the explosion. I took a drink of the water and it seemed to revive me somewhat.

I looked out over the trench rim. The court appeared deserted. Then I noticed that we had company just outside the court entrance, but it wasn't live company. Another German had paid the price of war, even though he was in our hands. He sprawled on his back, one leg drawn up and both hands stiffly clawing the air as though he had fought to the bitter end for his life. His face was contorted in pain. He must have been near forty and was almost bald. I looked for signs of the wound that had caused his death but could see none, although his left eye was terribly swollen, leading me to believe that a piece of shrapnel had gone through his eye into his brain. Strangely, though, there was no sign of blood.

As I was looking at the dead German, Major Oliver appeared over from the lawn.

'Hello, Sir.' I greeted him, 'What's the news now?'

'I just thought I would let you know that the 2nd Army is going to put down a barrage, and I really mean it this time!' he replied. 'Keep your heads down in about an hour's time. Another thing, the Guards Armoured Brigade and some of the 43rd Division are just over the river from us, so everything's going OK.'

'About time too!' I couldn't help saying, although I said it with a grin. 'OK, Sir, don't worry about us keeping our heads down, we can do that all right, if nothing else.'

Major Oliver went cheerfully on his way spreading the good tidings. What we didn't know at the time was that, although the 2nd Army unit was across the river on the far side, there was no hope of their crossing over and supporting us. Heavy fire by the enemy was preventing them from crossing over to reinforce us, although several gallant attempts had been made. As a matter of fact, a company of the 43rd Division did get across at heavy loss and established themselves in a tiny perimeter covering the river crossing. This little beachhead was to help us beyond description the night we fell back. I shall always remember the great efforts the 43rd Division and the Guards Brigade made to relieve us.

I noticed that two of the German prisoners were talking to the officer in charge of the court, a member of our division, although I believe he was Polish. I watched and saw the officer nod and say something. He walked back to a trench and called out. The guard who had escorted them down to the well appeared, slinging his Sten gun.

The two Germans surged eagerly out of the court and made for the little shrapnel riddled hut opposite the entrance. I saw them reach up and tear away at the wooden planks forming its walls. So that's it, I thought. They've got permission to rip down the hut for wood to put over their trench. Well, here goes. I jumped out and hurried across, and joined in the demolition work. I thought I could work fast, but those two prisoners put me to shame. I had a hard job getting hold of two long planks. In less time than I would have ever credited, the hut vanished. Only the concrete foundation remained with a few splinters of wood to indicate that a hut had ever stood there. The pipe with a tap on the end stood out ridiculously, the only part left more than three inches high.

I broke the two planks in half and these made excellent added protection above our heads with more earth piled on top. For the first time since the shelling and mortaring had begun I began to feel reasonably secure. True, loose earth fell in greater quantities than before whenever a missile landed near, due to the piled up soil on the roof, but we felt pretty snug. We had two tins of food left, half a tinful of water and a little more in our two water bottles. I even began to lose my worst fears of the shelling.

It was late that afternoon when a new sound fell upon our ears. A long smooth moan, somehow different from those to which we had become so accustomed. In a long drawn out descending arc, the invisible missiles wailed down to burst with a thunderclap explosion about half a mile beyond the pavilion and the tennis court in the direction of Oosterbeek. For a moment I thought that the Germans had now moved artillery around between us and the river. Up until now, the shells had been coming in from directions covering three quarters of a circle. Now the circle appeared to be complete.

Another salvo crossed the heavens and then a thought flashed through my head. British shells! Our shelling! The barrage! At last. The second salvo burst heavily. Heavenly music to our ears, but a music that caused my spine to tingle and make me shiver as I listened to the deep sigh marking the path of the speeding missiles.

Again and again the ground shook under the violent concussions of the bursting shells. They came in with a methodical whistle, the resultant explosions sounding like an immense door being slammed shut in a vast hall. I heard excited voices coming from nearby trenches. Louis and I were excited, too. The aid we had waited so long for was beginning to materialise. Why, by tomorrow some of that artillery might even be across the river and moved into our positions, giving us the full support we needed so desperately.

The smiling face of Major Oliver appeared over our trench.

'Hear those guns?' were his words of greeting.

'Yes, they are ours, aren't they?' I replied.

'They certainly are,' went on Major Oliver, 'and they will be shelling tomorrow as well.' He left to spread the great news throughout the park.

Almost as suddenly as it had started, the shelling stopped. Well, it hadn't been much of a barrage, but at least it was a heartening sign. Even those few salvos must have given the enemy something to think about and a headache, literally.

Scarcely half an hour had elapsed since the 2nd Army's shelling when three Typhoons appeared over the area. Only yesterday, three of these same aircraft had sent their death dealing rockets into selected enemy positions, and now they were back to repeat their performance. As before, they circled the battle area and, as before, enemy machine gunners (they were too low and too fast for heavy AA) desisted from opening up for fear of bringing the destructive wrath of the Typhoons down upon their specific positions. Evidently, the enemy did not wish to display heroism against those imposing aircraft.

I watched the leader flip over and start down, and held my breath as the searing rockets raced ahead of the diving plane, leaving thin trails of smoke to mark their path. An ominous rush of air came above the roar of the Typhoon's motors. The plane levelled off and climbed; the rockets tore on to burst with pulverising concussions close by the area where only recently 2nd Army shells had been falling.

The second Typhoon was already on its way down before the rockets of the first had exploded. Delivering its salvo of missiles, the second Typhoon climbed rapidly. Again, the earth trembled under the tearing blast of concentrated high explosives. Dirty black smoke hung over where the first rockets had hit, and the smoke from the new batch mingled in.

The third Typhoon swept in lower than the others and pumped its rockets on down. Somewhere a machine gunner opened up, but the Typhoon swept on and up unfalteringly. The released carriers of death bored on towards their target, until they too disappeared with a thunderous roar.

Almost before the last machine had climbed up and away, the leader was bearing down fast for his second run in. More machine guns clattered out this time. For a second, I saw the Typhoon stagger as though struck, but it kept going, releasing another batch of rockets that streaked through the air with a noise like a mighty wind sweeping over high mountains. Involuntarily, I shivered as I listened to those messengers of death speeding down to blast more of the enemy into oblivion. With a breath of relief, I watched the Typhoon climb away from the chattering machine guns and the arching tracers, flashing red as they reached their steel claws skyward.

The second and third machines bored in relentlessly, without swerving once from the ever-increasing smoking and burning tracers that climbed swiftly up to meet them as they came in lower and lower. Again the air vibrated with the shock of fired rockets on their way.

Heavy explosions shook the ground, and again smoke spiralled upwards from the target area. The Typhoons did not linger this time but sped away swiftly to their home bases, having fulfilled their tasks with unswerving devotion.

As their motors faded into the distance an infuriated enemy stepped up his artillery barrage which had temporarily ceased while the Typhoons had been over the area. The park echoed with the thunderous crashes as shells and mortar bombs struck trees while still in flight. These explosions, although not making the ground tremble as did the missiles striking directly down into the earth, nevertheless sounded far louder. I was thankful for the shelter we had built over our hole in the ground.

Intermittently the queer 'Crackers', missiles fired into the park which exploded continuously for short periods, sounding exactly like rifle fire, added to the confusion. It was some time before I learned what those peculiar missiles were. At first I had an idea that snipers had infiltrated into the park during the night (several had, so I was told by a captain who was talking to us one day during a lull in the shelling) then after I knew what they were, they worried me no longer and were just a waste of ammunition by the enemy, as far as I was concerned. Like all psychological weapons, once the secret is out and one thoroughly understands them, their power is completely lost.

Night was approaching, and an overwhelming feeling of tiredness came over me. For a week now we had slept for very short hours each night and it was beginning to tell upon us. For the men in the trenches around the perimeter it must have been even worse, for they had not even our opportunity for sleep. They were constantly on the alert for an enemy who might slip through their lines at any time during the hours of darkness, or even daylight, to reach their prime objective, the Hartenstein Hotel divisional headquarters fifty yards from our slit trench. Some died on those attempts, and a few were taken prisoner.

Dusk brought an increase of firing around the perimeter. Idly, with eyes half closed in a longing for sleep, I listened to the cacophony of sound that ripped the air. For the first time, I tried to figure out what sort of casualties we must have been suffering, but gave it up straight away. There is no way one can figure that sort of thing out when one is pinned down in one area.

At long last, night drew her enveloping cloak over the surrounding landscape. A cool breeze played on my face as I watched the familiar objects fade behind the advancing blackness. The sky hung sullenly overhead, tinged with red reflected from conflagrations that raged beneath.

Shortly after night had fallen, the fierce steel-clad tanks driven by the enemy stirred uneasily around the fir wood and also in the direction of Oosterbeek. Their tracks clanked and squealed sluggishly. Motors noise rose and fell, protesting as they propelled the giants forward. Somewhere out in the black, an anti-tank gun coughed heavily, although I could not understand how the gunners could see anything through the enveloping darkness, nor could I imagine the enemy shifting their tanks towards our lines through thick woods that hid our men, waiting, ready. Perhaps some nervous gunner had fired.

The noise of the moving tanks continued for some minutes, then quiet reigned again. Even the machine guns and rifles had gone strangely silent, as though the men had collapsed of sheer exhaustion after seven days of almost continuous battle. Firing did, however, flare up from time to time and, more often than not, a short burst would start almost the whole of the perimeter into action. A battle would rage for some minutes and then die down again. The village of Oosterbeek itself was particularly active whenever the outbursts occurred. Grenades would burst with dull explosions, mingling with the violent chatter of machine guns. Flickering tracers would streak through the trees of the park as ricochets and bursts fired too high would pass over their intended targets.

The night turned colder and ate into my very bones. I shivered and shuffled my feet, and thrust my hands deep into my pockets, while my carbine rested on the parapet covering the court. I watched the glow in the sky which would flicker from time to time as a new building caught fire or a ravaged one would fall in a shower of sparks.

I was thankful when Louis emerged to take over. The pitch black interior of our roofed-in trench at least shielded one from the bitter wind, which stirred mournfully through the trees of the park as though the very dead were crying out against the ceaseless slaughter that went on day and night. I fell into an uneasy slumber in which I remained until I found Louis shaking me, telling me through chattering teeth that it was nearly dawn. I almost cried out with the pain as I moved my cramped and numbed limbs. My head was filled with what seemed to be a giant ball of cotton wool through which threaded an endless pain. My eyes ached in their red-rimmed sockets. 'Stand to' – how I hated that phrase! It stood for all that could be regarded as discomfort; coldness, wetness, lack of sleep, tension and alertness, when one's very brain cried out for rest.

My teeth chattered as I emerged out into the raw pre-dawn. Louis had left my call late, for the first signs of grey were stealing across the eastern horizon. I shivered, and tried to beat my arms in the confines of the trench. We were too worn out and cold to talk. I peered into the still almost invisible tennis court. Nothing stirred. The heavy smell of death lay on the chill morning air, tinged with the taint of high explosives.

In the village, gunfire broke out with sudden abruptness. The remainder of the perimeter was not slow in following up. The thunder of battle rose and fell, shifting from sector to sector. Monday, the 25th of September. How much longer would this go on?

Chapter 18

Portents of Doom

Full daylight was slow in driving out the night that Monday, September 25th, but at last it succeeded. I looked at the sky. Grey and sombre, portending rain. Well, I thought, we have been so lucky up until now that we could hardly grumble if we did have a downpour, although I would hate it. The air was damp and it had seeped right through to my skin. I shivered again and again, and longed to see just a few bright and warming rays of sunshine.

Immediately after stand down, we lit one of the last tablets of fuel. Thirstily I watched the water slowly come to the boil. In the second half of the mess tin, a few pieces of sausage sizzled in their own fat. The hot tea helped to drive out the coldness that seemed to start from way inside me. As full daylight arrived, the temperature rose considerably, and soon I only had a stiffness left to remind me of what a cold night it had been.

I listened to the firing on the perimeter dying down a little as I wiped around the two mess tins with some leaves. This morning the battle had gone on longer than usual. Possibly the enemy, warned by the 2nd Army's shelling yesterday, had decided that it was high time we were annihilated before reinforcements were brought over the river.

The mortaring and shelling by the enemy commenced early. Even the fortification of the warm food and hot tea could not prevent a wave of despondency passing through me as the now familiar scream of the deadly missiles beat in on my brain. Every two or three minutes my nerves would tense up as the air was split by the high pitched shrieks and wails, as the shells and bombs bored in on their path of hate and destruction.

By mid-morning the barrage slackened off, and once I timed nearly ten minutes without hearing one shell or mortar bomb falling in the immediate area. All the time, I was waiting to hear the whine of British shells coming in to smash the German positions, but up until now there had been no indication that we were going to receive that support.

On the other hand, the enemy put in a very heavy counter-attack from the direction of the much fought-over church in the village. I first noticed the increase in small arms fire beyond the pavilion on the far side of the running track, where the perimeter lay in this part of the sector.

I looked anxiously over the tennis court. Some of the prisoners had been out in the open, but now all but one had gone to earth. The solitary figure was dressed in a black SS uniform, and was one of the most evil-looking Germans it had ever been my misfortune to come across. His rank was that of a Sergeant Major. God help any of our men who had ever fallen into his hands, I thought, as I looked at him gazing out towards the sound of firing.

The crash of gunfire increased in ferocity. A heavy machine gun had joined in, almost drowning the weaker snarl of the light machine guns and the machine pistols. A Bren gun hammered out purposefully from the line of trees skirting the pavilion. Rifles cracked sharply and continuously. The black uniformed prisoner had moved forward to the wired-in side of the court that faced the sounds of battle.

The thunder of fire grew even heavier. At any moment I expected to see figures, bent double, appearing amongst the trees on the far side. I felt the perspiration form and drip off my brow. The German, still the only one exposing himself, suddenly began to call out, shouting with all his might, 'Kriegsgafangener hier, shiessen sie nicht.' ('Prisoners of War here, do not shoot') and repeated this. He clung to the wire and shouted once more. The noise of the heavy machine gun broke out thunderously near, indicating that the enemy were making headway.

I heard the sudden sigh and crack of bullets raking through the leaves of the tree just above my head. The heavy gun hammered out again. I shouted out, 'Get down, you bastard, or I'll shoot you!' The German dived for his trench. I ducked as stray bullets swept over, cutting through the foliage. I raised my head and fired towards a half bent figure running across among the trees on the far side of the track. The figure fell forwards and disappeared. A Bren gun pounded out, and the snap and snarl of the Stens rose to a feverish pitch.

Peering over the rim of my trench, I gripped my weapon with sweaty hands. The fight seemed to be gradually coming nearer. The staccato bursts of German weapons rose to a pitch of madness and seemed to have reached the very edge of the tennis courts, whilst unseen bullets whipped and cracked all around.

As I waited with heavily beating heart, I saw quick movements from the undergrowth and trees across the tennis court and then clearly I saw a German soldier in camouflaged uniform half rise, carrying a machine gun. I sighted quickly and fired and he jerked and pitched sideways. Nearby a Sten cracked spitefully and the German seemed to jerk again and lie still, just visible through the undergrowth.

Shouts and screams in German mingled with English across the court. I saw three further camouflaged German soldiers bent double, dodging among the trees and fired again – then they were gone. Almost as fast as it had built up, the firing suddenly petered out, until only sporadic bursts shattered the air. I looked over the parapet. Not a head showed. An intense stench of cordite drifted over from the line of trees in front.

As comparative quiet set in, I clambered out of the trench to stretch my legs. Some of the prisoners were doing likewise. Our intelligence officer went to the cage and I saw him talking to the Sergeant Major of the Wehrmacht, who stood at attention before him. The officer turned and, seeing me standing by the entrance, called me over.

'Staff, would you mind taking one of the men over to the remains of the pavilion to see if they can tear themselves off some planking? They are complaining that we are treating them worse than the Russians did. They say that even the Russians took them out of the firing zone when once they were prisoners. Of course, they don't know the position we are in, and we certainly can't tell them that we ourselves are surrounded and in a pretty desperate position. They might try something on if we did.'

'OK, Sir, I'm ready.' I replied.

'Well, take him along right now, will you – you might see something that's useful to yourself also while you're there.'

He turned and said something to the German Sergeant Major, who turned and, raising his voice in a parade ground fashion, bellowed out someone's name. A head appeared over one of the trenches. The Sergeant Major gestured fiercely. The man clambered quickly out of his trench and hurried over. The Sergeant Major rattled off at him in German so fast that I could not understand one word of it. The prisoner replied and then moved over beside me. I motioned him on in front and together we went out and skirted round the tennis court fence to get to the pavilion. As we neared it, I felt a little uneasy, for I remembered the recent attack aimed in the direction we were going. I also noticed the slashed and torn condition of the pavilion as we climbed up the wooden steps.

We walked over and went inside, the prisoner tearing at any loose pieces of wood. I watched him in silence, but did not take any wood myself for I considered that we had just about all we needed. I leaned against one of the walls with my carbine at the ready.

The prisoner turned to me and said in slow German 'I think I have enough, thank you.' At that moment, a trapdoor flew open in the floor. It happened so quickly that I had no time to move. I found myself staring into the muzzle of a revolver while a very deep Scottish voice called upon us to 'Raise your hands up, you ruddy Germans.' I was too startled to raise my hands as demanded. At the same moment the Company Sergeant Major, who had been covering us, recognised my uniform. 'What the bloody hell are you doing in here speaking German?' he asked. I explained that I hadn't been talking German anyway, that it was merely my escorted prisoner who had spoken.

'Well, get the hell out of here quick, or you'll get yourself shot up tailing that bastard around with you.'

'OK chum,' I couldn't help saying, 'keep your hair on.'

The prisoner bent down and picked up the wood he had dropped on the appearance of the CSM and his persuasive revolver. As we walked back, I could not help but mentally agree with the CSM that it was rather foolish to tail around with an enemy in an area where fingers were itchy on the trigger. I marvelled also at the absence of shells, but my marvelling was premature.

I saw the prisoner into the court and then returned to my trench. Louis greeted me with a grin.

'We haven't got much water left, Dusty.' he said. 'The can's about half full and my water bottle is empty.' I checked mine. Less then half full.

'Well, let's wait and see.' I suggested. 'We can always fill our water bottles with what's left in the tin.' Louis agreed.

About half an hour later we heard the first salvos from the 2nd Army units flutter and wail over. The slamming explosions echoed across the park. We stood up, listening to the speeding missiles as they moaned over and down. Grimly we smiled at each other. This was more like it. Somehow those shells seemed to have a more purposeful whine about them than the enemy ones. Perhaps it was because they were cutting over and slightly across our front, whereas we were on the receiving end of the German missiles, and did not hear their full flight as they curved in.

The shelling seemed to stir the enemy gunners, for they too stepped up their salvos. In ever increasing numbers they flailed in and down until the park shook and shuddered once more every few minutes. We crouched in the trench and listened to the shattering bursts of thunder as they exploded in the trees and the more muffled roar of those boring down into the earth, setting it shaking and trembling, sending down cascades of soil shaken loose from the sides and roofs of our trench.

Once I looked out of the opening by which Louis was half standing. The prisoners had abandoned their shuffling around the court and has disappeared well down into their trenches.

All afternoon, the British shells droned in at about fifteen minute intervals, nothing like the short intervals between the enemy's interminable shelling, but nevertheless, it was great to hear their spine-tingling flight, knowing in all probability our gunners were striving to register direct hits on the very guns that were pounding us within our isolated bridgehead.

My ears picked up the distant rumble of aero motors. I listened intently, but could not place them. I was puzzled because they sounded heavy enough for supply droppers, but were far too high. I came out of the shelter of the trench and stared up. Then I saw them, three flights of medium bombers, American built B-25.

They passed over a little to the east flying at around five or six thousand feet. The distant thunder of enemy AA broke out and I watched the sudden blossoming of the little grey-black puffs of smoke marking the exploding shells in the heavens. The Mitchells flew steadily along without deviating. At first, most of the AA bursts were way behind, but they rapidly began to range in.

Now the exploding shells were right among them. I felt a sudden tightening of my throat as I saw one of the machines, flying to the rear of one of the formations, break away and start down in a steep dive. A thin trail of black smoke trailed out after the falling plane which keeled over until it was in a vertical dive. The motors were running almost wide open. Faster and faster the machine fell, the smoke trailing behind in a straight line with the speed of the dive. In vain, I waited to see the tell-tale white parachutes blossom out.

I could hear the roar of the twin motors above the noise of the rest of the aircraft droning on and the grunting of the anti-aircraft guns. I was unable to tear my gaze away from the doomed machine as it plummeted earthwards at a speed I never thought would be possible for that type of machine without it breaking up on the way down.

Moments later, it vanished behind the distant trees. A muffled explosion reached my ears a few seconds later. A column of oily black smoke spurted upwards and hung in the sky. I estimated it must have fallen some miles away, around Arnhem. I dragged my eyes from the smoke that marked the pyre of a brave crew, and looked up at the formation still continuing on its way without taking evasive action.

I saw a cloud of bombs fall away from the bellies of the machines. I lost sight of them almost immediately, but followed their path downwards by instinct. The formation was already turning homewards before the bombs struck. The ground trembled for several long seconds and a deep muffled roar reached my ears. A few moments later the earth again shook and a second rumble drifted across. I estimated that the bombs must have fallen in the direction of Utrecht, north of Arnhem. The Mitchells vanished from sight still turning, pursued by the relentless flak that had already sent one of their machines to its doom.

Louis and I looked at each other without saying a word. In one way, I felt elated and yet in another I felt despondent. The enemy had been hit hard, that we did not doubt, but it had cost us several gallant men and a machine to do so.

We huddled down in our hole as the enemy methodically raked the park again and again from end to end with their mortars and shells. We listened to the wicked hum of shrapnel from the near hits and thanked our lucky stars again and again that we had built a substantial roof over our heads.

The afternoon wore on, and at one time I was pleased to hear the distinctive moan of the 2nd Army's shells boring in on the enemy. The subsequent explosions made me shiver, even though I knew they were falling on the enemy and not on us. The barrage was short lived, however, and very sporadic as though the gunners were conserving their ammunition.

We filled our water bottles from the biscuit tin and found that we had only a small amount left. However, I did not feel like another trip down to the well. The shelling and mortaring, although by no means paralysing, was fairly frequent, and sometimes very close. The small arms firing seemed to have crept in closer also; I had no idea what the situation was like down at the well either, and I didn't feel very keen on finding out. I had the feeling the British-held pocket was getting smaller and smaller. It was almost dusk, and I felt a little apprehensive about the whole thing. No, I would leave it until tomorrow morning when broad daylight would give me more courage.

I looked up at the first signs of evening setting in and felt drops of rain on my face. Well, it was here at last, I thought. The rain increased and beat down harder. Some of it trickled through the roof and I had to move slightly to one side to avoid a steady drip, drip that persisted at my end. I noticed that my waterproof gas cape which I had spread over our trench, underneath the wood and earth, was bulging a little where some of the rain was gathering.

I had a sudden brainwave and thought I would see how the rain water tasted off the gas cape. If the worst came to the worst, we could catch it in our biscuit tin. I tilted the bulge towards a slit in the cape and caught the little stream of water in my palm, and sucked in thirstily. I was almost sick, and spat the water out faster than I had taken it in. It was absolutely vile after being in contact with my gas cape. I knew then that I would have to be almost dying of thirst before I would sip that water again.

The rain slackened off and almost stopped and I looked up at the grey skies. The air smelt clean and fresh after the downpour, but it also accentuated the odour of the dead. The peculiar smell hung tenaciously on the air, as did the smell of cordite and other explosives. Undoubtedly we were in for more rain, and I began to think about trying to make our hole more waterproof.

As Louis and I stood contemplating our home, with one ear cocked ever on the alert for the first whisper of hot metal sliding swiftly through the air in our direction, a soldier came through from the path by the lawn. He crossed over towards us and coming right up close whispered quietly that we were to report to the Flight Commander's trench immediately. I wondered over the mysterious air exuded by the man, but he was moving off to the next trench before I could question him.

I picked up my carbine, having an idea that another patrol was in the offing. I didn't feel at all like patrolling at the moment, but one has no choice in such matters at a time like this. I guessed someone must be left to watch the prisoners, for there were trenches guarding the court at each corner and some alongside, although not all were occupied.

With Louis, I set off for the Flight Commander's trench. It was almost dusk now. Machine guns and rifles kept up a steady thunder on the nearby perimeter. Usually at dusk the shelling practically ceased, but this evening there wasn't much sign of that happening.

We reached the trench to find a dozen other men there already. More were approaching. I sensed something unusual, but was genuinely surprised when I heard about it.

Captain Walchli stood outside his slit trench, more unshaven than I had ever seen him. He looked at us rather grimly and said,

'Keep your mouths shut about what I'm going to tell you or you may muck up the whole plan.' We looked at him with a new interest.

'Well,' he continued, 'we've had it.' I felt the hair raise on the nape of my neck. We all crouched down instinctively as a shell howled in close by, but straightened up again after the explosion.

'Well, as I was saying,' Captain Walchli went on, 'we've had it. Tonight we pull out.

'It won't be an easy task, and we won't all get back over the river. General Montgomery has ordered our withdrawal. It has been found impossible to get men and supplies across the river owing to the enemy shelling and machine gunning. We ourselves cannot hold this bridgehead any longer, so back we go.'

He paused to let his words sink in. No one moved or said a word. All looked at him expectantly to hear the rest. Captain Walchli went on,

'The pull-out starts at 10 p.m. I want you all here at 8.30 p.m. The men on the far side of the house will begin the withdrawal. All the glider pilots are going to be put out as guides. It'll be pitch black tonight in the woods with this rain. Our flight will be the first guides, beginning right here in the park. Others will be spread out as far down towards the river as is practical. No one must leave before the last man is through. In other words, you will be the last men to leave this park. Get it?'
We did.

Captain Walchli continued, 'The last of the men should pass through by 11.00 p.m., but we will give them a few minutes over, and then we'll beat it. Another thing, we will be passing through enemy-held woods, so no talking. Put socks or some cloth over your boots. Nothing must clank, and blacken your faces if you like. OK, any questions?'

'Yes.' I replied, 'What about the prisoners?'

'Oh, yes,' said the Captain, 'I want two volunteers to stay with them until about midnight, or if the enemy arrives earlier, to get away as quickly as possible.' I looked at Louis and shrugged my shoulders. Well, it looked as though we were the unlucky men. I turned to Captain Walchli to tell him that as we were already on guard duty there, I supposed that we might as well continue to do so. Before I could open my mouth, a man whom I did not know said 'Mac and I will stay, Sir – we don't mind, and we would rather travel alone, anyhow.' I looked at him in surprise. Somehow I felt I would rather take my chance along with the rest in an organised party than risk trying to sneak through on my own. I didn't argue with him; for my part I was greatly relieved, as I was sure Louis was too.

'OK, then,' said Captain Walchli, 'be back here at 8.30 sharp.' The group broke up.

It was almost dark now. Louis and I hurried back to our trench. I looked at the few prisoners who were standing beside their trenches in the drizzling rain, looking a sorry lot. If they only knew, I thought.

I checked over my torn rucksack. It was practically useless, so I took out the change of underclothing and a few other odds and ends and dropped the rucksack in the trench. I stuffed the underclothing inside my smock, together with a few sweets I had over from the forty-eight-hour ration packs I had brought in with me. Night had set in and we had nothing to do but wait until the hour of 8.30 pm. We listened to the thunder of battle, which raged around the perimeter. The enemy's shelling and mortaring continued with unabated violence despite the fact that darkness had fallen. Missile after missile bored in and exploded to the accompaniment of falling trees and whirring shrapnel. The rapid bursts of light machine gun fire raged more fiercely than ever. The Brens tapped out their defiance in short bursts. For a while, I wondered if the enemy had learned of our intentions, and was making every effort to cave in our lines before we could form up for the retreat.

The 2nd Army shells had started to whine in also, adding their thunder to the din that already was almost terrifying. I began to hope and pray that I would not be hit during those last few hours. That would be calamitous after surviving for so many days amid the flying steel and blasts.

I checked to see if I still had my notes and drawings. They were still there, a little crumpled and muddy, but nevertheless safe.

As the minute hand of my watch moved nearer and nearer to 8.30 p.m. I felt my heart beat a little faster. I began to glance more and more frequently at the faintly illuminated figures on the dial. I didn't want to be a minute late. Louis was constantly looking at his watch also.

The last thirty minutes went by with agonising slowness. I felt the perspiration forming on my brow. My ears, now thoroughly attuned to the variations in the sound of falling shells and mortar bombs, began to register that the enemy's shelling was shifting to the woods between the park and the river. I felt even more certain that the enemy knew of our plans, and that we were in for it when we left the slit trenches in the park and penetrated the dark dripping woods towards the river.

The minute hand on my watch closed in on the half-hour mark. I looked at Louis through the gloom of our shelter.

'OK?' I queried. Louis replied 'Yes, I'm ready, and it's 8.30. Let's go!'

Chapter 19

Retreat Across the Rhine

We shouldered our weapons and clambered up over the edge of the trench. A steady drizzle was falling and a cold wind was blowing up. I shivered. I took one last look at the tennis court inside which nothing moved. We stepped out onto the path and made our way down to the Flight Commander's trench. Several other figures had already gathered there. The darkness was almost impenetrable, and I knew that it would be even worse in the woods. Gathered round Captain Walchli's almost invisible form, we listened to his latest commands.

'Nothing's altered, men' he said. 'The retreat starts at 10.00 p.m., as I said before. I'll put you out in your positions in half an hour to make sure that we are in our right places in plenty of time. Remember, no firing under any circumstances until the order is given. If you are fired upon, just lay doggo, unless you are forced to fire back. If the enemy gets even an inkling we are pulling out, God help us. He'll put down a barrage of artillery that'll probably wipe us all out. Well, that's all. If you haven't covered your boots, do so right now.'

He moved off to another spot, and Louis and I sat down on the edge of Captain Walchli's trench. I fished a pair of almost dry, and brand new, socks out from my smock. I had to rip them to get them over my boots. It almost hurt to do that – socks weren't easy to come by. After much tugging and pulling, accompanied by a stream of swearing, I managed to get most of the socks over my boots. I stood up and moved around. I felt a little strange, and sat down again on the trench parapet.

The rain increased and, between bursts of firing when a lull occasionally occurred, I heard the wind sighing through the broken and shattered branches of the trees. The cold wind played around my face, biting through my smock and battle dress, both of which were already very damp. I shivered.

A shell whirled down with a scream and fell in the park area. I slid quickly down into the shelter of the absent Flight Commander's trench. A lurid glow suffused the horizon of a moment as the thunder of the explosion rolled across. I shivered again, but not only because of the cold.

I glanced at my watch. Ten minutes to nine. Captain Walchli's voice floated softly down, saying,

'OK chaps, come on out. Let's go!'

With a heart that beat a little faster than usual, I pulled myself up and out, in company with two other men. The darkness seemed even more enveloping since I had last been outside the trench, while the rain dripped down continuously. We gathered around our Flight Commander. He called out one man, and assigned him to the very spot we were standing on.

'Right, Sergeant' he whispered to the man, 'You are the first one. When the men begin to file back here, direct them down in this direction.' He pointed out into the darkness. 'I'll post the next man about fifty yards further on, and this will be repeated for the next half mile to a mile down towards the river. Don't stay in the shelter of a trench, otherwise the men will never see you. You'll have to stay out in the open. When the last man passes through at about eleven, you tail on behind. That applies to each man I put out. And don't tarry, as there will be no other troops apart from stragglers, unless it's the enemy – OK?' The man acknowledged his orders, and Captain Walchli whispered for the rest of us to follow him.

We cut diagonally across the path, away from the farmhouse, and about fifty yards past where we had left the first guide we halted again. I was standing close by the Flight Commander. Peering through the darkness he recognised me, and said, 'OK, Staff, you take the next post. Go down to the edge of the park by the road, about another ten yards further on, and take up a position there. I want you to direct the men along the road in this direction,' and pointed towards where the entrance to the farmhouse lay.

'Right, Sir.' I replied. He vanished into the deep gloom with the rest of the men following closely behind.

I went forward slowly and alone, feeling my way carefully. Once I stumbled into a shallow crater left by a mortar bomb, but regained my balance and moved on. I came to the fence that bordered the lane. Most of it was down and lying across the lane, shattered by shellfire. Half off the road, I made out the dim shape of a jeep and I walked over to it. This, I decided, would make as good a site as any. I came up to the jeep and peered closely at it, wondering why it was abandoned. I soon learned why. The metal was riddled and slashed by shrapnel. All the tyres were torn to ribbons, and one wheel had buckled underneath the slanting body. In the faint light given off by a smouldering fire from across the lane, the mangled jeep presented a grotesque sight.

I sat on what remained of one wing, and stared out into the blackness of the park. The rain fell unheedingly upon me. The chilling wind cut through my now thoroughly wet clothing. Again and again I shivered. I felt terribly lonely after the company of Louis, and the almost impenetrable blackness of the park did nothing to help relieve this feeling.

I listened to the roar of battle across the far side of the park in the village of Oosterbeek and realised that within a few hours I would be away from that hateful village and its carnage of death.

From the direction of the river came the now almost continuous drone of shells from the 2nd Army's guns. They sighed and moaned over and down into the enemy lines on the far side of the park. Explosions followed that made the very ground tremble and shake under my feet.

The enemy's mortars and eighty eights were busy also. They slammed their shells and bombs across in retaliation against the woods through which we would have to pass, and the night was alive with their vicious explosions. Most of them howled down in the area slightly to my left and behind me as I faced the park, sitting on the jeep's wing. I was poised to fling myself to the ground should the direction of the shell's flight, from either side, change to my detriment.

Some of the British shells were falling short, that I could tell. Occasionally, the droning missiles coming in from across the river would bore in and down and burst

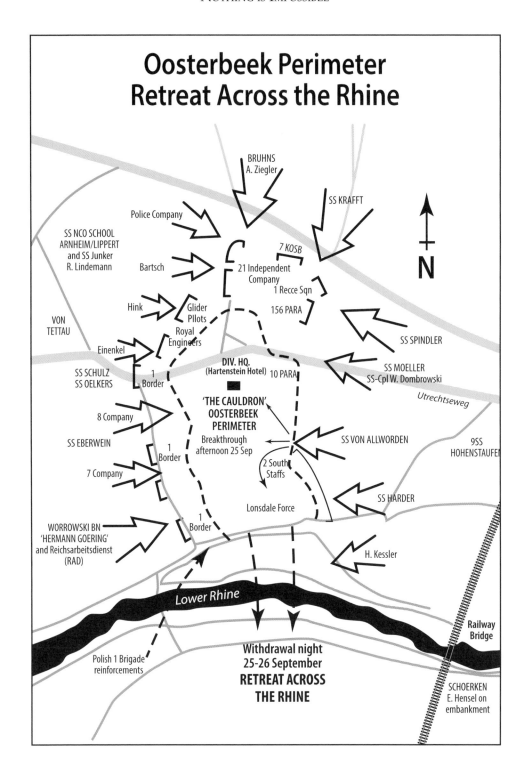

Oosterbeek Perimeter
Retreat Across the Rhine

short across the lane, some one or two hundred yards back. Falling branches and lurid flashes would follow each strike.

From the direction of the town of Arnhem a red glow silhouetted the trees ahead of me. The sky looked sullen and angry as though protesting against the useless slaughter and destruction. The low lying rain clouds accentuated the Dante's inferno that raged below.

I plunged for the ground as a shell drilled in. I fell on my face and clawed the ground in an effort to get half under the jeep. I couldn't worm underneath, and from the corner of my eye I saw the trees on my left suddenly stand out against a vivid red flash. Red hot metal fountained up and outwards from the centre of the burst. Darkness fell again almost immediately. The hair on my scalp tingled as I heard the ugly hum of spinning shrapnel.

I tried harder to squeeze under the jeep, and grazed my cheek in trying without success. A second missile howled in but burst a little further away. The warm sweat from my body mixed in with the cold penetrating rain on my skin under my clothes. Again the vicious hum of flying jagged steel. Again I hunched up in an agony of anticipation. And then it was over.

Limply, I eased my head out from under the jeep. I let loose a stream of curses to ease the tension that raged through me. At the same time, I became aware of a repugnant smell and cursed even louder when I discovered that I had plunged down into what I believe was cow dung. I cleaned off as much as I could, circumstances and light permitting, but without much success, a fact that I was reminded about many times later on by my comrades, who didn't consider me much of a comrade while the stench still clung to me. I would have cheerfully shot the animal there and then if it had been foolish enough to turn up at that moment, orders or not.

I glanced at my glowing watch dial and wiped off the rain that distorted the figures under the glass. Nine forty. In twenty minutes the first of the men would be approaching us if the retreat went off to time.

I heard footsteps moving softly towards me and then saw a dim figure. I quietly raised my carbine and covered it, my finger curling on the trigger. At the same time, I sank down on one knee in the deep shadow provided by the jeep's mutilated bodywork. Then I heard Captain Walchli's voice floating quietly over.

'Are you there, Staff?'. I relaxed, lowered my carbine and, rising up, called out softly in acknowledgement. He moved over to me.

'Are you OK, Staff?' he asked, 'I heard a couple of shells fall in the vicinity.'

'Yes, I'm OK, Sir.' I replied.

'Well, follow me.' he continued. 'We've changed the line of retreat a little as there are not quite enough of us to act as guides the way it is. I've got a new position for you.'

I followed closely on his heels, glad to leave the jeep area for more than one reason. We stumbled over the uneven ground, past the dark forms of shattered trees, until we came to a spot which I recognised as the farmyard, dark though it was. However, it was a little lighter than the place I had just left. Then I saw why. Across the yard the hayrick I had seen on my visits to the well was burning, throwing out a faint glow that lit up the farmhouse and yard. In the centre of the yard we stopped.

'OK, park yourself here, Staff.' said the Captain, and without further ado, crossed over to the farmhouse and passed in through the doorway. Then he pushed his head around the doorpost.

'Direct them out onto the road and tell them to turn left and follow it along until they come to the next guide, OK?'

I replied 'Yes, if I am still alive.' with a wry smile to myself. I was thankful for one fact, however, and that was that at least in this new position I was near some of my comrades, for I could hear Captain Walchli talking to them inside the farmhouse.

I looked apprehensively out towards the ring of blackness that lay beyond the glow thrown out by the hayrick. Across the way was the area in which the snipers were supposed to be lurking, unless they had been eliminated. The main enemy lines were only about three hundred yards away.

I listened to the missiles criss-crossing unseen in the night sky above. Instinctively, I half crouched and edged a little nearer the doubtful shelter of the farmhouse walls whenever a shell burst in the vicinity and shrapnel hummed down, striking with a deep thud into the ground and clattering on the broken roof of the house itself. The yard was covered with broken tiles and glass which crunched loudly under my feet whenever I moved.

At the sound of my movements, Captain Walchli peered out of the doorway and, seeing that I had moved over into the shelter of the walls, said in a most apologetic voice that, although it was uncomfortable for me to stand out in the centre of the yard with shrapnel falling around, I had better get back there, otherwise the column of men coming down through the park would not see me.

Reluctantly, I moved out into the centre of the yard again, feeling dreadfully naked and exposed and also alone. I peeped at my watch, and noted that it was five minutes to ten. Well, perhaps I wouldn't have too long to wait. The last man was timed to pass our spot in about one hour if the men were able to disengage and pull out on time.

The low rumble of artillery from across the river persisted and the shells fell in what I thought was an increasing number in the woods below the park. Some continued to whine overhead, falling on the far side of, and beyond, the park. Our artillery was really giving the enemy something to think about, which was part of the idea, I suppose, whilst with luck our withdrawal could be carried out.

Ten o'clock. I tensed and increased my vigilance. Captain Walchli had come out of the farmhouse and was standing in the shelter of the wall. We carried out a low conversation while I kept sweeping the surrounding blackness with a penetrating gaze, searching for the first signs of the men falling back. Five minutes went by, and then ten. I began to wonder if all was going to plan.

The drizzle continued to fall from the low red-tinged clouds. I peered anxiously into the blackness beyond the immediate vicinity of the yard. The footpath vanished into the deep gloom up towards the house. The minutes ticked by as I constantly glanced at the wet dial of my luminous watch.

10.15 p.m. I really began to feel uneasy. Then I heard a faint sound of muffled footsteps approaching through the darkness from the direction of the house. I tensed, waiting, silhouetted clearly against the glow thrown out by the still burning hayrick. If these weren't our men, my end was near. I was tempted to move into the shadow of the farmhouse wall, but Captain Walchli's warning beat inside my head. I felt warm beads of perspiration break out on my forehead, mingling with the cold of the rain.

With straining eyes, I stared hard. I saw the first figure materialise into the fringe of the glow. I called out a challenge. With beating heart, I awaited the reply. The dim figure stopped in its tracks and a wave of relief passed through me when the single word 'John' floated over in a low voice.

'Bull,' I replied. 'Advance to me.'

The dim figure moved into the centre of the glow and came over. His face was blackened, and around his feet was wrapped some sort of cloth. Behind him, at intervals, more men appeared out of the dripping night.

In a low voice I directed him on and without another word a long line of men began to file past me, their feet, although muffled by an assortment of cloth and sock coverings, crunched over the broken tiles and glass. The noise seemed excessive to my sensitive ears. It was clearly audible above the almost continuous thunder of exploding missiles in and around the woods just behind us. For two or three minutes the hunched and dim forms crossed the yard, each silhouetted for a fraction of a second against the glow of the burning hayrick, and then they were gone.

I felt better now that I had actually seen the first of the men going by. I eagerly awaited the next column. Smoke from the hayrick drifted across the yard, smelling almost pleasant. Occasionally, a portion of the stack, still untouched by the rain, would burst into a short-lived flame which was reflected on the whitewashed walls of the shattered farmhouse, throwing the surrounding park into an even deeper darkness.

A second column of men emerged from out of the gloom. I challenged again, and received the correct answer. The men filed past, moving as quietly as possible over the littered yard. A flame leaped up for a second as they passed, and I caught a glimpse of their haggard and worn faces, despite the dirt they had rubbed into their skin to help merge them into the deep black night. The flame died and the remainder of the column moved by. Not a word was spoken as the tired, weary men, still unbroken in spirit, toiled on to vanish past into the wet blackness of the night and to the river, and freedom.

As the last man disappeared out into the lane, I looked at my watch – 10.30 p.m. More shuffling men came out of the all-enveloping blackness, feet muffled, weapons held firm, but at the alert, held so that none could clash together. The rain increased, and now I felt its full force against my skin. I shivered as the wind stirred more and more. In my intense concentration on the men who arrived every minute or two out of the night, I hardly felt the numbing bite of the cold wind through my soaked clothes, but I shivered involuntarily all the same.

Still they came. In batches of five, in batches of ten, and sometimes in greater numbers, all shuffling silently along, some bent, some upright, some supporting others less fortunate than themselves, men wounded, but refusing to be left behind, the remnants of a proud fighting division. I felt a wave of bitterness pass through me. They did not complain. Yes, they had taken it, taken more than any soldier could be expected to take and still carry out an organised retreat. But they had also given it too as about one thousand five hundred German corpses testified, a figure that was admitted by the enemy later as well as confirmed by our own men. Yes, the enemy dead littered the woods, and the ruins of Oosterbeek and Arnhem, and the village of Renkum in and around which a detachment of our men had fought on until overwhelmed earlier in the battle.

10.45 p.m. In long and short lines the men continued to converge on this little battle scarred corner of the park. One column gave me quite a turn, emerging as it did from out of the blackness in the direction of the ploughed field beyond the well. I had sunk down on one knee when the leader appeared out of the gloom without warning, and I challenged with a throat that had suddenly gone dry, and only when the word 'John' came quietly but sharply out of the leader's mouth did the tension leave my body.

A shell burst close by as this column filed through. Without a pause, the line continued on, although in the light sent out by the hayrick, I saw every man turn his head in the direction of the explosion. I cringed a little as the flying fragments of steel whirred and ripped through the air, striking the now sodden earth with a deep thudding sound. The line bent over a little more, but kept going.

The small arms fire over on the far side of the house had all but ceased now. I wondered again if the enemy knew.

I could detect that 2nd Army shells were droning over our heads in increasing numbers and bursting beyond the house on the enemy positions. That would keep their heads down and help prevent them from learning that the front before them was gradually disintegrating as the men who had held the trenches for so long fell back to the river.

However, I noticed that more and more outbursts of firing were breaking out in the woods between us and the river and in the direction which the line of men were taking. Evidently our men were running into enemy patrols and positions. The rhythmic beat of a Bren echoed out in company with the cracking Stens, while in retaliation, the sharp and horribly fast enemy machine pistols and light machine guns blasted back. Grenades burst with heavy detonations deep down in the black dripping woods. Men were dying out there in their efforts to break out of the enemy ring, dying that those who followed might pass through the gaps torn in the enemy's line, paid for in blood.

Nearly eleven o'clock. I began to get restless. The number of columns was becoming less and less, and very infrequent. I had an idea that most of the men had passed through. Now the groups consisted of three, four or five men only. I stopped one leader and asked him if he knew how many more were behind him. He replied that he wasn't sure but that there were not many left, in fact they might all have gone.

I saw Captain Walchli at the door and passed on this information. He acknowledged it, but suggested that we stay a little longer just in case more might come. Somewhere out on the left a shell exploded and the sound of a tree crashing earthwards reached my ears. Another shrilled in and burst. That part of the wood had been receiving a lot of attention from one side or the other for the last hour. The sky over Oosterbeek had turned a deeper red as though fresh conflagrations were breaking out beneath. The horizon constantly flickered with flashes from bursting shells and mortar bombs.

At 11.15 I felt distinctly uneasy. Fifteen minutes over the allotted time. The sweat ran down the small of my back with the tension I was feeling. When I did eventually hear muffled steps approaching through the wind and rain-swept darkness, my stomach muscles tied themselves up in knots. I blinked the perspiration out of my eyes and with beating heart, waited in an agony of suspense. My relief was indescribable as a decidedly Cockney voice answered my challenge, forced out from the very pit of my stomach. Again, I asked if any more troops were coming.

'Not that I know of, chum.' was the weary figure's reply. 'If I were you, I'd get the hell out of here. I'm pretty sure that we are the last. At least, we were told that we were the last to leave the front on the far side of the park.'

I left the centre of the yard and crossed over to Captain Walchli. He listened to my report and nodded his head thoughtfully as he leaned against the wall just inside the doorway of the farmhouse.

'OK Staff, but just to make sure, we'll give them five minutes more. That'll make it 11.30, and then we'll march off.'

I returned to my post. Damn, I thought. I looked longingly towards the blackness into which the last line of men had disappeared. It would be horrible to get maimed by flying shrapnel at the last moment, or possibly killed, after having survived nine days of shelling and mortaring, small arms fire and aircraft strafing. I didn't want to lie here in this rain-soaked park, rotting beneath the leaves and tumbled branches like Jock. The smell of death hung closely over the park.

By 11.30 no other person had passed. We were alone. I knew it. Captain Walchli called out softly to me,

'OK Staff, let's go.' He stepped out through the doorway. I walked quickly over.

Several other men emerged from the farmhouse. I recognised some of them in the faint reddish glow. I caught a glimpse of Sergeant Hedman whom I knew pretty well, as he was an inmate of my hut back on Fairford aerodrome. We greeted each other in low tones and there and then decided to team up, for I had not seen him since we had been separated and appointed our allotted posts.

'OK men', said Captain Walchli, 'Let's go. No talking and don't bang your weapons together. Silence is essential. We'll try and catch up with the last column. Keep close together. We're going to find it pretty dark in the woods, so I think that it'll be a good idea if you undo the tails of your smocks, and each man can hold onto the one in front.'

Captain Walchli took a long look at the map he held, tilting it over so that the flickering flames that had burst forth on the hayrick could illuminate it. Then we were off. Out through the gate and onto the lane, where we turned left.

In silence, we tramped along in sock-muffled boots. The night seemed darker still, now that we had left the farmyard. The rain fell without respite. I had a vague idea of the route we intended taking, but soon lost my bearings after we turned off the lane and descended down a long track that plunged through thick woods. The darkness was impenetrable. I grasped the tail of Sergeant Hedman's smock while I felt the man behind me take a firm grip on mine. It was almost impossible to see the man in front, even though he was but an arm's length away.

From time to time we halted, and I could hear the rain dripping off hundreds of branches on either side. It was cold, bitterly cold, and I shivered time and time again. I found it hard to prevent my teeth from chattering. Whenever we did stop, it was accompanied by soft oaths that rippled back along the line as man after man bumped into the one in front who had halted unseen in the pitch black. Occasionally, a rifle would clank sharply against another when this happened. Hissed phrases such as 'Mind your bloody rifle, you just poked me in the eye with it.' and 'Quiet, you stupid oaf.' would break out.

On our left, shells drummed in and burst with monotonous regularity. The ground trembled whenever they fell near, accompanied by the sounds of falling branches as tree after tree fell victim to the flying steel and blasting high explosives. The blackness of the woods was broken by the bursts of flame from the explosions.

We halted longer than usual just after we had emerged from the woods. The distant fires in Oosterbeek and Arnhem threw a faint light into the clearing we had just entered. On our left, a tree-clad hill reared sharply up. I saw a line of dim forms approaching down the slope. We sank down on the saturated ground. I heard a faint whispered challenge from Captain Walchli in front. Somebody replied. We got up again. I looked at the line converging with ours. It seemed quite long.

We moved on with the men from the hill joining in as we passed. In one way I was relieved, for now I did not have the feeling of being the last, for men were still slipping down between the dark outlines of the trees and were now joining on the rear of our own line.

Plunging into the woods again, I lost sight of Sergeant Hedman and grabbed hold of his fast disappearing tail. We moved slowly, and the whole line was continually stumbling over fallen branches.

We came out of the woods once more and I glanced back at the way we had just come. From the direction of the park I could hear the almost constant sound of bursting missiles, and an angry red glare hung over the whole area. Lurid flashes would light up the thick woods for a moment, then die down again. The enemy were certainly blasting the park tonight. Well, you swine, I thought, you're too late, the birds have flown.

Ahead of us the night was split by the harsh crash of gunfire. We crouched down. A shower of tracers flashed diagonally across our front. A grenade burst heavily. There was a shout, and silence followed. We moved forward again, crossing what I made out to be, in the almost pitch dark, a vegetable garden. On our left I made out the dim outlines of a small building. We skirted the house and entered more woods. Slipping and stumbling, we made our way forward more by instinct than by sight. On through the saturated woods we went, the rain running off the overhanging trees and falling upon our already sodden clothing. My hands had gone stiff and numb from the icy impact of the rain.

Intermittent machine gun fire hammered forth from both flanks and in front. Sparkling tracers arched and bored through the darkness. The invisible line of men moved on slowly but surely. Once I stumbled into what I thought was a small shell crater. I plunged forward on my face and, swearing terribly, I lost my grip on Sergeant Hedman's tail. I dragged myself up immediately and lunged forward into the blackness, bumping into him more by luck than judgement. The man behind had also lost contact with me, but he soon caught up and I felt his grasping fingers clawing at my back as he found my smock tail.

Wiping the perspiration and cold rain from my forehead with an almost lifeless hand, I peered into the night. How much farther, I wondered? Branches whipped and stung my face as they sprang back from the invisible form of the man in front. Then we were out and clear of the woods. In the uncanny light thrown out by distant fires, we found ourselves tramping silently down a track that showed up rough and white against the wet black-looking soil on either side.

A skirmish was being fought a few hundred yards away on our right. Tracers flashed to and fro, accompanied by the echoing thunder of the shots. Some ricocheted and shot away into the night sky until they burned out and vanished. The fight continued, but the line of men ignored it. They had been ordered to avoid large scale fighting at all costs lest the enemy detect our retreat. In an all-out battle, we would be scattered and annihilated.

We kept on going, shuffling along in silence. Now the firing was behind us. A farm building, squat and of a dirty white colour, loomed up out of the night. We passed this silent and deserted dwelling and crossed over a tramway track.

I looked back. We were well out of the woods now. Its great dark mass faded away to either side and behind us. About a mile along on the right hand side of the woods towards Arnhem, a huge mass burned furiously, which explained the comparative lightness that hung over the wide stretch of field we were about to cross.

We started to file across the field, which felt wet and soggy under my boots. We only covered about fifty yards when I saw the dim form of Sergeant Hedman stop and sink down. At least in this faintly illuminated field we didn't crash into each other every time we stopped.

I followed suit getting down on one knee. Staring hard into semi-darkness ahead, I could make out a dim mass of men lying down about two or three abreast and vanishing into the gloom towards the far end of the field. The minutes ticked by and I lay down full length on the sodden ground. I found that we were lying alongside a wire and post fence that disappeared into the distance. Some of the wire close to me had been broken, as was the post close by my head.

As my eyes became more accustomed to the darkness I could make out that the level ground in the near vicinity had been shelled and mortared, for craters were scattered around. I felt uneasy at the sight, for there was no way of telling how fresh they were. God, I thought, if we get caught out here in the open, we will be blown to pieces.

There was not a scrap of cover. Only the shallow shell and mortar craters offered slight but totally inadequate protection. Not even a ridge of earth, if the enemy started to machine gun the field.

I hoped and prayed we would not be here long. So far, we had made good time, and halts had amounted to only a few minutes each. I peered at my watch's illuminated dial, distorted by the rain that dripped off my sleeve. 1.00 am. Hell, it was cold. Wet as I was, I could feel the even worse coldness of the sodden earth beneath me.

Five minutes went by without a move. Behind, I could hear the continuous rumble of bursting shells on the woods and beyond in the direction of the park. Shells from the 2nd Army guns droned by high overhead, unseen as they sped on their destructive errand.

I suddenly became aware of a pair of tracers that started from where I estimated the far bank of the river to be, which passed silently overhead and down into the woods some distance behind. They always came over in pairs about half a mile apart and parallel to each other. It was not until I was back over on the other side of the river at Nijmegen that I learned that they were tracers fired by two Bofors guns and intended to mark a path for us through the woods. To stray outside the limits marked by the tracers meant stumbling into the areas being shelled by the 2nd Army. Somebody had neglected to give this information out to us.

With startling suddenness, a Very light arched upwards about two hundred yards to our right and from slightly behind where the deep blackness of the woods merged with the grey of the field. At the peak of its flight, an eerie greenish light burst forth. It hung there for several agonising seconds. Blast, I thought, as I buried my head in the crook of my arm in order that the light colour of my face, which I had neglected to blacken, would not show up against the dark mass of ground on which I lay. If they spot us, we're finished. The Very light plunged earthward and went out.

From the same section of the woods, a machine gun broke out with its harsh stutter. Clearly, the shattering burst echoed across. I watched reddish-gold tracers curve up and down in their trajectory. They converged on the point where I estimated the head of our column must be, unseen away up ahead in the dripping rain. I sweated out the agonising seconds as I waited to see of the machine gunner would swing around his lethal stream of death.

The burst stopped. I waited tensely. Half a minute passed. The machine gun stuttered forth again in a long measured burst. Just short of the column head, the sparking tracer bullets struck the ground and ricocheted up into the dark sky. It was weird, first watching the fiery tracers dart across and then to hear the rapid explosions of the gun firing. It took a second or so for the sound to reach my ears.

The line ahead heaved like a serpent. In front of me, Sergeant Hedman rose up without a word and moved forward. I dragged myself up out of the quagmire of mud and followed closely on his heels. Before we had covered ten yards, the dim forms ahead sank silently down again. I dropped down just as a second Very light curled upwards and burst into full light. The hateful glow hovered for minutes, seemingly, although in point of fact it was merely seconds. I pressed my face against the saturated ground without noticing the numbing impact. I pushed my carbine forward to cover the direction of the light with hands numbed with cold.

The flare went out and the machine gun tapped methodically. I knew by now, with a feeling of relief, that the machine gun must have been firing on what is known as 'fixed lines'. This means that the machine gun is set up, usually by daylight, to cover a certain objective. Then at night, when no targets are visible, the machine gun is fired off along those set lines.

The men in front rose silently again, and I immediately pushed myself up and off the soggy ground. Less than fifty yards further on I saw the dim forms sinking down again. I followed suit, lying close alongside Sergeant Hedman. Hell, I thought, it will be dawn before we even begin to cross the river if we go on at this rate, and the dawn will bring down an avalanche of fire and steel from the unseen enemy. Yes, we had to get clear of the river before the first grey tinges of dawn lit the eastern horizon.

The rain fell without pause. My body had long since stopped rebelling against its cold embrace, but I could not help but shiver whenever the bitter wind increased in velocity and swept across the open field. I tried to move my numbed fingers with which I gripped my carbine so tightly. It was painful, terribly so.

I turned my head and looked back whence we had come. Between one and two miles back in the woods around Oosterbeek came the low rumble of exploding shells. The sky over the woods lay tinged with a deep red, reflecting the numerous fires that burned and smoked, despite the ceaseless downpour of rain.

Shells from our own guns on the far side of the river kept up their support, the missiles droning and sighing over with thin whispering voices that tailed across the night sky, unseen in their deadly passage. As the sound of their flight faded away into the distance, there came back the echo of their rumbling explosions. Yes, the enemy was being harassed, even as he himself was putting down his barrage on the park and surrounding area from which we had just fallen back.

The woods on either side of our avenue of escape were on fire in several places. In the direction of Arnhem lay the largest conflagration of all. The reddish glare that flickered and danced lit up the low lying clouds that scudded over the stricken town as though they too were fleeing this epic scene of death and destruction.

I looked forward as my ears caught the almost imperceptible sound of men moving. I rose again and stumbled along behind. We covered some ten yards and then flopped again in the muddy grassland. Another Very light climbed up into the night sky, casting its brilliance over half the field. I froze in the attitude of turning my head, as I looked out over the field towards where the darting tracers of the enemy machine gun were coming from, stuttering out at fixed intervals.

In the weird greenish glow of the flare, I could make out several deflated parachutes still attached to containers and baskets, relics of one of the supply drops. I didn't have to figure out why they were still lying there untouched. They were outside the perimeter, and undoubtedly the enemy had the field well covered by day and night. To walk out in daylight would have been one of the quickest ways to commit suicide.

The flare died out after lingering for what seemed an almost interminable period of time. I relaxed and sprawled on the ground, peering ahead, wondering what was keeping the line from moving just a little faster.

I looked at my watch. Between two and three a.m. Not many hours left until dawn. I still had no way of actually telling just how far from the river we were, although I suspected that it must lie at the far end of the field, some two hundred yards further on. But two hundred yards is a long way when moving only ten to fifty yards every twenty minutes or so.

For a while, I watched a lone tracer that periodically bored in from our left flank, on the opposite side to that where the machine gun lay. It would curve in and sigh past a good twenty feet over our heads and disappear into the blackness on our right flank. Whoever was firing was aiming far too high. As long as he kept on that aim I did not mind.

Then every nerve went taut. I felt my stomach bunch up. I didn't even turn my head towards the sound that swept down on us like an express train roaring through a tunnel. Oh God, no, not again, I thought. The roar rose almost instantaneously to a shriek. I screwed myself up on the ground and clawed into the mud, trying to bore my way on where it would be impossible to do so. I buried the left side of my face into the soft yielding ground, eyes wide open, as I waited for the impact. The shells screamed down in quick succession, passing low over our line, and I died a thousand deaths in those brief moments.

They burst on the far side of the wire and post fence, about fifty yards away. Vivid flashes lit the field for a moment. From the core of the explosions, I watched the white hot shrapnel blossom forth like a fountain. Perspiration exuded from every pore in my body as the angry hum of flying steel filled the air. It struck the earth around with a dull soggy sound.

Before the thunderous roll of bursting high explosives died away, another salvo was on its way in. I hugged the ground closer, my inner feeling crying out in agony for shelter, just a few inches below the level of the ground.

Again they howled down with a wail like that of a banshee. Again my muscles tied themselves up in knots. I forgot the bitter cold and the numbing rain. My nerves, exaggerating the danger of the moment, made me feel that I could almost reach up and touch the missiles as they streaked down and over with a sobbing scream. The ground shook and trembled under the vicious impact of the bursting shells. Again, the vivid flashes lit up the immediate area.

For a moment, I thought that the enemy could not help but see us silhouetted against the glare of the explosions, but that thought was driven from my mind as a further salvo cut down into the field. Hell, the swine knew. We'll be cut to pieces – with the river in sight. The last few yards and we were to die without being able to do a thing about it. What a finish, to die on this muddy stretch of field, probably blown to shreds.

I fumbled around, seeking a hole. Just a little hole, that's all I wanted. Some place to hide away from those searing jagged steel fragments. The bastards, why couldn't they have waited just one hour more? From out of the black wet night, another batch bored in with the first faint ominous whispering, rising to a crescendo that caused my spine to tingle and the hair on my nape to rise and prickle. Thunder filled the air again along with the whirring steel. One piece sliced low over my head and struck the ground alongside. Somewhere down the line a man cried out.

I lay there hunched up, awaiting the next salvo. The minutes passed, but nothing happened. I turned my head and fearfully peered back whence the shells had come, quivering in anticipation. I started as the machine gun chattered out its measured burst. Red tracers carved their set paths over the blackness of the field, bouncing off the ground and climbing into the wet night sky.

Thank heaven, I thought. Maybe it was just a fluke. Maybe they suspect, but don't know for sure. The Bofors tracer shells slid by on either side. The British shells continued their destructive flights. We got up again and moved forward. I prayed for the river bank to come into view.

We covered nearly a hundred yards this time. Eagerly I stared ahead, where I could now make out what appeared to be the hedge bordering the field. The Rhine must lie beyond that hedge. I peered at its dim outline hungrily, like a drowning man clutching at a straw. Salvation lay beyond that hedge. I didn't mind taking a chance at fighting, but being blown to pieces by shells was another matter.

I listened intently and, above the low rumble of battle, I picked out the faint sound of a chugging motor. Boats! That was the only explanation. I felt a thrill of elation run through me.

As the tension caused by the shelling began to ease, I became aware of the cold once more. My teeth began to chatter and I shivered almost without pause. The sodden clothes clung to my skin. The rain had almost stopped, which was one blessing, although it didn't help much now that we were wet through and through. If we had to swim the river, we couldn't get any wetter. In fact, it might even be a little warmer.

I became aware of another flare shedding its light silently over the field. Now that I had moved forward, the point where the flare burst into illumination was well behind me. I lay perfectly still except for the bouts of shivering over which I had no control.

My God, I thought, I shall never, never forget this night that is, if I survive. The chances seemed about fifty-fifty at that moment. We still had to cross the river yet, and I had an idea that it was under fire.

We were very near the point where the tracers from the machine gun were striking close to the head of the column. Even as I watched, I saw two men, impatient of waiting, rise up and step into the darkness at an angle that would take them across the field of fire of the machine gun. I guessed that they were fed up with waiting for the boats and were going to swim for it. The river was reputed to be about a quarter of a mile wide at this point and with a very swift current. Seeing that my limit was about fifteen yards, I would not stand much of a chance if I had to swim for it

The men vanished from sight and I turned my eyes to the front again. How much longer? Up again, forward several yards. The gap in the hedge was visible through the gloom, tantalisingly near. Now I knew what a rabbit feels like when it is mesmerised by a snake. I couldn't take my eyes off that gap.

For nearly fifteen minutes we lay thus. The low chugging sound of motors came and went periodically. I heard some of the enemy shells whine over and smash down somewhere beyond the river bank. The machine gun blasted out, the echoes floating across in the wake of the sparkling and glowing tracers. In the position where I was now lying, the tracers seemed to bore straight in towards me, curving slightly away at the last moment to strike the ground some fifty yards short. I no longer looked upon them as a menace. Nothing else mattered except for me to pass through that gap ahead.

The close-packed line of men rose once more and, with beating heart, I found myself less than twenty yards from the hedge. One more hop would take me through. For a moment, I looked back at the woods, half expecting the enemy to re-commence his shelling of the field. Give us just half an hour more, I thought.

I peered anxiously at my watch. I made a rough calculation and came to the conclusion that dawn would break in about one and a quarter hour's time. We had to get across by then, or else forever forgo the crossing in an organised style. After the dawn, it would be every man for himself and the devil take the hindermost.

I could hear the throb of motors a little more clearly now, but I was puzzled by the fact that they sounded so distant. With the hedge bordering the river only some twenty yards or so in front, I should have been hearing them much louder.

Ah! At last, at long last! I quickly heaved myself up off the sodden earth. With beating heart and hope in my breast, I reached the gap in the hedge. The machine gun hammered out a parting message as I stepped through. I peered ahead, seeking the lapping waters. Yes, there they were, but not where I had expected them to be. We were on a high bank, and I could see a steep muddy slope that led down to the river's edge some two to three hundred yards away. I was momentarily disappointed, for I had led myself to believe that I would find the waters at my feet.

We halted just through the gap. Somebody called out in a low voice to get down as the enemy were lobbing shells into that area from time to time, and that they expected a full strength barrage at any moment.

I crouched down in the slippery mud, made worse by the many boots that had churned it up since the retreat had begun. It started to rain again, a fact that I now barely noticed. I looked down into the gloom and, by the faint reflection thrown off by the distant fires, I could make out little groups of men at intervals down the side of the muddy bank, awaiting their turn to move forward into the boats. The boats, yes, where were they? I strained my eyes into the night. I couldn't hear the motors any more and wondered. Now I could make out that the foot of the bank consisted of irregular masses of rock that merged in with the swirling waters of the Lower Rhine.

I lifted my eyes and looked at the dark mass of the far bank where I made out a single pinpoint of light, subdued, but there right enough. A guiding light for the boats, no doubt. Between ourselves and that far bank, the inky black waters of the Rhine flowed swiftly towards the sea, many miles distant.

The wind blew colder still in the exposed position that we now occupied, and I found myself shivering almost without pause. The crest of the far bank was silhouetted from time to time by a flickering light that danced to and fro; flames from the muzzles of the 2nd Army guns pounding the enemy back in the Oosterbeek area. Somehow, crouched down just beneath the summit of the bank, I felt that we had broken out of the cloak of terror of the German shelling; but that was just an illusion, for their shells, and especially their mortar bombs, could seek us out just as easily as if we were back there in the soggy dark field behind.

A path led down at an angle across the muddy bank, and this we began to descend at a low word of command. Stumbling and slipping, I followed the man in front. My whole body was numb with cold and my clothes clung closely to my skin, a sodden mass of cloth. I half dropped as, behind, I heard the awful wail of shells falling. They burst with loud shattering explosions in the field we had so recently left. Hell, the swine, they are at it again. We stumbled a little faster.

We reached the jumbled mass of rocks. I bruised my leg against a protruding rock, but hardly felt the stab of pain that ran through it. I could now hear the lapping waters of the river. We climbed over the rocks and walked out onto a mass that jutted out like a jetty into the swirling black waters, gleaming slightly under the reflection from the many fires behind us.

We stood on the edge of the rocks with the cruel wind cutting through our sodden clothes, while the rain drove against us with no respite. I leaned on my carbine, feeling utterly weary. About three hundred yards away, fiery tracers cut down from the top of the bank into the river. An occasional shell exploded into the river, the fountains of water momentarily illuminated. Overhead at frequent intervals our shells sobbed past. Another salvo of enemy shells shrieked down on the field behind us. Poor devils, I thought of the men still waiting to move up to the river's edge.

I rubbed the rain off my watch dial and peered down at it. About one hour of darkness left. Hell, we were lucky, that is, if the boats were still coming over.

The faint white light across the turbulent waters burned fitfully, as though the wind was moving the carefully hooded lens from one side to the other. I stared hard at the waters and thought I could discern a dark mass moving in towards us, and the next moment it was bumping against the rocks. A Canadian voice floated out of the darkness, 'OK fellas, hop in and make it snappy. I've got several more journeys to make before all your pals are picked up.'

The boat had ridden up on the rocks and, despite the choppy waters, she remained still. We stepped into the boat and it rocked violently with so many getting in at the same time. It was as though a weight had been lifted from my mind. It just didn't seem true. Everything was going according to plan. The Canadian asked if any of us could row. I don't think he got one negative reply. I put my carbine down in a little space that I could find among the men that crammed the boat. I seriously began to doubt whether it would float with such a weight on board. Fumbling around, I found an oar which I pulled out from under the mass of men after a short struggle. The Canadian warned, 'Row as fast as you can, fellas, and make as little noise as possible. This isn't a healthy spot, Jerry has been shelling and mortaring the river periodically, and I have an idea that one of those periods is just about due. They've already got several boats - more by luck than judgement, though.' he added, as if he had thought that he had said too much.

We pulled on the oars. Nothing happened. The boat didn't move an inch. I forgot the cold and wet as I pulled hard at the oar. Someone swore softly under his breath. I could hear the men breathing heavily. More perspiration ran down my forehead and broke out on the small of my back. The boat was too far on the rocks and too loaded for rowing to float her free.

Staff Sergeant Jerry Spellman, who was one of the men nearest the rocks, jumped out and applied his massive bulk to the prow of the boat. She moved and gradually slid off. Jerry hurriedly jumped back in among the mass of men. The boat floated free with the waters almost breaking over her gunwales. Damn, I thought, I've had it if she sinks halfway across. The swift current caught her and twisted her around.

'Row, you bastards, row!' came the voice of the Canadian at the helm.

We rowed. After a few abortive attempts, during which we floated away down parallel with the bank, we got her around. I guessed that some of the men who now had oars in their hands had never rowed a stroke before this moment. Time and time again I was drenched by the icy waters of the river being thrown back from wildly splashing oars. I thought we were making an appalling noise, but I doubt whether it was heard above the general din of the distant shelling and machine gunning.

I looked down river and watched the tracers from a machine gun striking the dark waters several hundred yards away. Some of the tracers bounced up from the surface and burned away into nothing high in the dark sodden sky. The distant river bank, some mile or so farther on down, seemed to take on cliff-like proportions.

The prow of the boat swung first one way, then the other, and it was a very erratic course that we steered for the opposite bank. At one time, the guiding light disappeared altogether as we drifted too far to one side and moved outside its hooded beam. We picked it up again pretty soon. I felt the terrific tug of the fast flowing current, and was sorry for anyone trying to swim for it.

My blood froze suddenly as I heard a salvo of shells howl down into the river on our right. Lurid flashes lit the dark waters for a split second. However, they were too far off to harm us.

'See what I mean?' came the voice of the Canadian from the stern of the boat. We rowed faster still until I felt the sweat run down my back in a continuous stream. Hell, I thought, this is some quarter of a mile. In all probability, we rowed nearer half a mile against a strong current, if our zigzag course was taken into consideration.

We were lucky, for we appeared to be crossing during a lull on the part of the enemy's shelling and mortaring. Just one salvo so far, and we had covered over half way, I estimated.

Behind us, deep back in the woods, there still echoed the sound of small arms fire, although it was getting less and less. Above the noise of the bursting shells and mortar bombs, which drifted over to my ears in a muffled roar, I could pick out the sharp bursts of machine gun fire and the crack of rifles. They seemed tiny, far away and insignificant, but they indicated that desperate last stands and last savage efforts to break through the enemy ring, were being made by isolated parties.

As I rowed, my heart went out to those men who were fighting so hard in those almost fathomless black woods. Many were destined never to reach the Rhine river that night or any other night. Their lifeless shattered bodies would lie in those rain-sodden woods for days and nights unnumbered, perhaps forever, individually unsung, but as a whole glorified, if that is any compensation to their loved ones.

The dim outline of the far bank was drawing near. The light burned more steadily. I was panting with my efforts. We edged the boat around against the plucking current and fought to bring it up parallel with the light – the light that was a symbol of hope and rest after the last nine hectic days.

Another promontory of rocks similar to that which we had embarked from on the far bank behind us loomed up, jutting forth from the deep black waters. We bumped into it. I felt a wave of exaltation pass through me.

We were across. We had made it, thanks to the boatmen.

Chapter 20

Out of Arnhem

As we stumbled, exhausted, from the boat, a small group of figures who were gathered on the rocks held out helping hands. I eased my stiff limbs out over the side and felt my feet on hard rock once more. In the almost pitch darkness, I stumbled and caught my leg for the second time that night against the unyielding rock. Again, I hardly felt the ripped skin and bruised flesh. Why should it matter; I was across.

It was like stepping into a new world. It gave me the false impression, just as the river bank had done on the far side, that here we were safe from shells. A vain hope, as I was reminded of by one of the dim figures who had greeted us, saying,

'Right, men, get a move on. Follow the white tape over the bank and down onto the road, then turn right and continue on to Driel, which is the Divisional rendezvous, and don't linger or bunch; we've been mortared several times tonight already.'

We didn't need any spurring. We had had enough of mortaring to last us for a very long time.

I scrambled up the steep muddy bank between the tapes, which only just showed as an indistinct blur, having been trodden into the slippery mud by hundreds of boots before us. I reached the top of the bank and paused there for a few seconds while I took one last look at the inferno of the Arnhem area.

Immediately below lay the black, sinister-looking waters of the Lower Rhine river which had claimed so many lives. Beyond the river, the opposite bank stood out clear cut against the glow of numerous fires. To the left and right on the far bank conflagrations burned steadily in the woods, half a mile or so back from the river.

It was over Arnhem itself and around the village of Oosterbeek that the largest conflagrations raged. The low lying rain clouds were bathed in a blood-red bath, like some unnatural sunset. From the direction of the Hartenstein Hotel and Oosterbeek came the ceaseless thud, thud of bursting missiles, still ravaging the already torn and tortured ground.

Drawing a deep breath, I turned my head forward again and stepped off the brink of the bank to go slithering and falling down the sides that fell away at a steep angle. I slid easily down through the mud and struck the bottom of what I took to be a half dried up dyke or wide ditch. I scrambled to my feet and followed the dim leading figure up over a smaller bank. I groped forward and suddenly found myself walking on solid hard road once again.

It seemed darker still, now that we were down on the road beneath the bank. I caught up with the scattered line of men in front who showed faintly through the gloom ahead. Visibility was about ten yards. A thin drizzle still fell and the wind turned stronger. In the relief of being across, that didn't seem to matter any more.

The road along which we were marching and stumbling appeared to be a raised one with ditches or dykes on either side, while the bare looking fields vanished away in all directions as far as my limited vision could tell.

The men in front, about five of them, began talking in low voices. I could make out Sergeant Hedman and Lieutenant Palmer. I was pleased to hear friendly voices once more. I caught up with Sergeant Hedman and we were both glad to get together again.

A reaction now began to set in after the terrible nervous tension of the last few days. The reserve energy and mental fortitude I had summoned up for the retreat over the river now began to fail as my tired brain registered that the task was over, or nearly so.

I felt weary, dreadfully weary. My legs ached, and where my soaking wet trousers had rubbed against the inside of my thighs, the skin was raw and burned like fire and made every step an effort. The muscles of my legs sent stabs of pain from deep inside with every movement. These had gone unnoticed up until now, but the false sense of security that now enveloped me brought them to the fore as we lurched along through the dark wet night.

We had been marching for nearly fifteen minutes along this narrow, twisting and slippery lane which was supposed to be taking us to our rendezvous at Driel. During all this time, not a solitary figure had passed us. It was strangely quiet this side of the river except for the periodical bang of our guns farther back as they continued to fire across the river at unseen targets. I noticed, however, that the tempo of the artillery had fallen off considerably since we had begun the crossing of the river. I could still hear a muffled rumble from the Arnhem area, but even now it was beginning to take on the shape of a bad dream.

The wind moaned across the open spaces and my teeth chattered as the drizzle, driven on by the wind, whipped against my already numbed face and penetrated deep into my sodden clothing. Damn, I thought, how much farther is this blasted Driel?

We rounded a bend and tramped up a straight stretch of road. Most of the cloth on the men's boots, including the new pair of socks I had put on over my boots, had worn through and now our footsteps were no longer entirely muffled.

The first grey of dawn was breaking. I shivered at the thought of how close we had come to being left on the other side of the river to be exposed in the approaching daylight. We had crossed with less than one hour to spare. In the faint light I could make out the almost imperceptible outlines of some buildings bordering the road ahead. At last, I thought, this must be the village.

My thoughts were rudely shattered by a sudden deafening outburst of firing by a heavy machine gun a few yards ahead in the still clinging darkness. I found myself in a ditch alongside the raised road with water up to my waist. I crouched down in the foul smelling, weed-encrusted water and peered desperately into the dim dawn. Hell, I thought, we've walked into something all right. The faint outline of the road was deserted, all of our party being in the ditch. The machine gun crashed out again, the reverberating echoes beating across the open fields.

In front of me I heard Lieutenant Palmer calling out with all his power, 'Friend, friend, airborne troops from over the river.' I heard someone answer in English, and saw Lieutenant Palmer's dim figure clambering up out of the ditch. I followed suit. A figure was crossing the road from one of the buildings which I could just make out on the far side.

Lieutenant Palmer, after a few brief words with the other man, turned and called out, 'It's OK, men, it's one of 43rd Division's Vickers firing across the river at the enemy. We're just jumpy, that's all.'

We tramped on through the silent and seemingly deserted, village. So this is Driel, I thought as I looked at the shadowy buildings still barely recognisable in the slow creeping first light of the dawn. I began to make out the outlines of army trucks lying under nets, tucked away against the walls of the buildings. I felt a slight thrill at the sight. Here was evidence of a ground army with all its heavy equipment.

We passed the monstrous shape of a German Tiger tank lying half off the roadside. I could see its shattered track twisted up in a heap, dark as it was. The long barrel of its gun still pointed ahead as if challenging all comers to pass its shattered carcass.

Just after we had marched through the village, we came to an entrance of a farm. Two lamps burned in shielded tins on either side of the posts between which passed a churned up track of mud. A voice called out as we drew level, 'All airborne troops in here.'

This was it at last, food, rest and, most of all, sleep. How deluded I was!

We staggered through the mud and found ourselves at the rear of a mass of men who had reached here before us. I looked over their heads and saw that they were gathered before a barn-like structure, in the doorway of which a lamp flickered uncertainly. Hundreds of men were jammed in the small space. Cold and shivering, we took our place at the back. Within a few minutes more men had stumbled in through the gates and were now pressing us into the already tightly packed mass of men.

The minutes passed by, and no one moved. We had learned that we were to be given a mugfull of hot tea and a dry blanket at this point and that thought kept us going. I felt weak and exhausted and but for the fact that the mass of men literally held me up or I would have sagged to the ground. From the looks of the men's faces around me, now visible in the grey of the dawn, they were all in much the same condition. Utter exhaustion was reflected on most faces.

The men, who had been patient up until now, began to get in an ugly mood. Curses flowed freely on the cold morning air. Shouts began to go up: 'Come on, get your bloody finger out!' 'What the hell's holding you up?' 'Why don't you just dish the things out? We're fed up and tired!'

Tired was the word. My legs felt like buckling at any moment. A man passed out on my left. Two others broke through the jammed mass, carrying him away into a first aid tent pitched on one side of the yard. Every wounded man being helped in through the gateway was given, quite rightly, priority.

Every minute lifted the veil of darkness a little more. An officer came along and in all stupidity called out to the seething mass, 'Now get a move along there. When Jerry finds you all gone from over there he'll shell this place to blazes.'

With all disregard for rank, the men, infuriated, shouted 'Why the hell don't you get your men moving then?' and other remarks that at any other time would have been treated as insubordination of the worst type. The officer faded out of the picture. I think he now realised that the men's nerves had been stretched beyond all normal endurance, and that they weren't taking anything from some damn officer who had not been over there.

The threat of shelling had stirred something inside me. The experience of being shelled would haunt me for the rest of my days, especially the sound of the German 'Nebelwerfers'. Sergeant Hedman and I forced our way out of the jammed mass and made our way around to the rear of the barn. To hell with waiting there, I thought. There must be some place else where we can get the stuff. They aren't making any progress in there.

We found a door and peered in, to find ourselves looking in on a scene of piled blankets and several men milling around pulling and heaving at the piles and pouring out tea into mess tins. I would have given a great deal for a cup of that steaming hot tea.

I called out to a corporal who was sitting close by the door marking figures on a sheet. He looked up and came over.

'Look here Corp,' I said, 'just give us a blanket each, and to hell with your tea.' He protested at first, but I pressed him again and he gave in, handing us out two blankets. Just like the army, I thought, to have all the men crowding around one tiny entrance, when they could make use of several and get rid of the crowd quicker.

With dry blankets tucked securely under our arms, we fought our way through the milling mob, telling some enroute of the source of our supply. That corporal sure was going to be pestered from now on.

Reaching the gate, I asked the man there where we had to go now. I had visions of walking a little way out of Driel and resting up in some sort of shelter.
'Go straight on down that road,' he said pointing beyond the village, 'and keep on going until you reach the next village named Elst.'

'And how far is Elst?' I asked.

'About four miles.' was his reply. A wave of dismay ran through me.'Four miles?' I echoed. 'Hell, I don't think I could make one mile, let alone four.' We thanked him and moved out onto the road where we paused.

Four miles, I thought. Four miles through the cold half light with the bitter wind blowing and the driving drizzle, and in these sopping wet clothes. I cursed long and bitterly.

'Well, I suppose we may as well get going.' said Sergeant Hedman wearily. I nodded, and we trudged off down the muddy and slippery road in the wake of others who had already started out. I was to find that that long straggling line extended right into Elst. We must have been among the last one or two hundred men, for the other eighteen to nineteen hundred survivors had already set out for Elst.

Within the first half mile my legs ached agonisingly. More skin wore off the inside of my thighs by friction with the sodden trousers that clung tenaciously to them. My limbs were rebelling at every step, sore and stiff like a piece of machinery that has run dry for lack of oiling and is on the verge of seizing up. I forced myself on, every step a mile of agony.

We were crossing open heathland now, and the wind blew strongly, cutting over the raised and exposed road. On each side dykes ran parallel with the road. It was terribly exposed and the rain made the most of it although, luckily for us, it was now but a slight drizzle. However, the wind made sure that every drop penetrated home. Visibility was now up to half a mile but broad daylight was slow in coming. The half light clung on persistently.

In the distance I picked out the faint outline of two houses standing isolated in this stretch of deserted road. To me they represented a haven. There we might find rest and sleep, and shelter from the hostile elements.

I forced my rebellious legs on. Every yard was a nightmare. I was staggering more than walking. I clung on tenaciously to my carbine. That I meant to keep wherever I went. We came up to the houses. My head whirled. I leaned against a hedge that surrounded the first house.

We prepared to go up to the door and knock, when I heard the sound of a jeep's motor break into life and tick over quietly. The next moment the shape of the jeep came edging out from the shelter of the house wall. Wildly we moved towards it.

I called out to the driver asking him where he was going. If he was heading for Elst, we might just as well get aboard and be taken to where shelter had been organised. One of the dim figures inside the jeep let out a hiss for quiet. The jeep was on the road now, its nose pointing the way we were heading. I reached the driver's seat, and peered in under the canvas hood. About four men were squatting inside. I looked again, for I recognised them as airborne men with their blackened faces and muddied and torn uniforms. The driver said, 'We're pinching this jeep, so hop on the roof quick if you're coming, because we're going.'

Sergeant Hedman was already pulling himself up onto the roof. I followed suit, painfully levering myself up. The canvas hood sagged under our combined weight, but held. All scruples had been cast aside. I hoped the rightful owners would not wake up and discover their loss.

The jeep started off with an awful jerk, and I was almost thrown off. I clutched wildly at the rounded edge of canvas and managed to hang on with by my nails. They splintered, but held – I had to hang on. I couldn't walk another step. I was utterly exhausted, more so than I had ever been in my life.

Sprawled out on the hood I tried to regain my strength. The jeep was swaying from one side of the road to the other in the most alarming manner. The road was narrow and muddy, that I knew, but I seriously began to doubt whether the man driving had ever driven before, and this I later found out to be the case.

I saw another jeep approaching from the opposite direction and steeled myself. Our jeep swerved its erratic course towards the deep ditch on our side of the road. We teetered along its edge for several yards and the other jeep roared by terribly close.

We reverted to the centre of the road. Every few yards we passed small lines of stumbling men, who waved and shouted madly at us to stop and give them a lift. Our driver kept going. More than once I thought he was about to run down the gesticulating lines of men with their blankets wrapped around them, looking in the half light like figures from another world. I caught the sound of curses as we roared on past them unheedingly. The next second their shouts were lost in the wind that whipped and tore at my frozen body. I lay on my carbine to hold it down, afraid to let go my precarious grip on the canvas sides for fear I would be hurled off.

Another jeep raced towards us. This time our driver half swerved and stood on the brakes violently. By a miracle I clung on, but the jeep jerked and leapt ahead almost as soon as it had stopped. This was too much for me. My grip was torn loose and I fund myself toppling off the back of the jeep. I fell heavily onto the road and rolled over.

I staggered to my feet. The jeep had stopped again a few yards further on. I lunged forward and grasped hold of a projection and tried to pull myself up, but my strength failed me. I hung on as the jeep started with a jerk once again. My feet dragged on the road. Above my head I saw Sergeant Hedman appear at the rear of the lurching canopy. He reached down and, grasping my left arm, pulled with all his failing strength. I fought to heave myself up with this new aid, and only just succeeded in clambering on.

I lay on the heaving roof, the air sobbing through my lungs, hearing Sergeant Hedman telling me that he had my carbine. I groped for it and thrust it underneath me. The sweat beneath my clothes felt warm against the coldness of the rain that lay against my skin. I closed my eyes for an instant and wondered how much more I could take. Salvation was at hand, however. A few minutes later, after passing some burned-out vehicles on the side of the road, we reached a crossroad just outside the village of Elst.

Seeing the village in the new full dawn, I slid off the jeep as we stopped. Sergeant Hedman followed. The others got out and the driver drove the jeep into a grove of trees alongside the road. I was thankful the nightmare journey was over. Looking back the way we had come, I could see a long line of men shambling along both sides of the road; not in organised parties, but just little individual groups, drooping figures swaying and stumbling as they converged on Elst that September morning. Out of the hell of Arnhem, these survivors had lived to fight another day.

With the end in sight, I summoned up my last reserves of strength and with Sergeant Hedman walked into the village which bore signs of battle. We walked on through, limping but with a thankful feeling of having made it. On the far side we were directed into a field in which lay large numbers of tents and marquees.

We stumbled on over the duckboards laid down across the mud and were directed into a large marquee where we found a hot mug of Bovril awaiting us. I swallowed the liquid greedily. A new flow of life passed through me as the hot Bovril coursed down. We must have looked a sight, even to the men here who were used to seeing soldiers come out of the line. Indeed we were unshaven, filthy and bloodstained, with our muddy uniforms, sodden and torn, unrecognisable as such.

Hardly had we finished when a man poked his head into the tent.

'Some more Ducks (DUKWs) leaving for Nijmegen in five minutes. Anyone here ready to go?' The MO looked at us and said,'That means you. All the airborne are to concentrate there.'

We got up and moved out after thanking the medical men. They gave us a few cigarettes and I lit one, feeling grateful, although I am not a real smoker. There are times, however, when a cigarette is an invaluable comfort.

Broad daylight had now set in. Outside, I looked up at the high sides of the Ducks, the amphibious trucks which have played such an effective part in this war. I wondered if I had the strength to climb up.

Seizing hold of the edge above my head, I pulled myself up slowly, one foot resting on the rear wheel. One of the men who had been watching came over, saying as he did so, 'OK, chum, I'll give you a hand.' I felt his hands on my feet and the next moment I was toppling over the side underneath the canvas that covered in the top of the Duck.

I sprawled there leaning against the side. Others came in under the canvas, most of them with the aid of the same man who had helped me. The vehicle gradually filled up. In the gloom under the canvas I managed to grin at Sergeant Hedman.

The Duck vibrated as the engine sprang into life. A minute later we rolled over the soft ground and out onto a road. I pulled myself up, curious to see the type of country we would pass through. Tired as I was, I wanted to see it – I might never get the chance again. We were bowling along a road banked high above the surrounding landscape. Dykes ran along on either side. More than once we passed other stationary Ducks which had skidded and slipped off the slippery road down the sides of the banks. Other trucks and an occasional tank flashed past my restricted gaze, burnt and blasted on the line of the 43rd Division's path of advance to the river.

On either side of the road, the flat level low-lying land stretched away, looking bleak and desolate in the morning light. The rain had stopped and the sky was clearing. I listened to the roar of the Duck's motor and marvelled at our escape. The ordeal was over and we were on our way back.

We were now entering the outskirts of Nijmegen, I was informed by a 43rd Division man who was riding along with us. I peered forward at the town which had been mentioned repeatedly in our briefings but which I had not yet seen. Nijmegen, the objective of the 82nd US Airborne Division.

Road back to Nijmegen

Here, I learned later the story of the operation as experienced by the 2nd Army troops. The US 82nd Airborne Division had fought a pitched battle with the enemy and had prevented them from blowing up the bridge.

By the afternoon of the 19th, just over forty-eight hours after they had dropped and formed their perimeter, they had been linked up with by the spearheads of the 2nd Army, consisting of the Guards Armoured Brigade. Together they had taken the bridge intact after a fierce struggle, with the American troops crossing the river in rubber boats under a hail of fire from the enemy, which had inflicted very heavy casualties, to take them in the rear and seize the northern end of the bridge.

At the same time the Guards Armoured Brigade, spurred on by the American paratrooper's valiant efforts, punched forward from the south side of the river and crossed the bridge, linking up with the American party holding the far side. That was on the 20th.

By the 21st the Guards Armoured Brigade had surged forward from the bridgehead north of Nijmegen towards Arnhem, but had been stopped dead at the village of Bessam by a strong anti-tank defence thrown up by the enemy.

The Germans farther south of Nijmegen, behind the Guards Armoured and the 82nd Airborne, had counter-attacked against the narrow corridor at Son, but were repulsed. That same day two thirds of the Polish Parachute Brigade were dropped north and northwest of Elst, in the direction of Driel, with the hope of ferrying themselves across to reinforce the remnants of our division holding the perimeter at Oosterbeek.

At the same time, the enemy on the north side of the river, the same side of the river as we were on fighting on at Oosterbeek, seized the Heaversdorp Ferry, almost opposite Driel, thus cutting us off completely from the river and preventing the Poles from crossing in any large number.

The next day, on the 22nd, the enemy counter-attacked heavily and completely cut the narrow corridor driven up from the Eindhoven area to Nijmegen by the 2nd Army. The scene of the counter-attack was between Uden and Vehgel, south of Grave. The road remained cut until the following day, the 23rd. The 43rd, with the Guards, continued to attack fiercely, but were unable to break through Elst. The balance of the Polish Brigade was dropped on this day north of Elst.

On the 24th the enemy again cut the corridor and supply lines between Uden and Vehgel. This counter-attack was more serious than the last and the road remained cut all that day and into the next, the 25th. By the 26th, the road was cleared, but not until the afternoon, and we were greeted with the news that the road was again cut as soon as we arrived in Nijmegen. Having seen the might of the 2nd Army in guns and trucks as we had driven along, the news came as quite a shock to us. Up until now we had been under the impression that the whole corridor was solidly held, and expanding all the time.

On the 23rd, some of the Poles had been ferried across. The enemy had lost the Heaverdorp Ferry, but were still holding on close by and were able to put down heavy and accurate fire on anything that moved across the river.

By the 24th, a gallant company of the Dorset Regiment had made a determined effort to break through the enemy lines and at great cost succeeded in doing so, reaching the river's southern bank and linking up with the Poles. That night they managed to ferry across a few men, but none succeeded in reaching the 1st Airborne troops around Oosterbeek. The ferrying had to be abandoned at daylight because of intense fire from the enemy.

By this time, General Montgomery had abandoned his idea of landing the 52nd (Air Portable) Division which he had intended flying in by air transports on to Deelen airport, planned to be held by the 1st Airborne Division. The restricted perimeter into which we had been forced made the plan entirely out of the question, since the Germans still held the airfield. The 43rd Division was still fighting in and around Elst, and the selected men of the Dorset Regiment had made their courageous dash for the river.

General Montgomery made the decision that the 1st Airborne Division should be withdrawn from the Arnhem area on the following night, that of the 25/26th, and this we had carried out as I have recounted. By dawn of the 26th, a small number of men still on the north bank of the river had to give up the idea of crossing. These consisted of men of the 1st Airborne Division and of the Dorset Regiment, the men who had formed the small bridgehead on the north bank of the river. Most of them were cut to pieces as they lay on the fields between the woods and the river, as daylight broke. Some were taken prisoner, but not many. The battle of Arnhem was over.

Chapter 21

Nijmejen - and Home

We drove on through the streets of Nijmegen with its tree-lined thoroughfares. It was great to be back where houses stood again, and civilians thronged the streets. We stopped somewhere near the centre, in front of what had been a school. The Duck disgorged a mass of filthy, soaked and limping soldiers, a part of the 2000 survivors of the more than ten thousand originally sent in. I knew I was lucky; I was one of the two thousand odd men who had made their way back from the embattled pocket around Oosterbeek.

Into the dining room of the school we went. The room was already full of men from our Division who had reached here before us. Forms and tables were set up in every spare foot of space. We filed past a table, and each was handed a large glass of rum; I swallowed without once taking my lips from the glass. The liquor burned its way down my throat and sent a warm glow through my whole body, except my legs, they still remained stiff and numb with cold. It made me feel better immediately.

I was told to find a table, which I did, and an orderly brought over a plate of hot food. It was wonderful to see a clean white plate with wholesome, well-cooked food upon it. Sergeant Hedman sat opposite me, eagerly devouring his food. I ate until I was full, and swallowed mug after mug of hot sweet tea. I was at peace with the world.

Finishing our meal, we were guided upstairs and shown into a bare-walled room jammed with two tier wooden bunks. I sank wearily down on one and stripped off my sodden shapeless trousers, black with mud, together with my boots, which had squelched the whole time since we had left the park. I eased my sore and aching feet from their muddy grasp, and peeled off socks that fought to stay on my feet. I was torn between the desire of dropping flat on the bed and sleeping, of finding some place to wash off the mud that clung to all parts of my body. My eyes made up my mind for me. They closed, and I was fast asleep.

Many hours later I awoke, it was late afternoon. I looked at my watch to find that I had slept eight hours, and felt a different man. True, I ached in every limb still, and my eyes were still sore, but my head was almost clear, and already I felt better. I got up and went in search of water. No showers were available, but plenty of cold water flowing into large washbowls. Men were sluicing their naked bodies down regardless of the water flowing all over the floor. Idly, I wondered how much the ceiling below would take of this sort of treatment, as I took my place, naked as the day I was born, and let the cold invigorating water cascade down my filthy body.

I shaved with a battered razor and blunt blade lent me by another fellow. I didn't get all my beard off, but at least I could move around without scaring the life out of any kids I might run across outside.

Returning to my bunk, I sat on the edge and looked at the sodden shapeless mass of clothing on the floor. No, I wasn't going to put those on again. I wrapped a blanket around me, as many others were doing, and went in search of something dry to put on.

We were informed that a truck was coming in about half and hour with new clothing. We waited near the entrance, feeling like Red Indians in our get-up. I didn't care. I was warm, and I was fed. What more could I ask?

Word got around that the truck was here. In company with several other blanket-clad men, I went down the steps into the road. People stared and smiled at us. The truck was about fifty yards away, and we hobbled over to it. I got a brand new pair of trousers, together with underwear and socks, but no boots. I also received a new shirt, and felt quite proud of my new outfit. My original battle blouse (jacket), although wet, was still wearable. This was the first time I has ever got anything out of a quartermaster's store without signing for it.

Hobbling back into the building, I quickly donned the clean dry clothing. It was marvellous, feeling the warmth of the garments against my skin which, up until only a few hours ago, had been numbed with the cold rain that had soaked my clothing through and through.

During the evening, in company with Sergeant Hedman, I went for a stroll through the town. It was good to be alive and walking around the tree-lined streets, looking in the windows of shops, some of which had been shattered, with the goods piled up inside. I was surprised that the objects displayed had been left intact, but, after all, we were still on Allied territory – if it had been German territory – well, that would have been a different story. We got down as far as the bridge that had seen such bitter fighting and which had cost so many American and British lives. Shattered war materiel still lay at the approaches. We returned to the school, only to find that our quarters had been moved. We had to report in to what was the old barracks, used recently by the enemy.

We took up our beds and walked, literally. I didn't approve of the move for several reasons, the most prominent being that I suspected the enemy must be well acquainted with the barracks, and would quite rightly assume that we would make use of it. Yes, it was just the target for a pin-point bombing raid.

That night, as I suspected they might, the Luftwaffe raided the town. They were mainly after the bridge, but failed to get it. They did, however, score almost a direct hit on the school we had just vacated, wrecking what had been the kitchen. As a matter of fact, some of our men were still in the building when the bombs fell. They took a sudden dislike to the place and move over to the barracks. To our pent-up nerves, it seemed that the enemy was bent on hounding us without respite.

Our building rocked from the blasts of the few bombs dropped by the enemy planes. Through an open doorway, I watched the shadowy shape of one of the raiders swoop low overhead with golden red tracers from our guns criss-crossing his path. The roar of his motors blanketed out all other sounds as he passed over, almost skimming the rooftops.

I slept under the eaves that night, but many others moved downstairs to the ground floor, as they did not think it wise to be up three stories while the Luftwaffe prowled the night skies overhead. I was too tired to hear but the first of the outbursts of AA firing and bombs falling. I slept deeply that night. Not even the Luftwaffe was going to keep me awake.

There was no hateful 'Stand-to' the following day. That was a thing of the past for the time being. I slept on until nearly mid morning. During the day, the Luftwaffe carried out more attacks against the bridge. This time they came in from the opposite direction from that expected, but they didn't catch our gunners off their guard. They came in low, but were fought off and missed the bridge with the bombs they dropped. I strained to catch a glimpse of the house-hopping planes attacking the bridge less than half a mile away, but couldn't see a thing. It was tantalising to hear the thunderous roar of their motors, and the crash of the AA and yet not be able to see anything.

It was here at Nijmegen that I heard my first enemy jet plane. The German machine came whining down with a long drawn-out thin whistle that grew louder every second. For a moment my blood froze in my veins, for it sounded for all the world like a huge bomb screaming down straight towards the barracks.

Sergeant Harry Cole, who had been standing by my side, simply vanished like a streak of lightning into one of the air raid shelters built in the grounds of the barracks. Poor Harry – in his haste he burned his hand on one of the stoves being used by some civilians who had lost their homes in the recent battle of Nijmegen, and had made the shelter their dwelling.

Then the jet was gone, leaving an odd silence hanging over the town. The jet got nowhere either, another miss. I thought that we had got away from shelling too, but I was to learn otherwise during the day, not that we were endangered in any way, for they were falling too far away. They were enemy guns firing from the Siegfried Line, the northern edge of which terminated only a few miles away to the northeast. Nijmegen was within easy reach of the big guns in the line. The all-too-familiar moan of a shell crossing the heavens rent the air every fifteen minutes or so. Looking out of a window, I could see dirty grey-black clouds of smoke blossom upward and outwards from the buildings in the northeast section of the town, followed a second or so later by the thunderclap of the explosions and the trembling of the floor underfoot. Somewhere, deep down inside me, the sounds stirred an internal emotion. What I had just undergone was too recent in my memory to forget.

About midday, we were summoned together in the barrack square, and great was our joy when we learned that we were being returned to England at all possible speed. In fact, the lorries were coming in to pick us up some time in the early afternoon. We were also reminded that the road had been cut until yesterday evening, and that it could happen again, therefore every man was to go fully equipped, at least with arms and ammunition, if nothing else. That suited us; to get back to England we would fight our way through any blockade the enemy might lay across our route back.

After several false alarms, a long column of lorries swung into the tree-lined barrack square. Spirits were at tops, although in my heart of hearts I was sorry for the men of the 2nd Army who had been out here for so long, many of them since D-Day, with no hope of home leave for some time to come. They looked at us with unveiled envy from the doorways of the buildings as we happily climbed aboard the lorries that were to take us on our first leg home, back to England. We were to drive to Brussels, and from there Air Transport Command would fly us back to our bases in England.

To reach the Brussels area, we had to drive back down the narrow corridor that stretched between fifty and sixty miles to Eindhoven. In several places, especially around Uden and Vehgel, where the enemy had more than once counter-attacked and cut the road, the area was still under enemy artillery fire and subject to penetration by enemy patrols. Sixty miles of corridor blasted and cut out by the 2nd Army, spearheaded by the Guards Armoured Brigade while we had been entrenched at Arnhem. Burnt out tanks and trucks lay scattered along our route as we left Nijmegen behind.

A short way outside the town, we passed the scene of the 82nd US Airborne Division's landings. In the fields alongside the road, and even in orchards, lay scores of WACO gliders with an occasional Horsa glider. They lay there in all positions, facing in all directions, and in all states of disintegration from complete gliders down to shattered masses of fabric and tubular steel framework. On the whole, it looked a very good massed landing, which appeared quite concentrated. Hundreds of multi-coloured parachutes also decorated the landscape, scattered over the fields like a disease on the face of the fresh green countryside – a disease of death.

We drove on down the twisting road and passed through Grave. South of Grave we came across signs of battle where the enemy counter-attacks, which had cut the road earlier on, had been fought to a standstill. A line of our trucks lay alongside the road or pushed off into fields, burnt-out, bullet-riddled hulks, the price of a thinly stretched supply line with practically unguarded flanks. Tanks were there also, both the enemy's and ours. The burnt and rusting carcasses were there in abundance. The long eighty eight millimetre guns of the huge German Tiger tanks seemed to droop despondently, like the lifeless long neck and head of some prehistoric monster – torn and blasted hulks of steel that would never fight again.

The roaring column of trucks, of which we were but one unit, slowed down to a halt for the first time since leaving Nijmegen. Vehgel and Uden were behind us, villages that bore the scars of recent battle. We stayed there for some minutes, the engines ticking over. Ahead, I thought I heard the sound of an occasional explosion, but I couldn't be sure above the noise of the motor. I also thought I could pick out the not too distant crackle of small arms fire. The perspiration bega6n to break out under my new battle dress for the first time. I took a firmer grip on my carbine and sat there in silence, together with the others, under the canvas body cover which restricted our view outside.

The gears clashed and we were away again, picking up speed, excessively so, I thought. I soon learned why. We thundered through a village and swung around a corner following the main road. We had not gone more than two hundred yards when I saw a cloud of dust and smoke geyser upwards from the village we has just passed through. A direct hit on the road. I wondered how the trucks behind us were faring. We rounded a bend hiding the road out of the village from direct view. As we sped on across the flat landscape, I saw periodical clouds of smoke rise from the battered village as the enemy put shell after shell down onto the road and its vicinity. Luck seemed to be with us. I never heard the explosions above our racing engine.

All that afternoon we raced along the none too wide Dutch road, on through Son and, eventually, we were rolling through the streets of Eindhoven. People waved to us as we thundered through the narrow streets, throwing back the echoes of our roaring motors. I peered around the canvas covering and looked at the great Phillips Radio works which appeared about three quarters intact to me, but I could not tell what the inside condition was like.

We had reached the end of the corridor and were in an area that no longer held enemy troops for many miles on either side. Eindhoven, with the waving girls, dropped away behind and we drove on towards the nearby Dutch-Belgian border. We soon reached and crossed the border with nothing but a few strands of barbed wire, and an unmanned striped pole and guard box, to mark the place where the boundary of one country ended and another began. We sped on down a well-built concrete road over heathlands that stretched away on either side. We passed a large battery of enemy eighty eights pointing their ugly, long sand-coloured snouts skywards, their evil death-dealing power a thing of the past now. Silently they poked skyward, a symbol of defeat. AA guns that never again would belch forth flame and steel at our planes passing over on their errands of destruction.

It was evening by the time we reached historic Louvain and rumbled to a halt outside a large building that I suspected of being a girl's school by the signs that were painted on the doors. It had also been used by the Germans as a barracks as the various signs pinned up and the rather crude murals that had been painted on the wall of what was the dining room.

I found great pleasure in being able to press down a switch and see the flood of light blaze forth. Each little thing like that made me realise that we were really getting back into civilisation once more. Electricity had been missing at Nijmegen. We stayed the night in the big building, and again I slept well. Here we were not even pestered by the Luftwaffe, although a rigid blackout was in force as periodical raids had been made on the area.

I was up early next morning. It was fresh and springlike, and it was good to be alive and kicking. No start was indicated before ten a.m. so, with Sergeant Hedman, I went for a walk around the famous old town with its historic buildings. I was fascinated by the piles of fruit on the barrows of the stall keepers in the market place. I learned that they could not commence selling until a certain time, despite the fact that they were all ready. A policeman hung around to see that the order was carried out. Women began queueing even as we watched. An old woman in charge of a stall smiled at us and said something we did not understand. I was eyeing a huge pile of grapes, a fruit that our people back in England had not seen for a very long time.

The old woman picked up two large bunches of grapes and held them out to us. The policeman looked and then turned his back. I was embarrassed because of the people waiting for selling to start, but they were smiling also, so I took a bunch, as did Sergeant Hedman. I pulled out some Belgian money to pay, but the old woman waved it aside; she wouldn't take a cent. A deep feeling of warmth over the kindness of the old lady passed through me, and I thanked her profusely. The policeman turned back again and smiled approvingly.

I bought a few postcards and a couple of souvenirs and returned to the building. We got back just in time to join a gathering of our men in a shady courtyard. General Browning, our Divisional Commander, was there and he gave us a talk on the battle of Arnhem, its purpose and what we had achieved.

'All had not been in vain,' he said. 'although not completely successful, the operation has done much, and has cost the enemy heavily.'

The trucks rolled up and we embussed. We roared on over the Belgian landscape, through industrialised villages with tall chimneys, some of which still sent smoke eddying skywards, despite the destruction wrought around them. On through the narrow village streets, more often than not roughly paved and steep.

It was early afternoon when we reached Brussels Airport. It lay five miles or so short of the great city, and I was rather disappointed that we did not pass through it, or better still, stop there for a few hours, but the thought that we would be back in England that very day, with luck, made up for any such disappointments.

The long line of waiting Dakotas sent a thrill of anticipation through me. Much bantering talk flashed to and fro among the ranks. Home was but a few hours away now.

We had to wait nearly two hours, at the end of which time we had become a little impatient. Home was so near and yet so far away. Many things could happen to prevent us emplaning and taking wing to England.

But at last we were climbing up the metal steps and through the wide open doorway in the side of the plane. Good old Daks, the most reliable plane ever built. The fact that they burned easily under fire, because of not having self-sealing fuel tanks, was no fault in their design of construction. They were originally a civil plane, not made for war but, nevertheless, they served faithfully and well in that role when called upon to do so.

We had an American crew flying us back, and they were only too pleased to do the task. We, for our part, felt entirely at ease in the hands of these able men.

It was stuffy and somewhat warm inside the Dakota, about which hung the peculiar smell of dope that is always associated with planes, even metal ones. The starters whined and the engines roared into life, setting the whole fuselage trembling with their power. I strapped myself down in the ridiculously small indentation that represented a seat in the long aluminium benches that ran along the length of the body on both sides.

Then we were rolling down the hard packed runway, with the ground, which I could glimpse through the small round porthole, flashing by faster and faster every second, until it dropped below as we soared up and away from the airport.

I caught a glimpse of the outskirts of Brussels, but I was on the wrong side of the fuselage to get a good look at the city. I didn't mind. I was going home!

We droned on over the Belgian countryside, lifting and dipping as the bumps took hold of us. Above the roar of the motors, I could hear the sharp swish and whistle of the slipstream past the window by my side. We crossed over into France, although there was no way of telling by looking at the landscape. The little villages, marked by clusters of tiny red roofs, drifted by slowly underneath. The fields below looked tranquil from the height we were flying at. So different from those rain-sodden fields back in Holland at Arnhem. I couldn't forget those days. One minute they would be way back in the far corners of my memory, then they would flash to the fore in all their awful reality.

The pilots passed back word that we would be crossing the French coast in two or three minutes. Eagerly, we peered through the restrictive portholes, and beyond the shiny stretch of metal wings and protruding engine nacelles.

Slowly, almost imperceptibly, the grey Channel came into view. It had turned cloudy, and we were flying just above the intermittent woolly mass that seemed to stretch into infinity. But there were gaps through which I saw the cliffs of France slide away, to be replaced by an endless stretch of sparking waters, capped with white horses, indicating that all was not as smooth as our height would have led us to believe.

The beauty of the sky was not lost upon me, and I marvelled at the white cumulus masses that towered up for thousands of feet above the height at which we were flying. I also marvelled at the deep valleys between the rolling mist which now sped past beneath our wings, giving occasional glimpses of the grey waters below. But above all, I longed to see the white cliffs standing guard on our shores, or else the wide stretches of sands on the south coast around Romney and Rye, with the Martello forts dotting its curving shores.

I strained ahead of the immediate beauty searching eagerly, and at last it appeared – not the white cliffs, as I had half expected – but whitish golden sands backed by the rolling green fields of Kent. England! We were home! My heart beat faster, and I felt my eyes become moist. There she was, lying so quiet and peaceful, so different from the land of turmoil across that narrow strip of water we had just crossed.

The powerful motors of the Dakota carried us on over the lovely English landscape, looking like a fairyland from the air with its rolling hills and wooded dales, with little grey and red roofs peering out shyly from the sheltering masses of green foliage. The church spires jutting up proudly from the soil that had borne them for so long.

As we passed south of London, over my home county of Surrey, I was able to pick out familiar landmarks, and a quiet joy flowed through my whole body. I longingly watched those landmarks slide away behind. If only we could have landed at some aerodrome here, but that was not to be, for we were bound for our bases in the West Country. What matter, they were all in England. Why, by tomorrow I might even be home.

We reached the Newbury area and were told by our pilot that we would be landing at Ramsbury, which was their home base. Ramsbury I knew to be about twenty miles short of our aerodrome. Well, that was near enough.

We circled once, and I felt the wheels go down, shuddering in the slipstream, followed by the flaps with an even greater drag. The roar of the motors died, and the sharp whistle of the slipstream could be heard clearly above the low rumbling of the engines.

I tensed for the touchdown. It was perfect, and seconds later we were slowing to a halt on the runway. At the dispersal point we stopped. The door was opened and I dropped down onto the green grass of England once more. A feeling of exhilaration swept over me. We were all smiling stupidly, but happily. Home again, really home. Nothing could stop us now. The sun was shining and large white clouds drifted across the blue sky, lovely weather for late September. Eleven days ago we had taken off from a spot close by for what had turned out to be a somewhat disastrous operation, that can never be denied, even by those who make a habit of turning every defeat into a victory by long self-defending speeches. The war seemed infinitely far away. Arnhem just a bad dream, but a vivid one.

We lay on the grass, shielding ourselves as best we could from a cold wind that had sprung up. The sun had now gone behind the clouds. We waited for over an hour. It would soon be dark now, where were the trucks? We knew that we were back in England now for certain, always waiting.

Our American pilot passed by, and was amazed to see us still there. He was quite indignant about the whole matter, and told us to hop back in the plane and he would fly us over the last remaining miles to our field. We thanked him and jumped aboard. A few minutes later we were circling the familiar aerodrome of Fairford. It was almost dusk, and the runway lights were already glowing yellow through the dim evening light.

We touched down and slowed to a halt and, after deplaning, watched the plane roar forward again and take off into the gloom, its navigational lights shining brightly. A minute later it was gone and we trudged over to our huts, huts which now contained many empty beds that never again would be claimed by their previous owners. It was strange, entering that bare-walled building. It would never be the same again. Something would always be missing. I sank down on my bed and rested my head in my hands. Who would have thought that so much could happen in so few days? I looked up. But we must go forward until the end. This was just one episode in the long trail that might stretch ahead for many years yet. Yes, we must go on, and on.

For a moment I thought of those left behind, lying under sodden, rain-swept soil of Oosterbeek with its falling pine needles, and those who had been wounded with no chance of crossing the river with us, and those who had fallen into the hands of the enemy unwounded. But they would be avenged. Unbeknown to me at that time, we were destined to cross the Rhine again, this time to land on German soil.

This time victory would be undisputed, the enemy would be overwhelmed; the end was in sight.

Operation Varsity

Operation Varsity (24 March 1945) was the largest airborne operation in history to be conducted on a single day and in one location, involving more than 16,000 paratroopers and several thousand aircraft.

The objective was to cross the Rhine River, capture key territory and disrupt German defences aiding the advance of Allied ground forces. The British 6th Airborne Division was ordered to capture the villages of Schnappenberg and Hamminkeln, clear part of the Diersfordter Wald of German forces, and secure three bridges over the River Issel. The U.S. 17th Airborne Division was to capture the village of Diersfordt and clear the rest of the Diersfordter Wald of enemy forces. The operation was successful, with both divisions capturing Rhine bridges and towns that could have been used to delay British ground forces.

The airborne gliders landed in landing zones P, O, U and R under considerable anti-aircraft fire. The landing was difficult due to a great deal of haze and smoke resulting in a number of pilots being unable to identify their landing areas and losing their bearings. However the majority of the gliders survived, allowing the battalions of the brigade to secure the three bridges over the River Issel, as well as the village of Hamminkeln, with the aid of the 513th Parachute Infantry Regiment.

V. Miller Operational details:
- Glider chalk No. : 5
- Glider: Horsa Mk1- Serial No. RN545
- Glider Squadron: 'G' Squadron
- Departure airfield: Great Dunmow, Essex, England

- 1st Pilot: Sgt V. Miller
- 2nd Pilot: Sgt McGordon (RAF)
- Unit: Oxfordshire & Buckinghamshire Light Infantry (Major Gilbert)
- Tug Aircraft: Stirling Mk IV - R.A.F. 190 Squadron (1st Pilot Officer Bliss USAAF)

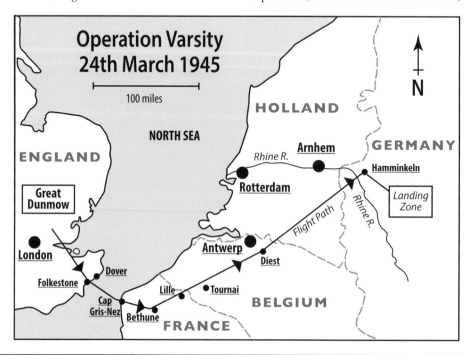

Chapter 22

Preparing for Wesel

As soon as I was back at Fairford I realised that things would never be the same again. So many faces were missing. Most of all I missed Tom. I visited the 'Nags Head' Inn in Letchlade. As I tramped down the twisting lane towards the village, I thought of Tom and his little MG and of our nightly visits to Letchlade, Swindon, Cirencester and all the other old towns and villages that saw us so frequently.

Never more would we go racing through the lanes of the Cotswolds with the wind whipping over the exposed seats of the low-slung powerful MG. This was my last visit to Nag's Head after my return that I could face without Tom. Flying had come to a halt despite the fact that new Horsas were arriving every day to replace those lying derelict and burned out on the fields of Holland.

On the 23rd of October, I climbed into the cockpit of a glider for the first time since we had flown into Arnhem. We were moving, leaving Fairford forever. The European campaign had shifted eastward and we also were moving eastward in England to shorten our operating range as much as possible, a range that stretched some of the towing aircraft to their limits. A plane towing a heavily laden glider eats up fuel.

I had Sergeant Hedman as my co-pilot. We stuck together after that last night at Arnhem, for it had made a bond between us that could never be broken. As we climbed up over Letchlade I took one last look at the village which had given Tom and me so many happy memories. The tall grey spire of the lovely village church slid by underneath and then was gone.

Our new aerodrome was Great Dunmow in Essex. I was happy to be there as it was very convenient for London. Bishops Stortford was but a few miles distant and that town was as pleasant as any I have known.

At Great Dunmow, whenever the prevailing weather permitted we took to the air. Mass landing exercises held precedence. We even carried one out during a small snow storm. Needless to say, the storm completely upset the exercise as visibility was reduced to nil. Even the birds weren't flying that day. We thought we could beat the snowstorm by several hours, but it fooled us.

The fatal year of 1944 bowed out and dropped back into the past. 1945 burst in upon us. The frequency of the mass landing exercises increased. Our High Command was determined that we should be on our toes in precision landings for the next operation as and when we might be called upon to carry it out. I didn't mind; I was enjoying myself flying high over the English countryside with the thunderous roar of the slipstream in my ears, one of hundreds of gliders in the air, moving in a long column with the occasional distraction of a mock fighter attack by the RAF Mosquitos and Typhoons.

Early on in the year we had a sudden influx of new crews. Included in the pilots arriving at our aerodrome, and all other aerodromes under our Wing, was a large proportion of RAF pilots, most of whom had been trained in the USA for bomber and fighter duties.

Apparently, our casualties at Arnhem had been so heavy, approaching 80%, that the RAF had been called upon to help us out. There were not sufficient of our own pilots being turned out at the training fields and, although we did not know it, the Rhine Crossing was looming nearer and nearer every day.

Quite naturally, a large number of the RAF pilots were rather fed up at being transferred onto glider flying. Their dreams had been of swift fighters darting through the heavens or of powerful heavy bombers thundering through the dark nights to pour down death and destruction onto the enemy below; and now, here they were on the slow lumbering gliders with the prospect of landing on enemy territory and engaging immediately in infantry fighting on the ground.

There were a few, however, who had actually volunteered for the job, but they were the exception rather than the rule. Despite their disappointment, the RAF pilots put their hearts and souls into the flying side of the game and did a magnificent task when the time arrived. I shall always be proud of my association with them all; they were a grand lot.

January and February came and went. In February I had the pleasure of meeting Captain BG again, my first pilot of the African and Sicilian days. He, who had gone over to Italy when I had returned home from North Africa, was as delighted at seeing me as I was at seeing him. Good old Bouch, one of the best and a man whom I shall always remember.

I learned from him that he had returned to England just before the Arnhem operation due to medical reasons. He had tried hard to accompany us on the operation, but the MO was adamant. However, he was not to be outdone. If he couldn't fly a glider in, he would at least fly over the battle area, and that is just what he did after persuading a re-supply pilot to let him accompany him on one of the drops. He admitted that there were times when he began to doubt the wisdom of volunteering to go on the trip. A Dakota on one side and another in front went down in flames that day. He only went on one of the drops and I cannot say that I blame him for declining further trips during that battle. Yes, Captain BG was a good officer and liked by all.

Every day the map of Europe showed a change. By now the Canadians and British had fought their way up to the Rhine through the hell of the Reichwald Forest battle and the floods around south of Arnhem. They were still short of the Rhine in the actual Arnhem area however, and held positions just north of Nijmegen. Further south, the US Army had already pushed up to the Rhine, and now the Allied Armies were massing all along the west banks ready for the plunge across. But where on the length of the Rhine would the crossing be carried out? I was vitally interested, for I knew that wherever it was, we would be in the thick of it.

It was a great day when we learned of the Remegen bridge being seized by the US Army over the Rhine, far to the south of the British sector. But somehow I knew that it was not sufficient. It was too far south to affect the British sector. No, we still had a part to play, of that I was convinced.

The intensity of our exercises increased. More and more gliders, including large numbers of the new Horsa Mark II, were arriving. We examined the first Mark II that landed in our field with great interest. It was a vast improvement over the old faithful Mark I, the principal improvement being the fact that the whole cockpit and nose could be swung open by the operation of two levers just behind the cockpit in the main part of the fuselage.

The nose-opening operation took less than a minute to carry out, and in a short few minutes, the heavy cargo of guns, jeeps and so forth could be rolling down the ramps and out through the wide open nose. When I thought of the terrific struggle we had with the removal of the tail section of our glider at Arnhem, I marvelled at the possibilities of the Mark II.

On the 7th of March, we carried out the most concentrated mass landings to date. The flight lasted two hours over several course headings, one of which brought us almost to the shores around the Wash., I watched with beating heart that day as the thin grey line of the North Sea grew steadily nearer and nearer. I knew that any day now we might be crossing that strip of coast to continue out over to enemy held territory, in all probability to Germany. That day, we turned a mile short of the sandy beaches and droned back to the base that had been selected for the mass landing known as 'Exercise Riff-Raff'. It was the last exercise carried out by the whole Wing before the Rhine crossing.

March the 20th 1945 saw us cut off from the outside world. Once again we were forbidden to step over the aerodrome boundary. Within me, for the last few days I had known it was coming. On the Rhine river banks, the 2nd Army had been laying down the largest smoke screen in history. The pall of dense smoke stretched the

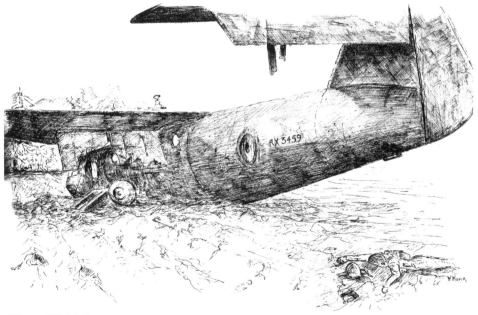

Horsa RX 3459

whole length of the Army's front, hiding the movements of the troops and guns and all the paraphernalia of war as they moved up for the assault.

Further south, the US Armies were poising themselves for a plunge across the river in their sectors. Day and night bombings by the RAF and USAAF were being stepped up to an incredible intensity. Communications, airfields, cities, docks, in fact everything that presented a military target was pounded without pause. As the hour of the Rhine river crossings drew near, the medium bombers and fighters confined themselves to blasting targets close in the rear of he opposite bank of the Rhine. AA positions, of which there were many, received especial attention.

We were now in the familiar confines of a briefing room once more. An air of expectancy and of confidence filled the large hut. This was to be the death blow to the enemy. They also sensed, or knew, that an operation was brewing, for periodically fighter bombers had slid across the night skies to attack our glider-packed fields.

Once I had watched the speeding black shape of what I believed to be a Messerschmitt 410 roar low over our airfield with guns hammering, the tracers darting forth like fiery tongues ahead of the racing machine. I had been travelling in London around the aerodrome perimeter track in a lorry after returning from a pleasant weekend at home. It was the sharp thunder of the fighter's guns, heard above the noise of the lorry's motor, that had prompted us to stop quickly and take cover. We also lost more than one Stirling bomber returning from a night supply drop to the underground forces in Denmark, Holland and Norway.

I will always remember the terrible rushing sound that had penetrated into one of the local pubs in Great Dunmow one night. It was about 9.30 p.m. The roar of the circling Stirling's engines, home again after completing its mission, could be heard above the chatter in the smoke filled bar.

Suddenly, the harsh blast of machine gun fire broke out sharply in one long burst. The bar hushed. We heard a thunderous rushing noise like the beat of a thousand birds' wings. Then a rocking explosion and silence, except for the rapidly fading drone of the enemy 'Intruder' fighter departing for home.

We all hurried out through the blackout curtain and stood in the main street. An angry red glow with intermittent flickering flames silhouetted the buildings of the village. The fire must have been over a mile away. We learned the following day that the Stirling had burned almost the second it was hit. Only one man got out in time by parachute – the rest perished.

Although the enemy's victories in this manner were the exception rather than the rule, it still had a disturbing effect upon the men, and although we knew from reports that the enemy's air force was practically destroyed, these demonstrations of his power, minute though they were, made us realise that they were still capable of operating against us.

Now, on the 21st of March, we were assembled for a briefing on an operation which would prove to be the last we would carry out in this war. Other small-scale airborne assaults were carried out later, such as the landings in Greece and on Rangoon, but not by the men who were now in the British Isles.

'Germany – this time you will be landing on the soil of Germany.' The voice of the briefing officer rang out clearly through the hut. The electric atmosphere that had prevailed grew even more intense. The briefing officer continued; 'Two airborne

Divisions will be taking part in this operation, the British 6th and American 17th, the date – Saturday the 24th. The divisions will have several objectives, including the capture of the high ground of the Diersfordter Wald and the village of Hamminkeln itself together with bridges over the Issel River east of Hamminkeln.

'The primary task will be the clearing of the high ground of the Diersfordter Wald in which the enemy has concentrated large numbers of troops and guns. In the north of our sector will be the German 7th Parachute Division and in the south the 84th Infantry Division, both under strength. Their only support is some hastily improvised troops consisting of one specially trained anti-airborne company and units of the Volksturm, the equivalent of our own Home Guard. Unlike the Arnhem operation, the divisions will be landing close to, and in many cases, almost on top of, their objectives.

'The enemy has concentrated a considerable amount of AA in the area but these will be receiving attention from tomorrow onwards from medium, light and fighter-bombers. Thirty minutes before you land, the RAF will be going in to give the positions a final strafe.' He paused for a moment to let this information sink in. The proverbial pin could have been heard to drop at that moment.

He went on, 'With regard to interference by enemy aircraft, this will be at the most slight and, in all probability, negligible. All nearby aerodromes, ten in all, will receive a concentrated bombing and strafing which should destroy practically all, if not all, aircraft of the enemy. Those that do manage to get into the air will be met by overwhelming numbers of our fighters. In fact, I think you can entirely discount any action against you by the Luftwaffe, but that does not mean you must not be on the alert for fighter attacks.

'2nd Army troops, consisting of the 15th and 52nd Divisions will be crossing over the Rhine during the night before your morning landings. This completely reverses the normal Airborne/Land Army tactics which have been followed up until now. It may in fact take the enemy by surprise, although we do know that they have been taking stringent action to forestall airborne landings in the area chosen by the High Command for your operation.

'The landing zones, as you will see from the map here, are about eight miles from the Rhine. This means that you will always be under the protection of the 2nd Army's medium artillery firing from the west bank of the Rhine. By the time you are completing your landings the units of the 2nd Army, who will have crossed over in the hours of darkness preceding, will have advanced two or three miles inland, leaving only five to cover before linking up with the airborne landings. However, it will be five miles of wooded country. It is estimated that contact will be made within twenty four hours, possibly less, and possibly a little more, but certainly no more than forty eight hours.

'Your route will be as follows,' he continued. 'Squadrons will take off and after forming up will rendezvous over Hawkinge, in Kent.' He traced the route with his finger, following the line of a length of red ribbon that started from our aerodrome at Great Dunmow.

'The course continues on over Hastings, across the Channel, striking land again at Cap Griz Nez near Calais. From there, you continue on to Bethune where the lift will turn eastward, passing south of Brussels. You will be crossing over a small stretch of Holland and so on over Germany to the Rhine and your landing zones.' He stopped.

I stared with fascination at the spot where the red ribbon terminated between the two towns on the Rhine named Emmerich in the north and Wesel in the south. I switched my eyes back to the briefing officer as he finished up saying, 'You will have fighter escort on the last leg of the flight. This is the biggest airborne operation planned to date and will consist of about 1300 gliders and involve 1700 powered aircraft, including towing tugs and paratroop droppers. In addition, 250 planes will be dropping supplies to you within a few hours of the landings. That's all. You will receive further briefings from your Squadron Commander, Met officer etc.'

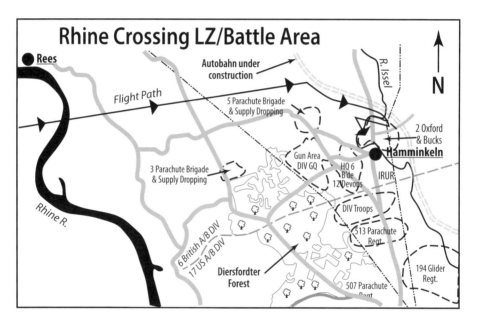

Our Squadron Commander took the briefing officer's place and proceeded to outline in more detail the actual tasks of our own squadron, breaking down the squadron into its flights and allotting each one its own landing fields.

At the conclusion, we all got up and moved onto the platform in order to study the maps and aerial photographs more closely. I paid particular attention to the photograph on which was marked an 'R' in red pencil showing a landing zone consisting of a field several hundred yards long and about half as wide – my particular field. I noticed that the end over which I would be making the approach had two houses.

Farm buildings were shown down each side of the field. All buildings were reported to house enemy troops – a cheerful thought.

By now I had been joined by the sergeant who would be acting as my co-pilot. He was one of the RAF replacements, a Sergeant McGordon, a very charming and conscientious fellow and above all a very skilful flyer and a dependable one at that.

I could not have wished for a better man. I knew Mac slightly, and we had got on well from the first.

Actually, I felt a little embarrassed at being in the position of captain of the glider and having Mac, who was a fully-qualified RAF pilot, as co-pilot. However I am sure that he understood the situation and knew that I knew he was just as capable of being first pilot as I was.

A spirit of eagerness pervaded the room. Excited voices rose and fell as points were argued out. Tug and glider pilots got together to iron out any differences or doubts existing. Co-operation was one hundred percent perfect. If ever there was an air and army team welded together, it was the RAF Troop Carrier Command and the Glider Pilot Regiment.

Mac and I sought out our tug pilot. To my surprise, he turned out to be an American pilot named Flight Officer Bliss, complete with American uniform. We learned that he had been a volunteer with the RAF before the United States had come into the war.

Recently he had been transferred back to the USAAF but as he had been flying with a British squadron for so long, he was finishing up his tour of duty with the RAF at Great Dunmow before leaving the RAF for good. He was a fine fellow and gave us one of the best tows I have ever experienced, from which I deduced that he had been towing gliders for a long time. His crew was a mixed one consisting of an Englishman, an Australian and a Canadian – a wonderful team, emphasising the unity between the Allies.

For the next half hour, we studied the maps again and again and carefully analysed the excellent aerial photographs. The maps had been carefully prepared and showed all the known enemy positions marked in various coloured inks. Power lines and telegraph poles, with their accompanying lines, were prominent. Many crossed our landing runs. I looked carefully at the village of Hamminkeln, one of our objectives. It wasn't very big but boasted two fair sized churches whose graceful spires stood out clearly in the photos. Our landing field was about half a mile from the outskirts of the village.

I noticed that the 3rd Parachute Brigade would be landing in an area on the edge of the western part of the Diersfordter Wald, while the 5th Parachute Brigade would be about one and a half miles from the village. In the fields (which were mostly ploughed) to the west, north, east and south of Hamminkeln were the landing areas of the 6th Air-landing Brigade, which we were bringing in by glider.

To the south east of the village, between it and Wesel, was the landing zone of the 17th US Airborne Division. On the whole it looked a very formidable and concentrated landing, which would have the backing of the 2nd Army surging forward but a few miles away on the great day.

The 2nd Army's artillery was to give the landing area a final heavy barrage to soften up the defences and to make one last strike at the many reported AA sites before we arrived. The barrage would be kept up until thirty minutes before we were due in.

The murmur of voices filled the room with navigators poring over maps with their crews. All their necessary equipment lay spread over the bare planked tables, protractors, computers, pencils, rulers and code books. Sharpened pencils traced lines across multi-coloured maps. The flight of a great air armada was taking one further step towards its materialisation.

Gradually, the briefing room emptied and Mac and I returned to our hut. The air was cool and clear outside after the stuffy smoke-laden atmosphere of the hut. It was a wonderful day with the sun shining through a mass of towering white clouds that moved majestically across the blue skies.

Well, this was it. We had waited a long time, and now the day was at hand. Perhaps this would be the final battle for the Airborne or perhaps there would be more yet. Other rivers lay athwart the army's advance before it could be said that Germany was completely overrun and defeated, but the Rhine was the greatest barrier of all. To cross the Rhine successfully meant sealing the fate of Germany, of that there was no doubt.

Back in the hut we found a batch of chattering glider pilots. The air of uncertainty that had been hanging over our heads was no longer there. Now we knew that we were on to something. The air that had replaced the one of uncertainty was one of 'Let's get it over with now.'

Already the officers of the troops we would be carrying had arrived on the 'drome and were in conference with our squadron commander. Some of the heavy equipment, such as six-pounder anti-tank guns and jeeps was already arriving. They would be loaded up tomorrow. The troops would not arrive until the day of the take-off.

Mac and I had been allotted thirty fully armed troops together with a hand trailer, so we were confronted with no loading problems. With the platoon we would be carrying, we had been ordered to attack and clear the houses surrounding our field. Five other gliders were designated to land in the same field, and together we should all make quite an effective fighting unit.

That night as I lay in bed I mused over the day's excitement. Tomorrow, the 22nd, we would start collecting together our G 1098 battle equipment and would also attend a more detailed briefing regarding exact landing zones and action after landing. This briefing would not be held in the main briefing room on the aerodrome but in a hut set aside especially for such occasions on our living site.

The 22nd was a busy day for us all. Trips to and from the Quartermaster's hut, with a long wait in line for each set of items which had to be signed for with meticulous care. During the month of January, I had attended a short three-week course on sniping at Watford in Hertfordshire. It had been pleasant there and I learned a great deal.

I had really volunteered because its proximity to London meant that I might have a chance to visit my wife to be Doreen. Now I found that I was to draw a sniper's rifle, complete with telescopic sight. I had hoped for a Sten gun, even though it had its drawbacks regarding the ease with which dirt could foul up the mechanism and magazine springs and its comparatively short range of accurate fire, but I had no choice and I was issued with a sniper's rifle.

In addition, I drew two hundred rounds of .303 ammunition in bandolier form together with two fully loaded magazines for a Bren gun and half a dozen No. 36 hand grenades.

We were issued with two forty-eight hour ration packs and one tin of iron rations consisting of some foul-tasting concentrated chocolate, tasting more like a well known brand of laxative than something pleasant as would be expected. A complete change of underclothing and an entrenching tool completed my issue.

We attended the squadron briefing that afternoon. Major Caroot was very thorough and nothing was left to chance. The planning seemed perfect and left no loophole for the enemy to take advantage as far as I could see. We sat on the long wooden forms listening to the Major and closely scrutinised the excellent sand model on the floor which represented the area in which we would be landing. The field in which Mac and I would touch down stood out clearly together with the surrounding buildings.

The Major droned on. 'You all know the general plan and we went over briefly our squadron and flight tasks yesterday. Today we will go through them in even more detail. We will be supplying thirty-six gliders, and that means seventy two crew. Six more crews and the necessary gliders will be held ready in reserve. I want this operation to be one hundred percent perfect and I want every man to do his best, as I know you will.'

The Major continued. 'Gliders, one to six (I felt my heart skip a beat) will land here.' He pointed to the field that I had been ruminating about, on and off, for the last twenty four hours with such intensity.

'Seven, to twelve will land here ....' He went on and on, each man present drinking in every word that fell from his lips. He ended up by stating that all glider pilots would stay with their loads once they were down until the initial tasks allotted the troops were completed, and then we were to rendezvous at a farm which I had noticed lay less than a mile from where we would touch down. At least we wouldn't have to march far.

OK I'll hand you over to your flight commanders now for their say.' Smoking had been permitted, as was always the case when briefings were on, whether it was the real thing or just an exercise, and the hut was thick with the fumes, forcing us to open all windows before settling down to listen to our respective flight commanders.

Outside, I could hear the guard walking round and round, keeping a sharp lookout to see that no unauthorised person came within listening distance of the hut.

I listened intently to our Flight Commander as he outlined the part our particular batch of gliders would play. Every word sank deep down into the core of my brain as he went on to explain that gliders one to six would have the task of clearing out the buildings around the edge of the field in which we were to land. We would accompany the troops that we were carrying into the assault, then, unless the local situation decided otherwise, we would rendezvous at the farm to await further instructions.

After the briefing broke up, I took another look at the photographs showing my landing field. I calculated that there would be about twenty to thirty seconds when we were coming in on the final approach, including the touchdown and landing run, when we would be extremely vulnerable to the enemy troops in the buildings alongside and at the end of the field. Assuming that we would land down the centre of the ploughed field, that would leave about seventy-five to one hundred yards on either side to which could be added another ten yards or so to allow for the set-back of the buildings. That distance isn't much if a defending soldier is anything of a marksman.

Well, I thought, someone has got to land there, and in all probability there will be others landing in even worse areas regarding close proximity to the enemy. It is the first sixty to ninety seconds or so between the approach, touchdown and the vacating of the glider that leaves the glider utterly helpless and at the mercy of any enemy troops in the immediate neighbourhood.

This applies equally to the paratroopers as they float earthwards, including the short time it takes them to release their parachutes and shed the harness and to take up defensive positions. In addition, there is the time it takes for them to get to another parachute, which may have floated down independently, carrying their arms and equipment.

When gliders are carrying heavy equipment, the vulnerability is even more pronounced as, even at the best of times with the use of the new Mark II Horsas and the Hamilcar gliders, a minute or two elapses before they are unloaded and their men and equipment are ready for action, more often than not in an exposed position due to the open space required in which to land the glider.

I left the hut with mixed feelings. The first excitement of the pending operation had worn off, and now I began to examine it in a more sober fashion. I weighed the pros and cons of the whole thing and finally came to the conclusion that the overall picture presented a better chance of success than any other operation so far attempted.

The weather continued fine, but with rather more cloud about than I would have wished. Well, we had another two days yet and it was predicted that fine weather would be our ally.

More heavy equipment was arriving on the airfield, that is, heavy as far as the airborne is concerned – Jeeps, guns and trailers. Mac and I decided we would look over the glider we had been allocated. I knew that it would be a Mark I, as all Mark IIs had been naturally allotted to crew who were taking in the guns and jeeps, and we were carrying troops only plus their small hand trailer.

I felt quite confident and not a little high spirited as I crossed over the wide expanse of grass towards the long line of gliders lying around the edge of the field. Tomorrow they would be marshalled ready for the takeoff on the 24th. We soon located our glider with the official number RN 545 marked on the fuselage together with our chalked number 5 as per the blackboard in the briefing room.

I was glad to find that she was a fairly new issue. This we knew from the official number. Any glider with the prefix R could be considered pretty new. The numbers of the older gliders, of which there were still a large number, mainly began with the letter D.

We checked over the controls and found that we had struck lucky as regards lightness on the control wheel. Gliders could be very heavy on the controls, making flying them almost a nightmare and certainly an excessive physical strain on a long flight. Our flight to Germany would take about four hours.

We went over the glider thoroughly and were completely satisfied. I climbed down the steps onto the grass and looked around at the other huge black shapes whose ominous shadows were to fall over the German homeland in the very near future.

Most of the glider pilots were out on the field. Apparently, we had not enough of the Mark IIs to take all the heavy equipment and the Mark Is were also being utilised for that purpose. This entailed the terrific struggle of easing the jeep and six-pounder guns through the lowered door in the side of the glider, which formed a ramp.

For a moment, I watched a nearby glider crew struggling alongside the gunners of a six-pounder and the driver of the jeep as they fought to literally lift the vehicle around the corner formed by the opening in the side. I crossed over and added my strength. It took us another fifteen minutes to get the jeep in. Time and time again, just when we thought we had manoeuvred the jeep through the narrow opening, we found that some small projection was preventing the vehicle being pushed in the last three inches or so that would enable it to be moved down inside the tubular-shaped fuselage.

I was sweating at the end of the struggle and my back and arms ached, but I didn't mind; I felt I was contributing just a little more to the success of the operation. Mac and I returned to our mess for a well-earned tea.

Friday, the 23rd of March 1945 arrived and we were briefed again and then drew further driblets of equipment. I had another look over our glider, just to make sure we had not missed anything. I wrote several letters, for I was not sure whether we would have time on the morrow; we would be far too busy making last minute arrangements and attending final briefings.

The weather remained fine. An atmosphere of tenseness prevailed. Tomorrow was the day. Nothing could stop us now, unless the weather failed us. There wasn't much chance of the 2nd Army beating us to it as they had done at Caen, Versailles and Tournai. We were completely committed.

That evening, many made the best of it at the mess bar, despite a warning from our Squadron Commander. I spent a few hours at the mess but drank in extreme moderation, as has always been my policy when an operation was pending. Mac took it easy as well.

The mess that night rang with the usual bawdy songs to be heard whenever men of the services get together before a big do. It was a great thing in the way that it helped to relax the pent-up feelings of those concerned and broke up the morbid atmosphere that most likely would have otherwise prevailed.

I was back in my hut by nine o'clock checking over my equipment and rifle together with the ammunition. I didn't want to get caught off balance tomorrow through negligence on my part. Errors on a battlefield, more often than not, are the last ones that a man ever makes.

A silence had settled over the hut. The men were busy at various tasks, mainly cleaning and assembling their weapons, while others wrote a last letter which would be posted twenty four hours after we had left. One or two just read or sprawled on their beds looking up at the ceiling with unseeing eyes through the curling smoke of cigarettes.

For a moment I paused to wonder what thoughts were passing through each man's head. None showed their thoughts outwardly, whatever they were. All kit bags had been stacked against the walls of the hut to be stowed until our return, each neatly labelled, just in case.

I rolled into my bed about 11 o'clock and fell into a light sleep. I was awake again less than five hours later before the official reveille which was timed for 4.00 a.m. The lights of the hut were still burning, indicating that the latecomers from the mess had not troubled to switch them off for the few remaining hours left before they were to be called from their beds again.

It was still dark outside and I felt dog tired, but I knew the feeling would wear off with the coming dawn. I felt a queer constriction within me as I realised that this was the day for which we had been waiting so long. Even back in the days of the invasion of Europe, the dim thoughts of future operations had hinged around the crossing of the Rhine, like a symbol marking the end of German power.

As I dressed in the thick sleepy atmosphere of the hut, a hundred thoughts whirled through my head on their chaotic course. In a few hours we would be winging our way across the peaceful English countryside with the multitude below wondering at the mighty air armada thundering past overhead in a seemingly endless line. Over the Channel, on over France, Belgium and Holland to a landing over the Rhine. Hundreds of gliders at a time swinging in for landings, swooping and turning to avoid the flak thrown up from the ground below. Glider after glider swooping in to touch down and race across the trim ploughed fields, grinding to a halt in a cloud of dust, or maybe flame. Watching out for other gliders sliding in from either side, the ones coming down directly over your head, or the machine darting in underneath just on your last hundred yards' run-in.

The raising of the sliding door, the men hurling themselves out free of the confines of the glider to hit the soil of Germany, ready to engage the enemy. The nerve-wracking seconds when you aren't quite sure of the reception in your immediate area. The whistle and crash of the succeeding gliders swooping in all around, bringing more and more men and equipment in the biggest concentration of airborne forces ever mustered.

I hurried over to the wash house with those thoughts chasing one after the other through my sleep-starved head. I washed and shaved, following the usual routine. Might as well go in with a clean shaven chin. It might be the last shave for some time to come – I was thinking of Arnhem then.

God, I hope it won't turn out to be another Arnhem. No, not this time – the odds were too much in our favour for that to happen. We just couldn't lose this time. Many would die, that fact had to be faced. Well, I wasn't going to be one of them. I suppose that last thought was in everyone's mind – we all thought we were impervious to shot and shell – until we got it. Well, what the hell, we could only wait and see. Yes, wait and see, that was the army's motto and that went for any army, whether it was Allied or enemy.

I returned to the hut with Mac, still feeling woolly in my head, but the cold water had helped. How I hated being up at such an early hour. Foolish as the thought was, I always wondered why the devil the army couldn't stick to regular hours. Why the heck did men have to fight and prepare to fight at such ungodly hours?

Mac and I collected together our haversacks, arms and equipment and made our way through the still-reigning darkness to the mess hall. Others had beaten us to it but many more were yet to come. It was lively in the brightly lit mess. Fresh eggs and bacon awaited us – the usual farewell meal. The tea had plenty of sugar and milk in it too – well, why shouldn't it? The cooks knew that a fair percentage of the men wouldn't be coming back to fill their bellies at this mess again.

The WAAFs serving us smiled in a wan way and bid us luck as we filed past them picking up the plates. The men cracked jokes with them and the atmosphere cheered up a little. Behind the WAAFs, the cooks stood smiling benignly. We told them to have a meal ready for our return or else....

Soon the mess was filled with the chatter of many voices. The first faint glimmer of dawn was creeping in through the windows. I felt more alive after sipping the sweet hot tea. Breakfast over, we went off to the briefing room for a final weather check. We met our tug crew there and exchanged banter, especially with the rear gunner to whom we gave strict instructions where to point his four guns that poked out backwards towards the glider when in flight.

The weather was going to hold good. Cloud would be encountered all the way to the coast, but its base was just above our flying height, which was 2,500 feet all the way to Germany. If cloud was encountered below our flying height, we were to fly on the 'angle of dangle' instrument, which was supposed to be a very efficient instrument to fly on when visibility was nil. Sometimes they worked, and sometimes they didn't.

Our intelligence officer got up and gave us a final report. He cheerfully informed us that the AA defences had increased but that fighters would be going in after them before we landed.

Chapter 23

To the Rhine

We left the briefing hut in the half-light of the coming day. Already the RAF crews were out warming up the mighty engines of the Stirling bombers that in a short while would be towing us across the skies over Europe. One after the other, they coughed into life and rumbled deeply in the morning air.

With the heavy rucksack on my back, plus two hundred rounds of ammunition in bandoliers draped around my body, fifty odd rounds in the Bren gun magazines, six grenades, my rifle and its accompanying telescopic sight and, last but not least of all, my tin hat perched on my head, I felt more like the proverbial knight of old, encased in heavy armour than the supposedly lightly armed 20th Century airborne soldier. The straps of the rucksack were already biting into my shoulders and we were just starting out. At least I wouldn't be wearing it while flying.

At a point where the perimeter track passed the back of the mess, we stopped. Here a truck would be picking us up and taking us around the perimeter track to the gliders. The marshalling point of the gliders was a good mile from the mess and time was short. I looked at my watch – 6.45 a.m. Take-off was at 7.15 a.m. for the first glider and tug – half an hour. If the truck came up within a minute or two, we should have twenty minutes or so to chat with our load and check over the glider.

Although dawn was setting in, it was still too dark to see more than a few hundred yards. The marshalled aircraft were too far away to pick out with the eye. We waited and waited. I began to get uneasy and felt the sweat break out all over me. Where the hell was the driver? It was nearly seven o'clock. Damn and blast him. If we had known how long he would be we could have walked around. At ten past seven he came roaring up to halt with a screech of brakes. We piled in cursing him for his lateness. I never found out what had held him up, all I knew then was that it would be a close shave. No time for a talk with the passengers on post-landing action, much as I would have liked. You couldn't discuss things once you were airborne; the thunder of the slipstream prevented anything but a shouted conversation with your nearest passenger.

We lurched and swayed around the perimeter track at a record speed, which at any other time would have ended up with the driver being under charge. He was spurred on by our dire threats and curses.

We stopped with a jerk alongside the long line of black gliders marshalled ready at right angles to the runway. On the far side of the runway were massed the huge Stirlings. The motors of the first two were already turning over ready for the take-off. Men were milling around the first glider attaching it to a tractor to tow it onto the runway. I hurried down the line, with Mac panting after me, and reached our glider indicated by the chalked number 5. I was perspiring freely from my efforts and cursed the driver again and again.

I estimated that I had five minutes left before we would be towed onto the runway. I threw my equipment through the open doorway and clambered quickly up the portable steps. The lieutenant in charge of our load met me as I stepped in. I had a hurried word with him before making my way through the connecting door to the cockpit.

Mac was still outside ready to check that the elevators and rudder swung in the correct directions as I worked the wheel and rudder bar controls in the cockpit. I gave Mac the appropriate signals as I swung the wheel over first one way and then the other and kicked the rudder bar, first left and then right. I got the OK signal from Mac and saw him dive for the steps to enter the fuselage. Panting, he sat down on the right hand seat and strapped himself in.

I swiftly carried out my cockpit check of the instruments, running my eye over the altimeter for correct setting, air pressure gauge, compass setting, and worked the release lever to see that it moved freely.

Out of the corner of my eye I saw the huge tail of the glider directly in front move forward, swinging slightly from side to side. Damn, I thought, we are next and we aren't ready, not quite. Feverishly, I placed the maps of the route in order of flight on the ledge in front. I fumbled around and found the straps, slipping them over my shoulders and over my thighs, thrusting home the locking pin after pulling the webbing together tightly.

The first combination was already roaring away down the runway. I could not see them off owing to the line of gliders in front being in the way, but the rising thunder of the Stirling's motors penetrated sharply through. I felt a faint tremor. The operation was on – the huge armada that was soon to be droning its way over Germany had started to spread its wings on the early morning air. Due to the excitement of the last ten minutes or so, I had hardly noticed that the grey dawn had turned into almost full daylight.

A tractor raced up and swung around under our nose, its coupling bar bumping and crashing behind it. The glider in front was being towed out onto the runway. The Stirling was already there, its four propellers spinning in shimmering discs in the early morning sunlight. Men darted forward, two towards the glider and two more to the Stirling's tail.

Each pair of men thrust the plugs on the end of the tow rope into the sockets on each of the glider's wings and in the Stirling's fuselage.

The ground crew scrambled down the steps they had placed under each of the Horsa's wings and dashed back to the side of the runway taking the steps with them. The controller was already waving his yellow discs slowly from side to side above his head as the massive Stirling eased forward with rumbling motors to take up the slack. As soon as the rope tightened, the controller whipped down the discs and with a mighty burst of power, as the pilot thrust forward the throttles, the Stirling surged forward smoothly with the Horsa being drawn swiftly along behind on the end of 300 feet of rope.

I didn't see the take-off being completed for, hardly had the combination began to roll down the runway, then our towing tractor moved forward and, seconds later, we were being swung around onto the runway facing into wind with our Stirling tug already there. Vaguely, I noticed the tail unit of the Stirling quivering under the slipstream blast from the four engines and the vibration from the slowly-turning power plants waiting to be unleashed in a mighty surge of power, thousands of horsepower at the tips of the pilot's fingers.

I was gripping the wheel tightly with my left hand while with the other I clasped the brake lever down on my right. This was it! The great moment! In two minutes we would be accelerating swiftly down the runway that stretched away up front straight ahead, slightly undulating and then, in about a mile, rising into the air to take our place amongst the mightiest airborne armada of our time.

Beads of perspiration trickled down my forehead and ran down my cheeks. My heart was beating hard. I blinked the sweat from my eyes. Out of the corner of my eye I saw the ground crewman on my side thrust the rope plug into the socket on our port wing. I knew that another man was doing the same on the other side. The men on the far end of the rope emerged from under the tail end of the Stirling and dashed back through the slipstream thrown out by the whirling blades of the great black bomber, clutching their caps as they did so.

The men under the wings were gone now. My throat and mouth were terribly dry. The intercom broke into life and the voice of the Stirling pilot came back clearly over the connecting wire asking if all was well. I released my hand from the wheel and placing the microphone against my mouth acknowledged, 'OK for takeoff' having given Mac a quick glance of inquiry and received the thumbs-up signal from him. Mac was listening in and knew what was going on. God, how I hated the suspense of the take-off where an operation was involved! Once we were airborne, I knew that I would feel OK.

I glanced outward and gave the thumbs-up signal to the controller who had been standing ready with the discs motionless above his head. He swung the discs down and up. I gripped the wheel again with a sweat covered hand and fingers and wrapped my right hand around the brake lever tighter.

The Horsa shivered and trembled violently as the Stirling's engines revved up and the slipstream came twisting back. With fascinated eyes I watched the snake-like rope straighten out. It tautened and the Horsa bucked lightly against the restraint of the brakes. The yellow discs fell. The voice of the tug pilot came back clearly 'Brakes off, number two.' I slammed the lever forward and heard Mac confirm the action.

Through the walls of the cockpit, I heard the Stirling's motors rise to a note of thunder. The Horsa shook violently under the new lashing of the slipstream. We surged forward swiftly under the powerful pull of the tug. I freed one hand from the wheel and waved at the swiftly receding line of men and WAAFs lining the runway to bid us farewell.

The runway beneath our nose began to reel away faster and faster. The tail of the Stirling swung gently from side to side, and I compensated with rudder. The swing ironed itself out as both the tug and glider gained speed and the increasing slipstream began to make the rudders more effective while the pressure on the wheel and rudder bar increased.

The cockpit was now filled with a thunderous roar which made ordinary speech impossible. I watched the flickering air speed needle creep up. Fifty, sixty, seventy mph. Still we hugged the runway. The green grass on either side of the concrete strip blurred by. Seventy-five mph. I eased back on the wheel. The Horsa, heavily laden as it was, rose smoothly free of the runway. It would have kept on climbing, but I eased it down to within a few feet of the concrete in order to give the Stirling the best chance of rising by allowing the tug pilot to gain take-off speed, about one hundred and ten mph.

The slipstream flailing back from the four spinning propellers of the Stirling came bouncing back off the runway, striking forcefully under our fuselage and wings. The wings fought to drop as the stream of air hit first one and then the other. Sheer physical effort is usually needed to hold a glider level on takeoff and this time was no exception.

My shirt clung to my back, soaked with perspiration. The end of the field loomed nearer and nearer. The airspeed was now over one hundred miles per hour, while the runway seemed to be rolling by at an incredible speed. The Stirling left the ground at last, rising swiftly up higher and higher. The hedge bordering the flying field slid past under our nose some hundred or so feet below. I caught a glimpse of a few reserve gliders parked around the boundary slipping past, and then we were climbing up into the fresh early morning while the dew still lay around on the rolling fields below our spreading wings.

My struggle with the wheel and rudder slackened as we climbed free of the turbulent slipstream and took up our correct towing position just above the corkscrewing slipstream from the tug's four propellers. A feeling of relief passed through me. The tension of the take-off eased away and once more I felt in my element, the air. It was as if a bond had fallen away each time my wheels left the troubles of terra firma and we rose swiftly up through the clean crisp air and the celestial glory of the towering white clouds which drifted so unconcernedly across the blue skies above the troubled earth.

I relaxed and watched the altimeter needle move around the dial – 200, 300, 400, 500 feet. We were flying through smooth air now, and the Stirling seemed poised motionless, suspended between heaven and earth, although I knew the labouring engines were pulling us through the air at some 120 miles per hour and lifting us higher and faster every second.

I looked across at Mac and nodded. He took over the controls. The glider never deviated one inch from her position – good old Mac – a wonderful flyer. I looked back through the communicating door and gave the thumbs-up to the men seated back in the fuselage. They grinned back and replied in like manner. The lieutenant grinned and shouted something about a 'nice takeoff'. I turned back and looked out through the side perspex window.

The peaceful fields of Essex moved slowly past underneath. Some of the villages huddled in the valley were still blanketed in the morning mist, hidden except for the grey spires and towers of the churches, which projected through the smooth white masses. The whole landscape looked fresh and green, far removed from war and the grim task which we had set ourselves.

I looked at the altimeter and saw that we had now reached 1200 feet. I lifted my eyes and stared ahead. A long irregular line of gliders and their parent tugs straggled out ahead climbing steadily upwards. They were heading for the turning point where we would form up. Then we would return on a reciprocal course bringing us back over our home base from where we would start out on our first leg.

It was getting slightly colder. The smooth air rasped past outside the cockpit with a high-pitched tone. Still we climbed, 2000 feet now. Only 500 more and we would level off. Ahead, I could see the first combinations going into a left-hand turn. They were forming into pairs in echelon, that is one combination flying slightly behind, to one side and above the other.

The leaders completed their turn and were coming back towards us, slightly higher than we were. The last mile or so seemed to rush up and flash by. We went into a turn, cutting in sharply in order to team up with the combination that had taken off before us. We made it and were riding in our correct position within two or three minutes, reaching our assigned altitude of 2500 feet and levelling off, air speed 145 mph.

The ground below seemed far off now, entirely disconnected from us. I almost felt like singing as I watched the remainder of the squadron, still climbing up in the opposite direction as we headed back for the airfield. Then we were over it and turning onto our first course.

I felt a slight pang of regret as I watched our base slide by under our nose, but forgot it almost immediately. We headed almost due south, and I noticed that my pencil line across the map passed close to Gravesend on the River Thames. I knew the town slightly and eagerly awaited its appearance. I was thwarted, however, for we passed to the east of it and as I was sitting on the port side it was impossible for me to see it. The river passed underneath, a silvery thread with which I was well acquainted.

Then the fields of Kent were before me. Kent had always been one of my favourite counties, and I always experienced great pleasure whenever the opportunity of flying over it presented itself.

I was glad that Mac was at the controls, for I was able to marvel at the beauty of the Garden of England flowing past slowly underneath. So peaceful and unhurried, I thought of the landscape unfolding its panoramic carpet below. Twisting streams meandering through the valleys. The little grey stone buildings nestling snugly around the village churches. Our height, if anything, enhanced the wonder of that lovely county which is also so enchanting from the ground.

I raised my eyes and looked ahead. My pleasant thoughts were rudely shattered by the sight of the long line of gliders and tugs stretching away in front, all the machines, except the very nearest, seemingly poised motionless on the morning air. Those near dipped and swayed in a gentle see-sawing motion. The vast armada flew on, displaying a power in the air that could not be denied. The very numbers tended to dispel any fears that I might have had. If we were afraid, I was sure that the enemy over the Rhine would be undergoing even worse pangs of fear the moment our air fleet appeared over their heads and the great black shapes wheeled and swooped down on their purposeful task.

I took over from Mac, who seemed grateful for the chance to peer down at the last English fields we would be seeing for a little while, perhaps forever. It was a pleasure to be flying our Horsa, so smooth and light. Just the slightest movement on the control column, or on the rudder bar every few seconds, was sufficient to keep our glider dead behind the four-engined plane hauling us through the Kentish skies. I watched the tail of the Stirling rising and falling very slowly, and carefully followed through its every variation of height and course. By doing this, the rope never tautened or slackened beyond the permissible margin, thus ruling out the possibilities of a broken rope and a forced landing.

Idly, I watched the rear gunner of our tug swinging his gun turret from side to side, sweeping the peaceful English skies with the menacing barrels of his four .303 machine guns. Well, it was good practise and showed that the rear gunner was on the alert.

The dull roar of the slipstream beat in ceaselessly, rising and falling as we climbed and dipped gently. I felt Mac tapping my right arm and looked across at him for a moment. He pointed downward and ahead. I leaned as far forward as I could without disturbing the control column and possibly causing a dive. I searched the landscape below and then spotted the object of Mac's interest. One of the Horsas had broken free and was gliding slowly but surely for the ground. The tug that had been towing it was turning in a big circle over the spot. I watched the glider diving earthward towards a large ploughed field. No landing under fire for that crew and passengers.

I lost sight of the glider just before it touched down, as we had flown past the spot. I forgot the incident as I watched a long stream of Hamilcars, towed by Halifax four-engined bombers, converging towards us about two miles away on our starboard. It was a heartening sight, and Mac and I exchanged grins.

The coast was ahead. I could now see where the green fields of Kent ended and the cold looking waters of the Channel began. Folkstone was hidden by a layer of cloud. We had turned onto our second leg. A queer constriction closed around my chest and heart as I watched the white cliffs fall away behind us. Some thirty miles ahead of us lay the French coast but a fairly heavy mist hung tenaciously near the water and visibility was down to about ten miles at the most, probably even less.

We roared on over the Channel at a steady air speed of 145 mph – height 2500 feet. I signalled for Mac to take over which he did immediately. I checked on the map and estimated that we should sight the coast of France within about twelve minutes. Sitting back, I relaxed, gazing down at the waters of the Channel which looked as smooth as a mill pond, an impression that was a deceptive one brought about by the height at which we were flying. I noticed a boat steaming along below leaving a long wake stretching out far behind. Probably one of the rescue ships that we had been told would be patrolling our route, just in case of forced landings in the Channel.

I swept my gaze around the skies. Alongside, below, above and away far out ahead stretched the immense line of gliders and tugs, silhouetted against the grey waters of the Channel below or the towering white cumulus clouds above whose roots lay about five hundred feet above us.

Directly below, about five hundred feet lower, I picked out a Hamilcar towed by a Halifax, both machines appearing motionless against the waters beneath as we were both flying along at identical air speeds. For several minutes I watched the clear-cut wings of the Hamilcar, idly speculating as to its load.

I glanced at my watch. Should see Cap Griz Nez in two or three minutes now.

I felt my heart beat a little faster as I strained hard to penetrate the white mist that clung so persistently to the waters below. It was impossible to pick out the true horizon for the mist merged indistinguishably with the distant sky.

Then, through the mist, I picked out the hazy outline of the French coast. At last! A minute later the white cliffs were standing out sharply through the mist. At the same moment I saw that one of the Hamilcars had broken free from its parent tug. I stared in fascination as I tried to judge its height above the Channel, trying to gauge whether it had sufficient height to clear the cliff tops of Cap Griz Nez. We were steadily overtaking the falling machine and we lost sight of it as it slid by underneath our nose.

French Coast Ahead

The shell-and bomb-pitted soil of Cap Griz Nez was directly underneath us now. I searched the area for signs of the long distance cross-Channel guns which had been shelling the Dover area on and off for the past two or three years, but could not pick them out, so well were they camouflaged. Now they were lost to the enemy, taken by the Canadians as they advanced up the coast from the Normandy bridgehead.

On our left was the town of Calais, around which we skirted, for it was still occupied by enemy troops, who continued stubbornly to defend the port. Low lying cloud over Calais prevented me from catching a glimpse of it.

We altered course by about ten to fifteen degrees to port and continued on over the lovely wooded landscape that spread out before us. Between the woods stretched huge tracts of farmland while little red-roofed villages lay scattered below in profusion.

I noted mentally what fine landing zones those huge un-hedged fields would have made if our cross-Channel invasion across the Straits of Dover had been made last year instead of in Normandy. History has shown, of course, that in actual fact the extremely strong defences thrown up by the enemy in the Calais area would have made an operation there highly dangerous. Nevertheless, I realised that from the point of view of airborne landing zones it was the dream of every airborne operation come true. There was room for our mighty stream and many others to land in those fields below.

The neat red-roofed farms and the huddled villages went by underneath the roaring majesty of our huge armada. How those French people must have looked up and wondered, even accustomed as they were to seeing vast squadrons of bombers and fighters flying past overhead.

Thirty minutes after we had crossed the French coast, the town of Bethune slid up to meet us. Here our stream turned due east. Mac followed our tug around into the turn, holding a beautifully co-ordinated bank. We straightened out and I motioned to him that I would take over if he was tired, and he nodded. I expect he was keen to get a look at the countryside flowing past underneath. The pilot actually at the controls has very little time to watch the landscape below, except for hastily snatched glances.

I gripped the wheel once more and placed my feet on the rudder bar. We were in the 'low tow' position, that is, below the tug and clear of the slipstream, and had been since just before we had crossed our aerodrome after forming up. I trained my eyes on the gently swaying tail of the Stirling and the ceaselessly revolving turret of the rear gunner. Actually, if anything, it was slightly less fatiguing having the plane silhouetted against the clouds and blue sky rather than the ground as is the case when one is in the 'high tow' position above the towing plane and its slipstream.

Mac was peering closely at the maps showing the route and I could see him out of the corner of my eye tracing the course with his finger. It was then that I saw our first fighter plane escorting us. It came racing up alongside, showed its belly for an instant, then dived away like a meteor. I took my eyes off the tug for a moment and glanced through the side window. A feeling of elation ran through me as I picked out a large flight of Typhoons cruising along a little higher than us and on the same course.

I glanced back at the tug to make sure we were not drifting off from him and then looked out again. Another flight of fighters was speeding along not far below us. I looked up directly above and ahead and there, sure enough, was another flight of some twenty or thirty fighters. Magnificent, I thought. We certainly have got some protection. I didn't have to call Mac's attention to the planes; he had already spotted them and grimaced back to me approvingly. It certainly was a morale booster to us all.

Ten minutes later we passed Lille well to the south. I could pick out the sprawling town, although the haze that hung over the area prevented any clear picture of it. We droned on eastward and less than ten minutes later were crossing over the French-Belgian border, although there was no way of telling it except by checking the map. If I had been able to scan the ground below carefully, I would probably have been able to pick out the striped pole and hut on the roads leading from one country to the other. At the moment, I was devoting all my attention to the Stirling in front.

The first big town we passed over or near in Belgium was Tournai and it was here that I handed back to Mac again. Un-strapping my safety harness, I got up out of my seat for the first time since we had strapped ourselves in on the airfield. I straightened out my stiff back and, after bending over Mac and telling him where I was going, stepped through the communicating door into the main part of the fuselage.

The men seemed glad to see me. Some raised their hands in salutation and grinned at the same time. Some just grinned, but one or two didn't look so good and only managed the ghost of a sickly smile. The noise inside the fuselage was terrific as the slipstream rushed by, beating on the wooden walls of the tubular body. I grinned at them all and waved back. I always tried to look completely at ease when speaking to the men we carried, for I believed they had a very critical eye on their pilots, in whose hands they were. I tried, therefore, to instil confidence in them.

I managed a few shouted words with the officer in charge above the noise. One of the men opened up a large Thermos of tea and poured me a cup. I didn't want to take it as we had a flask of our own in the cockpit, but he insisted. I accepted with a feeling of gratification, for it exemplified the spirit that bound together all men of the airborne, regardless of rank or branch.

I made my way back to the cockpit, holding onto projections as I did so for the glider was beginning to heave and roll as we ran into bumpy weather. In the cockpit, I pulled out the Thermos flask we had brought with us and poured out a mugfull of hot tea for Mac. I then slid into my seat and re-strapped myself in. I motioned to Mac that I would take over and he relinquished the control wheel and slipped his feet off the rudder bar. Undoing his straps, he bent down and picked up the mug from which tea was splashing due to the wallowing motion of the glider. I think he was looking forward to the hot liquid, for if he felt anything like I did before I had swallowed the hot tea moments before, his throat must have been absolutely parched.

The peaceful Belgian countryside spread out below showed no signs that not a long time before the Allied armies had been rolling forward over it, pursuing relentlessly the remnants of an all-but-broken German Wehrmacht. I took my eyes from the tug in front for a moment and glanced at the map. I saw that we were flying just south of Mons. Mons! The scene of fierce fighting between the British and the Germans in the 1914-1918 War.

If only those hundreds of thousands of sightless eyes buried down there below us could have seen our mighty armada thundering steadily onwards to give battle to the very same enemy against whom they had fought nearly thirty years ago! Would they have held sorrow in their eyes to think that all their efforts and supreme sacrifice had been in vain? Or would they have watched the mighty stream passing over their graves with a hope that this time the enemy would surely pay in full and never again be given the chance to rise and carry their flaming banner of hate and destruction across the face of war-torn and shattered Europe?

Mons and its tragic memory fell behind and soon we were drawing up parallel with Brussels. I had hoped to catch a glimpse of that great city, but we passed some fourteen miles to the south over a great tract of wooded country known as the Foret de Soignes. A distant heat haze prevented my seeing even the outermost suburbs.

About two minutes later we turned onto a fresh course some forty five degrees to port. I made a swift mental calculation and reckoned that we had about 130 to 140 miles to go; that would be about one hour's flying time at our present ground speed.

We were now flying over vast tracts of farmland with little clusters of farms standing out clearly from the brownish ploughed soil. Between these lay stretches of bleak looking moorland and occasional forests. The roaring of the slipstream drummed on incessantly, seemingly a permanent part of my life now. The glider rose and fell as we rode the air-pockets. The hot upward-swirling currents of air known as thermals increased as the sun rose higher and higher. The turbulent currents, meeting the cool layers of air above our flying level, were forming more and more towering cumulus clouds, beginning their birth as a little whisp of white mist and ending up as clouds piled one upon the other, billowing up for thousands and thousands of feet. This cloud formation took hours to mature and was too slow for us to see actually happen. All we saw was the ultimate masses of vapour in all their full-grown majesty.

We had been flying for nearly three hours now and we began to take over for each other with greater frequency as we were both beginning to feel the mental and physical strain the flight entailed. I felt tired and yet I knew that the flight was only the first part of our task. On the ground ahead lay, in all probability, an even greater test of mental and physical strength.

Every mile nearer the Rhine brought an increase in the tension and the constriction which tightened more and more across my chest. The perspiration, which had been oozing from every pore in my body since dawn, now began to increase. My underclothing clung sickeningly to my body, saturated with sweat. My eyes were tired and gritty and an ache flitted to and fro across my eyeballs with the constant concentration on the wallowing tug ahead. My fingers and wrists also ached from the long strain of gripping the wheel and following every dip and rise of the Stirling while my legs were cramped and the muscles protested at every movement on the rudder bar.

Tirlemont loomed up and faded away behind, and Diest appeared ahead through the haze on our port. Diest was the last town of any size we would see this side of the Belgian-Dutch border. From time to time we had carried out a short conversation with Flying Officer Bliss in the tug. Now his voice came softly over the intercom telling us that we were approaching the Dutch border, which confirmed my own map reading.

Mac was at the controls again at the moment and I eagerly traced our route across the map showing the last few remaining miles over Belgium. Then we were over Holland. Holland once again. For a moment it brought back sharp memories of our last visit to that country and its disastrous ending.

Casually, I noticed that the name of the first Dutch village over which we flew was Budel. Between fifty and sixty miles to go, less than half an hour's flying. I felt my heart beating faster, as it always did on such operations, when the last remaining miles were unreeling away beneath our wings. My nerves became more taut with each succeeding minute. Mac would be flying the glider all the way until the pull-off when I would take over for the landing. I wiped the sweat off my brow and licked my dry lips.

The flat landscape of Holland crept slowly past underneath. The villages were becoming less and less frequent as we ploughed on across the narrow appendix-shaped part of Holland with the German border drawing nearer every mile we traversed.

Ahead, I suddenly saw a thin, winding silvery line emerging from out of the haze. I pinpointed it on the map, the Maas River. In a few miles the border would be crossed, and we would be over Germany proper with the Rhine being the next river to cut across our course. The Maas, looking so quiet and peaceful, slid past under our nose. I felt the constriction within me tighten even more and found myself gripping my jaws together like a vice. I held onto the map with sweating palms and fingers as I tied in every road and village on the ground below with those shown on the map.

Just after we crossed the Maas River, Flight Lieutenant Bliss' voice came over the intercom 'Nine minutes to go.' The hair on my neck tingled. We were closing in on the target area and I glued my eyes closer to the map, scanning the landscape below as it floated by. Now was the time. Those last few miles had to be traced carefully in order that we would pull off at exactly the right spot and know that we were in range of our correct landing zone.

The village of Weeze was ahead and now we were crossing the Dutch-German border. I had a feeling of elation for a moment as I looked down on German territory for the first time. So this was Germany. It didn't look any different from Holland at this point but I knew well enough that the people were different, even if there had been a certain amount of intermarriage close to the borders. Weeze was the first German village over the border and the first one I had ever seen. From the 2500 feet we were flying at, I couldn't see whether it had been badly damaged or not.

The long formation was turning about twenty degrees to starboard over the village and Mac eased into a turn following our tug. This was the last leg. The many changes of direction since we had set out from England had been a deceptive measure by which it was hoped the Germans would be deceived as to our ultimate target area until the last few miles.

Hamminkeln lay at the end of this leg with less than eight minutes to go, we had been informed over the intercom. Even the Horsa acted as though it was tired out. It rose and fell, the rope slackening and tightening under the uneven pull. The dull roar of the slipstream rose and fell in sympathy with the wallowing flight, or so it seemed to my dulled senses, dulled perhaps through the tremendous concentration of map reading I was carrying out. Nothing else mattered. Pinpoint map reading was the most vital thing at the moment. We wouldn't get a second pass at those fields if we were wrong the first time.

I didn't have to worry about flak here, for our armies occupied the ground right up to the banks of the Rhine. Beyond the river would be a different story; even so, we would only have about four or five minutes to come within range of enemy AA. For a moment I took my eyes off the ground and looked at the long line of black machines stretching away in front, drawing closer and closer to the Rhine every second.

I turned my eyes down and forward again. A large tract of forest land was sliding up towards us. I identified it easily as the Hochwald and the far side of it lay only four or five miles short of the Rhine. Once more I raised my eyes and tried to pierce the haze. My heart was beating like a sledge hammer. The salty tang of sweat was on my tongue when I tried to pass it over my lips to relieve the terribly parched feeling there.

Then I caught my first glimpse of the Rhine. The silvery barrier loomed up out of the haze. For several moments I couldn't take my eyes off it.

'Six minutes to go.' I dimly heard the words coming over the intercom. The Rhine grew larger. I searched for signs of the crossing by the 2nd Army that had taken place a few hours earlier on, but could see nothing. The river appeared strangely deserted. I had expected to see masses of small boats crossing and re-crossing the river under fire but nothing seemed to be disturbing the quiet waters. I picked out one or two barges, moored against the far shores but there was no activity around them at all. They were some of the flak boats we had been warned that we might encounter. Either they had been put out of action or captured, for no fire was directed up against us from them, or if there was, I never noticed it.

For a moment, I was seized with an uneasiness that whirled within me, saying that the 2nd Army's advance must have been checked and that no river crossings had taken place. Then I realised that we were flying over the Rhine at a point a few miles to the east of the main river crossings of the Army and as I was occupying the left hand seat I could not see away to the right. Mac, flying from the right hand seat, may have glimpsed the crossings from his position, although I expect he was fully occupied with holding the Horsa steady behind the tug.

The roar of the slipstream was drumming in my senses like the thunder of a distant waterfall. My stomach muscles had gone terribly taut – we were entering the area where we could expect flak at any second. More perspiration broke out all over me, while my pulse beat madly. There seemed to be a hammer tapping rapidly inside my head and my face felt flushed.

The Rhine river was directly below us now and my eyes were searching ahead for signs of the Diersfordter Wald, the belt of high wooded forest, and the landing fields that lay beyond. A kind of shock went through me as I peered desperately down and forward. Where the outline of the Wald should have stood out clearly etched was just a murky haze that defied me to penetrate and locate pinpoints. The internal tension was terrible. I could feel my nerves stretch to breaking point. God, I had to locate our area.

At the same time I saw an irregular line of Dakotas and Halifaxes, already heading back from the dropping zones, on our port side. They had been the first aircraft over the landing zones, dropping paratroopers. A few red and golden tracers were curving up from the ground below, while grey-black balls of smoke began to burst in the sky. At that moment I saw an ominous reddish flame belch forth from one of the Halifaxes. Fascinated, I watched it rapidly gain ground, accompanied by thick black smoke spewing out and trailing behind.

The Halifax started to nose over and I saw several objects break away and tumble earthwards. White silk billowed out and, with relief, I knew the crew were safe. The Halifax fell swiftly to the earth, striking the ground just short of the river, which was now behind us. I caught a last glimpse of oily red-tinged smoke shooting skyward as the Halifax ploughed in, then I could see it no longer.

At that moment, for the first time, I felt the absence of parachutes. I knew that we would have no chance of bailing out if our glider was hit, for we did not carry parachutes, in common with our passengers. Yes, if our glider was hit, we would have to ride the flaming, shattered wreck down to earth and destruction.

Those thoughts were fleeting ones, for the urgency of the moment drove all others out of my head except one. I had to find out our position. I knew what had happened, or at least I thought I did. The combined shelling of our landing area by our 2nd Army guns, the laying down of the smokescreen on the west bank of the Rhine and the bombing of the city of Wesel to the south had produced a dense blanket of haze and smoke over the whole landing area and beyond the outer limits. I could only pray that a gap would show up through which we could dive down.

'One minute to go.' - I didn't even bother to acknowledge. Hell, I wish I was as certain as the navigator in the Stirling. I looked at the gliders ahead of us. They were breaking free and swooping and diving through the haze. Enemy tracers laced the sky, mingling with the high explosive shells bursting at all levels.

The towing planes were turning quickly for home as soon as the gliders had released into free flight.

Frantically, I searched the almost impenetrable haze below. I could now dimly make out the faint shape of the Diersfordter Wald. My body had gone indescribably taut. I forgot all about the searching fingers of steel thrown up by the enemy which could tear straight up through the thin wooden and fabric construction of the glider. Every effort was channelled into finding our landing zone.

I heard the voice from the tug, which seemed very far away, saying again and again 'OK, Number Two, this is it – good luck.' I acknowledged.

I placed my hand on the red-topped release lever but refrained from giving the sharp tug that would send the rope dropping away from the sockets in the wings and release us into free flight. Where the hell was the field? God, I can't see a thing. An agonising whirl of thoughts began to cascade through my head. The haze still obliterated the countryside below. A green light was flashing madly from the astro-dome on the Stirling. Evidently, as I did not pull off, the navigator was under the impression that the intercom had gone wrong.

I gripped the red knob tightly and pulled, calling out a farewell to the Stirling crew just before I did so. I felt a sharp jerk as the two rope ends fell away from the port and starboard wing sockets. We were free! The Stirling continued straight ahead for a few seconds and then went into a shallow dive to the left.

I shouted in a hoarse voice to Mac that I would take over. He nodded. I placed my feet on the rudder bar and my hands, sticky with sweat, on the control wheel. I glanced at the air speed indicator which stood at 140 mph. Height 2600 feet – we had gained a little.

We kept straight on, cutting across the smoke-enshrouded area. Our speed fell off rapidly and now we were down to ninety mph with only a thin high-pitched whistle accompanying us. Gone was the thunderous deafening roar of towed flight. Our fate was in our own hands now.

Chapter 24

Landing Over the Rhine

I called out to Mac asking him if he could see anything. He shook his head and grimaced. I could see the sweat running down the side of his face. Then ahead I saw fields through the obscuring haze, but by now we had overrun the furthermost boundaries of our landing zones. That I knew, for almost directly underneath, cutting across our course, was the unmistakable shape of the unfinished Autobahn that skirted the area one or two miles to the east.

However, I welcomed the sight of the road for it gave me something to line up on. I turned sharply right and followed a parallel course, eased back on the wheel and settled our airspeed at eighty mph. The haze was on Mac's side now and I had to look across the cockpit to see the landing area. Mac was peering through the side windows with great intensity.

A bead of perspiration traced its course down my cheek, causing an itch that was almost unbearable. I longed to rub my hand hard across my cheek but daren't take my hand off the wheel. From the corners of my eyes I saw bursting AA shells, tinged with flame, speckling the haze and fume-filled air.

Our height was rapidly decreasing and the altimeter needle passed the 1500 foot mark. I cursed inwardly, damning the smoke with all my heart. Little glimpses of landscape were becoming visible now that we were getting lower. A line of tracers fountained up directly ahead. I threw the wheel over and kicked on the rudder bar. They passed us by, terribly close.

I suddenly remembered the men behind and I turned my head for a moment, forcing a grin to spread across my face and then turned back to the front immediately. I knew we must have passed our field for I estimated we had been gliding almost two miles on the cross-wind leg. With a shout of warning to Mac to watch out for other gliders, I put the Horsa into a steep right hand turn, letting the airspeed rise up to over 100 mph just for safety. After all, we had a fully laden glider on our hands and I didn't want to take a chance on stalling in a low speed steep turn, stable as a Horsa glider was known to be.

We headed back on a reciprocal course. The altimeter was registering just over 1000 feet. Not much height left and still no signs of our zone. A glider slid right across our nose going down into the depths below. I had to ease over and up to miss his great black body flashing by. I cursed him through parched lips. The area, hidden beneath the haze, was now on my side and I peered vainly down. Where the hell was the field? I saw some anti-aircraft shell-bursts blossoming forth a little on our left and in front. They hardly registered on my brain. The landing field, where was it?

Now we were at 800 feet and eighty-five mph. Well, we had better turn into the wind now, irrespective of what lay below. We would have to take a chance. These thoughts raced through my mind in the last minute or two since we had cast free of our parent tug. The time had passed interminably.

Then, as though a miracle was being unfolded before me, I saw a clear gap in the murk below. It was just over on our left and through it I caught a glimpse of at least two gliders on the ground. This was it. This would have to do. At least we would be landing near some of our own men. Mac had also seen it and was pointing excitedly down. I nodded and put the Horsa into another steep bank to the left while Mac applied half flap.

I straightened the Horsa out and headed down directly towards the gap. The altimeter showed 500 feet. Air speed ninety mph. I eased back a little to eighty-five mph. The nearer we approached the ground the more the haze seemed to lift. Now I could plainly make out the field we were heading for. I stared hard. No, it wasn't possible. But it was true. It was the very field we had been detailed to land in. There, sure enough, were the two houses bordering the near end of the field and there were the farm buildings on each side. It was miraculous. Some guardian angel must have been watching over us.

At the same moment I realised that we were too high. We would overshoot the field. Mac had now applied full flaps. I dropped the nose a little and the airspeed built up, I eased back on the wheel again. The two houses loomed up nearer and nearer. I held the Horsa at eighty-five mph.

Now at 200 feet, we were about 400 yards short of the houses. With a shock, I suddenly glimpsed the tail unit of a Horsa protruding out of the roof of the left hand house. It had evidently plunged straight down into the building and its shattered remnants lay all around. The houses were almost underneath us now and we were down to about fifty feet. I saw two or three figures in field-grey half kneeling just outside the right hand house. Something cracked viciously above the smooth whistle of the slipstream. I winced slightly but held the Horsa steady. The bastards were firing at us. Another second would see us clear.

Landing Zone outside Hamminkeln

The roof loomed right up underneath and we flashed over by a good twenty feet. Now the brown ploughed soil was racing up towards us. I levelled off and we floated swiftly across the ground, the airspeed still reading eighty mph, and we were already half way down the field. Ten feet below us the furrows streamed backwards. I pumped the control wheel a little and we settled lower, skimming the ground.

The end of the field loomed up and then, to my horror, I saw power cables stretched across our path. They were suspended from heavy wooden poles, thicker than telegraph poles. A road ran across our landing run at this point and the power line followed this road. The cables rushed up towards us. For a moment, I toyed with the idea of pulling back on the wheel and trying to climb over the black power lines, but I realised that it would mean a stall on the far side. We just didn't have enough speed to climb. I held the Horsa steady on course, just clear of the ground. In alarm I saw the dangling cables loom up menacingly just over our cockpit. I eased the wheel forward and just at that moment our wheels hit. Fortunately, they struck a split second after we had passed under the cables. It was the road we had touched. Simultaneously, I felt a slight tug on the left side which pulled us around almost imperceptibly.

We bounced off the road two or three feet into the air (which might have proved fatal if it had happened a few feet before the power cables). Another ploughed field bordered the far side of the road and we again touched down. This time we stayed on the ground. I felt our wheels sinking into the soft furrows and a small cloud of dust rose for a second and whipped past the cockpit.

I slammed on the brakes, locking them to the last notch. The glider shuddered as it bounded forward over the field, slowing up every second. The airspeed fell away – sixty, fifty, forty mph.

I was already tearing off my straps before the glider came to a halt. I heard the sliding door in the fuselage being raised as we slowed down and stopped. As my ears recovered from the roar and whistle of the slipstream that had been beating into my head for the last few hours, I picked up a new sound. The familiar stutter of machine guns and the crack of rifle fire. It spurred me on.

I snatched at the maps and photographs on the front ledge. Mac was already on his way out through the connecting door. I could hear the soldiers rushing out through the lowered side door. I picked up my sniper's rifle, clawed my way out of my seat and plunged through the connecting door. I had left my rucksack under the first passenger seat and, finding it, tugged it free. Something cracked sharply through the wooden side of the glider. Another bullet snapped through. I lunged for the open door and literally threw myself out. I stumbled and fell down the ramp, landing on my face on the brown soil of Germany.

Inside the glider I could hear some men unshackling the hand trailer. The rest of the men were already out on the ground forming a defensive circle around the glider. I joined them. Panting, I pushed my rifle forward, leaving my rucksack lying on the ground beside me. This was no time to put it on my back.

I found myself looking over the field towards the road we had just flown across and the houses beyond. I shouted to the officer that they were the houses we had to clear, for in all probability he hadn't got his bearings, not being able to see the area as we came in to land as we pilots had. His view had been restricted to that afforded by one of the small eight to ten inch portholes. He shouted back an answer, but I couldn't hear what he said above the clamour of battle.

The bullets continued to zip and crackle past, mostly striking into the wooden sides of the Horsa behind me. Some ploughed into the ground alongside with a queer thucking sound. I had an idea the shots were coming from the houses at the far end of the field and bringing up my rifle I sighted through the telescopic sight. The distant windows appeared larger through the lens, but I still couldn't make out any human target.

Selecting one window, I set my range and squeezed the trigger. The rifle jumped with the recoil and my ears were filled with the first thunderous crash of the explosion that sent the .303 bullet speeding towards the black opening some 600 yards distant. The strong smell of burnt cordite drifted back as I drew back the bolt and rammed home a second cartridge. Again I brought the window into my sights. Again I squeezed gently on the trigger. The rifle bucked sharply and my ears rang with the crash of the explosion. I didn't know whether I was hitting anything but at least it would be a deterrent to the enemy if they were firing out from the window. I fired three more shots in rapid succession.

I paused to thrust a new clip of cartridges into the magazine. The rifle was warm in my hands now from the searing blast of the bullets as they sped down the barrel. Something whined by unpleasantly close to my head and I ducked instinctively.

I glanced across at the officer in charge of the troops. I didn't like this exposed position at all. All the cover we had was the shallow furrows where we lay. The nearest hedge lay some three hundred yards distant, while between the houses and our position was nothing but about the same distance of open ploughed ground with the road bisecting it some two hundred yards away.

What I dreaded most of all was the enemy ranging his mortars on the huge target presented by the Horsa a few feet behind us. We wouldn't have a dog's chance if they opened up on us with those hellish weapons.

I was saturated with sweat and my legs felt unreasonably weak, a fact with which I had first become aware as I had jumped clear of the glider. The strength which had kept me going during the flight seemed to have failed me. I wiped the sweat out of my eyes and prepared to fire on the house again.

The air just above my head was split by a rapid swish, swish, swish, followed almost immediately by the distant stutter of a machine gun. This was worse than the rifle fire. Before I could fire again, I heard the officer in charge call out something which I didn't catch. I saw the man beside me rise up on his knees and then start forward. Grabbing my rifle, I pushed myself up. Hell, it was an effort, my legs seemed dead. For a moment they buckled but I recovered. The men around me were moving forward. I grabbed my rucksack with my free hand and half slung the heavy object over my shoulder. I couldn't get it on my back unless I stopped and put down my rifle and I wanted to keep up with the rest.

I dimly heard the officer shouting something about extending outwards and I veered away from the man on my right. As I did so, he gave a peculiar cry and spun around, dropping in a heap. It came as a shock to me and I halted immediately and doubled over to him. One look at his bloody head told me that he was beyond aid.

The bastards! A malevolent fury swept over me, driving out the fatigue I felt.

I doubled up after the irregularly spaced line of men advancing over the field towards the houses. The enemy's fire continued to snap and crackle around us. We were nearly at the road now. My heart was going like a sledgehammer, while perspiration ran down my face.

Mac came up alongside me suddenly and I was thankful. I had missed him when we started to advance over the field and I had been worried although I had had no time to check up on him. I panted out a request for him to help slip my rucksack straps over my shoulders, which he did immediately. I noticed that Mac didn't have his rucksack. Apparently, he hadn't stopped to pick it up when he was on his way out of the glider.

We reached the road and doubled across it. On the far side was dug a series of slit trenches, probably as a precaution for the enemy soldiers as they crossed over the exposed farmland, in case of attacks by our aircraft.

The line of men dropped down into the holes under the shouted orders of the officer. It would give us a breather before the final assault on the houses. I couldn't find a free slit trench, although Mac was lucky. I did, however, locate a large shell hole just forward of the road and dropped down into it. Wriggling up to the summit, I peered forward towards our objective, which now lay about 400 yards distant. Thrusting my rifle forward, I sighted and fired off the first round. I thought I could pick out a small patch back inside the room lighter than the dark of the window. I fired again. The pale blur disappeared.

I shot a quick glance around and noticed all the others remained under cover. They, too, were firing on the houses. All around arose the crackle of small arms fire, echoing to and fro across the open farmlands. The greatest amount of firing was coming from the direction of the Diersfordter Wald which lay some two miles behind us. The distant explosion of grenades punctuated the small arms fire. I fired until I had used up my second magazine and then paused. My rifle felt quite hot and yet I had only fired a comparatively few rounds.

I looked around, keeping my head just above the rim of the crater, for enemy bullets continued to rake the area, but they seemed to be lessening. I picked out another party of our men some two hundred yards away beginning to advance outward from the road toward the houses. The men with whom Mac and I had advanced opened up, giving covering fire to the party stumbling over the ploughed field on our right. Having reloaded, I pumped shot after shot through alternate windows and through the black gap that marked the doorway.

Before the men advancing on the house had got within a hundred yards of it a man in grey-green uniform came slowly out of the doorway, waving a large white flag. I felt a thrill go through me. Hell, they were soon giving in. It would save us the trouble and the inevitable casualties of going in after them. I peered through my telescopic sight at him to get a better view, but it didn't help very much.

The firing directed at us from the house had now stopped, but I was aware of some shots coming in from my left. An outbuilding of one of the farms flanking the field lay about 100 yards away and I thought they were being fired from there. I looked back at the figure waving the white flag and saw that two of our men had reached him and were following him into the house. A few minutes later several more men emerged through the doorway with their hands clasped behind their heads. Well, that was that.

At that moment a shadow fell across my hole and I looked up. For a moment my heart stood still, for half crouched in the rim of the hole was a soldier - not a British one.

For a second I was frozen, my rifle was pointing away in the opposite direction and I knew I could never swing it around in time to cover him. In that split second the soldier stared back at me, standing stock still. Apparently, he had only just spotted me lying there in the shell hole. He was carrying a long tubular weapon over his shoulder. And then it struck me like a thunderbolt – he was one of the American paratroopers with a bazooka anti-tank weapon.

I was now glad that my rifle had been pointing the other way, for in his strange overalls and with his paratrooper's helmet, he looked for all the world like a German soldier at first glance. He had recognised my uniform at the same moment for he nodded his sweat-lined face and dropped down on one knee just outside the shell hole.

He said something about 'that goddam sniper' and peered towards the outhouse. Without another word he doubled forward towards the building. I swung my rifle around and sighted on the outhouse. As there were no windows, there wasn't much to fire at. Whoever was shooting from there was using minute holes in the walls or roof. I found what I thought to be one of the holes and fired.

The paratrooper had got within range now and I saw him aim the unwieldy contraption at the building. Next second came a roaring explosion. Smoke and flame enveloped the outhouse. The building burned steadily and soon I heard the crackle of exploding small arms ammunition coming from the holocaust. I didn't see the enemy sniper come out and guessed that he must have been hit when the missile exploded. The last I saw of the paratrooper, he was heading past the burning building, I presume looking for further victims.

For the last few minutes, I had been watching a Horsa glider that had come to rest only about a hundred yards away in front and a little to my left. At first, there was no movement, but now I noticed that several men were working on the nose, which had been damaged in the landing. The front wheel had collapsed and part of the underside of the cockpit had caved in. It was a Mark II, but the crash had prevented the nose from being swung open in the normal manner to permit the load inside to be driven out.

I had almost forgotten Mac in those last few hectic minutes and now I turned and called out to him. He shouted back and grinned. Mac was certainly taking it well considering it was his first action, and furthermore that he had not been trained as an infantryman but as a pilot, apart from the quick ground training that had been given to all the RAF men joining just before the operation.

There was a violent explosion in front of me. I crouched down in the shell hole. My body had gone strangely rigid. In that second, the horror of the mortaring and shelling at Arnhem came back to me. The knives of fear turned in my chest for a moment. So this was it. Here at last was the beginning of the destructive rain of high explosives I had been anticipating all the time since our wheels had touched down on the soil of Germany. Almost immediately after the explosion, I realised that something had been missing. Yes, the whine and scream of the falling missile. Why hadn't I heard it?

I pulled myself up level with the rim of the crater and peered over towards the wrecked Horsa for the explosion had sounded right on that spot. I half expected to see some of the men who had been milling around the glider lying still and silent on the ground, caught by the blast of high explosive. I stared hard, for the men were there alright but they weren't lying scattered around on the ground. They were all standing up very much alive and, what was more, they were in very nonchalant positions around the nose of the glider from which arose a trailing whisp of smoke.

Then, like a bolt from the blue, it hit me. It hadn't been any German missile bursting. It was merely that the men had placed some explosives, that were carried in the glider, by the nose and had blown the front clean away to enable them to drive out the jeep and gun that were inside the fuselage. This explosive was carried for just such an emergency, only normally it was used to blow the tail half off of a Mark I Horsa glider if the four bolts that held it in place became jammed.

It was a great relief to me, and I inwardly cursed myself for being so jumpy. I felt my body relax and looked over at Mac. He was just raising his head over the slit trench. His face bore a somewhat alarmed expression which quickly passed as he too recognised the source of the explosion.

I heard the officer in charge of the men we had brought in calling out to me and I looked over towards him. He told me that as the house had been cleared he was reporting to his company HQ. Was I coming? I told him that we would report back to our Squadron HQ rendezvous as originally instructed at our briefing now that the initial task had been completed. He shouted something about, 'Thanks for the lift, we'll be off' and waved his hand in farewell. I replied in like manner and watched him clamber out of his trench and assemble the men in single file, keeping several paces between them. With a word of command, they moved off down the road towards the village.

The rattle of small arms fire continued to roll across the fields. Sullen explosions of grenades, and some mortar fire, also echoed over. A sharp battle was being fought in the Diersfordter Wald between the Rhine and our landing zones. To the northwest I could hear the troops of the 5th Parachute Brigade engaging the enemy. I noticed that the haze, which had so imperilled our landing, was lifting a little, although it was still quite thick overhead. For some strange reason, it did not cling closely to the ground but started at what I estimated to be one or two hundred feet up.

The roar of the jeep's engine breaking into life brought my attention back to the glider. The men had cleared away the last splintered remnants of the cockpit and now the jeep was easing its way down two short ramps which were hardly necessary in this case due to the bottom of the glider's fuselage resting on the ground on top of the shattered nose wheel.

Calling to Mac, I got up and crossed over towards the glider. The jeep was outside now, together with the six-pounder gun, and the men were clambering aboard. I doubled over the last few remaining yards and asked the two pilots accompanying the gun crew if they were heading for the rendezvous. I didn't know them but I knew that all glider pilots would ultimately end up at the pre-arranged rendezvous. They answered in the affirmative.

The jeep was already full so Mac and I had to find a place on the gun. I lodged myself on as securely as possible for I knew that it wouldn't be a very comfortable ride, but I had no idea the nightmare it would turn out to be as we lurched across the fields to the rendezvous.

Stray bullets continued to buzz around angrily at intervals and I wasn't sorry when the driver let in the clutch and eased the jeep out onto the road. We turned right and bowled down the hard macadam road. I crouched lower as the wind whistled past and hoped that no sniper would be able to line up his sights on our racing jeep and gun.

We passed the farm building, still burning from the American paratrooper's shot. Smoke swirled and drifted over the road. Then we were free of its obscuring cloud and roaring along between the ploughed fields that stretched away on either side. The smooth ride along the road did not last long. Within a quarter of a mile from our starting point we slowed down and swung off the road onto a bumpy track to our left.

Mac and I were pitched and tossed about and it took all my strength to hang on and avoid being hurled off under the bouncing wheels of the heavy six-pounder gun which would crush the life out of us with no effort at all. The driver seemed to have forgotten, or chose to ignore, that he had a human cargo perched perilously on the anti-tank gun he was towing behind the jeep.

We were now skirting a line of trees which lay on our right. They were conspicuous by their presence for trees were scarce in this area. A mile or so away the Diersfordter Wald more than made up for this scarcity. It was also notable for the fact that it was the Squadron rendezvous, or so it had been arranged. We kept on going past the shady stretch of trees. The brown dust rose in clouds behind the spinning wheels of the jeep, enveloping us in its choking grip. I coughed and blinked my eyes, not daring to let go even one hand to wipe away the powder-like soil that got into my eyes and burned like hell.

I began to question the wisdom of begging the lift. To avoid a comparatively short march, we were risking our necks on this bouncing juggernaut, being nearly stifled to death and running the risk of being fired upon without knowing that it was happening, for the noise of the jeep's engine drowned out all other sounds. However, we had no option but to hang on grimly and pray that the journey would be short lived.

We swung sharply to our left and then right again, my hands slipping on the smooth frame of the gun as we did so. We came to a halt with a jerk and I slid off, staggering clear. I ached in every bone from the ride, even though it had lasted but a few minutes. Mac limped up alongside me.

Wiping the dust from my eyes, I surveyed the area. We appeared to be in a courtyard of a farm. Quite a number of our men were already there but I couldn't see any from our squadron. There were a number of German prisoners lined up against a nearby wall, with their hands still clasped behind their heads. I looked them over with interest for a moment. They were a sorry looking lot but I guess all prisoners of war look like that. I ought to know from personal experience.

Some looked quite frightened as though they were very unsure of their future. It was their ages that amazed me. I guessed that they ranged from sixteen to sixty, even older in a few cases. Many were regular soldiers and some were of the Volksturm, the equivalent of our Home Guard. Most of the Volksturm men had arrived complete with kitbags which seemed to indicate that they had packed ready to surrender the moment things got a little bit rough and not in their favour. No doubt they fired until our men got within a few yards and then emerged out from their defences which had kept them pretty safe until the menace of bayonet or a grenade had changed the outlook.

They may have been kids just out of school and old men hardly capable of marching at the double, but they were quite able to sight down the barrel of a rifle from a static defence position. Yes, some of them may have been old enough to be my grandfather, and some still young enough for school, but I could find no shred of pity for them. Kids! Many of our men were lying out there in the furrows, victims of a bullet from a gun fired by those 'kids'.

I turned away and asked one of our men standing guard over them the name of the farm and which of our troops were occupying it. He told me that the Air-landing Brigade HQ had established itself here. That told me that it couldn't be our squadron's rendezvous.

Then we ran into one of our Flight Commanders. I was glad to see him and he likewise appeared very pleased to see us. He told us that none of our men had yet reached the strip of trees which was our rendezvous and suggested that we dig in around the farmhouse here. He was going into Hamminkeln village which lay about a mile away to see if he could contact any of the other Flight Commanders, or our Squadron Commander if possible.

Mac and I scouted around the outside of the farm buildings seeking the best spot to dig in. Mac didn't seem too keen to dig himself a trench but the memory of Arnhem was still strong within me and digging in was among the foremost of my thoughts. We had been down nearly two hours now and, from the shelling and mortaring point of view, it had been strangely quiet. I had an uneasy feeling that the enemy must be re-grouping for a counterattack and I didn't want to be out in the open when that happened.

On one side of the farm, which consisted of several solidly constructed buildings, we came upon an orchard bordered by a hedge. Unfortunately, there was no fruit upon the trees since it was only March and, furthermore, if by some miracle fruit had been hanging from the trees this early in the month the shelling by the 2nd Army would have stripped and destroyed it before we arrived, as some of the shattered trees bore mute testimony.

Our great find however was not fruit but a number of ready-dug trenches alongside the hedge. For a moment I hesitated before jumping down into one, thinking of booby traps but then reasoned that the enemy would never have had time to carry out that task before we landed. I had an idea that the prisoners lined up in the nearby yard had been the recent occupants of these trenches and they certainly wouldn't have had a chance of booby-trapping them.

I was puzzled a little, for they were rather shallow and normally the enemy always dug very effective trenches. The fields of fire were excellent, as I perceived with a shock when I looked through the gap in front, carved out of the hedge by its former occupants. I found myself gazing, without a shadow of a doubt, upon my very own glider squatting serenely on the ground not more than two or three hundred yards away. God, what a target we must have presented as we came in, especially after we had stopped. A man in this very trench with a machine gun could have wiped us all out with a few well-aimed bursts. The only conclusion I could come to was that our salvation had been the capture of the men just before we touched down by some other airborne troops who had landed shortly before we had.

I proceeded to deepen the trench and soon learned why the Germans had dug only so far. I had removed about one foot more of soil when I noticed water seeping in. So that was the reason. I cursed softly and shouted out a warning to Mac in the next trench to give up digging any deeper. I was wasting my breath for Mac hadn't been digging at all, he had been merely resting – sensible fellow.

Clambering out, I prepared to move further down only to find that a platoon of machine gunners had taken over the remaining trenches. In one way, I was glad of the added firepower of a heavy Vickers machine gun but on the other hand it meant that I would have to remain in the same trench into which more and more water was oozing. I went in search of wood and had to tear down a door from an outbuilding. After breaking it down into its original planks, I soon provided myself with a very effective duckboard system, which worked quite well. On top of the wood I piled a mass of straw out of a barn and I was happy once more.

I paused and cocked one ear skywards. Yes, I had not been mistaken. The faint rumble of aero engines reached me. I peered up but could see nothing through the blanket of haze hanging low over the battle field. Mac was staring up at the sky in an expectant manner.

Across the fields came the stutter of small arms fire, and the distant crash of exploding mortar bombs. A few AA shells were bursting unseen in the haze above our heads as the thunder of motors increased. I was standing up outside my trench now trying to pierce the sight-restricting haze. The engines sounded familiar with their low pulsating beat, indicating that they were parachute droppers or glider tugs. At least they were ours, of that I was sure.

Now they were directly overhead and their roar filled the heavens. But still the haze prevented my seeing anything and also undoubtedly prevented the men up there from seeing their dropping and landing zones. I felt sorry for them for the visibility was probably even worse than when we had come in. And we had probably added a little smoke of our own to the already polluted atmosphere.

I suddenly became aware of the low-pitched whistle of a glider descending. Then, out of the haze, the black form of an American WACO glider appeared, swooping down in a swift turning glide for earth. It took on its true dark grey colour as it broke through the haze and I could see the white star plainly on its wing and side. It must have been down to 200 to 300 feet when I first caught a glimpse of it.

Now I saw something that I had heard mentioned in shop talk back at the mess but had never actually seen. From the tail of the glider a white parachute suddenly streamed out and blossomed open with a crack. The glider appeared to be almost stopped dead by the first tug of the parachute and then went on down, slowing rapidly under the drag of the straining silk billowing out several feet behind. In a matter of seconds it had vanished down into the ploughed field on the far side of the farm buildings and I lost sight of it. Even before it had disappeared, a second WACO came swiftly down out of the overcast. This one was coming in much faster than the first and literally wailed over the farm, the wind shrieking through the metal bracing on the tail unit. A white chute burst open behind the racing glider and that too disappeared from sight behind the buildings.

The roar of engines continued past overhead. Another WACO, ghostlike, flitted through the haze and turned steeply, cutting down sharply from the base of the overcast. It swept past overhead with a high-pitched scream. I dived for the trench as short stabs of flame spurted from the sides of the glider and the staccato crash of automatic firing blasted the air. The hot lead whispered and snapped around as the men within the glider sprayed the ground streaming past underneath less than two hundred feet below. I crouched in my trench cursing the men who were flailing the ground around with their lethal humming missiles.

Being shot at by the enemy is bad enough but being fired on by your allies is even worse. The firing stopped as the glider sped on over the farmhouse.

Seconds later I recovered from the first shock and realised that they were not at fault one bit. For one thing, I shouldn't have been standing up outside the trench like a damn fool and secondly, I guessed that they had spotted the grey-green clad forms of the German prisoners in the yard just over the wall from us without knowing they had surrendered. Poking their gun muzzles through the WACO's fabric, they had given us everything they could.

I straightened up and as I did so heard an awful rending crash away up ahead in the direction of where the glider had just vanished. I knew they had been travelling too fast. I only hoped that the crash was not as bad as the noise indicated. It must have happened over a quarter of a mile from where we were dug in.

Before the last of the unseen tugs droned past overhead, I saw two more WACOs on their way down. One was on fire and I watched with fascinated horror as the flames rippled along the fabric-covered fuselage. It dived in about half a mile away. The other glider made a good landing and I last saw it bouncing along over a ploughed field in a cloud of dust before it vanished behind a distant hedge.

Actually, the American gliders had been detailed to land on the far side of the village of Hamminkeln about a mile from where we were but, as I knew from experience, it must have been almost impossible for the glider pilots guiding their machines earthwards to pick out their correct landing zone through the pall of smoke covering the battlefield.

A peculiar silence settled over the area after the last tug had wheeled onto its homeward course and the last glider had settled to earth amid a cloud of dust of its own making.

All around the battle continued to erupt spasmodically, but it seemed to me that it was slowing up. The bursts of fire became more and more irregular with one exception and that was from the direction of the Diersfordter Wald. Our men there seemed to be having some difficulty in cleaning out the heavily wooded area, which wasn't surprising.

Mac and I got out our rations and set up our little methylated tablet stove. Now seemed the time for a mess tin of tea or at least a liquid that looked like tea and did in fact bear a strong resemblance to that refreshing drink.

To celebrate, we opened up a tin of sausages and within a few minutes we were enjoying our first meal on German soil. Somehow, I felt elated. The whole job so far had turned out far easier than I had expected. I may have lost a few pounds through the almost ceaseless perspiring and sweating since we had taken off from our home base back in England but that wouldn't do me any harm.

I felt ten times better after the tea and was ready for any further action, should it come. I had been cleaning my mess tin when a shadow fell across my trench. Looking up, I expected to see Mac and instead found myself staring at a young boy of about seventeen or less, dressed in a very ill-fitting jacket and trousers. For a moment, I looked at him. He smiled and said something in a tongue entirely unfamiliar to me. Summoning up the little German I knew, I asked him if he was in fact a German.

He seemed very agitated at this question and appeared to be vigorously denying my accusation. Then he spoke very slowly in German and at last I understood. He was a Russian boy who had been taken from his father's farm at Kiev three years before and had been forced to work on the farm which lay just behind us.

I invited him to sit on the edge of my trench and we tried to carry out a sensible conversation which, I am proud to say, went off quite well. The scant German I had learned in the past was proving very helpful now. I offered him some of the remaining sausages that were still in the tin. He accepted gratefully and without waiting to cook them started eating. The tea he declined.

I asked him how he had been treated and he replied that he had got along fairly well, but they never let him forget that he was the slave and they the masters. They fed him pretty well to make sure that he was able to do a good day's work, I suppose. They never beat him, although the farmer had threatened him from time to time. I also asked him if they were Nazis and whether they approved of Hitler. He didn't think they liked Hitler, for they never spoke of him nor had any pictures of him around. They were in fact, he said, very religious Catholics. Four brothers owned the same number of farms around the area.

He was terribly pleased that we had liberated him and tended to lay the whole matter to my credit alone. I should have felt flattered, but I could not help grinning at him for I had arrived at the farm after it had been captured and had had nothing whatsoever to do with his 'liberation' in actual fact. However, it seemed to make him feel good, so I didn't disillusion him.

He asked whether we would like any milk and I accepted his offer. Fresh milk would be most welcome. He got up and prepared to hurry back into the farm. He was free of his shackles now and felt like a king. The position of master and slave had been reversed with a vengeance. As he doubled off towards the farmhouse, I called out for him to bring back some hot water so that we could have a wash and also some fruit if he had it. I fancied apples, and he told me that they had plenty of them in the cellar.

Mac and I sat back in our trenches, feeling lord of all we surveyed. This was the life. We had acquired a faithful batman by the looks of things.

'Russky', as we had already named him, was back within five minutes. He was a little downcast, telling us that he couldn't get any milk as all the other soldiers had already taken it. He did, however, have the hot water and some apples. He watched us happily as we crunched away at the apples, after having washed away some of the dirt ingrained into our faces and hands. I felt wonderfully fresh after the sluice of hot water and even contemplated shaving, but laziness won out and I was content with the wash. After all, I had shaved earlier on during the morning.

Whenever firing would break out around, Russky would cock his head on one side, listen, and say 'Deutches soldaten kaput.' Usually I would agree, but at times I wasn't so sure when I picked out the terribly fast Brrrrrrrp of the enemy's machine pistols, and guns.

Later on in the afternoon, Russky left us after promising faithfully to come back. He even told me that he was coming back to England with me when we returned. I didn't say anything, but I knew that the army would be strongly disinclined to allow Mac and me to take such a person back with us.

I turned my attention to the ploughed field in which lay my glider. For some time, a thought had been ticking over in the back of my mind. I wanted a parachute to take back home to my soon-to-be fiancee Doreen, and by heck I was going to have one by hook or by crook.

The bait for me lay in the form of a bright orange supply chute lying less than two hundred yards away out in the open field. Telling Mac to wait, I opened my jack knife, picked up my rifle and crawled through the hedge then, straightening up on the far side, set off at the double, half bent over. No other person was in sight and I felt rather naked and alone. Well, most of the firing was at least half a mile away from the sound of it, and in many cases farther still. I stumbled over the rough furrows and at last reached the prize I sought, panting with my exertions as I knelt down beside the deflated parachute. Grasping the shroud lines, I hacked at them with the knife to free the chute, with the sweat dripping off my brow as I did so.

Slashing through the remaining lines, I hastily bundled up the orange mass. I was a little disappointed, for I had found that the fabric was rayon and not nylon. It was much coarser than I had thought but it was better than nothing. Later on I might get another chance of a silk or nylon chute.

I straightened up with the whole chute half bundled and half dragging in the furrows. Something whined by and struck the ground soggily. I cringed for a moment and then set off hell for leather back to the hedge. I think I broke the two hundred yard record on that sprint back and felt quite weak when I crawled through the hedge and dropped down into the comforting shelter of my hole. Having got my breath back, I examined my loot with pride.

Mac was all for going out on another trip. His desire for the soft silk of a chute had been aroused but mine had been temporarily dulled. I agreed to go out in about half an hour as the situation might have changed by then. Opening my rucksack, I stuffed the gaudy rayon into it, or at least I tried, but it was too bulky to go in with the items I already had. I was, however, ready to sacrifice my spare set of underclothing if necessary, but decided I would wait awhile and see how things panned out. Meanwhile I bundled the chute in a corner of my hole, clear of the oozy bottom.

I felt the urge to wander so, with Mac to keep me company, I set out. We passed through the farmyard and, as we did so, I noticed that the number of prisoners had increased. Some of our men were eagerly searching through the belongings of the latest arrivals, with an eye to souvenirs, no doubt.

Mac and I continued on down a dusty track towards the clump of trees that had been earmarked as our rendezvous. It was deserted. About three hundred yards further on we spotted a house and decided that that would be our objective.

We approached it with caution for, although firing had ceased in the immediate neighbourhood, one could never tell. The house had been severely damaged by shellfire and most of the roof was missing. Mac covered me while I kicked open the door. Actually, it didn't take much kicking for it was hanging on by one small piece of hinge. I wasn't worrying about booby traps, for I knew our landing had been too quick to allow that to have been carried out. I did proceed with caution, however, for there was just a chance that the house might still hold one or more of the enemy. Mac joined me and we went through room after room, seeing nothing but piles of plaster on the floors from the shattered ceilings. The house was fully furnished and it looked as though the owners had departed in a hurry for some food still stood on the kitchen table. As I looked at the piles of blankets and tablecloths inside the cupboards, I thought of how useful they would be back home where such things were so strictly rationed.

The house was silent and deserted and I felt very uneasy somehow. Through the shattered walls I could hear the chatter of small arms fire in the distance and the thud of exploding missiles, but undoubtedly it was gradually dying out. I was glad to emerge from the house again into the clean fresh air. A peculiar heavy smell had been permeating the house.

I breathed deeply and decided that I had had enough house inspecting for the time being. In any case, there was no other house within a mile or so, apart from the farm buildings. We retraced our steps back to the farm.

We tried to find someone who could give us further orders as to what to do, but none of our officers were around. OK, well, we were in our slit trenches on the orchard. Mac was restless over wanting to obtain a white silk or nylon chute so we again set out over a nearby ploughed field. This time the enemy didn't interfere with our search.

I spotted a white chute within two minutes. I almost missed it but my roving eye picked up a spot of white lying between the furrows a few yards off on my right. I hurried over and was very pleased with my discovery. Not only was it a fine chute of soft textured nylon but it had not fully opened. It was, I suspected, one of the auxiliary chutes carried by the American paratroopers and it had burst out of the pack after striking the ground, probably as the paratrooper had shed it. The nylon had burst out and now it lay in neatly folded layers along the furrow. All I had to do was roll it up, a matter of seconds, and cut off the long trailing nylon shrouds. I had a neatly folded bundle, instead of a great ungainly mass as I had with the fully opened orange chute earlier on.

Mac was a little envious of my find so we continued the search with redoubled energy. I came across a beautiful soft mottled chute used by our own paratroopers and bundled that up also, having in mind the lining of my trench to help keep out the cold that was sure to descend upon us with the coming of darkness.

I cannot remember whether Mac was successful or not in his quest but shortly afterwards we returned to our slit trenches. I made sure of stuffing the white chute well down into my rucksack. With so many men around I fancied that I would be minus that chute in a very short time if I left it lying around in the open. The mottled chute I put into the trench and now I was in possession of a well-lined hole.

Mac suddenly made up his mind that he ought to have his rucksack so, crawling through the hedge, we tramped across the ploughed field towards our abandoned glider. I approached it with a feeling of satisfaction. When it was so quiet that I could revisit the glider in which we had landed, things must certainly be going well in our favour.

Reaching the machine, I waited outside while Mac clambered up the ramp and into the fuselage to search out his rucksack – if it was still there. It was. I think Mac was greatly relieved at finding the rucksack still there intact.

While he was inside, I strolled around the glider and then I discovered why I had felt a slight tug to the left as we had come in underneath the power cables. The left wingtip was missing and the inner wooden construction was plainly visible. About eighteen inches had been sheared clean off by one of the poles supporting the cables. On the port side of the fuselage, near the top and just behind the cockpit, several jagged flak holes were evident. There were at least two clean round holes also, which I attributed to the marksmanship of the soldiers who had fired at us as we swooped low over the houses on our run-in.

On the whole, we had been extremely lucky, for dotted around the fields I could make out a number of crashed and wrecked gliders. Some had just made bad landings but many of them had been hit by flak. Now they lay there, silent and deserted, like the carcasses of a flock of crows which had descended on the wide open fields and had then been destroyed.

We set off back to our slit trenches and, on the way, passed the twisted and crumpled form of a German soldier lying lengthwise along a furrow. I knelt down and half rolled him over to make sure that he was dead, although I knew within me there was no doubt for no live human can lie the way he was. A burst of machine gun fire must have hit him, for his chest was just a ripped mass of spongy looking coagulated blood.

A feeling of pity went through me as I looked at that shattered remnant of a man. Some mother or wife would never see her son or husband again. Many more lay still in the oppressive afternoon heat and many more would join them before the sun set, bringing in the spreading cloak of night. I rolled his body face downwards again amid the discoloured, blood-stained earth. Already his body was exuding the strange smell of death.

We headed back and with a feeling of relief I dropped down into the shelter of my hole. I drank deeply from my water bottle and looked around for our friend Russky to refill it. He seemed to have disappeared, at least temporarily, so I got up and walked over to the farmhouse. The interior was dark and gloomy.

Clumping over the stone floor, I found myself in the kitchen. An old woman looked up from a chair on which she was sitting. I asked her for water. She nodded and got up. She appeared to have become accustomed to us soldiers by now although she did show traces of being uneasy. She worked on a hand pump and water spurted forth from the spout. I held my water bottle under it and then filled a cup. The water was very cold and refreshing, drawn up as it was from the depths of the earth. I thanked her, and she smiled faintly.

Passing in through another room, I found myself in a large barn-like attachment to the house. It was even darker in here. I peered around and found that I was in a cowshed. Several of the animals were in there. I noticed that other inmates had joined them – the German prisoners. They lay there in sullen silence as I passed down between them.

Coming out into the bright afternoon sunlight, I blinked. The first man I saw was an American pilot. I went up and spoke to him. He was looking dishevelled and not a little weary. He told me that he had been flying a paratroop-carrying plane and that they had been hit by flak and had caught fire. All the paratroopers managed to bale out and he and his crew had followed just in time.

'Look' he said, 'I can show you my machine from the yard.' I followed him to the stone wall running along one side. He pointed behind the farm and there, amid several gliders, lay the skeleton of the burned out Curtiss Commando 46 he had been piloting (the C-46 served a similar role as its counterpart, the DC-47 but was not as extensively produced).

The pilot looked at the twisted wreckage with a far away look and his voice trembled.

'God, I thought we would never get out of it – flames everywhere.' He turned and walked back to the farmhouse and I started back for the trench.

As I crossed over the yard, I caught sight of Russky. He was talking with one of the intelligence officers. At the same moment he caught sight of me and his face lit up. He called out something, and I walked over to the two of them. As I came up to them the officer turned to me and sighed.

'This kid says you liberated him or something, but I'm not sure of him. He's got no papers and tells me that they are at another farm where he used to sleep.' I told him of our meeting with the Russian boy and the officer nodded his head.

'Well, I'll tell you what, Staff. Can you take him over to the farm where he says his papers are and then bring him back here - are you free to do that?'

'Certainly, Sir.' I replied. 'I can take him over. I'm just waiting to hear from my squadron as to where we should rendezvous.'

With Russky, I set out across the ploughed fields again. We talked as best we could. Suddenly, he drew something from his pocket and thrust it at me. I took it and found that it was a beautifully made automatic cigarette lighter of aluminium. I didn't want to take it, but he insisted. I had nothing that I could give him in exchange but he didn't mind – he appeared happy enough that he had found his freedom.

As we approached the road, I noticed something hanging from the shrouds of a parachute draped over the heavy cables stretched between the poles, the same cables under which we had swept during our landing. As we drew near, I could make out that the object was the lifeless form of an American paratrooper swinging gently to and fro like a suicide at the end of a rope. I went right up to him, just to make sure, but he was dead. I almost felt sick as I looked at his face, half of which had been torn clean away together with most of his head. I tried to pull down the limp form but the chute was too well entangled up in the cable and I couldn't reach up high enough to cut the shrouds. We left the corpse still swinging slowly to and fro and set off across another field towards a farmhouse about half a mile away and in which, Russky kept reiterating, were his papers.

We stepped onto a dusty track which made easy going compared with the endless furrows of the ploughed fields. We came to a spot which must have had quite a shelling from the 2nd Army's guns before we had touched down. Craters were in profusion, some of them the largest I had ever encountered. Scattered around the edge of one of the deep, wide craters lay a number of dead cows. One appeared terribly grotesque, lying on its back with the four legs stiffly pointing skywards. It had already swelled to nearly twice its normal size. The guts of another lay spilled out over the brown soil and the smell of death was strong on the afternoon air.

I held my breath against the sickly smell and hurried past. Russky told me that he had been out in the middle of the fields when the first shells of our barrage had screamed down. He had run like mad for the farmhouse where we had first met him and had hidden along with the German family in what they termed their bunker, or shelter, while the bombardment continued.

We reached the farmhouse at last and found that a seventeen-pounder gun of ours had been parked nearby under a camouflage net. The crew had taken possession of the house. Russky went inside while I sat down on a shattered fence. Looking out from the top windows were two young frauleins but they weren't any beauty contest winners and my interest soon faded. They stared down with indifference at first and then, after a while, began giggling.

One of the crew drifted over to me and we started chatting away. Another came up and joined in. Russky came out through the doorway and our talk terminated. Just before we left the first man to whom I had spoken warned us not to go on any further as the enemy were supposed to be occupying the woods that lay about three hundred yards away beyond a low stone wall. I thanked him and told him that we were heading back in the opposite direction.

Russky and I walked back down the track, stepping to one side to let a jeep and trailer roll past. As it slowed down to pass us I caught a glimpse of its gruesome cargo of corpses whose lifeless boots stuck stiffly out of the rear of the trailer. They moved slightly as the trailer bumped over the ground giving the illusion, for the moment, that live bodies lay under the blanket. After the cloud of dust caused by the jeep had settled, we tramped off once more.

I was glad to get back into my trench after delivering Russky to the intelligence officer. Mac was boiling up some tea and I was thankful for the mess tin-full he passed over to me. I leaned back in my trench and listened to the sporadic sound of small arms fire echoing to and fro across the open fields.

It was now late afternoon and still we had no word from our squadron. We had spent the last hour talking with the sergeant in charge of the Vickers gun in the adjoining trench. To ease the burden of the men handling the Vickers, Mac and I had agreed to take on a watch during the night. I had never fired a Vickers but I knew how to operate one, and the men soon refreshed my memory and showed Mac the ropes. In any case, they would awaken if action started.

Chapter 25

On German Soil

The familiar form of our Flight Commander came into view and we learned from him that most of our flight had now gathered at the farm, and were in fact digging in about one hundred yards away in the farm yard. We went over with him, for I was anxious to see who had survived and who had not.

I was very glad to see so many familiar faces although several were missing, but that didn't necessarily mean that they were casualties. Mac and I decided that we may as well stay in the trenches we already occupied instead of digging in alongside the rest and this was agreeable to our Flight Commander who promised to send us word the moment there were signs of the whole flight moving out.

As we stood talking, my ears picked up the distant roar of low flying aircraft coming from the direction of the Rhine. In company with the others, I moved out away from the farm walls to try and pick out the approaching machines – they were ours, of that I was sure, for the engines had that familiar beat. The men, who had been searching a new batch of prisoners, finished their task and also looked up. The prisoners gazed skywards with a perplexed look upon their faces. They had been allowed to lower their arms, having been thoroughly searched.

And then I saw them. A long, spread-out line of four-engined machines, racing towards us at less than two hundred feet in most cases. For a moment I could not place their unfamiliar outline but, when they were less than half a mile away, I recognised them as U.S.A.A.F. four-engined Liberators. The thunder of their motors filled the heavens as they roared down upon us.

Most of them were approaching a little to our right, but two or three were heading straight for us. We cheered and ripped out our yellow Celanese identification triangles. Frantically waving the yellow signals, we tried to catch the eyes of the bombardiers. I guess they were flying excessively low to avoid the thick haze that still hung over the battlefield, with its base around two or three hundred feet above the ground.

Now they were directly overhead travelling fast – almost too fast for the purpose of dropping supplies. Their bomb bays gaped wide open, revealing neatly packed lines of supply containers. As I watched, the first speeding machine released its load and the containers curved forward, down and away from the bomb bays, the silk streamed out behind, bursting into full bloom as the powerful slipstream snapped open the chutes. Parachutes of all colours, red, blue, yellow and others started to emerge. Almost before the parachutes had fully opened, the cylindrical containers hit the ground, bouncing and rolling until brought up short by the dragging of billowing silk. We cheered even more, waving our red berets and yellow triangles wildly.

A second line of Liberators came boring in behind the first wave. These gained height a little before dropping their loads of multicoloured silk and containers. I knew that the men around me were cheering but the thunder of the motors was so loud that I couldn't hear their cheers. An infuriated enemy had opened up with chattering machine guns and I could detect some of the gunners in the Liberators firing back. Guns crackled murderously from both sides. More chutes blossomed forth with almost unbelievable rapidity.

I turned and looked at one of the German prisoners who was staring up at this demonstration of Allied air power. 'Well, what do you think of that?' I shouted above the roar of the motors. The German looked across at me and just said one word; 'Propaganda.' For a moment I was nonplussed and then replied. 'Yes, but very effective propaganda.' The German turned his sneering face skywards.

I watched one machine flying lower than the rest, way out on our right over towards the farm that I had recently visited with Russky. From the woods beyond the farm house, in which I had been warned the enemy still lurked, came a longer than usual vicious burst of machine gun fire. The Liberator staggered, nosed up a little and then dived earthwards out of sight. A dirty, oily column of smoke shot skywards, flecked with flame. I couldn't hear the noise of the explosion above the roar of the engines. For a moment I stared at the flaming pyre. At least one American crew had made the supreme sacrifice. They were far too low to have baled out.

A louder roar than usual brought my eyes back to the sky ahead. A lone Liberator was swooping straight towards us in a shallow dive. As it flashed by at some 150 mph and at less than one hundred feet I caught a glimpse of the bomb aimer inside the perspex nose of the aircraft. Along with the rest I waved madly at him and in reply he gave the 'V' sign with his fingers. Then the plane was gone in a thunder of sound that trailed off sharply as it vanished from sight, still flying at less than one hundred feet.

The supply drop was over. A feeling of exhilaration still flowed through my veins. That fast, low supply drop had been one of the most inspiring sights I had witnessed during the whole of the war. So swift, so sudden and so forceful. The whole drop couldn't have taken more than two or three minutes. Although, without doubt, it could not have been carried out according to the rules laid down for supply droppings, it had been almost one hundred percent successful from what I had seen. Most of the containers had shot forth from the bellies of the Liberators like bombs from a Stuka and the strain on the parachutes snapping open must have been terrific, nevertheless they had held and the drop had been accomplished. After all, Liberator crews were bombers under normal conditions and this had been a special job for them. Two hundred and fifty Liberators had been assigned to the re-supply drop but I myself saw only about twenty or thirty, owing to the thick haze and restricted view available to me.

After the murderous supply drops at Arnhem, when such heavy losses had been suffered by the gallant RAF crews from the curtain of fire and steel thrown up at them, this drop seemed to have gone off too easily.

The machine gun fire which had been directed against the low flying Liberators trailed off and an uneasy silence settled over the area. Already jeeps were bumping their way across the endless furrows to pick up the precious containers still lying there attached to the brightly coloured deflated parachutes. I watched the men hack at the shroud lines and heave the heavy containers up onto the jeeps before jolting their triumphant way back to headquarters.

A thick pall of oily smoke still hung over the spot where the Liberator had crashed and burned. I turned to find the American pilot, to whom I had been talking earlier on, standing nearby. He was staring out with an ashen look on his face towards the distant smoke. A low stream of muttered curses fell from his lips. He turned slowly on his heel and walked away with shoulders that sagged. There was nothing I could say.

It was now late afternoon and the first shades of evening would soon be enveloping the battlefield. I sat on the edge of my trench with my feet dangling inside, chatting away with Mac who sat perched similarly on his trench. I was feeling a little puzzled at the way the whole area had gone so quiet.

Yes, it seemed strange, for we had now been down on German soil for nearly half a day while the 2nd Army troops had actually been over the Rhine since the early hours of the morning. I quite expected a full scale enemy attack to take place in the coming hours of darkness but felt fully confident at meeting it. To reach us, the enemy would have to cross over some wide stretches of open ploughland and we should be able to stop them dead, even in the dark. Moreover, we had the support of the medium artillery of the 2nd Army way back on the far banks of the Rhine and, by now in all probability, batteries were already across the river on this side.

Our armies now had a foothold across the Rhine into Germany proper, and as yet no counter-attack had developed, that is, no action in any great force. However, we did learn that one of the bridges over the Issel on the far side of Hamminkeln had been blown by our men to prevent a strong local counterattack, led by Tiger tanks, from crossing the river.

At that moment, I heard the second, and last, enemy jet plane I was to hear throughout the war. The first had been at Nijmegen during the Arnhem operation. I stiffened as I heard the faint banshee-like sigh of the machine whining up from over the Issel river. It was flying low and going very fast and I only caught the merest glimpse as it streaked over the ploughed fields about a quarter of a mile away on my left. The brief look I did get, however, was enough for me to recognise the machine as a Messerschmitt 262, one of the latest of Germany's twin-engined jets. My close study of aircraft recognition charts back in England had not been in vain, although there was no benefit from it apart from an inward satisfaction of having recognised the plane as such. The Messerschmitt disappeared rapidly towards the Rhine river and its high pitched whine faded away. I assumed it was out either on a reconnaissance of the 2nd Army's crossings or a more purposeful task of trying to bomb the pontoon bridge riding the swiftly-flowing currents of the Rhine.

The machine gunners in the adjoining trench cleared a better field of fire through the hedge. I strolled over to the sergeant in charge and we drew straws to see when each man would go on watch. I drew from 11.00 p.m. to 1.30 a.m. With Mac and me taking part in the watches, the time had been reduced from two to one and a half hours for each man.

We 'stood to' just before dusk and I peered out, ever watchful, into the deep of the evening. Slowly, the clear-cut furrows lost their outlines and the gliders farther out, standing motionless like giant prehistoric monsters, gradually merged into the falling cloak of darkness. The warmth of the day faded and the chill of night took over. I began to shiver and drew part of the mottled chute around me as I gazed out into the dark open space on the far side of the hedge. No stars shone forth to shed their friendly light – friendly to us defenders, but not to any German who had to worm his way forward over the deep furrows to seek out our perimeter defences.

After 'stand down', I sat for a while beside Mac talking quietly, but soon I was seeking the comparative warmth of my trench and the enveloping folds of the chute. In the next trench a man stood guard over the Vickers and peered out into the almost impenetrable blackness.

As I lay in the bottom of my trench with my head and shoulders resting against one earthy end, I listened to the muffled rumble of our artillery, which seemed to be laying down a barrage to the north. I guessed it must be in the Rees and Emmerich neighbourhoods, some ten miles away. In those areas, the British and Canadian troops had stormed across the Rhine in their sector and had firmly established themselves on the east bank, but they were meeting very stiff resistance. The noise had been going on for some time and continued with unabated fury. Sometimes the tempo increased to a maniacal fury as though a thousand giants were beating the earth with as many bolts of lightning and their accompanying thunder. Flickering flashes illuminated the horizon formed by the walls of my hole as if a violent electrical storm were raging away to the north. It was a storm alright but a man-made one of steel and fire, raking and blasting the soil of Germany as it had never been scorched before in all its bloody history. The enemy, who had dealt out so much fire and destruction to others, was undergoing the same terror and devastation himself, only on a scale that far surpassed any Prussian dream of hate and death.

As fresh batteries added their fury to the holocaust already raging, the ground beneath my body trembled as if in agony, although many miles separated us from the hail of shells pulverising all in their path. The angry horizon flickered more than ever as hundreds of pieces of artillery belched forth flame and death from their red hot muzzles.

Once, I shivered uncontrollably as my mind drifted back to those days at Arnhem, when we, and not the enemy, had been subjected to a concentration of artillery and mortar fire, not anywhere so bad as that which tore asunder this very night, but which had lasted far longer than this barrage would ever do. The terrible destruction that must have been wrought to the north this night would shatter any defence the enemy might put up. Yes, in a matter of hours I knew the barrage would stop, having done a job that would enable the infantry and armour to advance, at least for a short way. Then our artillery would move up and again blast the enemy, and so on and so on, until the end.

For a moment I felt almost a pang of pity for the enemy who I knew must be crouching, shivering in their slit trenches and in their pillboxes, as batch after batch of our shells whined and screamed down on their positions, killing, maiming, driving men to babbling wrecks, as the all-engulfing horror of the artillery fire snapped their last shreds of reason. Then, thinking of our men, and of Arnhem, I hardened my thoughts and wished our gunners all the slaughter they could hand out to those men who stood between us and peace, and home.

Above the sullen rumble of the north, I picked out the menacing roar of low flying aircraft. I raised myself up and gazed up into the darkness, following the droning motors across the night sky. They must have been flying around a thousand feet of so, which was pretty low for bombers at night. The enemy planes curved slowly over our positions. There weren't many – not more than four or five at the most. One circled our positions while the others flew on towards the artillery that was blasting away at the enemy without pause.

About two miles away, I watched golden and red tracers start to climb slowly up into the night sky. They reminded me of the firework displays I used to watch at the Crystal Palace before war broke out. At the same moment, the enemy bombers dropped the first ghostly looking green flares. They appeared to float motionless in the sky, hanging menacingly over the heads of those who fired up the golden red tracers, as if in retaliation. One of the planes was diving down, its motors roaring louder and louder. It levelled off and climbed away. I heard the faint whisper of the first bombs dropping earthwards. Vivid red flashes lit the horizon, blotting out the gunfire flickers for a second or two. The ground shook and the sound of heavy explosions reached my ears. They had fallen about a mile away.

More tracers climbed silently skyward followed later by a faint boom, boom, boom, boom drifting over the fields. The gleaming spears of fire criss-crossed in the dark skies seeking out the enemy bombers. Again the distant, almost imperceptible, whisper of bombs going down and again the shuddering explosions, preceded by flashes of deep intensity.

Another flare blossomed out. The nearby hedge stood out in sharp relief and I could see clearly the long lines of dark furrows and, in the distance, the faint outline of our Horsa glider crouching on the ground like a monster of a forgotten age. A machine gun on my left clattered out and red tracers darted up wide of the flare. The gunner fired a second burst and the tracers seemed to pass right through the flare, but it kept on burning. The bomber dived and levelled off.

This time, the bomb fell with a harsher note. The flash that followed the strike was more illuminating and the ground shook just a little more than before. Golden tracers from the Bofors gun shimmered up on an almost endless fountain of bursts. The flickering pinpoints of the AA explosions dotted the night sky, but their sharp thunder was lost in the general sound of the distant artillery barrage.

The bombers droned off and soon all was silent again except for the ceaseless rain of shells being hurled into the enemy lines many miles away to the north. Suddenly, I felt tired and, before I realised it, had fallen into a light slumber. I awoke with a start later on with the sound of a machine gun beating out savage bursts somewhere on the village outskirts. A grenade flash lit the horizon of my trench. An enemy machine pistol chattered out sharp and deadly on the night air. Another grenade explosion and then silence. I closed my eyes and slept again.

I was awakened at eleven o'clock by a dim figure. It was one of the gunners asking me in an apologetic way if I would mind taking over the Vickers. I shook my head to clear away the cobwebs of sleep and managed a light-hearted reply.

It was cold, damned cold. I shivered as I loosened myself from the enveloping folds of the mottled chute and stood up. The boards underneath squelched as I moved around and I marvelled that I was still dry. I followed the weary figure of the gunner over to where the squat brutal-looking bulk of the Vickers gun poked its barrel through the gap in the hedge.

The gunner turned in and curled himself up in the trench next to the machine gun pit. I sat on the edge of the pit and gazed out into the blackness beyond the Vickers' muzzle. Beating my arms to and fro, I tried to bring back some warmth into my stiff and cold body. It also helped to keep my eyes open, which threatened to close at any moment.

It was quiet in our area, incredibly so. But to the north, the 2nd Army's artillery drummed continuously, accompanied by the endless flickering from their distant muzzles. I looked up at the skies and was rather surprised to see one or two stars glinting through the misty haze that still clung tenaciously over the battlefield.

I stiffened, and my eyes switched back front again as the night was split by the harsh crash of a long-drawn-out machine gun burst coming from somewhere on the outskirts of the village. Peering out through the hedge, I watched an intermittent line of tracers curving low across the ploughed fields in front. I had nothing to worry about for they were too far away and were, in any case, cutting across my front at right angles.

A crackle of fire answered the first burst. Interestedly, I watched the short lived skirmish being fought out. Somehow, I felt strangely detached and aloof from the criss-crossing darting tongues of flaming bullets as they sought their objectives. Then, as suddenly as it had started, the firing stopped.

However, it had brought me more on the alert and as the time wore on my eyes ached with the constant scanning of the blackness around. I almost began to imagine dim forms slipping along the furrows, bent double, creeping closer and closer. Beads of sweat broke out on my forehead. I eased myself forward close behind the Vickers. Blast these hallucinations! They always happened when one had to concentrate so hard, peering into nothing. I licked my lips and wished I had brought along my water bottle. Can't go back for it now.

I glanced at my watch and groaned to see that I had only been in position for just under half an hour. Still over one hour to go and the fog of sleep was already striving to overcome my resistance. I rubbed my sore and tired eyes and shook my head. This wouldn't do.

Again I tensed. I thought I could pick up a faint rustling sound in the enveloping blackness. My stomach muscles had gone hard and taut. I hardly drew in a breath. Was I hearing things again? I leaned forward over the Vickers and my fingers closed over the trigger. I peered into the dark until my eyes hurt with the intensity. A film of perspiration broke out all over my face and I felt my hands go moist.

There it was again, a faint, almost imperceptible sound. I couldn't quite place it, except that I knew it was just over the far side of the hedge, somewhere out there among the furrows.

Through a parched throat, I called out sharply the password of the night and tensely awaited an answer. Nobody replied but the faint moving sounds continued. I felt the hair on my neck rise and whole of my scalp tingled. I spat out another challenge, making up my mind that if no answer came this time, I would sweep the area with fire. Still no reply.

Then I saw a faint shadowy mass slightly on my right and about fifteen feet away. Instantly, I swung the barrel round, trained it on the mass and began to squeeze the trigger. Even as I did so, the muscles of my fingers froze. In that split second, my eyes had telegraphed a message to them, preventing that last fraction of an inch that would have sent a thunderous burst echoing out into the night, bringing everyone in the area out of his uneasy slumbers in a matter of seconds.

The tenseness flowed from my body and my stomach unravelled its knots. I cursed myself for a jumpy fool. The massive bulk moved nearer, revealing itself more clearly as a straying cow. I relaxed and, for the benefit of the cow's ears, spoke slowly and deliberately, emitting a long stream of curses. The cow paused about five feet away and I sensed it looking at me. Maybe she understood part of what I was saying, for she suddenly turned and lumbered off and swiftly vanished into the night.

After the cow incident, the night seemed to lose much of its menace and time and time again I grinned at myself at the thought of how close I had come to sending a stream of bullets into the hide of that fat Jerry cow. I kept up a vigilant watch, however, for occasionally a blast of gunfire would echo sharply across the open land and angry tracers, in a golden stream, would flash for a few seconds. Then silence would fall again. It did, however, indicate that enemy patrols might be on the prowl and I wanted to live and see the light of another day.

The last few minutes of my guard duty seemed to draw to a close in agonising slowness. As the illuminated hand of my watch drew level with thirty minutes past midnight, I rose and stretched my cramped limbs. After taking one deep penetrating look around, I stumbled over to Mac's trench and shook him into wakefulness. He was next on the list. Mac yawned and mumbled something, and huddled up once more. I had to shake him again before I brought him into some sort of wakefulness.

He got up and, in a half daze, weaved his way to the machine gun nest. The keen night air outside his trench and the uncertain walk had brushed away most of the cobwebs of sleep from his head. He nodded when I asked him if he felt OK and well awake. I told him of the cow, in case it came wandering around again, and then crossed over to my own trench.

It felt good to be nestling down between those four earthy walls amid the enveloping folds of the chute. The boards squelched in the water but I was clear of its soaking action, thanks to the wood and depth of straw I had placed over the muddy, watery bottom. I fell asleep almost immediately.

It seemed that I had only been asleep for a few minutes when I was awakened by someone roughly shaking my shoulders. I awoke with a start. It was still dark and I found myself looking up at a dim figure who was saying 'Stand-to, Staff.'

'OK, thanks.' I mumbled. The figure vanished and I heard him fumbling around Mac's trench, telling him the same tale of woe. For a moment, I lay in the dubious warmth of the chute and then forced myself up. A wave of damp cold air struck me as I rose above the edge of my trench. My teeth chattered at first and I shivered violently. The parachute had been a great help, but my body still felt damp and cold, while my right foot seemed to have gone to sleep and most of my right leg was numbed into insensibility. It took several minutes of rubbing before some semblance of life flowed back into it.

I leaned on the edge of the trench, upon which lay my sniper's rifle, and peered through the hedge. Hell, it was cold, a damn sight colder than it had been during my watch up until past midnight. I rubbed by hands together violently and called softly out to Mac. I couldn't see him but his sleepy voice came back out of the darkness. It was one way of keeping my eyelids open and I think Mac appreciated that point also. I would have given a week's pay there and then just to have been able to slip back into the folds of the chute at the bottom of my trench and close my eyes for another hour.

Then the first almost imperceptible streaks of light began to appear on the eastern horizon. At last dawn was on its way in. I stopped talking to Mac. It was too much of an effort. My soggy head couldn't keep up with the words that dripped from my numbed lips. Besides, I was sure that the dawn would bring in the long-awaited enemy counter-attack. I prayed that they would wait just a little while longer, until our vision was expanded just a little bit further out over the ploughed fields, then we would be able to cut down, with comparative ease, anyone attacking over the wide open spaces.

I remembered Arnhem, when each and every dawn had brought an outbreak of furious small arms fire around the defensive perimeter and the first mortar bombs and shells of a new day had screamed in on their deadly missions. I wondered how my body would react to the enemy's shelling. My stomach tightened up at the thought.

It grew lighter and my wonder grew with it. Then, on our right, came the first burst of machine gun fire. It hammered out sharply on the early morning air. It was still too dark to see more than a hundred yards out in front. A splutter of rifle fire retaliated. An enemy 'burp' gun rasped horribly fast somewhere out in front. Bammm - bammm - bammm -bammm - bammm replied a Bren, cutting heavily across the dawn.

From the depths of the Diersfordter Wald behind us, my ears picked up the echoing crash of more small arms fire. Then silence fell again. Tensely, I awaited the next move, but nothing happened. The dawn gained ground. Peering through the hedge, I watched the shadowy bulk of our Horsa take shape slowly through the rolling patchy mist that hung low over the earthy furrows. First it was grey and then, as the sun rose higher over the eastern horizon, the glider took on its familiar shade of black. The shadows of night appeared to be fleeing faster and faster before the advance of day. Now I could see clear across to the road and, beyond that, the distant blurred outline of the woods near the Issel river.

Still I awaited the rain of fire and steel I expected to burst upon us at any second. Then broad daylight was here and I knew the enemy had missed their chance. I just couldn't believe it. Sporadic firing broke out from time to time, but no general battle was joined. I really began to believe that the enemy was finished. If the 2nd Army was on time, their first elements would be linking up with us within a few hours. Although I did not know it, forward elements of the 2nd Army had already contacted our units which were nearest to the Rhine in and around the Diersfordter Wald.

We stood down with the breaking of full daylight and, with the warming rays of the sun beating down with a promise of a warm day to come, my spirits rose like a thermometer in an oven. Mac was also feeling good. He must have had an idea that all this talk about airborne units having a bitter fight the whole time had been a lot of hot air but, without doubt, this operation had been an overwhelming victory with everything on our side.

Something warm inside me was needed and Mac and I decided that there was but one answer. We got a fire going, and soon the inevitable brew was bubbling away merrily. The war seemed far away. It almost began to be a novelty if we heard a shot fired. I had a jovial word with the men around the machine gun and told them of my near mistake during the night. I was chided for not having knocked off the cow.

The sergeant in charge of the Vickers knew that we glider pilots would be returning to England as soon as the situation permitted, whereas the 6th Airborne Division had been allotted the task of spearheading one of the columns across Germany as soon as the 2nd Army had strengthened its bridgehead over the Rhine. With this in mind, he gave me his wife's telephone number and asked me to call her on my return to England to let her know that he was safe and sound. I made it one of my first tasks on my return.

The hot tea and food had made me feel tops. I was ready for anything and, although the desire to get back to England was strong within me, I would have been ready to go forward with the men of the 6th Airborne with a willing heart if we should be called upon to do so. I had always wanted to see Germany and now here was my chance.

The morning wore on uneventfully, except for occasional outbursts of shots from the Diersfordter Wald, and from the direction of the Issel river. At one time, the firing grew quite fierce over near the woods in front of the river. Mingling in with the rapid bursts of small arms fire, I heard the muffled explosions of artillery. I stood by the edge of my trench and gazed over towards the sounds of battle. But that too died down eventually and an unnatural silence settled over the area.

With Mac for company, I prowled through the farm into the yard where our flight was dug in. Still no news of moving yet, although it was rumoured that we would be joining the rest of the squadron which was already established in the village, having taken over several buildings there, so we were informed. This last item of news aroused interest within Mac and me, for we both preferred the shelter of a house to that of a trench, always providing, of course, that the enemy didn't start his shelling and mortaring.

We returned to our trenches and found the Vickers gun crew dismantling their weapon preparatory to moving off. The sergeant in charge told me that they had orders to proceed to one of the bridges over the river to give support to one of the coup de main parties that had landed the day before and who had captured the bridge. A German counter-attack was suspected to be in the making, as the men holding the bridge had heard several tanks moving around on the woods just over the far side of the river.

For a moment I thought of going with them. They were a likeable lot of fellows but then the desire to be with the squadron when they moved off back to England arose strongly within me, and I watched them march away without offering my services. I reiterated my promise to the sergeant to call up his wife on my return to

England and then they were gone, skirting around the hedge.

Just before they had left one of the men told me how they had fared on their landing. Apparently, they had been hit by flak as they circled over the pall of dust and smoke above the landing zone. Both pilots had been hit and the glider had gone into a dive. One of the pilots had just managed to almost level off before they had ploughed into the furrows. Most of the soldiers had been partly stunned by the impact which had completely wrecked the front of the glider, killing, he believed, both of the pilots. The machine gun platoon had fought their way out of the wreckage and one of their men had been sniped at and killed just as they began forming a defensive perimeter around the glider.

I had pumped the man to find out if he had known the names of the pilots for he told me that they too had taken off from Great Dunmow and I felt slightly sick at heart at the thought that two of my fellow pilots were lying out there gazing upwards with sightless eyes.

He hadn't known who the pilots were, except that they had been one army and one RAF pilot. As soon as the detachment had vanished from sight, I picked up my rifle, walked back through the farm and then out across the ploughed field. Near the far edge I easily picked up the glider I was looking for. It looked bad, with its nose, or what was left of the nose, buried in the soft brown earth of the furrows.

As I came up to it I could see that most of the cockpit had disintegrated under the force of the impact. Shattered plywood, metal and fabric, mixed in with jagged pieces of perspex, lay scattered around. The fuselage, from the open ramp door to the tail, appeared almost intact although the woodwork was slashed and torn in places where the flying steel of the bursting shell or shells had torn through. I looked at the wings. They too were rent in several places and mixed in with the larger gashes made by shrapnel, were numerous little neat round bullet holes. They had certainly run into a packet and I noted how lucky the machine gun crew were to escape.

I found one of the pilots lying there underneath a mottled parachute. The shapeless bulges under the silk could only mean one thing. Kneeling down, I gently pulled back the chute. I had been ready for a shock but I winced as a mass of tousled hair came into view, followed by a face so waxen and twisted up in pain that I couldn't recognise it. I braced myself and pulled the chute further back away from the lifeless hulk of flesh.

There was blood splashed over the smock, stomach wounds by the look of it. Then I found what I wanted – the little strip of leather sewn over the left breast pocket under the spreading RAF wings. A smear of blood masked part of the name but I knew who lay before me. The last syllable was enough. To make sure, however, I wiped part of the smear off and there, written in his own hand, was the name. I felt sick within me. Of all persons, it had to be him. Damn and blast the Germans – the swine.

As I stood looking down at his twisted body, I remembered how he only just married a few weeks ago. Never had time for a honeymoon. A WAAF at another airfield. One of the best men that ever breathed too. Always ready with a smiling welcome. His hair, normally so plentiful and wavy, had taken on a curious wiry appearance but it was the look of agony on his face that hurt me most of all.

I draped the concealing silk over his face once more and stood up feeling as bitter as I had ever felt, feeling the same way as I had on first seeing the battered form of Jock back at Arnhem. Why was it the best men always seemed to get it?

Taking one last look at the shapeless mass, I turned and walked around the glider, seeking the other pilot. On the far side of the fuselage I found another ominous irregular lump underneath an orange supply chute, measuring up just right for a corpse. Bending down, I drew back the coarse rayon cloth. A man in khaki lay there sprawled on his back. The bullet had hit him squarely in one temple and had emerged out on the other side of his head, tearing a large piece of flesh, skin and bone out during its exit. The nearside hole was neat and round but evidently the bullet had turned as it had ripped its way through the man's skull, thus causing the frightful wound on the opposite side. He never could have known what had hit him.

This must be the man the gunner back in the trench had told me about, but where was the other pilot? I dragged the chute back over the lifeless body and picked up the cherry-coloured beret that the man must have been wearing, laid it on top of the chute and then continued my search for the other pilot. Idly, I speculated whether the man lying dead under the orange chute would have died if he had had his steel helmet on. Judging from the point of entry of the bullet, I did not think that the tin hat would have saved him. I reset my steel helmet more firmly on my head, and crossed over the furrows to the far side of the glider.

I never found the other pilot and assumed that a burial party must have passed by and had room for just one more corpse on their litter of jeep. On my return to England I learned why I had not found the co-pilot. A medical unit inspecting the crash before I had reached the scene had found the three bodies and one of them had shown signs of life. They had picked him up and had in fact saved his life. I didn't have a chance to visit him in hospital but I did hear that he had many broken bones in addition to his wounds, but he recovered.

I walked on over the ploughed field to the nearest side and turned off, following a thick hedge back in the general direction of the farmhouse. A hundred yards along the hedge I came across four Germans who would never again awaken to the sound of a bugle, or anything else for that matter. I think they must have been caught by a burst of machine gun fire. Two of them lay in a tangled heap, one half on top of the other. The other two were sprawled at about two-yard intervals as though they had been running for the shelter of the hedge, and had been cut down as they did so. Three of them wore the very long overcoats used by German troops.

One looked as though he could have done with a good shave and a wash but he wouldn't have to worry about that annoying task again. His mouth hung open, showing a row of uneven yellow teeth. Coagulated blood trailed from his mouth down over his chin. He looked a murderous creature even though he was dead. Death had been more kindly to the other three. They looked quite calm and restful, although the sodden looking dark stains scattered over their uniforms belied the peacefulness and indicated the violent death they had died. One of the men was in fact a mere boy.

I stepped over the bodies lying athwart the path and hurried on. I knew it was no use searching them, someone had been there before me for at least two of the pockets were turned inside out and left so by the men who had gone about their gruesome task.

Back at the farm, I took in a swig of cool water and relaxed on the edge of the trench. I felt glad that I had checked up on the glider, otherwise it would have many days before I could have put aside the thought that I should have gone over there to make sure.

My attention was diverted to the sky as I caught the drone of high flying aircraft. The haze had all but lifted this day and I could see way up into an almost blue cloudless sky. I squinted and shaded my eyes with my hands. Yes, there they were. Obviously fighters by the way they were turning and speeding. They must have been flying around eight thousand feet but even at that height I was able to recognise the familiar outlines of the enemy Focke-Wolf 190s. They went into a circle, not a big one for there were not more than about five. I wondered at their purpose for they were flying too high to hope to make a surprise strafe attack.

Then I felt a thrill go through me for from the direction of the Rhine I picked up a line of at least ten planes racing up towards the circling 190s. As they drew closer overhead, I made out the blunt wings of Typhoons. It looked as though we were in for a grand front seat view of a first class dog fight.

The Typhoons closed in on the circling enemy and soon the sharp crackle of gunfire penetrated earthwards. The noise of zooming motors rolled lazily out on the warm afternoon air. The Typhoons dived again and again on the tight circle of 190s. Our fighters seemed to form up in a higher circle above the Germans and then peel off one at a time to bear down on the enemy on a shallow dive from behind. A long rasping burst, borne faintly on the air, and then the Typhoon would be curving away, down, and up again to its place once more in its circle.

After the third attack had been delivered, one of the enemy 190s fell off into a dive which grew steeper and steeper. A thin plume of smoke trailed out behind the falling aircraft. The roar of its motor, sounding faint at first, grew louder and louder until it was filling the whole vault of the heavens. Faster and faster the fighter plummeted earthwards, the sound of its motor rising to a high pitched scream. Fascinated, I watched its meteoric flight down. The gap between the earth and the plunging plane grew rapidly less and less and then it dived in at a fantastic speed. I estimated that it must have been doing somewhere around five to six hundred mph. It struck earth about two or three miles away. Black smoke spiralled skyward and mushroomed out in a spreading cloud. Seconds later, a noise like a muffled thunder rolled across the flat landscape. I did not see the pilot bail out unless I missed him as I watched the plane diving earthward.

High above, the dog fight continued with unabated fury. The sound of motors rising to a tortured scream and then fading away. The noise of guns being fired sounded like a giant ripping a piece of canvas in half, high in the heavens. Another plane dropped out of the fight and headed back towards the Rhine in a fast shallow dive. A Typhoon this time. Then the fight broke up with the enemy aircraft hightailing it back into the heart of Germany. The Typhoons took up the chase and in a short while the sky was clear and silent once more. It had been strangely invigorating, being in the position of spectator, watching the silvery machines turning and diving high up in the blue sky – the roar of straining engines in long drawn out bursts of power– the crackling blasts of gunfire drifting down through the thousands of feet.

My thoughts turned to the ground battle, such as it was. What was happening? Would we still come under a counter-attack before the 2nd Army arrived to give its support? Why no enemy shelling and mortaring? We had been told that the enemy would probably fight like madmen to defend their homeland, even if they were outgunned, outnumbered and outmanoeuvred. The Rhine was the last barrier to the heart of the Reich and we had breached it.

The troops around were in good spirits. Even the prisoners appeared to be relieved to be out of the battle, and fear and suspicion had been replaced by an air of indifference and, in some cases, arrogance. For them the war was over.

Around midday, Mac and I opened up two cans of rations and prepared a meal. Some of the prisoners standing around nearby sniffed the air and licked their lips, but we ignored them. It would have taken several cases of rations to have been able to give every prisoner even a slight semblance of a meal.

Having finished eating, we called on our Flight Commander again, but still no further orders. We prowled around the area, trying to glean more information, but without success we returned to our trenches, talking of all subjects under the sun.

It was about mid afternoon when we heard a distant sound that caused us both to cease talking and listen intently. From the direction of the Diersfordter Wald came the muffled sound of clanking tracks and rumbling motors. Tanks! We looked at each other. The noise grew louder. The men around had paused in their tasks also and were listening intently.

The sprawled farm buildings prevented our seeing along the road to the forest. The men who had been standing around suddenly had a yearning to see the inside of their trenches. I slid down into my hole and peered over the top. The noise stopped at a point I estimated to be half a mile away. There was silence for several minutes, and then the motors started up again and the clanking of tracks became more audible.

Although I had hardly dared myself to believe it, I guessed that the tanks must be the first of the 2nd Army's. Not a shot had been fired which, without doubt, would have happened if they had been enemy tanks. Nevertheless, I was playing safe and remained in my trench to watch. A sniper's rifle is hardly the weapon for a duel with a tank.

After the long, fruitless wait we had endured at Arnhem, I just couldn't convince myself that a link-up had been made so soon, even though it had been promised. Excited voices called from trench to trench.

The harsh rumble rapidly approached the farm. Tracks squealed on the road. The motors died down and the tanks clanked to a halt. I still couldn't see them. Voices shouted on the far side of the farm buildings and the engines coughed into life again. The next moment, I saw the long snout of a gun poke its way around the farm entrance, followed by the great steel hulk of the tank itself. Slowly it manoeuvred its way into the farmyard. Another followed in close on its heels. They stopped under the lee of a wall and Mac and I, in company with several other men, scrambled out of our trenches with joy and elation in our hearts.

The tank crews were already clambering out of the steel clad monsters. We reached the side of the tanks just as the crew dropped to the ground while we crowded around them and shook hands. The tank men looked begrimed and tired, but they too seemed very glad to see us and insisted that our landings had paved the way for them, enabling them to break out from their river bridgeheads with confidence and ease. We, in turn, were delighted to have their support and made no bones about declaring it. Although events were proving that we of the airborne had mastery of the battlefield, the addition of a few heavy tanks completely turned the scales against the enemy.

The two tanks didn't stay long and within fifteen minutes they were rumbling out through the farmyard entrance. They turned down the road towards Hamminkeln, raising a column of dust as they did so. We waved to the crewman of the rear tank whose head projected out of the open turret, and then they were gone. The heavy smell of hot oil still hung on the air over the spot where they had halted briefly. The interiors of those machines must have been hotter than a hothouse.

Chapter 26

Hamminkeln

So the link-up had been effected. If our morale had been high before the tanks had arrived, it was positively bubbling over now. Ten minutes later the same two tanks came clanking back up the road from the village and continued on towards the Diersfordter Wald. Presumably they weren't needed even down in the village sector and were probably returning to make a verbal report to their commander.

Shortly afterwards, another tank rolled up the road from the direction of the Diersfordter Wald. This time the men stayed a little longer and we gleaned further information. The crew told us that our area would be full of 2nd Army men and equipment by the following day. They themselves were, in fact, a reconnaissance unit seeking the best possible lager areas in the vicinity. The men in the tank had crossed over the Rhine the night before and after a short sharp battle on the fringe of the forest, had penetrated into it. They had nothing but praise for the paratroopers who had almost completely cleared the enemy from the depths of the Diersfordter Wald. Actually, they had linked up with the first elements of the airborne troops late yesterday afternoon.

We examined their tanks with great interest for it was not very often that we men of the airborne had a chance to see such heavy equipment. Smoke from the hot engines drifted out around the motionless hulk of armour.

The officer who had been riding in the tank came out from a conference in the farm with the airborne commander. A minute later the tank's powerful engine burst into life. With clanking and squealing tracks, the monster turned and rumbled out of the farm back to the Diersfordter Wald area

A short while later, my high morale received a sharp setback. From the direction of the Issel River came the distant thud of enemy guns firing, followed almost immediately by the blood-freezing, long drawn-out wail of shells in flight. For a moment my whole body stiffened and a peculiar shock ran through me. However, I knew instantly from the fluttering course the shells were taking, unseen across the sky, that we were in no danger. With my ears, I followed the descending flight of the shells.

They struck squarely among the belt of trees about three hundred yards away. With a dry mouth, I watched smoke spurt upwards, once, twice, thrice. Three succeeding explosions rolled across, like thunderclaps on a sultry summer afternoon. As the noise of the explosions died down, I heard the sound of tumbling branches. Again came the dull reports of the guns in the woods on the far side of the Issel. Again the spine-tingling wail ending in a rasping shriek followed by shuddering explosions. More smoke billowed upwards and outwards from the line of trees. Inwardly I thanked our lucky stars that we had not, after all, rendezvoused in the trees where the missiles were, even at this moment, bursting. A crackling fire took hold in the trees and blue-grey smoke drifted out over the ploughed fields. Inside the distant undergrowth, I could see the hungry red flames licking away.

I suddenly felt old and tired and the fear of shelling and mortaring that had been imbued in me at Arnhem arose within me. I prayed that the enemy gunners would not alter their range to bring those death-dealing shells screaming down amongst us. The farmhouse, I felt, one of the largest in the area, was bound to catch the attention of the gunners.

A third salvo whistled in and once more the trees were ripped and shattered by the flailing steel from the bursting high explosives.

I felt the perspiration breaking out on my forehead as I waited for the next salvo. But apparently the enemy gunners were satisfied, at least for the moment, for no further shells followed. I began to relax and watched the smouldering fires that raged within the narrow strip of woods.

As if in retaliation, we heard the first British shells sigh over from the direction of the Diersfordter Wald. They wailed down on the enemy positions on the far side of the Issel River. The sharp explosions from the bursting shells was the sweetest music my ears had heard for many a day.

For several minutes, salvos split the heavens apart as they tore through the air above our heads. Even though I knew them for British shells speeding on their way to deal death and destruction out to the enemy who, up to a few minutes ago had been hurling shells into our positions, I couldn't help but shiver at their menacing note. There was something so deliberate, so imminent, so irresistible about their song of death. I knew then and there that I could never become mentally immune to artillery fire and the closer it fell, the more the hands of terror would squeeze my heart. Arnhem had left its mark on me forever.

The guns fell silent and the black clouds of oppression seemed to lift. The afternoon was sunny once more. Then, as if not to be outdone, the German artillery opened up again but this time they had a different target and used a different type of shell.

I heard the distant sound of the gun being fired. There followed a faint whispering tearing sound and the next moment a black cloud suddenly spewed forth into the air over the village of Hamminkeln. The sharp thunderous crash of the explosion drifted over. The enemy were using air-burst shells, hoping no doubt to catch some of our men wandering through the streets of the village. The air-bursts would send down a shower of red hot steel slivers tearing and hacking down anyone in their path.

For a moment, a wrathful looking puff of black smoke hung there and then the gentle breeze that was blowing carried it off. Before the smoke of the first shell had vanished, another took its place. Again, the air vibrated with the impact. A third shell burst with a jarring crash. I wasn't so sure now that I would care to billet in the village after all.

The air-bursts went on periodically for several minutes and then stopped as suddenly as they had started. A dark thin film of cloud had formed over the village like a symbolic cloak of death. I waited to see if the 2nd Army's guns would retaliate but they remained silent. No doubt they had to prepare for far more important targets.

A little while later we got word that it had been reported that the Germans were massing in the woods for a counter-attack across the river. Tanks had been sighted taking up positions and infantry movements had been observed. That may have been the cause of the 2nd Army's guns opening up a short while before. No doubt they were trying to break up the concentration. A few minutes later, we witnessed the support the guns were getting in breaking up the enemy's concentrations.

A flight of Typhoons appeared over the area and began circling the positions of the enemy guns, tanks and troops. I knew what was coming, for the unmistakable outlines of rows of rockets were visible under the wings of each plane.

I got ready for a first class show. Several enemy machine guns chattered into life against the circling Typhoons. Red tracers darted up but the planes kept on turning. I counted three Typhoons. Then the leader started down from a point almost dead overhead of our positions. He went down in a shallow fast dive. At about two hundred feet he levelled off and at the same moment I saw the tell-tale streaks of smoke race out ahead. I could see distinctly the outline of the rockets bucking slightly as they bored down. The awful shoooooosh as they ripped on down came to me across the intervening space. The noise grew to a hollow roar and then the first batch disappeared into the wooded area. Violent explosions ripped the afternoon apart as though a giant was slamming-to the gates of the very heavens themselves. An ugly pall of smoke rose up and hung over the target area. The Typhoon curved upwards out of range of the enemy tracers which still speared upwards in furious retaliation.

Before the first Typhoon had levelled off again, a second one was bearing down on the enemy. Again I watched the rockets stream out in front of the diving Typhoon. To the Germans crouched in their foxholes the powerful rushing noise of the rockets flashing down on them must have seemed like the beating of a thousand wings of the Angels of death.

The shocking explosions beat out on the afternoon air and more smoke shot skywards, mingling with that of the previous explosions. If there were enemy tanks in the woods as reported, they were certainly receiving pressing attention. The third Typhoon raced in with its messengers of death and destruction. The clatter of the machine guns had ceased and the Typhoon released its rockets without interference. The missiles ripped through the air and vanished into the woods.

The Typhoon which had led the attack was already starting down on its second run-in. This time I thought I heard the low cough of cannon from the plane as well as the roar of the released rockets. Maybe the pilot was letting them have everything just for luck.

The remaining two planes followed suit and then climbed up to circle the inferno that raged below them of their own doing. The machine guns of the enemy cracked spitefully again and the Typhoons made off back towards the Rhine.

We talked excitedly of the last few minutes, showering praise on the RAF pilots who must have done a first class job if they had placed their rockets in the right area, and we were pretty sure on that point. About fifteen minutes later we heard the drone of a light aircraft coming over from the direction of the Rhine and then I saw a low-flying artillery spotting plane of the type that had a top speed of not much more than 100 mph.

The machine cruised over towards the woods on the far side of the Issel river at a height that appeared to me nothing short of suicidal. A pall of smoke still hung over the area recently beaten up by the Typhoons and the light aircraft circled over and around it. The burst of machine gun fire that I had been anticipating since the plane approached from the river suddenly ripped forth. I saw the angry red tracers smash up into the little plane. It staggered for a moment and then dived almost vertically for the ground. Levelling off about fifty feet up it came racing across the ploughed fields. It roared up towards our farmhouse and suddenly shot up into a climb and levelled off at about two hundred feet, wiggling its wings as it did so. I was relieved to see that the pilot appeared unhurt. Its drone faded away quickly as it headed back to report, no doubt.

It was now late afternoon so I decided to call upon our Flight Commander again. I found half of the trenches empty and learned that he had left for the village about half an hour ago and since then the men in the trenches had received orders to proceed to the village independently. Most of them had already left.

I hurried back to Mac with the news and we made short work of getting our belongings together. Shelling or not, I preferred to be in the village with my own flight. Mac felt the same way. I slipped on my rucksack and found that the weight of it had considerably increased due to the complete white parachute and the pieces of the orange rayon one I had packed into it.

We skirted down the hedge and cut across the corner of a ploughed field to another hedge where we came upon a seventeen-pounder anti-tank gun so skillfuly camouflaged that we were almost on top of it before we recognised the powerful tank-destroying weapon. We bandied a few words with the crew who were lazing in some foxholes dug close by before moving on.

As we left the gunners and started out across the large ploughed field in front that stretched all the way over to the road leading to Hamminkeln, Mac and I decided to split up. In this way we reckoned that we stood a better chance of picking up a white chute that Mac was so eager to lay his hands on. We arranged to meet again on the outskirts of the village.

I plodded on across the open field, passing as I did so two gliders. The first one was just a shattered mass of wreckage and only the tail unit retained some semblance of a flying machine. Even the seats, in most cases, were just a splintered mass of plywood and had spilled out amongst the furrows. Canvas safety belts, torn from their moorings in the fuselage, lay everywhere entangled in the slivers of the destroyed wooden fuselage. The area was clear of corpses. Evidently, the burial parties had made a call. I was certain that not many, if any, of the occupants of the glider had lived to see the sun set that day.

The second glider was almost intact. The port side undercarriage had buckled and collapsed and a long furrow stretching out behind the motionless machine testified that the glider must have come in rather fast. The ramp door lay wide open, resting on the ground and for a moment I saw in my mind's eye a mass of men erupting from the machine as it slid to a halt in a cloud of brown dust – the crackle of gunfire – the defensive circle – and then the advance.

About one hundred yards past the glider, I came across the motionless body of one of the 'Master Race'. He lay lengthways along a furrow face downwards with his two arms thrown out in front, the fingers of each hand clutched convulsively into the brown earth as though he had sought to tear life from the very soil for which it had been given. The ground around was saturated with his life blood. I eased the body over with a boot and it took considerable effort to do so.

An unshaven face, frozen in an expression of agony, stared up at the sky with sightless eyes. The good earth fell away from his open mouth with the movement. He must have been screaming as he fell with a burst of red hot lead tearing the life from his body and his mouth had gouged up the earth like a spade. The front of his uniform was just a pulpy bloody mass and I gave up the idea of going through his pockets to check on papers and so forth. I pushed the body over onto its face again and moved on towards the road. For a moment, I mused over how he had been caught out right in the middle of the ploughed field and could only conclude that he must have been making for the very trenches I had been occupying up until now. Men tumbling from one of the gliders swooping in for a landing had cut him down. No-one thinks of taking prisoners in those first few seconds on enemy soil. A man in grey-green uniform in those critical moments is a dead one, if caught within a rifle sight.

I felt not the slightest compunction for the shattered remains of the man I had just paused to look down at – just the feeling that that was one more German who would never again fire a weapon.

I reached the edge of the road and waited for Mac to catch up with me. He saw me sitting there and came over. He hadn't had any luck yet. I got up and we started to walk down the road towards the village. Suddenly I felt uneasy and said so to Mac. The road was deserted, and so was the whole landscape for that matter. Not a figure stirred anywhere yet I knew that our men were scattered in and around the village.

Well, we had to get on into the village. We stepped out and soon came up to the first house. Despite the news that our men were in the village, we proceeded with caution and I fixed my bayonet. The front door of the house hung right off the top hinge. Mac kept watch as I approached the open door at the side. I slipped in quietly and Mac followed.

Carefully we edged our way into the first room. A deep silence hung over the house. Outside, I heard a faint crackle of small arms fire in the distance but that was all that broke the silence. A scene of chaos met my gaze. I knew then that some of our men had already been through the house. Every drawer had been turned out in the search for souvenirs. We proceeded upstairs but found nobody, only untidy masses of clothing spilled out on the floors from the drawers.

Coming downstairs we searched the cellar but drew a blank there also. We left by the back door and it was a relief to emerge out into the afternoon sunlight. We tried the adjacent house with the same result, the only difference being that this one was even darker than the first.

The next house appeared to be the local policeman's home from the inscription that I saw in the wall beside the front door. I was even more cautious in entering that building but, like the rest, it appeared deserted. Mac and I walked quietly into the first room and there found ample evidence that the local police were thoroughly addicted to Nazism for the sign of the swastika was very prominent. We moved silently into the next room and as we did so I froze in my tracks and my heart beat a little faster. From the depths of the cellar I heard the low sound of voices.

I tiptoed towards the door marking the top of the steps down into the cellar. I paused again and listened and then relaxed and breathed again for an unmistakable Cockney voice came floating up to my ears. I am certain that it is only the English soldier who can cram so many foul words into one English sentence. I grinned to myself as I listened to the oaths dripping from the man's lips. Between the curses I heard the splintering of wood.

Quietly I descended the steps and came upon two bent figures in familiar camouflaged smocks feverishly endeavouring to break open a solid looking trunk with their bayonets. Not wanting to alarm them too much, for they might be itchy on the trigger, I called out 'Any luck?'. They both spun around, grabbing for their rifles but stopped as they recognised me in the dim light.

'Not so far, Staff.' said one of the men, 'But I'm going to get this bloody f***ing chest open or die in the attempt. I'm certain that there's something good in it.'

'You had better be a little more watchful or you might really die in the attempt.' I replied, thinking of how easily I had sneaked down on them. As an NCO I should have frowned on the brazen attempt at looting but, like most others, I chose to ignore the two soldiers. Such rules are laid down in army manuals, but are rarely enforced. Furthermore, I had no love whatsoever for the one-time inmates of the building or for any other of the village dwellers if it came to that.

I climbed out of the cellar and met Mac who had been upstairs while I had stolen down on the men in the cellar. We passed through the kitchen and I espied an alarm clock, which would prove an asset both here and at home. My rucksack weighed a little more as we stepped outside the building once again.

We decided that we would check through one more house before making straight for the centre of the village. It seemed that all the residents had fled at the first signs of our landing although where they could have gone, at such short notice was beyond me, unless they had made for the village church; and that is exactly what they had done, as we found out later.

Just as we were about to enter the house, three of our men came staggering out under a weird assortment of 'acquired goods'. One was almost bent double under the weight of a beautiful table model radio. I reminded him that the battle was not yet over, even though things were quiet. However, he hung onto his radio and swore that he would take it wherever he went and that he was going to get it back home, even if he had to carry it all the way in his arms. Actually, I saw the funny side of it as I watched him lurch up the road away from the village. I had an idea that he wouldn't carry it far despite his original ideas – a few miles marching carrying the weighty radio would cure him of that.

By now we had almost reached the centre of the village and the familiar red beret and steel helmet began to become more evident. I began to understand why we had found nothing in the houses we had searched.

We found our Flight HQ in the very place that I might have expected – the village inn. There was much handshaking and cheerful greeting, but many faces were absent – not that I attached much to it for the time being as I realised that they could still be with their passengers in some cases.

It was hot and my throat felt parched, so my first words were a demand for some beer. One sergeant, smelling strongly of drink, said apologetically 'I'm sorry, old chaps, but the bloody place has run dry.'

'You greedy lot of bastards,' I replied, 'Mac and I are dying of thirst.'

He chuckled a little, tipsy-like, and replied 'Better to die that way than with a bullet through your body – see the joke?' I did, but didn't appreciate it. However, he made up for his sin by informing us that the shop across the road had a barrel of beer left and that the owner was most generously ladling it out to the lads – with a little persuasion perhaps – but nevertheless, he was busy filling the glasses.

It didn't take us long to locate the shop with the barrel. We were met with a series of greetings varying in intensity. Sergeant Thomas, in his usual uncouth way, called out 'Make way for that drunkard Dusty. He'll finish the barrel in two ticks.' The title didn't exactly fit me, although I am proud to say that I can do my share of drinking whenever called upon to do so.

Sergeant Thomas turned and shouted onto the back room 'Come out you bloody German and tip the barrel.' A little wizened man came scuttling out from the rear room. I'm sure that he didn't understand a word Sergeant Thomas was yelling at him but I suppose he knew what was wanted. He smiled benignly at me as he tilted the barrel, a glass under the spout. I could see that there wasn't much beer left so I was ready for another before the old man had lowered the barrel down. He took it in good part however – he didn't have any option, I suppose. 'They are all on me,' went on Sergeant Thomas. I thanked him for his generosity.

Mac had his share also, but didn't receive quite so much good natured abuse from Sergeant Thomas as he wasn't familiar with him. 'OK, Thomas, thanks for the beer; we'll be seeing you. We have to report in to the Flight Commander. Know where he is?'

'Yes, back in the inn someplace.' he replied.

We didn't find our Flight Commander – he was with the Squadron Commander apparently, but we found his second in command, an RAF officer, Flying Officer Featherstone. He was one of the best and everyone liked him. He was typically RAF and didn't care much for the discipline the army had applied to him and, in turn, he hated handing it out.

He was glad to see us and told us to dump our rucksacks someplace and find ourselves a corner in the inn. It was good to be back amongst the Flight again, they were a real good gang. One of the first things we did was to find a couple of mattresses upstairs and bring them down to a ground level room. Next, we drew some furniture across the window. I had an idea it would help deflect any grenades that the enemy might have an urge to throw in on us during the night or by day if they put in an attack. I just left enough room to give a field of fire outwards.

Now was the chance for us to have a good wash and shave. The dust of the fields was thick upon me and the sweat running down my face had carved lanes through the dirt. My beard didn't help any either. We found plenty of water in the kitchen and I made the best of it.

As I was shaving, I heard the rushing sound of a shell. It burst like a thunderclap somewhere over our heads and the shrapnel clattered sharply against the roof tiles. Some glass tinkled as it fell into the road outside with the concussion and the impact of flying steel. Damn those air-bursts, I thought. Well, we were safe enough in the inn. Another shell burst thunderously overhead. More shrapnel flailed around. I finished my shave and sat down on the mattress to rest my tired bones. A few minutes later the shelling stopped. No more than four shells had come in.

Outside, the jeep and trucks of the 2nd Army were beginning to roll through the village in increasing numbers towards the Issel River and the broad plains beyond. It was a comforting sound and I lolled back and listened to the periodical rising and fading engine notes just outside our window. We knew that we were no longer just a pocket of men holding defensive positions inside enemy lines, we were now an integral part of the powerful 2nd Army.

My complacency received an unpleasant jolt a few minutes later. Without warning, a thunderous crash of heavy machine gun fire broke out and reverberated through the village. I jumped to my feet and grabbed my rifle and steel helmet. The sound of firing seemed to be just around the corner. I just couldn't make it out. How the hell had a patrol managed to penetrate through to the village across the fields in broad daylight without being spotted by someone?

I bumped into Staff Sergeant Nigel Brown. His face bore a look of surprised annoyance. If I know 'Nidge' Brown, he was sleeping soundly when the firing had broken out – or else drinking.

'The bastards, why can't they let a chap have a rest for a few minutes?' were his words of greeting to me. He was carrying a Bren gun in one hand and his steel helmet in the other.

Lieutenant Cartwright was in the bar of the inn and I heard his strident voice calling us all to meet him there. As we passed the kitchen I caught a glimpse of Staff Sergeant Hodge shaving.

'Come on, Bluffer.' I called out to him.

'Oh, to hell with them.' replied the Bluffer, 'I'm going to finish my shave while the water's still hot.' I didn't stop to argue, not that it would have done any good for he held the same rank as I did and didn't have to listen to me if he didn't want to.

The strident clamour of the machine gun hammered out without pause as if it was running on an endless belt of ammunition. In the bar, about ten of us gathered around the tall figure of Lieutenant Cartwright.

The gay atmosphere that had hung over the inn was gone and the air was heavy with tension. In a few precise words, the lieutenant divided us up into two sections, naming 'Nidge' Brown to command one of them. I came under his command which suited me. As I listened to Lieutenant Cartwright rap out his orders, the thought crossed my mind that the machine gun firing must mean one of two things. Firstly, and most likely, an enemy patrol had infiltrated into the village or, secondly, that it was a machine gun set up as a booby trap, timed to fire at a given time.

Our section had been ordered to search the houses immediately across the square from the inn. The other section was ordered into a position about one hundred yards away. At a final order from the lieutenant we filed towards the door.

'Nidge' paused for a moment, after peering cautiously out into the now deserted square. A second later, he was high-tailing it across towards the old stone church. I followed a few paces behind. The firing sounded terribly loud and near now that we had left the shelter of the inn. It echoed and re-echoed through the village. We crouched against the church wall while 'Nidge' got ready for the next dash, which would bring us to the first of the two houses we had to search. I remember noticing how all the army trucks had come to a halt with the drivers piling out of the cabs, their rifles at the ready. One man had crawled under his vehicle and was feverishly scanning the now deserted street.

With a sudden scurry of boots, 'Nidge' Brown darted across the intervening space, moving at a speed that was almost phenomenal for him. Under normal circumstances, 'Nidge' was loath to move at more than a snail's pace at any time. I even found time to grin to myself over his energetic efforts. Bending double, I dashed across after him. By the time I had reached the house, 'Nidge' had kicked open the door and was sliding quickly in around the doorpost.

As I plunged through after him, the firing stopped dead. Inside the house was darkness, broken only by shafts of daylight through the damaged walls. I could hear the other two men following me in. We went through the house room by room, but all was deserted. The machine gun burst into life again.

With 'Nidge' still in the lead, we came out of the house again. Keeping close to the wall, we scuttled into the next house. Finding nothing on the ground floor, we commenced to climb the narrow stairs leading up to the next floor. The machine gun fire sounded muffled in the house and I knew we were on the wrong trail, at least as far as that particular machine gun was concerned.

The air-bursts had done their work well on this house. The stairs were covered with plaster and broken brick that crunched under our boots in an alarming manner as we sought to steal quietly upwards. The bedrooms were empty, leaving only the attic to search. 'Nidge' cautiously mounted the wooden steps, holding his Bren gun at the ready. The Bren was hardly the weapon for house warfare where speed of moving the barrel around in a circle in split seconds might mean the difference between life and death.

I was panting from my efforts and the sweat rolled down my face in rivulets. My whole body felt saturated with perspiration and the clothes clung tenaciously to my skin. Grit from the fallen plaster got in my mouth as I followed the slow but sure progress of 'Nidge's' boots up the steps within a few inches of my nose. I had slung my rifle and held a number thirty-six grenade at the ready with one finger hooked through the pin. I reckoned I could do more damage with that than the one shot I might be able to get off with my rifle.

My sweating was for nothing as I found out when I saw 'Nidge' haul himself up into the attic, laying the Bren on the floor before he did so. I pushed the pin of the grenade, which I had drawn out a little, back in again. I clambered up after 'Nidge' with the other two following me. It was light in the attic at any rate for the simple reason that three quarters of the tiles were missing due to the recent air-burst shelling.

We crawled into positions which gave us an excellent field of fire. Through my gap in the roof between the joists, I could see way down the street that lead out of Hamminkeln towards the Issel River. Below me the trucks were still standing motionless with engines stopped.

Not a figure was in sight. I tried to locate the source of the machine gun fire which beat up clearly from somewhere down on our right and began to wonder why the barrel hadn't burnt out with such a prolonged burst of firing. Again and again I swept the area with a penetrating gaze, but couldn't pick up the slightest sign of movement or tell-tale whisp of gun smoke.

From the direction of the road entering into Hamminkeln from the Diersfordter Wald, I heard the heavy rumble and clank of a tank above the noise of the machine gun. I watched closely, not feeling at all sure as to whose tank it would turn out to be. I breathed a sigh of relief when I recognised the shape of a British tank swinging ponderously around the corner to halt in the square. Its huge gun snout swung slowly from side to side as though scenting its prey. With a rising engine note, it suddenly squealed around and thundered off down a side street. At the same moment the machine gun stopped. The silence was almost painful.

Sprawled out on the dusty tile and plaster covered floorboards, I drew in a deep breath and relaxed. For the first time I noticed how heavily my heart was beating against my ribs. I looked across at 'Nidge'. He was still staring intently down the barrel of his Bren with a strained expression on his face and his moustache, which never looked very trimmed at the best of times, looked more bedraggled than I can ever remember. The beer stains didn't do much to enhance it either.

We waited for several minutes until we noticed that the truck drivers were beginning to emerge from their places of concealment and were starting up their engines. 'Nidge' decided that we should return to the inn.

Crunching our way back over the litter, we descended the stairs and emerged into the fresh air, free of plaster and brick dust. 'Nidge' was swearing profusely about the 'idiots who get you out on a wild goose chase after waking you up from a deep sleep'.

We filed across the square into the inn to find the other section was already back. Nobody seemed to know what all the noise had been about. Maybe the tank had scared the enemy away, that is, if they had ever been here at all. We promptly forgot all about the incident. I took a deep drink of water and sat down on the edge of my mattress. Mac had wandered off and I had lost my desire for a rest.

Getting up, I went out of the inn, grasping my rifle firmly and turned off along the road down which I had seen the tank go a few minutes before. It was only a matter of about two hundred yards to the edge of the village. I leaned against a wall and looked across the fields in front. About eight hundred yards away was the beginning of a large wood where the enemy was supposed to be entrenched. It was, in fact, their nearest line to Hamminkeln. On the other side of the village, we had almost complete control as far as the Rhine, eight miles or so away. Between where I was standing and the woods, men of 6th Airborne occupied their positions in front of the enemy lines, although there was nothing to indicate that either the enemy or our men were there.

From behind me across the road I suddenly heard some of our men burst out laughing and shouting out 'Get hold of him, you stupid oaf.' I crossed over to the other side of the road and looked over the hedge. Just as I did so, I heard the crack of a revolver and at the same moment saw one of the flying officers of our flight dashing madly across the field in pursuit of a fleeing chicken, which screeched horribly each time the revolver in his hand kicked and belched flame. I almost fell over with laughing. The terror-stricken chicken met its end as I anticipated. The officer fired and the chicken's head literally disappeared in a puff of feathers. The headless body kept on going for a few feet under its own impetus and then rolled over, still quivering. The triumphant flying officer reached it and proudly held up the decapitated chicken.

A chorus of derision met him. 'What the hell do you think you were doing - five shots to knock him off – where did you learn to shoot?'

'OK, I'll do better on the next one, just you watch.' he replied. He advanced on a shed and immediately there was a terrific squawking, as though the chickens divined the purpose of his visit. They suddenly erupted out of the shed and the flying officer immediately selected one to pursue. I laughed again. I just couldn't help it. The tears rolled down my cheeks. The revolver cracked twice and he missed. The frantic chicken reached a wall and finding that it couldn't get by, turned and tried to dash back past its pursuer. Instinctively, he brought the barrel down instead of firing and hit the chicken squarely across the neck. It gave one short squawk, tumbled over, and lay still.

I walked back to the inn for I knew from my watch that if was almost stand to. Even though all appeared quiet and we were well back from the enemy, the procedure would still have to be carried out.

Flying Officer Featherstone met me and enlightened me that I was being made one of the section commanders. We went out into the back garden of the inn and I was shown my sector. Again I found myself in an orchard. I mused over the fact that the Germans in this area must be fond of apples.

My section was rather a small one consisting of three other men including Mac. We had one Bren gun, one rifle and two Stens. We worked out the positions offering the best field of fire and dug some shallow trenches. It was almost dark now and we should have been standing to several minutes ago. We had dug in about two hundred yards from the rear of the inn, facing towards the woods I had been studying earlier on.

I reconnoitred out front as best I could in the fading light and obtained a good idea of the terrain. After stand down we returned to the inn. Our Squadron Commander had decided that there was no need for everyone to remain out in the open. Two guards would take up posts and patrol round the inn. We would all take a turn to defend our HQ. Two hours for each pair. I was due to go on with Mac at midnight until 2.00 a.m.

We had chicken that night, cooked superbly by a couple of our own pilots. At first, the old lady of the inn had been persuaded to start broiling the chickens, but a short distant burst of gunfire, just after dark from the direction of the woods, half a mile away, had put her in a jittery state and she had begged to be allowed to go down into the cellar. We didn't stop her. In a way, I felt a little sorry for her, for she must have been all of sixty years old.

The dinner was served by the hands of no less than mine host Herr Hans Neu, proprietor of the inn. Hans Neu had been a member of the Nazi Party. I had perused his Nazi Party member book earlier on when I had first entered the inn. The book had been left lying on the table after Lieutenant Cartwright, who incidentally spoke fair German, had checked over it. No doubt mine host had followed Hitler in more than one way, even his moustache had been cut to simulate faithfully the Fuhrer's.

Judging by the hate that filled his eyes and the harsh look upon his face, he did not relish at all the task we had set him, that of serving us dinner. Silently he poured beer into our glasses and from the look he gave each of us as he passed, it was evident that his only regret was that it was German beer he was giving us instead of deadly poison.

However, to give him his due he had laid the table beautifully, considering that we had arrived without prior notice. A clean white paper-like cloth had been spread on the table and genuine silver gleamed upon it, throwing back a soft reflection under the persuasion of the golden candlelight. Idly I wondered how much of that silver he would still possess on the morrow, and no doubt the same question was also troubling him.

As soon as he had filled our glasses he returned to the counter.

Lieutenant Cartwright told him to start serving the food but Herr Neu seemed most unwilling to perform this act of servitude. Lieutenant Cartwright drew his pistol and banged it on the table, saying 'Serve!'

Herr Neu did so without further ado, then returned to the counter and stood there in the shadows glowering at us. Lieutenant Cartwright told him that he could beat it out of the room now; we didn't want him staring at us all the time. We could refill our own glasses.

Even in the dim light, I could see Herr Neu's face turn a deep red and the veins on his neck swell up. In a half pleading and half domineering voice he replied that he was the master of the inn and wouldn't be ordered out of his own room.

Lieutenant Cartwright toughened up on him and a minute later Hans Neu was slinking from the room, muttering curses and looking ripe to have a fit any minute. 'The Nazi swine.' said the lieutenant. I cannot say that I had any sympathy for Herr Neu. We ate heartily and quickly dismissed Herr Neu from our thoughts. It was an excellent dinner and our fellow pilots deserved full credit for the preparation of the meal.

Somebody had found three or four bottles of wine and these were uncorked. There were about fifteen of us and the wine didn't go far but we made the best of it, eking it out with some beer. I never found out where the beer came from, for when I had first entered the inn I had been told it was dry, and quite genuinely so. Somebody must have uncovered Herr Neu's reserve beer stocks since then.

Feeling suddenly terribly tired I made for the room where my mattress had been spread out. I stretched out on it and closed my eyes. The events of the day flitted through my tired brain. Dimly, I heard the distant chatter of a machine gun and I opened my eyes. The chatter stopped. I mused over how strangely quiet the whole sector was. We knew from information passed on to us that the 2nd Army and our 6th Airborne troops brought in by us had not yet broken out of the Issel River area. That was due to take place sometime tomorrow – or so we were told. A fog of sleep began to creep over me. My eyes closed, and I slept.

Chapter 27

Home Again

At midnight I was awakened by one of the two men who had been keeping watch since ten o'clock. I tried to clear my sleep-sodden head. I shook Mac into a sort of wakefulness and together we put on our steel helmets, I shouldered my rifle, and we moved down the passage to the doorway. From rooms on either side came the deep breathing and occasional snore of men resting peacefully in the arms of Morpheus.

We stepped outside into the square. A silvery moon overhead bathed the area in its bright cold light, at the same time casting deep shadows wherever buildings interposed themselves between it and the ground.

Mac and I had drawn lots for the posts. I got the permanent one just outside the door of the inn. Mac drew the patrol. He vanished into the shadows of the nearby walls on the first leg of his patrol after a few sleepy muttered words.

I shivered under the seeping cold and began to shuffle up and down outside the inn to keep warm. It was strangely quiet. For all the noise that reached my ears I might have been on guard duty down on Salisbury Plain in Wiltshire back home, except for the low rumble of artillery that drifted down from the north around Rees and Emmerich. Evidently, the Canadians and the British in that sector were still meeting with stiff resistance.

I kept in the shadows, for I was not sure of the attitude of the people of Hamminkeln as yet. We had heard varying stories of the type of resistance the people of Germany were putting up. Some said it was negligible, while others told tales of our men being found dead at the break of dawn with a knife between their ribs. I didn't intend to give them any chance.

The church across the square took on a singular beauty in the bright moonlight, half of it looking as though a blanket of snow lay upon the ancient stonework while the other half was lost in the deep impenetrable shadows. No sound came from it although I had learned that most of the villagers had taken refuge there during the landings and had remained there since. Unfortunately for the village dwellers their own artillery, as I had witnessed, had fired in a number of airbursts, and one of the shells, before bursting in the air, had struck the church tower with disastrous results, causing several fatal casualties among the occupants.

The streets were utterly deserted. No longer did 2nd Army trucks and tanks roll through on their way to the Issel River. It was like a ghost place through which the spirits of those destroyed in the recent battle roamed, flitting from door to door – the fantasy of a sleep starved mind.

Overhead a myriad of stars twinkled like a thousand jewels set in a vast expanse of black velvet while the queen of them all, the moon, hung motionless, casting her cold beams down in majestic splendour, softening the field of battle, now so silent. The haze that had proved so deadly to us had long since dispersed.

For a while I watched the faint distant flickering gun flashes to the north. It reminded me of the Northern Lights. I stamped my feet as lightly as possible and waited for Mac's soft footsteps. The chat we had every few minutes was a great relief from the boredom.

From the hinterland beyond the Issel River I picked up the faint drone of approaching aircraft. My head cleared a little and I welcomed the diversion. The aircraft – I calculated there must be three – circled over the village at what I estimated to be about a thousand feet or so. All remained quiet and no anti-aircraft fire was directed up at them from the fields hidden out there under the cloak of night.

I moved around, trying to get the moon behind where I thought one of the planes could cross over. Only once was I successful and then the black shadow silhouetted against the pale glowing disc was so quickly gone that I never had a chance to identify it.

The flares I had been expecting ever since the planes began circling suddenly blossomed forth into an eerie greenish-white light that floated almost motionless over the silent earth below. Another followed almost immediately, adding its weird menacing light to the one already hovering over what I guessed to be the farm area where I had been earlier on in the day. No longer were the bivouacked vehicles of the 2nd Army and the 6th Airborne Division hidden in the darkness as they lay massed at the approaches to the Issel River. The dropped flares must have illuminated some targets.

The planes circled once more and then I heard the leader boring in on a long straight run-in. The first bombs fluttered down their sighing path. A vivid flash lit up the outskirts of the village momentarily. The ground quaked under the impact of the explosives. Another batch whistled down – a little louder this time. Again the crimson splotches against the dark canopy of night, followed by the earth-churning blasts. And then the night, blacker than ever.

Another flare burst out almost over the same position. The planes came in again. This time they were met by probing fingers of the defending AA. The golden red tracers climbed upwards with illusory slowness. Light explosives coughed in the sky. The bombs wailed down. The tracers continued to criss-cross the dark heavens. The bombs burst heavily. Engines strained as the planes climbed sharply away after releasing their loads of death. Then the planes were gone, their motors fading away back deeper into Germany. Silence settled over the fields around Hamminkeln once more. A splutter of gunfire raked the far side of the fields towards the Issel River. Low speeding tracers dripped across the open ploughland. The skirmish was short-lived and peace returned quickly.

I looked at the illuminated dial of my army issue wristwatch. Half an hour to go. God, how I longed to close these heavy-lidded eyes of mine. Mac slid up out of the gloom and joined me. We talked of anything to keep our eyes open. Hearing a faint shuffling coming down the passageway of the inn, I turned to find Flying Officer Featherstone checking up. I grinned to myself as I noticed the acquired slippers on his feet and the revolver dangling from a very loose belt – typically RAF.

How's it going, Staff?' he asked me in a voice that I thought was surprisingly alert for the ungodly hour it was. 'OK, Sir, nothing to report, except that I feel as though I could sleep for a week.' He vanished back into the depths of the inn. Twenty odd minutes later Mac and I followed after our relief had been awakened and had taken our places. I was asleep within two minutes or so after my head touched the mattress.

Half an hour before dawn we were again aroused for stand to. I felt drunk with the lack of sleep and literally staggered outside with my section into the moonlit garden at the rear of the inn. Cold and disgruntled, we crouched in the shallow trenches, waiting, watching until the first faint light of the grey dawn flushed the eastern horizon. Monday the 26th March 1945. With tired inflamed eyes, I watched the distant trees of the woods around the Issel River take shape out of the enveloping night as it fled before the approach of day.

I had to marvel at the glory of the dawn – the flaming scarlet that superseded the soft pink that had followed the first grey. As each succeeding minute forced the still invisible sun higher and higher, the uncertainty of the night faded more and more until at last a new day was born and we stood down.

With the arrival of broad daylight, much of the sleepiness that had held my whole body within its grasp began to leave me. A sluice under the cold tap in the kitchen did wonders and soon the aches had left me. The only uncomfortable feelings were ones of hunger and thirst.

These were quickly remedied by the self-appointed cooks, and by eight o'clock I was sitting outside against the wall of the inn, still poundering the quiet dawn we had witnessed. Hardly a shot had been fired.

The only pangs of regret I felt for the villagers occurred at this point when I saw a slow procession of solemn faced men and women emerge from the church, bearing a pall. They were utilising a stretcher on which I could make out a thin shrunken figure under the grey army blanket that lay across it. As the procession drew level, I saw a pair of old and tattered shoes, such as might be worn by an aged woman, hanging lifelessly over the end of the stretcher.

Close behind the shrouded figure came a girl of about fourteen years, crying as though her heart would break. Her head was bent and she carried a lighted candle taken from the church. I had an idea that the figure under the blanket must have been the girl's mother. I learned later that the old lady had been one of the several civilians killed by the shells fired from the guns of their own kinfolk. Such is the tragedy of war - it had no respect for age or sex.

After the sad procession had vanished around a nearby corner, I walked over to the church and, mounting the steps, went inside. At first, I was taken aback by the stench. Evidently the people had either not been allowed, or had been too frightened, to leave the church. Old women, old men, children and babies had made the church their temporary home, but even in the House of God they had not been immune from the surge of war, as the gaping shell hole in the roof bore mute testimony. They looked up at me with apathy written all over their faces. A baby squalled and the mother tried to comfort it. I turned and walked out from the gloomy depths of the church into the bright morning sunlight.

As the morning wore on, desultory firing broke out from the Issel River area but nothing serious developed, and still we waited for further orders.

In the village, our men had come across a house in which all the foreign farm workers had been herded and among them was a youth of Russian origin who had been working for no less a person than Hans Neu, mine host. I attached myself to this youth for I had an idea that he might know of any hidden stores of drink our Nazi innkeeper might still have in his possession.

Sure enough, my persistence was rewarded, for once I had convinced the Russian that Hans Neu no longer dominated the scene and, furthermore, that he never would in the future, I was eagerly shown down the steps into the cellar. It was dark down there but the Russian youth led the way with a flickering candle held aloft. Underneath the inn were at least three cellars and in one I noticed an oil lamp burning. Frau Neu's anxious face peered out at us as we passed by.

In one corner of the furthermost cellar the Russian pulled aside several large empty beer barrels and pointed towards a series of shelves. In the vague candlelight, I made out the dust-covered necks of several bottles. However, on closer inspection, I found that there were no more than about six or seven but that was better than nothing, considering the inn had been thoroughly gone over by our men before Mac and I had arrived. Vanishing into the nearby shadows, the Russian bent down and returned with four more bottles. Then he indicated to me that there was not one single bottle left – we had secured the lot.

Back in the bar I was met with cheers as I laid my finds on the counter. I kept back two and left the rest for whomever came first. It was good wine and I thoroughly appreciated it as I leaned back in a chair and kept my glass filled. Halfway through the second bottle I became distinctly drowsy. I picked up the bottle and made my way to the open door – I was feeling stifled in the bar. A 2nd Army tank came rumbling up the street and stopped with a squealing of tracks outside. A dusty and tired-looking NCO looked down at me and asked if water was available. I told him it was and at the same time passed up the remainder of the wine to him. He accepted it with pleasure. Returning to the inn, I laid down on my mattress, fading away into oblivion.

I awoke about midday. There seemed to be something going on for I could hear excited voices calling out. My head felt thick and little stabs of pain flashed through it. I closed my eyes again, but curiosity overcame me and I got to my feet and went into the bar.

The gang were there in force. I asked what all the excitement was about.

'You mean to tell me you don't know?' the Bluffer said, 'What the hell have you been doing? We're going back home! Starting off in about an hour's time. I'm all ready to go myself. You'd better get your stuff together.' No other news could have cleared my head quicker. All the same, I made for the kitchen and doused my head under the tap.

An hour later, we assembled in the village square. It was hot and dusty. Some of the men had acquired a considerable amount of 'excess baggage' and our Flight Commander had no alternative but to stand up and say,

'Look, I don't care what you thieving bastards have got hold of, but for heavens sake put it somewhere where it won't show. If the Divisional Commander comes by, he'll throw a fit, and give me hell.'

I couldn't help smiling as I looked around at the miscellaneous articles adorning the men. One was trailing a huge beautifully chased sword. The funny part was that he was extremely short and, despite all the efforts he made, the tip of the scabbard continued to dig into the dusty road. Another was actually carrying a leather-covered travelling case and it certainly didn't look like any army issue.

For a few minutes the men wrestled with their equipment, and I must say that they made a remarkably quick job of disposing of their possessions so that they weren't visible to the eye at a casual glance.

'Right,' went on the Flight Commander, having critically watched us re-adjust our kit. 'We are going to march through the Diersfordter Wald and have a rendezvous with our lorries near the far side. It's about eight miles and I hope some of you scrounging lizards will notice the weight you are carrying before we make it. Actually, the march is not too bad; as I said, it's only eight miles – you're lucky.' All his chiding had been good natured but he had to be careful of course. At that moment, a voice chimed up from our group saying,

'You had better check your pack, Sir, that parachute's beginning to billow out.' A burst of laughter went up from the crowd as he slipped off his rucksack and made the straps more secure.

Straightening up, he called out 'OK, chaps, let's go, I want to get home again, even if you don't. We'll join the squadron at the crossroads.'

At the crossroads, we met up with the rest of the squadron under Major Priest. Jeers and greetings flew to and fro as we waited to form up for the march. Men of the units we had flown in belonging to the 6th Airborne Division looked at us enviously and a few passed over hastily scribbled notes for onward transmission to their relatives in England. The 6th Airborne Division was remaining to join in the final drive across the Reich. Some of the 2nd Army men were also standing around and I felt even more sorry for them, for many had been over in Europe since D-Day without seeing home again, and here we were, heading for home after only a few short days on German soil.

We formed up and after a whistle blast from Major Priest, began the long trek back to England. I took one last look at Hamminkeln. Somehow I knew that I would remember that village for all time, along with many others I had seen on the long trail that stretched from England to North Africa, Sicily, Holland and now Germany.

We tramped along the open road that led to the Diersfordter Wald. From the direction of the forest came truck after truck of the 2nd Army, each accompanied by a rolling cloud of dust that enveloped us with its clinging film. It got in my ears, throat and nose and before we had gone half a mile. I was plagued by a terrible thirst. It was rough going, but none of us cared for we were heading home once more, while the whole of the 2nd Army was streaming deeper and deeper onto Germany in the opposite direction.

As we marched up the road, we came upon new sites of the landings with gliders strewn in all directions and in various stages of disintegration, from slight damage to splintered matchwood. One lay completely burned out, with only the vague outline of charred wood and the burnt and twisted remnants of a six-pounder gun and a jeep to define it.

Scattered among the Horsas were a number of the giant Hamilcar gliders in which had been brought the powerful seventeen-pounder anti-tank guns and their towing units. In nearly every case, the huge nose lay wide open to one side, leaving the inside visible like the gaping maw of some prehistoric monster.

Yes, shattered gliders lay everywhere, bearing out the fact that the pall of smoke had, in many cases, effectively blotted out the landing zones for us men of the Airborne that fatal Saturday morning. However, very often the damage, which may have appeared bad to the untrained eye, was in point of fact superficial and probably had not seriously affected those within the gliders.

The further we marched away from Hamminkeln, the more signs of the 2nd Army we came across. I was amazed at the mass of vehicles parked in the fields on either side and especially around the groups of isolated farm buildings. Tanks, heavy trucks, jeeps, ambulances, guns of all calibres – the dream of every airborne man.

Whenever we reached one of these lagers that had been pitched near some of our gliders, we noticed that the men had made full use of them. Improvised clothes lines hung from machine to machine, while the interiors of several had been made into very effective living quarters.

I peered ahead and saw the tantalising shape of the Diersfordter Wald. It never seemed to get any closer. Already the straps of my heavily weighted rucksack were cutting painfully into my shoulders and the words of our Flight Commander sounded in my ears, 'I hope some of you scrounging lizards will notice the weight you are carrying before we make it.'

The sweat rolled down my face and I could feel other rivulets oozing down my spine. I tilted my helmet forward to try and keep the sun off my hot face. I longed for a cool drink of water but knew it wouldn't do me any good in the long run and, what was more, it was impossible to reach back and un-strap my water bottle without first stopping and slipping off my rucksack.

Now the dark forbidding mass of the Diersfordter Wald at last loomed up close and a few minutes later we entered its cool shade. We turned off the dusty road and made our way down between sloping banks along a rough rutted lane covered with lichen and moss. At any other time its beauty would have inspired me but at the moment, although I was glad of its shade, I longed to be through the deep woods and sitting in the trucks that would speed us to, and over the Rhine westward, and home.

A short while later we halted, and as I sank down on the soft grassy sward I thought I could never rise again. I wiped the burning sweat off my brow and licked my parched lips. My clothes clung to me, and the smell of perspiration exuded from every part of my uniform. I lay back on the bank and watched a line of lurching and swaying trucks grind past, heading towards Hamminkeln.

Then we were on the march again. On through the deep woods; up and down dale, sometimes in the cool shade of the towering trees and sometimes under the hot burning sun striking down through gaps in the thick foliage. Past wrecked German war material. Once we passed one of the deadly eighty eight millimetre artillery pieces blown clear over onto its back, now a useless hunk of metal. Around the deep crater, close alongside the gun, were the shattered and seared stumps of what had once been proud trees matured through the ages. Other trees farther away from the centre of the explosion had suffered sorely, the white flesh of their trunks showing where the red hot slivers of steel had ripped and torn the bark away in a frenzy of fury and destruction.

It was strange that the sight of those shattered things of beauty aroused more pity within me than all the German corpses I had seen in the past few days. To me, those trees were possessed of life and beauty, suffering destruction because man must fight; helpless bystanders, caught up in the mad whirlpool of war.

A little while later we overtook a long column of German prisoners being herded through the forest by a number of paratroopers who had had the unenviable task of rooting the enemy out of their well camouflaged and dug-in positions in the forest. Some of the paratroopers had acquired horses and were riding them barebacked in among the prisoners, urging them on at a stumbling trot under threats and curses, backing them up with the bared blades of their killing knives which they waved around in an alarming manner, although purely as a threat.

The sight of that surging mass of bewildered and beaten grey-green clad figures being driven on to the rear boosted our tired bodies. Our men caught the spirit and every time one of the paratroopers sent out a war cry, driving the prisoners on a little further, a shout of approval rose from our ranks. At each cry, the prisoners would throw fearful glances over their shoulders as they stumbled on as though expecting to be cut down at any minute. Maybe they expected the same treatment as they had dealt out to some of our men as we learned later on.

The seething mass of prisoners was driven into a nearby clearing, and soon the goading shouts of the paratroopers faded away behind us. Then we emerged onto a well paved highway, where, a little way down on the left, parked under the overhanging trees, I saw a line of trucks with the familiar Pegasus sign on their identification plates. Our march was over.

The drivers, sitting by their vehicles in the cool shade thrown down by the verdant foliage of the trees, rose and greeted us as we approached. We recognised some of them and they seemed as pleased to see us as we were to see them.

We broke ranks and eased our tired bodies down onto the mossy bank. Water bottles appeared and, along with the rest, I uncorked mine and drank sparingly. We had finished our march and were at liberty to slake our thirst. I wiped my sweaty brow with a cool leaf from a giant fern growing nearby. It helped to remove some of the clinging dust.

As we had marched through the forest, I had been vaguely conscious of sporadic firing going on in the woods on either side but had taken little notice of it. Now, as I lay back easing the aches from my body, I became more aware of the sharp rattle of small arms which shattered silence of the deep gloomy depths of the forest around. Actually, it was nothing to be alarmed at. It merely meant that a few last stragglers of the enemy troops were being flushed out and rounded up. I closed my eyes under the influence of the afternoon heat and the softness of the mossy soil underneath. My thoughts drifted to home. When would we reach there? Why, it might even be tomorrow!

Suddenly, I heard someone call out sharply, 'Hey, look out, there's some Jerries coming through the woods.' I snapped my eyes open and rolled over instinctively behind a nearby tree, grabbing for my rifle as I did.

'It's OK, Dusty.' went on the same voice, 'They are coming out with their hands up to surrender.' I was already peering around the bole of the tree and I watched a little band of grey-green figures making their way through the trees towards us with their hands well above their heads. Two of the drivers were already approaching them with their rifles at the ready. Another driver nearby informed us that the enemy had been coming out of the woods singly and in little groups all morning to give themselves up.

At that moment we got the word to mount the trucks and didn't need any second bidding. This was the moment we had been waiting for ever since we had learned that our task in Germany was over and that we were returning home.

Then we were rolling down through the tree-lined lanes back towards the Rhine, over which we had crossed only a few days ago by other means. The roar of the engines was like music in our ears. Every turn of the wheels beneath us was taking us nearer and nearer home.

The ride through the Diersfordter Wald was uneventful and, a few miles further on, we broke out of the forest. Minutes later we halted on the banks of the Rhine. Peering round the canvas top of the truck, my eyes fell upon the river once more. The sun sparkled on the quietly lapping waters and the words 'And gently flows the Rhine' passed through my head. For a moment, my thoughts drifted back to that night at Arnhem when we had made our crossing under fire on that wet night in September, six months ago. This would be a different crossing from that.

2nd Army engineers had erected a pontoon bridge across the river at this point and a churned up, dusty track led down the bank to the beginning of the fragile looking bridge. We had to wait several minutes to allow an eastbound convoy of trucks to sway and wallow their way across the unsteady structure.

On both sides of the bare earthy banks, several Bofors anti-aircraft guns had been dug in. For the moment they were idle but I noticed that their crews were continually scanning the skies for the approach of any hostile aircraft.

The last of the east-bound convoy of trucks cleared the bridge and ground up the churned bank towards us, sending out a rolling cloud of dust as it did so. Our engine, which had been stopped, broke into life again and we edged slowly down the bank towards the near end of the bridge.

As the weight of our trucks bore down on the wooden planking I felt the pontoons give and sink a little. It was a queer feeling as we slowly rumbled on over the bridge, a feeling as though we were riding the waves themselves. I must confess that, for a moment, I felt a little pang of anxiety as I looked out over the open back of the truck at the cold waters of the Rhine slapping loudly against the pontoons which, in turn, floated up and down with the motion of our progress. The eastern bank receded more and more, and I remember noticing how bare and muddy the whole shoreline looked.

We reached solid ground on the far side and crept up the steep bank away from the pontoon bridge which now stretched away behind us. Somehow, crossing over the river gave me the false sense that we had crossed over the borders of Germany and were now in a different country. Actually, the border lay many miles away ahead of us.

At the top of the bank we turned off onto a hard macadam road and, picking up speed, bowled swiftly on, passing more vehicles and guns enroute to the Rhine and the heart of Germany.

The first town we came to, named Xanten, had to be bypassed. A temporary road had been cleared through the outskirts. The centre was just a mass of rubble and shattered walls with a few blasted tree stumps to remind one that it had once been quite a pleasant town. Never before had I seen such a sight of desolation and utter destruction. No civilians moved amongst the pulverised stonework. Xanten had been made the centre of a strong defence by the Germans to prevent our troops reaching the Rhine in that sector and it had paid terribly for that privilege. My last glimpse of Xanten, after we had lurched and swayed through the shattered outskirts, was the view of a very ancient but strongly built windmill. Most of the top had been blown away together with the sails but the thick, strong lower stone and brick structure had withstood the shelling, although several gaping holes in the sides indicated that our artillery had blasted it into a useless hulk. Owing to its height, I guessed that the enemy had used it for an observation post until the top had been forcibly removed.

We rolled along the flat straight road that led through Kevalier and on to a little village, hardly touched by the iron fist of war, called Twisdeten. Here we turned into what appeared to be a rest camp set up by the 2nd Army and which, in the meantime, was being used as a transit camp for us.

We debussed and sought our tents. No one knew how long we would be here. It might be a day, or on the other hand, it might be a week or even more, we were told, depending on the transportation available. No airfields were in the vicinity and we would have to drive on into Belgium or Holland to reach the planes which would take us back to England.

It was almost dusk and, along with the rest, I turned in onto the straw palliasses spread out on the tent floor. A few of the more energetic hitch-hiked into the town of Kevalier we had passed earlier on, about five or six miles back on the road to Xanten.

The next day it rained, and rained hard. We knew there would be no flying and resigned ourselves to at least another day at Twisdeten. The field turned into a quagmire and all we could do was shiver in the tents and play cards. By this method a large amount of the souvenirs changed hands in a remarkably short space of time. It was one way of whiling away the long hours.

The following day dawned fine and clear and by midday the muddy field had almost dried up. I went out and sketched a nearby windmill with one of the few remaining pieces of paper in my possession. Afterwards I explored the mill in company with Mac. The war had passed by this building and the surrounding area. The villagers of Twisdeten had been very lucky.

Afterwards, I went off on my own and explored the village itself but could find nothing to inspire me to sketch. I did, however, locate a farm where I acquired several eggs, a fact that delighted my tent comrades.

The next day we were on the road again, rolling westward towards the German-Belgian border. We had about one hundred miles to go before we reached Helmond in Holland which was our objective for the day.

The miles passed by under our spinning wheels. We roared down the road parallel to the Meuse River but crossed over before we reached the Dutch town of Venlo. It was picturesque country through which we were passing and the day was in harmony with our spirits, bright and sunny, with but a few majestic white clouds floating serenely in the blue heavens.

The stench of petrol and oil was always in our noses, but we didn't care. The tyres whined on the road surface and village after village loomed up, echoed to our thundering motors, and then fell away behind; villages with strange sounding names such as Maasbree, Panningen, Deurne, until at last we were edging our way through the pretty streets of Helmond.

At Helmond we were billeted in another rest camp but this time it was in a brick building, a magnificent place which had at one time been a school, I believe. With Mac, I spent a pleasant evening in Helmond where we visited several of the local inns. A good night's sleep followed and I was raring to go when the dawn of the next day broke in all its glory.

We hung around until midday and eventually our trucks turned up. Eagerly we climbed aboard and took our farewell of the pleasant tree-lined streets of Helmond with its quaint, typically gaily painted Dutch houses.

Twelve miles out from Helmond, we entered the familiar town of Eindhoven. The people there were now used to the sight of truckloads of soldiers roaring through their city, and this time we got nowhere near the enthusiastic reception we had received as we had when passing through there on our way back from Arnhem that tragic September last.

On through the outskirts of the city, now almost back to normal. Around the bend, past the Phillips Radio factory and down the straight road towards Valkenswaard. We had been told at Helmond that the aerodrome from which we would be taking off was now to be one just outside Eindhoven, and it wasn't long before we swung off the main road onto the aerodrome itself.

We got out and stretched our legs on the sandy soil of the airfield. Wrecked German aircraft still littered the field and I found great interest in examining the nearby remains of a Focke-Wolf 190.

About half a mile away, a number of Dakotas were lined up in a very promising way. A few minutes later we were marching down towards the aircraft with a lilt in our steps. The last stage was in sight.

The pilots met us just short of the aircraft. They were Americans and seemed pleased at the chance of returning us to England. No time was wasted and our pilot packed in as many as he could with safety. Inside the familiar Dakota, I strapped myself in with the single safety belt dangling from the seat. The crewman closed down the doors and immediately I heard the whine of the self-starters on the engines. With a shuddering roar the two motors broke into life one after the other.

I felt the pilot release the brakes and we moved slowly forward, taxiing around the edge to the far end of the field. Our pilot evidently intended to get the longest run for the takeoff and I can't say I blamed him when I glanced around at the pile of equipment and men packed inside. The Dakota is a wonderful plane, far exceeding all the expectations of its designers and operators, but even it has its limits.

We swung around into wind, a slight pause and then the mounting roar of the motors as the pilot pushed the throttles all the way open. The concentrated horsepower hidden under the engine nacelles took up the strain and we began to roll down the runway. Slowly we picked up speed but still the tail clung tenaciously to the ground which was flashing by at ever increasing speed. Faster and faster. The machine shook and vibrated and I could feel it straining to lift the tail off the ground. The noise of the motors had risen to their peak and now our fate was in the hands of the pilot. For a few moments I had my doubts as, from the limited view available to me out of the small round porthole-like windows, I estimated that the far end of the field must be rapidly approaching and we still weren't airborne.

The pilot literally dragged her off the ground nose first, the obstinate tail clinging to the ground up until the last second. We rose sluggishly into the air and crossed low over the far boundary. I wiped away the film of sweat that had gathered on my forehead and watched the sandy tree-covered airfield surroundings drop farther and farther away beneath.

I heard the motors throttled back and we settled into a steady climb. At last we were really on the way, nothing between us and England except the unlikelihood of engine failure.

At about two thousand feet altitude we levelled out and I looked down at the flat Dutch countryside moving slowly by under our wings. I relaxed back in my aluminium seat, undoing my belt as I did so and, closing my eyes, thought of the weeks ahead. With luck, we would get two weeks leave. The steady drone of the two powerful engines outside on the wings, driving us swiftly homeward, combined with the gentle wallowing of the machine in the slightly turbulent air, lulled me into a doze.

I came to with a start a short while later. We were already over Belgium and before long would be over French territory, well on the way to the Channel, and beyond that – England. We had climbed higher – I could tell for it was chilly and the landscape looked at least five thousand feet below. It appeared very flat from the height at which we were flying. Then we were over France. The landscape appeared exactly the same, but the little sprawled out villages seemed to have roofs that were a little redder, and stood out more from the vast surrounding stretches of ploughed land.

Then the long-awaited Channel came into view. A thin grey line crept up over the horizon and a few minutes later I was looking back at the receding coast of France. We were descending slowly now. The increased pressure on my eardrums told me that.

A heavy blanket of cloud appeared ahead and under us. I lost sight of the white capped grey waters of the Channel as the filmy mist of cloud slid between them and our machine. We sank down until we were skimming low over the top of the white shroud, and sometimes even through it from time to time. Beads of moisture formed on the round porthole and were whipped back by the slipstream blasting past the outside of the thin shell of metal that lay between us and space.

I tried to pierce the layer of cloud below for a glimpse of the approaching English coast. A turmoil of feelings surged within me – that peculiar feeling that rises within every man on his return to the country of his birth. It seems to be a mixture of anticipation, joy, pride and heartfelt relief.

We began to let down through the whispy white mist that swirled around in an enveloping blanket. Rain slashed past the windows. The Dakota lurched and swayed in the turbulent currents. For a second we passed through an open patch of cloud and rain and I caught a momentary glimpse of a sandy beach and flat desolate fields beyond, then the cloud closed in again.

We went into a slight diving turn. Outside, the rain whipped past as we curved through the white rolling misty clouds. I crossed my fingers and hoped our airspeed kept up and, furthermore, that there were no cliffs in the vicinity. That glimpse of land I had caught was enough for me to know that we were down below a thousand feet.

We came out under the clouds still turning. Immediately below the churning waters of the Channel heaved and swirled. We levelled out at about 800 feet and as the nose swung round and straightened out I saw the sandy stretch I had glimpsed earlier on. My heart beat a little faster and I felt a warm grateful wave of emotion pass through me. My homeland.

Again we went onto a turn. Evidently the pilot was getting his bearings. Again the grey waters of the choppy Channel pivoted below our tilted wing. The wind buffeted and shook our machine but the pilot held the turn against the driving elements.

Now we were heading in once more and this time we crossed over the sandy strip of coastline at around five hundred feet. It was a desolate spot with a few summer bungalows dotted here and there. I tried hard to place the spot but couldn't. As we were heading for the West Country, I was thinking more in terms of the stretch of coast between Littlehampton and Selsey Bill but I soon learned I was way out. The co-pilot of the Dakota came through the connecting doorway and informed us above the roar of the motors and the slipstream that we were crossing over Dungeness on the Kentish coast, about sixty miles east of where I had supposed we would cross.

The rain passed and the sun shone forth through the clouds above us. We turned to starboard and commenced flying up parallel to the beaches. Less than five minutes later we were circling the green expanse of an airfield. This time I was right in my guess for it was Lympne Kent airfield under our turning wings.

We straightened out and I lost sight of the field. Now we were coming in on the last leg. The pilot throttled back and the noise of the engines faded away to a low rumble. I felt the drag of the flaps going down and our nose dropped a little more. A road bordering the airfield slid by fifty feet under our wings; the green grass of the field raced past, rising nearer and nearer. We skimmed over the grass, now speeding by in a blur. A gentle bump and we were down, rolling swiftly over the wet grass, sending the spray up past our windows as we ploughed through the dips. I felt the brakes go on and we slowed down gradually to a stop, starting almost immediately to turn off to our dispersal point. I breathed a deep sigh of relief. We were safely down, thanks to the skill of our American pilots. Bumping our way across the turf, we stopped at last outside some hangars. The pilot cut the engine switches and they died, bringing the great swirling propellers to a halt.

The co-pilot swung open the door and the fresh clean air of England entered the stuffy fuselage, bringing with it the scent of newly cut grass. The steps were lowered and we descended one by one down onto the soil of our homeland once more. It was great to feel solid earth under my feet and no words can describe the feeling of exhilaration I felt at that moment.

The air was clear and cool. Overhead, thunderclouds rolled by with the sun bursting out every now and again. Behind us was the chaos of Germany. Here was peace and life – not death and destruction. True, England had suffered in her turn, suffered deeply, but the hand of war had passed by and now tranquillity had settled over the enchanting landscape once again after six years of terror and destruction.

We walked with springy steps around the perimeter track to the mess where the staff served us an excellent lunch. In peacetime, Lympne had been the home of flying clubs and the signs were still there in the form of the clubhouse and the setting of the garden around the mess building.

I took the opportunity of finding a telephone box at the entrance to the airfield and made a telephone call to my dear Doreen, my girl friend for over a year and shortly to become my fiancee, then wife. The emotion from my surprise phone call was overwhelming to Doreen, because she had already seen at the local cinema newsreel films of our landings and had guessed I was there. The relief of my call was overwhelming for her.

An hour later we took off again. The weather had cleared and now bright sunny skies smiled down on us as if to welcome us home again. The beautiful Kentish countryside looked fresh and green after the thundery showers and here and there I was able to pick out a familiar village or two, for I knew well the course we were taking. Little villages, nestling snugly in the rolling Wealden countryside. Twisting, meandering streams and rivers spanned by ancient grey stone bridges. Graceful church spires peeping skywards from amongst the huddled cottages and green fields. Century old woods in a riot of green foliage as spring took hold. The rolling downs with their tree-studded slopes and the neatly hedged fields of varying colour contrasts. Such is the beauty and lure of Kent and Surrey too, my own home county adjoining Kent. In Surrey, the fields looked even greener than in Kent and the villages exuded more charm, but perhaps I am prejudiced.

Surrey was behind us now, and Hampshire came up under our wings. Half an hour later we were circling over the home base of our Dakota pilots in Wiltshire. For the second time that day I watched the flaps come down and braced myself for the slight shock of landing.

Back at the dispersal point, the engines died. It was journey's end. We tumbled forth in the gathering evening and found to our pleasure that we were really expected this time, unlike our return from the Arnhem operation. A hot drink and sandwiches awaited us in one of the huts. Fifteen minutes later, we were in trucks being driven swiftly through the lanes to our old training camp at Fargo, near Amesbury, nearly twenty miles away.

I had that old feeling of loneliness as I entered the hut allotted me. I knew that many faces would be forever missing from our mess back at Great Dunmow. Wearily, I slumped down on the bed I had selected and flung my kit in a corner.

Although I did not know it, we had completed the last operation that we glider pilots in England would be called upon to carry out. Shortly after our arrival at Fargo, we heard rumours that another operation had been planned for a landing around, of all places, the Kiel canal, a positive hotbed of anti-aircraft guns, the object being to seal off the German troops in Denmark. However, it came to nothing.

Our task was done. Never again would we spread our wings to strike at the heart of the enemy. The Regiment had striven to live up to its motto 'NOTHING IS IMPOSSIBLE'.

In 1946 I received my discharge from the army after nearly six and a half years. I left the service with mixed feelings. For those long years, I had become accustomed to the friendship and the invisible bonds that exist between fellow soldiers.

Now we had to face the future – of returning to civilian life where such bonds, if they are there, are far less binding. On the other hand, the thought of being free of the petty, but sometimes very necessary, discipline of the army was overwhelming. To be home. To be able to go where one wanted. To do as one liked, within reason, of course. To sleep at night undisturbed, knowing that the next night one wouldn't have to be outside in some bitterly cold field, watching, waiting. They may seem small things to desire to some people, but to us in the services, they were terribly important, and to have them was to have everything – the peace of civilian life.

Epilogue

There had been other operations by airborne forces, but on a much smaller scale. In 1943, two gliders had been towed to Norway by two Halifax tugs, their objective, to destroy the heavy water plant that the Germans were known to be operating in that country. Heavy water could be used in the production of the atomic bomb. The operation ended in failure, with one glider lost in a snow storm over the Norwegian coast, and the other crashed badly on the mountainsides.

What damage, if any, the men in the glider that crashed had done to the heavy water plant I do not know, for very little has ever leaked out about the operation. Before that, in February 1941, six Whitleys took off from Malta loaded with paratroopers. They headed for the Italian mainland. Their task was to destroy an important aqueduct over the small river known as the Tragino. They were successful in carrying it out.

Then, in February 1942, 6 officers and 113 men dropped from Whitleys into northern France at a place called Bruneval to seize and bring back some vital radar equipment the Germans were known to be developing and using in that area. The raid was completely successful.

The first airborne operation of any size, however, was launched on North Africa in November 1942 in conjunction with the invasion by Allied troops from the sea. The operation was entirely a paratroop one, with no gliders used. About 350 paratroopers were dropped. Their exploits are a story in themselves and this book is not concerned with the amazing battle which that gallant band of men fought.

Then followed Sicily (the first mass glider operation by the British), Normandy and, on the 15th of August 1944, a small force of gliders accompanied a host of paratroopers on their drop into southern France near Cannes. The glider pilots, incidentally, were my old comrades of No. 3 Squadron who had gone over to Italy before my return to England from North Africa. Arnhem and the Rhine crossing, the remaining two European operations have been dealt with in this book.

In 1945 a small band of airborne troops dropped in Greece near Athens with great success.

Our comrades in the Far East must not be forgotten either. One of the most daring airborne operations of the war was carried out in Burma when a mass landing was made in the heart of the jungle, well behind the Japanese lines. The landing itself was disastrous, most of the gliders being shattered almost to pieces in the insufficiently cleared jungle clearing selected for the operation. Despite this setback, the men carried on, waging a very successful battle against the Japanese lines of communication in that area.

And now, after two weeks' leave, we were back at an East Anglian aerodrome. Our eyes were turned to the Orient. A number of us had been earmarked for the final assault on Japan and her conquered possessions, most of which she had already lost under the heavy attacks launched by the United States and Australian troops. However, the advent of the atomic bomb and the ensuing surrender of

Japan, cancelled all plans for that theatre, and now we turned our eyes towards peace and home. For us the struggle was over.

Yes, the airborne have blazed their trail of glory and sacrifice across the deep vault of the heavens and over the blasted soil of Europe. Spawned from this war, their memory will live on forever and new men will ever come forward to take over and carry on the unfurled flag with the sign of Pegasus upon it, fluttering proudly in the breeze of freedom, ever ready to spread their wings over Europe again – or even further if the call should come 'Defend thy home by attack.'

They did not die in vain.

Between its formation in 1942 until the end of the war in 1945, casualties for the Glider Pilot Regiment were among the highest in the British Army. Of the approximately 3900 glider pilots trained, 3300 actually saw action, with 551 dying in action - 17% plus 220 wounded in action and 550 prisoners of war or missing. The total of all casualties - 40%.

Afterword

After the war, Victor married the love of his life Doreen Curthew-Sanders, who was born in Orange, New Jersey, USA. Doreen was the recipient of the parachute Victor risked his life to obtain. With squeals of joy and laughter, she opened the billowing parachute given as a gift in the front lounge amid friends and family and proceeded to make plans to sew her wedding dress. Rations being what they were, Victor knew what this volume of white silky fabric would mean for his betrothed, and had been willing to risk all just to make it possible for her.

Victor and Doreen were married in 1947, with Doreen wearing her wedding dress made from the precious parachute. After the wedding they briefly moved to New York in the States, where Victor worked for Doreen's father in an Import/Export business. They returned to England in 1951.

They were a well matched couple, as Doreen was an accomplished artist just like Victor, and they had much in common, including a deep love of art, nature, animals and the beautiful English countryside. She offered him the comfort and security of a loving home, something he desperately longed for after so many years of military service and the horrors of war.

She dearly wanted children, and over the next few years they produced three sons, Christopher, Peter and Timothy.

They built a home in Warlingham, Surrey, next to Kingswood, which was a financial challenge and sacrifice, but it offered them the privacy and seclusion they desired. That cottage and lovely garden was their special little piece of paradise and provided an ideal place to raise their family and enjoy a good life.

Fortunately Victor found a suitable job, first as an Export Manager for Innoxa, a cosmetics firm in London, then in a sales position in the 1970's for Innoxa's Industrial division that allowed him the physical and mental freedom he needed, working from home. He would spend days happily traveling the back roads of England calling on clients. He was not someone to be tied down to a desk in an office.

After the war, he found it difficult to easily blend back in with society and suffered with what we now recognize as Post Traumatic Stress Disorder. Deeply haunted by wartime memories, Victor relived his experiences with recurrent recollections shared in the form of stories with his friends and family. Almost immediately after demobilization, he started writing what was eventually to become this work, painstakingly inking his pencil sketches drawn in battle.

He also began to 'train' his children at a very young age in the arts of war, taking them into the woods to teach them hunting, tracking skills and self-defense. Frequently neighbors would see them marching with picket fence boards slung over their shoulders for guns, while marching in cadence for long hours. He taught them how to demobilize vehicles, set traps, read maps, and to be resourceful and anticipate the unexpected. The father wolf was going to make sure his cubs were prepared in case the world returned to wartime madness again.

After all, England, Europe, and the world were now being drawn into a disturbingly serious Cold War that had people marketing bomb shelters and planning for nuclear holocaust.

Victor also kept in touch with many of his old colleagues such as Nigel Brown, by joining the Glider Pilot Regiment Association and regularly attending Regimental evening dinners.

As a member of the GPRA he was contacted by Cornelius Ryan as part of the author's research for the book 'A Bridge Too Far,' and Victor was interviewed and went on to lend his precious manuscript.

When 'A Bridge to Far' was published in 1974, Victor was invited to the Dutch Embassy in London where he was presented with a signed copy. In appreciation for the use of Victor's valuable personal account of his experiences at Arnhem, the book was dedicated: 'For Victor Miller, Who Made this Book, With Thanks, Cornelius Ryan'.

In 1977 Victor was invited to the British film premier of 'A Bridge Too Far' in London. In the movie, if you look carefully at the beginning frames, as the gliders are being towed to leave for Arnhem, you will see 'Dusty Miller' chalked on the side of the nose of one of the lead gliders.

Much to Victor's despair, Doreen died of an aneurysm in 1987. From that time onward, the joy in Victor's world closed down around him. He hung her wedding dress on his bedroom door and would not allow it to be moved until the day he died at the age of 78 in 1997.

Post Script

SERGEANT TOM HOLLINGSWORTH
'G' Squadron, No.1 Wing, The Glider Pilot Regiment
Army No.: 14276776

Victor obviously knew that Tom had been left behind at the Hartenstien Hotel, but did not find out what happened to him until many months later.

On the last day of the battle at Arnhem, Tom became badly shell-shocked and was detailed to help dress the wounded at the Hartenstein Hotel. There he stayed with his charges until the end when they were captured. Tom (POW No.118316) was transported to Stalag XIB in Germany, arriving on the 4th of October 1944. Two days later, he was dead.

In the book "*We fought at Arnhem*" written by Mike Rossiter, he describes how Ron Jordan REME who was captured at Arnhem and sent to Stalag XIB, witnessed the tragedy:

"Ron quickly found out how dangerous their situation might become. There were regular air raids both night and day, but there were no air-raid shelters for the prisoners. If a daytime raid took place, their orders were to return immediately to their huts and stay there until the all clear. Shortly after Ron arrived the sirens sounded for a daylight raid. A force of B-17 Flying Fortresses flew overhead, their condensation trails gleaming in the sun. Many of the prisoners took their time getting back into the huts, wanting instead to watch this magnificent sight, but the guards became increasingly agitated, telling them to hurry. Suddenly a shot rang out from one of the guard towers. Sergeant Hollingsworth, the glider pilot who had commanded Ron's small unit on the perimeter of Oosterbeck, fell dead. His beret rolled on to Ron's feet. With rifle butts, the guards forced them through the doors of the hut , leaving Sergeant Hollingsworth dead on the ground."

The following article by Roderick de Norman was publish in the Glider Pilot Regimental Association's magazine *The Eagle*.

The Shooting of Sergeant Hollingsworth, Glider Pilot Regiment, 6th October 1944

On a hillside in northern Germany, overlooking the Luneburg Heath, lies the Becklingen War Cemetery. Therein lies the graves of some 2,402 Allied servicemen, many of whom had died, not as a result of battle but as Prisoners of War. A number of these deaths were from the ranks of those captured at Arnhem, many badly wounded. One death, however, remains unclear. It is that of 14276776, S/Sgt Thomas Hollingsworth, 1st Wing, The Glider Pilot Regiment. He was shot on the 6th October, 1944 by a guard at Stalag XIB, not many miles to the west.

Why was Sgt Hollingsworth shot? Was it a justifiable shooting and if not, was any brought to book for the killing? I hope to answer some of these questions in this article and put to rest a mystery that has remained for forty-seven years.

Stalag XIB was one of the three main POW Camps to be found in Wehrkreis (Military Region) XI and was located adjacent to the German barrack complex at Oerbke/Fallingbostel. These barracks had been built to house transit training formations, using the new training grounds and ranges at Bergen-Belsen. As with all such projects, it was built on a grand scale and reflected the huge expansion that was taking place within the German Army in the mid-thirties. To build such a large barracks, a large work force was required on a twenty-four hour basis and so a workers camp of wooden huts was also constructed. When war broke out these huts were found eminently suitable for POWs and the first prisoners, Poles, arrived on the 12th September, 1939. [1]

By September 1941, the meagre German records show that Stalag XIB was responsible for 54,581 prisoners. The majority of these, 51,760, were in Arbeitskommando or Working Parties, and were mainly drawn from those captured in Europe including France, Belgium and Poland. There had been a small British contingent there during mid-1941 but it was not until the middle of 1943 that a full time "staff" of British POWs arrived mainly to administer the ever growing number of British arbeitskommandos that were to be found within the Wehrkreis. The senior British NCO was RSM Wickham of The Buffs, and he soon became the "Man of Confidence", administering an ever increasing number of prisoners as the Germans had to evacuate their camps in the East, in front of the Soviets. These problems were small compared to what happened on the 4th October 1944 when the first train load of badly wounded and battle-weary British and American airborne troops arrived from Holland. Among them was S/Sgt Hollingsworth. Two days later, he was dead.

Tom was born in 1922 and first joined up at the age of seventeen as a lieutenant in the LDV or Home Guard. On being called up, he did his basic training with the Kings Shropshire Light Infantry before volunteering for the fledgling Glider Pilot Regiment. Initially he was based near Cromer before moving to Fairford.

For Operation Market, Sgt Hollingsworth flew as second pilot to SSgt Miller. Their passengers were a number of the War Correspondents assigned to the operation, among them Alan Wood and Stanley Maxted. Soon after landing S/Sgt Hollingsworth and his pilot were detailed to help defend the perimeter at Divisional Headquarters. As the defensive line shrank and casualties mounted, S/Sgt Hollingsworth became badly shell-shocked and was then detailed to help dress the wounded. Staying with the wounded until the end, he was thus captured and transported to Stalag XIB at Fallingbostel.

By the time Stalag XIB was liberated, on the 16th April 1945, the shooting of an unarmed prisoner should have been a single incident among many horrific tales for Stalag XIB ended its days as a stinking, disease-ridden cess pit. To the British prisoners, however, the shooting soon symbolised the evil of the Germans. RSM Lord, in a recording quoted in his biography [2], summed the killing up thus:

"POWs are reluctant to move quickly and when an air raid sounded - I think three days after we arrived - the men went into their huts, but one glider pilot S/Sergeant was rather slow moving in... A German sentry did no less than shoot him, and he died. This had a profound effect as the news spread around and I am quite sure it steeled the men's determination to withstand such treatment."

There were other shootings in the camp right up to liberation and James Sims, in his excellent book "Arnhem Spearhead", recalls: "... if we were too slow at pulling up the blackout boards at night the Germans fired through the walls of the hut." [3]

The treatment of all POWs at Stalag XIB had been so horrendous, especially with regards those from Arnhem, that the Judge Advocate Generals office commenced inquiries with regards to war crimes. Many of the camp guard staff were, by this time, prisoners themselves - some in England, others in Germany. The inquiry commenced taking formal evidence during the late autumn of 1945, not finishing until the summer of 1946. Luckily today, the papers from the inquiry can be found in the Public Record Office at Kew. They reveal the difficulties the investigators had in trying to bring to justice the guard that shot S/Sgt Hollingsworth, indeed, the difficulties in trying to find out in what circumstances he was shot.

One of the first to give evidence was RSM Lord. His sworn statement was used as an annex to that of RSM Wickham. Interestingly enough, RSM Lord made no mention of the shooting although a copy of a list of complaints was drawn up by him in December 1944, for onward transmission to the Red Cross. Heading that list was the death of S/Sgt Hollingsworth. Not long after this, more direct evidence of the shooting was given by Captain Wells, RAMC, also captured at Arnhem. In a very long and detailed account of the medical conditions in the Stalag [4] the following was stated in paragraph two:

"A glider pilot sergeant suffering from an acute anxiety state due to battle exhaustion... was not admitted to hospital. He was later shot and killed by a German sentry because he had not entered a shelter during an air raid owing to his inability to understand the German sentry's order to do so."

It would appear from later reports, that the above evidence was sufficient to class the shooting of S/Sgt Hollingsworth as murder. This in turn meant that a separate investigation had to be undertaken.

From all the evidence of the ex-POWs interviewed, a detailed list was produced of the camps' German staff. Once names were known, detailed searches were made of the numerous POW and Internment camps both in Germany and Britain. Investigators faced a formidable task. One of those first interviewed was ex-Hauptmann Langhans, the camp 1C or Officer in charge of Guards and General Quartering. Langhans had been working at XIB since the 27th January, 1940. One of the first comments he made was as follows:

"... during my five years activity at Fallingbostel I am able to say that 15-20 POWs of various nationalities were shot by the guard personnel... In addition, 20 prisoners were shot at but not killed and some 15 or 20 POWs were injured by members of the Stalag personnel... with punches, kicks, blows with sticks and with bayonets." [5]

Langhans went on to say that it was he who drew up the guard orders and that he had always insisted that, during an air raid, all prisoners should remain in their huts and if they refused, the guards would open fire with live ammunition. He also added:

"Further, the guards were made aware of an order issued by the OKW (Army HQ) to the effect that warning shots were forbidden."

Langhans was the man who wrote the orders but he was not the man who pulled the trigger. Indeed, the authorities were still not clear why Sgt Hollingsworth had been shot. They continued their questioning, now amongst some of the German NCOs. One of the first was a man named Wordel [6]. He had been a corporal and present at the shooting. He stated in his affidavit, taken on the 6th May, 1946, that there had been an air raid warning and all prisoners had been ordered into their huts as there were no shelters. Three POWs appeared not to do so. "I called to the sentry", Wordel said, "see to it that they all go into the huts. Don't stand there like a crowd of bloody fools." Wordel went on to describe how he turned his head and just after, a shot rang out. "I called at once for medical orderlies and a stretcher in order to take the wounded man to the Russian doctor nearby" he continued. As for the sentry, Wordel described how he just slung his rifle and "continued on his rounds." The Germans, apparently, did hold a brief enquiry, led by the camps legal officer, Wordel again:

"I reported everything that had happened... and was questioned as a witness by the prosecuting officer, a Hauptmann. The Hauptmann dismissed me and said the guard had acted correctly."

By this stage of the investigation, the British were treating the shooting as a murder. Information as to the identification of the guard responsible was still not forthcoming. Further leads were obtained however, thanks to a chance remark made by a German prisoner in POW Camp 2226. The prisoner stated that a former company commander of 426 Guard Battalion, formerly stationed at Stalag XIB, mentioned that one of his men had shot a British sergeant. An investigating team eventually tracked down the former Hauptmann concerned but he denied all knowledge of the matter. He was dually arrested but contemporary records go no further. [7]

What, then, was the outcome of the investigation? The records of the subsequent military trials concerning Stalag XIB show that the case mainly concerned the inhumane treatment of the Arnhem prisoners, especially those wounded. Only one of the eight defendants, Langhans, was also charged with the murder of S/Sgt Hollingsworth. He was acquitted. What is evident, however, is that Hollingsworth was probably very badly shell-shocked. Being shouted at in German would probably not have registered. There were probably many like him, suffering the mental exhaustion of the Arnhem battle as well as what is termed today as the Shock of Capture. To the Germans, he was not wounded and therefore had no need to be in the camp hospital. That decision cost S/Sgt Hollingsworth his life

Since writing this article, the author has been in contact with Peter Hollingsworth, Tom's brother, and would like to record his gratitude for the subsequent help given to him. Thanks must also go to Major John Cross for his assistance.

1. See "Orts-Chronik von Falling-bostel" Vols I & II. Reprinted 1987. p.230.
2. See "To Revel in God's Sunshine." Richard Alford. 1981. p.46.
3. "Arnhem Spearhead" by James Sims. Sphere Books Ltd. 1981. p.140.
4. See Judge Advocate Generals (JAG) papers - PRO - WO 235/231
5. See above.
6. See PRO papers WO 208/4675.
7. See PRO papers WO 208/4616.

The following information has been provided by Tom's brother Peter:

Tom Hollingsworth was born in Shropshire in 1922, the son of Thomas and Gladys Hollingsworth of Wood Green, Wednesdbury, Staffordshire. They later became the Mayor and Mayoress of that town.

Tom first joined up at the age of seventeen as a lieutenant in the LDV, or Home Guard, and was then called up for National Service at the age of eighteen in the King's Shropshire Light Infantry at Copthorne Barracks, Shrewsbury.

When the Glider Pilot Regiment was formed the following year, he volunteered and was sent to Cromer in Norfolk to train as a pilot; after qualifying, he was posted to G Squadron. Later he was transferred to Fairford in Gloucestershire from where he flew to Arnhem.

We at home knew that he had been captured in September and had been writing to him and sending Red Cross parcels to the camp - it wasn't until the following February that we learnt that he was dead and all the letters were returned. You may imagine the distress that this caused. It was particularly so for my parents as they were by then the Mayor and Mayoress of Wendnesbury and had to carry on with their Civic duties under such terrible conditions.

Shortly after the war ended, Jean, my sister, and I went to the Gaumont cinema in Wednesbury to see a film about Amhem called "Theirs was the Glory". We were amazed to see a sequence in the film where the gliders were approaching the drop zone and the tow rope from the towing Dakota was released. The camera turned to the pilot, and we saw Tom, who had been killed after the battle four years earlier.

The story doesn't however end there. Much later when the film A Bridge Too Far was made, the battle was re-enacted with actors such as Sean Connery, Richard Attenborough, and Robert Redford etc. A sequence early on showed the gliders preparing for take off. As the first glider pulls round onto camera the names are there on the side. Sgt Pilot Dusty Miller, Sgt Pilot Tom Hollingsworth. This was from records held in the Imperial War Museum. Clips of both films have been used countless times on television in war documentaries and so in a funny sort of way he is likely to live on long after the rest of us have gone.

My brother Peter I visited Peter Hollingsworth during the additional research for this edition and Peter has many personal family letters regarding Tom, including one written to his father dated 30th April 1945 from Sergeant W.A. Webb (Army No. 1450029), who had been a passenger in Tom & Victor's glider and who was also taken prisoner at Arnhem.

"I saw Tom helping to dress the hundreds of wounded then pouring in doing some really sterling work. I think he thought too much of others, disregarding personal danger and so I think got shell-shocked rather badly. I never saw him after this alive I'm sorry to say.

LETTERS FROM TOM HOLLINGSWORTH

```
                              R.A.F. Station.

                              Fairford. Glous.
Dear Dad,

        I know you would not expect me to be silly in
writing this letter, and I am therefore going to keep
it in quite a normal vein.

        I realise as I write how much worse it is for
those left behind, but I ask you not to take it too
badly, remember you have mother, John, Jean and young
Peter to look after.

        My first wish that I shall ask you is that you
pull the family through the shock: no one is to go into
mourning for me, as I think it is all wrong to advertise
any personal sorrow.

        I am not making any will, but I would like you
to see that the following requests are carried out:-

        1.   John is to have my car, as I think it will
        perhaps be a little more reliable than his own.
        he is to dispose of it when or how he likes, when
        he can get one more to his liking.

        2.   Jean is to have my War Saving Certificates
        in the hope that one day she may find the money
        useful setting up her own home.

        3.   I want you to sell the Motor Cycle, the money
        obtained to go to Peter, also my Lydenberg Shares,
        which I hope will have shown a little profit by
        then.     The Balance of my banking account, silver
        Cigarette Case and Gold Watch are also for Peter.

        4.   To Mary for such long and faithful service
        I enclose cheque for £50, and hope that she will
        remain with the family for many years to come.

        5.   To Mrs Ward £10 as an appreciation of the
        good work she has done and for many a good laugh.

        6.   Anything else of mine I want you to dispose
        of in the best manner possible, I suggest that my
        clothes go to the most needy cases in Wednesbury.
```

- 2 -

Well Dad, I think that covers all my requests, as
for you Dad if I was to write pages I could never thank you enough
for what you have done for me.   Perhaps I have never shown it,
but I am immensely proud of you   What son would'nt be? and I
know that when you retire you will have something to look back
upon both as a father and as a public figure.

My greatest wish I have never fulfilled, I wanted
to be as great a success in life as you have been.   Perhaps I
got away to a very slow start, but then I was always slow
settling down, and I know that I have given more than one
reason to worry about me.

I should have liked to have carried on the business
in our name, perhaps now John will do that, as I should hate to
think that of it passing out of the family after you have spent
your life building it up.

My feelings at the moment are very mixed.   When I
first went into the Army I had a dread of fighting and I became
bitter towards the type of life I was leading, everything was
directed towards one purpose, learning to hate Germans, but in
the last six months I have passed the stage of fear and I am quite
prepared for anything, because I know my job and I know I can do it.

If I die, I along with thousands of others will be
remembered for a time, but then our names will only be remembered
on a memorial.   In my opinion until all the countries are prepared to share their benefits, there will always be war, and men will
die every few years for the "fight against evil".   Thats why I feel
so cynical about this war as perhaps you did in the last.   Perhaps
the real reason that I haven't come through this lot is because
God never intended me to, for it is only when you really probe deep
into your thoughts there is someone who does control our destiny.

Please remember that, and I am sure it will be a great
comfort to you and all those at home I love so dearly.

All my love to you Dad, Look after Mom please.

All my very best love and wishes.

Tom.

R.A.F. Station,

FAIRFORD.

Dearest Mom,

For over a quarter of an hour I have sat at this table trying to think how I can best start this letter. It is so very difficult for me, for it isn't every day you have to write under these circumstances.

The main thought running through my head all the time is that you mustn't worry about me. I know it is very easy for me to say that, but how else can I put it? Worring about what has happened won't help, and you will only upset yourself and everybody else.

Please don't think that because I am writing this letter that I have made up my mind that something will happen to me but I must prepare myself for it, and I feel certain that although you have never admitted it you have realised that something may happen to me, and have prepared yourself for it, but you or nobody else can save me from my fate because God has planned that.

Let me show you what I mean. Two of my friends were taken off one of the operations we were doing. They were put on night flying same night, and they were both killed when a Stirling hit them whilst they were on the ground, so you see Mom it is just fate.

Naturally you will only get this letter in the event of my not returning from an operation. I have asked Dad not to wear mourning and I ask you to do the same, because it only advertises a personl loss.

I have been very fortunate in life, a decent education and a lovely home, and altogether a very full life, so really I have no regrets about anything that may happen to me.

Don't worry Mother dear will you.

All my very best love.

Tom.

Appendix One

PUBLIC RELATIONS UNIT - ARNHEM

MAJOR OLIVER

Major Oliver commanded the Public Relations Team during the Battle of Arnhem. This unit consisted of himself, as a Public Relations Officer, two BBC civilian broadcasters (Stanley Maxted and Guy Byam), two newspaper journalists (Alan Wood of the Daily Express and Jack Smyth of Reuters), two censors (Captains Brett and Williams), three men of the Army Film and Photographic Unit (Sergeants Mike Lewis, Dennis Smith and Gordon Walker), and four signallers (Butcher, Cull, Hardcastle, and Noon).

For his conduct during the Battle, Oliver was awarded the Silver Star: By direction of the President, under the provision of AR 600-45, 22 September 1943, as amended, the Silver Star is awarded to:

Major R. W. R. Oliver, British Army, for gallantry in action from 17 September 1944 to 26 September 1944. Major Oliver was in command of the group of correspondents assigned to cover the activities of the First Airborne Division (British) in the airborne invasion of Holland. He enabled the correspondents to radio their stories to the outside world and, in addition, he made the wireless sets available for operational military messages, since all other sets were rendered useless in the landings.

The following article was printed in *'The Newspaper World'*, on the 10th June 1945.

Major Roy Oliver, 31-years-old British regular army P.R.O., who was in charge of the war correspondents at Arnhem, has been awarded the U.S. Silver Star.

The official citation described how Major Oliver enabled correspondents to radio their stories to the outside world. "During this time," it continues, "the party was under considerable enemy fire and Major Oliver was wounded. In the withdrawal to, and crossing of, the Rhine, he was again wounded and lost his boat, necessitating his swimming the remaining distance, carrying film negatives, still photographs, and radio discs of the operation. His coolness under fire and marked devotion to duty are highly exemplary."

Alan Wood, who covered Arnhem for the Daily Express and had also worked in New Guinea and China, told the Newspaper World:

'Oliver is quite unique among P.R.O.s. In my experience a P.R.O. is either the occasional dud who has been weeded out of a fighting unit, or a professional soldier who knows nothing about journalism, or a journalist who knows nothing about soldiering. Oliver is a professional soldier who has been at Tobruk, who landed on

D-Day, went to Arnhem, and has been in almost every tough spot during the war. It gives war correspondents confidence having an old soldier with them. At the same time, Oliver is keenly interested in their work and always putting up suggestions for stories they should follow up'

'The job he did at Arnhem must be the most brilliant success a P.R.O. has had during the war. Never before have war correspondents been given the chance of getting out regular despatches under such difficult circumstances. Only on returning to London did I learn how good was the job he did. No news at all of the First Division got to London or to Corps headquarters through operational signals for two days after we landed. Oliver succeeded in getting his little P.R. wireless set working just before midnight on the day we landed. So, the first two days the only news the Corps Commander, Churchill, Montgomery or anyone else had of how the First was getting on was through the despatches of Stanley Maxted, of the B.B.C., and myself. Later on his P.R. wireless set was used almost entirely for operational messages.'

ALAN WOOD

Alan Wood the Daily Express reporter carried into Arnhem by Victor and Tom, sent the following reports published in the newspaper on 30th September 1944:

"Our glider pilots where Staff Sergeant Miller and Sergeant Hollingsworth. And we had another reserve pilot , the man who refused to be left behind. His name is Sergeant Webb and a little while ago he was grounded because of eye trouble. But somehow he managed to get permission to come "just to help with unloading at the other end."

The M.O. came round half an hour before take-off giving out air-sickness pills. We climbed aboard and found an English wasp which had wanted to come to Holland playing inside the pilot's Perspex. "Let him come " said someone "No fear – not going to risk him stinging you just as you're landing" they told Sergeant Miller.

Then the take-off, riding high above the tow plane, with a goodly company of Stirlings and Horsas spread around us like a swarm of birds stretched out to the horizon. We sat in the wooden fuselage of the glider, rather like a railway train and with something like the same noise as the air swept past , smoking and reading the Sunday papers.

"Damn no Nat Gubbins today" said the captain. The major was reading a novel by Daphne du Maurier.

On and on over England and the Channel: three gliders were ditched in it with destroyers rushing up to them. There was no hostile note of ack-ack when we crossed the coast from the sunny North Sea. We went over flooded country, pretty red-roofed houses waist deep and half drowned in water.

And then the flat fields of un-flooded Holland proper. We saw no living thing Dutch or German. The streets of the towns were deserted. Ack-ack opened up with a few black puffs on the left . An Oerlikon gun struck sharply against our wooden tail like someone rapping heavily on a door. One Stirling fell with its elevator plane cut off. But that was all.

Then the excitement as we got nearer and nearer to our landing zone, about eight miles west of Arnhem. We dropped the tow rope, lost speed with a jerk and the pilot steered round a tree , over a hedge and smacked down to a perfect skidded landing on a turnip field.

Perhaps a dozen gliders were there before us and dozens more came tumbling and toppling down after us. Two collided nearby. The glider under us crashed into some trees. One with a heavy lorry on board nosed over and ended upside down."

. . . .

Quote from newspaper article,
by Alan Wood 'Daily Express' Arnhem 1944

'If in the years to come,
you meet a man who says,
"I was at Arnhem",
raise your hat and
buy him a drink.'

Appendix Two

GLIDERS

General Aircraft GAL.48 Hotspur Mk II
General characteristics
- Crew: 2 pilots
- Capacity: 8 troops
- Length: 39 ft (11.89 m)
- Wingspan: 45 ft 10¾ in (13.99 m)
- Height: 10 ft (3.05 m)
- Wing area: 272 ft² (25.3 m²)
- Empty weight: 1,661 lb (753 kg)
- Maximum take-off weight: 3,598 lb (1,632 kg)

Performance
- Maximum speed: 90 mph (145 km/h)
- Landing speed: 56 mph (90 km/h)
- Range: 83 miles from a 20,000 ft release (134 km from a 6,100 m release)
- Wing loading13.23 lb/ft² (64.6 kg/m²)

WACO Aircraft Company CG-4A
(Cargo Glider-4A) Hadrian
General characteristics
- Crew: 2 pilots
- Capacity: 13 troops, or quarter-ton truck (Jeep) & 4 troopers
- Length: 48 ft 8 in (14.8 m)
- Wingspan: 83 ft 8 in (25.5 m)
- Height: 15 ft 4 in (4.7 m)
- Wing area: 900 ft² (83.6 m²)
- Empty weight: 3,900 lb (1,769 kg)
- Loaded weight: 7,500 lb (3,402 kg)
- Useful load: 'Troop Carrier (2 crew & 13 passengers): 4197 lb';
  'Cargo Carrier - Jeep (2 crew & 4 passengers, 1 Jeep Car): 4197 lb'
  'Cargo Carrier - 75 mm howitzer (2 crew & 3 passengers, 1 Howitzer,
  18 rounds ammunition): 4197 lb'
- Max take off weight: 7,500 lb (3,402 kg)
- Max take off (Emergency Load): 9,000 lb (4,082 kg)

Performance
- Maximum speed: 150 mph
- Cruising sped: 72.6 mph
- Stalling speed:: 49 mph
- Wing loading: : 8.33 lb/ft² (40.7 kg/m²)
- Rate of sink: Approx 400 ft/min (2 m/s) at tactical glide speed
  (IAS 60 mph, 96 km/h)
- Landing run: 600-800 feet (180-244 m) for normal three-point landing.

Airspeed AS 51 Horsa Mk1
General characteristics
- Crew: 2 pilots
- Capacity: 25 troops (20-25 troops the "standard" load)
- Length: 67 ft 0 in (20.43 m)
- Wingspan: 88 ft 0 in (26.83 m)
- Height: 19 ft 6 in (5.95 m)
- Wing area: 1,104 ft² (102.6 m²)
- Empty weight: 8,370 lb (3,804 kg)
- Loaded weight: 15,500 lb (7,045 kg)

Performance
- Maximum speed: 150 mph on tow; 100 mph gliding (242 km/h/160 km/h)
- Wing loading: 14.0 lb/ft² (68.7 kg/m²)

TUG AIRCRAFT

Armstrong Whitworth Albemarle
General characteristics
- Crew: 4
- Capacity: 10 paratroopers in ST
- Payload: 4,000 lb freight (1,820 kg)
- Length: 59 ft 11 in (18.26 m)
- Wingspan: 77 ft 0 in (23.47 m)
- Height: 15 ft 7 in (4.75 m)
- Wing area: 804 ft² (74.6 m²)
- Empty weight: 25,347 lb (10,270 kg)
- Loaded weight: 36,500 lb (16,556 kg)
- Max takeoff weight: 36,500 lb (16,590 kg)
- Powerplant: 2 × Bristol Hercules XI radial engine 1,590 hp (1,190 kW) each
- Propellers: De Havilland hydromatic propeller

Performance
- Maximum speed: 230 kn (265 mph, 426 km/h) at 10,500 ft (3,200 m)
- Cruise speed: 148 kn (170 mph, 274 km/h)
- Stall speed: 61 kn (70 mph, 113 km/h)
- Range: 1,300 ml (2,092 km)
- Service ceiling: 18,000 ft (5,486 m)
- Rate of climb: 980 ft/min (5.0 m/s)

Armament
- Guns: 4 × .303 in (7.7 mm) Browning machine guns in dorsal turret.

Short Stirling Mk IV
General characteristics
- Crew: 7 (First and second pilot, navigator/bomb aimer, front gunner/WT operator, two air gunners, and flight engineer)
- Length: 87 ft 3 in (26.6 m)
- Wingspan: 99 ft 1 in (30.2 m)
- Height: 22 ft 9 in (6.9 m)
- Wing area: 1,460 ft² (135.6 m²)

- Aspect ratio: 6.5
- Empty weight: 46,900 lb (21,274 kg)
- Loaded weight: 59,400 lb (26,944 kg)
- Max. takeoff weight: 70,000 lb (31,752 kg)
- Powerplant: 4 × Bristol Hercules II radial engine1, 375 hp (1,025 kW) each
- Propellers: Three-bladed metal fully feathering propeller
- Propeller diameter: 13 ft 6 in (4.1m)

Performance
- Maximum speed: 282 mph (454 km/h) at 12,500 ft (3,800 m)
- Cruise speed: 200 mph (320 km/h)
- Range: 2,330 ml (3,750 km)
- Service ceiling: 16,500 ft (5,030 m)
- Rate of climb: 800 ft/min (4 m/s)
- Wing loading: 44.9 lb/ft² (219.4 kg/m²)
- Power/mass: 0.093 hp/lb (0.153 kW/kg)

Armament
- Guns: 8 x 0.303 in (7.7 mm) Browning machine guns: 2 in powered nose turret, 4 in tail turret, 2 in dorsal turret

Douglas C-47 Skytrain /Dakota (USA design)
General characteristics
- Crew: 4
- Capacity: 28 troops
- Payload: 6,000lb (2,700Kg)
- Length: 63'9" (1943m)
- Wingspan: 95' 6"(29.41m)
- Height: 17'0" (5.18m)
- Wing area: 987 ft² (91.7sm)
- Empty weight: 18,135lb (8,226Kg)
- Loaded weight: 26,000lb (11,793Kg)
- Maximum take off weight: 31,000lb (14,0621Kg)
- Powerplant: 2 x Pratt & WhitneyR-1830 twin wasp radial engines

Performance
- Maximum speed: 244mph (360 km/h) @ 10,000' (3,050m)
- Cruise sped: 160mph (257 km/h, 139kn)
- Range: 2,575km (1,600m, 1391nm)
- Service ceiling: 26,400' (8,045m)
- Rate of climb: 10,000' (3,050m) in 9.5mins

ARMAMENT

PIAT – Projector Infantry Anti-Tank
Manufacturer: ICI Ltd & various other companies.
Overall Length: 39" (990mm)
Weight: 31.7 lbs (14.4kg)
Projectile Weight: 3lb (1.35 kg)
Muzzle Velocity: 450 ft² (137 m/s)
Effective Range: 109yds (100m)

Sten Gun - Regular Mark II:
- Overall Length: 30" (762 mm)
- Barrel Length: 7.8"(197 mm)
- Weight: 7.1lb(3.2 kg)
- Effective range: approximately109yds (100m)
- Cartridge: 9 x 19mm Parabellum
- Capacity: 32-round detachable box magazine
- Muzzle Velocity: 1,198 ft/sec (341m/s)
- Action: Blowback-operated, open bolt

M1 Carbine - American Manufacture
- Overall Length: 35.6"(900mm)
- Barrel Length: 18.0"(460mm)
- Weight: 5.2lb (2.4 Kg) Empty
- Weight: 5.8lb (2.6 Kg) loaded with sling
- Action: Gas operated rotating bolt
- Cartridge: 0.3 Carbine
- Capacity: 15 or 30 -round detachable box magazine
- Muzzle Velocity: 1,990 ft/s (606m/s)
- Rate of Fire: semi automatic
- Sights: Rear sight: Flip or adjustable. Front sight: Wing protected post

Lee Enfield No.4 Mk 1 (T) Snipers Rifle
- Overall Length: 44" (111mm)
- Barrel Length: 25.2" (640mm)
- Weight: 8.8lb (4Kg)
- Action: Bolt
- Cartridge: .303 Mk Vii SAA Ball
- Capacity: 10 round magazine, loaded with 5 – round clip chargers
- Muzzle Velocity: 2,441 ft/s (744m/s)
- Rate of Fire: 20-30 aimed shots per minute
- Sights: No.32 3.5x telescopic with windage adjustment
- Effective range: 550 yd (503m)
- Maximum firing range: 3000 yd (2,743 m)

Mills Bomb - No.36 Hand Grenade
- Weight: 11.0lb (765 g)
- Diameter: 2.4" (61mm)
- Length: 3.74" (95.2mm)
- Filling: Baratol
- Detonation: Percussion cap & time delay 4 second fuse

6 Pounder Anti-Tank Gun (designed: 1940)
- Barrel Length M III – designed for glider use with a narrow carriage: 8'4" (2540mm)
- Weight: 2,520lb (1,140Kg)
- Crew: 6
- Shell: 57 x 441mm R
- Calibre: 2.24" (57mm)
- Breech: Vertical sliding block
- Carriage: Split tail

- Elevation: -5° to +15°
- Traverse: 90°
- Muzzle Velocity: 2,600 ft/s (792 m/s) with AP shot
- Effective firing range: 1,650yd (1,510m)
- Maximum firing range: 5,000yd (4,600m)
- Sights: No.22c ×1 magnification and 21° field of view

75mm Pak Howitzer (USA designed: 1927)
- Overall length: 12'1" (3680mm)
- Barrel Length – designed for glider use with M8 M1A1 carriage: 4'6" (1380mm)
- Weight: 1,439lb (653Kg)
- Height: 3'1" (940mm)
- Width: 4'0" (1220mm)
- Crew: 6+
- Shell:
- Calibre: 2.95" (75mm)
- Rate of fire: 3-6 rounds per min (sustained)
- Breech: Horizontal block
- Recoil: Hydropneumatic constant
- Carriage: Box trail - dismantling
- Elevation: +5°to 45°
- Traverse: 6°
- Muzzle Velocity: 1,250 ft/s (381m/s)
- Effective firing range: 9,600yd (8,778 m)

Ford GPW 1/4 ton 4x4 (USA designed 1941)
- Length: 131" (3327mm)
- Width: 62" (1,575mm)
- Height: 72" (1,829 mm) reduced to52" (1,321 mm) with top down
- Wheelbase: 80" (2,032mm)
- Style: 2 door
- Layout: Front engined, rear/4 wheel drive
- Engine: 134 cu in(2.2lt)
- Transmission: 3 speed manual
- Curb Weight: 2,293lb (1,040 Kg)

Universal (Bren) Gun Carrier (designed 1934)
- Length: 144" (3650mm)
- Width: 6'9" (2060mm)
- Height: 5'2" (1570mm)
- Weight: 3t 16cwt (3.19 t) un-laden
- Engine: Ford V8 petrol
- Suspension: Hortsmann coil
- Fuel capacity: 20 gal (91 Ltr)
- Operational range: 150 miles (250 Km)
- Speed: 30mph (48 Km)
- Crew: 3
- Armour: 0.2" – 0.4" (7-10mm)
- Armament: Bren gun or Boys anti-tank rifle
- Secondary armament: Vickers machine gun, M2 Browning machine gun, Piat, 3" mortar, 2" mortar

MG 42 (Maschinengewehr 42)
- Overall Length: 44" (1,120mm)
- Barrel Length: 21" (533mm)
- Weight: 21 lb (11.57kg)
- Effective range: 219 – 2,187yd (200-2,000m)
- Maximum range: 5,140 yd (4,700m)
- Cartridge: 7.92 x 57mm
- Feed system: 50 or 250 round belt feed
- Rate of fire: 1,200 rounds/min
- Muzzle Velocity: 2,477 ft/sec (755 m/s)
- Action: Recoil operated
- Sights: telescopic or iron

Nebelwefer 41 (15cm NbW 41) - *6 Barrel battlefield rocket artillery launcher*
"Moaning Minnie"
- Barrel Length: 51" (1300mm)
- Barrels: 6 (non-rotating)
- Weight (Empty): 1,19lb (540kg)
- Carriage: Split tail
- Crew: 6
- Ammunition/Payload: H.E. Smoke, Chemical
- Calbre: 5.9" (150mm)
- Rate of fire: Cyclical 1-4-6-2-3-5 @ 36 rounds p/min
- Effective rate of fire: 6 projectiles @ 10 sec. 3 x 6 projectile salvos per 5 min
- Range: 2,710 yd – 7,721yd (2,478m – 7,060m)
- Action: Remote control - electronically fired
- Velocity: 1,122ft/s (342m/s)
- Elevation: -5° /+ 45°
- Traverse/Rotation: 360°
- Sighting Mechanism: SC35 or SC38 protractor quadrant

MG 34 (Maschinengewehr 34)
- Overall Length: 48" (1,219mm)
- Barrel Length: 24.7" (627mm)
- Weight: 26.7lb (12.1kg), 42.3lb (19.2 Kg) with tripod
- Effective range: 1,312yd (1200m))
- Effective range: 1,312yd+ (1200m+)
- Cartridge: 7.92 x 57mm
- Feed system: 50 or 250 round belt feed or 50/70 round drum
- Rate of fire: 1,700 rounds/min
- Muzzle Velocity: 2,500 ft/sec (762m/s)
- Action: Open bolt/recoil/rotating bolt
- Sights: Iron

Panzer IV Ausf H (Tank)
- Length: 19'5" (5.92m)
- Length gun forward: 23' (7.02 m)
- Width: 9'5" (2.88m)
- Height: 8'10" (2.68m)

- Weight: 25.0t
- Crew: 5
- Armour: 0.39"- 4.46" (10-88mm)
- Main armament: 2.95' (7.5mm) Kw K40
- Secondary armament: 2x Maschingewhr 34
- Engine: Maybach HL 120 TRM V12
- Transmission: 6 forward, 1 reverse
- Suspension: leaf spring
- Fuel capacity: 100 gal (470lt)
- Operational range: 120 miles (200Km)
- Road Speed: 26 mph (26 Km)
- Off road speed: 9.9 mph (16Km/h)

Panzerkampfwagen VI Tiger Ausf.E (Tank)
- Length: 20'9" (6.32m)
- Length gun forward: 27'9" (8.45m)
- Width: 11'8" (3.56m)
- Height: 9'10" (3.0m)
- Weight: 54t
- Crew: 5
- Armour: 0.98' – 4.7" (25-120mm)
- Main armament: 1 x 88mm KwK36 L/56
- Sights: Leitz Turmzielfernrohr TZF 9b
- Secondary armament: 2 x 7.92mm Maschinengewhr 34
- Engine: Maybach V12
- Suspension: Torsion bar Fuel capacity: 540lt (118gal)
- Operational range: 68-121 miles (110-195 Km)
- Speed: 28.2 mph (45.4Km/h)

Sd.Kfz. 250 (Armoured Half-track Personnel Carrier)
- Length: 15'0" (4.56m)
- Width: 6'5" (1.94m)
- Height: 5'5" (1.6m)
- Weight: 12,800lb (5,800Kg) loaded
- Crew: 2 + 4
- Armour: 0.22' – 0.57" (5.5 – 14.5mm)
- Main armament: 1x 7.92mm Maschinengewhr 34
- Ground clearance: 10" (285mm)
- Engine: Maybach 6 cylinder water cooled
- Transmission: Maybach VG 102128H - 7 forward+ 3 reverse
- Suspension: Torsion bar
- Fuel capacity: 30.8 gal (140ltr)
- Operational road range: 190 – 200 miles (300 – 320Km)
- Operational off road range: 110-120 miles (180 – 200Km)
- Road speed: 47mph (76Km)

Appendix Three

Operational Statistics

After the war, Brigadier 'Shan' Hackett commander 4th Parachute Brigade at Arnhem said "Our Glider Pilots were not only very high grade airmen – I believe that the Glider Pilot Regiment was the finest body of soldiers that the British Army produced in World War Two "

Operation Ladbroke 9th July 1943

This was the first large-scale Allied airborne operation mission involving gliders and parachute troops. The 1st Airlanding Brigade, using 136 Waco and 8 Horsa gliders on 9th July 1943, carried out the operation. The objective was to secure the Ponte Grande Bridge and await the ground forces for invasion of Sicily.

V. Miller's Operational details:

- Glider: WACO GG-4A
- Chalk No.: 110
- Departure airfield: Airfield F,Goubrine No.2, M'Saken,Tunisia
- 1st pilot: Capt Boucher-Giles
- 2nd pilot: Sgt V. Miller
- Unit carried: 'H' Company 1st Battalion Border Regiment (6pdr anti-tank gun & crew)
- Tug aircraft: Albemarle, No. P1389 ,38 Wing RAF
- Tug pilot: Squadron Leader L C Bartram, 296 Squadron
- Landing zone: 2, Sicily

British

- General Bernard Montgomery commanding 8th Army
- Major General Hopkinson commanding 1st Airborne Division
- Lieutenant Colonel Chatterton commanding 1st Battalion Glider Pilot Regiment
- Brigadier Philip Hicks commanding. 1st Airlanding Brigade a force of consisting of 2075 men.
- 65 gliders released too early by the towing aircraft and crashed into the sea, drowning approximately 252 men.
- Only eighty-seven men arrived at the Pont Grande Bridge. Casualties:
- Killed: 313
- Missing or wounded: 174

Italian

- Vice Admiral Primo Leonardi commanding:
- 206th Coastal Div, 385th Coastal Battalion, 121st Coastal Defence Regiment, 1st Battalion, 75th (Napoli) Infantry Regiment, 4th Infantry Division (Napoli).
- Losses unknown

Operation Market Garden 17th September 1944

Sunday 17th saw 500 gliders and 1,500 aircraft with the 1st Airborne Division taking the northern of two routes. The aircraft armada stretched for 94 miles (150 Km) in length and 3 miles (5 Km) in width. Fighter escorts of 371 Spitfires, Tempests and Mosquitos protected the fleet of aircraft.

Over 117 anti-aircraft positions along the Market Garden flight path were bombed and strafed by 212 Thunderbolts, 50 Mosquitos, 48 B-25 Mitchells along with 24 Bostons bombing military facilities around Nijmegen, Deelen, Ede and Kleve.

German fighters and anti-aircraft fire was minimal. The Allies lost 68 aircraft and 71gliders from all causes, along with 2 RAF and 18 USAAF fighters.

V. Miller's Operational details:
- Glider: Horsa Mk1 Serial Aircraft No.No. PW 780
- Chalk No.: 440
- Serial No.: B18
- Airborne block: No.56
- Departure airfield: Fairford, Gloucestershire, England
- 1st pilot: Staff Sgt V. Miller
- 2nd pilot: Sgt T. Hollingsworth
- Squadron: G , CO Maj R Croot
- Flight: 24, CO Capt R. O. Walchi
- Unit carried: HQ 1st Airborne Division Public Relations Team - Major Oliver,Capt Brett (censor) , Signalmen Butcher, Cull, Hardcastle & Noon, Army Film & Photographic Unit No.5: Sgt D.M. Smith, Sgt G. Walker, Army Press Team: Alan Wood (Daily Express), Stanley Maxted (BBC), Jeep & trailer & No.76 wireless set
- Tug aircraft: Stirling 190 Squadron RAF
- Tug pilot: Squadron Leader L C Bartram, 296 Squadron
- Landing zone: Z, Wolfheze

Glider Pilot Regiment: 1,334 Pilots flew 667 Gliders (all types over 3 lifts) British

- Field Marshall Bernard Montgomery commanding 21st Army Group
- Lieutenant General B G Horrocks commanding XXX Corps ground forces
- Lieutenant General F A M Browning's commanding 1st Airborne Corps
- Brigadier Roy E Urquhart commanding1st Airborne Division.
- 1st Airborne Division: 10,095 men, 2 GPR Wings, 2 Parachute Brigades along with artillery, anti-tank, Royal Engineer, Royal Army Medical Corps and Royal Army Service Corps units
- Killed in Action: 1,485
- Captured: 6,525 (over 3,000 wounded in action)
- Safely withdrawn: 3,910

The Glider Pilot Regiment suffered the highest proportion of fatalities with 17.3% killed during the battle of Arnhem:

1 Wing GPR: Lt Colonel Ian Murray (A, B, D, G Squadrons)
- 131 KIA (29 no known grave)
- 253 POW

2 Wing GPR: Lt Colonel J.W. Place (C, E, F Squadrons)
- 228 KIA (17 no known grave)
- 466 POW

RAF:
- 68 aircraft sot down from 36 & 38 Group.
- 160 aircrew KIA
- 80 aircrew POW
- 79 air dispatchers KIA
- 80 POW

USAAF:
- 27 aircrew KIA
- 3 aircrew POW

110 Allied fighters shot down supporting Operation Market-Garden.

German

- Feldmarschall Walter Model commander Army Group B.
- Obergruppenführer Wilhelm Bittrich commander II SS Panzer Corps with 8,500 men.
- Heer Kampfgruppen, Kampfgruppe 'Spindler"Kriegsmarine & Luftwaffe personnel.
- Waffen-SS soldiers under the command of Kampfgruppe 'von Tettau'.

Casualties- German information is incomplete, but II SS records show:
- Killed 1,300
- Wounded: 2,000

In addition the Dutch civilians suffered approx 433 killed during the battle.

Operation Varsity 23rd-24th March 1945

The largest airborne operation of WW2 with 1,348 gliders, 1,625 transports, along with 889 escort fighters delivering 22,000 airborne troops over the Rhine. The air armada stretched nearly 200 miles and took two hours and 37 minutes to pass any given point. 80,000 British and Canadian troops crossed a 20-mile stretch of the river with 2,153 more fighters covering ground operations.

V Miller's Operational Details:
- Glider: Horsa Mk 1
- Chalk No.: 5
- Serial No. RN545
- Departure airfield: Great Dunnmow, Essex , England
- 1st pilot: staff Sgt V. Miller
- 2nd pilot: Sgt McGordon (RAF)
- Squadron: G, CO Maj M W D Priest
- Flight: 24, CO Flt Lt Haig
- Unit carried: Oxfordshire & Buckinghamshire Light Infantry (commanded by Major Gilbert Rahr)
- Tug aircraft: Stirling Mk IV
- Tug pilot: Flight Officer Bliss (USAAF) 190 Squadron RAF
- Landing zone: R, Hamminkeln, Germany

British
- Field Marshal Sir Bernard Montgomery Commander 21st Army Group.
- Brigadier Hugh Bellamy commander 6th Air Landing Brigade.
- Colonel ~George Chatterton commanding GPR.
- 6th Airborne landed 7,220 men.
- 420 Horsa and Hamilcar gliders.
- 752 C-47's, 42 DC -54's
- Fighter cover with 213 RAF and 676 US 9th Air Force planes.
- 56 planes were lost during the operation. 240 planes flew a re-supply missions following on the glider landings of which 16 were shot down.

Casualties for 6th Airborne:
- Killed 590
- Wounded or missing 710
- GPR: 101 KIA

German
- General der Infanterie Günther Blumentritt commander 25th Armee.
- 1st Parachute Army consisting of 2nd Parachute Corps, 86th Corps, 7th Parachute Division (4,000 men) and 84th Infantry Division (4,000 men).
- XLVII Panzer Corps

Casualties- German information is incomplete
- POW Approx 3,000

Acknowledgements

Drawings

All drawings from originals created by Victor Miller - Copyright Victor Miller

Maps

Miller / Moran Design Corporation - Copyright Moran Design Corporation

Photographs

No. 1   Cardwell's Keep , Queens Royal Regiment Barracks, Guildford , Surrey
         as it is in 2014 - Archive/Copyright - C. Miller 2014

No. 2   Troops await to board a WACO CG4A in Tunisia for Operation Ladbroke
         9th July 1943 - Archive/Copyright - Imperial War Museum CN1002

No. 3   Author's sketch of his own glider crash-landed at night, Syracuse,
         Sicily - Archive/Copyright Victor Miller

No. 4   Author's diary map drawn a week after his landing in Sicily, showing
         area around the Ponte Grande - Archive/Copyright Victor Miller

No. 5   Author's diary map drawn a week after his landing in Sicily, showing
         area around the Ponte Grande - Archive/Copyright Victor Miller

No. 6   G Squadron , Glider Pilot Regiment. The Author is in the middle row,
         7th from left, Tom Holligsworth is in the top row 5th from left
         Archive/Copyright Victor Miller

No. 7   Author - centre left,standing by his Horsa in the summer of 1944 at
         RAF Fairford, Gloustershire, with Tom Holligsworth, far left
         Archive/Copyright - Peter Hollingsworth

No. 8   Author's pilots log book showing page for Operation Market Garden
         Archive/Copyright Victor Miller

No. 9   Author at controls of his Horsa glider on route to Arnhem - Archive/
         Copyright - Imperial War Museum - clip from cine film A70 169/1-7

No. 10   Tom Hollingsworth at controls of his Horsa glider on route to Arnhem - Copyright - Imperial War Museum - clip from cine film A70 169/1-7

No. 11   Picture taken by Sgt Smith through the author's cockpit, showing flack bursting just below the Stirling tug as they cross the Dutch coast on the way to Arnhem - Archive/Copyright - Imperial War Museum - BU1160

No. 12   RAF reconnaisance photo of Landing Zone Z at Wolfheze , showing the author's Horsa in the top right of the field on 17th September 1944. Archive/Copyright - Imperial War Museum - CL1173

No, 13   14:00 hrs on Sunday 17th September, the author was filmed by Sgt Walker with Sgt Webb, Dutch nurse from the Asylum at Wofhezen, Author, Maj Oliver - Archive/Copyright - Imperial War Museum - clip from cine film A 169/1-7

No. 14   The author marched past the body of Major General Kussin lying by his car, killed by Bren gun fire at the crossroads near Wolfheze. Archive/Copyright - Imperial War Museum - BU1155

No. 15   One of the author's glider passengers, War Correspondent Alan Wood typing his despatch, cigarette in mouth, while troops in the background consult a map near Oosterbeek, 18th September 1944. Archive/Copyright - Imperial War Museum - BU 1146

No. 16   View from near the tennis court, Hartenstein Hotel, Oosterbeek. Archive/Copyright - Imperial War Museum - BU 1144

No. 17   1st airborne division soldiers use parachutes to signal allied supply aircraft in the grounds of the Hartenstein Hotel 23rd September 1944. Archive/Copyright - Imperial War Museum - BU 1119

No. 18   Irene Reimann who the author spoke to, a German WAAF telephonist of Luft-Nachrichten-Regiment 201, the unit manning the headquarters bunker of the Luftwaffe's 3 Jagd-Division. She was captured in civilian clothing on the first day. - Archive/Copyright - Imperial War Museum - BU 1096

No. 19   Author's own copy of a reconnaisance photograph showing the landing zone and which he used whilst navigating to land at Hamminkeln. Archive/Copyright Victor Miller

No. 20   Nazi Party Armband & Membership book taken by author as a souviner in Hamminkeln - Archive/Copyright Greg Woodward

Bibliography

Mike Rossiter - *We Fought at Arnhem* , Transworld Publishers 2011

Daily Express - Alan Wood – 30th September 1944

Roderick de Norman - *The Eagle* – Glider Pilot Regimental Association
pegasusarchive.org

Peter Hollingsworth and family